Wild and Woolly

EDWARD BOREIN

Wild and Woolly

AN ENCYCLOPEDIA

OF THE *Old West*

BY *Denis McLoughlin*

1975

Doubleday & Company, Inc., Garden City, New York

We are grateful to the following authors and artists for their
permission to reproduce, in both the text and on the endpapers, line
illustrations from their fine books:

Harold G. Davidson: *Edward Borein: Cowboy Artist*

Harold McCracken: *The Frank Tenney Johnson Book*
                      The American Cowboy
                      The Charles M. Russell Book
                      The Frederic Remington Book

Thomas E. Mails: *The Mystic Warriors of the Plains*

Designed by Wilma Robin

Library of Congress Cataloging in Publication Data

McLoughlin, Denis.
  Wild and woolly.
  Bibliography
  1. The West—History—Dictionaries. 2. The West—
Biography. I. Title.
F591.M155   978′.003
ISBN 0-385-00237-8
Library of Congress Catalog Card Number 73-83655

from THE AMERICAN COWBOY

PREFACE

This encyclopedia is not intended as a reference work on the United States of America, nor is it professed to be a complete coverage of every article, person, or event that existed or occurred during the rip-roaring era of western expansion; the former task is outside the scope of this book, while to accomplish the latter would require more pages at one's disposal than are included in a complete set of the Encyclopaedia Britannica.

The harvesting of subject matter for the entries has been confined to that vast area west of the Mississippi that stretches from the forty-ninth parallel to the Rio Grande. Dreary entries on government policy have been avoided, and Presidents, Civil War battles, and minor exponents of political skulduggery are mentioned only when their inclusion is essential to the narrative of an entry. You will, however, find entries covering most aspects of the Wild West, and while a number of these are, of necessity, rather short, others are of considerable length. Both types of entry frequently include cross references that link them with one or more other subjects.

That's the Preface out of the way, and now, if you are interested in what ARMITAS or BERDACHES might be, or about the pros and cons of gunfighting, the myth of MURIETTA, and the vigors of the VIGILANTES, get on with it, for this book is for you.

Wild and Woolly

CHARLES M. RUSSELL

ABALONE A sea snail, the shells of which are used by many Indian tribes for decorative purposes; the Indians would make long journeys to the Pacific Coast to collect these shells, which, although unattractive on the outside, are a blaze of pearly color within.

ABBOTT, DOWNING & COMPANY Coach-building firm founded by Leon Abbott and Lewis Downing. The plant covered a five-acre lot at Concord, New Hampshire, and employed a labor force of three hundred craftsmen who worked a six-day week of fourteen hours a day. The firm's most famous creation was the Concord stagecoach, and these coaches were used by most of the major overland mail and passenger companies during the turbulent era of western expansion. These vehicles were not confined to the North American continent, however, for many were exported to both Australia and South Africa. (See CONCORD COACH.)

ABILENE, KANSAS The first of the Kansas trail towns to make an impact on the imagination. In 1867 it consisted of little more than a dozen log dwellings and the inevitable saloon, but by the following year it was a wide-open lawless cattle-shipping center. A combination of circumstances made this possible: An Illinois stock dealer named Joseph McCoy wanted to buy cattle from the Texans; there was water (the Smokey Hill River) and good grazing land in the vicinity of Abilene; nearby Fort Riley ensured the unlikelihood of Indian attacks; and the Kansas Pacific's iron was crawling west from Kansas City. McCoy threw up business premises and a hotel he named The Drover's Cottage, and let it be known that he was in business. The hotel was still unfinished when the railroad and the first trail herd reached Abilene, and for the next 4½ years the town was the main cattle center of Kansas. During its heyday twenty or more saloons, bearing such picturesque names as The Alamo, Applejack, Old Fruit, The Pearl, and the Bull's Head Tavern operated around the clock, while anything went in the vice area—sometimes known as the Devil's Addition, which was situated on the outskirts of the town, and it was not until 1870 that Tom Smith (latterly of the New York City Police Department) was made marshal and brought a modicum of law and order to the town. In 1868 seventy thousand head of cattle passed through Abilene on their way to the packing plants of Chicago, and by 1870 the number had increased to three hundred thousand. These numbers may have reached astronomical figures if Abilene had remained king of the cow towns, but it was not to be, for in 1871 the Atchison, Topeka and Santa Fe Railroad reached Newton, sixty-five miles south of Abilene, and for a variety of reasons—not the least of which may have been the Texans' desire to cut their saddle polishing by almost a week— the cattle-trading center moved south, and most of Abilene's wealth and the majority of its colorful characters moved with it. (See SMITH, "BEAR RIVER" TOM.)

ABSAROKEE INDIANS
Indian name of the Crow Indians. (See CROW INDIANS.)

ACOMA INDIANS A tribe of Pueblo Indians who have occupied Acoma for the past thousand years. They are a peaceful crop-rearing community who have remained at peace with the white man since 1700. Prior to this time, and after originally establishing friendly relations with the Spanish priesthood in 1581, they had trouble with the Spanish military. In 1598 a number of soldiers who were on an exploratory mission under the command of Juan de Zoldivar were killed by the Indians, and in 1599 Zoldivar returned with reinforcements to punish the people of the mesa. The invaders were

armed with cannons, and when the smoke of battle had cleared, five hundred Indians were dead and their town lay in ruins. The Acomas rebuilt, and in 1628 Father Fray Juan Ramirez, a Franciscan missionary, extended the hand of friendship without having it amputated. He lived with the Indians for more than two decades, and during this period a church was built, but on Ramirez' death in 1664 the whole Pueblo nation rose against the Spaniards and the mission was destroyed, and it was not until 1700 that peace was again established. However, in spite of all the bloodshed, the Acomas remained Christian converts and the church was rebuilt, and both it and the town remain tourist attractions to this day.

ACOMA, NEW MEXICO A Pueblo city dating from the eleventh century which remains occupied to this day. It is built on a four-hundred-foot-high sandstone mesa and boasts terraced houses, rock reservoirs for catching rain and snow, and a Franciscan mission.

ADAIR, JOHN   Partner of Charles Goodnight from 1877 until Goodnight's death in 1885. (See GOODNIGHT, CHARLES.)

ADAMS, ANDY Cowboy and author who is best known for his *The Log of a Cowboy,* first published in 1903. Adams, a boss rider on the Chisholm Trail, wrote further books, but none of them had the success of his first effort. Adams, who was born at Columbia City, Indiana, on May 3, 1859, died at Colorado Springs, Colorado, on September 26, 1935.

ADAMS & COMPANY Banking and express company that was originally known as The New York & Boston Express Company, establishing itself as Adams & Company in 1841. Their main source of revenue was from the California gold fields, and by 1851, after absorbing the rival firm of Livingstone, Wells & Company some six years earlier, they had expanded until they were the paramount company in their field, and it was not until 1852 that a serious rival, in the form of Wells Fargo & Company, was born. The latter company rapidly grew in size and ambition, and when a run on the banks occurred in San Francisco, only Wells Fargo reopened, and Adams & Company retired from the western lists.

ADOBE An earth used for making sun-dried bricks. Chopped straw is added to reinforce the product.

ADOBE WALLS An ancient Spanish settlement in the Texas panhandle whose entire population was wiped out by Indians, and which was a crumbling, deserted ruin of a place in 1874 when a party of buffalo hunters and freighters came along to re-establish the site. This latter Adobe Walls, consisting of a few sod buildings, a saloon, and two stores, has gone down in western history as the place where a handful of hunters successfully withstood the assault of a large war party of Kiowa-Comanche on June 27, 1874. (See BATTLE AT ADOBE WALLS.)

AHVOTE A young Paiute brave who in 1890 had to track down and kill his own brother when the latter had turned renegade and murdered a U. S. Mails carrier. This barbaric practice was the outcome of a working agreement between the red man and the white man: If the tribe executed its own renegades the Paiutes would have nothing to fear from the law or the U.S. military—that is, no punitive action would be taken against the tribe if the chief dealt with any of its members who sinned against

the whites. Ahvote's fratricidal action evidently preyed on his mind, for until the killing he had been well liked by the residents of Eldorado, Nevada, whereas afterward he became more morose with the passing of the years, and in 1897, when his squaw sought livelier companionship, the Paiute ran amok. Rightly or wrongly, Ahvote blamed two local teamsters for luring his woman away, and on May 12, 1897, he aired his grievance with gunfire. When the smoke cleared the town had the bodies of the two suspected teamsters plus those of four innocent bystanders left on its hands, and of Ahvote there was no sign. However, the old "working agreement" was still in force, and a short time afterward, Ahvote paid for his crimes at the hands of one of his kinsmen. The murderous Paiute's father, his uncle, or his brother are variously reported as having committed the deed; but whoever, it was poetic justice of laureate proportions.

ALAMO, THE Originally the Alamo was the Church of the Mission of San Antonio de Valero, a fortified settlement established by the Spaniards on the outskirts of the Presidio of San Antonio de Bexar. The mission covered about three acres, and the protecting wall (which was ten feet high) and all the buildings were made of stone. The whole fortress was built as an industrial school for the Indians, and they were taught weaving, building, and stock raising within its walls. The building of the church commenced in 1744 (some twenty years after the rest of the mission had been in use), and it was completed in 1757, but within five years the roof and twin towers collapsed, and although an attempt was made to repair the building, it came to naught. The church was to remain in this "decadent condition," for after a placid beginning, relations with the Indians began to deteriorate, so that by 1805 a

company of soldiers who had been detailed to protect the mission found themselves obliged to take refuge inside the
fortress. It was around this time that the
mission lost its high-sounding title and
was merely referred to as "the Alamo."[1]
During this period, internal troubles
shook New Spain, and by the time the
colonists separated from their European
motherland in 1821, numerous Americans had settled on the Spanish land
north of the Rio Grande. Clashes between the two sets of nationals were frequent, and on October 28, 1835, a detachment of Americans under the joint
commands of Colonels Bowie and Fannin
raised their colors over Bexar. It was a
short-lived triumph, for in February 1836
an army of 5,000 Mexican troops under
the command of Antonio Lopez de
Santa Anna was sighted, and the Americans, with their women and children, retired to the Alamo. The defenders—
approximately 180 men—withstood the
siege and bombardment for twelve days,
but at dawn on March 6, Santa Anna
mounted his final attack, and by nightfall, the fortress was his. None of the
women or children was harmed and
Santa Anna allowed them safe conduct,
but little quarter was given to the men;
they were killed to the last man, and their
bodies thrown onto a funeral pyre.

Below is a list of the known dead, with
place of birth given where possible.

Lieutenant Colonel Commanders:
Bowie, J. (Georgia); Travis, J. B. . . .
Aide-de-camp: Despalier, C. . . . Colo-
nels: Washington, J. (Tennessee) . . .
Captains: Baker, W. C. M. (Missouri);
Blair, S. C. (Texas); Blazeby, W. (Loui-
siana); Bonham, J. B. (South Carolina);
Carey, W. R. (Texas); Evans, S. B.
(Missouri); Forsyth, — (New York);
Gilmore, — (Tennessee); Harrison, —
(Tennessee) . . . Adjutant: Baugh, I. G.

. . . Quartermasters: Anderson, —;
Burnell, —; Melton, E. . . . Lieuten-
ants: Dickinson, A. (Louisiana); Jones,
J.; Kimball, G. C. (Texas) . . . Master
of Ordnance: Evans, R. (Ireland) . . .
Sergeant Major: Williamson, — . . .
Surgeons: Michison, D.; Pollard, A.;
Thompson, — . . . Ensign: Jameson,
J. B. . . . Privates: Autry, M.; Baker,
J. (Texas); Ballantine, R. W.; Blair, J.;
Bourne, D. (England); Brown, —;
Burns, S. (Ireland); Butler, — (New
Orleans); Cochran, —; Cottle, G. W.
(Texas); Crockett, D. (Tennessee);
Crossman, R.; Cummings, W. (Penn-
sylvania); Cunningham, R.; Davis, J.
(Texas); Dimkin, R. (England); Dunst,
J. (Texas); Ewing, J. L.; Fishback, W.
(Texas); Fuhbaigh, W. (Texas); Gar-
rett, I. G. (New Orleans); Halloway, S.;
Harris, — (Kentucky); Harris, J.
(Texas); Hawkins, — (Ireland); Hays,
J. M. (Texas); Howell, D. W. (New
Orleans); Huskell, C.; Hutchinson, —;
Ingram, — (England); Jackson, T.
(Ireland); Jackson, T. (Texas); Johnson,
L. (Texas); Johnson, W. (Pennsylvania);
Kent, A. (Texas); Kent, D. (Texas);
Kiddeson, —; King, J. G. (Texas); King,
W. (Texas); Lewis, W. T. (Wales); Linn,
W. (Massachusetts); Martin, A. (Texas);
McCoy, J. (Texas); McGregor, —
(Scotland); Miller, T. R. (Texas); Mil-
saps, I. (Texas); Mitchell, E. T.
(Georgia); Moore, R. B.; Muselman, R.
(New Orleans); Negging, G. (South
Carolina); Nelson, — (Texas); Nelson,
E. (South Carolina); Parker, C. (Mis-
sissippi); Robinson, — (Scotland);
Rose, — (Texas); Rusk, —; Ryan, —
(Louisiana); Sewell, M. L. (Texas);
Simpson, W. K.; Smith, C.; Starr, R.
(England); Stuart, —; Summers, W. F.
(Texas); Sutherland, W. D. (Texas);
Thomas, R. A. M. (Texas); Thurston,
— (Kentucky); Tumlinson, G.; Valen-

---

[1] A colloquialism derived from the fact that an elite company known as "la compañia
volante del Alamo de Parras" occupied the building for a considerable period.

tine, ——; Ward, D. (Texas); Wells, W. (Tennessee); White, I.; White, R. (Texas); Wilson, D. (Texas); Wright, C. (Texas); Zanco, D. (Denmark) . . . Clerk: John, ——.

The walls and buildings of the fortress no longer remain, but the ruins of the church are still preserved as a National Monument.

ALASKA Not exactly a Wild West state, but as it got a fair share of colorful characters from the western states, when gold was discovered in its Klondike region in the 1890s, it is included here. Originally a Russian fur trading outpost until the Russians sold it to the United States in 1867 for $7,200,000, it became the forty-ninth state, and the largest, in 1958. The Alaskan Highway, a ribbon of highway that passes through Alberta, British Columbia, and Yukon Territory, links it with the rest of the continental United States. The capital is Juneau.

ALDER GULCH Gold was discovered in this area on May 20, 1863, and the inevitable rush started. On June 7 of that same year, land was claimed for a townsite, and by 1864 the town—Virginia City, Montana—was a rip-roaring gold camp with a high rate of homicide. (See BEIDLER, JOHN XAVIER; PLUMMER, HENRY; and VIGILANTES OF MONTANA.)

ALGONKIN Name of an American Indian language group. Western tribes in this family include Arapaho, Blackfoot, Cheyenne, Gros Ventre, and Plains Cree.

ALLEN, CHARLIE A miner who was murdered by shotgun while camping in the Bitterroot Mountains of Idaho in October 1863. His killers were brought to justice and hanged on March 4, 1864. (See MAGRUDER, LLOYD.)

ALLENTOWN, OREGON
Gold camp of southwestern Oregon established in the early 1850s. Never achieved anything more than camp status and no longer survives as a "ghost."

ALLIN-SPRINGFIELD RIFLE A .50-caliber breech-loading rifle. The first guns of this type to reach troops in Indian Territory arrived at Fort Kearney, Nebraska, in June 1867, when Red Cloud and his Sioux were on the warpath, and there were 700 rifles and 100,000 rounds of ammunition in the consignment. Until this time the troops had been using muzzle-loaders, which took some time to reload, and it was undoubtedly the rapid fire of the new rifles that saved the day at the Wagon-box fight on August 2, 1867. (See WAGON-BOX FIGHT.)

ALLISON, CLAY Ranch owner, alcoholic, and a neurotic psychopath of the worst order, whose least objectionable habit was to strip himself naked, thunder up and down the street on his white horse, and then invite the dumfounded residents into the nearest saloon for a drink. That's the sunny side of the man. Not so funny: a duel to the death with bowie knives in a freshly dug grave—a duel that Clay won, but a wound from the fight left him with a lifelong limp. Even so, he didn't impress Wyatt Earp, who on a summer morning of 1877 at Dodge City, Kansas, cleared his Buntline Special faster than Clay could draw his piece, and forthwith ordered him from the town limits. Others were not so lucky. In Cimarron, New Mexico (Clay's home ground), Clay shot town marshal Pancho out of office when the latter tried to talk him out of shooting out the lights in Hank Lambert's saloon. Yet another marshal, Charlie Faber, got a slug through the heart after requesting Clay and his brother to remove their hardware—not an unnatural request, for they were at a dance at Las Animas, New Mexico, at the time.

In a lighter vein (for the reader, not the victim), there is the story of the dentist who in error extracted a wrong tooth from Mr. Allison's wolfish jaw, and of how Clay trussed the luckless dentist to the chair and in retaliation removed three of the unfortunate man's teeth without resorting to the use of anesthetics. The number of notches Clay was alleged to have in his gun butts varies between fifteen and twenty-one, yet he didn't live to become a notch on anyone else's pistol, as is the usual case with characters of his type. Mr. Allison had a most unnatural-natural demise; returning to his ranch in his buckboard, he fell from the wagon and the rear wheels broke his neck. This last incident occurred on a July day in 1877. He was thirty-seven years old at the time, and some say gloriously drunk, which, if correct, possibly makes him the first drunken driver to hit the headlines, for the local sheet gave him an unearned send-off. The editor may have had his tongue in cheek at the time, for he wrote: "Clay Allison knew no fear. To incur his enmity was the equivalent of a death sentence. He contended that he never killed a man willingly but only out of necessity." (See COLBERT, CHUNK.)

ALLMAN, JOHN   Former U.S. cavalryman of Tennessee extraction who went on one of the West's worst killing sprees in the summer of 1877. It started over a poker game in the cavalry barracks at Prescott, Arizona, when, to emphasize his argument, Allman shot two sergeants dead. He escaped after killing Dave Groat and Bill Epps, two members of the posse that was hard at his heels. While on the run, Allman killed two woodcutters. This was in August 1877, and two weeks later he walked into a Yuma saloon; killed Vince Dundee, the bartender; and

made off with the cashbox takings and as many bottles of whiskey as he could carry. Shortly afterward, Deputy Sheriff Ed Roberts saw Allman in a Williams, Arizona, saloon, and went to make an arrest. It was the deputy's last earthly and official act, and Allman fled from the drinking den with pistol smoking. Too many lawmen were biting the dust, so Sheriff Ullman of Coconino County called in a few fast guns who called themselves "Outlaw Exterminators, Inc.," deputized them forthwith, and told them to get on with it. Allman's sand was running out now, but over the next few weeks he endeavored to live up to his reputation. Thomas B. Dowling, a sheepherder, was killed for his gun and ammunition; thirteen-year-old Ida Phengle and a twelve-year-old Hopi girl were kidnaped for whatever they had to offer—some say Allman "liked 'em young." The girls were released after the killer had taken what they had to offer (some say it was rape), and now Allman had a Hopi war party at his heels. But Allman was not to be scalped or emasculated, for Clay Calhoun of Outlaw Exterminators beat the Hopi to the quarry. Calhoun came upon Allman on October 11, 1877, and the old Indian cliff dwellings in which the outlaw had taken refuge echoed to the roar of Colt revolvers. Calhoun brought the body of Allman back into Holbrook, Arizona, the following day. The corpse had four bullet holes: groin, stomach, chest, and mouth, all in perfect alignment. Calhoun is reported to have said, "liquor and women got Allman," but we think it was those neatly spaced holes. (See OUTLAW EXTERMINATORS.)

ALTA, UTAH   A small mining town at the foot of the Rustler Mountains of Utah. In its heyday (the early 1870s) Alta possessed twenty-six saloons and possibly the largest cemetery in the West for a town of its size—the latter having more than a hundred gun-law victims within its precincts. In 1873 a stranger to the town promised to resurrect all Alta's dead for a not exorbitant fee, but after carefully considering the offer the townies turned it down and instead gave the stranger a community collection totaling $2,500 on his undertaking to leave Alta for all time. The town is now naught but a ghost.

ALVORD, BURT   Deputy sheriff of Cochise County, Arizona, who in the 1890s teamed up with another deputy named Billie Stiles and formed the Alvord-Stiles gang. In 1899 Alvord became a constable at Willcox, Arizona, and under this respectable cover he and Stiles organized several holdups. These two phony lawmen, together with other members of their gang, were captured after their holdup and robbery of a Southern Pacific train near Cochise on September 9, 1899. In jail, Stiles obtained privileges by ratting on his buddies, but he put these privileges to the common good by turning the tables on their jailers and releasing Alvord and the remainder of the gang. Stiles drifted to Nevada after the jailbreak, but Alvord formed a new gang and made an attempt to rob the El Paso–Southwestern train at Fairbanks, Arizona. Unfortunately for the bandits, Sheriff Dell Lewis happened to be in the vicinity, and although the gang escaped, one of its members was seen to be hit in the gunfight that ensued. Burt Alvord became either a corpse or a will-o'-the-wisp after this last recorded holdup by the gang. A decomposed body was found shortly afterward, and it is reported that it was identified as Alvord. Other reports, however, placed him in Latin America, Jamaica, and other points south.

AMERICAN EXPRESS COMPANY   In 1850 three competing express and banking companies—Livingstone and Fargo; Wells & Company; and Butterfield, Wasson & Company—merged and became known as the American Express Company. At this time the foremost people in the banking-express business were Adams and Co., a firm that was skimming the cream from the California gold fields; in 1852, to compete with this firm, the American Express Company formed a subsidiary company, Wells Fargo & Company. This offspring established itself in California the same year, and in 1855, after a run on the San Francisco banks, it expanded until it was without serious rival. Further mergers and takeovers occurred until the American Express Company had fingers in most of the bullion-filled pies of the continent. The American Express Company's business has continued uninterrupted to the present day. It runs an armored car service in New York, and to own an American Express credit card is to possess one of the foremost contemporary status symbols. (See ADAMS & COMPANY; BUTTERFIELD OVERLAND MAIL COMPANY; PACIFIC UNION EXPRESS; PONY EXPRESS; and WELLS FARGO & COMPANY.)

AMERICAN FUR COMPANY   Organized in 1808 by John Jacob Astor, the company traded for pelts with both buckskinned trapper and Indian alike. Their original headquarters was directly across the Minnesota from Fort Snelling (an Army fort built in the V formed by the junction of the Minnesota and Mississippi rivers), but a few years later the firm had trading posts in Oregon, and in 1849, when Fort Laramie was built in Wyoming Territory, field operations were started in that area. The executive head of the company was Ramsay Crooks, and its chief buyer was Kenneth McKenzie, "King of the Missouri." Of the trappers who owed loyalty to the company the more notable were Jim Beckwourth, Lucien Fonatelle, and Étienne Provost.

AMERICAN HORSE
The white man's name for Wasechuntashunka, an Oglala Sioux chief who fought many engagements with the U.S. military in the Montana-Wyoming areas. His last battle occurred on September 9, 1876, when his camp[2] was attacked by Captain Anson Mills and a force of two hundred men. The Indians surrendered when their chief was wounded and their ammunition almost gone. American Horse had a severe abdominal wound, and he died that night in the camp of his enemies.

AMERINDS   A contraction of "American Indians" (corny, but no doubt very scholarly).

AMOS, FRED   A California road agent who was tried and convicted for stage robbery. On hearing his sentence he requested that Judge King play him a game of seven-up, double or nothing. The request was granted, but it wasn't Fred's day; he lost and got twenty years in San Quentin, instead of the ten the judge had originally passed down. Not much of a biography? Agreed, but you can't have much when you get twenty years.

ANDERSON, "BLOODY" BILL
The most vicious of Quantrill's guerrilla leaders. In 1862, when Bill was twenty-two years old, the Anderson family—father, two brothers, three sisters, and an uncle—were running a small farm at Aubrey, Kansas. On March 7 of that year Quantrill raided the town, an act that brought Union troops into the area, and four days later Bill's father and uncle were hanged as Confederate sympathiz-

ers. Bill dropped his manure fork, or whatever, and rode out to join Quantrill, a notorious character who plundered, murdered, and raped in the name of the Confederacy. In 1863 Anderson's three sisters were placed under arrest by General Ewing of the Union Army, who suspected them of spying for the rebel cause. The prison they were confined in collapsed, and one of the girls was killed,[3] a tragedy that is sometimes given (rather belatedly, one might think, as Bill was well blooded before this time) as the spark that ignited the killer's blood lust. Anderson took part in the Lawrence, Kansas, massacre of 1863, and the band under his command is believed to have killed more people on that day than any of the other columns under Quantrill. Bloody Bill became hostile to Quantrill in that same year, and Anderson was in complete command of the murderous band that looted Centralia on September 27, 1864. Male prisoners were stripped and shot out of hand. This stripping was evidently done for ignominious rather than sodomistic reasons, for female prisoners are known to have been disrobed for more practical purposes. In the latter half of 1864 Bloody Bill and his band held up and looted a train, but the sand was running out now, and on October 27, 1864, Anderson was shot dead by Union troops. After his death it is alleged that a pair of women's scalps were found attached to his horse's bridle, while it is known that a silken scarf bearing fifty-three knots was taken from the pocket of his buckskins. The scarf is believed to have belonged to one of his sisters, and the knots are said to have been a record of Bloody Bill's personal score of victims since the jail incident of 1863. (See LAWRENCE MASSACRE and QUANTRILL, WILLIAM CLARKE.)

---

[2] Located at Slim Buttes, South Dakota.
[3] Of the three girls, Jenny, Mary, and Josephine, it was the latter who died. After this tragedy, Jim Anderson, the younger brother, joined Bloody Bill's band.

ANDREWS, JESSE   Better known, and gone down in history under the alias of "Buckshot" Bill Roberts. Andrews was a small man, a mere 5 feet, 4 inches in height, and he didn't weigh more than 112 pounds with his gunbelt strapped on. He had long years in the Regular Army as a first sergeant, during which period he saw service in both the Civil War and the Indian campaigns, yet he is remembered mainly as a victim of the Lincoln County, New Mexico, War. He arrived in Lincoln County from Texas (where a buckshot wound received while serving in the Texas Rangers had rendered his left arm partially useless), and he had built up a small ranch in the Ruidosa Valley by the time the shooting started. Andrews was friendly with Major Murphy, a leader of one of the warring factions, but although it is recorded that an Andrew Roberts ("Buckshot" was a man of many names) rode with the posse that murdered J. H. Tunstall (an Englishman who was Murphy's most serious business rival), the little ex-soldier professed neutrality. Neutrals were evidently suspected in those warring days, for when "Buckshot" paid a visit to Doc Blazer on April 4, 1878, and a gang of anti-Murphy men, led by Dick Brewer and including Billy the Kid, happened to be hanging around Blazer's premises, little cordiality appears to have been shown. Charlie Bowdre shot the new arrival in the stomach, a mortal wound, yet "Buckshot" worked his Winchester from the hip—the only way he could fire the weapon—to good effect. He shot Jack Middleton through the lung, blasted a finger from George Coe's hand, and had the rifle barrel rammed into Billy the Kid's stomach when it misfired. Andrews tossed the gun down and staggered into the building, where he found a .50-caliber buffalo gun, which he used to blow off the top of Dick Brewer's head. The gang had had enough, and when they withdrew, Doc Blazer sent for a surgeon to tend the dying Andrews. But a burial detail would have done instead, for the little fighting man died thirty-six hours later, and Doc Blazer had both him and Brewer buried behind his premises.

ANGEL, PAULA   Hanged by the vigilantes in New Mexico for murder. As far as we can ascertain, Paula, Cattle Kate, and a girl named Juanita were the only women to suffer hanging at the hands of vigilante bands. (See JUANITA and WATSON, ELLA.)

ANGELS CAMP   Multiracial mining camp born of the 1849 Gold Rush. Named after a miner named George Angel. It was sited, among a rash of other such settlements, in Calveras County, California, an area plagued by roving bands of Mexican outlaws during the early 1850s. Mainly of interest as being the site of Mark Twain's famous Jumping Frog story. (See MURIETA, JOAQUIN.)

ANTELOPE   Hollow-horned hoofed mammal, a subfamily of which exists in the American West. (See PRONGHORN.)

ANTRIM, CATHERINE   Wife of William H. Antrim. Catherine's early life is vague, but it is known that she was born in Ireland, spent some years in New York before moving West, and was a widow with two teen-age sons when Antrim married her. In the Santa Fe, New Mexico, *Book of Marriages,* the date of her second marriage is given as March 1, 1873, when she gave her name as Catherine McCarty. Her two sons acted as witnesses, and their names are given as Henry McCarty and Joe McCarty. Henry, the younger of the two, was later to become known as "Billy the Kid." Shortly after the marriage, Antrim left Santa Fe with his bride and stepsons and the family settled in Silver City, a mining community in the southwestern corner of the territory, and it was here that Catherine contracted what was known in those days as "galloping consumption." She was bedridden for months and died on Thursday, September 16, 1875, when she was in her thirty-fourth year. (See ANTRIM, WILLIAM H.)

ANTRIM, "KID" One of the many names under which the little killer known as "Billy the Kid" masqueraded. (See McCARTY, HENRY.)

ANTRIM, WILLIAM H. An Indiana man who was born at Huntsville on December 1, 1842. He joined the 54th Regiment of Volunteers when he was nineteen, but although the Civil War was in progress, he saw no active service, and he was honorably discharged a few months after his enlistment. Most of his adult life was spent as a miner, operating in the Silver City–Georgetown areas of New Mexico. Antrim married when he was twenty-nine, but was a widower within eighteen months. The latter years of his life were spent with relatives in California. (See ANTRIM, CATHERINE.)

APACHE INDIANS More than nine hundred years ago, nomadic bands, of possibly Asian origin, filtered from the far North of what is now the continental United States and settled in the Southwest and in northern Mexico. The Spaniards named these people "Apaches," and at that period the Navahos were included in this all-embracing name.[4] The main tribes were the Chiricahua, Jicarilla, Mescalero, San Carlos, White Mountain, and Kiowa-Apache, and of these only the last mentioned was a plains tribe. The others roamed the arid desert lands of Arizona and New Mexico, farming oc-

casionally and committing armed robbery ceaselessly, although it must be noted that "armed robbery" was the white man's name for their depredations; to the Apache, it was a normal mode of life. They are recorded as sometimes living in pueblos, but their nomadic existence made the wickeyup (similar to an inverted bird's nest and composed of like materials) more suitable, as it could be considered expendable when they decided to move on. The Apache were numerically inferior to the great plains tribes to the north, yet they caused the white man relatively more trouble, and for every Apache who fell in the wars and skirmishes of the 1800s, two soldiers lost their lives. It was not until 1886 that they were finally subdued and confined to the various reservations in Arizona and New Mexico. (See CHATO; CHIRICAHUA APACHE; COCHISE; GERONIMO; JICARILLA APACHE; KIOWA-APACHE INDIANS; MANGAS COLORADO; MESCALERO APACHES; NATCHEZ; NANA; SAN CARLOS APACHE; VICTORIO; and WHITE MOUNTAIN APACHE.)

APACHE KID A sergeant of Apache scouts based on the San Carlos Agency and under the command of Al Sieber. When the kid was twenty years old his father was murdered, and under Apache law the Kid was expected to avenge the killing. This he did, and he was arrested for murder, but he was acquitted. Disgusted with the verdict, the local Indian-haters had the Kid rearrested together with seven other Apaches on the charge of murdering a whiskey peddler. The Apaches denied the charge—which may have been trumped up—but were found guilty and sentenced to eight years apiece, and on November 1, 1889, they found themselves bound for Yuma Penitentiary under the escort of Sheriff Glen Reynolds and his deputy, W. H. "Hunky

[4] Apache de Nabaju.

Dory" Holmes. Things didn't go hunky-dory for the lawmen, for en route to the prison they were overpowered and shot dead, and their prisoners escaped. Seven of the renegades were soon recaptured, but the Kid was, from thence onward, to remain at liberty, and for the next five years he left a bloody trail across the territory. Utterly ruthless, even for an Apache, he took countless squaws and cut their throats when he grew tired of them, while the number of prospectors he murdered, or white girls he abducted, raped, and killed will never be satisfactorily established. The reign of terror ceased in 1894, and many let it be known that it was their unerring aim that had brought about this peaceful state of affairs, but as there was a five-thousand-dollar reward on his head (literally) at the time, and no one brought this trophy forward, most of these claims can be written off as groundless. Only one such claim is worthy of mention here. A prospector, Edward A. "Walapai" Clark (a man whose partner, Bill Diehl, had been killed by the Kid in 1889), one night spotted an Apache trying to steal his mare. Clark fired his Winchester, and the Indian lurched off into the darkness. The next morning the prospector followed a trail of crimson spots into the desert and found a bloodstained headcloth, such as are worn by Apaches, but there was no sign of a body. We could accept this as the authentic full stop to the Kid's career, for he may have found some almost inaccessible spot in which to die, but unfortunately for this belief, the Kid is reported to have been seen and spoken to in Mexico many years later.

APACHE PASS   A narrow defile that runs through the Chiricahua Mountains in the southeastern corner of Arizona. Originally named Puerto del Dado (Doorway of Dice), the pass was the scene of a wagon-train massacre and numerous skirmishes between the U.S. military and the Indians. (See BATTLE AT APACHE PASS.)

APPALOOSA   A breed of horse originally developed by the Palouse Indians of Idaho and eastern Washington; hence the breed is variously referred to as Palousian or Appalousian as well as by the more common Appaloosa. Later the breeding was taken over by the Nez Percé Indians, who used them for war and ceremonial purposes, the natural decorative quality of the horse making it ideal for the latter use. Appaloosas are white with a sprinkling of black or occasionally brown, irregular spots—markings that, oddly enough, can be felt with the hand. They average 4 feet, 10 inches in height, weigh anywhere from 800 to 1,000 pounds, and are frequently seen in the circus ring.

ARAMBULA, JOSÉ FRANCISCO VILLA   Mexican general and revolutionary who crossed the Mexico–United States border with several hundred troops on March 9, 1916, and raided the town of Columbus, New Mexico. A battle between Villa's forces and 250 U. S. Cavalrymen who were stationed in the town raged for a short time, and then the raiders returned to Mexico, but not before many buildings were in flames and seven U.S. soldiers and eight townspeople had been killed. An expedition consisting of three cavalry columns (one of which was the 7th, of Custer fame) under the command of General John J. Pershing pursued the Villistas into Mexico, and although they failed to capture Villa, they scattered his armies and shattered his power. In 1923 Pancho Villa was assassinated by a gang of his fellow countrymen, and on September 13 of the same year, Jesus Salas Barraza was sentenced to twenty years' imprisonment for his part in the killing.

ARAPAHO INDIANS   A tribe of buffalo-hunting plains Indians who were allied to the Sioux and Cheyenne. In the 1600s they were located in what is now northern Montana, but by the 1800s they had worked their way south, and their tepees were scattered over western Kansas and eastern Colorado. The Arapaho were a fighting tribe, and apart from many minor raids against the whites, they took part in two of the major U. S. Cavalry–Indian engagements: the Fetterman fight and the Battle of the Little Big Horn. Their dress was typical of the plains tribes: buckskins embellished with beadwork and porcupine quills, a chest protector made of dozens of the latter frequently being used as body armor. The Arapaho and their allies, the southern Cheyenne, were finally settled in Oklahoma.

ARBUCKLE, HENRY The only man on record as having used a train to rout an Apache war party. Arbuckle, an engineer, won an old 0-4-0-type engine named "Little Emma" in 1882 in a Fourth of July crap game at Pueblo, Colorado. Showing great enterprise, he had Little Emma freighted to the copper mining area of Clifton, Arizona, where he used her to haul ore for the Lazensky Company. It was in 1884, and during one of these hauls, that Arbuckle sighted a large war party of Apaches filing through a narrow cut through which the train had to pass. Arbuckle lashed open the throttle and plowed into the Indians before they could escape from the steep-sided defile. It was a complete rout, and if the Indians had been intent on raiding Clifton, Little Emma most certainly saved the day. That it was a war party, there can be little doubt, for on arriving at Clifton the engine was found to be smeared with war paint as well as other, more gruesome, reminders of its charge.

ARIKARA INDIANS Also known as Arikaree, Rickaree, and Ree Indians, and sometimes called "Corn Eaters." They are an offshoot of the Pawnees, and from 1650 to the late 1800s they were located in the Dakota area, although there is evidence that some elements of the tribe traveled far South during the 1700s, for the tribe had guns by 1773, which the aforementioned wanderers had evidently bartered from the white men (possibly Spaniards) somewhere on their travels. The Sioux were their deadliest enemies, and as the Arikara were a minority tribe, in 1850, they formed a defensive alliance with the Hidasta and Mandan tribes. It was possibly this hatred of the Sioux that made the Arikara eager to assist the white men in their campaigns against such Sioux chiefs as Red Cloud and Sitting Bull. The Arikara served as scouts in the U. S. Army, and fifty of their number accompanied Custer on his fateful march into the Big Horn country in 1876. The Arikara lived in dome-shaped earth lodges, and wore the usual fringed buckskins and buffalo robes of the plains tribes. Today they have small holdings in Montana, and their numbers are reduced to a few hundred.

ARIKAREE INDIANS (See ARIKARA INDIANS.)

ARIZONA Southwestern state known as the Apache State. It covers an area of 113,909 square miles, and in its northern half are such scenic wonders as the Painted Desert, the Petrified Forest, and the Grand Canyon of the Colorado. Originally it was Mexican territory; most of it was ceded to the United States in 1848, with the Godsden Purchase added in 1853. It remained a territory, and was the "last frontier," until 1912, when it became the forty-eighth state. Fifty-five thousand of its first settlers—Apaches, Hopis, and Navahos—still reside within its boundaries. Phoenix is the state capital.

ARIZONA CATTLE COMPANY
Known as the A. L. Bar outfit; brand *AL*. It was founded in 1883 by John W. Young, a son of the Mormon leader, and was one of the largest spreads in Arizona. The main ranch buildings were at Fort Rickerson (about ten miles north of Flagstaff), and its cattle ranged over an area of more than eight hundred square miles. The company went out of business in 1899. (See PLEASANT VALLEY WAR.)

ARIZONA RANGERS   A body of men formed by Captain Burton C. Mossman to combat lawlessness in the territory. They were organized in 1901, the pay was $120 a month, and the force consisted of fourteen men. The Rangers were disbanded in 1910. (See MOSSMAN, BURTON C.)

ARIZONA STATE PRISON
The Territorial Prison at Yuma, which after 1912 became the State Penitentiary. (See YUMA PENITENTIARY.)

ARKANSAS   Absorbed into the United States in 1803 as part of the Louisiana Purchase, it became the twenty-fifth state in 1836. Country of the illicit still (the "likker's" been known to make eyeballs bleed—ugh) and all that doggone feudin'. It covers an area of 53,102 square miles and is referred to as the Bear State or the Wonder State. Little Rock is the capital. Please note that the last syllable, "sas," rhymes with "paw."

ARKANSAS TOM   Alias of a member of the Doolin-Dalton gang. (See DAUGHERTY, ROY.)

ARKANSAS TOOTHPICK
A stiletto-type dagger that got its name from the fact that hillbillies usually favored this kind of weapon.

ARMADILLO   A small, armored mammal, which in the United States was confined to southern Texas until the present century. This fast-burrowing little animal's diet usually consists of insects, and almost invariably the female gives birth to quadruplets, which are always of the same sex. In the Southwest baskets are made from their shells and sold as curios.

ARMITAS   The name means "short leg-armor," and they were a type of chaparreras (chaps) that were both short in length (just below the knee) and light in weight. They were at one time popular on the warmer cattle ranges of California and Nevada. Sometimes known as "chinks."

ARNOLD, PHILIP   A prospector who together with John Slack, a fellow prospector, succeeded in pulling off one of the greatest hoaxes in the West. With money accrued from a successful mining deal, Arnold visited Europe and purchased fifty thousand dollars' worth of precious stones from Amsterdam; on his return to the States he and Slack "salted" a barren area of Wyoming with the stones. By subtle underacting they allowed stories of their "find" to "leak" out, and were finally persuaded to allow independent observers to see the field after stipulating that these observers be led to their find blindfolded. Rubies and sapphires as well as diamonds were found in great numbers, and then everyone wanted to get in on the deal. "Everyone" · included such notably shrewd characters as Baron Rothschild and Astbury Harpenden of London, England, and Arnold and Slack "reluctantly" accepted six hundred thousand dollars for a two thirds share in their find. The bubble burst when an astute geologist realized that the stones had already been worked by hand. Efforts were made to recover the six hundred thousand dollars but they were unsuccessful, so the investors gave hollow laughs and wrote it off to experience. It is quite likely that a few stones still remain in that "salted" area of Wyoming.

ARONDONDO, PEDRO
Gambler and cardslick who traveled the Colorado circuit in the 1800s. In the summer of 1889, in Canon City, Colorado, a cowboy named Red Ivan accused him of stacking the deck, and as such talk—whether true or false—was regarded as "fightin' words" in that time and place, the inevitable gunfight occurred three days later, when Arondondo's and Ivan's tempers had been fanned to killing pitch by the locals, who were no doubt eager to see some action. It was a routine shootout, and Pedro was sent on his way with a bullet between his eyes. Not so routine were Pedro's actions over the forty-eight hours preceding his dramatic demise. During this period, and after consulting his tarot cards, he had bought an off-the-peg black suit and ordered a neat headstone with a chiseled inscription. The cards must have been an honest set, for the finished stone was ready for delivery some hours before it was needed, and the inscription read: *"Pedro Arondondo, born 1857—died 1889, from a bullet wound between the eyes fired by Red Ivan."*

ARROYO A dried-out streambed found in desert areas. An arroyo becomes a watercourse after heavy rains, but the water rapidly subsides, and the temporary riverbed dries out and becomes an arroyo once again. The term, which is Spanish, is used mainly in the southwestern states.

ASSINIBOINE INDIANS A Siouian tribe of buffalo-hunting Indians who kept relatively to the same area—west and northwest of Lake Superior—from 1650 until the 1800s. George Catlin, who visited the Tribe in the early nineteenth century, described them as "tall, graceful in their movements; and wear their pictured robes of buffalo hide to good effect." Catlin also stated that they wore their hair to a very great length, but that the length was produced by gluing additional switches and was not necessarily the owner's own growth.[5] The Assiniboine were tepee dwellers, and they cooked their meat by dropping heated stones into water; their name, given to them by the French, is derived from this practice and literally means "stone boilers," although on occasion some writers have translated the name into "pot boilers"—an error that may have given rise to the report that the tribe members were cannibals at one time.

ASTOR, JOHN JACOB A German who was born near Heidelberg on July 17, 1763. He arrived in New York City in 1783, penniless but enterprising, and by 1808 he had accumulated sufficient capital to organize the American Fur Company. A few years later his trading posts were firmly established across the continent and he became the United States' first recorded millionaire. Expeditions financed by Astor reached into the far Northwest, and his trading headquarters in Oregon became the site of the present-day city of Astoria. His latter years were spent in buying land in New York that became extremely valuable, and he died there in 1848. Not to be confused with his later namesake, who was drowned in the *Titanic* disaster of 1912.

ATCHISON, TOPEKA AND
SANTA FE RAILROAD The second-

[5] This artificial lengthening was practiced by many tribes.

longest railroad in the United States, surpassed only by the Southern Pacific's 13,656 miles of track. Work started on the railroad on October 30, 1868, at Topeka (Atchison, oddly enough, was ignored by the company), and on April 26, 1869, the first official train, a "Picnic Special," ran a return trip over the first seven miles of completed track. By September of the year treble this distance had been laid, and seven years later they were on the last lap and battling (gunplay and other skulduggery) with the Denver and Rio Grande over right-of-way through the Raton Pass, the only logical way into New Mexico and so to Santa Fe. The railroad, which had once been referred to as "starting nowhere and going nowhere," had over 12,569 miles of track in 1970. Originally known as the Atchison, Topeka and Santa Fe Railroad, it is now known as the AT and SF Railway, a shortened version of which is Santa Fe Railway.

ATEN, IRA   Joined the Texas Rangers when he was twenty, and during the next six years rose to the rank of captain in Company D of the Frontier Battalion. Over the year 1888–89 he was both a Texas Ranger and sheriff of Fort Bend County. He resigned from the Rangers in the fall of 1889 and spent some time as sheriff of Castro County before becoming manager of the giant XIT Ranch, a position he held for ten years. In the early 1900s he settled in California and invested in property. Aten died at El Centro, California, on August 5, 1953, at the age of ninety-one years.

ATHABASKAN   American Indian language group. Mainly confined to Canada, although the Apache, Hupa, and Navaho belong to this family.

AUDUBON, JOHN JAMES
Artist and naturalist who was born in Haiti and educated in France, and settled in the United States in his late teens. He made hundreds of paintings of American bird life, and these, accompanied by a text he had written, were issued as a four-volume publication by a British publisher. During his travels in search of feathered subjects he met numerous frontier characters, notable among whom was James Bowie. Audubon died in 1851 at the age of sixty-five.

AURORA, NEVADA   A Nevada gold town that was founded in 1860. It had four years of glory, but during this short period its graveyard received sixty-five tenants, half of whom were gunshot victims. By 1864 the gold seams were running out and people began to drift from the town, although some remained and managed to eke an existence from the mines until 1881, when water flooded the shafts (as it did in many other mining areas) and further mining became impossible. The buildings were of stone and brick, but what remained of these was razed by junkmen and vandals in the late 1950s.

AUSTIN, NEVADA   Another Nevada gold town with a similar life cycle to Aurora (see above), although as yet it hasn't completely reverted to the desert, for the International Hotel is still open for visitors. Austin was rather more cultured than many of its contemporaries, and miners' daughters were sent to private schools to be taught French and classical dancing. However, the town possibly wasn't too effete, for as there is no mention of males attending these select establishments, it can only be assumed that effeminate sons were shot out of hand.

AUSTIN, TEXAS   State capital of Texas. Named after Stephen F. Austin (1793–1836), founder of the first American colony in Texas. Austin is located on the Colorado River in eastern Texas, approximately 150 miles WNW of Houston. Main industry is food processing, and the city is an educational and artistic center.

AUZA Mexican general who led an expedition against the Comanche in 1793. It was partially successful, inasmuch as his slaughter of Comanche braves weakened the tribe for some years.

AVERILL, ELLA WATSON A girl who was lynched alongside James Averill. (See WATSON, ELLA.)

AVERILL, JAMES (JACK) In the early 1880s Averill arrived in Carbon County, Wyoming, and settled on the banks of the Sweetwater. Under the Homestead Act this was quite legal (his claim is on record and is dated October 29, 1880), but as he had chosen a site used for grazing by the UT, Bar 11, and Hub and Spoke outfits, the cattle barons didn't take kindly to his arrival. Even so Averill prospered, and by 1882 he was running a saloon-store and was postmaster for the area. Unfortunately, Averill, who was a well-educated man and should have known the meaning of diplomacy, began writing a series of anti-cattlemen letters to the press, and in 1888 he had a onetime girlfriend join him who forthwith set up a comfort station for lonesome cowboys on an adjoining lot. The cattlemen had no quarrel with this range bagnio (they were a broad-minded lot in minor matters), but when their cowboys got to trading company cattle for favors rendered they saw red, and in July 1889 eleven cattlemen paid a visit to the Averill supermarket. Averill and the girl were taken to a group of cottonwoods and lynched forthwith. There were five witnesses to this atrocity:

a fourteen-year-old invalid boy named Gene Crowther; three adult settlers—Frank Buchanan, Bob DeCory, and Ralph Cole; and the younger son of Averill and the girl. Of these, DeCory and Cole disappeared without a trace. Crowther died in the home of one of the cattlemen, and the child was shot and left for dead. Only Buchanan survived unscathed, and he left the country. (See AVERILL, TOM; CROWTHER, GENE; JOHNSON COUNTY WAR; and WATSON, ELLA.)

AVERILL, TOM Son of James Averill and Ella Watson, who, as he was five years old at the time of the lynching of his parents, must have been born some four years prior to their reunion on the Sweetwater. After the lynching, the child was taken to an abandoned dugout, chained to a stump, and shot in the neck. Luckily he was found by a band of Sioux, who took him to Pine Ridge Reservation, where he recovered and was reared to manhood as the adopted son of Chief Iron Tail. Tom joined the Buffalo Bill Wild West Show in 1896 when he was twelve, and he toured Europe with the show in 1899. He left the show in that year, and by 1900 he had managed to join the U. S. Army and was stationed in China with the 14th Infantry during the Boxer uprising. On leaving the forces he became a rodeo cowboy and was touring the shows for many years. Tom Averill was still alive and well in the late 1950s when he was writing factual articles for *True West* magazine under the name of Buffalo Vernon, and we are indebted to him (and the magazine), for the major portions of this entry were adapted from his writings. (See AVERILL, JAMES, and WATSON, ELLA.)

AZTEC LAND & CATTLE COMPANY Organized between 1883 and

1884, with headquarters on the Little Colorado River near St. Joseph. It was known as the Hash Knife outfit, and was one of the most famous spreads in Arizona Territory. In its heyday it possessed over eighty thousand head of cattle. The company failed about 1900, but its brand ⏄ lived on until around 1910. (See PLEASANT VALLEY WAR.)

FREDERIC REMINGTON

BACA, ELFEGO A Latin American who most certainly bore a charmed life. Baca was born in 1865 at Socorro, New Mexico, and his first recorded adventure occurred two years later, when he was kidnaped by Apaches who, for some unaccountable reason, returned him unharmed within two days. By the time he was nineteen, and after spending some years as a ranchhand, Baca was sporting an unofficial deputy sheriff badge, and on November 30, 1884, while wearing this tin, he arrested a cowboy in San Francisco, New Mexico, for a breach of the peace. The victim's friends, fellow riders of the Slaughter spread, frowned upon this arrest, and on that same evening they set out to get the "dirty little Mex." Guns were fired, and the cowboy foreman was killed when his horse fell and rolled onto him. This gave the Slaughter men an excuse to hold a drumhead court, which found Baca guilty of murder, and on the following morning eighty armed men, with lynch-ing in mind and under the leadership of an Englishman named Bill French, attacked an ancient cabin wherein the self-appointed deputy had taken refuge. The gunplay started at 9 A.M. and continued until sundown the following day when Elfego was taken into protective custody by his friends. Over this period around four thousand bullets had been poured into the shanty, and fire and dynamite had been used in an attempt to flush Baca, yet he remained unscathed and his guns had accounted for eight victims, three of whom required the professional service of a mortician. Baca was tried twice for the killings and was acquitted each time. The rest is anticlimax, although it would be sufficient for most men. After his acquittal he was elected sheriff of Socorro County, and during this term of office he arrested many a baddy without having to resort to gun-play, for the outlaws were only too will-ing to give themselves up when confronted by a man of Baca's reputation.

Later years saw a little action; he was run down by a fire truck, stabbed by a lunatic, carved by a knife artiste, and survived three automobile wrecks. Over these routine years he had become a lawyer, a profession he was active in until his death in 1949.

BACK JOCKEY A leather flap that is situated behind the cantle of a saddle and rests on the saddle skirt.

BACON, ELIZABETH
Elizabeth (or "Libbie," as she was affectionately known) was born in Monroe, Michigan, in 1842, and as her parents were solid financially, the first twenty-one years of her life were spent in the sheltered world of private school and embroidery circles. On February 12, 1864, Elizabeth married George Armstrong Custer, an extrovert cavalry officer of the Union Army, and for the next twelve years of her life she traveled from fort to fort with her husband. On June 25, 1876, General Custer and his command died violently on the Little Big Horn, and Elizabeth spent the remainder of her life writing and lecturing on frontier Army life. The best-known of her writings is *Boots and Saddles*. Almost fifty-seven years of widowhood were to elapse before Elizabeth, on April 6, 1933, was to be reunited with her husband. (See CUSTER, GEORGE ARMSTRONG.)

BADLANDS Not the place where the bad men go. They are arid regions wrinkled by deep gullies, and are valueless as either farming or pastureland. Badlands occur in quite a few of the western states—the Dakotas, Utah, etc.

BADMAN FROM BODIE A figure used by American mothers to frighten their offspring into line during the latter half of the nineteenth century; small wonder, for he must have been a far more real figure than such mythical figures as bogeymen and such. (See BODIE, CALIFORNIA.)

BAKER, CULLEN M. Sallow-faced Tennessee-born killer whose parents moved to Cass County, Texas, when Cullen was four years old. At sixteen the youth was an underweight, whiskey-drinking gun bully of near-zero literacy. In 1854 he married a young girl named Jane Petty, who at seventeen was a year senior to the gun-happy Baker. In 1858 Cullen shot and killed a man named Bailey, and Baker and his wife and small daughter hurriedly left Texas and settled in Arkansas. His wife died there in 1860, and Cullen dumped his child with a grandparent. Two years later, and after stabbing a man to death in Arkansas, Baker was back in Texas, where, luckily for him, the Bailey incident appears to have been forgiven or forgotten, and in 1862 he married a local lass named Martha Foster. The Civil War was in progress now, and the newly married deadbeat was conscripted into the Confederate Army. During these years of strife our bullyboy appears to have made like a shuttlecock; he deserted the rebel cause, and after killing two Union soldiers at Spanish Bluff, Texas, he joined the Union Army for a short spell before deserting and swelling the ranks of some Confederate irregulars.[1] Twelve months after the war ended, Baker's second wife died, and that same year—after a short but ostentatious period of mourning—he was running his eyes over the no doubt subtly padded curves of a girl named Belle Foster. But Belle, who was no relation to his second wife, didn't deign to

[1] Confederate sympathizers who carried their form of guerrilla warfare into the postwar years. Any "nigger" or "damned Yankee" was, in their opinion, a legitimate target for their guns. Wild Bill Longley was a member of this gang for a short period in 1868.

notice Baker, for all her attentions were confined to a crippled schoolteacher named Thomas Orr. The slim gunman never forgot or forgave this affront to his vanity, and this was to lead to his undoing. In 1867 Orr married Miss Foster, and Baker, probably in an attack of spleen, shot a grocery store owner dead during a petty argument over a bill. Federal troops went out after Baker, but Baker, who was leading a small gang of farm looters at this time, managed to avoid arrest. This was not without bloodshed, for within the next twelve months the wanted man shot dead five soldiers: a captain, a sergeant, and three troopers. Thoughts of Belle were still in Baker's mind, however, and in December 1868, at gunpoint, he dragged Orr from the arms of Belle—dramatically speaking, but nearly accurate—and hanged the schoolteacher from a tree. Luckily for Belle, Orr was found before he expired, and the following January he and three friends caught up with Cullen. Orr and his little posse of honest men were not gunfighters, so they can hardly be blamed for opening up and killing Baker before he had chance to uncork.

BAKER, FRANK Baker, part Cherokee, was a member of the Murphy posse which, under the leadership of Billy Morton, foreman of the Dolan cow outfit, shot down and killed John H. Tunstall, an act that started the bloodletting in the Lincoln County, New Mexico, War. Baker and Morton were run to earth on Tuesday, March 5, 1878, by Dick Brewer and his party of eleven gunnies—all Tunstall men, one of whom was Billy the Kid, and were taken into custody for their part in the slaying. The Brewer party arrived in Roswell, New Mexico, with their captives on Saturday, March 9, and Morton registered a letter with Ash Upson, acting postmaster at the time. At Roswell, Brewer let it be known

that he and his men were taking their prisoners to Lincoln, New Mexico, where they would be charged with the murder of Tunstall. The cavalcade did set out in the general direction of Lincoln, but Baker and Morton were killed en route. The rest is based on the alleged statement of Frank McNab, a member of Brewer's posse who returned to Roswell the following day and had words with Upson. When in the vicinity of Aqua Negra (some twenty miles west of Roswell), Morton snatched a pistol from the holster of one of the posse and shot its owner dead. He and Baker then made a break for it, but they had been allotted slow horses (their mounts had been shot from under them at the time of their arrest), and both men were soon overtaken and killed. Billy the Kid is usually given the credit for the shooting of Baker. (See LINCOLN COUNTY WAR; MCCARTY, HENRY; and UPSON, ASH.)

BAKER, JOE Leader of a small gang of desperadoes who confined their earlier crimes to Texas. Until 1894 the gang consisted of three men: Mr. Baker and two other characters, who were known only as Buck and Six Toes. In that year they were joined by a Texan named Bob Herring, and a short time later, Baker masterminded his biggest job, the stealing of thirty-five thousand dollars in gold. The gang fled to Oklahoma and holed up in the Wichita Mountains, and it was here that the gang began to lose its "togetherness." Joe was "all ag'in'" the newcomer getting a slice of the golden jackpot and planned to shoot Bob Herring and have done with it. Bob, however, got the drop on Baker, Buck, and Six Toes, and after relieving them of all their hardware and horses, he headed North with the gold and more or less all their worldly goods. From then on, Baker and his buddies shared but one obsession: Get Herring. The three men split up, and Baker headed North for Montana, where sometime later he was seen trying to steal a horse. If he'd been walking all that time one is tempted to sympathize, but if Joe sought to use this hard-luck story when caught in the act, the sheepherder to whom the mount belonged couldn't have been too impressed; least, it seems that way, for he shot Joe Baker dead. (See HERRING, ROBERT.)

BAKER MASSACRE Occurred on January 23, 1870, in northwestern Montana, when Colonel Eugene M. Baker, who had been ordered from Fort Shaw to apprehend the killers (Blackfoot Indians) of a white fur trader, came upon a small band of Indians who were camped along the north bank of the Marias River near what was to be the present-day town of Shelby. Baker, who was in command of four detachments of cavalry and a platoon of mounted infantry and who was known to be a "jug a day man," immediately gave the order for an all-out attack on the village; this despite the protests of his civilian scouts, who realized that the camp had been isolated because of an outbreak of smallpox among its inhabitants, mostly the aged and some number of sick children. The village's headman, Chief Heavy Runner, became one of the first victims, and by the time the soldiery had completed their butchery, more than 170 men, women, and children had either been clubbed or shot to death. Well after the infamous event, Colonel Baker was called before a court-martial, where he was completely exonerated of any wrong. Paper justice was satisfied, and as there are no reports of any of Baker's troops coming down with smallpox, it appears that nature also failed to equalize on this occasion.

BALLARD RIFLE
A single-shot breech-loading rifle that was based on the Ballard patent of November 5, 1861. The rifle was manufactured by the Martin Firearms Company and was chambered for .32-, .38-, or .44-caliber cartridges.

BANDANA The cotton, linen—or, occasionally, silk—neckerchief worn by the cowboy. Like most cowboy equipment, it was purely functional, and as it was frequently used as a towel, handkerchief, or sweat rag, it was also known as a "wipe." When worn bandit fashion it protected the rider from trail dust, and when passed over the crown of a hat and tied under the chin it would keep a stetson anchored in high winds or protect the ears from frostbite during winters on the northern ranges.

BANNACK, MONTANA On July 28, 1862, gold was discovered at Grasshopper Creek, and Bannack sprang up almost overnight. The town was utterly lawless, for the local sheriff was the leader of its criminal element, and it is reported that a knifing or a shooting occurred nightly in Cyrus Skinner's saloon. Vigilantes finally resorted to counterviolence until some measure of order was restored. In books you may find Bannack located in Oregon and Idaho as well as Montana, and, while this may be confusing, each location is correct, for territorial boundaries hadn't been firmly established in the early 1860s. In 1862 the town was in Oregon; the following year saw it in Idaho for a short period, while Montana became its permanent residence in 1864, and it became the territorial capital for a time. Most of the town has now returned to the brush, but a few derelict buildings still survive. (See BEIDLER, JOHN XAVIER; PLUMMER, HENRY; and SLADE, JOSEPH A.)

BANNOCK INDIANS
A minority tribe of plains-plateau dwellers

who have been settled in the southern Idaho region for the past three hundred years. The Bannock made buffalo hunting excursions to the Great Plains, but their culture and living standards were inferior to those of the true plains tribes, and buffalo never became their staple diet. Wickeyups were used for shelter, although on occasions earth lodges would be built for winter quarters. Their present home is the Fort Hall Reservation in Idaho.

BANNON, DAVE   Of interest only inasmuch as he became both killer and a corpse within the space of two merging gunshots. The town was Bodie, California, and the setting was a local saloon in September of 1880. Guns were flashed when Bannon got into an argument with a man named Ed Ryan, and powder was burned at such close range that both combatants collapsed to the floor with the holes in their shirts still smoldering.

BANTA, CHARLES ALBERT FRANKLIN   Lawyer and newspaper owner of Arizona's frontier period. Banta, who was born in Warwick County, Indiana, on December 18, 1843, had been a Civil War soldier, muleskinner, and itinerant printer by the time he reached Arizona in 1873. He founded five of the territory's newspapers, and although his life may appear tame when compared with some of his contemporaries, he had at least two brushes with death during his Arizona period: On one occasion he was captured by Apaches and only saved from being burned at the stake by the timely arrival of the U. S. Cavalry, while in 1884 he received a bullet in the neck as a clincher to a political argument. Banta died on June 21, 1924, while an inmate of the Pioneers Home at Prescott, Arizona.

BAPTISTE, JEAN   Born in 1805, the son of Touissant Charbonneau—a French-Canadian fur trapper, guide, and interpreter—and a young Shoshone girl named Sacagawea. William Clark of the Lewis and Clark Expedition financed the child's education, and on completing his schooling at St. Louis, Jean could speak many languages. His middle years followed a similar pattern to those of his father, but by the late 1860s, Jean must have realized that only one of these pursuits was worthy of full-time application, for around that time he settled on the Wind River Reservation with three copper-skinned concubines and an almighty gleam in his eye. (See CHARBONNEAU, TOUISSANT, and SACAGAWEA.)

BARBED WIRE   Invented by Joseph Glidden, an Illinois farmer who made his first length with the aid of a coffee grinder and a grindstone and who was granted a patent on November 24, 1874. Production began in 1875, but it was not until a twenty-five-dollar-a-week salesman named J. W. Gates got into the act and introduced it to the rangeland that sales began to boom. In later years the drummer was known as Bet a Million Gates, and it is not to be wondered at, for the King Ranch alone had fifteen hundred miles of the barbed wire fencing erected. The wire comes in many varieties, one of which incorporates wooden blocks with protruding spikes, and at the present time many collectors are willing to pay two dollars for eight-inch lengths of the rarer types.

BARBER, SUSAN MCSWEEN   Friend of Billy the Kid and heroine of the Lincoln County, New Mexico, War. Susan, together with her husband and the Kid and his gang, withstood a three-day siege when, in July 1878, the McSween home became the focal point of a gun battle between the warring factions. Alexander A. McSween was killed on July 19—the climax of the battle—but over the days previous to this instant widowhood, Susan's periodic piano playing, repetitious renderings of "Home, Sweet Home," could be heard during lulls in the gunfire; courageous recitals with all that lead flying around, and although they failed to "still the savage breast," they must at least have lent a somewhat genteel touch to the whole bloody carnival. Susan eventually remarried and spent the latter years of her life in White Oaks, New Mexico, and although the town is now a ghost town, her headstone can still be found in the local cemetery: "1845, Susan McSween Barber, 1928."[2] (See LINCOLN COUNTY WAR.)

BARNES, SEABORN Born in Tarrant County, Texas, in 1853, Barnes grew up into a tall, scraggy individual with an antipathy toward honest toil. Between lengthy rest periods he tried his hand at cow work and pottery making, but neither of these oddly diverse occupations must have been to his liking, for when he was twenty-four he joined the Sam Bass gang of bank and train robbers. On April 10, 1878, Seaborn was wounded during the Mesquite holdup, and although only flesh wounds, the scars were still fresh when he received his final dose of lead, for Seaborn was shot dead by Texas Rangers at Round Rock, Texas, on July 21, 1878. (See BASS, SAM.)

BARTER, DICK A Britisher who settled in California during the gold boom of 1849 and who became known as "Rattlesnake Dick," after an unsuccessful effort at prospecting in the Rattlesnake Bar area. This failure made Rattlesnake see the light: Why dig for gold when mule trains loaded with the stuff

were threading the mountain trails daily? With the Yreka Mine's eighty-thousand-dollar mule trains in mind as a target, Barter organized a gang and laid his plans. His No. 1 man, Cyrus Skinner, and a gang of lesser lights would attack and loot the train, after which they would rendezvous with Rattlesnake Dick, who would have pack mules waiting to carry the cumbersome wealth to a safe place. The actual robbery went without a hitch, but when Cyrus and his sweating band reached the rendezvous, there was no sign of the man who had masterminded the caper, for the worst of British luck had overtaken Rattlesnake, and he had been tossed into Auburn jail on a charge of mule theft. Skinner buried half the gold, and with lightened loads he and his men hightailed for Folsom and some decent loose living, but although they reached the former, Wells Fargo detectives prevented them from savoring the latter; Skinner was made DOA, and all his men were captured. A short time later Rattlesnake Dick broke jail, and for the next three years he kept himself solvent by committing numerous stage robberies. The end came for this misplaced Britisher in July 1859, when he was shot dead by a posse of lawmen while trying to avoid arrest.

BASSETT, CHARLES E. Friend of the Earps and Bat Masterson, and a leading light in Dodge City, Kansas, law-enforcement circles. Bassett was half owner of the Long Branch Saloon for a short time. In 1877 he was elected sheriff of Ford County, with Bat Masterson as his deputy, but in January of the following year positions were reversed when Bat became sheriff. While holding this office Bassett took on the job of city marshal at a hundred dollars a month, a position that had become vacant when

2 McSween is spelled incorrectly on the tombstone.

Marshal Ed Masterson was shot dead in April 1878. Although Bassett made, or took his part in numerous arrests while serving as a lawman, he never killed a man. In 1883 he was a member of the Dodge City Peace Commission. The manner and date of his death are not known.

BASS, SAM The illiterate leader of the short-lived Sam Bass gang. Sam was born in Lawrence County, Indiana, on July 21, 1851, the youngest of a family of ten children. He left home when he was eighteen, and after a twelve-month stint in a Mississippi mill, he arrived in Denton County, Texas, in 1870. Over the next four years, Bass had several honest jobs, but after buying a sorrel mare in 1874, racing and gambling seem to have gotten into his blood. In 1875 he left his current employment (in the service of county sheriff W. F. Eagan) and devoted his time to running horse races and dallying with the local pinups. That summer he wandered around the Indian Nations (Oklahoma) with his sorrel, and as it was a fast horse, he didn't do too badly. By December of that same year he was cooking up get-rich-quick schemes with a certain Joel Collins in San Antonio, Texas. In August 1876, Bass and Collins placed a 50 per cent deposit on five hundred head of beef steers, and with the help of a man named Jack Davies, they reached northern Kansas with the herd and made a quick sell. This could have been classed as honest toil, but when they failed to settle up with the Texas cattlemen who had let them have the cattle on deposit, their enterprise became little more than a glorified form of rustling. Loaded with *dinero,* the trio arrived in Deadwood, Dakota Territory, and here Collins built himself a house that became the scene of one long orgy. Whiskey fumes filled the air, and lush lovelies filled the beds

until the three men were near insolvent again. There was only one thing such high livers could think of to do, and working on the principle that anything comes cheaper in quantity, they pooled their remaining cash, built a saloon on the premises, and imported a choice selection of hard-bitten prairie flowers; the Collins-Bass-Davies brothel *cum* saloon was ready for business. This red-light emporium has been described as "the most degraded den of infamy that ever cursed the Earth," a sentiment evidently shared by the majority, for it did a roaring trade. The three pimps, however, were guzzling up the bar profits and gambling away the above-decks takings faster than the lucre was rolling in, so, following the suggestion of one of their girls named Maude, they recruited three of the bordello's most regular clients— Bill Heffridge, Jim Berry and Tom Nixon —and as a six-man gang proceeded to knock off a number of stagecoaches. Their holdups were many, and on one occasion a driver was killed, yet they only netted a hundred dollars from this chain of crimes, and it was not until they robbed a Union Pacific train at Big Springs station on September 19, 1877— a robbery that netted them sixty thousand dollars in gold coin—that the gang could be considered "big time."

With ten thousand dollars in each man's saddlebags, the gang split up, and Sam Bass returned to Denton County, where he recruited Henry Underwood and Frank Jackson. This gang pulled two stage robberies before its ranks were reduced to two by the arrest of Underwood, and it was not until Bass built up a heavier mob that he really got back into his stride. On February 24, 1878, Bass, Jackson, new recruit Seaborn Barnes, and others robbed the Houston and Texas Central at Allen station. This robbery was followed in rapid succession by three others: the Houston and Texas at

Hutchins on March 18, the Texas and Pacific at Eagle Ford on April 4, and the Texas and Pacific at Mesquite on April 10. Mesquite was the gang's last job. Wanted fliers had been rolling off the presses for months without interfering with Bass's activities, but now the county sheriffs, Pinkertons, United States marshals, and the Texas Rangers were all putting pressure on the gang, and posses were keeping them forever on the move. Around this time one of the irregulars of the gang turned informer, and when Bass, Barnes, and Jackson arrived in Round Rock on July 21 with a view to robbing the town bank the following day, the lawmen were waiting. The outlaws got off the first shots, and Deputy Sheriff Grimes was killed and Deputy Sheriff Moore wounded by the fusilade, but Barnes was shot dead as he mounted his horse, and although Bass and Jackson got clear of the town, the outlaw leader had a wound in the back that was to prove fatal, and later that day a company of Texas Rangers found him lying under a tree dying. Sam Bass' grave can still be seen at Round Rock, and the "Ballad of Sam Bass" is still a Texas favorite.

BATTLE AT ADOBE WALLS
At dawn on June 27, 1874, more than a thousand Indian horsemen came out of the sun and attacked this small buffalo hunters' settlement in the Texas Panhandle. The attacking force was led by Chief Quanah Parker, and consisted of Kwahadi Comanche, Kiowa, and Cheyenne—a flying wedge of the finest light cavalry the world has ever seen, and had they caught the hunters unprepared, as was their intention, the result would have been a massacre rather than a battle. Unfortunately for the Indians, however, one of the sod buildings had partially collapsed during the night, and

the white men, after being awakened by the noise, had remained up and about, so that on hearing the thunder of hoofs they had grabbed big-fifties and met the initial attack with a barrage of lead. Around thirty men and one woman (a Mrs. Olds, wife of one of the businessmen) were at Adobe Walls at the time. Twenty of these were buffalo hunters, two of whom (Bat Masterson and Billy Dixon) were to leave their marks in western history. Indian attacks were mounted and repulsed for three days until, on the evening of the twenty-ninth, Quanah Parker, who had himself been wounded in the arm, withdrew his forces. The Indians had lost the cream of their mounted warriors in the repeated attacks, while the white men had only three dead on their hands, a couple of brothers named Shadler and another hunter. Aftermath: Two days after Quanah Parker's withdrawal, and possibly during a whiskey-swilling victory celebration, Mrs. Olds became a widow when her husband accidentally shot himself.

BATTLE AT APACHE PASS
A band of Apaches led by Cochise and Mangas Colorado attempted to dry-gulch a detachment of U. S. Cavalry in the pass[3] in July 1862 when the soldiers were checking on the water supply of a spring in the area. The troopers under the command of Captain Thomas L. Roberts had ridden ahead of the main command—twenty-one supply wagons with escort, in search of water, and were met with a withering hail of Apache lead as they approached the spring. The Indians had thrown up stone breastworks on the slopes of the pass, but by late afternoon the soldiers were within two hundred yards of the spring and were safely ensconced within the stone corral of the old Apache Pass stage sta-

[3] A narrow defile running through the Chiricahua Mountains in southeast Arizona.

tion. A howitzer that had accompanied the troops could now be used, and Captain Roberts ordered a few dozen shells to be lobbed in the rear of the Apache redoubts. That was the end of the day's fighting, but much the same thing happened on the following day, when the wagons and the rest of the escort arrived, only this time, and faced by a second howitzer, the Indians retired for good. The Army authorities were quick to realize the importance of the spring, and on July 28, 1862, Fort Bowie was established to ensure access to its waters.

BATTLE AT BEECHER'S ISLAND
A battle that took place in 1868 on the Arikaree fork of the Republican River in western Colorado. At first light on September 17, a large war party of Sioux and Cheyenne attacked the night camp of fifty civilian volunteers who were out Indian hunting under the command of Major George Alexander Forsyth and Lieutenant Frederick Beecher. More than a thousand warriors were in the attacking force, and Forsyth had no other choice but retreat. He and his men covered the four hundred yards that separated them from the Arikaree, and fording the shallow waters, took refuge on a tiny sandbar that squatted in midstream. Here the men dug in, for all of their horses had been systematically shot dead by the Indians, and all hope of making a run for it had been abandoned.

Sporadic firing continued throughout the morning, and at noon half a thousand mounted braves streamed from the hills in an all-out attack. The white men, mostly veteran hunters and frontiersmen, held their fire until the island vibrated with the drumming of hoofs; then they broke the charge with a deadly barrage from Spencers and handguns. Indian dead bloodied the waters, and Lieuten-

ant Beecher and a doctor who had accompanied the expedition lay dying as the red men retreated to the hills. Roman Nose, mightiest of the northern Cheyenne war chiefs, led a further cavalry charge around 6 P.M., but the attack broke up when he was fatally wounded, and his warriors carried him from the field. By now the besieged party had two more dead and numerous wounded who were incapable of working guns, and when darkness fell, Forsyth, who was himself a serious casualty, got volunteers Jack Stillwell and Hank Trueau to leave the island in an attempt to bring reinforcements from Fort Wallace, 125 miles away. The following night, after a day of sniping, two more of the command, Allison Pliley and Jack Donovan, were sent on a like mission—a journey that turned out to be unnecessary, for the first two volunteers had gotten through, and a few days later, when Pliley and Donovan were nearing the fort, they met Colonel L. H. Carpenter and his relief force of seventy black troopers of the 25th Infantry, who were already heading for the Arikaree. Carpenter's "Brunettes"[4] arrived at the island on September 27, and although their guns were not needed, for the Indians had melted away on the twenty-second, a field ambulance they had brought along most certainly was. During the five-day siege Forsyth's band sustained thirty casualties, five of which were fatal, while the Indians fared infinitely worse, with over seventy dead and an unknown number wounded.

BATTLE OF SAN JACINTO
Fought at the junction of Buffalo Bayou and the San Jacinto River in southern Texas on April 21, 1836. The opposing forces were crack Mexican troops under General Antonio Lopez de Santa Anna

---

[4] Not a derogatory term, for they gloried in the title and were one of the crack regiments of the U. S. Army.

and a ragged, bobtailed army of Texans led by General Sam Houston. The Mexican general had in the region fourteen hundred troops in his command, while the Texans had little more than half that number, yet by catching the Mexicans around siesta time, Houston succeeded in gaining a magnificent victory, which gave Texas her independence and at the same time avenged the Alamo disaster of two months earlier. Only seven Texans were killed in the fighting, a battle that left the Mexicans with over six hundred dead. The great Santa Anna was among the four hundred prisoners who were taken, and although he expected to be shot, Sam Houston treated him fairly leniently; twelve months in the "brig" and then he was tossed back to Mexico. Aftermath: Texas became the Lone Star republic, with General Sam Houston as its first President. (See ALAMO, THE.)

BATTLE OF WASHITA As the white men won this "battle," it was referred to as such, although in this instance the word was little more than a euphemism for massacre. (See WASHITA MASSACRE.)

BATTLE OF WOUNDED KNEE Four Hotchkiss guns, all of which were pumping explosive shells into a crowd of Indians—men, women, and children—at the combined rate of two hundred rounds a minute; this was a battle? (See WOUNDED KNEE MASSACRE.)

BATTLE ON THE LITTLE BIG HORN When it entered the softly inclined valley of the Little Big Horn in the Montana Territory on June 25, 1876, the 7th Regiment of U. S. Cavalry was at full strength: 666 well-equipped officers and men, plus Indian scouts and white civilians who acted as guides and interpreters. By nightfall over a third of its ranks were dead and the remainder pinned down by an overwhelming number of Sioux and Cheyenne. In that year an all-out attempt to crush the North Plains Indians was being made by the U. S. Army, and during the early days of June—the Moon of Making Fat—more than six thousand fighting Indians had gathered in the Little Big Horn Valley for a united stand against the pony soldiers and walk-a-heaps (infantry) who were being sent against them. The Indians, mainly Sioux and Cheyenne, with smaller groups of Arapaho and Gros Ventres, were under the political leadership of Sitting Bull, who had numerous war chiefs at his disposal: Crazy Horse, Rain-in-the-Face, Gall, Hump, Fast Bull, Crow King, and Black Moon, to name but a few. Lieutenant George Armstrong Custer was in command of the 7th, and on the morning of June 25, having received intelligence that a large encampment of hostiles lay directly ahead, he split his command into three battalions: C, E, F, I, and L troops remained with Custer; A, M, and G were commanded by Major Reno; and D, H, and K were led by Captain Benteen. Following orders, Benteen and Reno crossed Ash Creek, a small stream on the regiment's southern and left flank, and the separated detachments paralleled Custer's line of march as he led the attack on the village; in theory the three columns were to converge on the encampment and hit the Indians in a treble-headed attack. So much for theory. The Indians were not taken by surprise, as Yellow Hair expected, for three battalions of cavalry stir up a lot of dust, and as the buckskinned Custer led his detachment toward the village in column of two, first at a canter, then at a gallop, three thousand Sioux and Cheyenne hit him like a tornado. Within five minutes the troops had been compelled to dismount, and as clumsy walk-a-heaps they straggled up a hillside to regroup around the regimental colors and troops guidons. Custer no doubt expected Reno and Benteen to arrive with reinforcements, but the other arms of his command were already pinned down by overwhelming forces of Indians, and no help was forthcoming. Thirty-six-year-old Custer and all his shattered force were already huddled on the banks of the Styx. Half an hour later it was all over, and squaws were straggling from the village to work on the dead. Bluffs prevented Reno and Benteen from seeing Custer's defeat, but the rising cloud of dust and smoke that hung over the valley, and the rattle of small arms that crescendoed, thinned out, then died during late afternoon, must have been evidence enough of his plight and possible defeat, yet dug in and immobilized as they were by surrounding hordes of painted warriors, there was nothing they could do, and if the warriors who had annihilated the main command had crossed Ash Creek, it is almost certain that none of the regiment would have survived that day. But the Indians had won one battle, and as is their nature, it was sufficient unto the day; energies could now be dissipated in less dangerous activities: scalping, looting, victory dancing, and coup talk. Reno and Benteen managed to survive the night, and at midday on June 26 Sitting Bull recalled his braves, and the greatest concentration of warriors the plains had ever seen began to break camp and go their separate ways. The casualties, both red and white, are listed below.

Custer Battalion
200 killed[5]

Reno Battalion
36 killed and 26 wounded

Benteen Battalion
11 killed and 29 wounded

Sioux Indians
21 killed; no. of wounded unknown

Cheyenne Indians
12 killed; no. of wounded unknown

BATTLE ON THE ROSEBUD In retrospect this battle can almost be said to be a dress rehearsal for the Indian victory on the Little Big Horn—a fight that occurred only eight days later, and only twenty-five miles to the northwest of the Valley of the Rosebud in the Montana Territory. On June 17, 1876, flying columns of mounted Indians attacked General Crook's command as it cantered along the west bank of Rosebud Creek. Over a thousand troopers, cavalry and mounted infantry, rode behind Crook that morning, yet the attacking Sioux and Cheyenne managed to drive wedges into the command and break it up into separate detachments. The darting spearheads of Indian cavalry kept Crook's forces on the defensive until that evening, when, as suddenly as they had appeared, they withdrew and drifted off into the twilight. It was an Indian victory, a small one but a victory nonetheless, for they had only eighteen wounded at the close of the fight, while Crook had fifty-seven dead and wounded on his hands. Truly a rehearsal it would seem, for the Indians who had given Crook a drubbing were from the most formidable encampment the West had ever seen, a camp that sheltered the massed might of both the Sioux and Cheyenne, and whose tepees squatted like a thousand anthills in the Valley of the Big Horn. The Indians were to have a far greater victory before the Moon of Making Fat had waned. (See BATTLE ON THE LITTLE BIG HORN.)

[5] Save for a Crow scout and Captain Keogh's horse Comanche, there were no survivors. Markers now stud the hillside on which the command perished.

BAT-WING CHAPS
Sometimes called "flap chaps." Protective leg coverings made from leather. They have open legs that are wrapped around the limbs, then snapped together behind the flaps. (See CHAPARRERAS.)

BAXTER SPRINGS, KANSAS
The first of the Kansas trail towns. It is situated in the southeastern corner of the state, and during its year as the main cowtown, 1866, it was the northern terminal of the Shawnee Trail.

BEACHY, HILL Proprietor of the Luna House, a hotel and a stage station in Lewiston, Idaho Territory, who in 1863 turned amateur detective to track down the murderers of his best friend, a pack-train owner named Lloyd Magruder. Certain circumstantial evidence pointed to four men who had stayed at the Luna House for one night prior to their leaving the territory. With a companion, Beachy followed the trail of this suspect quartet through Washington and Oregon before finally overtaking them in California, where he had them arrested. On December 1, 1863, Beachy arrived back in Lewiston with his four prisoners—James Romaine, David Howard, Chris Lowery, and Bill Page—and had them charged with the murder of his friend. Knowing that the evidence against the men was rather weak, Beachy went to work on Page, who appeared to be the most pliant member of the gang, and by the time the trial arrived, Beachy had succeeded in getting a confession. On January 23, 1864, Romaine, Howard, and Lowery got thumbs down from the jury, while Page was given a chance to turn over a new leaf. Page was most likely given his freedom for having "talked" and so helped to convict his buddies; but then again, perhaps the jury had a sense of humor. On March 4,

1864, the three convicted men were hanged in a ravine just outside Lewiston, and this last act in the Magruder affair was witnessed by around ten thousand people. (See MAGRUDER, LLOYD.)

BEADLE AND ADAMS New York City publishing firm whose dime novels were sold in all the eastern states and peddled by train "butchers" throughout the cruder western areas. The firm entered the cheap paperback field in 1860 after an advertising campaign that numerous lesser men have been copying ever since. In the fall of that year, an intriguing query—"Who is Seth Jones?"—appeared in the newspapers and on the billboards, and a few days later, *Seth Jones, or The Captives of the Frontier* was released to end the suspense. Selling more than five hundred thousand copies, it was the first dime novel to successfully feature a Wild West background, and the author, a young schoolteacher named Edward Sylvester Ellis, was immediately commissioned to write four more; a paper deluge of frontier violence was on the way. Ellis and a writer named Colonel Prentice Ingraham were to become Beadle and Adams' most prolific writers, although Buffalo Bill Cody immediately comes to mind when dime novels are mentioned, and he did in fact write[6] a few while in the Beadle and Adams stable. Below are a few of the magnificent titles, almost short stories in themselves, which the firm published during its heyday:

Deadly-Eye, and The Prairie Rover,
by Buffalo Bill   No. 24
Fancy Frank, or Colorado, or The Trapper's Trust, by Buffalo Bill
                           No. 158
Kansas King, or The Red Right Hand,
by Buffalo Bill   No. 1,038

---

[6] They were ghost-written.

*The Dread Shot Four, or My Pards of
the Plains,* by Buffalo Bill
                                        No. 973
Adventures of Wild Bill, the Pistol Prince,
by Colonel Prentice Ingraham
                                        No. 354
*Night Hawk George, and His Daring
Deeds and Adventures in the Wilds
of the South and the West,*
by Colonel Prentice Ingraham
                                        No. 39
*Bowie Knife Ben, The Little Hunter of
the Nor'west* by Oll Coomes
                                        No. 29
*Theyendangea, the Scourge, or The War
Eagle of the Mohawks,*
by Ned Buntline   No. 14

Non-Westerns; early "kitchen sinks,"
etc.:

*Honest Harry, or The Country Boy
Adrift in the City,* by C. Norris
                                        No. 52
*Smart Sim the Lad with a Level Head,
or Two Boys Who Were "Bounced,"*
by Edward Willett   No. 36

*Hydrabad, The Strangler, or Alethe,
the Child of the Cord,*
by Dr. J. H. Robinson   No. 70

(Was the above a dramatized account of
a bad birth?)

*The Cretan Rover, or Zuleikah
the Beautiful,*
by Colonel Prentice Ingraham
                                        No. 85

The firm of Beadle and Adams, which
once operated from 98 William Street,
New York, no longer exists, but many
of their dime novels can still be obtained
from firms specializing in early Americana. The launchers of good old Seth
were not alone in this field. (See DIME
NOVELS.)

BEAN, ROY Best remembered as the
"law west of the Pecos," although Bean
was pushing sixty when he settled in the
area. Prior to this time his record is
rather vague, and the fact that this earlier
period of Bean's life reads like extracts
from the *Police Gazette* speaks for itself.
Mexico, circa 1845: killed a local badman and quickly left the region (Bean,
a native Kentuckian, was around twenty
at the time). San Diego, California,
1850: got thirty days for killing a man in
a duel. Los Angeles, California, year unknown: killed a Mexican in a row that
revolved around the attentions of a local
belle, and was strung up for the offense
by friends of the deceased. The girl cut
him down after the mob had left, or so
Bean reported when he regained his
wind; could be true, for he had rope
burns on his neck until his death.
Mesilla, New Mexico, 1861–: formed a
band of guerrillas, ostensibly to help the
Confederate cause, but who were known
locally as "The Forty Thieves"; married
Virginia Chavez, a very young but cultured chick with Canary Island ancestry
who produced two male and two female
Beans for Roy before she left his house
and board for good. So, from small beginnings . . .

In 1882, bearded, rum-soaked, and fat
(he could only fasten the top button of
his waistcoat), Roy Bean arrived in the
tent town of Vinegarroon with a copy of
the 1879 edition of the *Revised Statutes
of Texas,* a mission, and two passions.
The mission was soon within his grasp:
Bean was appointed justice of the peace,
and from then on he could levy fines
when he was short of cash, and hang
folk when he was short of patience. His
two passions were "likker" and a woman
whose fading magazine photograph he
had been carrying around for years; the
first was easily slaked, the latter never.

Judge Roy Bean moved to Langtry,[7] a whistle-stop on the Southern Pacific track, and here he built himself a court-house, which was little more than a saloon with a built-in jury box. Roy named this 20-foot-by-14-foot seat of justice "The Jersey Lilly" (a semiliterate sign painter's error, not ours). Here juries imbibed deeply before considering a verdict; Bean spent the fines he collected on wholesale-price booze, and an enjoyable time was had by all bar the defendant. The justice charged five dollars for conducting an inquest, and a similar amount for performing the marriage ceremony. Bean usually ended the latter service with a somber ". . . and may God have mercy on your souls," and at the same time let it be known that at any time thereafter, for a further five bucks, he would "unmarry 'em iffen it didn't take." Killings were frequent, and although Bean could hang a horse thief without batting an eye, if any of his pals faced a murder charge before his bar (the word is used in both its judicial and alcoholic sense), he could be lenient. When a drinking buddy was charged with the murder of a Chinese laborer, Roy ruled that as there was no mention of "Chinese; homicide of" in the *Revised Statutes of Texas*, it couldn't be a crime, therefore the man must be acquitted; and on another similar occasion, ". . . the Mexican shouldn't have gotten in front of the gun my friend happened to be firing." A strain of macabre humor runs through these events, and as the following anecdote suggests, Roy probably excelled in this vein. One sultry day, a man—one of those irritating strangers who seem to have been forever passing through the West—dropped dead in front of "The Jersey Lilly," and the judge,

who had been lending a boozy atmosphere to his surroundings on the front porch, clumped down his three board steps to act as coroner. After pronouncing the man dead, and after a search of the corpse's pockets had turned up a revolver and forty dollars, Bean shed his coroner role and legally pocketed the loot by confiscating the gun and handing down a posthumous fine of forty dollars for carrying a concealed weapon. Judge Roy Bean's most precious moment came in the spring of 1888, a season when the girl whose tattered picture he carried in his pocket played in San Antonio, but although the aging judge arrived at the theater in fresh raiment, free of alcoholic fumes, and got a front-row seat, no one would introduce him to the thirty-one-year-old actress who had plagued his mind for years. Sadly, the judge returned to Langtry, where he was to rule for another eight years before finally overstepping his authority; in 1896, after a count of votes registered for Bean proved their number to be well in excess of the people in his bailiwick, he was removed from the bench. Yet Bean was far from finished. In 1896, to stimulate sales of his dollar-a-bottle stock, Bean promoted a fight between Bob Fitzsimmons and Peter Maher. The fight, which was staged on a sandbar in the Rio Grande and won by Fitzsimmons, had the distinction of being photographed in Kinetoscope. Private citizen Bean staggered on for six more years, and had he lived but a few months longer he would have met the woman of his dreams, for while touring Texas in 1903, Lily Langtry visited the saloon *cum* courthouse where he had once ruled. Bean's "Jersey Lilly" is still standing. (See LANGTRY, LILY.)

[7] Roy Bean claimed that he named the place in honor of the girl "in his wallet." The unromantic Southern Pacific dignitaries state that it bears the name of one of their stodgy top brass. There is still dispute over the christening, but we favor the old scallywag's version, and to hell with the debunkers.

BEAR COAT The Indians' name for General Nelson A. Miles, an officer whose winter topcoat was made of rough bearskins.

BEARS Carnivorous mammals that are really gigantic members of the dog family. Two species, featuring many varieties, roam the western states of America. The black bears, which are the more common, are referred to as brown or cinnamon bears when their color deviates from the norm, grow to a length of five feet, and may weigh up to five hundred pounds. Their diet isn't strictly carnivorous, and they will eat berries, honey, and birds' eggs as well as the meat from deer and other game. Dish-faced bears are, on the whole, the more formidable of the two species, and the larger varieties can bring down a buffalo with ease. Sizes range from four feet to the giant Kodiak,[8] which can reach ten feet in length. A variety whose hair is interspersed with gray, or is totally gray, is known as the grizzly. Grizzlies can reach a length of over nine feet, and although they were at one time numerous west of the Mississippi, they are now almost extinct. Dish-faced bears are omnivorous eaters and have a similar diet to black bears; neither species truly hibernates, but in the colder regions they will retire for long periods of rest during the late fall and winter months.

BEAR SPRINGS FIGHT Occurred on May 5, 1871, in Arizona, when a party of Chiricahua Apaches led by Cochise trapped a detail of the 3rd U. S. Cavalry in the Whetstone Mountains. The Apaches, who were being pursued by Lieutenant Howard Cushing and twenty-two men, succeeded in ambushing the troopers in a small canyon near Bear Springs. In the five minutes of fighting that followed, Lieutenant Cushing and ten of his men were killed. The remainder, a sergeant and eleven other enlisted men, only survived by making a speedy withdrawal.

BEAVER The largest of the American rodents, sometimes reaching four feet in length. They are dark brown in color and have heads similar to squirrels. The large tail is gray and naked, and roughly paddle-shaped. "Busy as a beaver" means just that; they fell trees and dam rivers, so creating ponds in which they can live and rear their young. When their artificial pond silts up, the beaver move out and start work on a new site. The passion for beaver hats in the nineteenth century greatly reduced the little animals' ranks, but luckily the fashion petered out before they were all extinct and now they are increasing once more. The tribal organization of the beaver, inasmuch as they all work for the benefit of the whole community, can almost be said to be superior to that of humans, while their weather forecasting makes the meteorological office dullards appear only fit for damming streams; the little beaver knows the height to which spring floods will rise a good nine months in advance. Beaver give birth to between two and eight kittens, and they look after their youngsters for at least eight months.

BECKETT, ROSE A teen-ager who, together with her sister Mary, was kidnaped for a "fate far worse than death" by a notorious procurer named Sam Purdy. The girls who had "been stolen" —to use the parlance of the day—in their hometown of St. Louis, Missouri, were transported by flatboat to Natchez, Mississippi, and here they were put on the

---

[8] The largest carnivore alive; yet despite its size, the Kodiak is completely unaggressive. Coloring varies from black to light cream. It is found on Kodiak Island, which is off the Alaskan coast, so it can hardly be classed as a "western" bear.

auction block with some seventy other pieces of merchandise. The lasses couldn't have been too bad, for while some of the bordello-bound girls brought only $125 per unit, Rose and Mary were knocked down for $200 apiece. The girls, whose only outlook now was being knocked up, were taken by their new owner and installed in his New Orleans house of good repute, sexwise. That could have been their sordid end; but a gentleman named Carlos White was already working his way through an endless chain of brothels, etc., in search of the girls. Mr. White found them in The Swamp, an out-of-town joint where the stock was well guarded, and although he was no doubt pale and weak by then, he had sufficient strength and armament to kill one of the girls' guards and "buffalo" the other, so that both he and the sisters could escape through a window. Rose and Mary were later reunited with their parents. Carlos? Oh, well; let us just say that the practice he must have put in during his search evidently stood him in good stead, for he settled in Louisiana, and today, although he is long since dead, one fifth of the families in the state who bear his surname also have him in their family tree. (See PURDY, SAM, and WHITE, CARLOS.)

BECKWITH, ROBERT Member of the Murphy faction in the Lincoln County War of 1878. Beckwith is credited with the killing of Alexander A. McSween during the siege of the latter's home on July 19, 1878. Beckwith himself was killed by Billy the Kid before the day was out. (See BARBER, SUSAN MC-SWEEN, and LINCOLN COUNTY WAR.)

BECKWOURTH, JAMES P. Buckskinned, hair plaited Indian fashion, part-black mountain man who was born around 1800, and whose lying anecdotes made it difficult to sort out the man from the legend. We do know he was a trader and a trapper, and if his stories are to be believed, he was the greatest Indian fighter and squaw lover the West has ever seen; he claimed credit for wiping out thousands of Blackfoot when others believed smallpox to have decimated the tribe, and he confessed to going through eighteen wives—eight of whom he possessed at one time—and hundreds of mistresses in his active lifetime. In his late prime Beckwourth was guiding parties of migrants across the Sierras, and he made quite a pile out of this. The canny mulatto made a pact with the storekeepers of Marysville, California; he would bring all the migrants to the town instead of bypassing it and going on to Sacramento if the merchants gave him six thousand dollars for each delivery. The townsmen agreed, and Jim used the money to build up a ranch in the foothills of the Sierras. After settling on the ranch he resorted to a spot of rustling to increase his stock, and in 1855 he was forced to leave California a few hoofbeats ahead of the vigilantes. After tarrying and trading in St. Louis for some years, he headed for Colorado and went into business at Denver. City life palled, however, and by 1860 he was trying his hand at being a frontiersman, and it was during this period, when he must have been ready for a pension, that he acted as guide to Chivington, an expedition that ended in the infamous Sand Creek Massacre. (See BONNER, THOMAS D., and SAND CREEK MASSACRE.)

BEECHER'S BIBLES In 1845, during the pro- and antislavery riots in Kansas, Henry Ward Beecher, a Massachusetts preacher, advocated that all migrants should possess a rifle; henceforth the term "Beecher's Bible" was a synonym for "rifle."

BEECHER'S ISLAND   A narrow sandbar in the Arikaree River of western Colorado. A fight took place here in 1868. (See BATTLE AT BEECHER'S ISLAND.)

BEESON, CHALK   Co-owner of Dodge City's famous Long Branch Saloon and friend of Wyatt Earp and Bat Masterson. Chalk was also the organizer of the Dodge City Cowboy Band.

BEHAN, JOHN   Sheriff of Cochise County, Arizona, from 1881 to 1882. Behan only served this one term of office, but as Tombstone was the county seat, and the time was during the town's most turbulent period, he appears in western histories with a frequency that is denied more notable lawmen. The appointment was worth thirty thousand dollars a year if you happened to be corruptible, and Behan may have been. He was a friend of "the cowboy element" (the contemporary parlance for outlaws), and during his term of office he became part owner of the Dexter Corral and Livery Stable at Tombstone, with John Dunbar, the county treasurer, as his partner. In 1882 a grand jury indictment faced Behan, and he hightailed from the county before a full investigation into irregularities that had occurred during his term of office could be completed. In 1887, and while employed as a turnkey at Yuma Prison, Behan killed a Mexican during an attempted jailbreak. A picture of Behan made during his Tombstone period shows a slim-faced man with thinning hair and the "gunfighter" mustache of the period. (See BENSON STAGE MURDERS; EARP, WYATT BERRY STAPP; and O. K. CORRAL.)

BEIDLER, JOHN XAVIER   Born in Mountjoy, Pennsylvania, on August 14, 1831, of German and American parent-age, Beidler was later to become the most zealous vigilante the West has ever seen. Whether this stemmed from a law-abiding nature or from a morbid desire to hang as many men as possible will never be known, although photographs of Beidler taken during his "long rope" days tend to swing one to the latter belief. He was short, fat, and pompous, with a set, uncompromising face whose lips are hidden by a drooping, untrimmed mustache—little in fact to suggest that the "milk of human kindness" pumped through the man's veins. In dress he seems to have favored off-the-rack suits and a giant sombrero, the latter lending him the appearance of a giant toadstool. Beidler's first recorded adventure seems to have occurred when he was twenty-one years old, and after already being a man of many trades: shoe-, brick-, and broommaking, to name but three. He was then in Kansas and a member of a vigilante posse that had routed a gang of border ruffians, and at that time it cannot be denied that he had a sense of humor, for after a howitzer loaded with printer's type had been used against the ruffians, and while the victims were picking type from their persons, he was heard to remark that "at least it would teach them to read." Beidler then became a saloon owner, and for the next few years he ran the People's Saloon in Atchison, Kansas, but by 1863 he was staking claims in the Alder Gulch region of Montana, and it was in this lawless area that Beidler left his most emphatic mark. Over the next two years vigilante Beidler was in at the hangings of dozens of owlhoots who had infested the gold camps; Plummer, Slade, Helm—you name them, Beidler was there. In 1886 he was appointed collector of customs for Montana and Idaho, and he died in the former territory[9] on January 22,

[9] Montana became a state in 1889, a few months before Beidler's death.

1890, at Helena, where he had finally settled. (See VIGILANTES OF MONTANA; in this entry you will find the names of many victims of vigilante justice who have separate entries and can be linked —by hemp, usually—with Mr. Beidler.)

BELFILS, LOUIS E. An itinerant French watchmaker who, in 1855 and when he was twenty-four years old, stumbled upon a fabulously rich gold strike in southern Oregon. Then comes the rub: Indians attacked Louis and he had to leave his strike and head for the mining camp at Selina. The strike is now one of the "lost mines" of the West, for although Louis searched for years, the exact location eluded him, and when he died in 1900 and his son took up the quest, the younger Belfils had no better luck. The watchmaker's son died in 1955, but others are no doubt still searching, knowing that somewhere between lat. 42° 10' and 42° 20' N and long. 123° 40' and 123° 50' W lies the big bonanza.

BELL, J. W. Deputy sheriff who was killed by Billy the Kid when the latter escaped from the Lincoln County jail on April 28, 1881. (See McCARTY, HENRY.)

BEMIS, CHARLES A. New England gambler who became a saloon owner at Warren, Idaho, and who in 1872 made western history by winning a beautiful Chinese girl in a poker game. Bemis continued gambling—possibly in hopes of building up a harem—and when he was wounded in a gunfight that broke up a poker game, his 1872 jackpot nursed him back to health. When fully recovered, Charlie and his mistress settled down on a small homestead on the banks of the River of No Return, and here they made quite a good living selling chickens and vegetables. The little gambler finally married his winnings,

and when he died in 1922 aged seventy-four years, his widow became the possessor of the little farm. Most likely Bemis had their relationship made legal so that the girl wouldn't be left destitute or returned to China in the event of his death. (See NATHOY, POLLIE.)

BENDER, JOHN Moronic son of William and Ma Bender who, in spite of his low IQ and lunatic laughter, played no small part in the family enterprise: murder, presumably with a robbery motive. (See BENDERS.) If you have done as the contents of the parentheses suggest, read on. After the family's disappearance, some authorities believe that John may have been killed by Kate and the Old Man, and if the family did escape the wrath of Colonel York's men, this theory seems reasonable, for a half-wit like John would have been little more than dead weight when both speed and inconspicuousness would have been all-important. (See BENDER, KATE; BENDER, MA; and BENDER, WILLIAM JOHN.)

BENDER, KATE Daughter of William and Ma Bender, and sister of the moronic John. At the time of the family's first recorded appearance, Kate was a copper-tressed, hazel-eyed lovely who had just flushed into young womanhood (ample and well-distributed "flushing," if contemporary reports are to be believed). Kate was a self-confessed mystic; she told fortunes and had handbills printed that advertised her psychic powers. The lass, however, was not without physical accomplishments, for as the leading light of the family business, she was something of a knife artiste. Kate drew crude figures of men on the walls and used them as targets for her blade, but that was merely practice, for Kate was the throat-slitting cog in the family machine. (See BENDERS.) You've read as suggested? Good! Around 1889 the onetime neighbors of the Benders were visited by a deputy sheriff from Texas, who handed them a photograph to peruse; as they perused, the man gave them a tale. He had recently married a woman who was adept at reading fortunes, and as everyone knew about the soothsaying Kate by that time, he had brought the matter up before his spouse, who, in turn, had brought up a forty-five and told him to desist; all very odd, and naturally he was suspicious. . . . Well, the neighbors figured it could be Kate iffen you allowed for another eighteen years of flushing. The lawman departed and was never heard from again. Had the Texan gotten saddled with Kate, rather than the reverse? And if so, did she remove him? Some more: In the early 1920s the San Francisco newspapers reported the death of an elderly woman and at the same time suggested that the deceased may have been the notorious Kate Bender. Of such stuff are legends made. (See, BENDER, JOHN; BENDER, MA; and BENDER, WILLIAM JOHN.)

BENDER, MA   No Christian name has ever been mentioned, found, or imagined; maybe just as well, for any flowery feminine nomenclature would have sat badly on Ma. She was built like a grouse that has been grounded for years; her hair was a straggly white mop, and she could speak only German. Ma could have been little more than an accessory before and after the fact when Pa and their brood were bloodletting. (See BENDERS.) Right; now you can carry on. The fate that is alleged to have overtaken the half-baked John is believed by some to have accounted for Ma —the motive evidently being transport difficulties in the latter instance. It's possible, for neither Kate nor the Old Man appear to have been troubled by squeam-

ishness. (See BENDER, JOHN; BENDER, KATE; and BENDER, WILLIAM JOHN.)

BENDERS   Whence they came, no one knows; but come they did. They threw up a 30-foot-by-16-foot shack on a ridge in Mound Valley, Kansas, put up a large sign that read "Groceries" and smaller ones that let the traveling public know that meals and liquor were also available, and then they were ready for business. The Bender family had arrived: Ma, Pa, John, and Kate—three gruesome ghouls and one luscious one. The shack was only a one-roomed affair, but a burlap drape that hung from the ceiling beams divided the interior into two areas of privacy: a saloon *cum* eatery and the family's domestic quarters. Kate did the cooking, ran the saloon (a plank and trestles served as a bar), and showed a few curves at the front door when business was slack. Groups of patrons and local residents who were known were allowed to dine and leave with little more than gastronomical disturbances;[10] lone strangers rarely. Should an unknown traveler happen to come in for a meal and an eyeful of Kate when the place was free of other diners, he would be seated with his back to the curtain, and Pa or John would slam him with a hammer when his head molded the burlap. Kate would then cut the victim's throat, and united, they would get the corpse into a 6-foot-by-5-foot pit under the floorboards and so out of the way. The Benders had three years of success; then in March 1873 they killed a certain Dr. York and stirred up quite a mess of trouble for themselves. The doc was reported missing, and his brother, Colonel York, clouded up the dust at the head of a posse in search of the defunct aesculapius. The posse halted at the Benders' and questioned Kate. Yes, she had seen

---

[10] Reports suggest that Kate was the attraction; her cooking was lousy.

the doc and even watered his horse, but that was all she knew; perhaps the good colonel would like to return alone some time to have his whiskey dregs read? Yes, ma'am; the colonel needed no second bidding: He would return! The posse thundered thataway, and the Benders were not around the following morning. Later, a wagon with their "Groceries" sign on board was found abandoned near Thayer, Kansas, and the ticket agent at the local depot said he had sold four tickets to an old man who had a fat woman, a youth, and a girl with him. Could these travelers have been the Benders? Not if the following theory is correct. Rumor hath it that somehow Colonel York's suspicions were aroused while questioning Kate, and that he did return to the shack, but not alone as requested. The posse wiped out the family and burned[11] the bodies nearby, after which York and three of his men disguised themselves and went through the ticket-buying routine. As none of the bodies of the Benders' victims had been found at the time of the alleged cleanup and there was no evidence against the family, why did York have them all killed? And if he had found damning evidence of guilt, why should he and his men cover their tracks? None of the posse ever talked, so this whole theory can be written off as a colander of surmise. The deserted shack was not searched for some time—which rather points out that the Benders had aroused no suspicions in the Mound Valley region; but searched it was eventually, and the corpses of a seven-year-old girl and eight men were found buried in the rear garden. The bodies were viciously mutilated, and as it was estimated that the Benders had probably only netted a thousand dollars from their crimes, it was assumed that a lust for money wasn't their

only motive. After the whole grisly story had gotten around, numerous folk came forward with stories of how they had escaped from the Benders' clutches. (See BENDER, JOHN; BENDER, KATE; BENDER, MA; and BENDER, WILLIAM JOHN.)

BENDER, WILLIAM JOHN Hulking, beetle-browed, German immigrant who was the "Old Man" of the notorious Bender family. (See BENDERS.) Now carry on. If William John and the rest of his family didn't get "done in" in 1873, he most likely lived on for another eleven years, for in 1884 an aged character who answered to his description and who spoke with a German accent was arrested near Dillon, Montana, for a murder that had occurred in Idaho. The crime had taken place near Salmon, and the victim's skull had been crushed by a blunt instrument. The murder method, plus his prisoner's clamming up when "Bender" was mentioned, convinced the arresting officer, Deputy Sheriff Snook, that the man he had in custody was none other than Bender, Sr. The suspect was placed in ankle irons and tossed into the Salmon jail, but before Snook could check with the Kansas authorities, the old man was dead; he had tried to cut off his foot to escape, and subsequently bled to death. Snook had no ice house, so he tried to preserve the body in a calcifying pool while he awaited news from Kansas. Word didn't arrive, and on the advice of an anatomist who believed that the skeleton might "talk," Snook had the body boiled. Nothing was ever resolved, for by the time news arrived from Kansas, even his best friend wouldn't have known William John Bender. The skull, which was known locally as "Bender's skull," was on display in the Buckthorn Saloon at Salmon until Prohibition closed the place

[11] Alternatively, buried in a swamp.

in 1920. At some time during the next thirteen years the skull must have gone in search of liquor, for its whereabouts are now unknown. (See BENDER, JOHN; BENDER, KATE; and BENDER, MA.)

BENI, JULES A larcenous Frenchman who founded a trading post near Lodgepole Creek in 1850. Nine years later an overland stage halt was built nearby, and Beni was put in charge. The way station was an important one, being one of the very few that possessed a telegraph office, and almost overnight other buildings began to spring up in that northeastern corner of Colorado. First the four essentials of any western community: a saloon, a dance hall, a hotel, and a smithy. Then came the stores and places of lesser merit, and the clapboard cabins of settlers. The town was christened Julesburg in honor of its founder, and in 1860, when the hoofbeats of the Pony Express were first heard along the South Platte, Russell, Majors, and Waddell, organizers of this fast mail service put Beni in charge of a twenty-five-mile stretch of the run. Around this time Indians began attacking and looting the coaches, and as survivors of these raids described the marauders in terms that later Americans would use in respect of a three-dollar bill, the Frenchman came under suspicion as having organized the holdups. These suspicions must have been strong, for Jules was dismissed, and a certain Joseph A. Slade rode into Julesburg as his replacement. Beni didn't bother sticking feathers in his hair after that, but he robbed more coaches than ever out of sheer spite, and when he came upon Slade he blasted the new superintendent into the dust with a charge of buckshot. Slade, as tough a character as ever rode the West, recovered, and when his turn came to exact revenge, he pulled out all the stops. The killing of Beni was no Main Street shootout. Slade got the drop on the Frenchman and trussed him to a post. He then cut off his victim's ears before slowly shooting him to death with a precision that Fu Manchu would have appreciated. For years afterward Slade carried the dried-out ears in his pocket, and although they would have made ideal ashtrays, there is no record of him having used them as such. (See SLADE, JOSEPH A.)

BENSON STAGE MURDERS
The Tombstone-Benson stagecoach was held up and robbed on many occasions, and this entry, an attempted holdup, was chosen only because of its magnificent cast of characters. On March 15, 1881, the *Grand Central* coach of the Kinnear and Company, stageline was approached by four bewigged and false-bearded highwaymen as it slowed to cross an arroyo near Drew Station, and when Eli Philpott, the driver, failed to obey their command to halt, the bandits opened fire and killed him. Bob Paul, a Wells Fargo messenger who was riding shotgun, opened fire, but the shooting had stampeded the horses, and he had to drop his gun and grab the reins in an attempt to keep the Concord on even keel. When the coach arrived at Benson it was discovered that there was a second casualty: A passenger named Peter Roerig had been wounded in the fusillade, and he died soon afterward. The county sheriff should have been notified, but Paul, who distrusted John Behan, wired Deputy U. S. Marshal Wyatt Earp instead. Four unsavory characters who had suddenly left their usual haunts—Luther King, Bill Leonard, Jim Crane, and Harry Head—came under suspicion, and Earp deputized a posse and rode out into the scrub in search of the layabouts. Meanwhile Sheriff Behan had been informed, and he and a deputy tagged along in the posse's dust cloud. The dep-

uty U.S. marshal and his men—brothers Virgil and Morgan, Bat Masterson, Marshal Williams, and Bob Paul—overtook and arrested King on March 19. King had just finished admitting his part in the affair when Behan rode up and demanded custody of the prisoner. Wyatt, who was only too eager to lead his posse in search of the other miscreants, handed King over, and then he and his men thundered South. But their luck was out, and their quarry escaped across the Rio Grande. Dust and trail-weary, the magnificent six returned to Tombstone, only to learn on arrival that King had escaped, and that Wyatt, Paul, and Doc Holliday were now suspected of the bungled Benson job. Luckily these suspicions, which were later thought to be Behan-inspired, came to naught, for it was reasoned that "attempted" could hardly be associated with such men as Earp, Holliday, and Paul. (See BEHAN, JOHN; HEAD, HARRY; HOLLIDAY, JOHN HENRY; KING, LUTHER; and LEONARD, BILL.)

BENT'S FORT Can refer to any of the three forts that the Bent brothers— Charles, George, Robert, and William— built in southeastern Colorado between 1826 and 1853. All the forts were erected as trading centers, although each was sufficiently strong to have withstood a siege if the necessity had arisen. Their first fort was built in the shadow of the Rockies, but on the advice of their Indian friends, the Bents moved eastward, and in 1828 they built what was to become known as the Old Fort at the mouth of the Purgatoire River. Only William survived to see the last structure. This he had built near Big Timbers on the Arkansas in 1853, and it was more elaborate than the earlier efforts. It covered over an acre of ground, was built of stone, and had cannon mounted on each of its walls, while it sheltered a small army of trappers, hunters, scouts, etc. (See BENT, WILLIAM.)

BENT, WILLIAM Best known of the four Bent brothers, merchants and traders with Indians, Bent operated in Colorado in the first half of the nineteenth century. William was born in 1809, and fifteen years later he was touring the southeastern Colorado area as agent for the American Fur Company. William was well liked by the Indians, who knew him as "Washichuchee-kohlah" (the small white man), and during a lifetime spent among them he took at least two Cheyenne girls as wives, both of whom he successfully papoosed. In 1847, after hearing the news that his brother Charles, who had become governor of New Mexico, had been killed and scalped by Indians, Bent recruited a small army, and with the avowed intention of scalping every "Injun" they met, the band moved South. They didn't have to lift any hair, for by the time they arrived the culprits had been tried and were ready for hanging, a spectacle that William and company waited to witness. In 1852 Bent negotiated with the federal government with regard to the sale of the Old Fort, but he became so incensed at the long-drawn-out negotiations that he dynamited the property in disgust. He then moved on to Big Timbers, where he built the greatest of the Bents' forts. He lived here until 1859, in which year he was appointed Indian agent for the Cheyenne and Arapaho. On taking this appointment he leased the building to the government, which thereupon renamed the place Fort Fauntleroy; Fauntleroy! William musta spat. On May 19, 1869 William Bent died, leaving an estimated fortune of between $150,000 and $200,000. (See BENT'S FORT.)

BERDACHE A French term widely used by the Amerinds when alluding to men who wore women's clothing—that is, homosexuals. Most tribes looked upon these individuals with contempt, but the Illinois (just east of the Mississippi, so they have no separate entry) trained and groomed handsome young boys to become male concubines. White men usually referred to these abnormal types as "squaw boots."

BERNARD, HENRIETTE ROSINE A titian-haired beauty who was born in Paris, France, on October 24, 1844. In 1862 Henriette made the theater her career and adopted the stage name of Sarah Bernhardt. (See BERNHARDT, SARAH.)

BERNHARDT, SARAH European tragedienne who toured the western and middle western states of the United States in 1881. Miss Bernhardt was then at the height of her career and was undoubtedly the greatest tragic actress in the world, yet even so Sarah didn't rely on histrionic ability alone when it came to "draggin' 'em in"; after seeing her play *Camille* at St. Joseph, Missouri, the editor of an Atchison, Kansas, newspaper reported as follows: "Her dress was white . . . and cut so low in front that we expected every moment that she would step one of her legs through it." This wonderful girl—even by today's standards her photographs are really something—lost a leg in 1915, but she continued to tread the boards almost until her death, on March 26, 1923. (See BERNARD, HENRIETTE ROSINE.)

BIEDLER, X. Incorrect spelling of Beidler. (See BEIDLER, JOHN XAVIER.)

BIG CASINO The name by which Pat Garrett was known in his early Fort Sumner gambling days. This was to differentiate from "Little Casino," who was none other than Billy the Kid. (See GARRETT, PATRICK FLOYD.)

BIG FOUR HAT Style of Stetson with a medium-high crown: 6¼ inches in height, and having a 4-inch brim.

BIGHORN SHEEP Also known as the mountain or Rocky Mountain sheep. The bighorn is one of the largest species of sheep, with a fully grown specimen weighing about 300 pounds and standing 3 feet, 6 inches at the shoulder. The spiraled horns are massive, those of the big ram measuring up to 3 feet along the outside curve and having a diameter of around 16 inches at the base. Coloring varies with the locality, but a grayish-brown is the most typical shade. The bighorn is now virtually extinct in some areas—a regrettable condition that has mainly been brought about by trophy-hunting morons.

BIG-NOSE KATE A frontier whore, which possibly makes her a cut above a backward whore. (See ELDER, KATE.)

BILLY THE KID The West had many gentlemen who adopted or were known by this title. Throughout this book, however, when "Billy the Kid" appears in the text without further identification, it refers to the one and only Henry McCarty. (See McCARTY, HENRY.)

BING KONG Chinese tong that operated in the San Francisco area over the latter half of the nineteenth century. (See CHINESE TONGS.)

BISON As no one ever heard of Bison Bill, bison hunters, Chief Bison Hump, and the bison nickel, we can afford to ignore the scholars in this instance. (See BUFFALO.)

BLACK BART *Nom de guerre* of that poet laureate of road agents, Charles E. Bolton. (See BOLTON, CHARLES E.)

BLACKBURN, DUNC Leader of a gang of road agents who plagued the Deadwood, South Dakota, area in 1877. The gang stopped and robbed nearly all stages leaving Deadwood, and in the course of the robberies many of the drivers and shotgun messengers were either killed or wounded. Unfortunately, their crimes cannot be accurately ascertained, for the Joel Collins–Sam Bass outfit was operating over the same terrain at the same time, and on at least one occasion both gangs have been credited with the same crime; Wyatt Earp states that the Dunc Blackburn gang pulled the holdup in which Johnny Slaughter was murdered, while Charles L. Martin, in his "Sketch of Sam Bass the Bandit," is equally emphatic that Bass and company were responsible. Whatever, we do know that Dunc and his boys left the vicinity of Deadwood sometime during the early summer of 1877, and that the redoubtable Wyatt may have had something to do with their decision to leave. (See EARP, WYATT BERRY STAPP.)

BLACKFOOT INDIANS
Numerically strong tribe belonging to the Algonkin language group, and although they were at one time confined to an area north of the 49th parallel, they were firmly established in what is now northern Montana by the time the white man arrived on the scene. Like other warlike tribes that made the buffalo their commissariat, the Blackfoot lived in tepees and dressed in the elaborate beaded buckskins of the plains. Their name possibly dates back to their prehorse period, for prairie fires were not uncommon, and moccasins could easily have become blackened by the charred ground; there

are other theories, but this is probably the best, for in making sign talk for "Blackfoot," the right foot is raised and the flat of the hand is passed along its edge from heel to toe—rather as if brushing off dust. The Blackfoot are now on reservations in Montana, Saskatchewan, and Alberta. This tribe should not be confused with the Blackfeet Sioux, who are a subtribe of the Dakotas.

BLACKHAWK WAR Blackhawk, a war chief of the Utes who had accepted the Mormon faith, started hostilities against the settlers of central Utah on April 10, 1865, his provocation being the "slapping down" of a young chief of the tribe by one of the settlers. Cattle were stolen and people killed, and on April 12 the Sanpete militia, which had been mustered at Fort Gunnison and sent against Blackhawk, was routed by the Utes. Somewhat panicked, the settlers abandoned Fort Salina and gathered at Fort Gunnison farther north. A courier was dispatched to Fort Douglas at Salt Lake with the usual "Help! Come quickly!" message, but the U. S. Army authorities weren't interested; section thingumajig, paragraph so-so stated that they were only hanging around at Salt Lake to protect the overland mail, and that was that. On May 26 a settler's wagon was attacked in Thistle Canyon, and John Given, his wife, and four children were killed and scalped. In July the Utah militia retaliated with equal viciousness, and squaws and children were butchered when a surprise attack was launched against a small Ute village. The Indian raids continued: On October 18 a farming couple and their hired girl were killed and mutilated, and throughout the winter the settlers were harassed constantly. In June 1867, a skirmish occurred between the militia and the Utes, and in the course of the fighting Blackhawk was wounded. From then on the raids began to peter out, and in the summer of 1867 Blackhawk held a parley with the whites. The war chief, who was suffering from both tuberculosis and the effects of his wounds, was allowed to make peace and return to his people. The following winter the Utes' death chant echoed through the hills surrounding their encampment: Blackhawk was dead.

BLACK HILLS Located due west of the Badlands of South Dakota. The hills are not as oppressive as their name would suggest, although a covering of dark green pines do lend a brooding atmosphere to their appearance. The Sioux held the Black Hills[12] sacred, and when prospectors flooded into the hills after the discovery of gold in the area in 1874, the tribes gathered to give battle. (See CUSTER, GEORGE ARMSTRONG; BATTLE ON THE LITTLE BIG HORN; and BATTLE ON THE ROSEBUD.)

BLACK, JAMES Famous frontier cutler who was born on May 1, 1800, in Hackensack, New Jersey. Black ran away from home when he was eight and apprenticed himself to a Philadelphia silver-plate manufacturer whom he stayed with for ten years before moving on to Washington, Arkansas, and opening his own cutlery business. His work was evidently superior, for his fame spread, and in December 1830 he was approached by James Bowie, who wanted a knife made to his own specifications—not for sharpening pencils, but real "killing stuff." Black, who had a secret process for hardening steel, and whose blades kept their cutting edge indefinitely, responded bravely, and a month later fourteen inches of deadly man-carver was handed across the counter to a man who was to slice his way into the history and folklore of the West. Black had married by this time, and when his wife died in 1838 he was left with four small children. This was possibly too much for the man, for a year later he took to his bed, and while suffering the effects of an undisclosed illness, his father-in-law, who had always hated him, attacked him about the head with an iron bar. Black's dog drove the older man off, but although Black recovered from his illness, he was never the same again after that iron-bar shellacking. He lost his sight and forgot all his steel-hardening secrets, and when he died in the late 1850s he was an incurable imbecile. (See BOWIE KNIFE.)

BLACK KETTLE One of the most famous of the southern Cheyenne chiefs. Black Kettle tried to maintain friendly relations with the white man, yet even though an American flag fluttered above his tepee as an indication of his intentions, on two occasions his village was attacked and numbers of his people massacred. On the first of these occasions he lost his wife (November 29, 1864); and on the second, when Custer attacked his village on the morning of November 27, 1868, both he and his latest spouse were killed by the troopers. (See SAND CREEK MASSACRE and WASHITA MASSACRE.)

BLACK SHAWL Mixed-breed Indian girl who became the wife of Crazy Horse. Black Shawl bore the Oglala leader one child, a girl, whom they named "They are afraid of her," and who con-

[12] English translation of the Sioux *Paha Sapa* (the Sioux place their adjectives after nouns, so *"Paha Sapa"* actually becomes "Hills Black" on being anglicized). *"Pa Sapa"* is frequently found in fiction and non-fiction Westerns, but this is incorrect, for as *"Pa"* means "Head," *"Pa Sapa"* becomes "Head Black"—"Black Head."

tracted a white man's disease—possibly whooping cough[13]—and died in infancy. (See CRAZY HORSE.)

BLACK, WILLIAM   Known to be an alias of Wild Bill Longley. (See LONGLEY, WILLIAM P.)

BLAIR, EUGENE   Wells Fargo shotgun messenger who rode the box between Nevada gold camps in the 1870s. None of the coaches Blair rode was ever robbed, although attempts were made aplenty. Highwaymen died by the dozen, and as Blair was presented with a new gun for each road agent he had killed and his collection of hardware was reputed to be one of the largest in the West, the highways over which he traveled must have been literally fenced with Wells Fargo R.I.P. markers.[14] When there was a lull in the banditry, Blair, who must have gotten the gun collector's bug, would attempt to lure the baddies to their doom by broadcasting facts about real or imaginary gold shipments, and on at least one such occasion and when Blair had some of his boys along, three bandits who had taken the bait were met by such a barrage of gunfire that all hope of ever identifying the corpses was abandoned as soon as the smoke lifted. For all his years of riding shotgun on one of the toughest runs in the West—Aurora to Bodie—the hardcase Blair was never even wounded. (See BODIE, CALIFORNIA, and DAVIS, JACK.)

BLAKE, FRANK   Notorious horse thief and abductor of lissome lassies. Blake, who worked the "Horsethief Trail," from Arizona to Kansas, made the scene at Abilene in 1871, and although he is reputed to have been a friend of Wild Bill Hickok, who was town marshal at this time, this didn't prevent Blake from disrupting the peace by kidnaping a seventeen-year-old redhead named Bessie Fenner. Bessie was to join a tried and tested harem of two, whom Frank's rare form of kleptomania had picked up earlier. Bessie's father also disappeared around this time, and when Blake became suspect for the lifting of Miss Fenner, it was also assumed that he had killed[15] Old Man Fenner when the latter had stood 'twixt Frank's lust and the girl's honor. Posses followed Blake and the much-ravished females as far as Arizona, and here the girls—Lucy Griswold, Bessie Fenner, and a dark-eyed beauty known only as Chihuahua—were rescued. Blake, however, remained at liberty for some time longer, finally realizing that "crime don't pay" when he and three of his henchmen were gunned down and killed by lawmen near the present site of Apache Junction.

BLAKE, JACK   Recruited to the ranks of the Doolin-Dalton gang after the original Dalton mob had been wiped out at Coffeyville, Kansas, in October 1892. Blake, who was known as "Tulsa Jack," rode with the new gang until May 1895, at which time he was shot down and killed by lawmen. (See DOOLIN, BILL.)

BLAZER'S MILL   A large two-storied adobe structure located on the Rio Tularosa on the southern area of New Mexico. The building, which served as a sawmill, was owned by Dr. Emil Blazer, a retired dentist. The building is best re-

---

[13] Suggested because, although Black Shawl was tubercular, the child is said to have died from "another of the white man's diseases."

[14] No sentimentality here; the markers served as warnings.

[15] The body of Fenner was found, much later, in a dried-up streambed outside Abilene, but whether Blake had killed him will never be known, for had there been sufficient evidence against the man he was past the stage when he could be brought to trial.

membered as being the site of Buckshot Roberts' last stand. (See ANDREWS, JESSE, and LINCOLN COUNTY WAR.)

BLEVINS, ANDY Son of Mart Blevins, a small-time Arizona cattleman. Andy, who was born in 1862, spent the major part of his adult life peddling illicit whiskey to the Indians. Later he became a cattle rustler, and in the early 1880s he left Texas two jumps ahead of the local law and returned to northern Arizona, where, from then on, he adopted the alias of Andy Cooper. Andy was known to be a "man on the prod," and when sheepmen invaded the Pleasant Valley district he was only too eager to resort to gunplay in an effort to remove the woollies from the range. On September 2, 1887, a gang led by Andy shot down and killed two sheepmen—John Tewkesbury and William Jacobs—and a couple of days later Andy was heard bragging about the murders in Holbrook. Commodore Perry Owens, newly appointed sheriff of Apache County, who was in town with a warrant for the arrest of "Andy Cooper" on a cattle rustling charge, overheard these remarks, and when the wanted man retired to his parents' home, Owens went to make the arrest. Owens was probably one of the fastest and coolest gunfighters the West had ever seen, and Andy Cooper was shot dead when he resisted arrest. (See OWENS, COMMODORE PERRY, and PLEASANT VALLEY WAR.)

BLEVINS, MART Cattleman who in the 1860s settled in northern Arizona with his wife, five sons, and a young daughter. Mart is reputed to have drifted down from Canada, and prior to his Arizona period little is known of the man. His ranch at Canyon Creek was in a desolate area of Gila County—an ideal situation for the alleged cattle-rustling activities of his five sons. Mart Blevins dis-

appeared in July 1887, rumored to have been killed by Navahos whose horses he had stolen. Could be—but there is no evidence to support this. (See PLEASANT VALLEY WAR.)

BLUE DUCK With a name like "Blue Duck" it is hardly surprising that many writers refer to this gentleman as a "Cherokee half-breed" or a "flat-faced Indian," when in actual fact he was a white man whose adopted alias is the only name he left in the records. Blue Duck was a member of a three-man gang of small-time rustlers and stage robbers who at various times were an integral part of the Sam and Belle Starr gang, and Belle is reported to have been fond of a little Blue Ducking on the many occasions when Sam didn't happen to be around. This is more than likely, for when Blue Duck went on a drunken shooting spree in 1884 and killed a farmer named Samuel Wyrick, it was the amoral Belle who saved his neck: Blue Duck was arrested by marshals, tried, and sentenced to hang, but Belle, by employing the best legal talent her ill-gotten gains could hire, got his sentence commuted to life imprisonment. (See STARR, BELLE.)

BOBCAT A short-tailed, longish-legged member of the cat family which is common in most states of the Union. Bobcats can attain a length of 3 feet, 6 inches; color varies from an olive brown to russet brown that is liberally sprinkled with black markings. Their young, between two to four, are born in the spring. Bobcats usually prey on rabbits and other small mammals, but they have been known to be used by cattlemen in their war against sheep: A bobcat would be caught and released after a bell had been fastened around its neck; the tinkling of the bell would prevent the cat from stalking its natural prey, and from then on it would play havoc among the slow-moving woollies.

BODIE, CALIFORNIA The town where the "bad man" came from. Bodie was born in 1860, soon after gold had been found in the Mono Lake region of California, and like many of its predecessors, the town soon began to put on muscle, so that by 1870 it is reputed to have had a population of fifteen thousand. At this time thirty mines were in operation in the area, and three brewery companies, supplying more than thirty-five saloons, were working an around-the-clock schedule in their efforts to prevent the mineworkers from suffering the effects of drought. The sixty brothels, which were open twenty-four hours a day, kept an estimated eighteen hundred members of the gentler sex in full employment, and as it must have taken an astronomical number of clients to keep these lassies fully operational, the righteous element in Bodie must have been almost nil. Killings were frequent, and on many occasions stemmed from motives most trivial: who was first in a brothel line; to quiet opposition at a union meeting; to clinch an argument regarding a previous killing; and so on, and so on. The fact that Bodie had "a man for breakfast" daily aroused little comment, but when one Sunday passed into limbo without a corpse being made, the townsfolk were quick to point out the "Christian spirit" of the place. In 1932 a fire stripped most of the flesh from what was left of Bodie, and today it is nothing more than a ghost town. (See BODY, WATERMAN.)

BODY, WATERMAN Usually known as Bill Body.[16] Waterman discovered gold in the vicinity of Mono Lake, California, in 1859, and although he

perished in a blizzard that same year, the town that subsequently blossomed on the spot where he had made his strike was named after him. Admittedly, his name was spelled wrong, but the thought was there, and some fourteen years after his death, and when the townfolk of Bodie had built all the saloons and brothels they needed, further homage was paid to the man who had made it all possible. Body's body (sounds quaint, don't it?), or rather his bones, were dug up and his skull was given a place of honor in the Cosmopolitan Saloon. The skull can hardly have been contented here, for Waterman—who had an apt first name—had never been known to "touch a drop," so it gives pleasure to relate that in 1879, and during a further revival of interest in the man, all of Body's bones were collected and interred in a small casket over which a memorial shaft was to be erected after the hat had been passed around. Handouts were generous, and the marker was duly made; but then came Waterman's most tragic posthumous hour: President Garfield, the "miners' friend," was assassinated before the marker could be erected, and the crummy miners stole Waterman's memorial and erected it to Garfield instead. (See BODIE, CALIFORNIA.)

BOLTON, CHARLES E.
A scholarly, mustached gentleman who is reported to have been born in New York State, and who affected a curly-brimmed derby hat and a gold-mounted cane during leisure hours. When working he wore a long white duster coat, a flour sack with eyeholes over his head, while a double-barreled shotgun replaced the cane—for Mr. Bolton became "Black Bart" during business hours. As far as is known, no killings can be attributed to him, so although he was one of the most

16 Rhymes with "toady" (no insulting inference intended).

successful road agents to ever operate in the Mother Lode region of California, to many he will not appear half so colorful as some of the lesser lights who bungled their jobs with gunfire. The immaculate Bolton worked studiously at his chosen profession from 1875 until 1883, successfully robbing twenty-seven of Wells Fargo's coaches during this period. After each job he would leave a few lines of doggerel behind; an extract from one of these is given:

I've labored long and hard for bread,
For honor and for riches,
But on my toes too long you've tred,
You fine-haired sons-of-bitches.

BLACK BART the PO8

Black Bart's last robbery occurred near Copperopolis on November 3, 1883, and although he escaped from the scene, a blast from the guard's gun must have so unnerved him that he left an amazing variety of clues behind, and it was only a matter of time before he was caught. A derby hat, a case which had contained field glasses, a magnifying glass, and a sparkling white handkerchief, were handed over to James B. Hume, the local Wells Fargo Sherlock. Hume perused the square of linen through the lens the bandit had inadvertently provided and came up with a laundry mark that led, via ninety laundries, to 37 Second Street, San Francisco, where an elderly gentleman was arrested. This must surely be the only case on record in which cleanliness has led to the arrest of a western badman! Hume must have had a certain respect for the man whom he had put the collar on, for his official report on Bolton—if we exclude the robbery details—contains nothing derogatory: ". . . person of great endurance

. . . comparatively well-educated . . well-informed . . . good talker . . . exhibits genuine wit . . . few close friends, but those of first-class respectability . . . neat and tidy . . . proper and polite in behavior, chaste in language," etc. The judge may have paid some heed to this buildup, for Bolton only got six years, which amounted to little more than eleven weeks per robbery. Bolton was released from San Quentin four years later, two years having been deducted from his sentence for good behavior, and as he was around sixty at the time, he must have decided that three score years was a good age to retire, for nothing was heard of him again.[17]

BONANZA A successful enterprise or a run of luck, although in western jargon it was usually confined to a lucky strike in mining or prospecting.

BONNER, THOMAS D. A British journalist who settled in California for a time during the midnineteenth-century gold rush. Bonner, however, didn't do any prospecting, for he managed to have himself elected justice of the peace for the gold-rush town of Indian Bar. From then on Bonner was known as "the Squire," and no poor man ever lost a case when the Englishman presided. This didn't stem from any sympathy with the underdog, but from a more practical reason: Poor men cannot pay fines but rich ones can, and as Bonner collected a percentage of the court's take, it was to his advantage to hand down decisions that were certain to swell the judicial kitty. Bonner met Jim Beckwourth in the early days of 1852, and when Bonner was driven from Indian Bar in the fall of that year after a far too obvious miscarriage

[17] Wells Fargo is rumored to have made a settlement with Bolton on his release: a fat annuity, in return for which "Black Bart" promised to turn his back on crime for good. If true, it makes a happy ending.

of justice,[18] he sheltered at the aging mountain man's home until he could get passage back to England. During his 1852–53 winter at the Beckwourth ranch, he ghosted his host's life story, and on his return to London he had it published in serial form in a local newspaper under the title of *The Life and Adventures of James P. Beckwourth.* When it was published in book form in the States in 1856, Jim's pals "know'd he'd wrote it fer it were sech a pack o' lies." (See BECK-WOURTH, JAMES P.)

BONNEY, WILLIAM H. Billy the Kid undoubtedly used this name as an alias, but although Pat Garrett, and numerous others since, have stated that William H. Bonney was in fact the Kid's actual name, there is little evidence to support this view. The first book dealing with Billy the Kid, and the one with which we will concern ourselves (for later writers used it as a source of facts), was *The Authentic Life of Billy the Kid* by Pat Garrett. This book, which was ghosted by an itinerant newspaperman named Ash Upson, can have had little research put into it, for it came on to the market a bare fifteen months after the Kid had been shot down and killed by Garrett. In Chapter 1 of this work the Upson-Garrett combination gives the facts about the Kid's early life: that his name was William H. Bonney and that he was born in New York City on November 23, 1859. The only facts here are that Upson has lifted one of the Kid's aliases, added his—the writer's own—birthdate of November 23, and started a myth. The facts that need to be heeded when inquiring into the early life of Billy the Kid are those that were dug up in the 1950s and which undisputedly give his name as Henry McCarty. What made Henry McCarty dream up the William H. Bonney alias?[19] The "William H." isn't too difficult to dispose of, for his stepfather was named William H. Antrim. Bonney is the stumbling block, but if we cease to look upon it as a surname and take a more romantic view, it is possible to arrive at a solution that is at least feasible. Bearing in mind that the Kid was well liked by the *señoritas,* that he was only semiliterate, and that girls do use terms of endearment, could "Bonney" not be the Kid's rendering of a nickname that one of his girls may have given him? (See ANTRIM, CATHERINE, and McCARTY, HENRY.)

BOOT HILL A synonym for cemetery, the term originated in Dodge City around 1875, and it referred exclusively to a slight rise just northwest of the town that had become a temporary burial ground. Boot Hill had a short history, and because of this, few tenants. In 1878 the Prairie Grove Cemetery was completed, and in February of the following year the two dozen or so graves on Boot Hill were opened and their occupants reinterred in the new cemetery. Epitaphs that are alleged to have been burned onto the odd piece of lumber that served as markers on Boot Hill are of a somewhat humorous type: "Died of lead poisoning," and—for a past-tense rustler— "Too many irons in the fire." A new schoolhouse was built on the old Boot Hill site, but later this was pulled down to make way for a new city hall. Thanks to the movies and twentieth-century writers of Westerns, the term is now in general use throughout the modern West, so that no town with a violent or even lukewarm past can now afford to be without one— tourists, you know; in other words, the cemeteries of the 1800s have been re-

[18] Bonner had given judgment in favor of an impoverished but all too well-known crook.
[19] Some of the letters that are extant and that are known to have been written by Billy the Kid bear this signature. Others are signed "Billie."

christened "boot hills" and may have a sign to prove it. (See DODGE CITY, KANSAS.)

BOOT, JOE   Arizona miner who shares the glory with Pearl Hart for having committed the last stage robbery in the annals of the West. (See HART, PEARL.)

BOOTLEG PISTOL   Any type of single-shot under-hammer pistol that could be carried in the calf of a boot. They came in as many makes as calibers and were quite popular until the middle of the nineteenth century.

BORJOQUES, NARCISO
Californian robber and killer who is reputed to have always shot his victims through the head. In 1871 Borjoques murdered a rancher and his family and burned the bodies. This crime got Sheriff Harry N. Morse on his trail, but the killer was shot down in a saloon brawl and didn't live to be arrested. (See MORSE, HARRY N.)

BORNE, HENRY   Better known as "Dutch Henry," which seems to point to his being of German extraction, although little is known of Borne's early life. All that is known occurred after his leaving Custer's 7th Cavalry in the late 1860s. Borne got himself arrested at Fort Smith, Arkansas, for stealing twenty government mules (the most valuable animal on the plains) and was given a long sentence at hard labor. After serving three months, Borne escaped, and although he appears to have ignored mules from then on, he worked his way up until he was the most famous horse thief in the West. At the height of his career he had an estimated three hundred men working for him, and on at least one occasion he was sufficiently hard-faced to sell a lawman one of his stolen hay burners. In

1874 Dutch Henry was wounded while resisting arrest in the Ellsworth area, but there is no record of his having been tried or sentenced around this time. Four years later Bat Masterson had him arrested in Idaho, and brought him back to Dodge City to face charges of horse theft. Bat needn't have bothered, for when Dutch Henry came to trial, he was acquitted. But the horse thief's stars were beginning to darken, and a few months after his Dodge acquittal he was recaptured by the Arkansas authorities and returned to jail to complete his many long years of hard labor. Borne is reputed to have died in the early 1930s.

BOUYER, MITCH   Civilian scout attached to the U. S. Army. Bouyer, who was known to the Indians as "man in calfskin vest," was killed by hostiles at the Battle on the Little Big Horn.

BOWDRE, CHARLIE   Member of Billy the Kid's gang whose early life was spent as a cowhand on the New Mexico, Arizona, and Texas ranges. In the late 1870s he married an attractive Mexican girl named Manuela, and if letters of his that are extant do not bear the mark of hypocrisy, Bowdre seems to have wished to settle down. But it was not to be. During the Lincoln County War, he sided with the Tunstall-McSween faction and rode with Billy the Kid. In 1878 Bowdre saw action at Blazer's Mill, and after the war had worn itself out he continued his friendship with the Kid, and they went in for a spot of brand changing. These rustling activities were curtailed for Charlie by Sheriff Pat Garrett, who, at the head of a posse, trapped the gang at Stinking Springs on December 27, 1880. A gunfight followed, and Charlie Bowdre died from the effects of seven bullet wounds. Bowdre is alleged to be buried alongside Billy the Kid and Tom O'Folliard at Fort Sumner

—at least, the headstone says just that; but other sources state that only two bodies are interred at Fort Sumner, and that Bowdre is buried on the banks of the Rio Hondo. The river is 150 miles southwest of Stinking Springs—a long way to take a body in those days, so the headstone is most likely correct. (See ANDREWS, JESSE; LINCOLN COUNTY WAR; and McCARTY, HENRY.)

BOWEN, JANE The girl from Coon Hollow, Texas, who became the legendary sweetheart of John Wesley Hardin. Jane was fifteen when she met Hardin, and barely sixteen when they were married by a Methodist preacher in Riddleville, Texas, in September 1871. Jane gave Hardin three children, two girls and a boy: Jane; Callie; and John Wesley, Jr. Jane Bowen Hardin died while her husband was in prison, on November 6, 1892, aged thirty-six years. (See HARDIN, JOHN WESLEY.)

BOWIE, JAMES Soft-spoken aristocratic Southerner whose name will forever conjure up visions of knives. James was born in Kentucky in 1796, but the family moved to Catahoula Parish, Louisiana, when he was four, and he grew up in this area. In the local swamps he learned to rope alligators and then dispatch them with a butcher knife, and it was over this period that he became a champion of the knife, and for the rest of his days he preferred the blade to the pistol. When his brothers, both of whom carried firearms, queried his choice of weapons, James would neatly sum up his reasons with the remark, "A knife is always loaded." In 1818 James moved to Texas with his brother Rezin, and here they met Jean Lafitte and were introduced to the slave trade. At his headquarters on San Luis Island (off the Galveston, Texas, coast), the pirate explained the intricacies of selling "black ivory" in the States, and James and Rezin bought a quantity of the ebony merchandise at the going price of a dollar a pound and smuggled them across to the mainland by boat. In three years the Bowie brothers had cleaned up more than thirty thousand dollars, and they returned to Louisiana, where they went into partnership and opened the first steam mill sugar refinery in the state. This business prospered, and within five years they had sold out at a handsome profit, but by 1826 they were suffering the effects of financial malnutrition, and they resorted to selling forged land titles. The U. S. Supreme Court soon killed this racket, and James was forced to approach the local bank for a loan, but Major Morris Wright, the banker, turned down his request, and Bowie went away simmering. James came to the boil slowly. At that time local duels were fought on the Vidalia sandbar, a small island in the Mississippi, and Bowie inadvertently met Wright here on September 19, 1827, when both men were acting as seconds in a duel. Words were exchanged, and Bowie boiled over and disemboweled the banker with a neat one-two-three of his blade. Victorious, but not altogether popular, Bowie returned to Texas, and a few knife fights later he met Maria Ursula de Veramendi, a Castilian beauty who solved his money problems for a time when he married her at San Antonio de Bexer on April 22, 1830. Maria Ursula was the daughter of the Mexican lieutenant governor, a gentleman who was reputed to be worth a quarter of a million dollars, and who settled a fifteen-thousand-dollar dowry on his daughter's head. After the marriage James Bowie became known as a hard-drinking man, and even after the fifteen thousand can be assumed to have been spent, he still continued to be in ample funds. For years this cash came from the sale of silver bullion, and although Bowie let it be known that he had discovered a rich mine, it is far more likely that over this period he was robbing mule trains that transported the metal from the refineries.[20] About the middle of 1830 Bowie heard talk of an Arkansas cutler whose knives could "cut hickory for an hour and still remain an edge to shave with." James, whose mind must have been forever thinking up better methods of vivisection, visited the cutler, and by January 1831, James was in possession of the original Bowie knife.[21] He was soon to have legitimate targets for his new knife. As he was returning to Texas along the Southwest Trail our hero was set upon by three highwaymen, all of whom he killed in well under a minute. In the late spring of 1833, Bowie's wife and two children died in a cholera epidemic, and he returned to Louisiana. But the pull of San Antone was strong, and he was back there helping to kill "greasers" when the Texans revolted against Mexican rule in 1835. Bowie was commissioned colonel in the bobtailed army of settlers and frontiersmen that harassed the troops of Mexico, and although reports of his contemporaries state he was too selfish to ever be anything but a poor military man, he retained his rank until his death at the Alamo. Although he was killed by Santa Anna's men, Bowie can be said to have died in bed, for he was lying prone with a broken hip (he had fallen from a scaffold—builder's type) when the Mexican troops overran the Al-

amo on March 6, 1836 and put him, and every other male, to the sword. (See ALAMO, THE; BLACK JAMES; BOWIE KNIFE; and LAFITTE, JEAN.)

BOWIE KNIFE   The first Bowie knife was made in January 1831. James Bowie left a wooden prototype with an Arkansas knifemaker in December 1830, and four weeks later the cutler had his improved finished model ready for delivery. Knives bearing similarities to the Bowie knife had been manufactured in Europe for a hundred years before James made the scene, but the knife made in that January of 1831 was the king-sized killing tool of them all. It was 15 inches overall and 2 pounds in weight. The blade was 10 inches in length and around 2 inches across, and although the knife could be termed single-edged, a 2½-inch concave curve, which swept down from the brass fighting guard[22] to the tip, had been honed to razor sharpness as an added lethal touch. The hilt was of black walnut and the cross guard was about 3 inches in length, while the brass-mounted back of the blade was almost half an inch thick. Once the knife James owned became known, there were numerous imitations,[23] and at least a dozen cutlers have claimed the invention as their very own. Bowie knives were used as an all-around tool by most frontier folk—to slaughter hogs, cut wood, and eat with, but those imported from Sheffield, England, were evidently not intended for

[20] Bowie's "going to the mine" was probably nothing more than a polite euphemism for "going hijacking," for when he needed more bullion he would always take a gang of ten cronies along with him—quite a number to be allowed to know the whereabouts of a "secret" mine, one might think. Prospectors are still searching for Bowie's lost mine, but unless they find it the hijacking theory must remain valid.

[21] Rezin, eldest of the three Bowie brothers, is frequently credited with the invention of the Bowie knife, which he is alleged to have made by the dozen at his smithy. That an aristocratic Southerner should sweat himself silly in this pursuit seems rather odd, and how he ever found time to make all his cutlery among slave trading, sugar refining, and other less meritable enterprises is never explained.

[22] Brass, being softer than steel, held an opponent's blade when the back of the knife was used to parry a thrust.

[23] Much the same thing happened to Henry Deringer.

such homely chores, for they bore the engraved legend, "America Can and Must be Ruled by Americans"—a slogan obviously intended to provoke a wave of homicidal violence. (See BLACK, JAMES, and BOWIE, JAMES.)

BOZEMAN TRAIL   An overland route to the Montana goldfields that was pioneered by John Bozeman in the spring of 1863. The Bozeman left the Oregon Trail near Fort Laramie and followed a northwesterly course up into Montana before veering west and crossing the Big Horn River, then angling southwest to its terminal point at Virginia City, Montana. Five military posts guarded the trail over the 1865–75 period: Fort Laramie, then (working northwest) Fort Fetterman, Fort Reno, Fort Phil Kearny and Fort C. F. Smith.

BRADY, MATTHEW B.   Foremost of the early-day photographers. Brady, whose parents are believed to have been Irish immigrants, was born in Warren County, New York, in 1822.[24] Brady opened his first gallery in New York City in 1844—a mere five years after photography had become possible, and although he never took his camera to the far West, his portraits of notables who left their mark in this area is sufficient reason for his inclusion in this volume. During the Civil War Brady was official photographer for the Union armies, and the work of the master and his team over this period has to be seen to be believed, while the Andersonville atrocity pictures are similar in content to those taken at Belsen some eighty years later. Brady died in New York on January 15, 1896. The following are but a few of his sitters who have Wild West connections: John Brown, Sam Houston, Kit Carson, George Armstrong Custer, John C. Fremont, Washington Irving, Allen Pinkerton, Mark Twain, Lew Wallace, and Brigham Young.

BRADY, WILLIAM   Sheriff of Lincoln County during the initial stages of the Murphy-McSween feud. Brady was an old Army buddy of Murphy's, and it was a Brady posse that shot down and killed John H. Tunstall, McSween's partner, on February 18, 1878. Although the sheriff didn't accompany the posse on what turned out to be a murder mission, he signed his own death warrant by ordering his deputies to ride out that winter morning, for Tunstall was a friend of Billy the Kid, and vengeance was not long delayed. On April 1, 1878, Sheriff Brady and one of his deputies were killed by a hail of lead as they walked down a Lincoln street. This was an ambush killing by the Kid and his gang, and although Brady's death is frequently notched up to the Kid, it is impossible to say whose bullets wound up in the sheriff's back. (See LINCOLN COUNTY WAR and McCARTY, HENRY.)

BRAHMA CATTLE   Cattle imported from India for crossbreeding purposes. Texas Brahmans are a mixture of the original Indian stock, Longhorns, and Herefords; while their wild nature had prevented them from becoming popular as range stock, this selfsame trait has made them a must for rodeos.

BRANDING   Any method used to mark cattle or horses for ownership identification purposes, although it is usually done by a heated branding iron or a knife. In the latter case flaps or gashes are cut into the skin of the animal. Rump gashes are known as breeching, while cuts that allow folds of skin to hang from

---

[24] The year is taken from Brady's tombstone, but this is little to go by, for the same stone erroneously gives the year of his death as 1895. Brady himself stated that he was born in either 1823 or 1824.

the face or shoulders are called wattles, and those that allow skin to droop from the lower jaw or neck are called dewlaps. Ear marking is also done with a knife, but this form of marking is usually found in conjunction with a burned brand and rarely stands alone. Brands made by an iron can be altered by a rustler who used a little ingenuity and a running iron, but knife marks are more or less forgeryproof.

BRANDING IRON A tool for branding cattle or horses by burning a design on their hide. There are roughly two types: the stamp iron and the running iron. The former almost always has the complete brand design either welded or screwed to the shank, while the latter, which usually has a hooked end, can be used to make, or alter, almost any brand, and is therefore much favored by members of the rustling fraternity. At one time, in some areas, to be caught with a running iron in one's possession usually meant a quick one-way trip to the nearest hanging tree.

BRANDS A form of range heraldry that denotes stock ownership and that from simple beginnings became more and more elaborate in an effort to beat rustlers. A brand is usually composed of stock components such as a square, vertical bar; horizontal bar; circle; letter or part of a letter, etc., and the positioning of such components lends a descriptive adjective to the brand: A letter placed horizontally is termed "lazy," while if it leans to the right it is known as "tumbling," and angling to the left, "crazy." The permutations that can be made from these components are virtually limitless, but even so, many brands are highly original designs that ignore stock patterns. At the present time you can register a brand in Texas—whether you possess cattle or not—for around five dollars,

the only stipulation being that your design be unlike any other brand.

BRAZEL, WAYNE   Small-time rancher who rented pasture from Pat Garrett, and who was the self-confessed slayer of the ex-sheriff. Garrett was about to sell his ranch, and Brazel stated that a row developed regarding his terms of lease and that when Garrett reached for his gun, he shot Garrett in self-defense. Wayne Brazel was tried in April 1909, twelve months after the killing, and he was acquitted. Legend has it that Brazel was paid to accept responsibility for the murder and that a hired gun named Jim Miller did the actual shooting, and in this instance legend is most likely correct. (See GARRETT, PATRICK FLOYD, and MILLER, JIM.)

BRAZOS RIVER One of the main rivers of Texas, and one of the seven that had to be crossed by trail herds that followed the Chisholm or Shawnee trails north from San Antonio. The Brazos runs in a southeasterly direction from its headwaters in the Staked Plains, and drains into the Gulf of Mexico some forty miles southwest of Galveston.

BREAKENRIDGE, WILLIAM MILTON "Billy" Breakenridge was born at Watertown, Wisconsin, on Christmas Day 1846, and by the time he was sixteen he was serving in the 3rd Colorado Cavalry. After leaving the Army he tried his hand at freighting and prospecting, and although he had little success in the latter pursuit, he continued searching for his pot of gold until 1880, at which time he became a deputy sheriff under John Behan at Tombstone. This job consisted mainly of collecting taxes, but as Behan's bailiwick encompassed Charleston and Galeyville, camps whose populations were composed almost entirely of rustlers and gunmen, the job was no sinecure. Deputy Sheriff Breakenridge was either well in with the lawless element, or his reported psychological approach to the problem made the job a success; he is alleged to have arranged a meeting with Curly Bill Brocius (one of the most rip-snorting rustlers and gunmen in the territory) and to have requested that that gentleman act as his bodyguard, and Curly Bill is reported to have stepped out of character and obliged. Being a Behan man, Breakenridge was naturally opposed to the Earps, but this antipathy never developed into a brawl or an exchange of gun dialogue, which was probably as well for Billy, for no one has ever reported that he was fast with a gun.[25] In 1882 Breakenridge tried his hand at ranching for a spell, but by 1886 he was back behind the tin as a deputy U.S. marshal, and after the turn of the century he was employed as a special agent by the Southern Pacific Railway. Breakenridge died in a Tucson, Arizona, hospital on January 31, 1931. (See GRAHAM, WILLIAM B.; HUNT, ZWING; and RINGGOLD, JOHN.)

BREWER, DICK   Ranchowner and foreman of John H. Tunstall's horse ranch, and active participant in the Lincoln County War. Brewer was a witness to the murder of Tunstall; the leader of the posse that arrested Morton and Baker for the killing; and he was in at the shooting of the two prisoners by Billy the Kid. Mr. Brewer was voted "out" on April 4, 1878, when the top of his head was blown off by Jesse Andrews at Blazer's Mill. (See ANDREWS, JESSE; BAKER, FRANK; LINCOLN COUNTY WAR; and McCARTY, HENRY.)

BREYFOGLE, JACOB   Blacksmith cum prospector of German origin who has given people another "lost mine" to

find. Breyfogle prospected in the California gold fields then moved East to Virginia City, Nevada, in the early 1860s. In 1864 he wandered westward again, and somewhere in the Death Valley area of the California-Nevada border he is believed to have hit the jackpot. But herein lies the rub: Shortly after finding his bonanza Breyfogle was attacked by Indians. When he was found rambling around by another prospector named Yount some weeks later, although Breyfogle's pockets were loaded with high-grade ore, a crack from a warclub had somewhat emptied his mind. He was, in other words, badly orientated, and even after making a partial mental recovery, he was unable to backtrack and find what is now referred to as the "Breyfogle Lost Mine." That the semidelirious man's pockets were heavy with ore when he was found there can be no doubt, for Yount would never have spent time helping Breyfogle to search for the strike if there had been no tangible evidence of its existence, but at the time of writing, and although new generations are still searching, no one has staked a claim to Jacob's lost bonanza. Jacob's brother Charles C. Breyfogle is sometimes credited with playing the leading role in this little melodrama; this substitution no doubt lends a touch of refinement to the story, for Charles C. is on record as being an educated man, whereas Jake is reputed to have been a bit of a slob; but otherwise the story is the same.

BRIDGER, JIM   Possibly the most famous of the mountain men, Bridger was born in 1804 at St. Louis, Missouri, but eighteen years later his itchy feet had taken him to the region of the Shining Mountains. His main revenue came from trapping beaver, and by the time he was thirty-nine he had secured sufficient capi-

25 In 1925, when Wyatt Earp was seventy-six and Breakenridge was seventy-nine, the two elderly gentlemen met and talked over old times without any show of animosity.

tal to build his own trading post on the Green River of Wyoming. This center became known as Bridger's Fort, and he amassed a considerable fortune trading with the migrant trains that prairie-schooner'd along the Oregon Trail. Apart from getting a Blackfoot arrow lodged in his person in 1832—an act for which he never forgave the whole tribe—Bridger's relations with the Indians were friendly, and he married a Shoshone girl and had four children by her. During this prosperous period he bought a farm in Missouri and settled his family in this comparatively civilized area, but by 1854 this farm was all he had left. The Mormons objected to his selling of arms to the Indians, and in that year Brigham Young's "Avenging Angels" swooped down on Bridger's Fort and burned it to the ground. Bridger lost nearly a quarter-million dollars from this senseless attack, and for the next four years he struggled to obtain sufficient money to put his case before the government and have action taken against the Mormons. At the time of this financial stress, Sir George Gore, an Irish nobleman and pathological killer of wildlife, hired Bridger as a guide, but although the mountain man was glad of the money—and all the imported Irish whiskey he could guzzle for free—he was relieved when the government put a stop to Sir George's senseless slaughter, and the well-blooded knight and his retainers were almost forced to leave the country. In 1858 the authorities listened to Jim's pleas, and troops were sent against the Mormon citadel, but although these forces occupied Salt Lake City, nothing was resolved as far as Bridger was concerned, and he received no compensation for the outrage of four years earlier. Bitter and nearly broke, the aging pioneer joined the Army as a scout, and for

the next decade he either witnessed, or was involved in, many of the skirmishes along the Bozeman Trail (the Powder River Expedition of 1865 [which disgusted Bridger with its standing orders to kill every Indian over the age of twelve] and the Fetterman Fight of 1866, to name but two). In 1868 the Sioux under Red Cloud destroyed most of the forts along the Bozeman, and two years later Bridger was discharged from the Army with failing health. In 1871 this trailblazer[26] retired to his farm in Missouri where, his wife having died some years previously, he was looked after by his daughter Virginia. For years Bridger suffered from a plethora of complaints—goiter, rheumatism, and finally blindness, and in July 1881, in the presence of Virginia and after muttering "the Mighty One above has called me" in the Shoshone tongue, the old mountain man died. (See FETTERMAN FIGHT and GORE, GEORGE.)

BROADWELL, DICK   Onetime cowboy of the Halsell outfit of Oklahoma who joined the Daltons in their eighteen-month reign of terror. Young Broadwell was shot dead on October 5, 1892, while the gang was attempting a double bank robbery at Coffeyville, Kansas. (See COFFEYVILLE, KANSAS, and DALTON GANG.)

BROCIUS, "CURLY BILL"   Alias of a notorious badman named William B. Graham. (See GRAHAM, WILLIAM B.)

BRONCHO   Spanish for "rough, coarse," or "rude," but in western parlance it more specifically refers to a half-trained horse.

BRONCHO APACHE   An Apache who bears allegiance to no particular

---

[26] Jim Bridger was a tireless explorer, three of his "fust there's" being: South Pass, the Great Salt Lake (at the time he thought he had reached the Pacific), and the Yellowstone Park geysers.

tribe—that is, a brave who has severed his tribal connections.

BROOKS, WILLIAM   Known as "Buffalo Bill," Brooks was an Indian scout, buffalo hunter, and stage driver who became a famous lawman relatively late in life. Brooks was forty years old when he took the job of city marshal at Newton, Kansas, in the early months of 1872, but age[27] hadn't slowed his reflexes, and although he was wounded in a gunfight in July he tamed the town temporarily, so that his fame soon spread to Dodge City, and he was persuaded to leave Newton and try his hand at cleaning up the "cow capital" in the latter half of 1872. During his first month as marshal at Dodge he killed or wounded no less than fifteen hard cases, on one occasion wiping out a family of four brothers who ganged up on him for killing a fifth; Brooks used only four shots for this mass execution, so he was obviously no slouch with an equalizer. At least one of Brooks' killings while in Dodge was not a line-of-duty job, for he is known to have shot down a rival over the attentions of a dance hall girl, but the marshal was not reprimanded for this; either the City Fathers were afraid of the toughest man around, or they took the reasonable view that a sex-inspired killing was justifiable homicide. Women were the downfall of Buffalo Bill at Dodge, for after a row over a local young damsel with a very rugged character named Kirk Jordan, Brooks was forced to leave town; the marshal could face the light stuff—.45s and such—but he dived for cover when Jordan opened up with his Sharps "Big Fifty." Brooks paused only long enough to surround a quantity of whiskey before throwing in his badge and heading for the timber. Some years later Buffalo Bill Brooks

tried for the marshal's job at Butte, Montana, but he was beaten to the post by Morgan Earp. This evidently rankled the tamer of Newton and Dodge, for he let it be known that he would shoot Morgan on sight. Morgan accepted the challenge, and a few hours later the two men met on the main street in a rare but classical example of the western gunfight. Two shots sounded as one and Morgan clutched his arm as Brooks lost his clutch on life—a bullet in the body had ended the saga of Buffalo Bill Brooks.

BROTHELS   The bawdyhouses of the West, as opposed to the scattered cribs of the red-light districts' freelancers, were usually opulent palaces of basic entertainment. A few thumbnail descriptions of some such places are given below, but it must be remembered that although outstanding, they are not isolated examples, and similar places could be found in many of the larger cowtowns and mining camps. Tessie Wall's, San Francisco: an elaborate establishment of heavy-pile carpets, brocaded sofas, cut-glass chandeliers, gold-leaf tables, and tasseled draperies, a place of refined loose living where the clients were never drugged or robbed. Bull Run, San Francisco: If this place was still operating we would warn you to avoid it, for although equally grand, it was run by a gentleman named Ned Allen, and like many such places run by males—and possibly because they cannot take an active part in the profession—Ned endeavored to pull his weight by administering "mickies" to satiated clients and robbing them. A madame would rarely resort to this, for it was a surefire way of ruining her good name. Everleigh Sisters, Omaha: Graciousness and the last word in plush-inspired passion was also the theme here. Added refinements were a gold-plated pi-

[27] Forty was old for a gunfighter, for it is surprising how many were shot down in their thirties.

ano and a stained-glass ceiling, although the latter must have been for the staff's enjoyment, for such being the nature of things, it is unlikely that any of the visiting cowpokes noticed this splendid canopy. San Francisco is mentioned twice, and this could hardly be avoided, for in 1850 the city had a red-light area that would have made the similar quarters in Paris, France, look like a Methodist convention. French women were in great demand, and in the above-mentioned year five hundred cute Parisienne pastries were imported to give the place zest —a zest the entire population occasionally shared when a minor earthquake tremor would decide to collapse a bordello wall during a rush hour. By 1878 San Francisco appears to have been almost one big joyhouse, and in that year the perturbed City Elders conducted an on-the-spot inquiry with a view to passing legislation to curb the lewd goings-on. Things evidently didn't look quite so lewd from inside these lush emporiums, and after the investigation had been helped along by a few of the girls serving them drinks, etc., the graybeards must have forgotten all about such useless pursuits as bowling and bingo, for apart from a few remarks at after-dinner stags, nothing more was heard of the clean-up campaign. (See BULETTE, JULIA; DODGE CITY, KANSAS; and RED-LIGHT DISTRICT.)

BROWN, GEORGE W. Member of Henry Plummer's gang of road agents. Brown was arrested by vigilantes and hanged from a cottonwood tree for the crimes of multiple murder on January 4, 1864. (See INNOCENTS and PLUMMER, HENRY.)

BROWN, HENDRY Onetime whiskey peddler and buffalo hunter who was at the Adobe Walls fight, and who later joined the McSween faction as a hired gun during the Lincoln County War. Brown, who at this period rode with Billy the Kid, was in at the killings of Morton and Baker, and of Buckshot Roberts. At the end of the Lincoln County War Brown severed his association with the Kid and moved to Tascosa, Texas, where, of all things, he became town constable. This, however, soon palled, and he headed North to Kansas. At Caldwell he managed to get himself appointed deputy marshal, and after killing two men in a gunfight, he was promoted to marshal. He had the Caldwell star until 1884, in which year he leaped to the other side of the fence by organizing a raid on the bank at Medicine Lodge. Brown and three others hit the bank in April of that year, and Brown was responsible for the murder of the bank president, while another member of the gang killed a teller during the robbery. A heavily armed posse captured the four bandits after a long-drawn-out gunfight, and the prisoners were lodged in the local jail. During the night a large mob attacked the calaboose, overpowered the jailers, and dragged the four gunmen to a nearby tree where they were all hanged without further ceremony. (See ANDREWS, JESSE; BAKER, FRANK; BATTLE AT ADOBE WALLS; and LINCOLN COUNTY WAR.)

BROWN, JOHN Born on May 9, 1800, in Connecticut, John Brown had a variety of callings before he rose to fame as a violent political agitator. He first studied to become a Congregational minister, but gave this up in 1818 and tried his hand at soldiering. He soldiered on for more than thirty years before settling in a very unsettled Kansas in 1855. Pro- and antislavery feelings were rife in the region, and Brown, a militant abolitionist, became the guiding star of the antislavery movement. In 1856 Brown and some of his followers killed a gentleman named "Dutch Bill" and four other proslavery sympathizers on Pottawatomie Creek, and the following year he organized a retreat for runaway slaves in Virginia. In 1859 Brown made his biggest play, and he and his men seized the government arsenal at Harpers Ferry. The insurrectionists held the building for two days before they were forced to surrender by Lieutenant Colonel Robert E. Lee. The abolitionist was tried and found guilty of murder and treason—quite justifiably so, and he was hanged on December 2, 1859. John Brown's body is the one referred to as "mouldering" in the Union Army song of the Civil War years.

BRUER, DICK An error in nomenclature that appears in *The Authentic Life of Billy the Kid* by Pat Garrett. (See BREWER, DICK.)

BRUNETTES Nonderogatory term applied to regiments whose ranks were black; the 10th U. S. Cavalry, commanded by Colonel L. H. Carpenter, was known as Carpenter's Brunettes.

BRYANT, CHARLIE A member of the Dalton gang who was sometimes known as "Blackface" because of facial powder burns. Bryant took part in the gang's holdup of a Santa Fe express on May 9, 1891, but he hardly lived long enough to spend his share of the fourteen thousand dollars reported to have been stolen. Shortly after the robbery he was arrested by Deputy U. S. Marshal Ed Short and escorted onto a train bound for Wichita and the nearest federal court. Although handcuffed, "Blackface" managed to come into possession of a revolver en route, and both he and the deputy marshal died in the ensuing gunfight, which occurred in the train's caboose. If the testimony of the time can be believed, Mr. Bryant is one of the few western gunmen who bothered about

having his boots removed before drawing his last breath. (See DALTON GANG.)

BUCKAROO A word used throughout the West as an alternative to "cowboy." The word is derived from the Spanish *vaquero*.

BUCK GANG Short-lived gang that was extremely colorful in the racial sense. Rufus Buck, the leader, was a Ute Indian; Sam Sampson, Lewis David David, and Maomi July were Creeks; and Lucky Davis, the final member, was Creek and black. Their careers as holdup men and rustlers lasted but thirteen days, but during that period they completely terrorized the folk—both white and nonwhite—who were living in Cherokee Territory (Oklahoma). The downward path of these ne'er-do-wells commenced on July 28, 1895, when they murdered a deputy U.S. marshal, and once outside the law, and between holdups, they spiced their life of crime with a spot of rape. The gang captured a widow named Wilson and put her to the question five times, and a lass named Rosetta Hassan got the same treatment while her husband was held under the guns of the nonactive members of the gang, and after she had been threatened that "her . . . brats would be tossed into the creek iffen she caused too much fussin'." There doesn't appear to have been any rules of precedence within the gang, for although Rufus was undoubtedly the leader, Lucky Davis was the first to escort the reluctant Rosetta into the bedroom; neither does a "color bar" seem to have swayed their actions, for on at least one occasion a black was shot dead just for the hell of it. On August 10 they were tracked down by U.S. marshals and Indian police, and after a bloodless gun battle all five miscreants were arrested and taken to Fort Smith, Arkansas, for trial. They were brought before Judge

Parker in 1896, and a quintuple hanging was staged on July 1 of that year.

BUCK, RUFUS Leader of the notorious Buck Gang. (See BUCK GANG.)

BUCKSHOT ROBERTS One of the aliases of Jesse Andrews. (See ANDREWS, JESSE.)

BUCKSKIN Soft leather that at one time was made from deerskin, but is now usually made from the skins of sheep. The soft texture of the Indian buckskin was produced by having the squaws chew the skins for hours on end.

BUCKSKIN JOE Here we get three for the price of one, as it were, for "Buckskin Joe" can refer to Buffalo Bill Cody's horse, a mining camp in the Pike's Peak region of Colorado, or to the old prospector who discovered gold in that area.

BUFFALO The American name for a species of ox that is known as bison in Europe, and that at one time roamed both continents in large numbers. The buffalo is divided into two varieties—the prairie and the woodland—the latter being the larger of the two but inferior numerically. In the early 1800s the prairie buffalo could be counted in the tens of millions and was roughly divided into four great herds—the Northern herd, the Republican, the Arkansas, and the Texas, but by the end of the century only a few small herds had survived the indiscriminate slaughter by hide hunters and so-called "sportsmen," and today only a few thousand remain, all of which are located on government or private preserves. A recent English encyclopedia gives the European bison as being the larger animal, the vital statistics being given as 9 feet in length, 6 feet at the shoulder, and three-quarters ton in weight, yet Ivan T. Sanderson in his *How to Know American Mammals* states that the American variety can reach a length of 12 feet, be 6 feet at the shoulder, and weigh up to 1 ton. Obviously in one of these instances national pride is battling with scholarship, and we can only assume that an elastic tape measure and faulty scales must have been used by one of these authorities to salve their conscience. At one time an attempt was made to cross buffalo with range cattle, but although the offspring didn't look too weird, the enterprise was a commercial failure. (See CATTALO.)

BUFFALO BILL CODY One of the many Buffalo Bills who helped to almost exterminate the American buffalo, but undoubtedly the most famous of them all. (See CODY, WILLIAM FREDERICK.)

BUFFALO HORSES The cream of the Indian pony herds, they were horses specifically trained for hunting buffalo, and that were readily distinguishable among the plains tribes by a "V" notch cut into the tips of their ears.

BUFFALO HUNTERS A gang of footloose individuals who invaded the plains in their hundreds in the middle 1800s, and who only disappeared when the buffalo had been reduced to near extinction. They were tough men all, yet there was little glamor in their trade, and folk usually kept upwind when in their presence. Many were misfits who worked alone, but more often a hunter would employ some even lowlier type to do the skinning, etc., while he cooled his gun barrel. Almost any type of firearm was used by these men, but the Sharps "Big Fifty"—"the gun that shoots today and kills tomorrow"—was preferred to all other models. Sometimes the herds were attacked from horseback, but the usual practice was to pick off beasts from the perimeter of the herd; this was called a "stand," and an experienced hunter could blast away all day without stampeding the dumb critters. Buffalo were hunted for meat (for the railroad construction crews), for their robes, and then, when the hide market collapsed, for their tongues alone, and if you couldn't afford a gun (or couldn't hit a barn if you possessed one), you could always collect the bones and sell them for fertilizer. The skinners were the underdogs of the profession, but they were undoubtedly skilled in their work, and they could roll a ton-weight carcass over by using the decapitated head as a wedge. Earp, Hickok, Garrett, etc., were all buffalo hunters at some time or other of their careers. Sir George Gore and other European noblemen also slaughtered buffalo in large and senseless numbers, but as these types were merely trophy hunters who shot at anything that moved if it couldn't fire back, they can hardly be termed "buffalo hunters" in the strict sense of the meaning. (See CHIPS.)

BUFFALOING   The gentle art of bending a revolver barrel around an adversary's skull without homicidal intent, although occasions have been known where the whole effort has been ruined by the victim failing to recover. Wyatt Earp was one of the foremost practitioners of this anesthetizing art.

BUFFALO SOLDIERS   North Plains Indians' name for black troops.

BUFFALO VERNON   Colorful name used by Tom Averill, the latter half of which the Indians gave him. (See AVERILL, TOM.)

BULETTE, JULIA
Girl of part-French parentage who is believed to have been born in Liverpool, England. Julia, young and undoubtedly beautiful, arrived at Virginia City, Nevada, in 1859, and as there were more than six thousand men chasing a handful of women in the town, she went into the most obvious line of business. The enterprise flourished, and as Julia's capacity was naturally limited, within twelve months she was employing six other girls in an effort to thin the line. Her bagnio, which was known as Julia's Palace, was the last word in luxury. The furnishings were expensive and elaborate, French wines flowed, and the whole place reeked of rare Parisian perfumes. Miss Bulette, despite her profession (or possibly because of it), had the proverbial heart of gold, and during a fever epidemic she turned her palace into a hospital and pawned much of her jewelry and furs to raise money for the sick. When the sickness had passed and the bagnio had again reverted to its proper place in the scheme of things, the men of the town made her an honorary member of Engine Company No. 1 (the Fire Department). The female element sniffed at this, but Julia ignored these simulated cold symptoms, following the fire truck after each alarm and making on-the-spot coffee for the sweating firemen. In 1867 three trail lice entered Julia's Palace, ostensibly as customers, but when they had left, the place had been looted and Julia lay strangled to death. Virginia City responded magnificently—its inhabitants were nearly all males; remember? All mills, mines, and business premises closed down for the day of her funeral, and the local brass band playing "The Girl I Left Behind Me" led the cortege to Julia's final resting place, which, alas, was far outside the city limits, for the so-called "men of God" wouldn't allow the lass to be interred in hallowed ground. In 1868 a man named John Millais was arrested and charged with the murder. Leaders in the Church paid

him frequent visits while he was in jail awaiting trial, and, even sadder to relate, the respectable women of the town treated him as a hero; the saner element, who were in the majority, triumphed, and on April 24, 1869, Millais was hanged.

BULLARD RIFLE
Rifles manufactured by the Bullard Repeating Arms Company of Springfield, Massachusetts. The firm produced rifled muskets, carbines, and hunting and target rifles, and models could be obtained with round or octagonal barrels and in a large variety of calibers. The hunting rifles weighed 10 pounds and were 11-shot repeaters with lever action.

BULLBOATS   Coracle-type boats made from buffalo hide stretched over a frame of light wood. Their use was confined mainly to the Mandan and Hidasta tribes, and the boats could be put to a secondary use during heavy rains by inverting them and placing them over the smoke holes of the tribes' earth lodges. Catlin believed that the Mandan may have been of British or, more specifically, Welsh descent. One wonders if these coracles (among other European pointers) helped sway him toward this belief.

BULLDOZER
A single-shot, .41-caliber pistol made by the Connecticut Arms and Manufacturing Company. The gun had an octagonal barrel and was without trigger guard.

BULL DURHAM   Popular brand of granulated tobacco marketed in small muslin sacks that at one time had a packet of brown "roll your own" papers attached. The Bull trademark and the

latter half of the name are derived from England's Durham's Mustard.

BULLION, LAURA   This girl's surname is sometimes given as "Bullin," the confusion probably arising from the fact that during the time she was riding with the Hole in the Wall gang a gentleman named Bullin was also a member of the gang. The Pinkerton files give "Laura Bullion" as the alias of Della Rose. (See ROSE, DELLA.)

BUMMERS   Name given to an organized gang of thieves, rapists, and terrorists who more or less ran the town of Auraria, Colorado, from the middle 1850s until 1860, in which year a vigilante committee of ten townsmen and the local sheriff brought a semblance of law and order to the community by thinning the ranks of the Bummers with multiple hangings.

BUNTLINE, NED   Pen name of Edward Z. C. Judson. (See JUDSON, EDWARD Z. C.)

BUNTLINE SPECIAL   Nowadays any single-action .45-caliber Colt's revolver with a 16-inch barrel is referred to as a "Buntline,"[28] but the name can only be correctly applied to any of the five guns that Ned Buntline purchased and that had the name "Ned" carved into their walnut butt plates. Around thirty of these extralong-barreled revolvers were manufactured in 1876, and at a retail price of twenty-six dollars the guns—which were actually Peacemakers with overlong barrels—came complete with detachable shoulder stocks and hand-tooled scabbards. Bunt-

[28] In 1957 Colt reintroduced a long-barreled revolver, but although the model is called a "Buntline Special," it must be emphasized that it is only a replica of the original, and not an accurate replica at that, for the barrel is only 12 inches in length.

line presented a Special to each of the following: Wyatt Earp, Charlie Bassett, Bat Masterson, Bill Tilghman, and Neal Brown. Brown and Bassett kept their gifts in mint condition, but Earp, Masterson, and Tilghman cut their barrels down to their own specifications, each trimming his Buntline to 12 inches, 4½ inches, and 7½ inches, respectively. Earp carried his against his right thigh, and he is reported to have found it the ideal weapon for buffaloing truculent characters whom he had no desire to use up. (See COLT FIREARMS.)

BURKE, JEAN HICKOK
Name used by the daughter of Jane Cannary and James Butler Hickok after her mother's second marriage—which was to a gentleman named Charlie Burke. (See CANNARY, MARTHA JANE, and HICKOK, JEAN.)

BURKE, STEVE Insurance man who became a deputy U.S. marshal in the early 1890s. Burke remained a lawman for four years, over which period he took part in many gun battles. He was never wounded by lead, but while arresting Cattle Annie at Pawnee he lost much of his scalp hair, and for days afterward his face bore a Martian-canal pattern of scratches. Around 1895 he became a preacher of the Gospel, and he died in the 1940s while addressing an evangelist meeting at Paris, Texas. (See McDOUGAL, ANNIE.)

BURRO The Spanish name for "donkey," and one that is used throughout the West. Although burros are stubborn, they are a must for prospectors, for they can carry up to 300 pounds, a load that is nearly double that which the average cow pony can be expected to carry for any length of time. These long-eared, mousey-hided creatures are known to be able to swim, but they usually drown without making any effort to save themselves if they are expected to cross a stream. Their wanderlust is legendary, and a prospector who had searched for ore for fifty years is reputed to have admitted that thirty of those years had been spent searching for his burros, which invariably, however hobbled, wandered away whenever he hit the sack.

BURROW, REUBEN HOUSTON
Next to the youngest of the males in a family of five girls and five boys. Rube was born in Lamar County, Alabama, on December 11, 1854. His father was an illiterate moonshiner whose Christian name was Allen, and his mother was a successful backwoods faith healer named Martha Caroline, who had been a nineteen-year-old Miss Terry when she married Burrow in 1849. Rube and brother Jim, who were only semiliterate like the rest of the family, moved to Texas in 1872, but unlike most wanderers, Rube kept in frequent touch with his family and often enclosed money with his almost undecipherable messages— "analyzer" for Ann Eliza is but one precious example. For fourteen years Rube and Jim lived more or less tranquil existences in Texas. They had a small farm —small by Texas standards, for they wrote home about "planting 35 acreys of corn" and having a "few ooats sode," and in 1876 Rube married a lass named Virginia Alvison, who gave him two children before she died in 1880. He remarried in 1884 and Jim married two years later, and in that year, possibly because they had heard all about the glamorous and late-lamented Sam Bass, the two brothers left their cozy firesides and became outlaws. They specialized in train robbery, and a list of such crimes committed by them gives a good idea of their success and movements over the next twelve months.

December 1886: A train of the Fort
Worth and Denver at Bellevue,
Texas.
February 1887: A train of the Texas Pa-
cific at Gordon, Texas.
June 1887: A train of the Texas Pacific
at Ben Brooks, Texas.
September 1887: Repeat performance of
above.
December 1887: A train of the Texas
Pacific at Genoa, Texas.

After the last-mentioned robbery a
friend of the Burrows named Will Brock
was taken into custody, and at his subsequent trial he was given twenty-two
years for his part in the crime. The Burrows were now badly wanted by the
Pinkertons and other law-enforcement
agencies, and the two brothers returned
to Alabama to lay low. On January 10,
1888, having heard that the wanted men
had returned to Lamar, the local lawmen
surrounded what they believed to be the
Burrows home, but in the darkness the
posse circled the wrong house, and Rube
and Jim escaped. In February of the
same year the brothers were arrested by
the Montgomery, Alabama, police, but
Rube escaped after a gunfight in which
he killed a citizen. The older brother now
forgot train robbing for a time and concentrated on rescuing Jim. He recruited
a hard case named Lewis Waldrip to help
him in the enterprise, but on October 5,
1888, and before their scheming could
come to anything, Jim died in prison
from rapid consumption. On December
15, 1888, Rube and another man robbed
the Illinois Central at Duck Hill, Mississippi. A gunfight occurred during the
robbery and Rube shot and killed a passenger named Chester Hughes. In June
of the following year Rube killed an express agent in Alabama. This shooting
was merely to settle an argument and had
nothing to do with train holdups, but by
September the outlaw was back at his

profitable pastime, successfully looting a
train in Mississippi. After this robbery
Rube fled to the Florida swamps, and he
didn't surface again until September 1,
1890, when he held up and robbed a
Louisville and Nashville train at Floma-
ton, Alabama. But time was running out
for Rube, and when he made the mistake
of taking shelter in the home of a giant
black named Jesse Hildreth on October 7,
the man overpowered him and handed
him over to the authorities. The outlaw
was lodged in the Linden, Alabama, jail,
and sometime during that day he came
into possession of a revolver. This only
hastened his end, for although he managed to wound a guard in his escape bid,
that selfsame turnkey shot him into eternity.

BURTS, MATTHEW Member of the
Burt Alvord–Billy Stiles gang who is
known to have taken part in the Southern Pacific train robbery near Cochise,
Arizona, on September 9, 1899. After
this holdup Burts came under suspicion,
but as there was little tangible evidence
against the man, the lawmen involved resorted to strategy. Constable Grover of
Pearce, Arizona, appointed Burts as a
deputy, and when the outlaw's suspicions
had been lulled, a confession was talked
out of him when he had been gotten
gloriously drunk. Burts named all his
confederates, and all the members of the
gang were arrested. The talkative Matthew got a long term in the territorial
prison at Yuma, and on his release he
moved to California, where he went into
the cattle business. He was engaged in
this respectable enterprise until his death,
said demise occurring in November 1925,
when Burts was shot dead by a neighbor
after an argument over grazing rights.
(See ALVORD, BURT.)

BUSCADERO A type of gunbelt with
twin drop loops. When the belt is buckled

across the lower abdomen the loops are located on the left and right hips, and the holsters that swing from these loops hang lower on the thighs than is the case with the more common[29] waist-type belts. This undoubtedly makes for a faster draw, and although the word is derived from *busca*, which is the Spanish equivalent of "search" and therefore can be applied to a searcher or lawman,[30] it is occasionally met with as meaning just the reverse—that is, a fast two-gun man who is outside the law. A modern hand-tooled buscadero complete with twin holsters can be obtained for about forty dollars. (See FAST DRAW; GUNBELT; and HOLSTER.)

BUTLER, FRANK   Exhibition marksman who was outpointed by a young girl named Annie Moses in an Ohio shooting match. Frank swallowed his pride and did the best thing possible in the circumstances: He married the girl, and as her manager built her up into one of the greatest shooting stars the world has ever seen. From then on his career and fortunes were inextricably linked with Annie's. Frank, an Irish immigrant who had arrived in New York City in 1863 when he was twenty-three years old, had tried his hand at numerous jobs in the States—driving a milk wagon, following horses in the most menial sense, selling newspapers, and glass blowing—before taking up stage work. Trained dogs helped him out for a time, but he had made his name in the New York halls as a trick shooter by the time of the Ohio shooting competition mentioned earlier.

Butler died in Detroit, Michigan, on November 23, 1926, exactly twenty days after the death of his wife. (See OAKLEY, ANNIE.)

BUTTE   An isolated flat-topped hill that usually rises from a comparatively level plain and that is, more or less, a small mesa. Buttes are particularly numerous in Utah and Arizona, although somewhat better-known ones are to be found elsewhere. Two Nebraskan examples are Jail Rock and Court House Rock, both of which were used as landmarks by the pioneer migrant trains.

BUTTERFIELD OVERLAND MAIL COMPANY   One of the many stage lines organized by ex-stage driver John Butterfield. Plans for the Overland, which was financed by representatives of Adams & Company, American Express, and Wells Fargo, were drawn up in 1857, but it was not until September of the following year, and after the company had been awarded the government mail contract, that the coaches began to shuttle over their twenty-six-hundred-mile journey from Tipton, Missouri, to San Francisco. The Overland followed the wheel ruts of the old Jackass Mail, a sweeping curve to the south that was known as the Ox-bow Route.[31] There were 139 way stations along the route, and a cavalry detail escorted the coaches through the treacherous Apache territories of Arizona and New Mexico. Celerity, Concord, and Troy coaches, and either mules or horses were used by the

---

[29] Far more common in the Wild West. The buscadero, although used on the frontier, has only really come into its own with the advent of movies and television. Some buscadero-type belts used by present-day movie characters are, designwise, on the lunatic fringe. Nearly a whole steer hide would be required to make some of these latter-day articles, and on occasions the guns, which hang near their wearer's socks, have been observed to fly from their holsters when the script has called for their owner to leap onto his horse.

[30] A term mainly confined to the Southwest.

[31] This long, sweeping southern route was chosen in preference to the more direct central route because its climatic conditions made it operable throughout the year.

Overland, and if you were lucky, a one-way trip could be made in twenty-four days. The Ox-bow Route was abandoned at the outbreak of the Civil War, and the Butterfield route shrank until it was only carrying the mail from Salt Lake City, Utah, to Placerville, California, a third the distance of its original "longest stage run in the world." (See OVERLAND STAGE LINE.)

BUZZARD   A medium-sized bird of prey. The American species, which is known as the rough-legged buzzard and is feathered down to its toes, is up to 2 feet in length and has a wingspan of around 4 feet. Its diet consists of rodents and small game. The buzzard is not a carrion bird. This is emphasized, for in America there is a tendency to call vultures "buzzards." (See VULTURE.)

CHARLES M. RUSSELL

CADDOAN INDIANS Blanket nomenclature for Indians belonging to the Caddoan language group. The main tribes in this family were the Pawnee (Nebraska), Caddo (Texas), Wichita (Kansas), and Arikara (North Dakota). All these people were farmers, which necessitated their living in settled communities, villages whose dwellings usually consisted of beehive-shaped grass huts or earth lodges. (See ARIKARA INDIANS; CADDO INDIANS; and PAWNEE INDIANS.)

CADDO INDIANS Tribe of the Caddoan language group that in the early years of European settlement in North America were located in the area that is now known as Arkansas. Sometime prior to 1600 elements of the tribe moved westward across the Mississippi and settled in northeastern Texas to raise their crops of maize and melons. The progeny of this western division of the tribe are known as Plains Caddo, but although they adopted to some extent the horse culture of the plains and hunted buffalo as far west as the Staked Plains, they never became true nomads, and tepees were only used while on the hunt. Caddo farming settlements were composed of houses that had clay-on-wattle walls and grass roofs, or alternatively, beehive-shaped grass lodges. Some of these houses would be left without side walls, and these would be used during the hot seasons. Clothing, which was simple, was kept to a minimum, but when decorating their bodies with either paint or tattooing, the Caddo could be very elaborate. Friction between the tribe and the white man was comparatively rare, and during the latter half of the nineteenth century, hundreds of Caddo scouts served with the U. S. Army.

CALAMITY JANE Nickname of grim foreboding. (See CANNARY, MARTHA JANE.)

CALHOUN, CLAY Range detective, deputy sheriff, and U.S. marshal who in the 1880s was the top man of a group of lawmen who operated in the Arizona territory and were dubbed "Outlaw Exterminators, Inc.," by the press of the region. Clay, who was born in 1861, was married four times during his lifetime, and he was the last surviving member of Outlaw Exterminators when he died on November 21, 1948. (See ALLMAN, JOHN, and OUTLAW EXTERMINATORS.)

CALIFORNIA Western state with a thousand-mile coastline on the Pacific. The land was originally Mexican territory, but was ceded to the United States after the Mexican War and became the thirty-first state in 1850. Sacramento is the state capital, and the state is referred to as the "Golden State."

CALIFORNIA JOE A wanderer who should have at least retained his Christian name. (See MILNER, MOSES.)

CALUMET The Amerind sacred pipe. The bowls of these pipes were made of catlinite, and the stems, which were usually around two feet in length, were elaborately decorated and sometimes adorned with feathers. Red feathers were attached to war pipes and white feathers to peace pipes. (See CATLINITE.)

CAMEL IMPORTING COMPANY Short-lived enterprise that was organized in San Francisco around 1860. The company imported twenty Bactrian camels[1] with the intention of using these animals to freight silver for the Nevada mines, but although the U. S. Army had been using camels for years with a certain amount of success, opposition[2] from rival interests forced the Camel Importing Company to jettison its enterprise. (See CAMELS.)

CAMELS In 1848 the U. S. Army was toying with the idea of using camels in the Southwest, but it was not until 1855 that thirty thousand dollars was allocated to the Quartermaster's Department for the purchase of a number of these animals, and another year had elapsed before thirty-four of these "ships of the desert," which had been purchased in various Mediterranean countries, were disembarked on U.S. soil. These camels were quartered on Camp Verde, Texas (soon to become known as "Little Egypt"), and in 1857 a further shipment of forty-one beasts joined them. The U. S. Army now had the raw material to form a camel corps and a desert pack column—dromedaries for the former and Bactrians for the latter. This should have worked out in both instances, but it didn't. Theoretically, the advantages of a camel corps were many: Camels will not "spook" at gunfire; they can go for long periods without water; and the sight of them would cause American horses, and therefore Indian ponies, to turn tail and stampede; they were obviously just what was needed to settle the Indian problem once and for all. Yet for all of this, a charge of camel soldiers was never to make the American scene. Veteran cavalrymen whose legs were permanently calipered to horse dimensions were unable to stay on the beasts, while rookies who managed to stay on deck would become violently "seasick." These difficulties couldn't be overcome, so the "camel corps" project was abandoned, and the elite of the camel herd were downgraded and pressed into service with the Bactrian laborers. The pack trains were a success, and camel caravans were getting firmly established in the Southwest when the Civil War came along and, for some unknown reason, put an end to the venture. Why the Confederate forces didn't use

[1] A twin-humped species that is found in central Asia. Used mainly as a freight animal.

[2] Such as banning the Bactrians from using the streets of mining camps, and the allegations that the "furrin critters" caused stampedes among horses and cattle. The Army could afford to ignore such spanners being cast into its works.

these animals, which had multiplied considerably over the years, has never been explained. It is known that a few were sold and found their way into zoos and sideshows, but the majority were allowed to roam off into the wilderness. These wanderers are alleged to have turned many a hard-bitten buffalo hunter into a jellied wreck. In the main these hunters were an illiterate lot who may never have heard of a camel let alone seen one, so it is not to be wondered at that on sighting a "humped monster" they would stagger for the nearest settlement in a state of shock. As the years passed "monster" sightings were reported as far north as the Dakotas. (See CAMEL IMPORTING COMPANY.)

CANADIAN RIVER Easterly flowing river that winds through three states. From its headwaters in New Mexico's Sangre de Cristo mountains it meanders eastward across northwest Texas and on into Oklahoma, where it joins the Arkansas some forty miles west of the Arkansas state border. The Canadian is about nine hundred miles in length, and it is frequently mentioned in both factual and fictional literature of the West for, in Oklahoma, it had to be forded by trail herds using either the Chisholm or Shawnee trails.

CANDELARIA, NEVADA One of the better known of the rash of mining camps that sprang up in Mineral County, southwestern Nevada, in the 1860s. Candelaria was founded in 1865, and some fifteen years later, in its heyday, it supported two newspapers (*The True Fissure* and *The Chloride Belt*), both of which boasted of the town's eleven saloons,[3] half-dozen restaurants, and

two hotels, and, equally boastfully, of the many delights one might find in the Pickhandle Gulch area, where ten madames kept their premises of sin open twenty-four hours a day. Whiskey was sold by the gallon, and death could be bought for a chance remark. Fatal shootouts were commonplace, but as all the survivors of these engagements were acquitted on self-defense pleas, only seven murders are on record as having been committed during the town's life span, and no one was ever arrested for these seven crimes. Despite these hazards, Candelaria remained a thriving community until a decline in silver prices, and the consequent closure of some of the mines in the area, drove the majority of its citizens elsewhere in search of work. The town was a mere wraith of its former self by the early 1900s, but a little mining continued on into the 1930s, and it was not until 1949, when the last straggler left, that it became a fully qualified "ghost."

CANNARY, MARTHA JANE
Sometimes spelled "Canary," but whatever, this was the one and only Calamity Jane. Jane was born on May 1, 1852, at Princeton, Missouri. The family had a two-hundred-acre farm, and Jane lived here until her parents pulled up stakes and moved westward in 1863. It is not definitely known at what age this blue-eyed, sandy-haired girl left home, but in 1869 she was located in Cheyenne, and over the next few years her name became known throughout the frontier towns and forts of the West. Jane usually wore male attire and showed a preference for fringed buckskins—a choice of apparel in keeping with her on-and-off employment as a muleskinner and her equally masculine relaxations of hard

[3] Four of these saloons were the Roaring Gimlet, the Bank Exchange, McKissick's, and the Chloride.

drinking, cigar smoking, and tobacco chewing. In 1870 this undeodorized lass met James B. Hickok in the vicinity of Abilene, Kansas, and they were married before the year was out.[4] The marriage lines were written on the flyleaf of a Bible, and the Reverends W. K. Sipes and W. F. Warren conducted the ceremony.

Whether the "flyleaf wedding" was legally bulletproof is openly doubted by many,[5] but Jane evidently figured she was Mrs. Hickok, for when she gave birth to a girl child at Benson's Landing, Montana, in 1873, she launched it into the world as Jean Hickok. Calamity, forever footloose, soon had the baby adopted, and once more returned to her mule trains, and it was in this capacity that she joined the U. S. Army in 1875. Her life in the Army was short-lived, for when it was discovered that Jane, who had enlisted as a man, was of the weaker sex, she was tossed out on her buckskinned butt. This military action somewhat puzzles: Admittedly, photographs of Jane taken around this time show her in male attire, but her face and figure are far from masculine. Could it be that she was only discharged when the troops had grown bored with her? The following year we find Jane hanging around the heels of Wild Bill in Deadwood, Dakota Territory, and it is here that Calamity alleges that she gave Hickok a divorce so that he could marry Agnes Lake. Be that as it may, Jane continued to dog Bill's footsteps after his marriage to Miss Lake. But the Deadwood reunion was short-lived; a gun was fired at 4:15 P.M.

on August 2, 1876, and Hickok became a figure in history. According to Jane she was responsible for the arrest of the killer, whom she ran to earth in a butcher shop, but according to our Space Age debunkers, this was not so; perhaps they are right in this instance, for to our heroine of the moment, truth was elastic. Jane mourned Hickok in the Deadwood saloons—which is not to imply that her grief was anything but genuine—and even though she married a Charles Burke in 1885, Hickok was never to be forgotten. This second marriage didn't take, and although the couple were not officially separated until 1895, Jane had gone her own way well before this time. In August 1893 Calamity joined the Buffalo Bill Wild West Show, and after touring the eastern states, she visited England with the troupe. On their return to the States, Jane was bounced for excessive drinking. But show biz still beckoned, and in 1896 Jane was touring the Midwest with the Palace Museum Show. Between her acts, which consisted of giving a hectic account of her life—how she had saved Wild Bill from a gang of cutthroats and such guff—Jane found time to write her autobiography. Unfortunately there wasn't enough time for a thorough job, for Jane was kicked out of the show for being drunk and disorderly, and the volume remained a slim, incomplete affair.

At the turn of the century we find Calamity in a joyhouse, bedridden—by sickness, not trade—but by 1901, fully recovered, she had left the bawdyhouse behind her and taken a job with the Pan American Exposition. It didn't last. The

---

[4] This marriage is discredited by most writers on the grounds that a well-groomed dandy like the famed pistoleer would never have given a pot like Calamity a second glance. Maybe so; but then again, Hickok wouldn't always be smelling of cologne, for he jacked up his resources with buffalo hunting from time to time, and after having naught but buffalo in his sight for days, Jane may have looked pretty good.

[5] The U. S. Department of Public Welfare is not in the rank of these doubters, and in 1941, after examining the marriage lines and other evidence of identity, it granted Jean Hickok McCormick old-age relief, and listed her in the department files as the daughter of James Butler Hickok and Martha Jane Cannary.

wild and willful girl went on a bar-wrecking bender, assaulted two police-men, and was fired instantly. Billings, Montana, saw her the following year, but not for long: Jane shot up a bar and was escorted to the town limits. The West was getting tame, and colorful characters of the past were now regarded as delinquents. A juvenile delinquent with a figure like a roller coaster and wearing skin-tight Levi's may have been tolerated, but Jane had left the first flush of girlhood way back down the trail, and her detractors were now saying that she looked an old bag of seventy.[6] A hotel room in Terry (a town near Deadwood) is the setting for our final scene, for on August 2, 1903, Jane died here. The cause of death was pneumonia, and it is in the record that a few hours before her death, Jane made a final request: "Bury me next to Wild Bill." They were nice people, and they did. (See HICKOK, JAMES BUTLER, and HICKOK, JEAN.)

CANNIBALS An anglicized rendering of *cannibales*, the latter word being used by the Spaniards in the seventeenth century when referring to the man-eating Carib Indians of the Caribbean islands. Cannibalism usually stems from hunger or ritualistic motives, so when *Homo sapiens* appeared on the menu in the American West—a land well supplied with game—it must have been for ritual-istic reasons.[7] By eating a brave man, one absorbed his courage. It was also reasoned that none of his kinsmen would do you violence when they knew that one of their number was in residence behind your navel. Some of the Northwest coast tribes are known to have practiced can-nibalism to a small extent, while the

Tonkawas of southwestern Texas varied their diet with Comanche or gringo when-ever available. The large metal pot of the joke cartoons was favored in the south-ern regions, and cuts of human origin would be boiled with horse meat until a grisly form of "Irish stew" was ready for consumption. (See ASSINIBOINE IN-DIANS; DONNER PARTY; HELM, BOONE; PACKER, ALFRED; and TONKAWA IN-DIANS.)

CANOE A long, narrow, and some-times portable craft that is propelled by a paddle or paddles. The Amerind canoes used west of the Mississippi varied con-siderably in both design and in the mate-rials used in their construction, but they can be roughly classified into four re-gional types. The Algonkin of the northern plains used the familiar birch-bark canoe when this material was avail-able. These craft were easily maneuvered on water and were light enough to be transported long distances over land, but by 1800 the horse and the horse-drawn travois had become the backbone of the plains travel, and canoe building was virtually abandoned. In Texas and the southeastern gulf areas a dugout canoe made from a hollowed-out log was favored. This type was ungainly and heavy and could only be carried for short distances. The seed gatherers of California (the western region) were the builders of an ultralight canoe. Made from bundles of Tule rushes, these boats rode high on the surface and had a su-perficial resemblance to early Egyptian vessels. The Indians of the northwestern coastal areas built some of the largest canoes on record. These king-sized, elab-orately decorated seagoing craft could

---

[6] This is ridiculous, for photographs of Jane taken around this time show a not unpleasant, sombreroed woman in a dark dress who appears to be about forty-five to fifty; a bag maybe, seventy never.

[7] The hunger motive can only be applied when white Americans—such as Packer and mem-bers of the Donner party—turned to cannibalism.

carry about eighty rowers, and they were used for ceremonial, war, and whaling purposes. Cedar logs were used in their construction, the logs being hollowed out by fire, then shaped by steam. A separate piece was added to form an upswept prow, which gave protection when the boat was being used as a military landing craft.

C A Ñ O N   Spanish alternative for "canyon." This word is favored in the Southwest.

C A N T L E   A curved projection rising from the rear of a saddle.

C A N T O N,   F R A N K   M.   The real name of this gentleman, who, according to his own account, was born near Richmond, Virginia, in 1849, is unknown. Other names that have been glued to him over the years are Richard Horn and Joe Horner. During his early childhood the family moved to Denton, Texas, and when he was around nineteen, Frank went trail herding for a period before being employed by the Wyoming Cattle Growers' Association as a range detective. This was the beginning of an on-and-off lawman career that was to embrace nearly fifty years. In 1880 he was raising beef in Wyoming and in 1882 was elected sheriff of Johnson County, Wyoming, a position he held for two years before being elected "out." Shortly after this defeat, he was accused of the ambush murder of two ranchers, but at his trial he came up with a trump-card alibi and was acquitted. He next flickers as a leading light in the Johnson County War, after which, being no longer welcome thereabouts, he took up a job as superintendent at a meat packing plant, but by 1894 he was back behind the tin as undersheriff of Pawnee County, Oklahoma, and, a short spell later, as a deputy U.S. marshal for Oklahoma.

Three years later, he went North to Alaska to work for the North American Trading and Transportation Company, panning for gold, without success, in his free time. While in Alaska he arrested a baddie with a twenty-five-hundred-dollar price on his head, but after hearing that his prisoner had, a few days previously, rescued a married couple from an ice floe, Frank let the man free. In 1900 Frank was once more back in Oklahoma, where he was soon put in charge of the criminal investigation branch of the Texas Cattle Raisers' Association. When Oklahoma achieved statehood in 1907, its first governor, C. N. Haskell, gave Frank the job of adjutant general, an appointment he was to retain for nine years with Haskell's successors. The man known as Frank M. Canton died in 1927. (See CRAVENS, BEN, and JOHNSON COUNTY WAR.)

C A N Y O N   A large-sized but narrow gorge that has often been formed by a riverbed, and whose sloping sides are sometimes nearly vertical. The largest canyon in the United States, and the world, is the Grand Canyon of the Colorado. (See GRAND CANYON.)

C A P I T O L   S Y N D I C A T E   The name by which the Capitol Freehold Land and Investment Company is usually known. The company was founded by John and Charles Farwell, and after buying three million acres of the Texas panhandle, they surrounded the area with barbed wire and named it the "Ten in Texas" ranch, so named because it was supposed to cover ten Texas counties (some of which were larger than a few of the eastern states), but in actual fact the ranch only extended over nine. The first herd of cattle arrived in July 1885, and B. H. Campbell, the ranch manager, asked the strawboss of the herd to suggest an apt brand. The strawboss, a veteran of the trails named Ab Blocker, scratched his head, spat, then grooved XIT on the ground. At the peak of its operations the XIT outfit was running cattle on a further two hundred miles of range in Montana, and was the biggest spread in the history of the West. In the early 1900s the company began selling its land to settlers, and within a few years this vast cattle empire had dwindled into history.

CAPTAIN JACK The Modoc chief involved in the Modoc War of 1872–73. (See MODOC WAR.)

CARBINE A short-barreled rifle especially suited to cavalry use.

CARMACK, GEORGE W. A Californian who had the distinction of being the first man to discover gold in Alaska. Carmack had prospected in the West for more than a decade without success before striking it rich at the mouth of the Klondike River on August 17, 1896, but the bonanza was worth waiting for, and George had salted away more than a million dollars in gold in quick time. Carmack, who was born in 1860, died on June 5, 1922, at Vancouver, British Columbia.

CARPETBAGGERS A term that originated in America at the close of the Civil War. During its infancy the word was only applied when a person whose possessions would have fitted into a carpetbag went into speculative enterprises such as banking and real estate. Later the term was to embrace an even scurvier lot of rogues—to whit, any person who stood as a political candidate in a constituency where he or she was unknown.

CARSON, CHRISTOPHER ("KIT") Probably the best known of the long hunters and mountain men, those rugged individuals who bragged they were "ha'f hoss, ha'f alligator," and who roamed the Shining Mountains and beyond during the first half of the nineteenth century. Carson, who was born in Kentucky on Christmas Eve 1809, was persuaded to become an apprentice saddler when he was fifteen, but the trade wasn't to his liking, and two years later he joined a wagon train heading for Santa Fe. From here he moved northward, and within a few years he had become an experienced trapper, and like the rest of those buckskinned bullyboys, Carson, who was small in stature and bowed of leg, "talked tall." This youngster appeared at the mountain men's Green River rendezvous in 1835, and here he got into an argument with a veteran named John Shuman. A bit of Arapaho fluff named Waa-Nibe (Singing Grass) had built up pressures in these men, and the tough talk developed into a duel on horseback. Shuman, a red-bearded giant of a man whose jaws would have served as a bear trap, was confident of victory, but after the flintlocks had thundered, he was to bite the dust completely unpressurized, while Carson lived to marry the girl—a simple ceremony that consisted of a few disgusting goings-on under a blanket. A girl was born of the couple, and when Singing Grass died in 1842, Carson took the child to St. Louis to be educated. Here, and in that year, he joined the Fremont Expedition, which was to survey the Columbia River Valley region, and it was in the capacity of guide to "The Pathfinder" that Carson returned to the Far West. On completion of this mission he wandered South, and in 1843 he married a Spanish girl in New Mexico. The wanderer settled here for a spell, and in the early 1850s we find him driving sheep over the New Mexico mountains, across Arizona, and on into gold-glutted but meat-hungry California. A neat profit of thirty thousand dollars was made from this venture. But such pastoral activities were not to last forever, and when cannon boomed in the East, Carson joined the Union Army. The North must have heard about his "Indian for breakfast" bragging, for they made him a general almost overnight and told him to use the North Plains as his larder. General Carson's most notable military engagement occurred on November 24, 1864, when, with a force of four hundred men, he attacked a large village of Kiowa and Comanche near Adobe Walls, Texas. Compared with the later Adobe Walls fight, this battle was a fiasco. Carson's men managed to kill a few redskins who were confined to their tepees through reasons of health or old age before the cream of the village counterattacked and the soldiers were forced into ignominious retreat. After Lee's surrender, Carson soldiered on with the rank of brevet brigadier general. His duties? Unofficial peacemaker to the Northwest tribes—honest; no foolin'! The brevet brigadier general died at Fort Lyon, Colorado, in 1868, and his remains are buried at Taos, New Mexico. (See ADOBE WALLS; BATTLE AT ADOBE WALLS; FREMONT, JOHN CHARLES; and SHUMAN, JOHN.)

CARTER, NICK   Alias that was probably inspired by reading the exploits of a fictional detective of that name. (See CASHEL, ERNIE.)

CARTRIDGE BELT   A leather or webbing belt fitted with either ribbed loops or pouches in which cartridges can be carried. Loops are usually favored on leather,[8] and pouches on webbing. The former type is invariably worn by civilians, while the latter type is confined to military usage. Leather cartridge belts come in a variety of styles and widths, ranging from a narrow simple model with an uninterrupted row of loops—and therefore having no specific holster area —to the elaborate buscadero with its twin drop loops from which holsters can be hung. Midway between these examples, elaboratewise, is the cartridge *cum* money belt. This is made from a folded piece of hide and is of sufficient width to accommodate a double row of cartridges.[9] Money can be fed into the belt through a slit, which is usually located behind the buckle. (See BUSCADERO; GUNBELT; and HOLSTER.)

CARVER, WILLIAM   Onetime dentist who is usually referred to as "Doc" Carver, and whose career as a marksman made the Winchester .73 internationally famous. Carver, who stated he was Indian-born, gave up dentistry and took up shooting in the 1870s, and within ten years he was probably the finest exhibition marksman of the period. The press referred to him as "Deadshot Carver" and "the greatest shot in the world," and Carver must have been in complete agreement with the headlines, for he was confident enough of his ability to allow challengers of his prowess to blaze away with shotguns while he shattered the targets with a Winchester rifle. Doc toured England and Europe over the 1879–82 period, during which time he appeared before a few crowned heads on the Continent, and thousands of uncrowned heads at such places as Liverpool, Aldershot, Sydenham, and Sandringham in England. In the closing months of 1882 he returned Stateside with a profit of eighty thousand dollars, some of which he invested with W. F. Cody—a combination of show-biz talent that resulted in "The Wild West, Rocky Mountain, and Prairie Exhibition" being put on the road. The show was a great

[8] If the shoulder cartridge belts—that is, bandoliers—are ignored.
[9] This type was a great favorite with the Texas Rangers.

success, but the partners didn't see eye to eye, and at the end of the season the relationship was dissolved. The favorite target of the time was a hollow glass ball, said ball being tossed into the air and shattered—or missed—by a rifle bullet. Carver's greatest feat was to shatter 5,500 of such balls out of a total of 6,212—a marathon shootout that lasted over 7½ hours.

CARVER, WILLIAM Texas born[10] train and bank robber who rode with the Wild Bunch in the late 1880s. William, who was also known as Bill or Tod, participated in many of the gang's holdups, and although he was never a leader, he most certainly made his presence tell at the Winnemucca, Nevada, bank job of 1900; just prior to this caper, and on the outskirts of the town, Carver had been beaten to the draw by a giant skunk, and on entering the bank the fumes from his clothes took most of the kudos for subduing the staff. This evil-smelling one was thin of face and poorly dressed—off-the-peg suit, battered derby, and hobnailed boots; he looked like a bum. No sombrero or low-slung gun rig? Afraid not; for this was a transitional period over which the gunman of the plains was finally to deteriorate into the street-corner thug, who in turn became the organized gangster of the Prohibition period. William, like most of his kind, met a violent end. It happened on April 2, 1901: the death spot was Sonora, Texas, and the cause of death was gunshot wounds from the pistols of Sheriff E. S. Bryant of Sutton County and a three-man posse. (See ROSE, DELLA, and WILD BUNCH.)

CASHEL, ERNIE This character committed most of his crimes in Canada, but as his birthplace was Wyoming, USA, Ernie has been allowed to sneak between these covers. This ex-grammar school boy made his first appearance on the police blotter in Wyoming when he was nineteen years old. The charge was armed robbery, and the young gunman got two years. On his release in 1902, Cashel crossed the border into Canada, where, at Calgary, he promptly did a spot of paper hanging (writing bad checks) before heading westward. He got less than a hundred miles before he was picked up by the Northwest Mounted Police. The arresting officer immediately wired the Calgary police, and a short time later Ernie was being escorted back to Calgary by the chief of police of that city. Lawman and suspect traveled by train—a slow train, which Cashel left via the washroom window. The fugitive adopted Ellsworth as an alias, and under this name he was befriended by an aging rancher named Rufus Belt. Mr. Belt was repaid for his provision of board and lodging by a bullet in the chest and having his body tossed into a creek; robbery was the motive. The NWMP—who "allus git their man when there are no wimmen around" —trailed Cashel to a village near Jumping Pond, but too late: The young, good-looking American, who was now going under the name of Nick Carter, had left the village just as soon as he had exhausted its supply of female talent. The law finally caught up with Mr. Carter in a hotel room at Anthracite, and he was lodged in the Rocky Mountain Penitentiary to await trial. Ernie didn't have a prayer, and he was booked to leave this world, the stipulated time of departure being December 15, 1903. Five days before the hanging Ernie had a visitor: brother John, up from Wyoming. Brother John was evidently a practical lad, for shortly after his departure, the condemned man broke out of jail at gunpoint. Freedom was to be short-lived, but

[10] In Bandera County, a few miles west of San Antonio.

during this spell of liberty Cashel found time to write a letter to his pursuers: "Still in good shape . . . in spite of you Mounties. If you get me alive . . . tell Mr. Radcliffe [the hangman] to go back to Ottawa. . . ." On January 12, 1904, the Mounties got Cashel cornered in a small shack, and after a brief and bloodless gunfight, he was smoked out and arrested for keeps. Ernie Cashel had his belated appointment with Mr. Radcliffe on the morning of February 2, 1904.

CASSIDY, BUTCH   The tough but good-natured-sounding alias of Robert Leroy Parker. (See PARKER, ROBERT LEROY, and WILD BUNCH.)

CATLIN, GEORGE   American artist and explorer who devoted most of his adult life to portraying the Indian on canvas. In 1841 Catlin published a written and pictorial record of eight years spent in this endeavor. This publication, consisting of two volumes, is illustrated by four hundred engravings, which are covered by a text of great authority.[11] The strength of this work lies in the fact that Catlin reached the Indians years before the white invasion of the West. This resulted in the volumes becoming source books on the American Indian, for Catlin's illustrations are free from the bastardized costumery (store pants, trade blankets, etc.) that became prevalent when the white and red cultures interweaved. Catlin, who was born at Wilkes-Barre, Pennsylvania, on July 26, 1796, died on December 23, 1872, at Jersey City, New Jersey.

CATLINITE   Also known as Pipestone. A type of red stone found in Minnesota that is easily carved when first taken from the ground but that quickly hardens when exposed to the air. The quarries, located near the present-day town of Pipestone, were known to the Indians as the "Fountain of the Pipe," and although they were on Sioux territory, the area of the quarries was regarded as neutral ground. The stone was, and still is, used for the making of pipe bowls. Named after George Catlin. (See CATLIN, GEORGE.)

CATTALO   A buffalo-domestic cattle offspring. Charles Goodnight was the originator of this crossbreeding experiment, but although he built up a small herd of these animals, cattaloes were not a financial success, and the project was abandoned. (See GOODNIGHT, CHARLES.)

CATTLE   The cattle of the trail-herd days can be roughly divided into three types: Longhorns, crossbreeds, and Herefords. Of these the longhorn was predominant until the late 1800s. These lean animals were the results of three centuries of interbreeding, their forebears being the Andalusian cattle, which the Spaniards had allowed to run wild. This was the wild, raw material on which the cattle industry of the Southwest was built, for although these critters were not good beef producers, they were there for the taking, and one could become a cattle baron on a lariat string. To the cattleman the longhorn had two disadvantages: low hamburger content, as mentioned; and a "cussed" streak, which made them both difficult and dangerous to handle. This lean build and mean outlook were instrumental in extinguishing Longhorns from the American scene and introducing crossbreds into the picture. Crossbreds were of Longhorn-Durham or Longhorn-Hereford extraction, and they were sufficiently plump and docile to survive as

[11] Titled *Letters and Notes on the Manners, Customs and Conditions of the North American Indians* by George Catlin. Published by the author at Egyptian Hall, Piccadilly, London, in 1841.

an economical strain until the turn of the century. Herefords superceded the cross-breds, and the Herefords, which are both smaller and plumper than their predecessors, now dominate the American scene. (See BRAHMA CATTLE and CATTALO.)

CATTLE ANNIE An early-day juvenile delinquent. (See McDOUGAL, ANNIE.)

CATTLE KATE A lynch-mob victim whose maiden name was Ella Watson. (See AVERILL, JAMES; AVERILL, TOM; and WATSON, ELLA.)

CATTLE TRAILS Any trail which, through constant usage by cattle outfits, became the accepted method of moving beeves to shipping points or fresh pastures. (See CHISHOLM TRAIL; NORTHERN TRAIL; SHAWNEE TRAIL; and WESTERN TRAIL.)

CAYUSE An American cowboy term that is synonymous with horse. The word derives from the Indians of that name.

CAYUSE INDIANS A Northwest tribe belonging to the Penutian language group. The Cayuse are noted mainly for their horse-breeding and horse-trading activities, and for their early acceptance of Christianity. As early as 1833 they were observing the Sabbath, and a mission was firmly established on their land in 1847. In this year the Christian handshake was abandoned in favor of the grasped tomahawk, and the unfortunate personnel of the mission, both male and female, were massacred. The Cayuse were near kin of the Nez Percé, a tribe whose customs, dwellings, and costume were similar in all respects to those of the Cayuse. (See NEZ PERCÉ INDIANS and WHITMAN MASSACRE.)

CELERITY WAGON A lightweight coach of similar size to the Concord but of much lighter construction. Stageline companies usually confined celerities to branch routes or mountainous stretches, and they were rarely used for long hauls. The wagons had canvas roofs and side curtains. The latter could be adjusted across the unglazed windows to suit the prevailing weather conditions, and when they were closed and strapped into position the coach was, to all intents and purposes, canvas sided. (See CONCORD COACH.)

CENTER FIRE RIG A term applied to a saddle whose rigging is positioned centrally.

CENTRAL PACIFIC RAILROAD The Central Pacific was incorporated in 1861, but it was not until 1863 that this government-subsidized project started work on its first length of track. The iron crawled east from Sacramento, California, and by June 1864 passenger trains were shuttling over the first thirty-one miles of the Central Pacific's system. Pushing eastward, an army of sixteen thousand laborers blasted, leveled, and tunneled a right-of-way across the Sierra Nevadas, so that when they spilled out onto the comparatively level plain area of Nevada, they had left some fifteen tunnels and forty miles of snowsheds behind them. In mid-June 1868 the twin ribbons of steel reached what is now Reno, Nevada, and from here on one might think the tracks were merely unrolled from some giant drum, for a record track-laying feat of more than ten miles in under twelve hours was set up over this last stretch of track. On May 10, 1869, at Promontory, Utah (a spot designated by the government), the Central Pacific's iron was linked up to that of the Union Pacific's, and America had its first transcontinental railway. (See UNION PACIFIC RAILROAD.)

CHACON, AUGUSTINE A racial mixup with a fair injection of Apache. This heavily mustached, gangling misfit, whose stamping ground was the Arizona, New Mexico, and Mexico border area, is credited with around thirty notches, most of which were won north of the border. Chacon, at the head of a gang of Mexican deadbeats, would enter United States territory, murder and pillage, and then hotfoot back into Mexico. In 1896 he murdered Pablo Salcido at Morenci, Arizona Territory, but on this occasion he goofed in his getaway. The law got him cornered, and after a gunfight in which Chacon killed a deputy and was himself wounded, he was arrested and lodged in the county jail at Solomonville. At his trial he was sentenced to hang, and this should have been the end of the line for Chacon, but one of those beautiful *señoritas* who always seem to be around when a baddie is in trouble smuggled a hacksaw into his cell, and he cut through the bars and was off into the night. From then on Chacon's career was a repetition of notch-gathering incidents: a couple of sheepherders near Phoenix, Arizona; two prospectors near Solomonville; a stage holdup near . . . you get the trend; Augustine was going to have no gun butts left. By 1901 Arizona was fed up to the teeth with Chacon and his ilk, and in that year the Arizona Rangers were formed to clean up the territory, and one of their first assignments was to "get Chacon." Chacon must have noticed the rise in temperature, for he lay low south of the border where, legally, he was safe from the Americanos. But he hadn't reckoned on Ranger Captain Burton C. Mossman, a man who worried little over the niceties of international law. Mossman traveled to Mexico where he was able to locate Burt Alvord, an American who knew Chacon and who was also a fugitive from a Stateside murder rap. The Ranger had a proposition: "Take me to where Cha-

con is and I'll see that you [Alvord] are acquitted when you return to Arizona." Alvord agreed, and a short time later Mossman got the drop on Chacon and smuggled him North. The murder conviction of 1896 had gathered a little dust but it was still valid, and on November 23, 1902, Augustine Chacon was hanged at Solomonville. (See ALVORD, BURT; CHAVEZ, PEDRO; MOSSMAN, BURTON C.; and SLAUGHTER, JOHN.)

CHADWELL, BILL A Missouri farm boy who was born in 1857 and who lived a blameless, hard-working life until he was persuaded to join the James band in the summer of 1876. Bill had a short-lived career as a bandit, for he was shot to death when the gang was cut to pieces at Northfield on September 7, 1876. (See JAMES GANG; NORTHFIELD, MINNESOTA; and PITTS, CHARLIE.)

CHAMPION, NATHAN D. Champion was born on September 29, 1857, in Williamson County, Texas, and from a tender age he worked as a rider for various cow outfits. Sometime in the early 1880s Nathan reached Wyoming with a trailherd crew, and he must have liked what he saw, for he collected his pay and settled in Johnson County. He established headquarters in an old cabin that had been abandoned by the K.C. spread, and after a short space of time he had built up a small herd—a minor success story shared by numerous other homesteaders who had drifted into the area. The building of these herds was viewed with suspicion by some—namely, the big cattle barons of Wyoming, whose herds were being decimated by rustlers. These men, mostly absentee owners who headquartered at Cheyenne, brought Pinkerton operatives into the picture, and in quite a short time the barons were studying the private eyes' reports. Mr. Champion appeared in these reports, the intelligence being that he was the leader of the Red Sash gang of outlaws.[12] The law was of little use to the men in Cheyenne, for Johnson County juries, which were usually composed of homesteaders, were remarkably lenient with rustlers.[13] Hired guns seemed to be the answer to the problem, and in November 1891 Nathan had his first brush with these professionals. But Champion, who was no slouch with an equalizer, succeeded in driving the gunmen from his spread on this occasion, and it was not until six months later that he was to go down under a veritable hail of lead. In the early hours of April 11, 1892, silently and on a thin carpet of snow, a small army of gunmen took up positions around the Champion cabin, which, at the time, Nate was sharing with a buddy named Nick Ray. After breakfast Ray went into the yard to chop wood and was immediately cut down by gunfire. Champion managed to get the severely wounded Ray back into the shack, where, late in the afternoon, Ray died. By this time the shack was riddled with lead and Champion's gun had felled two of the invaders, yet he remained unscathed and was even finding time to write a blow-by-blow description of the siege.[14] Just before dark the cabin was fired, and Champion was forced to make a run for it. More than forty guns made liver spots of flame before his eyes, and he was dead before the echoes from the fusilade had time to fade. His guns and gunbelt were taken as souvenirs, and he was left with a "Rustlers Beware" notice pinned to his shirt. Twenty-eight bullets were later recovered from the corpse. (See AVERILL,

JAMES; JOHNSON COUNTY WAR; and WATSON, ELLA.)

CHAPARRAL   A name derived from the Spanish *chaparra*, a word that means "evergreen oak." The anglicized term is more elastic, and "chaparral" can be applied to any dense thicket that is composed of evergreen oaks, bramble bushes, or thorny shrubs.

CHAPARRERAS   Protective leg coverings that have their origins in Spain, and that, centuries later, found their way into the West via the *vaqueros* of Mexico. North of the border "chaps" can be roughly divided into two types: closed or batwing. The former type are pulled on like trousers and are, in most cases, similar to Indian leggings—that is, each leg is usually a separate unit, and they are frequently fringed. Batwings are wrapped around the leg and snapped into position, three or four fasteners being used for this purpose, and the legs are joined by a belt that fastened across the small of the back. This latter type almost always has pockets (in some instances these are replaced by built-in holsters) and is available in either leather or the undressed skins of goats or sheep; hairy chaps being favored on the colder northern ranges. Both types of chaps are still worn in the West, batwings being by far the more popular. (See ARMITAS.)

CHAPS   A shortened version of chaparreras. (See ARMITAS and CHAPARRERAS.)

CHARBONNEAU, TOUISSANT   Black-bearded   French-Canadian   fur

---

[12] Champion, like many other homesteaders of Texas origin, frequently wore a *vaquero*-type red sash, but whether such a gang ever operated, or that he was the leader, has never been established.

[13] Out of 180 cases brought to trial there was only a single conviction.

[14] This pathetic document is far too lengthy to be included here, but in it Champion had named Frank M. Canton as one of the attacking force—a name that was to be erased at a later date.

trapper and layabout whose main claim to fame is his association with the Lewis and Clark Expedition. In the early years of the 1800s Charbonneau was living in a Mandan village that hugged the banks of the Missouri a few miles north of where the present city of Bismarck, North Dakota, is located. When the Lewis and Clark party arrived at the village on October 26, 1804, Touissant was lucky enough to get himself hired as an interpreter by the outfit; very lucky indeed, for he had three copper-complexioned "wives" to support, and his knowledge of sign talk was only mediocre. The job paid twenty-five dollars a month and was to last for two years, and from the journals of the expedition[15] it would appear that Charbonneau may have been rather more of a burden than an asset. When not womanizing, he was utterly lazy; his shooting was wretched, and when traveling by boat he was invariably "seasick" whether the rivers be large or small. In 1811, five years after he had been paid off by Lewis and Clark, he was acting as guide and interpreter to a noted English wanderer named H. M. Brackenridge. Charbonneau's skills may have improved a little over the years, for he continued to get interpreting jobs, which helped to eke out the miserable pittance he got from his trapping. This French-Canadian may have been pretty small potatoes in his wood and Indian lore and marksmanship, but in one pursuit he most certainly excelled, for it is authoritatively stated that he was pursuing squaws until he was eighty years old; top that if you can. (See BAPTISTE, JEAN; LEWIS AND CLARK EXPEDITION; and SACAGAWEA.)

CHATO   Chiricahua Apache chief who was hostile during the Apache–U. S. Army wars that covered the decade 1873–83. Chato, whose name means "flat nose," was never among the big names of the Apache nation, and he rarely had more than two dozen warriors in his band—a band that was responsible for the murders of Judge H. C. McComas and his wife on March 28, 1883. On May 24, 1883, Chato returned to the San Carlos Reservation. His crimes were either overlooked or forgiven, and he was made a sergeant of scouts, a job that was to last until the latter months of 1886. In August 1886, the last organized bands of hostiles surrendered. These were the bands led by Nachez and Geronimo, and turncoats like Chato and company, whose Apache lore played no small part in bringing the wars to a close, may have figured they were in line for promotion. But the white-eyes of that period cared little about justice where the Indian was concerned, and Chato and the rest of the scouts were stripped of their uniforms and exiled to Florida with the rest of the Apaches.[16]

CHAVEZ, PEDRO   Pint-sized Mexican who was a member of Augustine Chacon's gang. In 1896 he and Chacon robbed the store of a Mr. Paul Becker at Morenci, Arizona, and during their getaway they murdered a citizen named Pablo Salcido. The law gave chase, and after a gunfight in which Chacon was wounded, both men were arrested. A joint trial was held, and hanging sentences were handed down. Chavez was lodged in Tucson jail to await his fate, but just prior to his scheduled execution,

[15] The journals refer to him as "Charbono," a phonetic rendering of the name.
[16] Some years later the Apaches were transferred to Indian Territory (Oklahoma). The authorities were either stricken with remorse—rather belatedly, one might think—or Florida seemed capable of experiencing a real-estate boom far greater than Oklahoma was ever likely to see.

he succeeded in making his escape.[17] It was a short-lived taste of freedom, for a posse under Sheriff Wakefield caught up with him in the Santa Rita Mountains, and he was shot to death while resisting arrest. (See CHACON, AUGUSTINE.)

CHEROKEE BILL   Colorful name for an off-color character. (See GOLDSBY, CRAWFORD.)

CHEROKEE BOB   Off-color character with a colorful nickname. (See TALBOTTE, HENRY J.)

CHEROKEE INDIANS   A southeastern tribe of the Iroquois group that can only be described as western Indians from around 1830 onward. During the late 1820s and on into the early 1830s the Cherokee were forcibly removed from the Carolinas and transferred to a stretch of land west of the Mississippi-Missouri —land that was later to become known as Oklahoma Territory. The Cherokee, who now dressed in the manner of the white man, were promised that they would be allowed to farm this land in peace "as long as waters shall flow." This should have read "until we stop your tap," for when white settlers began to invade the Indian territory in the late 1870s the U. S. Government did nothing to dissuade these trespassers—rather the reverse, in fact; and in 1889 the Indians were pressurized into selling their lands to the Great White Father at around $1.25 an acre—peanuts for sure. The Cherokee now live in the northeastern corner of Oklahoma, an area of the map in which flowing waters are conspicuously absent.

(See CHEROKEE STRIP and OKLAHOMA LAND RUSH.)

CHEROKEE STRIP   Alternatively referred to as the Cherokee Outlet, the strip was a section of Indian Territory (Oklahoma) which, by the treaty of 1866, had been set aside as the communal property of the Five Civilized Tribes—that is, the land was unassigned tribally. The strip survived until 1889. In that year the government bullied and brainwashed the tribes into selling this tract, and after the Oklahoma Land Rush, the strip was no more. Many an outlaw must have regretted the passing of the Cherokee Strip, for, being outside white jurisdiction, it had made a grand bolt-hole. (See CHEROKEE INDIANS and OKLAHOMA LAND RUSH.)

CHEYENNE INDIANS   Plains Indians of the Algonkin family. The Cheyenne[18] were originally farmers who lived in the area that was later known as Minnesota, but in the seventeenth century the tribe began a slow westerly migration, and by 1800 farming had been abandoned and they had adopted the manners and customs of the tepee-dwelling nomads of the plains. The Cheyenne had skirmishes with the Sioux until 1840, at which time a peace treaty was ratified between the two nations, a treaty that must have been negotiated by sign talk, for the Sioux and Cheyenne languages have nothing in common. Cheyenne dress and dwellings were similar to those of the other main plains tribes, and the Sun Dance ritual was shared by them, but the Cheyenne dog soldier societies and

---

[17] Security measures must have been pretty lax in Arizona jails at this period, for Chacon escaped from the Solomonville jail within days of Pedro's break.
[18] In early-nineteenth-century literature the spelling is given as "Shienne," but whatever the spelling, the word is pronounced like "shy Anne." By this time, after a transitional period of nearly half a century, the horse had become the accepted method of plains travel, giving the Indians an increased mobility that made it possible for them to use the buffalo herds as their commissary.

the practice of cutting off the hands (or forearms) of slain enemies were exclusive to the tribe, the latter peculiarity being responsible for the "cut hand" identification that neighboring tribes applied to the Cheyenne. The Cheyenne, with an average height of six feet, were the tallest of the plains tribes, and their war parties helped form the backbone of Indian resistance in the U. S. Army–Indian wars of the 1800s. They are now confined to reservations in Montana and Oklahoma. (See BATTLE AT BEECHER'S ISLAND; BATTLE ON THE ROSEBUD; BATTLE ON THE LITTLE BIG HORN; BLACK KETTLE; DOG SOLDIER; ROMAN NOSE; SAND CREEK MASSACRE; SUN DANCE; and WASHITA MASSACRE.)

CHEYENNE, WYOMING A town in the southeastern corner of Wyoming that became the cow capital of the northern ranges. Cheyenne, however, cannot be compared with the cow towns of Kansas, for it had little of their wildness. It was the headquarters of the Wyoming Cattlemen's Association and home of the Cheyenne Club, a verandaed building that had the distinction of being the first of such premises in the United States to be equipped with electric light. The club membership was composed of cattle barons who, when they weren't drinking on the veranda, could indulge in such innocuous pastimes as tennis and dancing. Yet these absentee owners whose herds stretched across Montana and Wyoming cannot be classed as effete, for when the occasion demanded, gunmen, from as far south as Texas, were imported to act as disciplinarians on the range. Cheyenne, which is the state capital, is still the cattle center of the Northwest, and its annual "Frontier Days" celebrations are nationally famous. (See CHAMPION, NATHAN D., and JOHNSON COUNTY WAR.)

CHICKAREE
A small red tree-squirrel that is found in most areas of the West.

CHIMNEY ROCK A two-hundred-foot-high pinnacle of rock in Nebraska that is the most famous of the landmarks used by the migrant trains of the nineteenth century.

CHINESE The Chinese invasion of the West began around 1849, the California gold fields being the gateway through which the Orientals found their way into almost every corner of the region. Color prejudice, which frequently led to riots, prevented the Chinese from ever becoming successful miners. Their claims were "jumped" and their bodies holed by lead with such frequency that they could never hope to go it alone as prospectors, so they turned from mining and took on menial jobs in the towns and settlements. The influx may have halted there, but in the 1860s the railroads, such as the Central Pacific, imported further Chinese as track layers. The advantages of employing the Orientals were manifold: They were of docile behavior, would work for lower wages than either the American or the Irish immigrant construction workers, and were quite happy with a bowl of rice. With the completion of the railroads thousands of these Chinese became unemployed and were forced to fan out in search of work. A few of the more enterprising opened opium dens, but the majority of them became either laundrymen or cooks. Racial prejudice made these people insular, and when they found themselves in sufficient numbers in such cities as San Francisco and Sacramento, they confined themselves to small areas that in time became known as "Chinatowns." (See CHINESE TONGS.)

CHINESE TONGS Tongs are mutual aid societies that are peculiar to the Chinese. The tongs of the Orient are outside the province of this book, it being sufficient to state that their origins go back into the first century of the Christian era and that for many centuries afterward they were little more than rebel and bandit organizations.[19] By the nineteenth century, large-scale outlawry was being abandoned in favor of that more subtle form of banditry known as Big Business, and tong funds—accrued from members' subscriptions—were being invested, and a member could avail himself of benefits that varied from an assisted passage to the New World, to refuge from the law should he become a fugitive; he also had the satisfaction of knowing that his remains would be taken care of in the event of his death. This was the type of secret society that took root on American soil wherever Chinese were in sufficient numbers, and they were to flourish, with slight modifications, from the 1860s until well into the twentieth century. In their lush years nearly thirty tongs were making their influence felt along the Pacific seaboard. Every major city on this coastline had at least one such society. The main incomes of all these tongs derived from one or more off-color enterprises, such as opium dens, prostitution, and the smuggling of slave girls[20]—pursuits that engaged fearsome rivalry in areas where more than one tong operated. San Francisco's Chinatown was the headquarters of six tongs (Big Kongs, Hop Sings, Yun Yings, Sen Suey Kings, Suey Ons, and Suey Sings—an awesome-sounding menu, to be sure), and numerous small strongarm groups known as Highbinder societies—a rather high-sounding title for gangs whose activities were confined to those fields of endeavor that require no capital outlay—blackmail, kidnaping, and contract murder. Little wonder that San Francisco was the scene of long wars for more than forty years. Rival tongs employed Highbinder killers to eliminate competition, and these fighting men (*boo how day*) were the hatchetmen of the tong wars. Split skulls were the order of the day and pitched battles were fought, and anyone with tong connections was liable to end up in an alley with a double profile. This state of affairs lasted until 1922. In that year pressure from the San Francisco Police Department resulted in a peace treaty being drawn up and signed by the six presidents of the tongs. The police kept the treaty with its signatures as a "big stick," and the tong wars were a thing of the past. (See LITTLE PETE.)

CHINKS A type of chaparreras. (See ARMITAS.)

CHINOOK A wind originating on the leeward slopes of mountains, particularly when confined to the eastern slopes of the Rockies. Such a wind is warm and dry, and as it is most active in winter and spring its presence, or absence, can have a marked effect on the northern cattle ranges.

CHINOOK INDIANS
Sometimes called "Flatheads," a name derived from their practice of molding their heads into a wedge shape. This is done in infancy before the skull bones have hardened, a wooden flap being hinged to the cradleboard in such a manner as to exert pressure onto the frontal bones. The Chinooks lived along the Columbia in Wash-

[19] The first tong on record was the carnation-painted Eyebrow Society. Other early tongs were the Yellow Turban Society, the Copper Horses, and the Fists of Righteous Harmony. The Boxers were an offshoot of the last-named.
[20] Chinese maidens without official U.S. entry permits. They became slave, brothel, and marriage-market merchandise.

ington and Oregon, and they were renowned as traders,[21] acting as middlemen in commerce between the Indians of the Coast and those of the plains. Their diet consisted of fish and small game. Wickeyups made from grass or bark were used for shelter. Chinooks belong to the Penutian language group.

CHINOOK TALK   A bastardized language embracing Chinook, French, and English words, that was used extensively in the Northwest to facilitate trading arrangements between Indians and white men.

CHIPMUNK   Small ground squirrel that has distinctive bands of light and dark coloring in the fur on its back. Chipmunks nest in holes in the ground,[22] and they are well distributed throughout the West.

CHIPS   Buffalo or cattle droppings that have been dried out by the elements. On the prairies where wood was scarce they were collected and used as fuel, and it was a lazy sodbuster who hadn't got a stockpile of these obscene scones outside his soddie by late fall. Of interest to the collector: These cakes, varnished and packaged under the trade name "Dung Ho!," could be purchased in the West in the mid-1960s. On the box lid they are described as being "An early American conversation piece . . . preserved forever in its natural state."

CHIRICAHUA APACHE   One of the three main divisions of the Apache nation. The Chiricahuas headquartered in a warm-springs valley that runs latitu-

dinally between the Chiricahua and Dragoon mountains of southeastern Arizona. (See APACHE INDIANS; CHATO; COCHISE; GERONIMO; and NATCHEZ.)

CHISHOLM, JESSE   A Cherokee half-breed trader who, inadvertently, was responsible for the existence of the main cattle trail between Texas and Kansas. Chisholm blazed this trail over the years 1864–66 while hauling merchandise from San Antonio, Texas, to Wichita, Kansas, and vice versa. The cow outfits, who later followed the same route, named the trail after its originator, and the name stuck. (See CHISHOLM TRAIL.)

CHISHOLM TRAIL   The main cattle trail between San Antonio, Texas, and Abilene, Kansas.[23] The trail covered a distance of almost six hundred miles as the crow flies, and it was more than fifty miles wide in places. Numerous rivers had to be crossed by trail herds using the route,[24] but good grazing and the fact that the trail was comparatively level counterbalanced this disadvantage. The northern half of the trail bisected the Indian lands of Oklahoma, but little Indian trouble was experienced by the cattlemen, for any war parties that might be encountered could usually be appeased by diplomatic means—a few head of cattle being cut out from the herd and handed over to the red men to guarantee safe conduct. This trail should not be confused with the Chisum Trail. (See ABILENE; CHISHOLM, JESSE; and CHISUM, JOHN S.)

CHISUM, JOHN S.   New Mexico cattle baron of the latter half of the nineteenth century. Chisum was born in Ten-

---

[21] Possibly an inborn skill that was further developed by early contact with the white trappers.

[22] In the colder areas they hibernate the winter away in these nests.

[23] The original trail terminated at Wichita, but in 1868 a livestock dealer named McCoy was instrumental in extending the trail north to Abilene.

[24] Moving north from San Antonio the major rivers, in order of crossing, were the Brazos, Colorado, Trinity, Red, Canadian, Cimarron, and Arkansas.

nessee in 1824, moving westward to Texas with his parents in the late 1830s. The family settled in Paris, Texas, and John grew to adulthood there. By the time he was thirty, Chisum was an established cattleman of Texas, and in 1867, when he decided to push West to New Mexico, his herd was more than ten thousand strong. Operating under the Long Rail and Jingle-bob brands,[25] he established headquarters at Bosque Grande, about forty miles south of Fort Sumner, and within a few years he was undisputed cattle king of New Mexico Territory. In 1872 he moved his ranch headquarters to the Roswell area (his South Spring Ranch), and by 1876 the Chisum herds were smothering the Pecos Valley region. Small ranchers accused him of swallowing up their stock, and Chisum retaliated by accusing them of rustling, a harsh term that meant much the same as the little men's polite euphemism. Chisum was undoubtedly plagued by rustlers but he evidently never had any idea "whodunit," for during the Lincoln County War he was friendly with Billy the Kid, a little outlaw who had helped reduce his herds more than somewhat. The cattle king never married, and the domestic side of his life was taken care of by his niece Miss Sally Chisum, a nifty lass who was much taken—no innuendo intended—by Billy the Kid. The South Spring Ranch was elegantly furnished, yet Chisum is reputed to have always slept in a bedroll that he kept alongside his bed. John Simpson Chisum died on December 22, 1884, and he was buried at Paris, Texas. (See CHISUM, SALLY; LINCOLN COUNTY WAR; and MC-CARTY, HENRY.)

CHISUM, SALLY The daughter of James Chisum[26] a brother of the New Mexico cattle baron John S. Chisum. In 1875 Sally left her home in Texas to run the domestic side of her Uncle John's South Spring Ranch, and it was here that she met such big names of the Southwest as Pat Garrett and Billy the Kid. In truth Sally has only been introduced into this volume because of her knowledge of these men, and the descriptions given below have been composed from her reminiscences as reported by Walter Noble Burns in his *The Saga of Billy the Kid*. Pat Garrett: A very tall, gray-eyed man who possessed a sureness of stride and a calm manner. He had a crooked smile, but this did not detract from his appearance, and he was remarkably handsome in spite of a melancholy expression which, after a few shots of liquor, would be replaced by a friendly glow as he became the life and soul of the party with his wonderful tales of frontier life. Billy the Kid: A well-groomed, sharply dressed young man who sported a white stetson, dark jacket and vest, gray shirt and trousers, and a natty black bow tie, a flower buttonhole occasionally being added to revive the somber tones. He laughed easily and had a clear-eyed look that enhanced his handsome, youthful features, and his hands were as small as a woman's. He was happy and good-humored, and politeness and courteousness—he removed his hat in the presence of ladies—added to his charm.[27] John Simpson Chisum: Not very loquacious but generous in the extreme, and having a soft smile, which remained on his face most of the time. He had good clothes but rarely wore them, so usually he could

---

[25] A double-knife brand consisting of a gash running from shoulder to flank, and an earmark that caused the member to droop.

[26] John Chisum had three brothers who helped him run the South Springs Ranch: James, Pitzer, and Jeff.

[27] Sally had a soft spot for Billy, to be sure. He was a frequent visitor at the ranch, sometimes staying for a week or longer, and during these visits he and the girl would go riding or fishing together, while some evenings would be spent chatting on the porch.

be mistaken for any humble cowhand. At no time did he carry a gun.

Miss Sally was at the ranch during the Lincoln County War, but sometime afterward she married Uncle John's bookkeeper, a man named William Roberts, and they set up home in Roswell, New Mexico.[28]

CHIVARRAS Leggings manufactured from either heavy-duty cloth or leather; a kind of poor man's chaparreras. The term is confined to the Southwest.

CHIVINGTON, JOHN M. Six feet, seven inches of Irishman, who, after years as a blacksmith *cum* preacher in Kansas, found his way into Colorado Territory and became an elder of the territorial outpost of the Methodist Church. In 1864 Chivington was given a commission in the Colorado Volunteer Forces and wound up in command of the 3rd Colorado Cavalry, a collection of rabble who had been organized to stamp out Indian uprisings in the territory. On November 29, 1864, Chivington's command attacked a peaceful Cheyenne village at Sand Creek and massacred its inhabitants. Women and children were shot and bludgeoned to death without mercy, and after the atrocity Chivington joyfully reported, ". . . unnecessary to report that I captured no prisoners." The saner elements were aghast, and the Methodist elder was court-martialed. Justice was blind that day and he was acquitted, but in deference to public opinion, he was relieved of his command. Years later this infamous character turned up in Denver, Colorado, and here he got the job of undersheriff, a position he was to hold until his death in 1894. (See SAND CREEK MASSACRE.)

CHRISTIE, NED A full-blooded Cherokee Indian who in 1885 turned his back on honest pursuits after killing a deputy U.S. marshal named Dan Maples. Until this time Christie had been a respected member of the Cherokee tribal legislature, but after the killing he disappeared into the Cookson Hills, and for the next seven years he was one of the most wanted men in the Oklahoma Indian Territory. Over this period he committed a variety of crimes, and a plethora of charges—ranging from whiskey peddling, through stock theft to armed banditry—were ready to lay at his door just as soon as the law discovered his whereabouts. Said door and whereabouts were discovered by U. S. Marshal Heck Thomas on November 1, 1892, when he and another lawman trailed Christie to a log fort near Tarlequah in the Cookson Hills. The fort looked damn near impregnable, so the two bloodhounds sent for reinforcements and a three-pounder field piece, and when the small army arrived "t' battle commenced." More than two thousand rounds of small-arms fire were soaked up by the logs, and the thirty rounds that were fired from the cannon had a disconcerting habit of bouncing from the logs and boomeranging back— a case of "Fire! . . . Duck!" After twenty-four hours of stalemate and a few fatalities among the attacking force, the stockade was finally breached with dynamite, and when shell-shocked Ned staggered through the smoke working his Winchester, he was cut down by officers. A photo of Mr. Christie shows a youthful mustached figure wearing a store suit. He is leaning against an old door with a lever action cradled across his arms, and he appears quite tranquil although somewhat wooden of pose.[29] (See THOMAS, HECK.)

[28] It was here that Walter Noble Burns interviewed her in 1924.

[29] Not to be wondered at, for the photo was made posthumously, and after the corpse had been allowed to harden in an artistic, pre-*rigor mortis,* arranged pose. This was a favorite practice in the West, where there was a healthy demand for these morbid "pin-ups."

CHUCK WAGON A covered wagon on which a chuck box has been installed. The chuck box is fitted at the rear of the wagon in such a manner that when the cover of the chuck box is lowered, a hinged support swings down and thus transforms the cover into a work table for the cook. Tin plates and cups and other feeding utensils, together with coffee, spices, baking powder, etc., are carried in fitted drawers that make up the main bulk of the chuck box. A leather boot, fitted beneath the rear running gear, is used to carry the heavy cooking equipment—mixing bowls and, frequently, a Dutch oven, while cumbersome victuals such as flour, potatoes, and sides of pork, plus the outfits' bedrolls, are carried in the wagon box.

CIMARRON COUNTY SEAT WAR In October 1887 Cimarron, Kansas, was voted the county seat of Gray County, a decision that didn't set well with a certain Mr. Asa T. Soule, a wealthy brewer of hop bitters who, for personal reasons, wanted the town of Ingalls as the county seat. Soule charged fraud and carried his case to the courts, and the political future of Cimarron and Ingalls hung in the balance for over a year without a decision being handed down—a year during which Cimarron hung on to the title of temporary county seat. By New Year's Day 1889 Asa was getting as explosive as his bitters. He reasoned that if he could lay his hands on the county court records and install them in the Ingalls courthouse, he would have it made. All he needed was some musclemen, and they came easy: A friend of his knew county sheriff Bill Tilghman, and by January 11 a gang of fast guns had been deputized—all nice and legal-like—and were ready to go after the thousand-

dollar reward that Asa was prepared to hand out when the records were in his hands. Within a few hours of getting their badges, more than a dozen hard cases—including Tilghman and such notables as Neal Brown and Jim and Tom Masterson—piled out of a wagon that had been drawn up outside the Cimarron courthouse. It was the wee hours of Sunday January 13, and the streets were deserted as Neal Brown and the Mastersons broke into the courthouse while the rest of the mob stood guard. The records consisted of a mountain of important-looking tomes and beribboned bumf, and the three active looters were forced to make many journeys to and fro, and as they hotfooted up the courthouse stairs for the last pile, the alarm was raised by some local night owl. Windows were flung up, and drowsy citizens raked the street with gunfire. Four deputies were cut down in the first barrage, and the unscathed members of the invading force tossed their wounded into the wagon, piled in after them, and beat a thunderous retreat. Their escape was a success, and the thwarted townies turned their attentions and gunfire in the direction of the upstairs rooms of the courthouse where, to all intents and purposes, three of the raiders were trapped. One citizen lay dead and three others had been wounded. Lynch talk was in the air that Sabbath, and with more than two hundred armed men pouring lead in their direction, the trio in the courthouse didn't appear to have a chance. But the trapped men were hard lads, and the thunder of guns and tinkling of glass continued until dawn the following day, at which time the besieged men were allowed to leave town under a flag of truce.[30] Asa got his records and Ingalls became the county seat until a further

[30] A leniency that can be explained. Bat Masterson, who was in Denver at the time, heard of his brothers' plight from a telegraph news item, and he immediately wired Cimarron that if his brothers were harmed he would descend on the town with an army of gunfighters the like of which the West had never seen.

election in 1893 handed the honor, and the records, back to Cimarron. So what about the dead citizens?; Well, er . . . six of the invaders were tried for the murder, but all were acquitted.[31]

CIMARRON RIVER From its headwaters in northeastern New Mexico, the Cimarron meanders in a generally easterly direction until it joins the Arkansas near Tulsa in northeastern Oklahoma. During its journey the river winds its way through four western states: New Mexico, Colorado, Kansas, and Oklahoma.

CINNAMON BEAR A color variation among brown bears. (See BEARS.)

CLAIBORNE, BILLY Young glory-hunter who after the death of Billy the Kid in July 1881 insisted that he be addressed by that title. Three men laughed at such grandstanding, and the three men died. Claiborne[32] was arrested after the third killing[33] and tossed into the San Pedro, Arizona, jail to await trial. On October 22, 1881, Ike Clanton, backed by Tom and Frank McLaury, rode into San Pedro and rescued the counterfeit Billy the Kid from custody. Four days later in Tombstone, Claiborne buckled on his two guns and showed his appreciation by standing alongside Ike and company at the O. K. Corral. Much powder was burned in that historic Earp-Clanton showdown, but Mr. Claiborne came through unscathed, mainly because he fled the area before anyone could get a bead on him. The buscaderoed Billy was to survive for almost a year. In the fall of 1882 he got "likkered up" in Tombstone's Oriental Saloon, and when Frank Leslie, the barman *cum* bouncer, ejected him from the premises, Claiborne went

for his guns. But Forty-rod had ruine his reflexes, and as he goofed in his gun play he must have seen Frank thum back the hammer, sight, and . . . A self defense verdict was handed down a the inquest. (See LESLIE, FRANK, an O. K. CORRAL.)

CLANTON GANG A more apt titl for this outfit would be Bandits, Inc., fo the enterprise run by N. H. "Old Man" Clanton was an amalgam of various out law bands whose combined strengtl sometimes numbered more than thre hundred. Cattle rustling was the gang main activity, although stage and bullion pack train robberies were undertake when the jackpot was sufficiently tempt ing. The Clanton Ranch at Lewis Spring near Galeyville, Arizona, was the gang headquarters, and all the cattle move ments in the southwestern area of Ari zona Territory were forwarded here b a network of spies that usually dressed a Mexican peasants and covered every wa terhole in the region. In July 1881 Ol Man Clanton received intelligence of a mule train that was freighting bullio through the Chiricahua Range, and a the head of a gang of cutthroats that in cluded such characters as Curly Bil Brocius and John Ringo, he ambushe the train in Guadalupe Canyon, slaugh tered the nineteen Mexicans who wer leading the animals, and made off wit seventy-five thousand dollars in silve bullion. A few weeks after this bloody affair, the Old Man and five of his mol were driving a herd, which had bee stolen in Mexico, through Guadalup Canyon when they in turn were am bushed by friends of the murdered mule teers. Clanton and four of his men wer dead within minutes, the only survivo

[31] I. W. English—the victim—now ceased to be a murder victim; self-defense anc accidental-death verdicts were kinda popular out West.

[32] Frequently spelled "Clairborne."

[33] The victim in this instance was a scoffer named James Hickey.

being a gunnie named Earnshaw. From then on Brocius became top man, and although Clanton's three sons (Ike, Finn, and Billy) and the term "Clanton Gang" still survived, as far as this entry is concerned, the Clanton Gang, as such, ceased to operate with the passing of the Old Man. (See CLANTON, JOSEPH ISAAC; CLANTON, N. H.; CLANTON, PHINEAS; CLANTON, WILLIAM; GRAHAM, WILLIAM B.; and RINGGOLD, JOHN.)

CLANTON, JOSEPH ISAAC   The loudmouth braggart of the Clanton clan. Ike usually served as a messenger boy in the Old Man's bandit empire, but on occasion he would be entrusted with a cattle-rustling detail, and he was in at the Guadalupe Canyon pack-train massacre. On October 26, 1881, Ike backed down at the O. K. Corral, but shortly afterward he is alleged to have made an attempt to assassinate Virgil Earp before hightailing south of the border. A few years later, and after the Earps had left Tombstone, Ike was back in the territory, and he and Finn were back in the cattle-rustling business. In 1887 a new sheriff[34] was elected in Apache County—the scene of the Clantons' activities—and his clean-up campaign swept Ike and Finn from the ranges in less time than it takes to say "they went thataway." The rustlers were trapped at their base camp on the Blue River, and Ike was shot dead as he tried to escape. (See CLANTON GANG; O. K. CORRAL; and OWENS, COMMODORE PERRY.)

CLANTON, N. H.   The "Old Man" of the Clanton gang. What the initials stand for at this late date is anyone's guess, for as early as 1880 his Christian names had been obliterated by the "Old

Man" brand. Clanton, who was a Texan by birth, lived a bent life from an early age, but his criminal activities were pretty small potatoes[35] until he settled in Arizona, where he emerged as a gang leader of ruthless ability. He located a homestead in the territory near Fort Thomas, and here he raised a brood of misfit sons and a herd from stolen stock. In 1879 a silver strike a few miles south of the ranch was responsible for a rash of mining camps springing up in the area, and the Old Man pulled up stakes and relocated near Galeyville, a wide-open settlement that was a satellite of the main camp at Tombstone. Here Clanton built up a rustling, bandit, and smuggling empire which within a few months was clashing with the Tombstone authorities almost daily. The Old Man, however, didn't live to see the showdown at the O. K. Corral, for he had been killed a short time earlier. (See CLANTON GANG; CLANTON, JOSEPH ISAAC; and CLANTON, PHINEAS.)

CLANTON, PHINEAS   Phineas, or Finn, must have been the weak member of the Clanton clan, for his press releases are mostly negative: absent at the Guadalupe Canyon massacre, absent from his paw's last rustling expedition, and absent from the O. K. Corral fracas. A shirker, no doubt, but after the O. K. shootout things became more definite. He was implicated in the murder of Morgan Earp, but nothing came of this, and a few years later he was up in Apache County rustling cattle with his brother Ike. Something became of this: Finn was arrested and given a long stretch in the penitentiary at Yuma. (See CLANTON GANG; CLANTON, JOSEPH ISAAC; and CLANTON, N. H.)

34 Sheriff Commodore Perry Owens.
35 Not wishing to sell the Old Man short, however, let it be known that he fled his native Texas in 1849 with a posse at his heels, and some years later he took leave of California with the vigilantes eating his dust. Obviously he was a "bad un."

CLANTON, WILLIAM Better known as Billy. The Old Man had a good offspring here and he knew it, and had Billy lived he would have made an excellent entry here. An accomplished rustler and horse thief at twelve; a killer who had been bloodied at Guadalupe Canyon by his early teens; and a corpse by his midteens. Authorities differ regarding his age at this crucial period, but it was no less than fifteen and no more than seventeen; whichever, a brief candle to be sure. He should never have toted a gun at the O. K. Corral. (See CLANTON GANG; CLANTON, N. H.; and O. K. CORRAL.)

CLARK, JIM Colorado specialist in robbery at gunpoint. He is reputed to have robbed the rich and given to the poor, a Robin Hood policy that is highly regarded in some quarters.[36] In 1895 at Telluride, Colorado, Jim managed to con the local council into hiring him as town marshal, but he didn't allow the appointment to interfere with his stand-and-deliver activities, and as these activities were an open secret, he didn't last long as a lawman. The council fired him, and because of his record told him to "git outa town!" Jim ignored the request and stepped up his one-man crime wave to make up for his lost paycheck. The rich element got fed up with him, and they passed around the hat to establish a Clark removal fund and let it be known that they wanted a removal man. They found one—a poor gent who needed the dough and didn't give a toss about Robin Hood—and a short time later a shot rang out as Clark stepped out of a beer joint. The ex-marshal jerked, then pulled himself together and wobbled across the street and into a brothel; poor Jim mustn't have realized

how bad he'd been hit, for he died in that joyhouse. And that, folks, is a story shot full of morals.

CLARK, WILLIAM A Virginia-born geographical expert who was co-leader of the Lewis and Clark Expedition of 1804–6. Clark, an ex-military man who had resigned from the Army in 1796 for reasons of ill health, was responsible for the publication of the journals of the Lewis and Clark Expedition in 1814, some five years after the mysterious death of Lewis. As a reward for his co-leadership of the expedition Clark was made brigadier general of the Missouri Territory militia and in 1822 he was appointed superintendent of Indian Affairs in St. Louis. He held this latter position until his death in 1838 at the age of sixty-eight. (See LEWIS AND CLARK EXPEDITION.)

CLARKE, MALCOLM
Onetime trapper who was firmly established as a fur trader by 1870. At this time Clarke, who had married a Piegan girl and had five children by her (two daughters and three sons), was living near Helena, Montana, with his family. Clarke was well liked by the Indians, who knew him as "Four Bears,"[37] and when friction developed between the Blackfoot and the white settlers in January 1870, he visited the tribe in an effort to prevent bloodshed. Clarke took his son Horace along; this was an unfortunate choice, for Horace was on bad terms with a member of the tribe, a brave named Ne-tus-cheo, who had been accused of horse theft by him. The alleged horse thief happened to be present at the council, and the peace talk never got under way. The Clarkes flung a few harsh words at Ne-tus-cheo and the Indian flung back lead, which

[36] Irrational, of course; only a stupid person would attempt to rob the poor.
[37] In his trapper days Clarke is reputed to have slain four grizzlies in one lone-handed encounter. Obviously a very tough *hombre* or very small bears; cubs, perhaps?

killed Malcolm and wounded Horace. (See BAKER MASSACRE.)

CLARKE, RICHARD A Deadwood, South Dakota, settler who took on the mantle of a fictional character named "Deadwood Dick." Dime novels[38] built around this nonexistent Dick flooded the country in the early 1880s, and after reading the publisher's line "Truth is stranger than fiction," the public may hardly be blamed for going in search of such a character. Mr. Clarke heard opportunity knock. Pint-sized and both long-haired and long-winded, he climbed into an ill-fitting suit of fringed buckskins and strapped on a .45; and that was how the West was won by Richard, for when he mosied out into the sunlight he was an immediate success. He obliged the reading public by giving substance— however pint-sized—to their paper hero, and he gave the town another character to add to its list of "people and places to see." This three-dimensional Deadwood Dick sold rusty old guns with phony histories, homemade scalps, and pin-ups of himself; he also had a short spell with the Buffalo Bill shows, and, for a time, a show of his own. Further Deadwood Dick romances were published after Mr. Clarke had emerged from obscurity, so he never had any need for a publicity department. (See BEADLE AND ADAMS and DIME NOVELS.)

CLEMENS, SAMUEL LANGHORNE Author who wrote under the pen name of Mark Twain. Clemens, who was born at Hannibal, Missouri, on November 30, 1830, didn't enter the West until he was over thirty years of age. Up to this time he had seen service as a Mississippi River pilot, and had, for two weeks, served as a lieutenant in the Confederate Army. After resigning from the retreating rebel army he moved to Nevada Territory. Here he was bitten by the prospecting bug, and for more than a year he tried his luck in the Esmeralda area with little success. Tired of mining, he moved to Virginia City, and here he found a job on the editorial staff of the *Territorial Enterprise*. During this journalistic stint he adopted the Mark Twain[39] by-line, and when he left the *Enterprise* in 1864 he continued to use this name. In 1867 his humorous novel *The Celebrated Jumping Frog of Calveras County* was published, and Clemens became famous overnight. Other well-known works of his include *Innocents Abroad*, *A Tramp Abroad*, *Roughing It*, *Tom Sawyer*, and *Huckleberry Finn*. Clemens died on April 20, 1910.

CLEMENTS, EMANUEL Texas cattle owner and trail boss who is usually known as "Mannen" or "Manning." Clements, aided by three brothers and two sisters,[40] raised herds in Gonzales County, Texas, then trailed them North to the railheads in Kansas. In 1871, while moving a herd North, and just after crossing the Red River, Mannen killed two men in his outfit, a couple of brothers named Joe and Dolph Shadden. After this double killing, the telegraph wires hummed, and when he arrived in Abilene, the town marshal was waiting with a pick-up order. If the trail boss who is quoted as saying, ". . . killing a

---

[38] A generic term: Deadwood Dick novels were published in Beadle's Boy's Library, and their price was half a dime. The author of these stories was Edward L. Wheeler, and eighty of his D.D. efforts were published.

[39] The riverboat influence here: "Mark twain" is a nautical term associated with depth sounding.

[40] Brothers Jim, Joseph, and Gipson (usually known as "Gip" or "Gyp"), and sisters Mary Jane and Minerva. These five—and, of course, Emanuel—were cousins of the notorious John Wesley Hardin.

man don't amount to nothing. I'd cut anyone down to breeches high with a sawn-off shotgun for three hundred dollars," had been as tough as some hero worshipers would have us believe, there should have been a gunfight here. But Mannen was a bigmouth who rarely tried anything if his bluster was met by a cool, level glance, and Marshal "Wild Bill" Hickok arrested him without incident. At the trial, Mannen told some yarn about the Shaddens trying to kill him, and he was acquitted on a self-defense plea. In 1874 Mannen oyezed around that he and his brothers were going to "tree" Wichita, and a few days later nearly half a hundred Texans rode toward town with the intention of carrying out this threat. A tall, mustached deputy marshal named Wyatt Earp blocked their progress on the wooden bridge spanning Cowskin Creek, and hoofs shuffled and pawed on the boards as the cavalcade came to a halt. Mannen was brandishing two .45s, but he paused and eyed the thin line of special deputies Earp had strung out along Douglas Avenue—maybe twelve to twenty men. Mannen had the edge, but he abandoned it by reholstering his gun, and after a few quiet words with Wyatt Earp he swung his horse around, and the small army of Texans cantered away. The end came for Emanuel "Manning" Clements on March 29, 1887. He was having a drink in the Senate Saloon at Ballinger, Texas, when he got into an argument with the city marshal, Joseph Townsend; guns were drawn, and Clements was "cut down to breeches high." (See HARDIN, JOHN WESLEY.)

CLIFTON, DAN Better known as "Dynamite Dick." Dan was a small-time rustler of Indian Territory who hit the big time after joining the Doolin gang in the closing months of 1892. Clifton was active in most of the gang's holdups, and was wounded (he lost three fingers) at the gunfight at Ingalls. Clifton, and a fellow outlaw named Ben Cravens, were tracked down by peace officers near Blackwell, Oklahoma, in November 1896, and Dynamite Dick was blasted into eternity in the ensuing gun battle. (See CRAVENS, BEN, and DOOLIN GANG.)

CLUM, JOHN P. Best remembered as a fearless frontier editor, although Clum, who was born on September 1, 1851, had been both an Indian agent and a lawyer before he settled down to a journalistic career. In his early twenties he served as Indian Agent on the San Carlos Reservation, resigning in 1877 when he found that his sympathy for his Apache wards was incompatible with the government's hardening policy toward the Indians. Two years later he bought a small publishing business and got his first taste of newspaper work. He liked it, and when mining camps began to spring up in the southwestern corner of Arizona Territory, he freighted his presses and equipment into Tombstone and founded the Tombstone *Epitaph*.[41] He was never short of copy here, for apart from minor killings—which were tucked away in the "Deaths Doings" column—there was constant friction between the Earps and the Clantons, frequent stage holdups, and an occasional headline-busting event such as the Guadalupe Canyon massacre or the gunfight at the O. K. Corral. On May 1, 1882, he sold his interest in the *Epitaph,* and a short time later he left the territory[42] and moved to Cali-

[41] The first issue of this daily and weekly publication was peeled from the handpress on May 1, 1880.

[42] Why he left is anyone's guess. It has been suggested that Clum, who always backed the Earps in his column, feared reprisals by the criminal element after the brothers left the ter-

fornia, where he became assistant editor on the San Francisco *Examiner*. (See O. K. CORRAL; TOMBSTONE, ARIZONA; TOMBSTONE EPITAPH; and TOMBSTONE NUGGET.)

COCHISE Chiricahua chief who until 1860 was not actively hostile to the white-eyes. In that year Cochise's band, camped in the Apache Pass and supplying firewood to the stage station there, was unjustifiably accused of kidnaping a half-breed boy named Mickey Free, and for the next eleven years Cochise's Chiricahuas raided, burned, pillaged, and murdered throughout the southern half of Arizona. During this period of carnage only one white man succeeded in establishing friendly relations with Cochise: a red bearded six-footer named Tom Jeffords. This man won the complete trust of the Chiricahua chief, and in 1871 he was instrumental in bringing his Apache friend's antiwhite campaign to an end. Cochise died in 1876, at the age of sixty-three years.[43] (See APACHE INDIANS; BATTLE AT APACHE PASS; FREE, MICKEY; JEFFORDS, THOMAS J.; and NATCHEZ.)

CODY, WILLIAM FREDERICK Plainsman and showman who was born at Le Claire, Iowa, on February 26, 1846, a son of Isaac and Mary Cody and the fourth-born of a family of five girls and three boys. In 1850 the family moved to Kansas, where Isaac established a home and a small sawmill business, and it was here that the head of the family died in 1857. This was a disaster, for although Pa's enterprise had been a near failure, it had brought in a little cash. In an ef-

fort to help out the family budget William, who could fork a horse as good as anyone, got a job as messenger boy with the firm of Russell, Majors, and Waddell, a firm of freighters whose Conestoga trains fanned out into the Far West from their home base at Leavenworth. Young Cody's duties consisted of carrying messages between these wagon trains, for which service he was paid ten dollars a week plus his keep. The West suited Cody, and by 1860 he had talked himself into a job with the Pony Express. During this stint Cody rode the Julesburg section of the line, and it was while in this service that he met James B. Hickok (who was to become a lifelong friend) and clocked up his saddle-polishing record of around three hundred miles in a little over twenty-one hours. Cody returned to the family hearth in 1861. The Codys were still impoverished in spite of the fact that Mrs. Cody had converted her home into a boarding house, and William took on temporary jobs in an effort to relieve the situation until the death of his mother in December 1863. Two months later he joined the Union Army, and he served with the 7th and 9th Kansas Regiments as a dispatch rider until the last few months of the war, at which time he was transferred to hospital duties at St. Louis. On being demobilized in 1865, Cody became a stagecoach driver, and by March 6, 1866, he had saved enough of his pay to marry Louisa Frederici, a girl whom he had met in St. Louis. The newlyweds tried running a boarding house, but this was a failure, and Cody returned to the plains in search of work. He found it: first as an Army scout attached to General

territory in May 1882. On the other hand, Tombstone may have held bitter memories for Clum, for sometime between his selling the paper and his leaving the area he is said to have suffered the loss of his wife and baby daughter. Apart from hearsay, there is no record of this, but the fact that Clum returned to Tombstone in 1930 and made an unsuccessful attempt to locate his wife's grave give substance to at least part of the story.

[43] As late as 1960 a chief of the Chiricahua Apaches was a great-grandson of Cochise.

G. A. Custer's command at Fort Larned, and then as a hunter for the Kansas Pacific Railroad. In the latter job, he got his first taste of fame, killing more buffalo in one day than the self-styled "Buffalo Bill" Comstock. Cody's score was sixty-nine against Comstock's forty-six, and from then on it was to be "Buffalo Bill" Cody whatever his employment. His fame spread, and in 1869, while he was employed as chief of scouts by the Army, he made the acquaintance of Ed Judson, a writer of dime novels who wrote under the pen name of Ned Buntline, and in December of that year "Buffalo Bill, King of the Border Men" was published in the New York *Weekly* under the Buntline by-line. This was the first of a deluge of Buffalo Bill yarns, and Cody soon found himself being invited to parties and luncheons, a social whirl that was to take him as far afield as New York and Chicago. In 1872 Judson took him to see a play in New York that had been adapted from one of the writer's B.B. stories, and a short time later Cody had been persuaded to tread the boards in person. From that time on —save for a short period in 1876, when he found time to return to the plains and lift the scalp of Yellow Hand—he was to devote his life to show business. His first major role behind the footlights was at the St. Louis Opera House, where he played himself in an epic entitled *Scouts of the Plains*. It was a lousy epic and he forgot all his lines, but a critic described him, somewhat fruitily, as a "beautiful blond," and the audience wanted more and more, and more and more. John M. Burke replaced Judson as Cody's manager, and the shows went from strength to strength. Money poured in, and by 1876 Cody settled his family[44] in a

palatial house in Rochester, New York. A few years later he built "Welcome Wigwam," a large house on the North Platte, and here he held drinking sessions with his freeloading pals until the place was little more than a glorified saloon. In 1882 the shows became outdoor spectacles that later included such props as the old Deadwood coach and a small herd of buffalo, both of which were chased around the arena by a party of "real live Injuns." These outdoor Buffalo Bill shows—periodically they were given different names—toured the United States and Europe, and by the early 1890s Cody was a millionaire. His domestic affairs, however, were a different story. His drinking and womanizing—and no mistake, he was in a class of his own at both pursuits—had by now given Louisa a built-in frown, and after being knotted into painful bends by some of her cooking, he accused her—probably unjustifiably—of trying to poison him. Louisa left instanter, and Cody started divorce proceedings almost as speedily. Shortly after this domestic upheaval, the show played in London, England, and here Cody proposed to an English actress named Katherine Clemmons, a siren whom he had fallen for during an earlier visit. He would marry her just as soon as his divorce came through; meanwhile, he would invest eighty thousand dollars in the furthering of her career. The divorce didn't come through, and Katherine married someone else. It was an embittered Cody who returned Stateside, but in 1902 the death of his daughter Arta brought about a reconciliation with Louisa. The following year business began to fall off, and within five years Cody was heavily in debt.[45] Pawnee Bill (Gordon Lillie), whom Cody had at one time employed,

---

[44] Louisa, daughters Orra and Arta, and son Kit Carson.

[45] This may seem incredible, but Cody was generous in the extreme, and apart from supporting all his kinfolk, he was also making regular allowances to Alexander Majors (his old employer) and others.

came to his aid, and the Buffalo Bill Wild West and Pawnee Bill Far East Show—a bastardized mix-up for sure—kept Cody from bankruptcy for a little while longer. The blow fell in 1913, and the joint operation was put up for auction to pay off a mountain of debts. Cody was now sixty-eight years of age, but there was still some iron in his aging frame, and he managed to raise enough capital to form the Cody Historical Pictures Company. This company, in conjunction with the Essanay Film Company, made a one-reeler cavalry vs. Indians movie on the Pine Ridge Reservation, but exhibitors showed a reluctance to book the film, and consequently it became a financial failure. The latter years of Cody's eventful life were spent traveling around the country with the Sells-Floto Circus. Over these years he was plagued by rheumatism and prostate trouble, and he could hardly stay in the saddle; he was a freak —a pathetic reminder of the West that had perished; but he knew it and he accepted it, and by accepting it he was—in this writer's opinion—taller than he had ever been before. On January 10, 1917, the old plainsman died, and the news of his death swept the World War I news from the headlines, an obituary fit for a king. He is buried on Lookout Mountain in Colorado, and a bronze equestrian statue of him in his prime stands over the grave. (See BEADLE AND ADAMS; CARVER, WILLIAM; HICKOK, JAMES BUTLER; JUDSON, EDWARD Z. C.; LILLIE, GORDON W.; and YELLOW HAND.)

COE, FRANK   Small rancher who sided with Billy the Kid during the Lincoln County War. He and cousin George had adjoining ranches in the Ruidoso Valley of southeastern New Mexico, and it was here that the two cousins first met the Kid in 1877. Frank survived the

Lincoln County War and lived to a ripe old age. Coe's present-day kinfolk still live in the area. (See LINCOLN COUNTY WAR.)

COE, GEORGE   Member of the Billy the Kid faction during the Lincoln County War. George was wounded slightly at Blazer's Mill, but he survived for many years, and he was the last survivor of the war when he died at Glencoe, New Mexico, in 1957. Some years before his death he had his reminiscences ghost-written and published under the title *Frontier Fighter*. (See ANDREWS, JESSE, and LINCOLN COUNTY WAR.)

COE, PHIL   Dapper-dressed Texan gambler—derby hat, gold-headed cane, the lot—who became acquainted with most of the West's disreputable characters while working the gambling circuit in the 1860s and early 1870s. To quote his contemporaries, ". . . he was tall . . . elegant and handsome . . . sported a neatly trimmed beard. . . ." In 1871 elegant Phil arrived at Abilene, Kansas, accompanied by nonelegant Ben Thompson, and there the two men formed a business partnership that resulted in the Bull's Head Tavern and Gambling Saloon being opened under their joint management. The portrait of a large bull was painted across the front of this building, a portrait that was to cause some controversy. It was too much bull; like its bull parts were kinda fearsome large. The townies who washed and shaved branded the sign as obscene, and Marshal Hickok was prevailed upon to use his influence in the matter of its removal.[46] Wild Bill had words with Phil and Ben regarding the "shame of Abilene," and the marshal gave them twenty-four hours to remove the bull, or parts thereof, before he took any further action. Further action oc-

---

[46] Hickok may have needed little persuading, for he is known to have had gambling trouble with Phil prior to this time.

curred the following day: Wild Bill strode across the street carrying a can of paint and a brush and painted out the offensive area of the portrait with a delicacy of touch that may have indicated latent talent. The bull was now a steer, and everyone was happy except Phil and Ben. A short time after this event, on Thursday evening, October 5, 1871, Phil Coe "radio'd" his whereabouts by firing a shot outside the Alamo Saloon. This was a breach of a town ordinance that forbade the carrying of pistols on the streets, and Wild Bill came hurrying out of the Alamo, his mustache heavy with beer suds and his silk sash heavy with guns. Phil said he had "jest been shootin' at a dawg," then swung the muzzle of his gun in the marshal's direction and fired two shots. A silly thing to do, for Hickok, who remained unscathed, traded two back, and Phil was carried from the field with two abdominal wounds that were to prove fatal within forty-eight hours.[47] (See HICKOK, JAMES BUTLER, and THOMPSON, BEN.)

COEUR D'ALENE INDIANS

A minority division of the Nez Percé whose home was in the Coeur d'Alene region of northern Idaho. (See NEZ PERCÉ INDIANS.)

COFFEYVILLE, KANSAS

Mercantile town in the southwestern corner of the state that has found its niche in western history as being the site of the Daltons' last robbery, a double bank job that took place on October 5, 1892. At nine-thirty on that Wednesday morning, the three Daltons, Grat, Emmett, and Bob, together with two other members of the gang, Dick Broadwell and Bill Powers, rode their horses into the town's plaza with the intention of robbing the Condon and First National banks. The hitching rails, which the gang had expected to find outside the banks, had been temporarily removed by workmen who were busy on the streets, and the bandits were forced to leave their horses in an alley that was more than a block away from the banks, a minor item that was to lead to their undoing. At nine forty-two, the bandits entered the banks; Grat, Broadwell, and Powers into the Condon Bank, and Bob and Emmett into the First National, which

---

[47] This is an extremely controversial shootout, for over the years the debunkers of Hickok have clouded the issue. Although these detractors usually agree that Coe did fire a shot outside the Alamo, they allege that Hickok had been waiting for an excuse to gun down Phil "nice and legal like" for some time, and on hearing the shot Hickok dashed out into the street and shot poor Phil down in cold blood, the assumption here being that Wild Bill could recognize the sound of Phil's gun when a cartridge was exploded therein. Does not this appear more feasible; Coe meant to kill Hickok, and, knowing that the lawman was in the Alamo, he fired a shot to flush him from the building and then . . . things went wrong for Phil. After this event, writers, for many years, inclined to the view that bull trouble and gambling were responsible for the friction between these two men, but by the 1960s sex had settled in the West—panties littered the chaparral, and the average cowpoke could recognize a bra from a pair of horse blinkers—so, in deference to public opinion, said reasons were abandoned and a woman angle was introduced into this segment of the saga of Wild Bill Hickok. The woman was vague at first—a whore from across the tracks or a dance hall girl —but within a few years, and after much research, the trollop brand was placed upon the bustled butt of a girl named Jessie Hazel. With variations the Jessie Hazel stories go something like this: Wild Bill, florid with passion, breaks into Jessie's room, only to find that Phil —who was no doubt showing her his elegance—had beaten him to it. Phil (and it must be noted here that over his years in print, this lad has developed a lot of type-set muscles) bounces Bill off the walls and then proceeds to strangle his somewhat groggy rival, but Jessie, not wishing to see her clientele reduced, intervenes and . . . well, so on and so on, etc. This makes for a good story, and as it is well known that Wild Bill spent much of his time in the boudoirs of the bawds, and that a girl named Jessie Hazel did exist, it all could be true.

was no more than fifty yards away across the street. All were armed with Winchesters and handguns, and Bob, Grat, and Broadwell were wearing false whiskers. The whiskers couldn't have been a very effective disguise, for a Coffeyville resident named Alec McKenna had made a tentative recognition of the mob as they strode from the alley, and when they entered the banks he kept his suspicious gaze flickering between the two premises. Meanwhile, the Condon detail had gotten bank vice president C. T. Carpenter and two of his staff under their guns and were waiting around for the vault's time lock to operate at nine forty-five. During this short wait, McKenna glanced into the bank and on seeing the gang's weapons, he raised the alarm. Residents grabbed guns, and pandemonium reigned; Grat forgot about the vault, and the three outlaws fled from the bank with guns blazing. Across the street Bob and Emmett spilled from the First National with more than twenty thousand dollars in loot, and Lucius Baldwin became the first fatal casualty in the battle when he tried to intercept them and was cut down by Bob's Winchester. Seconds later two more citizens[48] died as the gang made their bloody journey to the alley, which was to become a death trap. All five members of the band were to reach their horses before the barrage from the aroused citizens was to take its toll. From then on it was a confused montage of swift action. Marshal Charlie Connelly charged into the alley and traded shots with Grat, and both men fell dead; John Kloehr, a livery stable owner, killed Bob and Powers with some fast Winchester work; Emmett and Broad-

well leaped into saddles, but Broadwell was cut to pieces as he thundered from the alley, and Emmett[49] was swept from the back of his mount by shotgun blasts. The Coffeyville fight lasted about five minutes, but in that period four of its citizens had been murdered, and the Dalton gang had been reduced to a shambles. (See DALTON GANG.)

COLBERT, CHUNK   Chunk is a gunman with a nebulous background in spite of the fact that it would have been quite in order for him to carve eleven notches in his gun butts had he been so minded; leastways, that's what them old-timers outside the drugstore were spreading around way back. This fertilizer would never have made an immortal bloom of Chunk, for only one of his alleged victims is given a name.[50] So what's kept Mr. Colbert's name in print over all these years? Clay Allison shot him, that's what. It happened more or less thisaway:[51] Chunk came down from Colorado gunning for Clay. It seems that Clay had sliced a chunk out of one of Colbert's kinfolk way back. When and where? Don't bother us with dates and places, friend, they ruin the flow of action. Well, anyways: Chunk catches up with Clay at Clifton, New Mexico. They size each other up—count each other's notches, as it were—and decide to play it safe by settling their differences with a horse race. Chunk romps home well ahead of Clay, but Clay don't take it good and slaps the winner's face. Any fool can see there's a showdown coming; but not yet. The two killers tromp over to the Clifton House—maybe it's raining and they don't want to get all wet in a

---

[48] George W. Gubins and Charles T. Brown, partners in a shoemaking business.

[49] Emmett survived and was given a life sentence in Kansas State Prison.

[50] Walter Walled, who is alleged to have been shot down by Chunk in a dance hall at Trinidad, Colorado.

[51] Perhaps and maybe, for on occasion Chunk has an unnamed stand-in, and the drama —stirring coffee, flying lead, etc.—takes place in a different town at an earlier or later date.

street shootout—but whatever, they sit facing each other across a table, and Chunk and Clay grit "Make yer play,"[52] and they order ham and eggs with coffee and whiskey. Sickening isn't it? But it gets worse. Coffee is stirred with pistol barrels and the two men eat and eat and eat; on and on for two hours those two fast guns stir and eat. Then flame lances from rusty gun barrels: BANG! B-A-N-G! Chunk was the slow one, and he fell face forward into his last remaining mouthfuls of ham and eggs, with a bullet hole between his eyes. After *two hours*, "last remaining"? Yes siree, and Chunk was all chucky-egged up when they buried him out back; like they served mighty big helpings out West. (See ALLISON, CLAY.)

COLE, ZERELDA M. A girl from Kentucky who was to become famous— or infamous—as the mother of Jesse and Frank James. Zerelda, who was born in Lexington County, Kentucky, in 1824, married a Baptist minister named Robert James when she was seventeen. The newlyweds moved West and established a home in Clay County, Missouri, within easy reach of the town of Kearney. Here, over the years, three sons and a daughter were born: Alexander Franklin on January 10, 1844; Robert (who was to die in his first year) on July 19, 1845; Jesse Woodson on September 5, 1847; and Susan on November 26, 1849. In 1850 Zerelda was left to look after the children while her husband went to try his luck in the California gold fields, but the minister's luck was out; the life was too rugged for this man of the cloth, and he expired within a month of reaching

the promised land, leaving his widow with three mouths to feed. This task required aid, so Zerelda shopped around, and twelve months later she was tripping up the aisle with a fifty-six-year-old widower named Sims. After a little over three years this marriage ended in divorce, and in 1855 Zerelda married a Dr. Reuben Samuels. Four more children were to result from this union: Sarah, John, Fannie, and Archibald,[53] who were born in 1858, 1861, 1863, and 1866, respectively. The Civil War and, later, the activities of Franklin (Frank) and Jesse James were to cast a cloud over this marriage for years. Zerelda Samuels died in 1911. (See JAMES, ALEXANDER FRANKLIN; JAMES GANG; and JAMES, JESSE WOODSON.)

COLLINS, JOEL Joint leader of the ill-starred Bass-Collins gang. Collins was born in Kentucky, but when he was quite young his parents moved West and he grew to manhood in Dallas County, Texas. In 1876 Joel, who was holding down a good job as a cattle trader, met Sam Bass in San Antonio, and they became good friends. From then on Joel's saga is one of moral decay, a story of loot and loose women that can be found elsewhere in this volume. Collins was shot dead by possemen and soldiers at Buffalo Station, Kansas, on September 26, 1877. Money for a lot of loose living was found in his Levi's: ten thousand dollars, his share of the loot from Big Springs train robbery, which occurred a week earlier. (See BASS, SAM.)

COLORADO Western territory that became a state in 1876. Colorado is a

[52] After reading the events that follow, and remembering how the antagonists had tried to settle their differences peacefully (by a horse race), one wonders if witnesses may have erred in their reporting here; surely "Make yer pay" would have been more apt. If this assumption is correct, then Chunk could be termed the winner, for Clay is reported to have paid the bill.

[53] Killed by Pinkertons in 1875.

Rocky Mountain state, and Denver, the capital, is one mile above sea level. Gold was discovered in the territory in 1858, and towns sprang up as the "Pikes Peak or bust" brigade invaded the area. One such town—apart from the capital —is Central City in Gilpin County, and this is reputed to be the oldest living gold camp in the West. Buffalo Bill's grave, and a museum devoted to him, are situated near Golden, a town a short distance from the capital. The state covers an area of 104,247 square miles and is bounded by seven other states.

COLORADO RIVER   Formed in Colorado by the confluence of the Grand and Green rivers. The Colorado winds between the Rockies and the Sierra Nevada and travels more than two thousand miles before reaching the sea in the Gulf of California. The river is famous for its canyons and gorges.

COLT FIREARMS   After reading a few Westerns one might be forgiven for thinking that the Colt percussion and metal cartridge revolvers were the only handguns used in the West. Such a monopoly, however, never existed, for many many makes of multishot guns were in use before the first Colts came off the assembly line in 1836, and dozens of American and foreign arms firms were competing with Colt's Patent Firearms Manufacturing Company throughout the frontier years. Many of these rival firms turned out weapons that in some instances were superior to the Colt models yet, despite weaknesses in the springs and ejection mechanisms of the Colt metal cartridge revolvers, which led to frequent breakages, they became the most popular sidegun of the era, with probably a third of the gun-toting population relying on their "trusty Colt." A complete list and description of Colt's

percussion and metal cartridge revolvers and revolving rifles would take up most of this volume, so this entry will confine itself to the better-known models.

Paterson. Five-shot single-action percussion revolver. Trigger folded into the frame when the gun was uncocked. Octagonal barrel and no trigger guard. Various barrel lengths, and ranging in caliber from .28 to .40. Manufactured from 1836 to 1843.

Walker. Sometimes known as the Whitneyville Walker. Six-shot single-action percussion revolver of .44 caliber. Square-backed trigger guard and 9-inch octagonal barrel. The Walker was the largest and heaviest of the Colt handguns, being 15½ inches in overall length, and weighing slightly more than 4½ pounds. Two thousand of these guns were made in 1847.

Dragoon. Six-shot single-action percussion revolver of .44 caliber. Square-backed or conventional trigger guard. Round 8-inch barrel and hinged lever-action cylinder rammer. Very similar to the Walker but weighing 7 ounces less. Manufactured from 1848 until 1860.

Navy. Six-shot single-action percussion revolver of .36 caliber. Square-backed or conventional trigger guard. Octagonal or round barrel, 7¼ inches in length. Creeping lever ramrod. Frequently have brass trigger guards and backstrap, and naval scene on cylinder. Around 13 inches in overall length, and about 2 pounds, 10 ounces in weight. The first of the Colt handguns to have rifled barrels. Approximately 215,-000 of these guns were manufactured between 1851 and 1860.

Army. Six-shot single-action percussion revolver of .44 caliber. Conventional trigger guard and round barrel, which could be either 7½ inches or 8 inches in length. Creeping lever ramrod. Made on same frame as 1851 Navy, but with modified cylinder. Around 13 inches in length; about 2 pounds, 11 ounces in weight; and of very streamlined appearance. Manufactured from 1860 until 1872.

Frontier. Six-shot single-action metal cartridge revolver of .44 caliber. Conventional trigger guard and round barrel, the length of which depended on the model: the Cavalry model was 7½ inches; the Artillery model was 5½ inches; the Civilian model was 4¾ inches. Spring ejector rod located under barrel. Fluted cylinder. The first of the Colt sidearms to have a top strap. The long-barreled model (the Cavalry) has an overall length of 13 inches and weighs about 2½ pounds. Manufactured from 1873 until 1941, and reintroduced in 1957. From 1873 until the end of the black powder era (1890), 165,-000 of these revolvers were made.

Peacemaker. Identical to the Frontier model save for caliber and weight. Models and barrel lengths and history of manufacture are exactly the same, and Peacemakers are included in the 165,000 total of the previous entry. The Peacemaker was chambered for .45-caliber cartridges; this meant that extra metal had to be reamed from the cylinder, therefore it is slightly lighter in weight than the Frontier model.

A number of guns in all the above models had modified butts that allowed

for a shoulder stock in either wood or skeleton metal to be fitted. Over the years hundreds of Colt percussion revolvers were given cylinder conversions that permitted them to use metal cartridges.

Revolving rifles. Colt revolving rifles were percussion handguns with extra-long barrels and fixed wooden shoulder stocks, their frames and cylinders, in most instances, being similar to those of the handguns which happened to be contemporaneous—Paterson, Dragoon, and so on. The main exceptions to this trend of design was the Paterson of 1837. This gun was a .50-caliber hammerless with twin-ring triggers, the forward one of which was used to cock the piece. No more than a hundred of these guns were produced. By 1839 the Paterson factory was turning out a center-hammer model in .56 caliber that was available in five-, six-, seven-, or eight-chambered versions. This shoulder arm was manufactured for about six years. In 1850 Dragoon-type models with side hammers were available. The hammer modification was a safety precaution (see general remarks at end of paragraph), but by 1857 center-hammer guns were back in fashion. These guns, which were manufactured toward the end of the revolving-rifle era, were chambered for six shots and came in a choice of three calibers: .36, .44, or .56.

None of these weapons was a complete success. Chain reaction (ignition of all loads at the fall of the hammer), back-flash accompanied by particles of flying lead, and escaping hot gases were of little consequence in a handgun, but when such happenings occurred in a shoulder arm, the result could be disastrous. Side hammers, which were placed on the side of the piece that was farthest removed from the operator's face when the gun was in use, were introduced to combat this danger, but they couldn't prevent backflash and chain reaction from taking their toll. Burning clothing was a minor hazard, and scorched faces or blindness was an ever-present danger. The above-mentioned hand and shoulder arms were but a small part of the Colt output. Derringers, carbines, etc., were also manufactured over the period covered by this entry. At the present time the company manufactures automatic pistols, numerous models of double-action revolvers, and the world-famous Thompson submachine gun. (See BUNTLINE SPECIAL; COLT, SAMUEL; and DERRINGERS.)

COLT, SAMUEL   Inventor and manufacturer of a multiple-shot sidearm whose cylindrical magazine automatically revolved with the cocking of the hammer. Sam, who is alleged to have whittled his first model from a piece of wood during a voyage to India, took out his first patent in 1835, and by the following year Paterson Colts (so named because the plant was located at Paterson, New Jersey) were coming from the assembly line. They weren't the all-fired success Sam had imagined, and in 1843 the enterprise went bankrupt. Four years later he got a government order for one thousand revolvers—big skull-busting efforts for the Mexican War—and this gave him the opportunity to re-establish his business. Other models followed, and over the years the name of Colt became synonymous with "gun." Sam, who was born in 1814, died in 1862, and his passing was no doubt mourned by those individuals who had prospered as his products became widely used: to whit,

the morticians of the West. (See COLT FIREARMS.)

COLTER, JOHN   Trapper and mountain man who only began to leave his tracks in western history in 1803. In that year William Clark was combing Kentucky in search of recruits for the Lewis and Clark Expedition of 1804. Colter was one of the men chosen, and he has gone down in the records as one of "Clark's nine Kentuckians," although he was in fact born in Virginia in 1775. The expedition was to give Colter his first taste of the West, and he liked what he saw, so that on the return journey in 1806 he obtained permission to leave the expedition and went trapping along the Upper Missouri. From 1807 onward Fort Manuel—a newly erected fur-trading post —was to become Colter's headquarters. The fort was located at the junction of the Upper Missouri (Yellowstone) and the Big Horn rivers,[54] and in 1808 Colter left this base to accompany a large party of Crows on a hunting expedition. Unfortunately the Crows and the lone white man met an even larger party of Blackfoot who were out on a Crow-hunting expedition, and a full-scale battle ensued. The fight resulted in a stalemate, but during the action Colter had been observed to kill a Blackfoot brave, and from then on the whole tribe was out to lift his *otokan*. The following year a party of these warriors surrounded Colter and a fellow trapper named John Potts as they stepped from their canoe, and when Potts showed resistance, he was pincushioned with arrows. Waving the dead man's freshly lifted scalp, the Indians led Colter to their main camp, and here he was stripped of everything bar the hairs on his chest, etc., and told to "run." Remarkably decent of the Blackfoot, for they allowed him a five-

[54] Near the present-day town of Custer, Wyoming.

hundred-yard start before all the fit specimens of the tribe pounded after him on foot. The game got serious then, but although Colter was seven days' journey from Fort Manuel, he kept his spirits up —arrows and war clubs whizzing past his ears no doubt helped in this—and he figured that if he could reach the Madison River some six miles away he would stand a good chance of survival. Feet hamburger'd by prickly pear, body nicked by arrow flints, and no doubt looking pathetically comic, Colter pumped on. After five miles the tribe's four-minute miler began to overtake Colter, and the blood-stained white man turned at bay. The brave raised his spear but was tripped by Colter, who immediately grabbed the enemy weapon and used it to pin the Blackfoot to the ground. The pursuing tribesmen paused by their dead comrade long enough for Colter to make his escape, and seven days later he arrived at Fort Manuel. Twelve months later, he returned to the Blackfoot country with a large party of trappers, but once again the Indians made things hot, and after five of the trappers had been converted into little more than hairy trophies, the trappers were forced to return to the fort. This Indian problem evidently got too much for Colter, for he left the area late in 1809 and moved east to the Missouri Territory, where, in 1810, he married a young girl named Nancy Hooker. The newlyweds settled in a small cabin in Franklin County, and Colter did a little farming here until his death in November 1813.[55] (See LEWIS AND CLARK EXPEDITION and LISA, MANUEL.)

COMANCHE   The only equine survivor of the white men of the Battle on the Little Big Horn. This sorrel, which was purchased by the U. S. Army in 1868, became Captain M. Keogh's personal mount, and it was he who named it Comanche after it had been wounded in an engagement with the tribe of that name. Keogh rode Comanche on that fateful day of June 25, 1876, and after the battle the horse was found standing among the field of dead. Comanche was badly wounded, but veterinary skill saved his life, and he became the mascot of the 7th Cavalry until old age brought about his death in 1892. (See BATTLE ON THE LITTLE BIG HORN.)

COMANCHE INDIANS   Tribe of the Uto-Aztecan language group that left the Rocky Mountains regions of Wyoming around 1660 and moved South with the intention of getting horses. This intention had been partially realized by the early 1700s, when the tribe was located in the Kansas area, but it was not until they settled in Texas a few decades later that they became fully mounted and were able to pursue the nomadic life that is typical of the plains Indians. Tepees replaced more permanent structures, crop farming was abandoned completely, and the buffalo became the tribe's chief source of sustenance. At the height of their power—the first half of the nineteenth century—the Comanche were

[55] There was no money for a coffin or a decent burial, so Nancy merely placed Colter's parfleche onto the chest of the corpse, left the shack, and went to live with a brother in Illinois. She never returned, and more than a hundred years were to elapse before Colter's remains were to find a permanent resting place. In the summer of 1926 a steam shovel operating near New Haven, Missouri, scooped up a bundle of old bones and a leather pouch. The pouch had Colter's name branded onto it, and inside there were notebooks and fur-trading receipts that were still quite legible. Colter had been a big name in mountain man circles, and as such his name is part of the American heritage, so the bones were casketed and returned to the earth, and a decent headstone was provided to mark the grave.

probably the finest horsemen the world has ever seen,[56] and this ability, when coupled with their warlike disposition, made them the scourge of the southern plains. The Comanche raiding parties usually spared their female captives, for there was a good market for such merchandise: Copper-skinned girls would either be kept as slaves or traded as such, while fair-skinned maidens would always fetch a good price from the unscrupulous gringo or Mexican slave-traders who infested the Southwest. When dealing with these latter individuals the Comanche invariably raped their wares—a rather spoilsport gesture—before handing them over to their purchasers. The Comanche, whose destiny and acts of war were inextricably linked with those of the Kiowa, waged constant war with the Anglo-Americans from 1830 until they were finally subdued for all time in 1875. The tribe are now reservation Indians in Oklahoma. (See KIOWA INDIANS and QUANAH PARKER.)

COMANCHEROS
Mexicans, half-breeds, and a sprinkling of Caucasian Americans formed the ranks of the comancheros, a body of men who, either singly or in groups, traded with the Kiowa and Comanche of the southern plains. Their trading was usually illicit, and the comancheros were little more than fences who bartered trade beads and low-grade whiskey for cattle and horses that they knew to have been stolen. The majority of the comancheros were riffraff, and many of them were not averse to dealing in human merchandise.

COMSTOCK LODE Gold- and silver-bearing area in western Nevada. Gold was discovered in the region in 1859 by two penniless Irish miners named Peter O'Riley and Pat McLaughlin, but the lode was not to be named after these two sons of Erin, for an unscrupulous fast-talking character named Harry "Old Pancake"[57] Comstock conned them into parting with a large share of their claim, and after being known as Washoe's Diggings for a short spell, the Comstock Lode became its permanent name. Virginia City, Gold Hill, and Silver City were but three of the settlements that sprang up on the Comstock.

CONCHAS Spanish term for "shells," which, when used in the West, applies to those slightly concave disks of gold or silver that are used to decorate the equipment of both horse and rider.

CONCORD COACH This was the most efficient and elegant of all the coaches that were built to ply the western trails. The basic model, which had a twelve-foot wheelbase and weighed slightly more than twenty-one hundred-weights, retailed for around a thousand dollars, but extras could escalate this price considerably. The chassis (which was the over-and-under type and sloped toward the rear), running gear, wheels, and braking equipment were always painted in a brilliant yellow, but the body of the coach came in a choice of either scarlet or bottle green. The large windows, which were unglazed,[58] had adjustable curtains of either canvas or leather, and had armrests fitted into their bases. Interiors were plush lined and fitted with three upholstered bench seats and small candle lamps. More than a

---

[56] The Comanche guided their mounts by foot pressure, the single rein being used only as a brake. A Comanche innovation was the horsehair loop, which was plaited into the manes of their horses. This was used as an armrest when the rider slid from the back of his mount and rode against the animal's side.

[57] He is reputed to have lived on nothing but pancakes.

[58] Door windows were glazed.

dozen passengers could ride inside the coach with a certain amount of comfort, while over short journeys this carrying capacity could be doubled by daredevils who didn't mind riding on the roof.[59] The body of the coach was cradled on twin thoroughbraces,[60] which were attached to curved brackets located on the front and rear axles. (See ABBOTT, DOWNING & COMPANY.)

CONESTOGA WAGON The original "prairie schooner"[61] and the main freight vehicle of the western trails. Although these wagons had been built in the Conestoga Valley of Pennsylvania since the early 1700s, it wasn't until more than a hundred years later that they were to become numerous. The California gold rush of 1849 brought a great demand for Conestogas, a demand that was to increase in volume as the frontier was pushed ever westward. Over these middle decades of the nineteenth century, Studebaker—whose plants were located in Ohio and Indiana, and Lathans—with plants in Missouri and Iowa—were the principal builders of Conestoga-type wagons. A fully loaded wagon would carry three to four tons, and six yoked pairs of oxen were needed to keep them rolling along the trail.

COOK, BILL Oklahoma outlaw who was born in 1873 with one in eight of his corpuscles pure Cherokee. Bill tried his hand at range and farm work until he was twenty-one, at which age he formed a small gang and started a short career

as an owlhoot. He and his sidekicks were blamed for twelve robberies that were committed in Indian Territory (Oklahoma) over the next twelve months, and when Bill was arrested in New Mexico in January 1895 and returned to Fort Smith, Arkansas, to be tried by "Hanging Judge" Parker, Bill no doubt realized that things looked bleak. They were, but at least Parker couldn't find anything to hang him for, so after being found guilty on the twelve robbery counts, Bill was handed a forty-five-year prison sentence. (See GOLDSBY, CRAWFORD.)

COOK, DAVID J. "Never hit a man over the head with a pistol, because afterward you may want to use your weapon and find it disabled," quoth Mr. Cook at the height of his career, and the gentleman must have known what he was talking about, for he is reputed to have arrested some three thousand criminals during his years as a peace officer in Colorado. Cook, who was born in Laporte County, Indiana, on August 12, 1842, came to Colorado in 1859, after spending the first few years of his working life as an itinerant farmhand in Indiana, Iowa, and Kansas. Over the next few years he tried his hand at an assortment of jobs,[62] but in 1864, and while serving in the Colorado Cavalry, he was detailed for detective duties, and this must have been one of those rare instances in which the military fitted a round peg into a similar-shaped hole, for Cook reveled in his crime-fighting assignment, and when he

[59] This may seem incredible after seeing movies and television Westerns in which replica Concords are used; such replicas are, however, frequently only built to two-thirds scale.

[60] A number of rawhide thongs bound together to form a 3½-inch-thick leather spring.

[61] "Schooner" was apt in more ways than one, for the box, which was built on a slightly concave wagonbed, swept upward and angled outward at the front and rear like the prow and stern of a schooner, while the wagonbox was of such watertight construction that it would float across a river with ease.

[62] Prospecting in Gregory Gulch, 1859–61; farming in Kansas for a few months of 1861; and freighting in Missouri, 1861–62. He returned to Colorado in 1863 and joined the Army in that year.

was released from government duties in 1866 he continued this Army-inspired career. The civilian appointments of this 6-foot, 3-inch giant from the "Hoosier State" make a formidable list: city marshal of Denver, 1866–69; deputy U.S. marshal of Colorado Territory and the state of Colorado, 1873–80; chief of police of Denver, 1880–81; and superintendent of the Rocky Mountain Detective Association.[63] In 1882 Cook had a volume of his reminiscences published under the title *Hands Up! or Twenty Years of Detective Life in the Mountains and on the Plains.* This is a saga of murder, robbery, lynching, and shootouts that makes Garrett's *Authentic Life of Billy the Kid* seem like a bedtime story for squeamish infants. This Rocky Mountain bloodhound managed to survive all his shooting scrapes, and he died in his home at Denver on April 29, 1907.

COOLEY, SCOTT   Ex-Texas Ranger who became a leader of one of the factions in the Mason County War of 1875. Timothy Williamson, a friend of Cooley's, was shot to death by a mob while being taken to jail by Deputy Sheriff John Worley, and on hearing of this, Cooley blamed the incident on Worley and set out to avenge the death of his friend. This he did,[64] but the killing of Worley wasn't sufficient for Mr. Cooley, and he took part in further killings until the Texas Rangers finally clamped down on Mason County and put a stop to the bloodshed. Cooley was never arrested and what became of him is a mystery, although some folks say he died shortly

after the Mason County fracas. (See MASON COUNTY WAR.)

COONS, WILLIAM   The victim of a highly organized but unique lynching. Bill Coons settled down as a homesteader in Lincoln County, New Mexico, in 1879, and although he was known to indulge in a spot of rustling and hog stealing, this form of kleptomania, which was common on the frontier, wasn't to lead to his undoing. Trouble over water rights with a neighbor named John Flemming erupted into violence in April 1881 when Coons went to Flemming's home and shot the latter dead. Sheriff Pat Garrett investigated but could find no witnesses to contradict Bill's statement that "Flemming drew his iron fust"; in fact, Garrett could find no witnesses whatsoever. Flemming's friends put lynch talk in the air, but Bill also had friends, and in May they gathered around at his home to celebrate his forty-third birthday, and, at the same time, alleviate any fear he may have had regarding mob violence. The party got under way with Bill and six couples singing and dancing and guzzling much whiskey. Sometime later Bill noticed that his home was bulging at the seams, so he sat down to count heads: more than two dozen. Bad whiskey? No; for Bill recognized some of his victim's friends, and a few moments later his worst fears were realized. The newcomers, all of whom were male, drew pistols and at gunpoint locked all of Coons' supporters into one of the bedrooms. They then held a "kangaroo court," and witnesses were produced who stated that Coons had started

---

[63] Cook founded this organization around 1868. It was a kind of unofficial Interpol of the Rockies that covered the following states: Colorado, Kansas, Nebraska, New Mexico, Utah, Texas, Wyoming, Arizona, and California. In 1873, while head of this organization and a deputy U.S. marshal, he was appointed major general of the Colorado Militia; a busy little bee, no doubt, yet he still found time to dabble in real estate, and he was the proprietor of the Brunswick Billiards Hall and Saloon in Denver.

[64] Cooley shot down Worley outside the latter's home, and although he is alleged to have cut off his victim's ears and shown them around afterward, little credence should be attached to this, for it savors too much of an episode in Joseph Slade's career.

to empty his revolver at Flemming while the latter had his back turned, and that the last shot—the only one to take effect—had caught Flemming in the chest when he turned around to see what all the rumpus was about. Bill was found guilty and sentenced to be hanged forthwith, but in deference of the fact that it was his birthday, the "court" helped him finish off the remainder of his whiskey before sentence was carried out.[65] No one was ever arrested for ruining this frontier birthday party.

COOPER, ANDY
Alias of Andy Blevins. (See BLEVINS, ANDY.)

COPPERHEAD   A highly poisonous snake which is allied to the rattlesnake. Its scales are a coppery shade of red, and it grows to a maximum length of 4 feet. (See RATTLESNAKES.)

COPPERHEADS   A name which, during the Civil War, was applied to those Northerners who were known to have, or were suspected of having, sympathies with the Confederate cause.

CORDERILLA   Multiple mountain system that may be comprised of several ranges. In the West it refers specifically to those systems that are located between the Rockies and the Sierra Nevada.

CORNETT, BRACK   Louisiana-born outlaw who, at the head of a small gang, committed bank and train robberies in south Texas during the 1880s. A photograph of Brack shows him wearing two guns, but these didn't help him much, for after his gang had staged a train robbery near Austin in the fall of 1887 Brack was tracked down by Deputy Sheriff A.

Allee, who shot him dead when he resisted arrest. The shootout occurred on February 12, 1888, at a ranch near Pearsall, Texas, and Brack was twenty-nine years old at the time of his death.

CORTINA, JUAN NEPOMUCENA   Ginger-haired, pale-skinned Mexican whose family owned land and property both north and south of the border. Juan was born in Mexico in 1825, but a short time later his father died and he was taken by his mother to live on the family's Santa Rita Ranch near Brownsville, Texas. Mexicans were fair game north of the border, and the Cortina spread dwindled over the years as land grabbers whittled away at its perimeters. On reaching manhood Juan "whittled" back by killing a few of the opportunists who had settled on Cortina land, the result being that warrants were issued for his arrest. On September 13, 1859, Marshal Shears of Brownsville arrested one of Cortina's men in a saloon, but a moment later Juan strode through the batwing doors, severely wounded Shears, and escaped with his fellow Mexican. The citizens of Brownsville (and in fairness to Juan it must be stated that a large proportion of them were the sweepings of the South) began to reach boiling point; but the red-headed Mexican was to beat them to it. On September 27 he led an army of a thousand cutthroats of many nationalities into Brownsville. They captured Fort Brown from the U.S. military and the city hall from the nonresistant clerical staff, and proceeded to sack the town. All residents whom Juan had had trouble with in the past were shot out of hand, and the following day he issued an ultimatum to the townsfolk: "One hundred thousand dollars in gold or we burn the town to the ground." A more conserva-

[65] A tender farewell touch; an improvised band accompanied Bill to the nearest tree.

tive member of the Cortina family talked him out of this, however, and he withdrew his men to the outskirts of the town, where he could hold it in a state of siege. One man got through his cordon, and a few weeks later an army composed of U.S. troops, Texas Rangers, and civilian volunteers thundered to the relief of Brownsville. Cortina, whose army had increased considerably since his initial success, met the relief force at Palo Alto and whipped the daylights out of them, but in a return engagement in December, the Cortinistas were routed after a couple of dozen of their number had been killed. Cortina's force headed north, pillaging and burning as they moved, and on December 20 he captured Edinburg, Texas, and four days later, Rio Grande, Texas.[66] On Christmas Day a large force of Texas Rangers caught Juan with his chaparreras down and the Cortinistas, who were liquored up with the Christmas spirits, were forced to beat a hasty retreat across the border. Here, on friendly soil, Juan set up headquarters, and for the next fifteen years his outlaw legions raided the large ranches of Texas. By 1875 his men had rustled more than nine hundred thousand head of cattle out of the Lone Star State, but in that year the Texas Rangers "forgot" the international boundary and followed Juan back into Mexico, where they routed his forces beyond possibility of comeback. From that time on, Cortina confined his activities to politics, and he died peacefully in 1893.

COTTONTAILS A generic term that embraces no less than six varieties of rather short-eared rabbits that are known technically as wood hares. Like all rabbits they are extremely prolific, but their tails are rather larger than those of the European rabbit and, unlike the latter, they do not dig holes.

COUGAR More correctly referred to as the puma. (See PUMA.)

COUNTY SEAT WARS These were usually engineered by unscrupulous land speculators whose holdings became far more valuable if the embryo township in which they were located became the county seat. These wars were peculiar to Kansas, and in any county where two towns aspired to the designation of "county seat" and the decision was left to the electorate, speculators whose interests were threatened would pay bribes to fix the count, or hire gunmen to intimidate the pollsters. Civic-minded citizens attempted to prevent this by hiring known gunfighters to protect the polls, etc., and shooting frequently started when rival mercenaries met head on. Even if the election passed without bloodshed, parties whose interests lay in the losing town would rarely accept defeat, and in attempts to reverse the decision of the electorate they would go to ridiculous lengths: stealing the courthouse records of their rival, or, on at least one occasion, the actual courthouse buildings.[67] County seat clashes, which were confined to the latter half of the 1800s, occurred in Stevens, Gray, Garfield, and Wichita counties. (See CIMARRON COUNTY SEAT WAR.)

COUP French word for "blow." When applied to the American Indian it means strictly this, and although a coup could result in death for the recipient of the

66 On this occasion Juan collected a ransom of one hundred thousand dollars in gold.

67 Not quite as difficult as it may sound: In new towns the buildings would be of wooden frame construction, so it would be possible to jack them from their sites and move them away on wooden rollers.

blow,[68] counting *coup* was usually done with a light *coup* stick or the bare hands. Therefore a brave who had merely touched ten of the enemy during a battle could claim as many *coup* as one who had dispatched a like number with a hatchet. Pronounced "coo."

COURTRIGHT, JIM   They say he was born in Iowa around 1848, that he served as an Army scout during the closing year of the Civil War, and that after the war he painted G.T.T.[69] on the door of his home before leaving his native state. What his ma or pa or both said about his lousing up their front door will never be known, but we do know that a wizard with the six-guns was appointed city marshal of Fort Worth, Texas, in 1876, and that this was Courtright the man. Tall, dark-eyed and dark complected, medium brown hair worn overlong, and a drooping beer-filter mustache worn untrimmed; and one of the rare breed—an ambidextrous gunfighter; but, to quote Bat Masterson, "an ignorant bully of a man." He served as city marshal for three years, then moved West into New Mexico and got a job as guard with the American Mining Company. During a stint guarding the silver-ore trains, he killed two would-be robbers, and when news of the killings got around, he was offered a squatter-busting job by General A. Logan, a rancher whose rangeland was being overrun by these nesters. Courtright accepted, and he was put on the payroll as "ranch foreman." His duties were simple: lean on the squatters, and then, if they didn't take the hint, give them a gunfighter's salute. The

first squatters to get Colt's medicine were two Frenchmen who were either too stubborn to move or had been just too idle to learn English. The temptation to insert a long-drawn-out gunfight here was strong, but as the Frenchmen were most likely unarmed, any such dramatic boost to the narrative would be wholly inaccurate. Suffice to state that Courtright and a gunnie named James McIntyre—who was probably down in the Logan books as "foreman's secretary"—shot the Frenchmen dead. The surviving nesters went to the law, and the New Mexico authorities issued murder warrants that sent the two killers in search of safe retreats. McIntyre lit out for South America, but Courtright only got as far as Fort Worth, where he was arrested on October 18, 1884, but a few days later he escaped from custody[70] and fled to Canada. Two years later he returned to New Mexico and surrendered to the authorities. This was a good move, for by this time the killings were old stuff, and when he came to trial he got a "not guilty" verdict. After leaving the courthouse he returned to Fort Worth, and here he started the T. I. C. Commercial Detective Agency. This business was in no way competitive to Pinkertons or any of the other private-eye firms. It was merely the front for a protection racket, and Courtright became a parasite who lived on the monies he obtained from shaking down the proprietors of Fort Worth's numerous saloons and gambling halls. Bullyboy Jim had only one trouble spot on his collection rounds: the White Elephant Saloon, whose proprietor, one Luke Short, told him to "Go jump in the

---

[68] When a hand weapon had been used to deliver the blow. A *coup* was not credited to a brave who killed an enemy with a long-range weapon (bow, rifle, etc.); in such an instance the honor went to the first man to touch the corpse.

[69] "Gone to Texas"; this was common practice.

[70] Courtright was escorted to a restaurant for his meals, and during one such excursion a friend smuggled him a brace of pistols. With these he held his guards at bay while he escaped on a horse that had been left outside the eatery.

river" each time he called. One must never back down if one is to succeed in the protection racket—as any book on illicit careers will confirm—and Courtright was well aware of this. On Tuesday, February 8, 1887, Courtright set out to make a horizontal example of Luke, and at 8 P.M. he sent a man into the White Elephant to tell Luke that Mr. Courtright desired words with him outside. Short obliged, and in answer to Courtright's usual request, he came out with his usual watery reply. Suddenly Courtright shouted "Don't try to pull a gun on me!"[71] and reached for a gun on his right hip, but before he could trip back the hammer, Luke's opening shot had removed the thumb that had been busy with this task, and while Jim was wondering what to do next—maybe the border shift or perhaps to bring his left hip gun into play or maybe just run—two more slugs slammed into his chest, and as he staggered under their impact, Luke's fourth shot drilled his forehead. At the trial that followed, Luke was acquitted. (See SHORT, LUKE.)

COUSIN JACKS   Nicknames given to immigrants from Cornwall, England, who entered the West in the thousands to work in the gold and silver mines. Most of the mining camps had a fair share of these "Cousin Jacks."

COWBOY   Usually referred to as a "cowhand" in the West. These men, the proud ones of the cattle industry, are the riders who work cattle, a term that covers such chores as trailing, cutting out, roping, branding, and the rounding up of cattle. When you call them "cowpokes" smile, and make like you was jest kiddin'.

COWPOKE   Little skill and a poor sense of smell are the somewhat negative attributes required for this job. Cowpokes ride with the cattle during rail shipment, their job being to see that none of the animals lie down, as this can cause others to stumble when the train's brakes are applied. The only equipment needed is a small stick, which is used to poke the beasts.

COYOTE   Small North American prairie wolf that usually hunts in a pack. Coyotes are around 3½ feet in total length and have a brownish-gray coat that lightens to buff on the underside and cheeks and throat.[72] They are not dangerous to man, and when in captivity they make affectionate though somewhat unreliable pets. Pronounced "ki-otey," or "koy-otey," variations that are regional.

COYOTERO APACHE   One of the three main divisions of the Apache nation.

CRAVENS, BEN   Small-time outlaw of the Cherokee Strip. Ben, who was Iowa-born, moved into the strip in his late teens, and it was here that he started his criminal career by selling illicit whiskey to the Indians. Sometime later he turned his attention to cattle stealing, and although the number he stole on any given occasion never amounted to more than would fill a butcher's shop window, it was a far more serious offense than his earlier pursuit, and it got the law on his tail. Said law, in the shape of Frank M. Canton, caught up with Ben, and after a gunpoint arrest Ben was lodged in the Perry, Oklahoma, jail to await trial. But

[71] This was a fairly common piece of frontier dialogue, which meant little, as it could be either true or false. It was shouted with the intention of it being overheard by witnesses who would then assume that the shouter was acting in self-defense from then on.
[72] A very light-colored variety is found in the deserts of the Southwest.

Ben didn't wish to await any such procedure, and a few days later he broke jail and resumed his criminal career by committing a string of minor armed robberies. Ben usually worked alone, but in the summer of 1896 he teamed up with a like character who bore the colorful alias of "Dynamite Dick."[73] This was a short-lived partnership, for in November of that year Ben was recaptured after a long-drawn-out gun battle near Blackwell. He was severely wounded in the shootout, but he recovered to stand trial, and in January 1897 he was given a twenty-year stretch in Kansas State Penitentiary. This should have kept Ben out of the saddle for some time, but it didn't; he escaped once more,[74] and after a few small jobs he persuaded a young ne'er-do-well named Herbert Welty to join him in the robbery of the post office at Red Rock. After the robbery—during which the postmaster, Alva Bateman, had been murdered—Ben decided he would like to keep all the loot, so to save argument, he shot Welty down and left him for dead. After this Ben changed his name to Charles Maust, got himself a wife, and settled down to a spot of honest toil as a farmhand in Missouri. This tranquil period lasted until 1908. In that year he was arrested for horse theft under the name of Maust, but unfortunately for Ben, he was recognized under his true identity and was returned to Oklahoma to stand trial for the murder of Bateman. Welty, who had recovered and been given a long prison term, was the main prosecution witness, and Al Jennings was the attorney for the defense. Al must have put in a good plea, but although Ben escaped the death penalty, he was returned to the pen to complete his twenty years, and that, as far as this entry is concerned, is the end of Ben, for he didn't escape again,

and when he was finally released he settled down to live a respectable life, and who wants to read about a respectable life?

CRAWFORD, JOHN WALLACE
Better known as Captain Jack Crawford, the poet scout. Crawford undoubtedly did plenty of scouting for the U. S. Army during both the Sioux campaigns of 1876 and the Apache wars of some three years later, but he is far best remembered for his prolific output of verse. Tear jerkers were his forte, but publishers were not impressed with his work, and the poet resorted to having his work printed and bound at his own expense. He gave these delicately bound volumes away (some folks say he had to), but not before they had been suitably autographed. A mustached and Vandyked long-haired lad with a faraway look on his face (which may have been hammed for the camera) and a plethora of friends who suffered his recitations in watery silence—a suffering that didn't go unnoticed by Jack, or unappreciated, for he is known to have said, "I have been in the habit of reciting my poems and singing my songs whenever I could corral a squad of friends and old comrades possessing vitality enough to survive the affliction." The poet was a great friend of Hickok, and after the gunfighter's death he scribbled off a couple of rhythmical obituaries entitled *The Burial of Wild Bill* and *Wild Bill's Grave*. The first eight lines of the former epic swing along as follows:

Under the sod in the Prairie land,
We have laid him down to rest,
With many a tear from the sad, rough
  throng,
And the friends he loved the best.

---

[73] The alias of an ex-Doolin gang member named Dan Clifton.
[74] Cravens made a wooden gun, covered it with silver paper, and used it to bluff the guards.

And many a heartfelt sigh was heard,
As over the sward we trod,
And many an eye was filled with tears,
As we covered him with the sod.

Maybe it could do with a little turfing out, but Jack finally made his name with such stuff, and his song and recitation routine was to "slay 'em" on the music hall circuits for many years. Writers frequently refer to Jack as "a phony"; a phony what?

CRAZY HORSE   This blue-eyed Oglala Sioux war chief (*potanka*) with the light brown hair and the comparatively pale skin was, according to some West Point military instructors, the greatest Indian cavalry tactician who ever lived. The child who was to become Crazy Horse was born near Rapid Creek, Dakota Territory, in 1842,[75] the son of an Oglala holy man named Crazy Horse (Tashunka Witko) and a woman from the Brule division of the Sioux nation. During his early years the boy was known as Curly, but after taking part in a raid on an Omaha village when he was thirteen, he was given the name His Horse Looking. Two years later he was severely wounded while taking part in a similar raid, and as he lay convalescing, his father proclaimed to the village that from then on his son would be known as Crazy Horse, and that he—the father— would adopt the name Worm. When he was twenty-six Crazy Horse had a spot of woman trouble. He stole Black Buffalo Woman from her husband No Water, and No Water retaliated by shooting him in the face. Crazy Horse recovered, but he carried the scar resulting from this marital dispute for the remainder of his days. Shortly after this

shooting, he married a girl named Black Shawl, but a few years later he was smitten by love or lust and he took a second wife, a young half-breed who is usually referred to as "the Larrabee woman."[76] For most of his adult life Crazy Horse was in constant warfare with the U. S. Army. He served under Red Cloud (Mock-Peah-lu-tah) from 1865 until the latter signed a peace treaty with the whites in 1868. After this time, and until 1876, Crazy Horse was a war leader under the political leadership of Sitting Bull (Tatanka Yatanka). The number of skirmishes and battles in which Crazy Horse was actively engaged over this overall period 1865–76 are too numerous to be adequately covered in this entry, but most of the major engagements will be found elsewhere in this volume. When painted for war— lightning-flash marks and spots denoting hail—Crazy Horse would wear either the full body of a hawk attached to the side of his head or a war bonnet with buffalo horns and a dozen eagle feathers fanning upward and outward at the rear, and, on occasion, a red trade blanket would hang cape fashion from his shoulders. Crazy Horse reached the peak of his career as a war chief in 1876, and on June 25 of that year five companies of the 7th U. S. Cavalry must have heard his rallying cry[77] as the Sioux and Cheyenne swept down on them in the valley of the Little Big Horn. After this Indian victory thousands of U.S. troops were drafted into the Dakota-Montana area, and after a few minor skirmishes with the military, Crazy Horse came into the Red Cloud Agency in May 1877. At this time Black Shawl was suffering from advanced tuberculosis, and in August

[75] Various authorities give dates ranging from 1838 to 1849 inclusive, but 1842 seems the most likely, and all the ages of Crazy Horse given in the above narrative are based on this year.
[76] The name is also given as Larravee, Larrivee, and Larravie.
[77] "Come on, Lakotahs, it is a good day to die, a good day to die!"

Crazy Horse requested permission to take her to the Spotted Trail Agency, where medical treatment was available. He got a blank refusal; but this was Crazy Horse, and he did what a man should do: He left the Red Cloud Agency with his wife and got her safely to the Spotted Trail Agency, but he was arrested by Indian police and taken to Fort Robinson. On seeing the barred cells at the fort Crazy Horse is reported to have pulled a knife, but before he could use this alleged blade, he was seized by Indian police, and while these turncoats held him he was bayoneted by an infantry captain named Kennington. This occurred on the afternoon of September 5, 1877, and at midnight of that day Crazy Horse died. A Dr. McGillicuddy, Worm, and a 7-foot-tall warrior named Touch the Clouds were with the war chief during his last hours, and on the morning of the sixth, Worm had the body of his son taken away for burial. This was a secret burial, and the location of the grave remains a mystery to this day. The horned war bonnet he wore still survives, and there are numerous photographs still around that are reputed to be of Crazy Horse, although none of these has ever been authenticated.[78] (See BATTLE ON THE LITTLE BIG HORN; BATTLE ON THE ROSEBUD; BLACK SHAWL; FETTERMAN FIGHT; HORSESHOE STATION; JULESBURG FIGHT; LARRABEE, NELLIE; and WAGON-BOX FIGHT.)

CROCKETT, DAVID   Half hoss, half alligator, whiskey swiller supreme, shot extraordinary, keeper of tame bears and killer of wild ones, friend of the Indians and lifter of scalps; so this is a schizophrenic? No, this is Davy Crockett, "King of the Wild Frontier," teller of tall tales and probably one of the West's first comedians. He helped Andrew Jackson—or maybe it was the other way around—to achieve victory during the Creek War of 1817; he kilt forty-seven b'ars in one month, and, single-handed, chopped up a cougar with his good old shiv. No scars or trappings from these encounters adorned his person; but he did wear fringed buckskins and a coonskin cap, apparel that seems to suggest that he did shoot something. There was, however, beneath all this humbug, a man of stature. Davy was born in Tennessee on August 17, 1786, the son of a second-generation Irish-American and a girl from Maryland named Rebecca Hawkins. Davy had little schooling, but when he became fifteen he became a keen student of the basic mechanics of practical biology, and lasses of various creeds and nationalities were to be talked into giving their "all" by his homespun approach before he settled down with a Scottish girl named Polly Findlay. Polly is reputed to have been a direct descendant of King Macbeth, and this could be true, for after their marriage on August 8, 1806, she gave our Lothario a dog's life. In 1817 the thirty-one-year-old Crockett joined Andrew Jackson's forces, and Crockett no doubt killed a few redsticks (Creeks) in this mopping-up operation, which was a hangover from the Anglo-American War of 1812–14. He returned home the

---

[78] When Crazy Horse was dying Dr. McGillicuddy tried to take his photograph (some doc!), but the war chief turned his face to the wall, remarking to the effect that "no one must take away his shadow." Writers have used this incident to prove that Crazy Horse never allowed his photograph to be taken, but this of course is ridiculous; Crazy Horse was dying, and to an Indian *in extremis* his "shadow" would be something tangible, a very hold on existence; therefore the McGillicuddy incident only proves that the war chief did not want his photograph taken under the circumstances related. If this assumption is correct, then one of the half-dozen or so photographs going the rounds that are alleged to be of Crazy Horse may be a likeness of him.

following year to find that Polly had gone to join Macbeth and Davy was left without "a tender and loving wife," to quote his ghost-written words. Shortly afterward a buxom widow named Elizabeth Potter caught his roving eye, and a few months later Davy became the defunct Mr. Potter's legal successor. Over the next few years he began to take an interest in politics, and after serving as a magistrate for some time, he was elected to the Tennessee state legislature, and then in 1827 he was elected some more: to the United States House of Representatives, no less. On and off congressman was to be his lot for the next eight years, and then in 1835 the electorate voted him o-u-t for the last time. Colonel of Militia Crockett[79] told them what they could do with their stuffed ballot boxes and headed for Texas, where he was to have his finest hour. (See ALAMO, THE.)

CROW INDIANS A tribe belonging to the Siouan language family who are related to the Hidasta and the Mandan. Sometime in the 1600s they settled in what is now North Dakota and Montana, but with the introduction of the horse to the North Plains in the middle of the eighteenth century, the Crow took up horsemanship, and by 1800 they had become fully mounted tepee-dwelling nomads who relied almost exclusively on the buffalo and its by-products for food, clothing, and shelter.[80] Their hair was worn long and usually unbraided, while their buckskins were fringed and decorated with porcupine quills. Crow craftsmanship was superior to that of most plains tribes, and their elkhorn bows, which were frequently covered with

snakeskin, could drive an arrow completely through a fully grown buffalo. They were hereditary enemies of the Sioux, and when the Sioux and Cheyenne clashed with the U. S. Army—battles and skirmishes that covered more than a decade of the latter half of the nineteenth century—the Crow Indians hit back at their rivals by joining the Army as scouts. The Crow are now on reservations in Montana. (See CURLEY.)

CROWTHER, GENE   A fourteen-year-old[81] boy who is variously reported as having been: the adopted son of James and Kate Averill; a youth who was employed to carry messages for the couple; a cripple who lived with them; or an invalid they knew. On July 20, 1889, Gene was a witness to the lynching of James Averill and his wife, an infamous act that the boy had tried to prevent. On seeing the couple being forcibly removed from their homestead, Gene had run for help, and he and a neighbor named Frank Buchanan had followed the execution party to its destination where Buchanan had unsuccessfully tried to save the pair by opening fire from a nearby ridge. Immediately after the event, Crowther was captured by one of the cattlemen concerned in the lynching and taken to the latter's home. No one was allowed to see the boy, and before any of the lynch mob could be brought to trial, Gene died under mysterious circumstances.[82] (See AVERILL, JAMES, and WATSON, ELLA.)

CRUZ, FLORENTINE
Mexican-Indian half-breed who was a hanger-on of the Clantons and Curly Bill, and who is usually referred to as Indian

---

[79] An appointment picked up during his political years.
[80] A history that, from around 1750 on, applies to most of the tribes of the North Plains.
[81] Some authorities claim the boy was only twelve, although the majority incline to the age given in this entry.
[82] The cattlemen claim he died from Bright's disease, but the homesteaders said the boy died from the slow administration of poison.

Charlie. Cruz took nearly as long to pull a gun as he did to pull on his pants, and he was only given light work by the outlaws who plagued Tombstone when no one else was available. On March 18, 1882, he was employed as fingerman by the gunman who murdered Morgan Earp. Soon afterward a posse led by Wyatt Earp caught up with Cruz. Earp knew Cruz was no gunslick, so he gave him an edge: Cruz could start fumbling for his iron at the count of "one," but Wyatt would wait until the count of "three" before drawing.[83] Good enough. "One . . . er . . . two . . . er . . . three," and Indian Charlie was dead before he hit the ground. His gun was half drawn. (See EARP, MORGAN.)

CUMMINS, JIM Blue-eyed, sandy-haired stringbean of a man who was born around 1840. Cummins fought for the Confederacy during the Civil War, after which he became acquainted with Jesse and Frank James. For many years he was a hanger-on of the James gang although he never became a particularly active member, but after the train robbery at Winston, Missouri, on July 15, 1881—a crime in which Cummins is alleged to have taken part—he became untrustworthy,[84] and by the fall of that year Jesse was searching for him with murderous intent.[85] But the gang leader was never to catch up with Jim, and after Jesse's death, Frank James was wise enough to let bygones be bygones.

Jim Cummins died peacefully in a Confederate veterans' home. (See JAMES GANG.)

CURLEY A Crow scout who was the only human[86] survivor of the Custer battalion at the Battle on the Little Big Horn. Curley, whose Indian name was Ash-ish-ish-e, escaped by disguising himself as a Sioux (plaiting his loose hair and covering his Crow buckskins with a blanket taken from a dead Sioux) and taking part in the action against the 7th Cavalry. After the battle Curley made his way northward, and two days later he reached the confluence of the Big Horn and Yellowstone rivers, where Custer's supply ship—a government-chartered river steamer named the *Far West*—was waiting. Here Curley gave the outside world its first news[87] of the battle in the "Valley of the Greasy Grass." In 1913 Curley returned to the site of the battle with author Earl A. Brininstool, but although he pointed out landmarks for the writer, he could not be persuaded to talk of the actual engagement between the Indians and the 7th Cavalry. Curley died on May 23, 1923, and he is buried in the National Cemetery of the Custer Battlefield. Of passing interest: Curley's brother, White Swan, served as a scout with the Reno battalion, and he was crippled for life by wounds he received when the command was pinned down by Indians on June 25. (See BATTLE ON THE LITTLE BIG HORN and COMANCHE.)

---

[83] This may appear rather unsporting of Wyatt until one realizes that a medium-fast gunfighter could have drawn, shot a man dead, and downed a small whiskey in the time he allowed Mr. Cruz.

[84] To whit, accusing Jesse of the murder of a man named Miller.

[85] The search at one time led Jesse to a farm near Excelsior Springs. The farm, which had originally been Jim Cummins' home, was, at the time of Jesse's visit, owned by William Ford and his wife—a girl named Artello, who was Cummins' sister—and although Jim had "lit out" before Jesse's arrival, Jesse beat up the fifteen-year-old son of the Fords in an effort to find out the whereabouts of the boy's uncle. This was a stupid action on the part of Jesse, for the Ford clan never forgave him for it.

[86] A four-legged survivor was a horse named Comanche.

[87] Curley, who could not speak English, relayed his information by a mixture of sign talk and diagrams.

CURLY   Alternative spelling of "Curley." Both spellings are come across when referring to the Crow scout who survived the Custer battle and the young Crazy Horse. As both are phonetically the same, spelling is a matter of choice, but to avoid confusion, the shortened version is used in the entry on Crazy Horse, while we have given the Crow scout the superfluous "e." (See CRAZY HORSE and CURLEY.)

CURRY, GEORGE   An alias adopted by George Manuse, a gentleman whose nose was of formidable proportions, a built-in snorkel that was responsible for his nickname of "Big Nose" and "Parrott." (See MANUSE, GEORGE.)

CURRY KID   Alias of Harvey Logan. (See LOGAN, HARVEY.)

CUSHMAN, PAULINE   A lively Spanish-type beauty who is reported to have horse whipped men who doubted her virtue, and to have smashed crockery over the heads of those who wished to find out if there was any justification for the whippings. Pauline was born in New Orleans on June 10, 1833, of Anglo-Spanish parents, who, when their daughter was ten, moved northward and set up a trading post in Michigan. The family traded with the Chippewas, and by the time she was eighteen, and possibly because she was fed up with Chippewas with everything, Pauline left home and tried her hand at a theatrical career. This was a success, and Pauline toured the halls playing feminine lead to many of the matinee idols of the frontier and points east. In 1863, while touring the South during the Civil War, Pauline was

persuaded to become a Union spy by a northern agent who was "out in the cold" well behind enemy lines. Pauline knew numerous Confederate officers who must also have been gentlemen, for there is no record of any of them being crowned or horse whipped by Pauline, and from these gentlemen our heroine managed to get snips of "for your eyes only" stuff which, for a time, found its way to Union headquarters. For a time; then some southern cad lifted Pauline's skirt[88] and found some "Top Secret" drawings concealed in her drawers; the T.S. drawings concerned fortifications of the area—i.e., the area of hostilities, war-wise!—and things looked bleak for this early-day Mata Hari. The girl was tried and found guilty and she should have been shot, but Union sympathizers rescued her in the nick of time, and she was returned North to continue her interrupted career behind the footlights.[89] During the postwar years, Miss Cushman's name appeared on the billboards from New York to San Francisco, and it wasn't until 1879 that she gave up this career. In that year Pauline put an end to the controversy regarding her purity by marrying a roving-eyed rake named Jere Fryer, and the couple settled at Casa Grande, Arizona. The marriage wasn't a success, but while at Casa Grande, Mrs. Fryer got a reputation as an umpire at gunfights and became known as an animal lover. Before the year was out, Jere had been left to wash his own "smalls," and Pauline was trying to make a theatrical comeback. There was to be no comeback, and Pauline was forced to take on any jobs until her death in San Francisco on the night of December 6–7, 1893. At the time of her death, Pau-

[88] In line of duty?
[89] About this time she posed for Matthew Brady, and her photograph shows a dark-haired girl wearing a ground-length dress of frilled taffeta that is extremely elegant. The hair style Pauline favored is undatable, and if the portrait is so covered that only the head is exposed, this Civil War girl could be mistakenly labeled as a contemporary lovely.

line was employed as a cleaning woman, and she had no savings, but an organization called the Grand Army of the Republic hadn't forgotten her, and she was given a big funeral. Later, a plaque that reads "Pauline Cushman, Federal spy and Scout of the Cumberland" was attached to her headstone.

CUSTER, ELIZABETH The wife of George Armstrong Custer. (See BACON, ELIZABETH.)

CUSTER, GEORGE ARMSTRONG Controversial cavalry officer who was born on December 5, 1839,[90] at New Rumley, Ohio, and whose rank fluctuated considerably during his fifteen years of service. In 1861, after four years at the U. S. Military Academy at West Point, Custer was appointed a second lieutenant of volunteers in the Union armies. During the war he was promoted to captain after being cited for bravery at the Battle of Bull Run, and in 1865 he was holding the brevet rank of major general when he accepted the first flag of truce from General Robert E. Lee. Early the following year his regiment was engaged in policing duties in Texas, and over this short period Custer was accused of brutal disciplinary action toward both Southerners and his own men. He was, however, never brought to trial, and a short time later he was mustered out of the volunteers and joined the regular Army with a subsequent drop in rank: from brevet major general to captain. That same year, 1866, he was ordered to Fort Riley, Kansas, where, having been promoted to lieutenant colonel, he was

placed in command of the newly formed 7th Cavalry. Custer who, with his long, blond hair, has often been referred to as the "Last of the Cavaliers," adopted an Irish tune called "Carryowen" as the regiment's battle song and soon had his command whipped into shape. This "whipping into shape" may have been accomplished by extreme disciplinary action, for the following year Custer faced a court-martial for ". . . marching his men excessively, allowing two of them to be killed . . . all on a journey of private business,[91] excessive cruelty and illegal conduct in putting down a mutiny by shooting deserters." All these charges were, however, dismissed for lack of evidence, and Custer was acquitted. He rejoined his regiment at Fort Dodge, Kansas, in October 1868, and the following month the 7th Cavalry virtually wiped out a friendly Cheyenne village that was in winter camp on the Washita. At the close of this infamous engagement, Custer captured a beautiful Indian girl named Monahseetah, and although she couldn't speak a word of English, he decided she would make an ideal personal interpreter. The Cheyenne girl was closeted in his quarters, and it seems likely that she interpreted him well enough at his most passionate, for she was to share his lonely frontier life for many moons to come. In 1871 Custer's regiment was temporarily assigned for more or less policing duties in Kentucky, and it was not until 1873 that they returned to the plains, where, some three years later—on the Sunday of June 25, 1876—Lieutenant Colonel George Armstrong Custer and his immediate command were wiped out by Indians whom they had been sent to de-

[90] The eldest of five children born to Emmanuel and Maria Custer; the other children were Nevin, Thomas, Boston, and Margaret. Thomas and Boston died with their brother on the Little Big Horn.

[91] The "private business" was going AWOL to visit his wife, who reportedly was very ill, a military offense for which Custer had many a trooper shot.

stroy. When the buckskinned body of Custer was finally recovered, it was found to be unmutilated—save for a bullet wound in the temple—and his blond hair remained inviolate. This condition of the corpse has given rise to the belief that Custer died from a self-inflicted wound, for Indians will not scalp or interfere with the body of a suicide.[92] (See BACON, ELIZABETH; BATTLE ON THE LITTLE BIG HORN; BLACK KETTLE; 7TH CAVALRY; and WASHITA MASSACRE.)

CUSTER MASSACRE   Face-saving, yet erroneous, description of a defeat. (See BATTLE ON THE LITTLE BIG HORN.)

CUT-NOSE SQUAW   An Indian woman whose nose had been slashed for having been caught in adultery.

[92] According to many of the Indians who fought in this engagement, numerous cavalrymen committed suicide that day. This can easily be believed, for "saving the last shot for yourself" was not an uncommon practice when overwhelmed by Indians.

EDWARD BOREIN

D AKOTA HAT Style name for a stetson that differs from the Big Four Hat only inasmuch as the Dakota has a whipped brim. (See BIG FOUR HAT.)

DAKOTA INDIANS Usually referred to as Sioux Indians, a name which, although incorrect, has become acceptable through constant usage. Occasionally spelled "Dacotah" or "Dakotah." (See SIOUX INDIANS.)

DALE, MARIA VIRGINIA A saloon and dance-hall girl who married the notorious Joseph A. Slade. Maria, who is reputed to have been a beauty of generous curves, was an excellent horsewoman and a moderately good pistol shot, and on that night in March 1864 when she heard that her husband was going to be lynched, she buckled on a brace of pistols and thundered over twelve miles of mountain road in an effort to save him. Unfortunately for Maria —Joe, too, for that matter—she arrived in Virginia City after he had expired. Maria found him cooling off in a darkened room of the Virginia Hotel, and after giving the lynchers a magnificent tongue-lashing, she got down to making burial arrangements. These were somewhat unique; a tin coffin was made to her specifications, and when Joseph had been neatly arranged inside, Maria had it topped up with whiskey before the lid was sealed on. Joseph's pickled remains were then transported to Utah for burial. A short time later Maria returned to Virginia City, where, within a few months, she married Jim Kiskadden, a gentleman who had been an acquaintance of her late husband. (See SLADE, JOSEPH A.)

DALTON, EMMETT Born in Cass County, Missouri, in 1871. While in his teens he served as a deputy U.S. marshal, but in 1889 he left this law-abiding job and for the next three years his career was interwoven with the outlaw activities of brothers Grattan and Robert. After the Coffeyville showdown of 1892, and after recovering from wounds he had received in that bloody affair, Emmett was put on trial for the murder of George Cubine and Lucius Baldwin, a trial that resulted in his being sentenced to a life term in the Kansas State Penitentiary at Lansing. Emmett entered the prison on March 8, 1893, and the following year he married his long-time girlfriend, Julia Johnson, in the prison chapel. Julia had a long wait, but in 1907 Emmett was pardoned and the couple moved to California and settled in Hollywood. Here Emmett prospered as a building contractor, and, to a lesser degree, as a writer. Most of his writing was done for the movies— some of which he made brief appearances in—but his main literary work was *When the Daltons Rode*, an allegedly true account of the Daltons' activities. Emmett, last of the Coffeyville raiders, died on July 13, 1937. (See COFFEYVILLE, KANSAS; DALTON, FRANK; and DALTON GANG.)

DALTON, FRANK The eldest son of Louis and Adeline Dalton. Frank, who was born in the Daltons' colonial-style farmhouse in Missouri, became a U.S. deputy marshal working out of Fort Smith, Arkansas, in 1884. Three years later, brothers Emmett, Grattan, and Robert joined him in Arkansas, and they too became lawmen. Frank's character was beyond reproach, and had he lived, his sobering influence may have prevented his younger brothers from ever becoming bent, but on November 27, 1887, he was shot dead by a gang of whiskey smugglers, and shortly afterward Emmett, Grat, and Bob turned in their badges. Emmett is reported as saying that he and his brothers left Fort Smith because of graft and corruption in the marshal's office. There most likely was graft

and corruption until they left, for after Frank's death they are alleged to have become hand-in-glove with the criminal element.

DALTON GANG A gang of outlaws who began operations in the winter of 1889. The nucleus of the gang was the three Dalton brothers, Robert, Emmett, and Grattan, all of whom had been deputy U.S. marshals for a spell before taking to the outlaw trail. The early activities of the Daltons, which were confined to Oklahoma, were of a minor nature when compared with their later crimes, but even so, by the summer of 1890, their horse stealing and barn looting had made the territory too hot for their liking, and Robert, who was the undisputed leader, led his brothers westward to California. The Daltons' first known crime in California occurred on February 6, 1891, when four masked men took over the Southern Pacific depot at Alila and flagged down the San Francisco–Los Angeles express. George Radcliffe, the fireman, was shot dead when he resisted, but the four gunmen failed to break open the safe and had to flee empty-handed. A short time later Grattan was arrested and given a twenty-year sentence, but he escaped from his escort while being taken to jail and rejoined his brothers. California was now plastered with wanted fliers, and Robert wisely decided that they should return to Oklahoma before resuming activities. Once back in the territory the brothers established headquarters in a dugout near Kingfisher and began recruiting extra guns until the gang numbered seven:[1] the three Dalton brothers plus newcomers Charlie Bryant, George Newcomb, Charley Pierce, and Bill Doolin. On May

[1] Not an arbitrary figure, for the names given in the above narrative are only those of gang members who are known to have been engaged in the robberies concerned, but as all the gang wore bandana masks and sometimes numbered as many as ten, it is fair to assume that Doolin and Broadwell, and possibly others, took part in many of the gang's raids.

9, 1891, these seven looted the Santa Fe Limited at Wharton in the Cherokee Strip. The Daltons employed the same *modus operandi* in this robbery as they had in their earlier California venture, but on this occasion the holdup was a success: No one was killed, and the gang escaped with fourteen thousand dollars. A few days after the Wharton robbery, Charlie Bryant was shot dead in a gunfight, but before the month was out the reduced gang had successfully flagged down a Missouri, Kansas, and Texas train at Lelietta and escaped with nineteen thousand dollars. After this job, the gang split up and the three Daltons settled down in a small house at Hennessey. Sharing this domestic setting was Daisy Bryant, the late Charlie Bryant's sister and a girl whom Robert had quite a crush on. Passion probably ruled Bob for the next thirteen months, for it was not until June 2, 1892, that the Daltons, together with a character named Dick West, committed their next robbery. This was the Santa Fe express train job at Red Rock, which netted the gang a meager two thousand dollars. This modest amount didn't last long, and on July 15, 1892, the gang held up and robbed a train of the Missouri, Kansas, and Texas Railroad at Adair in the Cherokee Strip and rode off with seventeen thousand dollars after killing one man and wounding three others. During the same month the Daltons are reputed to have robbed a bank at El Reno of around ten thousand dollars, but this crime has never been satisfactorily laid at their door. Through August and September the Daltons lay low while Robert, between dalliance with Daisy, plotted what he hoped would be the crime

of the century: a double bank job at Coffeyville, Kansas. On October 4, Robert, Grat, and Emmett, with a new recruit (Bill Powers), and old hands Bill Doolin and Dick Broadwell, set out for Coffeyville, but the following morning Doolin's horse developed a limp and only five men rode into town. None of these five was to ride out again. (See BRYANT, CHARLIE; COFFEYVILLE, KANSAS; DALTON, FRANK; DALTON, WILLIAM; DOOLIN, BILL; DOOLIN GANG; NEWCOMB, GEORGE; PIERCE, CHARLEY; POWERS, BILL; and WEST, RICHARD.)

DALTON, GRATTAN Born in Cass County, Missouri, in 1864. Grat[2] became a lawman in 1887, but this was a short-lived career, and by the winter of 1889 he was riding the owlhoot trail with his brothers Robert and Emmett. (See COFFEYVILLE, KANSAS; DALTON, FRANK; DALTON GANG; and DALTON, WILLIAM.)

DALTON, LOUIS Member of a Kentucky family of wealthy plantation owners and father of members of the infamous Dalton gang. Louis, who served in the Mexican War of 1846–48, settled down in Missouri after his release from the Army, and here he married Adeline Younger[3] and set up home in a large colonial-style farmhouse in Cass County. By 1864 the Civil War had wiped out the Dalton family fortune, and Louis was forced to try his hand at farming, and, for a short spell, saloon keeping. In 1882 he moved his family[4] to Indian Territory (Oklahoma), and then six years later, onto a farm near Coffeyville, Kansas. Louis Dalton died here in 1889.

[2] History states that Grat was killed at Coffeyville, but as late as 1955 a ninety-four-year-old resident of Colorado Springs, Colorado, was proclaiming loud and clear that he was a Grat Dalton. This is of interest only inasmuch as it points out the ridiculous lengths to which some old-timers will go in an effort to have the spotlight turned their way. Others have laid claim to being Billy the Kid, Jesse James, Bob Ford, etc.

[3] A half sister of Colonel Henry Younger, father of the notorious Younger boys.

[4] Adeline and fifteen children, all of whom were born in the Cass County farmhouse.

AN ENCYCLOPEDIA OF THE OLD WEST

DALTON, ROBERT The first member of the Dalton family to shoot a man dead, a sordid crime that happened thusly: In the fall of 1888, Minnie Johnson, a cousin of Robert's and a girl whom he had been a-visitin', transferred her affections to a gentleman named Charlie Montgomery. Bob didn't take kindly to this, and the following spring he waylaid Charlie and shot him through the back of the head. The killer was wearing a lawman's badge at the time, and he claimed that he had caught his rival stealing horses, an enormous untruth that none of the neighbors believed, but for some unknown reason the authorities accepted Bob's version, and Charlie went down in the records as the victim of a justifiable homicide. Shortly after this miscarriage of justice, and after wooing a wench named Eugenia Moore for a spell, Bob turned outlaw, and for the next year or so he was leader of the Dalton gang. The end came for Bob on October 5, 1892, when he was shot dead at Coffeyville. He was twenty-four years old at the time of his demise. (See COFFEYVILLE, KANSAS; DALTON, FRANK; DALTON GANG; and DALTON, LOUIS.)

DALTON, WILLIAM Born in Missouri in 1869. In 1891 William had long since left the family homestead and was settled in California, where he was making a name for himself in politics. In February of that year his brothers, Robert, Emmett, and Grattan, held up a train at Alila, California, and after this robbery attempt William gave Grat shelter, but a posse was hard on the heels of Grat, and when they arrived at the front door, both William and the fugitive were taken into custody. Bill was lucky, for his political friends came to his rescue, and he was released without a stain on his character,[5] and by 1892 he had worked his way

up to become a respected member of the California legislature. Then came Coffeyville and the stigma of association, and Bill resigned from politics and returned to Kansas, where he joined the newly formed Bill Doolin gang. The ex-politician looted and killed with the Doolin mob until it was disbanded in the summer of 1895. Bill, who was now married, settled down to a spot of farming in Oklahoma, but on September 25, 1895, a posse surrounded his homestead, and he was shot dead by U. S. Marshal Loss Hart when the latter saw him reach for a gun. (See COFFEYVILLE, KANSAS; DALTON GANG; DALTON, LOUIS; DOOLIN GANG; and INGALLS, OKLAHOMA.)

DALY GANG A loose-knot gang that plagued the Nevada gold fields in the 1860s. The leader of these ruffians was a young gunslick named John Daly, a hard case who had drifted into Nevada from California. Associates whom he could call on for assistance when a spot of horse stealing or armed robbery was on the agenda were John "Three Finger" McDowell, Jim Masterson (no kin to the lawman of that name), William Buckley, Jim Sears, Irish Tom, and Italian Jim. In October 1862 Daly shot a man dead in Aurora, and two months later another gentleman fell before his guns in Carson City, but as both of these Daly-made corpses were of the criminal element, the law allowed Daly to go on his way unmolested. In the spring of 1863 Jim Sears, while doing a spot of free-lancing, stole a horse from a solid citizen named William R. Johnson, but before he could make his getaway, he was blasted into eternity by an employee of Johnson's. When the news of Sears' death reached Daly he decided to make an example of Johnson that would put the fear of God into the law-abiding element. On Feb-

[5] Even so, one cannot help but wonder, for *four* men did hold up the train at Alila, California.

ruary 1, 1864, the Daly gang finally caught up with Johnson, and in an exhibition of professional know-how, cut his throat and then set fire to the corpse. Daly had made his point, but it failed in its objective. He had sadly underestimated the temper of the honest folk, and they in turn were utterly fed up with the bum; the Citizens' Protective Association (a newly formed vigilante committee) took six of the Daly gang into custody before the six knew what was happening, and on February 8, Daly and three of his cronies were hanged outside Armory Hall in Aurora.[6]

DANCE HALLS Foot stamping to a fiddle accompaniment was a built-in fixture of the pioneers, so when they came to building settled communities a dance hall would get priority over such structures as restaurants, churches, and schools; it would, in fact, hold its own with such western necessities as saloons and honky-tonks. A simple dance hall would be little more than four log or sod walls with a canvas roof where a solitary fiddler would scratch out jigs while some old crone served drinks from a makeshift bar. Others, which were more or less saloons whose floor space would be kept free of tables and chairs, would probably have a trio of fiddlers and some hot-lips trumpeter, and perhaps the luxury of a piano. As women were scarce on the frontier,[7] dance-hall proprietors imported lasses for their establishments. These girls, who were frequently amazons of Teutonic stock, were hardly the silk and satin lovelies of Hollywood Westerns, but even so, they kept the cash drawers heavy, for customers considered fifty cents a dance a fair price to pay for the privilege of bulldozing one of these prairie flowers around a sawdust-covered floor. The term "dance-hall girl" is frequently used as a polite euphemism for "whore"; this is slanderously incorrect,[8] for any girl who was so inclined could easily have rented a crib and made far more money than these lasses in gingham and cheap print dresses. Dance halls were commonly known as hurdy-gurdy houses, and all were fully licensed. Dance halls should not be confused with honky-tonks, although a certain amount of dancing was sometimes carried out in the latter. (See HONKY-TONKS.)

DANIELS, JAMES Bowie knife bullyboy whose history is hazy until his arrival in the Montana gold fields in the 1860s, although he is alleged to have knifed a Frenchman to death in California before making the scene in Montana. This is quite feasible, for in 1865 at Helena he bowie-knifed a man named Gartley[9] to death during a quarrel over a game of cards. Vigilantes arrested Daniels, but instead of stretching his neck, they handed him over to the legal authorities, and at a subsequent trial he was given a three-year sentence. Daniels spent a few weeks in the territorial prison and then, for some unknown reason, he was released with a pardon. If Jimmy had possessed much sense he would have been a good boy after his release, but he wasn't;

---

[6] The four men hanged were John Daly, William Buckley, Jim Masterson, and John McDowell. Italian Jim and Irish Tom were released; could be that the vigilantes wished to avoid any international incidents.

[7] A scarcity which, prior to the importation of females and coupled with the Westerners' passionate desire for a jig, led to a rather odd practice: Half of the men at a dance would tie handkerchiefs or bandanas around their left arms, and these were the "women"; although this practice didn't cast any slur on a man's virility, one can only hope that it didn't lead to any disgusting horseplay after the ball was over.

[8] In most cases; there would, of course, be exceptions.

[9] Gartley's wife dropped dead when she heard the news of his violent end.

he went around threatening witnesses who had appeared for the prosecution at his trial, and he was only prevented from knifing a man named Hugh O'Neil in the back by the use of force. After this affair, the vigilantes decided Mr. Daniels had pushed his luck too far, so he was seized and hanged forthwith.[10] (See VIGILANTES OF MONTANA.)

DANITES Alleged to have been the Destroying Angels of the Mormon Church; the enforcers, terrorists, or murder squads who are said to have been organized by Brigham Young in an effort to eliminate specific individuals or groups who were in active opposition to the Mormons. A Mormon convicted or suspected of a violent crime was, at one time, invariably dubbed a "Danite" or "Destroying Angel," but whether such nomenclature was ever used by the Mormons, or whether a Danite cell was ever an accepted branch of the early Mormon Church, is most certainly open to doubt. When Horace Greeley questioned Brigham Young regarding Danites, Young denied any knowledge of their existence. (See MORMONS and MOUNTAIN MEADOWS MASSACRE.)

DAUGHERTY, ROY Usually appears in print under his aliases of "Arkansas Tom" and "Tom Jones." Roy was born in Missouri of highly religious parents, but although said parents succeeded in talking two of his older brothers into becoming preachers, they had little luck with Roy. In his early teens he left home and wandered into Oklahoma Territory to become a ranchhand. Over the next few years, he worked for various cattle outfits, and it was during this period that he became acquainted with Bill Doolin,

an outlaw who, at that time, was riding with the Daltons. After the Coffeyville disaster Doolin formed a gang of his own, and sometime in the fall of 1892 Roy joined this band of owlhoots. The self-styled Arkansas Tom rode, looted, and killed with the Doolin gang until his arrest at the Battle of Ingalls on September 1, 1893. In April of the following year, Daugherty went on trial and was sentenced to fifty years in the territorial prison at Lansing. If prison sentences meant anything, Roy would have been due out in the middle of World War II; but they mean little, and he was released on parole on November 6, 1910. His brothers were in no small measure responsible for his liberation, and it was probably due to their efforts that Roy was persuaded to live in peaceful co-existence with the law for the next six years; but in 1916 he had a lapse, and he was arrested for taking part in a bank stickup at Neosho, Missouri. This time the judge handed Roy eight years in the Missouri state prison, but he was a good lad behind the walls, and he was allowed back into circulation on November 11, 1921. A short time afterward he was suspected of a bank job that had occurred at Asbury, Missouri, and "Hold for Questioning" notices bearing his many names began to blossom on the walls of post offices and the various law-enforcement agencies' notice boards, but it was not until August 6, 1924, at Joplin, Missouri, that a young policeman got within arm's reach and Roy had a go at making a last stand. Now, Roy had been a middling fast man with a low-slung .45, but this was 1924 and guns were being worn either under the arm or in the back pocket of the pants, and he didn't stand a chance, for before Arkansas Tom or Tom Jones or Roy Daugherty could remember where he was keeping his iron, that city cop had

[10] According to Professor Thomas J. Dimsdale, Daniels was the last man to be hanged by the Montana Vigilance Committee.

shot all three of him dead.[11] (See DOOLIN GANG and INGALLS, OKLAHOMA.)

DAVIS, JACK   A Virginia City deadbeat and gambler who was suspected of numerous stage robberies in Nevada during the late 1860s. On November 4, 1870, Central Pacific's Train No. 1 was held up and looted of more than forty thousand dollars in gold at Verdi, Nevada,[12] and a short time later Jack Davis was arrested for participating in the robbery. He drew a comparatively light sentence in the penitentiary at Carson City, and on his release he drifted East until he reached Texas, where in the fall of 1876 he made the acquaintance of Sam Bass and threw in his lot with Sam's bunch of owlhoots. After leaving the Bass gang, Davis moved to New Orleans for a spell, but in 1879 he was back in Nevada holding up stages. But things were a little different than in the old days; the coaches now had double guards, and when Jack held up a stage at Willow station and wounded one of the guards, the second guard, a hard case named Eugene Blair, pushed the business end of a double-barreled scattergun into Jack's face and let him have both charges. It was impossible to recognize the bandit's remains, but Mr. Blair claimed it was Jack Davis, and most folks took his word for it.[13] (See BASS, SAM, and BLAIR, EUGENE.)

DAWSON, ROBERT   Member of the Gaspar Trammell gang, an organization that fenced goods for Jean Lafitte. After Lafitte's last act of piracy in 1816, Trammell and his gang left Galveston with two million dollars in silver, which they hoped to sell at St. Louis, Missouri. Two hundred miles north of Galveston, Mexican soldiers were sighted, more than two hundred men who were rapidly gaining on the heavily laden wagons. Trammell and his men dropped the silver into a lake before they were overtaken and cut down by the Mexicans. Only Robert Dawson escaped, and months later he reached St. Louis. Naturally, he told his story, and he named the lake: Hendrick's Lake, Texas. And that, folks, is the reason for this entry on Robert Dawson, for we like to let our readers know where they can lay their hands on a spot of lost loot from time to time.[14] (See LAFITTE, JEAN.)

DEAD MAN'S HAND   A hand of cards that consists of a pair of aces and a pair of eights. So called because Wild Bill Hickok was holding such a hand when he was shot dead. (See HICKOK, JAMES BUTLER.)

DEADWOOD DICK   There were many self-styled "Deadwood Dicks"[15] in the Dakotas, Richard Clarke, thanks to his own efforts, probably being the most notable of these dime-novel enthusiasts. (See CLARKE, RICHARD.)

DEADWOOD, SOUTH DAKOTA   Originally Deadwood Gulch, a mining camp founded during the Black Hills

---

[11] Roy was fifty-three years old at the close of his career.

[12] This is reputed to be the first train robbery in the Far West.

[13] We can hardly blame their acceptance of identity, for Blair was a mighty tough customer, but it might be safer to assume that what happened to Davis after his farewells to Bass can, at least, only be conjectured, for he is reported to have been seen in Nicaragua as late as 1920.

[14] Another reader may, of course, beat you to it. But we very much doubt it. Others have been searching for the past 150 years or more, and apart from a few bars of pure silver that have been recovered, the main jackpot is still there at the bottom of the lake.

[15] The "Deadwood Dick Library" of dime novels published by Beadle and Adams was responsible for this spate of soft-to-medium-boiled characters.

gold rush of 1875. As the timber-covered slopes prevented lateral growth, the town consisted of a narrow main street, the length of which only remained static for short intervals. Twelve months after the first tents and false fronts had been thrown up, the population was around the twenty-five thousand mark, and the number of saloons, sporting houses, cribs, and various other dens of iniquitous loose living had increased accordingly. In its early years Deadwood saw such notable western characters as Wyatt Earp, Calamity Jane, Wild Bill Hickok, Poker Alice, Sam Bass, Doc Holliday, and a collection of Deadwood Dicks, all of whom may have quenched their thirst at such places as the Bucket of Blood, Montana, or Nuttall and Mann's No. 10 Saloon;[16] watched visiting thespians or burlesque artists at the Gem or Bella Union[17] theaters; or tried their luck at the Green Front Sporting House. In 1879 the town was almost burned to the ground, and four years later more than half of its buildings were carried away by floods, yet the town survived these elemental setbacks, and today it is something of a tourist attraction with its Adams Museum, the site of Wild Bill's last gamble, and the graves of both he and Calamity Jane. (See CLARKE, RICHARD.)

DEADWOOD STAGE   Can refer to any of the four stagecoaches that Buffalo Bill Cody bought from the Marquis de Mores. Cody used them up, one at a time, in his Wild West shows, a coach being brought into service when its predecessor had become battered beyond repair, and as each coach had its turn in the arena it became known as the "Deadwood Stage."[18] (See DE MORES, MARQUIS.)

DEAF CHARLEY
Nickname of Camilla Hanks. (See HANKS, CAMILLA.)

DEAL, PONY   Small-time outlaw who was a member of the Clanton gang, and —at a later date—the Curly Bill gang. Deal was with Curly Bill when the latter shot Marshal Fred White, but although Deal was arrested by Wyatt Earp as an accomplice, he was released for lack of evidence. On January 6, 1882, Deal was one of the three men who held up the Tombstone-Bisbee stage, and that same year he was suspected of being the slayer of a tinhorn gambler named "Johnny Behind the Deuce." In neither instance was Deal prosecuted, and before the year was out, he was shot dead in a gunfight at Clifton, New Mexico. (See CLANTON GANG; EARP, WYATT BERRY STAPP; GRAHAM, WILLIAM B.; O'ROURKE, JOHN; and RINGGOLD, JOHN.)

DEARBORN   A lightweight four-wheeled family carriage with a canvas top and adjustable canvas sides; it is designed to be pulled by one horse.

DEATH VALLEY A desert valley located in California just west of the Nevada

---

[16] Hickok was shot dead while playing cards here.

[17] Leased in 1876 by an actor of international repute named Jack Langrishe, the Bella Union soon became one of the foremost vice emporiums of the West. Jack must have had rather liberal views, for after the curtain came down on each evening's performances—usually variety shows—the Cyprians of the town were allowed to ply their trade within the precincts of the theater, and after suitable financial arrangements had been made, one could dally with a doxie in any of the seventeen curtained boxes that flanked the auditorium.

[18] Each coach had an identity of its own: *Kitty, Deadwood, Medora,* and *Dakota,* names that the marquis had had painted on their side panels. *Kitty* is now in the Stagecoach Museum at Shakopee, Minnesota.

boundary. Death Valley,[19] which is flanked by the Funeral Mountains of the Armagosa Range on the east and the Panamint Mountains on the west, has a maximum depth of 280 feet below sea level—the lowest point of land in the Western Hemisphere. The valley has very little rainfall, and as any water that may collect becomes impregnated with mineral salts of a poisonous nature, it is unsafe to drink from any of the water holes in the area. The Paiutes knew the region as "Ground Afire"—an apt name, for temperatures can reach 134°F in the summer. Two small settlements, Stovepipe Wells and Furnace Creek, are located in the valley. (See SCOTT, WALTER.)

DEATH VALLEY SCOTTY An unusually successful desert rat. (See SCOTT, WALTER.)

DEER Individual species are described under separate headings. (See MOOSE; MULE DEER; WAPITI; and WHITE-TAILED DEER.)

DELANEY, WILLIAM E. Onetime suspected rustler who on December 8, 1883, was one of the men who took part in a robbery and massacre at Bisbee, Arizona. After the robbery Delaney fled South and holed up in Minas Prietas, Mexico. Here he adopted the name of Summers, but the alias didn't help him for long, and in the middle of January 1884 he was arrested at gunpoint by William Daniels, a Cochise County deputy

sheriff who had tracked him into Mexico. (See HEATH, JOHN.)

DELLA ROSE Sometimes given as an alias or nickname of Laura Bullion, while in actual fact the reverse is correct, Della Rose being the girl's correct name. (See ROSE, DELLA.)

DE MORES, MARQUIS A French nobleman who arrived on the American scene with more than three million dollars in the spring of 1883. The marquis soon put some of his cash to work: He bought forty-five thousand acres of land in South Dakota at less than a dollar an acre, built an up-to-date packing plant, and bought complete trail herds to keep it in full operation. Refrigerator railroad cars were used to get the meat to market in prime condition, and the latest machinery was used to convert the by-products into fertilizer. The marquis must have been a human dynamo, for in addition to looking after his business enterprises, he found time to supervise the building of a twenty-eight-room mansion and a small town on his Dakota rangeland.[20] In time he fenced his lands and built up his own herds, but this fencing in didn't go down too well in the West, and when three buffalo hunters protested their right-of-way by cutting his wire, the marquis resorted to violence: He shot one of the men dead and wounded his companions. De Mores was arrested and jailed, but after a long-drawn-out trial he was acquitted. Sometime in 1885 the marquis bought four stagecoaches and started a local stageline. He placed a newspaper editor named A. T.

[19] The town of the same name huddles the Southern Pacific tracks some twenty miles east of the valley.

[20] A full staff of domestics was employed at the mansion, while the main buildings of the town—which the marquis had christened Medora, after his wife—were the De Mores Hotel (two dollars a night and six dollars a week), a saloon, a theater, and a club for the De Mores employees. The mansion is now one of North Dakota's tourist attractions, and as the De Mores had never bothered to pack before they walked out, it is still furnished as it was when he and his wife left it more than eighty years ago.

Packard[21] in charge of this operation, and the stages began shuttling between Medora and Deadwood—a distance of two hundred miles—at regular intervals. Unfortunately this enterprise encountered too much competition, and within a short time of its inception the marquis closed his stageline and sold its four vehicles to Buffalo Bill Cody. The De Mores empire collapsed in the winter of 1887 when blizzards decimated his herds, and six months later the marquis and his wife and family retainers left the Dakotas, never to return. (See DEADWOOD STAGE.)

DENO, LOTTIE A professional lady gambler who is reported to have been sufficiently beautiful and cultured to have caught the eye of Doc Holliday,[22] caught and held it for years without any response from the copper-haired Lottie, a girl who always kept a card table between her satin-sheathed curves and the boys. Lottie was first heard of in 1876 at Jacksboro, Texas, where she was running a faro layout, and it was here that Holliday first noted her statistics, but he still hadn't made any headway by the following year, when Lottie had moved to the hide hunters' town of Fort Griffin. Miss Deno lived alone in a small house at Griffin, and as no man was ever known to have crossed its threshold, the hide men nicknamed her "Mystic Maude." Mystic Maude showed another side of her nature while at Griffin: When two gunmen shot each other to death in front of her layout, the copper-haired girl never batted an eyelid, and remained behind to count her chips when everyone else had fled. This cold-blooded lass, who once confessed she was a desperate woman, left Fort Griffin in the early 1880s and headed for . . . no one knows where. (See BENDER, KATE.[23])

DERINGER A single-shot muzzle-loading pocket pistol that was designed and manufactured by a Philadelphia gunsmith named Henry Deringer. This gun, which came in various calibers (.36–.50) and a choice of barrel lengths (1½ inches–6½ inches), was the original Deringer.[24] The barrels of these pistols are rifled and are made of iron, and almost invariably there is a "sunburst" design incorporating the letter "P" on the left side of the breech. Deringers also have the words "DERINGER PHILADELPHa" stamped on both the breech and the lock plate, and the forward end plate of the trigger guard is engraved with a pineapple design. When first placed on the market (circa 1850), these guns retailed for about three dollars each, but their price increased consider-

---

21 An ex-university graduate and baseball star who produced and edited *The Badlands Cow Boy*, a newspaper with a weekly circulation of around six hundred.

22 Doc finally settled for Big-nosed Kate (Kate Elder), a woman who was anything but "beautiful and cultured."

23 This is just a passing thought, for as far as this writer is aware, no one has ever connected Lottie Deno with Kate Bender. Lottie did, however, have a lot in common with Kate, a girl who disappeared three years before Lottie appeared on the scene. They were both copper-haired and were labeled as "mystics"; both are known to have been cold-blooded, and both appear to have had an aversion to men. Only four points admitted; but if it is borne in mind that good-looking women were extremely scarce on the thinly populated frontier, and that today it would be difficult—if not impossible—to find two copper-haired, cold-blooded female mystics with an aversion to men in a city such as New York or London, the four points are not without interest. Anyhow, read about Kate and see what you think.

24 These guns are now known as Deringer-derringers to differentiate them from the models of imitators—individual gunsmiths and firms who cashed in on the fact that Henry Deringer had failed to patent his model.

ably as supply failed to keep up with demand.[25] (See DERRINGERS.)

DERRINGERS Generic term for any single- or double-barreled[26] pocket pistol of large caliber, whether it be percussion or metal cartridge type. After Henry Deringer had established that there was a ready market for such a weapon, dozens of gunsmiths and arms firms began to turn out these easily concealed[27] pistols. Many of these guns are almost exact replicas of Henry Deringer's original model, while others are entirely different in design. Guns in the derringer class that have little in common with Deringer's pistols were manufactured by such firms as National Arms Company, Colt's Patent Firearms Manufacturing Company, American Arms Company, and E. Remington and Sons. The last-mentioned firm turned out the most popular model: an over-and-under double-barreled .41-caliber rimfire pistol that was in continuous production from 1865 to 1935. All derringers have a low muzzle velocity and are only accurate up to about six feet. (See DERINGER.)

DESERET The Mormons' name for their Promised Land, a New Jerusalem that is located in Utah, with Salt Lake City as its nucleus. Deseret means "Land of the Honey bee"—"honey bee" in this instance being synonymous with "industrious." (See MORMONS.)

DESTROYING ANGELS The alleged killer squads of the Mormon Church. (See DANITES.)

DEWLAP A cattle brand mark consisting of a flap of hide that has been cut in such a way that it hangs downward. Dewlaps are located on the front of the neck and under the chin.

DIAMONDBACK A species of rattlesnake. (See RATTLESNAKES.)

DIGGER INDIANS A label that is sometimes attached to any of the agricultural tribes of California and the Southwest; it shouldn't be, for it is a term of a derogatory nature.

DIME NOVELS The blood and thunders of an earlier era. Dime novels were magazine-sized (about 8½ inches by 11 inches) paperbacked books, each of which contained one long complete adventure story of about 30,000 words.[28] These novels covered almost every lurid aspect known to man; they could be set in any part of the known or unknown world or in nonexistent Ruritanian pastures, but for all this wide canvas, yarns with a Wild West flavor were by far the most popular. Quite a number of these romances were based— very, very loosely—on fact, although the majority were pure fiction. Beadle and Adams was the most prolific publisher of dime novels, but they were not without rivals, and brief details of three of their better-known competitors are given below.

Frank Tousey Publisher, 34–36 North Moore Street, New York, New York. Publisher of the Wide Awake Library, a weekly issue retailing at five cents a copy.

---

[25] The .41-caliber model with a 2½-inch barrel was by far the most popular.

[26] Pocket pistols with four barrels are occasionally referred to as derringers, but it is more usual and correct to class such multishot weapons as pepperboxes.

[27] Their only advantage over other small arms, for they had neither the accuracy nor the stopping power of similar-calibered but larger handguns.

[28] In books of sixteen pages (the most popular thickness); books of thirty-two pages may have stories running to more than sixty thousand words.

Tousey would occasionally bring out a "Special" at ten cents a copy; of these *The Life and Trial of Frank James*—a verbatim report of the trial—is one of the more notable.

John W. Morrison Publisher, 13–15 Vandewater Street, New York, New York. Publisher of Morrison's Sensational Series, a weekly issue retailing at five cents a copy.

Street and Smith, 29 Rose Street, New York, New York. Publisher of Diamond Dick Library, a weekly publication that retailed at five cents a copy.

The dime novel boom lasted from around 1870 until 1920, and the dime novels finally petered into oblivion in 1933.[29] (See BEADLE AND ADAMS.)

DIMSDALE, THOMAS J. An English professor and ex-Oxford graduate and an advanced consumptive who, in search of a healthful climate, entered the United States via Canada in July of 1863 and settled at Virginia City, Montana.[30] Professor Dimsdale ran a private school here for a time, but he abandoned this form of livelihood on being given a territorial educational appointment in the spring of 1864. In August of that year he became editor of the newly established *Montana Post,* and it was while at the editorial desk of this newspaper that he wrote the series of brilliant articles for which he is best remembered. These occasionally humorous but frequently hard-hitting reports were concerned with the violent lives and equally violent ends of some of the local desperadoes who infested the Montana gold camps, and of the vigilantes who were responsible for their eventual downfall. A collection of these articles, which ran in the *Montana Post* from August 26, 1864, until March of the following year, was published in book form in 1866 under Dimsdale's original title, *Vigilantes of Montana.*[31] (See VIGILANTES OF MONTANA and VIRGINIA CITY, MONTANA.)

DINERO   Spanish term denoting "money" that has crept into the conversational English of the Southwest.

DIXON, WILLIAM Better known as Billy Dixon, an Army scout and buffalo hunter whose activities were confined to the Staked Plains area of Texas. Dixon, who was born in 1850, started his plains career by freighting supplies for Lieutenant Colonel G. A. Custer during the latter's expeditions against the southern Cheyenne from 1868–69. In 1874, and after some years of independent freighting and hide hunting, Dixon joined up with a group of kindred spirits and went searching for buffalo signs in the Panhandle. They found Indian signs instead, and from June 27 until June 29 they were pinned down at Adobe Walls by Quanah Parker's feathered cavalry. Shortly after this engagement, Dixon was scouting for Colonel Nelson A. Miles, and in September of that same year Dixon and five others—a civilian scout

[29] The thick short story magazines, which, for some unknown reason, smelled of raisins, possessed lurid full-color covers, and were affectionately known as "the pulps," were responsible for the death of the dime novels. Of interest to collectors: There are still plenty of genuine copies of dime novels going around at a price of two to three dollars a copy.

[30] In this entry Virginia City has been located in Montana to avoid confusion. In 1863 it was in Idaho, but on May 26, 1864, during the period covered by the above narrative, Montana's territorial boundaries were established, and from then on Virginia City, Montana, is correct.

[31] The 1866 edition is now virtually unobtainable, but luckily the book has since been republished (1953) by the University of Oklahoma Press; it is Volume 1 of their Western Frontier Library.

named Amos Chapman and four troopers—were attacked by a war party of Kiowa and Comanche. The Indians succeeded in driving off the white men's horses, and Dixon and his companions were forced to take cover in a buffalo wallow.[32] Firing continued throughout the day, and by early evening one trooper lay dead and all but one of the besieged party had suffered wounds; what little water they had carried had long since gone, and ammunition was running low. Yet, an Indian massacre this was not to be; a providential flash flood drove the Indians from the area and filled the buffalo wallow with badly needed water. The following morning Dixon dragged himself from the muddy depression and went in search of help. Three miles from the wallow, he met up with an Army supply train, and the officer in command grudgingly[33] detailed a surgeon and two troopers to return to the scene of the fight with Dixon. Dixon's requests for ammunition and transport were ignored, and after the military medic had bandaged their wounds and the two troopers had given them a meager supply of hardtack, the men in the wallow were left with their position but slightly improved. Around midnight, and after nearly forty-eight hours in the wallow, a cavalry trumpet was heard, and Dixon and his companions were firing their last few rounds into the air when a patrol found them. After the Indians had been swept from the South Plains, and when the buffalo herds existed only in men's minds, Billy Dixon settled down to relive his past on paper, and these reminiscences, collected and edited by his wife shortly after his death, were published in 1914 by the P. L. Turner Company under the title *The Life of Billy Dixon.* (See BATTLE AT ADOBE WALLS.)

DOAN'S STORE A large mercantile establishment[34] that Judge C. F. Doan and his nephew Corvin erected on the Texas side of the Red River. The building was on the Western Cattle Trail, and most of Doan's trade came from the trail herd crews who usually tarried there before crossing the river.[35] Stock that could be purchased at Doan's included horse equipment, clothing, bedding, firearms, and whiskey. (See WESTERN TRAIL.)

DODGE CITY, KANSAS
In the summer of 1872 the Atchison, Topeka and Santa Fe Railroad, pushing westward, reached Buffalo City, a small whiskey peddlers' camp consisting of a few soddies and which was located on the Arkansas River some five miles to the west of the military reservation of Fort Dodge. Almost overnight makeshift saloons and gambling dens—housed in tents or dugouts—bloomed amid the soddies, and within a matter of weeks false-

[32] This skirmish has gone down in history as "The Buffalo Wallow Fight." Dixon was wounded in the ankle during the fight, and Chapman received a leg injury that necessitated the limb being amputated. The four soldiers in the engagement were Sergeant Woodhall and Privates Rath, Harrington, and Smith. Each of the six men who took part in the fight was awarded the Congressional Medal of Honor; in the case of Smith, the only fatal casualty, this was a posthumous award. The site of the fight is in northwestern Texas, some twenty miles south of the present-day town of Canadian.

[33] The only explanation for this shoddy treatment was that the supply train had been harassed by Indians, and Major Price—the train's commander—evidently wanted to get his column back to base as quickly as possible.

[34] Consisting of two buildings, one of which was of timber construction, while the other had walls of adobe bricks. Both had wooden pitched roofs.

[35] The ford became known as Doan's Crossing.

fronted buildings were going up on each side of the Santa Fe's tracks, and the settlement had been rechristened Dodge City.[36] This was to become the greatest cattle market on earth, a transient cowboy's paradise of brothels, saloons, dance halls, and restaurants that have led to its being variously referred to as the "Queen of the Cow Towns," the "Babylon of the Plains," or the "Wickedest Little City in America." Around 1876 the town had twenty saloons,[37] which catered to the thirst of its twelve hundred inhabitants; two theaters—the Comique and the Alcazar—where pneumatic wenches in pink tights raised the blood pressure of visiting waddies; and numerous dance halls and red-light emporiums,[38] where said waddies could let off steam. The wearing of spurs was permitted in dance halls, but in the ultimate resorts bawds bearing such colorful names as Hop-fiend Nell, Big-nosed Kate, and Scar-faced Lily would usually request their removal. During its boom years—roughly 1877 to 1887 —the population of Dodge never went much over the three thousand mark, for to many—Doc Holliday, Belle Starr, Luke Short, Wyatt Earp, and Bat Masterson, to name but a few—it was only a temporary residence. The Dodge City of today has a population of about fourteen thousand, and it is still a cattle center. (See BOOT HILL.)

DOGIE   An orphaned or otherwise abandoned calf. The word derives from the Spanish *dogal*—a tied-off calf.

DOG SOLDIER   Member of a Cheyenne warrior society. Initiates of the Dog Society were the professional soldiers of the Cheyenne nation, and as such the only duties they were expected to perform while in camp were those of a police nature. The policies and decisions of the society were not influenced by the tribal council, so it was not unusual for war parties of dog soldiers to be attacking settlers when the remainder of the tribe were not actively hostile. These independent raids got many a grizzled Army scout spitting out tobacco-juiced phrases about dog soldiers whenever he saw a Cheyenne, incorrect identification that in time resulted in the uninformed and the misinformed referring to all Cheyenne males as dog soldiers. Chosen dog soldiers would have a length of rope attached to their person when going into battle. On the free end of this rope, which was usually about ten feet in length, was tied a wooden spike, and if the warrior was forced into a defensive position he was expected to drive the spike into the ground and make a last stand within the area which the dog rope permitted—a circle of some twenty feet in diameter. When old age or wounds incapacitated a warrior who possessed such a rope, it was quite permissible for him to sell it to the highest bidder. The dog dance—a war dance of the Cheyenne—was performed by dog soldiers. (See CHEYENNE INDIANS.)

DOLAN, JAMES J.   Active participant in New Mexico's Lincoln County War. Dolan,[39] who was born in Ireland on May 22, 1848, at Loughrea, County Galway, entered the United States

---

[36] Named after Colonel Richard I. Dodge, commander of the nearby garrison.

[37] Some of the better-known saloons were the Green Front Saloon, Junction Saloon, Opera House Saloon, Alhambra Saloon, Long Branch Saloon, and Old Horse Saloon.

[38] A term that originated in Dodge City. When train crews of the Santa Fe visited the brothels they were in the habit of leaving their red lanterns outside the doorways of these places so that their whereabouts would be known, should any emergency arise; hence the term "red-light house," which later expanded into "red-light district."

[39] Dolan's name is sometimes given as John J. Dolan or John G. Dolan.

around 1866. Shortly after his arrival he joined the Army, and he served in the 37th U. S. Infantry until he was discharged in 1869. After leaving the forces he moved down into New Mexico, and here he became friendly with a compatriot named Lawrence G. Murphy, a gentleman who owned a trading post that was located on the military reservation at Fort Stanton. Dolan was employed by Murphy, and he worked at the post until May 1873, at which time the military authorities withdrew their concession after Dolan had taken a shot at one of the officers from the fort. Even so, the two Irishmen remained friends, and they moved from the reservation and opened separate stores in Lincoln, Dolan's being a large wooden structure that dealt in general merchandise. Around 1876-77 Dolan was hand in glove with Billy the Kid, inasmuch as Dolan was buying cattle from the Kid that he knew to have been stolen from the Chisum herds, but in 1878 Dolan rode with the posse that murdered J. H. Tunstall—a friend of the Kid's—and from that time on he and the Kid were on opposite sides of the fence. In 1879 Dolan was arrested for the murder of Huston Chapman, a Las Vegas lawyer who had been visiting in Lincoln, but although it is quite likely that he committed the offense, at his trial he won an acquittal. Dolan came through the Lincoln County fracas unscathed, and he died at Lincoln on February 26, 1898. (See LINCOLN COUNTY WAR; McCARTY, HENRY; MURPHY, LAWRENCE G.; and TUNSTALL, JOHN HENRY.)

DOLAN, JOHN A gentleman of low repute who was hanged by the Montana vigilantes at Virginia City on the night of September 17, 1864. The crime for which Dolan[40] was handed his "suspended sentence" was pretty small beer: the stealing of seven hundred dollars in gold from a friend with whom he had been lodging. The vigilantes, however, suspected him of far darker deeds, and as his friends were of the lower social orders (one of the same had been hanged some two months earlier), he was obviously executed as an example. (See KELLEY, JEM, and VIGILANTES OF MONTANA.)

DONAHUE, CORNELIUS
Cornelius was born at Philadelphia, Pennsylvania, in 1850, and he graduated from college there, but in his late teens, and after reading many dime novels featuring life on the plains, he moved to Texas and became an itinerant ranchhand. Pay was poor, so Donahue, who had a congenital deformity of the left foot that resulted in his being nicknamed "Lame Johnny,"[41] went in for horse stealing. He was never arrested for these early criminal activities, but by 1875 his statistics began to appear on "Wanted" posters throughout the Lone Star State, and in the spring of 1876 Donahue traveled North to Dakota Territory and settled at Deadwood. Donahue became well liked in the mining camp, and the year following his arrival he served as a deputy sheriff. This appointment must have firmly established his reputation, for when he turned in his badge, the Homestead Mining Company took him on as their bookkeeper. He may have prospered in this job without, let it be said, any manipulation of the books, but in the early days of 1878 he was recognized

40 Also known as John Coyle and "Hard Hat."
41 Lame Johnny Creek in the Black Hills is named after Mr. Donahue. The "Johnny" half of the nickname probably stems from the fact that Donahue used the alias of John A. Hurley after leaving Texas.

by a Texan who arrived in Deadwood, and when this bigmouth spread the word around, Donahue soon found himself both ostracized and unemployed. Realizing that honest employment was now a thing of the past, Lame Johnny went back to horse stealing, and within a matter of weeks the stock of hay burners at the Pine Ridge Indian Reservation began to dwindle at an alarming rate. Around this time Donahue was also suspected of a stage robbery, but when he was arrested by Captain Frank Smith (a livestock detective) at Pine Ridge in October 1878, it was for horse theft and nothing more. After the arrest Smith and his captive climbed aboard a Deadwood-bound stage, but midway between the reservation and the mining camp a masked man halted the coach and succeeded in spiriting Smith's captive away into the brush. A last-minute rescue? No, folks; the following day Cornelius "Lame Johnny" Donahue was found dangling from a tree. The how come, by whom, and what for of this lynching have never been satisfactorily established.

DONKEY
Usually referred to as a "burro" in the West. (See BURRO.)

DONNER PARTY The bearded man shielding his eyes from the last rays of the setting sun is flanked by a woman who holds an infant to her breast and by a small girl who crouches against his left leg; they are dressed in the manner of pioneers, and they have been imprisoned in the Sierra Nevada for more than half a century: a quartet in bronze who are anchored to a stone pedestal on which a plaque bearing the legend, VIRILE TO RISK AND FIND; KINDLY WITHAL AND READY TO HELP; FACING THE BRUNT OF FATE; INDOMITABLE UNAFRAID. There are no names on the plaque, but this is the Donner Monument,[42] a monument to the death of a wagon train.

The canvas of the wagons had once been ochre, but now, after five hundred miles of sun-scorched plains travel, it was bleached to the whiteness of bone. Since this California-bound wagon train had left Independence, Missouri, in May 1846, numerous landmarks had been raised—Chimney Rock, Scott's Bluff, Courthouse Rock, Red Buttes, and Independence Rock—and then fallen behind, and now, in July, the sixty or so wagons housing some three hundred souls were camped on the Little Sandy in southwestern Wyoming, and plans were being made for the remainder of the journey. Here the Donner and Reed[43] families proposed that the train would make better time by taking the Hastings cutoff, it having been agreed that Landsford Hastings would meet them at Fort Bridger to guide them over the route that bore his name. Experienced mountain men argued against this, and the majority of the pioneers decided to take the more usual route via Fort Hall in Idaho, rather than risk a comparatively little-used trail that crossed the Utah salt flats. George Donner was voted wagonmaster of the Hastings cutoff contingent, and he led twenty wagons and eighty-six pioneers southwest toward Fort Bridger. At Bridger it was learned that Hastings had left to guide an earlier party, and there was a

[42] Designed by sculptor John McQuarrie and unveiled in 1918. Three members of the Donner party—Patty Reed, Eliza Donner, and Frances Donner—were present at the unveiling ceremony.
[43] The Donner family was comprised of George and his wife Tamsen; their five children (Eliza, Frances, Elitha, Leanna, and Georgia); George's brother Jacob; the Reeds; James Frazier; his wife, Margaret; and their four children.

week of indecisive delay before it was decided to hire a Bridger guide named Juan Baptiste to pilot them around the southern end of the Great Salt Lake. A few days later at Weber Canyon a note was found blazed to a tree—a warning left by Hastings: The canyon was blocked by storm debris, and they would have to cross the Wasatch Mountains to reach the salt flats. Baptiste refused to accept responsibility from then on, but the train managed to get across the mountains intact, and on September 2 they were pushing out onto the dazzling white alkali flats. According to Hastings, crossing this parched area should have taken forty-eight hours. It didn't. It took almost a week, and before the flats were behind them, three wagons had been abandoned and more than a hundred cattle and oxen had been lost; and, even worse, food was running short. Paiutes began to run off stock, and their raids made it unsafe to venture far from the wagons. Hunting deer meat had to be abandoned, and on September 18 two men, Charles Stanton and William McCutchen, volunteered to push ahead on fast horses and try to reach Sutter's Fort in California; if they made it, they would attempt the return journey with provisions; if not . . . The two men rode off and the wagons continued their sluggish journey toward the distant Sierras, and somewhere over this lap of the trek four horsemen joined the Donner party—an apocalyptic trail crew that rode herd on the wagons as they swayed along to their appointment in Samarra. An old-timer named Hardcoop was struck down by illness, and he was left to die by the trail; a man named Wolfinger was murdered by persons unknown;[44] James Reed lit out for Sutter's Fort after he had been banished from the company for knifing a man to death,

and by the time the wagons circled in Truckee Meadows on October 18, tempers were stretched to the danger point, and stomachs were flat from hunger. On the nineteenth Stanton returned. He was accompanied by two of Captain Sutter's Indian guides and, far more important, they were leading a provision-laden mule train. The party tarried at Truckee Meadows, and as stomachs were filled and bodies rested, tempers became eased, but on the fifth day of their idleness ominous signs in the west forced the party into action: Leaden skies hung over the jagged barrier in their path, a gray mountain range that began to whiten as the oxen were being yoked. The prairie schooners snaked out of the meadows, a long, broken-boned finger pointing toward their last bulwark: the Sierra Nevada. Slowly the wagons ground upward until the snow was boottop high. At Alder Creek, George Donner's wagon lurched to a halt with a broken axle, and the remaining fifteen wagons skirted the immobilized Donners and pushed on until they reached what is now Donner Lake, and where there was a collection of abandoned cabins that had been built by earlier migrants. Here they waited for the Donners, and when they failed to arrive, Stanton returned to Alder Creek. George Donner and his brother Jacob were bedridden, and Mrs. Tamsen Donner was feeding them and her five children on strips of cowhide. Even so, Tamsen couldn't be persuaded to leave her husband, and Stanton returned to the lake. Blizzards bansheed down from the peaks, and by the end of November all the remaining oxen and cattle had been lost and the snowdrifts were over twenty feet deep. A man named Bayliss died of starvation, and panic began to spread in the camp. Improvised snowshoes were made

[44] Unknown at the time; before he died at Donner Lake a man named Joseph Rhinehard confessed to the crime.

and a party of fifteen, which included five women and had Stanton and the two Indian guides in the lead, set out for Sutter's Fort to bring help. Apart from Stanton this was a sorry party, and when he developed snow blindness he was left to freeze to death. The next to die were butchered and eaten, and when this obscene food ran out the Indians were murdered and stripped of as much of their flesh as the remainder could carry. In the middle of January what was left of this party—two men and five women—staggered into Sutter's Fort, and a short time later a rescue party of seven volunteers was heading out for Donner Lake. These seven reached the starving camp on February 19 to find that many more of the party had perished and that the survivors were eating soggy strips of meat from pots of unmentionable remains. Twenty-three[45] of these famished ghosts decided they were strong enough to be led out of that Sierra deathtrap, while the remainder, who were too weak to walk, huddled around their stoves and waited for a larger relief force, which was expected at any moment. The moments dragged on into days. Men, women, and children died, and the stewpots bubbled until early in March, when a large rescue party headed by James Reed (he who had been banished) managed to fight their way through the last of the winter storms. For most of the human skeletons at Donner Lake, this meant survival. But not for all; George and Jacob Donner died at Alder Creek while the rescue party was at the lake. Tamsen died the day after her husband, making sure that her five children would be taken out of the mountains when April thaws made the journey less dangerous before sinking into a sleep from which she never awoke. Of the

eighty-six people who followed George Donner, thirty-six perished, fourteen of whom were young children.

In 1927 a fifty-year-old man named Charles E. Davis suddenly gave up his job and devoted the next two years of his life to staking out every single mile of the Donner Party route. Davis seemed to possess an uncanny instinct as to where relics or traces of the party could be found, for during his self-imposed task he unearthed the graves of John Snyder (James Reed's victim) and those of two men named Hargrove and Halloran; the remains of five wagons; the skeletons of dozens of oxen; campfire sites that had been long since buried, and numerous household articles.

The last living survivor of this ill-fated wagon train, Isabella Breen, died in 1935.

D O O L I N , B I L L Arkansas-born cowhand who, prior to his becoming an outlaw, worked on the XL Ranch in Wyoming and later for the HX (Halsell) Ranch on the Cimarron River in Oklahoma. Bill got his first taste of easy money after joining the Dalton gang around 1891, and after the Coffeyville disaster in the fall of 1892, he formed his own gang. In the early months of 1894 Doolin got married (to a minister's daughter), and some twelve months later the gang split up for good.[46] At this time Doolin had a price of five thousand dollars on his head, and a short time later he was arrested by U. S. Marshal Bill Tilghman; the arrest took place in a bathhouse at Eureka Springs, Arkansas, and Doolin was transported to the Guthrie, Oklahoma, jail to await trial. The trial never took place, for Bill escaped in a mass breakout and fled to New Mexico, where, for a short time, he was given food and

---

[45] Some of whom died before reaching Sutter's Fort.
[46] No evidence points to the preacher's daughter having had anything to do with the breaking up of the gang; more's the pity.

shelter at the home of novelist Eugene Manlove Rhodes. Sometime in 1896 Doolin rejoined his wife, and they settled in a small house near Lawton, Oklahoma. The Doolins now had a young son, and Bill, who had been suffering from consumption for at least two years, may have decided to settle down, but in the middle of July, U. S. Marshal Heck Thomas thundered on the door of their homestead. Mrs. Doolin answered the door, and after exchanging a few words with her, the marshal pushed past her and went into the house. Seconds later a shotgun roared, and the following day the shot-riddled and emaciated body of Doolin was identified; headlines proclaimed that Thomas had shot him in a gunfight, and the marshal collected the five-thousand-dollar reward. Many years later the truth about the "gunfight" was finally established. Doolin was dead from consumption when Thomas entered the house, and the marshal knew this, for Doolin's widow had told him as much at the front door, but on entering the house Heck Thomas had made one of the quickest decisions of his life: With Doolin dead from natural causes there was no hope of a reward, so the marshal fired both barrels of his shotgun into the corpse. Callous? No, magnificent; for Heck Thomas finally persuaded[47] Mrs. Doolin to accept the five thousand dollars that he had intended her to have when he pulled the triggers of his scattergun. (See COFFEYVILLE, KANSAS; DALTON GANG; and DOOLIN GANG.)

DOOLIN GANG Organized by Bill Doolin in the fall of 1892. The gang consisted of Bill and nine others: "Bitter Creek" George Newcomb, Charley

Pierce, "Tulsa Jack" Blake, Oliver "Crescent Sam" Yountis, Richard "Little Dick" West, Roy Daugherty (who was better known as "Arkansas Tom"), Dan Clifton, George "Red Buck" Waightman and William (Bill) Dalton. In November 1892 the newly formed gang left their favorite mustering place—the small town of Ingalls in Oklahoma Territory—and rode north into Kansas, where they held up a Pacific express at Caney without suffering any casualties. Shortly afterward, in the spring of 1893, a bank at Spearville, Oklahoma, was looted, and a few days later the strength of the gang was reduced by one: Yountis was tracked down by lawmen at his home near Orlando, Oklahoma, and he was shot dead while resisting arrest by U. S. Marshal Chris Madson before he'd had time to spend any of his $4,500 share of the loot. During that summer the gang looted a Santa Fe express near Cimarron, Oklahoma, and pulled a double train holdup at Wharton in the Cherokee Strip. On September 1 thirteen U.S. deputy marshals traced the gang to Ingalls, and after one of the fiercest gun battles in the West, three of the marshals lay dead and Arkansas Tom had been arrested. Rewards ranging from $250 to $5,000 increased the pressure on the gang, and harried by marshals, the outlaws were forced to extend their area of operations. In 1894 a sheriff was killed during a raid at Canadian, Texas; Bill Dalton killed a state auditor named J. G. Seaborn when the gang looted a bank at Southwest City, Missouri; and a Pawnee, Oklahoma, bank was relieved of $10,000. In May 1895 the eight remaining members of the gang held up a Rock Island train at Dover, Oklahoma, after which Red Buck

[47] There has never been any hint of collusion between Mrs. Doolin and the marshal. Thomas had always had a certain amount of respect for Bill Doolin, and Thomas evidently didn't wish to see Doolin's widow destitute.

was banished from the band for doing a spot of promiscuous shooting during the getaway,[48] and Tulsa Jack was shot dead by pursuing officers. A few weeks after this reduction of their ranks, Doolin and his five remaining gunnies held up an express office at Woodward, Oklahoma, and escaped with nearly $7,000. The Doolin gang was now almost a thing of the past, and after Newcomb and Pierce had been mustered from its ranks—by accurate gunfire of a fatal nature—in July, the gang ceased to exist.[49] The fates of the four surviving members are dealt with elsewhere in this volume. (See CLIFTON, DAN; DALTON, WILLIAM; DAUGHERTY, ROY; DOOLIN, BILL; INGALLS, OKLAHOMA; NEWCOMB, GEORGE; PIERCE, CHARLEY; WAIGHTMAN, GEORGE; and WEST, RICHARD.)

DOUBLE CINCH A double band—usually one of horsehair and one of webbing—that is used to hold a double-rigged saddle in position.

DOWD, DANIEL Arizona stage robber and suspected rustler who took part in the infamous Bisbee Massacre of December 8, 1883. After this crime Dowd fled south of the border and holed up at Corralitas, a village in Chihuahua. The Arizona authorities had not overlooked this possibility, and "Wanted" notices printed in Spanish were circulated to all the Mexican border towns. They offered a fifteen-hundred-dollar reward for Dowd, and it was not long before his whereabouts were relayed to Deputy Sheriff Bill Daniels of Cochise County, Arizona. Daniels entered Mexico as a civilian in January 1884, and he succeeded in capturing Dowd that same month: He buffaloed the fugitive outside a *cantina* one night and spirited him back into Arizona to stand trial. (See HEATH, JOHN.)

DOWNING, BILL Reputed to be the alias of a gunman named Frank Jackson. (See JACKSON, FRANK.)

DRAG The tail end of a cattle herd that is being kept on the move.

DRAGOONS Originally infantrymen who were armed with muskets called dragons. Later the term came to be applied to mounted infantry, a definition that is apt when referring to the United States Dragoons of the last century. The American Dragoon regiments were organized in 1833, and they protected the trade routes and migrant trails against Indian attacks until 1861, in which year they were disbanded and the cavalry regiments took over their duties. Recruitment for the Dragoons was on a "foreign legion" basis, inasmuch as British, French, and German soldiers of fortune were admitted into the ranks without any embarrassing questions being asked. Uniforms were elaborate; short navy tunics with a row of brass buttons, sky blue trousers with yellow braided outer seams, leather shako with eagle badge,[50]

---

[48] An odd action admittedly. One can only assume that Doolin—who had married a minister's daughter a year previous to this event—may have been trying to improve his public image around this time for his wife's sake.

[49] The United States deputy marshals obviously *forced* them out of business. They did not disband *voluntarily* to take up peaceful pursuits as most reports—of a hero-worshiping nature, let it be noted—would have us believe. The only heroes in the above narrative were the underpaid lawmen of the period.

[50] This type of hat was probably issued in the 1840s. Catlin's drawings, which were made in the 1830s, depict the 1st Regiment of U. S. Dragoons wearing cocked hats, while at a later date (circa 1850), Charles Wimar was portraying Dragoons wearing brass helmets.

and white canvas webbing shoulder straps to take the weight of a musket and saber. Early armament consisted of flintlocks—a pistol and a musket—and a cavalry saber, but by the late 1840s breechloading carbines and Colt's Dragoon pistols were in use. There were few forts[51] in the area these troops patrolled, and more often than not they had to sleep rough, so the men were allowed to wear buckskins or almost anything they fancied when in the field.[52] (See COLT FIREARMS, subheading *Dragoon*.)

DRUMMER   A traveling salesman. The men who fanned out from the East and the Middle West with the mail order catalogues and the samples. John W. Gates was probably the most successful of these men; he sold barbed wire, while lesser men took orders for firearms, ladies' underwear, saddles, whiskey, and farming equipment. Somewhat lower in the scale were the foot-in-the-door types who hawked such dubious merchandise as patent remedies, mustache wax, unbranded liquor, enameled metal collars, paper ties, prize packages,[53] and lightning rods.

DRY GOODS   A term that embraces such merchandise as silks, linens, etc., and articles manufactured from such materials. A store selling such merchandise.

DRYGULCH   To assassinate a person from ambush.

DUCK'S FOOT PISTOL
A multibarreled pistol. (See MOB PISTOL.)

DUDE   Derives from the German *dudenkop*, which literally means "a lazy fellow." The anglicized contraction is used to denote an affected or foppish person, and, by association (as such a person is deemed unlikely to be skilled or experienced), a tenderfoot. The latter word is almost synonymous with "dude" in the western states.

DUGGAN, MART   A ten-minute egg who was appointed city marshal of Leadville, Colorado, in 1877 after the City Fathers had studied reports regarding his reputation: seven killings behind him, a mean disposition, a bullying nature, and a complete absence of fear; in other words, just the man for cleaning up a tough mining town. Duggan harassed the holy as well as the godless, yet as he rarely caused grievous bodily harm to the goodies, and he frequently *rigor mortised* the baddies, he was tolerated, and he retained his badge for eleven years. He may have retained it for another eleven years, but in 1888 he picked a fight with a gambler in a local den of vice, and his tenure of office expired in a fog of gunsmoke as said gambler shot Mart Duggan[54] dead.

DUGGAN, SANDFORD S. C.   Born in Fayette County, Pennsylvania, in

All these may only have been worn on ceremonial occasions, for there are numerous instances relating to active service in which the troops are known to have worn flat-topped peaked caps.

[51] Most of the military posts west of the Mississippi were built after the Dragoons had been disbanded.

[52] As an additional privilege, hair could be worn to shoulder length.

[53] "Prize packages" contained stationery, recipes, Paris fashion plates, a calendar, amusement and how-to-get-rich guides, needlework hints, and miscellaneous "padding" of a similar nature; they retailed at twenty-five cents, a price that showed the salesman a 200 per cent profit.

[54] Of all the marshals and miscellaneous lawmen this writer has come across, Duggan is the only one to have anything in common with that well-known television gunslinger, Matt Dillon. Their names have the same number of letters and their initials are the same.

1845. Duggan moved West in his mid-teens, a transient delinquent who established his whereabouts loud and clear by shooting a man named Curtis to death in a Black Hawk, Colorado, saloon. This was not a shootout but a cold-blooded killing, and Duggan found it advisable to flee the camp. A short time later he was settled in Denver and living with a young free-lance prostitute named Kittie Wells. Kittie provided Duggan with shelter, food, and money, and no doubt offerings of a more personal nature, in return for which he provided her with a few bumps to keep her in line. One night Duggan pistol-whipped Kittie almost to death. Crimes against women, whatever their profession, were regarded as downright disgusting out West, but luckily for Duggan, he was arrested by City Marshal Dave Cook and lodged in the local jail before a lynch mob could be formed that would have dealt with him in a more appropriate manner. The womanbeater's luck held, and when he appeared before Judge Orson Brooks the following day, he was freed on a technicality. Duggan didn't push his luck; knowing the verdict was unpopular with the miners, he fled Denver and rode East, not looking back until he reached Laramie City, an end-of-track town on the Union Pacific right-of-way. Duggan—or at least his immediate past—was unknown here, and he managed to get himself appointed city marshal. Sometime later a traveler who was acquainted with both Duggan and the Kittie episode arrived in Laramie City, a quirk of fate that resulted in the marshal being stripped of his badge and given twenty-four hours to "git outa town." In the fall of 1868 Duggan—most unwisely—returned to Denver, where he

immediately engaged in a series of nocturnal adventures of a stand-and-deliver nature. Reports streamed into the marshal's office, and within hours Dave Cook was hot on Duggan's trail, finally capturing him at Golden, a camp some eighteen miles from Denver. Cook returned safely to Denver with his prisoner, but a few days later, and while Duggan was being moved between jails, his escort was overpowered by a mob, and within a few minutes Sandford S. C. Duggan[55] was dangling lifeless from a cottonwood tree. (See FRANKLIN, EDWARD.)

DUGOUT Any type of building that is erected in an excavation so that little more than its roof is exposed above ground level.[56] Quite a few of the plains towns were originally dugout communities, the business premises of which had their signs—GROCERIES, SALOON, POST OFFICE, etc.—fastened to their roofs.

DULL KNIFE A chief of the northern Cheyenne who was active in the Bozeman Trail wars of the 1860s and the climactic North Plains Indian–U. S. Army engagements of the 1870s. In the spring of 1877 Dull Knife surrendered to General McKenzie, and in August of that same year the chief and his small band were escorted to the Darlington Reservation in Oklahoma. The sterile dust-land of the reservation was no place to live, and in September 1878 Dull Knife and a chief named Little Wolf, with some three hundred followers (two thirds of whom were women and children), left the reservation and headed for their homelands in Montana. After numerous engagements with the military, the two chiefs

---

[55] Whether Sandford had any blood relationship with Mart Duggan cannot be ascertained, but that they had geographical links and that Dave Cook knew both these men is an established fact.

[56] An antitornado precaution that was far from wasted on the Great Plains.

parted company a few miles north of Ogallala, Nebraska, and Dull Knife and about 150 Cheyenne headed for the sandhills in the northwestern corner of the state. Blizzards raged in the desolation of the sandhills, and Dull Knife and his band were little more than starving scarecrows when a "heroic" battery of artillery, which had been supported by the 3rd U. S. Cavalry, lobbed shells into their ranks and forced them to surrender. The survivors were taken to Fort Robinson and locked in a disused barracks, and here they remained, on meager rations, until January 5, 1879. On that day the commanding officer of the post stopped their rations completely,[57] and after four days without food the Indians broke out of their prison and staggered out into the snow. Homicidal maniacs in blue uniforms gave chase, and within a short time fifty Cheyenne—mostly women and children—had been bludgeoned or shot to death and their bodies left to freeze into grotesque poses in the snow. Dull Knife was not among the dead, and on the fifth of February he and a few survivors arrived at Pine Ridge Reservation and surrendered. The white men were calm now. Saner minds had taken over since that infamous day at Fort Robinson; there was no more talk of sending Dull Knife back to Oklahoma, and he and his handful of survivors were allowed to remain at Pine Ridge. Dull Knife died here in 1883. (See LITTLE WOLF.)

DUMONT, ELEANOR The alias of a professional gambler named Simone Jules. (See JULES, SIMONE.)

DUNN, ROSA Rosa, sometimes given as Rose, was fourteen years old and was living in Ingalls, Oklahoma, with her mother and stepfather in 1893, a year in which allegations concerning her association with outlaws got her a brief and unwanted position in the spotlight. None of these allegations can be proved or disproved, although it is an established fact that Rosa had met Bill Doolin and some of his gang at her brother's ranch on the Cimarron. From these brief encounters with baddies the stories have blossomed, and now, at first glance, this lass with a convent school education appears to have been little more than a juvenile delinquent of the "Gay Nineties." Rosa is variously reported as having been the girlfriend, mistress, or wife of "Bitter Creek" George Newcomb, and when this outlaw was wounded by marshals during the Battle of Ingalls on September 1, 1893, Rosa is supposed to have dashed to the fallen man's side with a rifle and ammunition and to have shielded him with her body until others of the gang could rescue him. United States Deputy Marshals Bill Tilghman and Chris Madson believed this story; Doolin and company said little; many said another filly had the feminine lead that day, while others state that no girl was active in the battle. Anyway, to get back to Rosa: This gun girl or much-maligned miss married a blacksmith named Charles Noble in 1897, and when he died a few years later, she remarried and settled in Washington, D.C. Little more was heard of Rosa, but she is known to have died in Washington in March 1956. (See INGALLS, OKLAHOMA; NEWCOMB, GEORGE; and ROSE OF CIMARRON.)

DUST BOWL An unnatural geographical feature that has been brought about by the plowing up of grassland in a region subject to high winds and little rainfall. Once the protective covering of grass has been removed, winds whip away the dry topsoil until only a barren

---

[57] This was done in a stupid attempt to "persuade" the Cheyenne to return to the Darlington Agency. Captain H. W. Wessells was the post commander at Robinson over this period.

wilderness remains. Dust bowls were inadvertently produced in Kansas, Colorado, Texas, and Oklahoma.

DUTCH HENRY One of the better-known horse thieves. (See BORNE, HENRY.)

DUTCH JOHN A victim of vigilante justice whose real name was John Wagner. (See WAGNER, JOHN.)

DYNAMITE DICK Alias of a member of the Doolin gang. (See CLIFTON, DAN, and DOOLIN GANG.)

THOMAS E. MAILS

E AGLE A large bird of prey whose feather-clad head distinguishes it from the bare-headed vultures. If we ignore kites, hawks, buzzards, etc., all of which may be described as "eagles," there are two species of true eagle that inhabit the North American continent: the golden eagle and the bald eagle. Both of these birds are sea eagles and have a wingspan of about 7½ feet. The bald[1] eagle is the national emblem of the United States, a choice of symbol that may be regarded as somewhat of a gaff, for whenever possible the bald eagle will bully smaller birds into giving up their piscatorial prey, while on other occasions it will resort to searching the littoral for any carrion that may have been washed ashore.

E ARMARKS Mutilations made on the ears of cattle for identification purposes. The marks are usually made with a knife. (See BRANDING.)

E ARP, JAMES Born in Hartford, Kentucky, in 1841, the eldest son of Nicholas and Virginia Earp. James joined the Union forces at the outbreak of the Civil War and was invalided out in 1863 after being severely wounded at Frederickstown, Missouri. This wound prevented him from ever becoming dextrous with a gun, and although he was closely associated with his brothers Wyatt, Morgan, and Virgil for the major part of his lifetime, he was never actively engaged in any of their spectacular exploits. James died in San Francisco in 1926. (See EARP, NICHOLAS PORTER, and EARP, WYATT BERRY STAPP.)

E ARP, MORGAN One of the gun-fighting members of the Earp family. Morgan, who was born at Pella, Iowa, in 1851, served as a deputy town marshal at Dodge City, Kansas, in 1876, and as a deputy sheriff headquartered at Dodge the following year. A short time later,

---

[1] The name is rather a misnomer, for the bald eagle is far from needing a toupee, its head having a thick covering of white feathers.

while serving as town marshal at Butte, Montana, Morg killed a hard case named Billy Brooks. In January 1880 he moved down into the Southwest and joined his brothers Wyatt, Virgil, and James in the nine-months-old mining camp of Tombstone. Here Morg got a job riding shotgun on the Wells Fargo coaches, a job that lasted until he was wounded in the shoulder at the O. K. Corral showdown. Late on the Friday night of March 17, 1882, Morg was playing a game of pool in Bob Hatch's billiards saloon on Allen Street when the windows of the doorframe exploded inward before a hail of flying lead; Morg's back was the target, and he dropped to the floor dying.[2] Wyatt, who happened to be present, carried his brother into Hatch's office and lay him on a sofa. A doctor was called but he was of little use, and after remaining conscious for a little over half an hour after being shot, Morg died during the first few minutes of Saturday morning; a .45 slug had shattered his spine. (See BENSON STAGE MURDERS; BROOKS, WILLIAM; CRUZ, FLORENTINE; EARP, NICHOLAS PORTER; EARP, WYATT BERRY STAPP; and O. K. CORRAL.)

EARP, NICHOLAS PORTER Born in 1813 at Wheeling, West Virginia, of parents of Scottish ancestry. In his middle twenties Nicholas was settled in Hartford, Kentucky, and there he married his first wife, a young girl who died shortly after bearing him a child, whom they christened Newton. In 1840 Nicholas married for a second time, the bride being a seventeen-year-old girl of English extraction named Virginia Anne Cooksey, who gave him seven children: James (1841), Virgil (1843), Martha (1845), Wyatt Berry Stapp (1848), Morgan (1851), Warren (1855), and Adelia

(1861). The newlyweds bought a plantation near Hartford, and Nicholas practiced as a lawyer in the town until 1843, at which time they sold their land and moved west to Monmouth, Illinois, where they purchased a farm and Nicholas served as a deputy sheriff until he joined the U. S. Army to fight in the Mexican War of 1846–48. In 1847 Nicholas was invalided out of the service. Three years later he sold the farm, pulled up stakes, and moved his family—the couple now had four children—to Pella, Iowa; Nicholas obviously had a psychological form of athlete's foot. The family remained here for fourteen years, but they moved West again in 1864 after Nicholas had been discharged from the Union Army, in which he had held the rank of captain while serving as provost marshal for Marion County, Iowa. This was their last big move, a wagon train epic that ended on December 19 at San Bernardino, California. Six days later the Earps were settled on a ranch they had bought on their arrival, and Nicholas began dreaming of buying further acreage. These dreams he put into practice, and years later he owned much of the land on which the town was built. The latter years of his life were spent as a magistrate on the county bench, and he died here at Colton, California, in 1907. (See EARP, JAMES; EARP, MORGAN; EARP, WARREN; and EARP, WYATT BERRY STAPP.)

EARP, VIRGIL Born in Hartford, Kentucky, in 1843. At the outbreak of the Civil War Virgil joined the Union forces, and he served with an Illinois regiment until the early months of 1865. In 1877, after spending a short time as deputy town marshal at Dodge City, Kansas, he moved to Prescott, Arizona,

[2] Morgan wasn't the only casualty; an innocent bystander named George Berry died from shock when a stray bullet struck him in the leg.

where he became part owner of a silver mine, and it was his glowing reports of mining possibilities that brought Wyatt, Morgan, and James into the territory during the winter of 1880–81. The four brothers settled in Tombstone, and after the death of the town marshal, Fred White, in 1881, Virgil was appointed temporary marshal. On December 28, 1881, and some three months after being wounded at the O. K. Corral, five shotguns roared on Allen Street, and Virgil fell to the ground riddled with buckshot.[3] He survived this fusilade, but he was crippled for life, and a short time after he left Tombstone. Virgil died of pneumonia at Goldfield, Nevada, in 1906. (See BENSON STAGE MURDERS; EARP, NICHOLAS PORTER; EARP, WYATT BERRY STAPP; and O. K. CORRAL.)

EARP, WARREN The youngest son of Nicholas and Virginia Earp, and as such he has been overshadowed by the derring-do of his older brothers. Warren, who was born at Pella, Iowa, in 1855, spent most of his early adulthood with his parents in California. In 1881, after the O. K. Corral gunfight, he arrived in Tombstone, where for a short spell he served as a deputy U.S. marshal while helping Wyatt track down the killers of Morgan. The Earps left Tombstone in 1882, and Warren didn't return to Arizona until 1900, when he became a cattle detective for the territory's Cattlemen's Association. A short time later, and while employed in this capacity, Warren was shot dead by two rustlers. (See EARP, NICHOLAS PORTER, and EARP, WYATT BERRY STAPP.)

EARP, WYATT BERRY STAPP The member of the Earp family with the

charmed life and the fastest gunhand; a one-man spectacular who became a legend before he reached his prime; and a man who has now been reduced to television corn, and who has become the butt of any hack who wishes to reduce such an outstanding figure to the writer's own sorry level. Wyatt, who was born at Monmouth, Illinois, on March 19, 1848, got his first taste of the West in 1864 when his family moved to California by wagon train. During this trip, and near Fort Laramie, the party had two encounters with hostile Sioux, and later while the wagons were being provisioned at Bridger's Fort, Wyatt, who hunted meat for the outfit, went on a few shooting and fishing expeditions with old Jim Bridger.

On arrival in California Wyatt became a driver for the Banning Stage Line, and later he worked for a freight company that operated between San Bernardino and Salt Lake City, Utah. By 1868 Wyatt had teams of his own and was doing subcontract work for Charles Chrisman, who was hauling freight for the Union Pacific's construction crews. At the expiration of this contract, young Earp returned to his birthplace, and in January 1870 he married a local girl named Willa Sutherland. A few months later Willa died in a typhus epidemic and Earp moved to Lamarr, Missouri, where for the next twelve months he did a stint as town marshal.

Over the years 1871–73 Wyatt's main income was to come from buffalo hunting, and it was over this period that he first met such characters as Wild Bill Hickok, Billy Dixon, Kirk Jordan, Bat Masterson, etc. In April 1875 Earp was appointed deputy marshal at Wichita, Kansas. While behind a badge at Wichita,

[3] The assassination attempt took place at midnight; the five shotgun wielders fired from the shelter of a partially erected building on Allen Street, and Virgil dropped to the ground outside the Eagle Brewery Saloon.

Earp had brushes with Mannen Clements and John Wesley Hardin; closed "Rowdy" Joe Lowe's den of iniquity—sometimes referred to as a "dance hall"; and pistol whipped the notorious Sergeant King into submission when that gentleman resisted arrest. When his year of office expired, Wyatt moved on to Dodge City, where he had been offered the job of assistant marshal, and in May 1876 he was deputized by the city marshal, Larry Deger.

Although Deger was the marshal, he was merely a political figurehead, and Wyatt had full authority when it came to hiring deputies, running the town, and sharing out the "kitty"—a bonus of $2.50, which was awarded to the marshal's office for each arrest. During this term—Wyatt's first as a lawman at Dodge —he chose brothers Morgan and Virgil, Bat and Jim Masterson, Joe Mason, and, for a short spell, Neal Brown as deputies to back up his play. Loaded shotguns were cached at trouble spots (saloons, etc.) and Wyatt established a "deadline" (this was literally the railroad tracks that bisected Dodge); as long as troublemakers kept their "hurrahing" and mayhem to the south side of these tracks, they had little to fear from the lawmen, but if they carried their shoulder chips and their hardware into the northern section, they could expect to be buffaloed and tossed into the cooler. Sometime during the height of the cattle season a writer named Ned Buntline visited the marshal's office in search of material for his dime novels, and he was so impressed by the lawmen of Dodge that he presented Wyatt and two of his deputies with custom-made Colt's Specials before hurrying back East. (Ned gave similar guns to two members of the Ford County sheriff's office, also located in Dodge.)

In the fall of 1876 Wyatt turned in his badge and headed for Deadwood in Dakota Territory with the intention of trying his hand at prospecting, but when he arrived, most of the likely spots had been staked, so he freighted firewood and had a short stint at riding shotgun for Wells Fargo before pulling out for Texas, where he hired out as a cattle detective. At Fort Griffin, while on the trail of Dave Rudabaugh, he became acquainted with Doc Holliday, a consumptive gunfighter who from that time on was to throw in his lot with Earp whenever possible.

In April 1877 Ed Masterson was shot down and killed at Dodge, and Mayor Kelley wired Earp to come North and grab a badge. Wyatt did as requested, and he started his tour of duty as an assistant marshal under the city marshal, Charles Bassett (Deger's successor), in July 1877. Shortly after his arrival, Wyatt forced a psychopathic killer named Clay Allison to back down and leave Dodge without resorting to gunplay, and gave a visiting cattleman named Tobe Driskill a dose of buffaloing *cum* calaboose treatment, which eventually led to gunplay. Tobe, who had only wanted to shoot up the town, was a wealthy rancher, and after his belittling experience he let it be known that a thousand dollars was waiting for the man who ushered Earp into Boot Hill. An attempt was made at this reward on the night of July 26. Wyatt was standing outside the Comique Theater when a horseman thundered up and began to squeeze a few shots off in his direction. Three shots missed Earp and whined through the doorway of the theater—three shots that caused consternation among the audience and prompted comedian Eddie Foy to break off singing "Kalamazoo in Michigan" and throw himself down on the stage—and then the lawman brought his Buntline into play and the rider spilled to the dust. The gunman, who was later identified as George

Hoyt, died from his wounds on August 21. Others are reported to have tried for the jackpot, but as Wyatt remained unscathed and his guns accounted for no further bounty hunters, these stories, although possibly true, are difficult to substantiate.

In September 1878 a party of hostile Cheyenne passed close to Dodge, and many of the citizens rode out to "git theirsel's an Injun." Earp refused to join this "likker'd up posse," and during their absence Tobe Driskill and a gang of armed Texan riders "treed" the town and got the lone lawman bottled up outside the Long Branch Saloon. This could have been the end of Wyatt's saga, but Doc Holliday came through the batwings of the saloon with two .45s at the alert, and after he had winged one of the cowboys in the shoulder, Wyatt had merely to buffalo one of the ringleaders and the danger was past.

After the Dora Hand slaying in the fall of 1878, and the Levi Richardson– "Cockeyed" Frank Loving duel, which occurred in the spring of the following year, Dodge became a comparatively quiet town, and Wyatt had little more to do than gamble his time away. Boredom smothered him, and after reading glowing reports of the rich silver strikes being made in Arizona Territory, he handed in his badge and headed for the Southwest, with Tombstone as his objective. James Earp and his wife and daughter left Dodge with Wyatt, and at Prescott, Arizona, Virgil and his wife joined the party. At Tucson, Wyatt was appointed a deputy sheriff by Charles Shibell (an old acquaintance who at the time was the sheriff of Pima County, an area that embraced Tombstone), and a few days later, on December 1, 1879, the Earps

arrived at their destination, a rough-and-ready mining camp which, although only months old, was already the stamping ground of such hard cases as John Ringo, Curly Bill Brocius, and the Clantons. In January 1880 Morgan Earp and Doc Holliday rode into town, and from that time on there was constant friction between the outlaw element and the Earp-Holliday foursome.

The activities of Wyatt and his brothers over their Tombstone period are too numerous to itemize in the space of this entry, as are the incidents that led up to that thirty seconds of carnage that has gone down in western history as "The gunfight at the O. K. Corral," but details of major events and brief histories of some of the characters concerned can be found under separate headings (see end of this entry). Suffice to say that during this skulduggery Wyatt was living with a girl named Mattie;[4] dabbling in real estate; occasionally riding shotgun for Wells Fargo; and was in possession of a quarter interest in the Oriental Bar and Gambling Saloon.

The O. K. showdown didn't still the guns of the opposition; in December, Virgil was shot down and severely wounded, and Morgan was murdered the following March. Wyatt, who until this time had preferred to buffalo delinquents, only throwing lead as a last resort, now went on what lurid private-eye novelists would describe as "the kill." Frank Stilwell, who was known to have been implicated in Morgan's death, was the first of the killers to fall before Wyatt's guns, a shootout that occurred in the railroad yards at Tucson, and for which—on a murder warrant sworn out by Ike Clanton—Sheriff Behan attempted to arrest Earp on his return to Tomb-

[4] This is not to suggest that Wyatt hadn't married the girl; he most likely had, but no record of this marriage has yet been unearthed. The Tombstone "Epitaph" invariably referred to the couple as Mr. and Mrs. Wyatt Earp.

stone. Wyatt ignored Behan, and at the head of a posse rode off in search of the others who had had a hand in Morgan's death. A short time later Wyatt's Buntline sent Florentine Cruz (alias Indian Charlie) to the Happy Hunting Grounds, and William B. Graham (alias Curly Bill Brocius) got the full and fatal charge from Wyatt's shotgun when the posse caught up with him at Iron Springs. Sheriff Behan continued to wave his warrant, and in May 1882 Wyatt and Doc moved up into Colorado and invited Behan to set extradition proceedings in motion. Behan tried, but the governor of Colorado refused the Arizona request, said governor being under the impression that Behan, and what was left of the outlaw faction, merely wanted Earp back in Tombstone for purposes of revenge, to whit, the assassination of Wyatt. Warren joined Wyatt in Colorado, and for a time they tarried at Trinidad, where Bat Masterson was running a gambling saloon.

For the next two years—save for a brief visit to Dodge in 1883 to help out Luke Short—Wyatt roamed the Colorado gold camps with Warren. In 1884 the brothers moved to northern Idaho and tried their luck at prospecting in the Coeur d'Alene region, but luck wasn't with them, and when their cash ran out that same year, Wyatt parted company with Warren and joined Lou Rickabaugh—his onetime partner in the Oriental Saloon—at El Paso, Texas. Here Wyatt built up a stake and had a bloodless encounter with gunman Bill Rayner before moving on to San Diego, California, where successful real-estate ventures enabled him to establish a small stable of thoroughbred racehorses. In July 1888 Mattie Earp died, and over the next few years Wyatt became quite a figure in the sporting world with a reputation of "gameness, squareness, and fair play."

At the close of 1896 Wyatt refereed the Sharkey-Fitzsimmons fight, and the following year he married Josephine Sarah Marcus, a girl of the Jewish faith who was thirty-six years old and whose family were prosperous merchants in the community. Early in 1898 the newly married Earps moved north to Alaska and Wyatt cashed in on the mining boom by opening the Dexter Saloon and Gambling Hall at Nome, but in 1901 they returned to California, where they outfitted for a prospecting trip into the mining area of Nevada. Goldfield, Tonopah, and most of the Nevada camps saw the Earps over the next five years, during which time their base was a saloon that Wyatt opened at Tonopah in 1902. For a brief period in 1909 Wyatt guarded bullion shipments for a Los Angeles bank, and over the next few years he and his wife acquired valuable oil and mining properties and spent their time between homes they had bought in Oakland and Los Angeles.

In 1927 Earp recounted his life story to western historian Stuart N. Lake, a series of interviews that was to cover two years and that may have stirred up old memories within Earp, for sometime in 1928 he returned to Tombstone for a last look around. Coca-Cola signs greeted him and the smell of hot dogs was in the air. No one knew him, and to the girl selling drinks and souvenirs at the entrance to the town's cemetery he must have been just another kindly old tourist, for until years later there was no possibility of her knowing that on that day she had been within arm's reach of one of the greatest gunfighters the West has ever seen. Wyatt Earp died on January 13, 1929. His wife Josephine, who had borne him two children (neither of whom survived childhood) during the early years of their marriage, died in 1944. For many years only the Marcus family and a few close friends knew the location of Wyatt's grave, but on the night of July 6–7, 1957, thieves stole the headstone from the plot—all 560 pounds of it—and the ensuing publicity turned the Hills of Eternity Memorial Park at Colma, California, into a western buff's paradise overnight. The Tombstone authorities had wanted Wyatt's ashes (his body had been cremated), but they disclaimed all knowledge of the robbery when questioned. At the time of this offense Roy Earp, a distant relative of Wyatt's, was an inspector on the Oakland Police Department. (See ALLISON, CLAY; BEHAN, JOHN; BENSON STAGE MURDERS; BUNTLINE SPECIAL; CLANTON GANG; CLEMENTS, EMANUEL; CRUZ, FLORENTINE; EARP, JAMES; EARP, MORGAN; EARP, NICHOLAS PORTER; EARP, VIRGIL; GRAHAM, WILLIAM B.; HAND, DORA; HOLLIDAY, JOHN HENRY; HOYT, GEORGE; KING, MELVIN; LITTLE WOLF; LOWE, JOSEPH; O. K. CORRAL; O'ROURKE, JOHN; RAYNER, BILL; RUDABAUGH, DAVE; SHORT, LUKE; THOMPSON, BEN; and TOMBSTONE, ARIZONA.)

EATON, FRANK Born October 26, 1860, at Hartford, Connecticut, and died April 7, 1958, at Anardarko, Oklahoma, at the age of ninety-seven years. Between these two dates plenty seems to have happened to Frank, and according to his reminiscences, *Pistol Pete, Veteran of the Old West*,[5] it most certainly did; his father murdered; gunfights galore—eleven notches on his gun; a deputy U.S. marshal; and an acquaintance of such big names as Jesse James, Pat Garrett, and Belle Starr. Well—er . . . let's just say that the book is well worth reading if only for its lively accounts of such folk as Garrett and the Benders, and its descriptions of bullwhacking, pistol priming, etc., for no records of Pete having

been a deputy U.S. marshal (which means little) or of all the gunfights he is supposed to have been in (which means much) appear to be available. However, Frank Eaton (alias Pistol Pete and Frank Goodhue) looked a grand old man in 1948 (riding a horse and wearing a genuine old-time gunbelt), so he may have done all the things he claimed. In 1956 Frank, and an old gent who professed to be Jesse James, put themselves at the disposal—or mercy—of a panel of Denver scientists who wished to probe into the mystery of the old-timers' longevity, and, as you already know, Mr. Eaton died two years later.

EDWARDS, GEORGE Alias of Bill Miner. (See MINER, BILL.)

ELDER, KATE Better known as Big-nosed Kate and occasionally referred to as Kate Fisher. In spite of Kate's addiction for cheap whiskey and the use of adjectives of an obscene nature, of her having a nose similar to that of an elephant seal's and being of formidable proportions, she was sufficiently attractive to men to carry on her chosen profession of free-lance whore until her untimely and shocking death. There are no reliable records relating to Kate's birth and early years, although there are numerous rumors that she was a Southerner and that she had known Doc Holliday many years before she met up with him in 1877. From 1877 until 1881 Kate's life was linked with that of Doc's, and this period is well documented. A short time after Doc had given her the boot, and while touting for clients in a Bisbee saloon, Kate was accidently shot to death by a crazed drunk. On hearing the shots Kate dove for cover, but her rotund rear must have remained magnificently vulnerable,

[5] Written by Eva Gillhouse and published by Arco Publishers Ltd. in 1953.

for a stray shot pierced that rotund rear and made an end of it for Kate. (See HOLLIDAY, JOHN HENRY.)

ELEPHANT During the California gold rush "Elephant" was more or less a synonym for the Mother Lode region. Example: A would-be prospector would answer that he was "going to see the elephant" if his destination was queried while en route to the gold fields. Later, the expression lost its geographical significance, and tenderfeet entering the West for the first time would use the phrase whatever their pursuits or destinations. On their return they would claim that they had "seen the elephant."

ELK European name for a species of deer called the moose in North America, while in North America the wapiti deer is usually referred to as the elk. (See MOOSE and WAPITI.)

ELLIS, ANNIE An acquaintance of many of the top-line gunfighters who were touring the West in the 1870s, Annie, who was born at Dolgelly, Wales, in 1845, arrived in the United States with her brother when she was thirteen years old. On arrival at Kansas City said brother failed to support Annie, and she was taken care of by a charitable institution until she was nineteen, at which age she married David Rule, an itinerant carpenter who was twenty-five years her senior. Around 1870 the Rules located at Abilene, Kansas, but they had little family life, for David's job—contract work on the Army posts—kept him away for long periods, and in 1871 Annie became friendly with Wild Bill Hickok, a randy, dandy cock-of-the-walk who found her a job in a restaurant—a hash-slinging position that helped Annie kill time during her husband's absences. A few years later Annie opened a boarding house at Wichita, which at various times

sheltered under its shingles such big names as Wyatt Earp and Bat Masterson. Dave was of course coming and going throughout this period, and in 1873 Annie gave birth to a child whom they christened Kate before Dave once more lit out. On this occasion his destination was Kansas City, with the object of making a bank withdrawal. He made the withdrawal, but almost before he'd time to riffle through the wad, he was murdered in his hotel rooms and the money changed hands; robbery being the motive for the attack. Annie, who had moved to Dodge City during this last—and final—absence of her husband's, now found herself destitute, but a short time later, after borrowing fifty cents for "milk for the little one," the newly made widow married a moderately wealthy rancher named George Anderson, and from confetti onward, her money problems were at an end. George gave her money to purchase property from Bat Masterson, and Annie opened a boarding house *cum* restaurant on Second Avenue that was patronized by Wyatt Earp, Bat Masterson, Luke Short, Bill Tilghman, and many lesser lights of the Kansas trail towns. In 1886, and after giving her two children, George left Annie, but when he died at the turn of the century she got enough money from his estate to help her over the remainder of her life. Annie Ellis Rule Anderson died in 1931. Quotes of Annie's, reported after her death, are of interest rather because of their conflicting nature than of their historical value, which is probably nil: regarding the early-day lawmen—Earp, Masterson, etc.: "They were gentlemen . . . they gave their enemies a chance"; "Bill Tilghman borrowed one of my dresses and disguised himself to escape the wrath of Wyatt Earp"; "They were all a bunch of cowards; none was brave"; "Bat Masterson was run out of town by an unarmed man";

"They were not like the racketeers you read about now." Annie evidently had her on days and her off days.

ELLSWORTH, BURT   Alias of flamboyant badman Ernie Cashel. (See CASHEL, ERNIE.)

ELLSWORTH, KANSAS   Located on the Smokey Hill River in central Kansas. From 1871 until the end of the 1873 season, Ellsworth was the main cattle-shipping center of the state. During these boom years, the main buildings in the town were the Grand Central Hotel, Drover's Cottage, Brennan's Saloon, and American House; events were reported in the columns of the Ellsworth *Reporter;* and Ben Thompson made himself generally obnoxious when he wandered from his headquarters in the Grand Central, where, for a time, he ran a gambling hall-saloon concession. The town is still very much on the map, but as a tourist attraction it is overshadowed by both Dodge and Hays cities.

EMPEROR NORTON   Self-styled Emperor of the United States of America. (See NORTON, JOSHUA.)

ESCARPMENT   An abrupt steep slope or an inland cliff. Usually caused by erosion, but can be the direct result of a fault.

ESMERALDA   Name given to that area of the Nevada-California mining region that embraced the camps of Bodie and Aurora. Evidently not all miners were illiterate, for the name is taken from Victor Hugo's *The Hunchback of Notre Dame.*

ESPINOSA, FELIPE NEVIO   In 1861 Felipe Nevio Espinosa and a handful of his kinfolk crossed the international boundary and wandered up into central Colorado with the express intention of killing six hundred Americanos—a hundred gringos for every Espinosa who had been killed in the Mexican War of 1846–48. Why Felipe, who had made his vow at the cessation of hostilities, waited so long before putting his bloody threat into operation is anyone's guess, but it is known that by the spring of 1863 the Espinosas had murdered twenty-six Coloradans, a mixed bag that included soldiers, prospectors, freighters, and sawmill workers, all of whom had been shot in the head, after which a sharpened stick had been forced into the wound. After these warming-up outrages the Espinosas found themselves being hounded by cavalry units, and Felipe must have gotten to wondering if his little band would ever reach its target figure, for he sent a message to the governor of the territory which, when boiled down to basic, went something like this: "We will stop our vendetta if you will give us a land grant of 5,000 acres and appoint us captains in the Colorado Volunteers. If you do not agree, we will kill a further 574 Americanos." The governor replied by putting a $2,500 reward on Felipe's head. The Espinosas went back into business forthwith, a Mr. Carter being their next gun-and-stake victim. Shortly after this murder a man named Metcalf staggered into Fairplay wearing a bullet hole the Espinosas had given him. Soldiers and posses thundered out of the town, and after finding two more bodies—the remains of two gentlemen named Leymar and Seyga—they spotted a lone traveler who looked a likely suspect and who decamped in the direction of Fairplay when they swooped toward him. The traveler was apprehended when he reached the town and a liquor'd-up mob marched him to the local hanging tree, but before they could lynch him a circuit Methodist preacher identified the man as John Foster, a respectable hotelowner from California Gulch,[6] and he was released with apologies. A newcomer, who arrived in the town on Foster's heels (well, almost) was not so lucky. Something about his person aroused the miners' suspicions (he'd most likely washed), and they dragged him from his lodgings and lynched him without ado. This poor fellow was later identified as a Mr. Baxter, a businessman who had had his journey permanently interrupted while en route for California Gulch. A short time later, a posse composed of vigilantes from Fairplay and California Gulch caught up with the Espinosas and succeeded in killing Victorio Espinosa. The posse immediately identified the corpse as Felipe's leavings and then headed for the nearest saloon to celebrate. Two more men were shot and skewered while the celebrations were in progress, and on September 3, 1863, Felipe and Julian Espinosa waylaid a buggy in which a Mr. William Philbrook and a young but evidently old enough girl named Dolores Sandez were riding. William escaped, but alas, the lass Dolores was raped. When the cavalry found Dolores and heard her tale they must have realized things were getting serious; a murder was one thing—rape was another; and although Dolores may have been delighted, or at least thankful for the difference, the soldiery were most emphatically not. The rotten greasers who had done the deed were having all the fun, and they must be made to pay. The Army called in a scout named Tom Tobin—a man who could maybe give the sex of a flea after studying its tracks— and a captain and fourteen troopers followed Tom into the wilderness. Tom lost the captain and twelve of his detail[7] while on the trail, but he managed to find the Espinosas. The scout and the two troopers whom he'd failed to lose flushed their quarry at Indian Creek, and Tobin brought down Felipe and Julian with two shots from his muzzle-loader. Immediately afterward he cut off their heads—the better to prove he'd done what he'd done—and on reaching Fort Garland he put in his claim for the reward. Unfortunately for Tobin, there was little money in the territorial till, and he had to be satisfied with some new buckskins, a gun, and fifteen hundred dollars. Some say the heads of Felipe and Julian were pickled and that later they were given a tour of the carnival circuit, but others say nay. A "nayer" is Kit Carson III, who stated in 1955 that the heads were buried at the back of Fort Garland shortly after being taken from their owners. K. C. III is probably right, for Tom Tobin was his maternal grandfather, and Kit was born at Fort Garland.

EVANS, CHARLES A very unlucky gentleman. In April 1875 Evans went on trial for his life, accused of the bludgeon murder of a nineteen-year-old youth named Seabolt whose body had been found in Indian Territory (Oklahoma). When found, the body was bootless, and an empty wallet had been found nearby. Evans, who had been arrested and charged on the purely circumstantial evidence of being in possession of the victim's horse, claimed at his trial that he had bought the horse from Seabolt, and he was acquitted. Then came the rub. Immediately after the acquittal the presiding judge should have signed Evans' release papers, but he failed to do this, possibly because he had handed in his resignation and was in an almighty

---

[6] A mining camp some thirty miles west of Fairplay. In 1878 California Gulch was renamed Leadville.

[7] He later claimed that he had done this intentionally, and he was most likely speaking the truth, for he wouldn't have had any desire to share the reward.

hurry to leave town,[8] and this oversight on his part meant that Evans had to languish in jail until a new trial could be arranged. In June of that same year, Evans came up before the bench for his second time. Judge Isaac C. Parker— later to become known as "The Hanging Judge"—presided, and the victim's father was in the courtroom; an unfortunate combination as far as Evans was concerned, as we shall see. Cocky, and confident of acquittal, the accused walked into court wearing a nearly new pair of shoes, which Mr. Seabolt immediately recognised as having belonged to his son. Open and shut. Charles Evans was hanged at Fort Smith, Arkansas, on September 6, 1875.

E V A N S , C H R I S T O P H E R Friend of George and John Sontag, California train robbers of the late 1800s. Evans, who owned a small farm, always denied that he had taken part in any of the Sontag holdups,[9] but after the Fresno robbery of August 3, 1892, he gave shelter to fugitive John Sontag and helped him fight off a pursuing posse. In June 1893 Evans was captured at Simpson Flats after an eight-hour gun battle in which he was wounded (blinded in his right eye) and a lawman was killed. On November 3, 1893, Evans was convicted of murder, given a life term, and lodged in the Porterville jail. Two weeks later he broke jail at gunpoint,[10] and he wasn't recaptured until February 1894, after which he was placed in the top-security prison at Folsom, where he remained

until he was paroled in the spring of 1911. His family had moved to Portland, Oregon, while he was serving his term, and he settled with them on his release. Chris Evans died at Portland in 1917, aged seventy years. (See SONTAG BROTHERS.)

E V A N S , J E S S E Friend of Billy the Kid for about ten years, Jesse, who was born around 1855, met the youth who was to become known as Billy the Kid in Silver City, New Mexico, sometime during the period 1869–71, and a few years later they were riding the range together. In 1876 these two boyhood friends were running a somewhat erratic business venture in Arizona—namely, cattle rustling and horse stealing. In 1877 Jesse was arrested by Sheriff W. Brady on a warrant sworn out by an Englishman named John H. Tunstall and that charged Jesse (and others) with the theft of the Englishman's horses. Jesse was tossed into a crude log jail at Lincoln, but he escaped within twenty-four hours and no one troubled to bring him in a second time. In February 1878 Evans was an active participant in the murder of Tunstall—one of his bullets struck the Englishman in the chest—but although he was indicted for the murder he was never arrested for the crime. Later that same year Jesse was working for a businessman-rancher, James J. Dolan, and exactly one year after the Tunstall murder and while still working for Dolan, he is alleged to have had his last meeting with Billy the Kid,[11] after

---

[8] Irate citizens had given the judge (a certain Judge Story, who was highly unpopular) until sunup to leave town.

[9] Naturally! Yet loot from the Fresno job was found on his farm.

[10] Pistols that had evidently been smuggled in by friends or relatives.

[11] After Tunstall's death Billy—who had become a close friend of the Englishman—had sworn to get his killers, so we must assume that at this meeting Billy spared Jesse because of their long friendship or perhaps because he knew that Jesse was his equal with a gun. He may, however, have told Jesse to leave the territory; or perhaps you like the idea of these two chums shaking hands and letting bygones be bygones. Only one thing is sure about this last meeting: Reports on it vary as to location and dialogue.

which Evans disappeared from the territory and—as far as is known—nothing more was heard of him. (See McCARTY, HENRY, and TUNSTALL, JOHN HENRY.)

EVANS, LOU Member of the Sam Purdy white slave ring. Lou, who acted as procurer for the outfit, was shot dead during an argument over a poker game that was being played on a riverboat at Natchez in June 1805. No one was ever arrested for this spot of good riddance. (See PURDY, SAM.)

CHARLES M. RUSSELL

FABER, CHARLIE   One of the many victims of Clay Allison's .45. Faber, who was town marshal of Los Animas and a deputy sheriff of Bent County, Colorado, was called to Frank Fayley's Olympic Dance Hall in Los Animas on the night of December 21, 1876, for the purpose of requesting Clay and John Allison (Clay's brother) to remove their hardware and to put a damper on their troublemaking. Faber entered the dance hall carrying a shotgun, but Clay spotted him first, and the lawman got two slugs in the chest before he could bring his scattergun into action, but before he fell he succeeded in emptying a load of buckshot into John Allison's legs.[1] Faber was dead before the smoke had cleared, but when Clay was charged with the slaying, no prosecution witnesses could be found, and he was released. (See ALLISON, CLAY.)

FALLON, CHARLES   Snaggle-toothed[2] horse thief who arrived at Lewiston, Montana, with a buddy named Ed Owens during the town's Fourth of July celebrations of 1884. Both men were heavily armed, although they had merely come to Lewiston to race a hay-burner that Fallon had led into town. Had Fallon won, little more may have been heard of either man, but he didn't, and after he and Owens had failed to drown their sorrows in a local saloon, they decided to take over the town—an unwise and whiskey-soaked decision, for they had only gotten around to killing one citizen and wounding another when an almighty barrage from the guns of the townies put twenty-one pieces of assorted hardware into their combined and liquored-up anatomies; R.I.P. Fallon and Owens. Fallon is believed to have been around forty years of age at the time of his death.

[1] An innocent bystander (he sure gets around) was also wounded by a few stray pellets.
[2] These teeth, which were rather pointed, are presumed by some to have been responsible for Fallon's sobriquet of "Rattlesnake Jake"; on the other hand, a rattlesnake skin hatband that Charlie sported may have led to the "Rattlesnake" tag.

FANDANGO A lively Spanish dance for two persons. Guitars and castanets are the usual accompaniment. Popular in the dance halls and *cantinas* of the Southwest. By extension, any lively affair —e.g., a riotous fight—may be termed a fandango.

FANNING A rapid-fire method of emptying a single-action revolver of its loads, the hammer being cocked and released by the palm of the free hand, which is agitated in a shuttlelike movement above the gun. It looks good on the movies—a good theatrical gimmick that is guaranteed to bring down the house—but its practice is not recommended when engaged in an actual shootout, for the rapid movement of the fanning hand drags the gun off target to such an extent that said target can hang around in comparative safety until the fanner's gun is empty, after which the showoff can be inexpensively accounted for by one studiously placed piece of lead; small wonder that in the well-documented annals of the West only one or two instances of fanning can be found. (See GUNFIGHTING and LOVING, FRANK.)

FANTAN Chinese name for a card game in which the winner is the first person to dispose of his or her cards.

FARGO, WILLIAM G. Born at Pompey, New York, on May 20, 1818. At the age of thirteen William was riding a forty-mile mail route, but it was not until many years later and after trying his hand as a grocer, then as a freight agent, that his name was to become inextricably linked with that of Wells. In 1843, and while employed as a messenger by the express firm of Pomeroy and Company, Fargo became acquainted with a fellow employee named Henry Wells, and in 1845 a business bond was forged between these two men that re-

sulted in the historic Wells Fargo chain of enterprises. William Fargo died in 1881. (See WELLS FARGO & COMPANY.)

FARO A gambling card game, the name of which derives from the fact that a portrait of a pharaoh was originally pictured on one of the cards. Reputedly of Italian origin, the game became popular in France in the late seventeenth century, and from here it spread to the French colonies in North America. A faro box and a layout are required for the game. The box spring releases the cards in pairs, and bets are laid as to whether a particular card will win or lose. Twenty-five releases are made from the box; the top card (soda) and the bottom card (in hoc) do not count.

FARRAR, ANDREW Teamster who got the drop on Joseph A. Slade but didn't live to tell the tale. How come? To be quaint but apt, this is how come. When Slade found himself looking into the muzzle of Andy's cap 'n' ball six-shooter he denounced the teamster as a yeller-liver'd sonofabitch (or somesuch) who was too scared to fight with his fists. Andy bristled as only the unshaven can and tossed his gun aside and—well, yes—the crafty Joseph shot him to death before he'd time to roll up his sleeves. There are other versions of this sad tale, but none is more sinister, and as it is an established fact that Slade did murder Farrar, the above—the most popular version of the killing—may well be correct. (See SLADE, JOSEPH A.)

FAR WEST A riverboat that was chartered by the government to act as a supply and mail-carrying vessel during the 1876–77 North Plains Indian campaign. The *Far West* was a small wood-burning sternwheeler with twin smokestacks, which over its period of government service was skippered by

Captain Grant Marsh. The boat acted as base for Custer on his last march, meeting the column at Fort Buford and, progressively later, at the mouths of the Powder, Tongue, Rosebud, and Big Horn rivers. When Custer left, leading his column south toward the valley of the Little Big Horn, Captain Marsh anchored at the mouth of the Big Horn to await news. On the twenty-seventh of July a Crow scout brought serious news, and Captain Marsh pushed his craft upriver until he reached the mouth of the Little Big Horn River—the nearest navigable point to the site of the Custer disaster. The *Far West* anchored here for a week, during which time the body of Custer and fifty-two wounded from the Reno and Benteen detachments, plus the badly wounded "Comanche," were brought on board. On July 3 Captain Marsh upanchored, and the *Far West* started on its record-breaking journey to Bismarck, a distance of 710 miles of treacherous waterway that was covered in 54 hours.[3] The arrival of the *Far West* with its shattered cargo confirmed an earlier "smoke and moccasin" rumor that Custer and his command had been wiped out. (See BATTLE ON THE LITTLE BIG HORN; CURLEY; and CUSTER, GEORGE ARMSTRONG.)

FAST DRAW "How fast with a gun were the old-time gunslingers?" This question, or a variation of same, frequently arises when the subject matter of

either a printed article or idle conversation revolves around the Old West, and while it is impossible to answer such a question with any degree of certainty, the following data and comments may help to throw a little light on the subject. Speeds of present-day gunslingers as recorded by such devices as the Dee Woolem electric timer and Fastair missile camera[4] are given as follows:

Nick Nicastro
    on 1959 television program 18/100 sec.
Rod Redwing
    on 1959 television program 23/100 sec.
Dee Woolem
    on 1959 television program 35/100 sec.
Nick Nicastro
    fastest speed claimed   5/100 sec.
Dee Woolem
    fastest speed claimed   11/100 sec.

Woolem and Redwing—both of whom teach the stars of Western movies the art of the fast draw—may be classed as professionals. Kelo Henderson, second lead in a 1959 television series "Twenty-six Men," could clear leather, cock, and fire in 27/100 second. Such speeds appear fabulous, and it has been claimed that the old-time gunfighters could never have matched these timings. Admittedly, the old-timers had no electronic timing devices, yet they did indulge in a timing practice that takes exactly the same time to perform today as it did in the 1800s. This is the practice of placing a coin on the back of one's gun hand when it is extended at chest level, then tilting the

---

[3] A record that has yet to be beaten. Much of the distance was along uncharted waterways, yet even so, Captain Marsh kept his boat under a full head of steam as it crashed through accumulations of river debris and skidded across sandbars.

[4] The Dee Woolem electric timer is a large clock with a single sweep-hand and a dial whose circumference is marked with a hundred divisions. A release button activates the sweep-hand, which is timed to make a complete circle in one second, while a noise-sensitive element in the clock causes the clock to stop when the gun is fired. The fast-gun artiste keeps the fingers of his gun hand pressing on the button until he is ready to go into action. The Fastair missile camera photographs both the gunslinger and the clock throughout the action at the rate of three hundred exposures a second. Colt's single-action revolvers are used in these beat-the-clock contests, and the revolvers are invariably carried in low-slung, buscadero-type rigs.

hand until the coin slides off, at which instant the hand is whipped down to the gun butt and the pistol is brought into play. The coin takes approx. 40/100 second to reach the ground from this height —about 52 inches if you're average height and not cheating by standing on a chair—and in this time (that is, before the coin hits the ground) an old-timer pistoleer would be able to get off his first shot. Slightly under 40/100 second, yes, but still slower than Mr. Nicastro and company. However, Nicastro and all the present-day leather slappers have their gun hands within a few inches of their gun butts before making their play, whereas an old-timer's hand would be more than two feet from his holster when the coin cleared it; in other words, when competing against the clock, the gun hand moves less than 18 inches throughout the whole action, whereas when using the coin device the gun hand has to cover more than twice this distance. Let us close by saying that while present-day professionals practice gunslinging to make a living, the men of an earlier era practiced the art to go on living; and that latter reason, as an incentive, cannot be surpassed. (See GUN-FIGHTING.)

FERNANDEZ, MANUEL Arrested, tried, convicted, and sentenced to hang for the knife murder of Mike McCartney, a Yuma, Arizona, storekeeper. The killing occurred in December 1872, and Fernandez was hanged on May 3 of the following year. Fernandez is of interest only inasmuch as he was a "first": the first man to be legally hanged in the territory of Arizona. (Arizona became a separate territory in 1863.)

FETTERMAN FIGHT At 11 A.M. on December 21, 1866, Colonel Henry B. Carrington, commanding officer of Fort Phil Kearny, received a message from lookouts who were stationed on Pilot Hill[5] that a woodcutting detail that had left the fort a few hours earlier was being attacked by "many Indians." Carrington immediately organized a relief force and placed Captain William J. Fetterman in command, and minutes later Fetterman—an ex-Civil War officer who had joined the garrison a month previously and a fire-eater who proclaimed that given eighty men he could ride through the whole Sioux nation—led his command[6] out into the frost-hardened wilderness. At this time there were probably more than two thousand of Red Cloud's Sioux within a five-mile area of the fort, yet when Fetterman arrived at his destination and found that the Indians had moved off, he erroneously believed that the approach of his column had put the hostiles to flight, and when a small detachment of mounted Sioux led by Crazy Horse broke cover and headed for Lodge Trail Ridge, Fetterman led his mixed command of cavalry and infantry in pursuit. The Indians zigzagged their ponies up the ridge and countermarched along the crest to throw a few insults at their pursuers before disappearing from the skyline.

From a vantage position in the fort, Carrington's binoculars soaked up the movements of both hostiles and Fetterman's detachment, and when he saw the silhouettes of cavalry and infantry follow the Indians over the skyline, he must have felt some annoyance and a little unease, for Fetterman had been given explicit instructions that he must not cross

---

[5] A natural vantage point located a few hundred yards due east of the fort. The hill was also used as the post cemetery.

[6] Composed of fifty infantrymen, twenty-seven cavalrymen, one lieutenant of cavalry (George W. Grummond), and two civilian volunteers (Isaac Fisher and James Wheatley) —exactly eighty men, but they failed to ride through a fraction of "the whole Sioux nation."

the ridge and thereby put his command out of visual contact with the fort. Meanwhile Fetterman was leading his men down the far side of the ridge in pursuit of Crazy Horse's red-blanketed braves, wind-whipped splashes of color that were drumming across the white wastes of the valley beyond. Suddenly the blankets swirled from their wearers' shoulders as the Indians wheeled their ponies to face the soldiers, and Fetterman ground his column to a halt as he realized the truth. But the sand had run out and there was no time for a withdrawal. More than a thousand Indians who seemed to appear from nowhere swept down on to the flanks of his troops, and in less than sixty seconds of impacting arrowheads, thudding warclubs, and the rattle of small-arms fire, Fetterman and his command had been wiped out to the last man. When the spasmodic crackle of gunfire reached his ears, Carrington organized a relief force to go to Fetterman's aid, but when this force, which was commanded by Captain Tenedore Ten Eyck, reached the crest of Lodge Trail Ridge, there was little they could do. The valley floor was swarming with hostiles, and Ten Eyck, realizing the folly of engaging such an overwhelming force, wisely kept his command hugging the skyline, where they waited until the Indians had left the area before venturing into the valley to recover the bodies of Fetterman's last command. (See PHILLIPS, JOHN, and RED CLOUD.)

FIESTA   Religious festival, holiday, or carnival; a fair. Spanish term which is used in the Southwest.

FIFTH WHEEL   Term used to describe a circular or semicircular metal plate that is part of the forward running gear of buggies and lightweight carriages.

FINK, MIKE   One of those types who asks you to place an apple on your head as a target and then shoots your head from under the apple; in other words, a real "fink." Mike, who was born at Fort Pitt, Ohio, spent only the last year of his life west of the Mississippi. Prior to this period—which was to be climactic in the most positive sense—he had been a keelboat captain on both the Mississippi and Ohio rivers, a nautical nuisance who spent all his spare time looking for fights in riverbank saloons. His name was used to terrorize children, and his guns were used to shoot cups of grog from the heads of fellow daredevils or, on one occasion, the heel off a cotton-picking black. That Hugh Glass beat Fink up for this heel-blasting offense may be only a rumor, but that Fink was arrested for this wounding and released after he had terrorized the court is a fact. By 1820 steamboat competition was pushing the flatboats and keelboats from the rivers, a fact that made Mike, who had never gotten around to buying a "smokepot," bristle more than a little. He bristled for two years, then blew his stack by ramming his obsolete keelboat into a head-on collision with one of the hated steamers. Both boats sank, and quite a few river travelers weren't around for roll call, but Fink was never arrested. He had, however, lost his means of livelihood—at least riverwise—so he climbed into a suit of buckskins and began to make like a mountain man.

Comes 1823, and Mike in his newly adopted role and with a friend named Carpenter, joins Major Andrew Henry's Missouri expedition in the capacity of fur trapper and meat hunter. Some of Mike's betters on this expedition were Hugh Glass, Jim Bridger, and Tom Fitzpatrick, real-stuff mountain men all. Of "worsers" Mike had none. So up the wide Missouri, where, at the mouth of the Yellowstone, a stockade was thrown up to serve as headquarters. The stockade was solemnly named Fort Henry, and Fink and Carpenter trotted off into the wilderness in search of pelts. Sometime during this search, woman trouble developed between these two men. The lass in question was way back in St. Louis —a thousand miles removed from sparking distance by any but the gods—but both men had evidently known her charms, and constant bragging as to who had had what, when, and where, coupled with the fort's rotgut liquor and a dearth of women, caused their friendship to split at the seams. The climax came after they had returned to the fort. Here Mike made friendly overtures to his buddy so that he could conduct an explosive symphony that would resolve the question as to who was going to do what in St. Louis once and for all. Carpenter accepted the laurel branch, and to show there was no ill feeling left, he allowed himself to be persuaded into putting a pot of whiskey on top of his head for Mike to shoot at. Mike took steady aim and blasted Carpenter from under the pot; the corpse had a bullet hole in the forehead, and a Hawken rifle had done the job. A few weeks later the fort's blacksmith, a man named Talbot who had been a friend of the defunct Carpenter, shot Mike Fink dead, so Fink never did get back to the delights of St. Louis.

FIREWATER A term for whiskey that derives from the fact that the Indians tested the peddlers' brew by throwing a sample of his tobacco-colored alcohol onto a fire; big blaze = heap good firewater.

FISHER, JOHN KING Usually referred to as King Fisher, the "John" being dropped when he reached adulthood and began to sally forth in flamboyant outfits: sombreros trimmed with gold braid, gold-embroidered vests, white silk shirts, scarlet sashes, and, after a raid on a traveling circus during which he killed a Bengal tiger, tigerskin chaps, were all in his wardrobe, while a pair of ivory-handled Colt .45s invariably dangled from his silver-mounted gunbelt, and the bells of his silver spurs let everyone know when he was a-comin' and a-goin'.

John King Fisher was born in Collin County, Texas, in 1854, the first child of Jobe Fisher and Lucinda Warren Fisher. Lucinda died when John was in his second year, and his father remarried and moved his family to Goliad, where Fisher, Sr. went into business as a freighter. John spent his school years at Florence, a town some 150 miles from Goliad, and during this period he lived with relatives who had settled in the area, only returning to Goliad when he was in his early teens and after he had completed his basic education. Shortly after his return to the family hearth he was arrested and indicted for horse theft, and on October 5, 1870, he was given a two-year sentence in the state penitentiary.[7] The pen was evidently overcrowded, for Fisher was released in February 1871 after serving only four months. From then on his companions were to be a motley selection of rustlers, murderers, rapists, and general deadbeats. Shortly after his release, King teamed up with a gang of Mexican rustlers, but after an altercation over the division of loot from their cattle-rustling operations, King shot three of the Mexicans dead and took

[7] On admittance to the penitentiary, King's official description was given as follows: 5 feet, 9 inches; 135 pounds; light hair; and brown eyes. Photographs taken some years later show him sporting a large mustache, which spreads across his face like the horns of a water buffalo.

over the whole enterprise. Some elements disputed this takeover, and a further seven men were to fall before Fisher's guns before he was firmly established as the leader of various interlocking bands whose area of depredations covered more than three counties and whose ranks sometimes swelled to over the hundred mark.

Once firmly in the saddle, King bought a ranch at Pendacia Creek (near the border town of Eagle Pass) and used it as his headquarters, and that he had formed a high opinion of himself by this time is apparent from the wording on a signpost he had erected alongside the road that led to his ranch: "THIS IS KING FISHER'S ROAD—TAKE THE OTHER ONE." During these "ranching" years King is reputed to have been hand-in-glove with Porfirio Diaz, the Mexican *insurrecto* who was later to become President of that country. Diaz brought stolen Mexican beef to the border, where he exchanged it for King's rustled stock. This was a judicious arrangement, for Mexican buyers never queried Texas brands, and the Texans weren't fussy when it came to buying stock that had been stolen south of the border. King Fisher had his brushes with the law, but public apathy was at such a sad low that these brushes merely caused him periodical inconvenience.

In 1875 he was arrested and charged with assault with intent to kill, but the prosecution could find no witnesses, and he was released. The following year, Captain Lee Hall and a body of incorruptible Texas Rangers arrested King on a murder warrant, but after languishing in jail for nine months—during which time he was allowed such extracurricular privileges as lasses and liquor—he was released for lack of evidence. Six murder charges and two horse-theft indictments ended up the same way, the last indictment being dismissed in 1881. These

legal pressures did, however, do some good; while King had been dickering with lawyers, and during the periods when judicial restraints had made it impossible for him to keep tight rein on his owlhoot empire, the gang had begun to split up, so that by the time the last indictment had been tossed out of court, there was no gang left to control. This state of affairs didn't seem to worry Fisher, and when he was offered the appointment of deputy sheriff of Ulvalde County (if the law couldn't harm him it may as well hire him), he accepted. In March 1884, and while in the state capital on official business, Fisher met up with a whiskey-soaked bullyboy wearing a hard hat, a miserable mustache, and a pantsful of guns: Ben Thompson, late of everyplace where trouble had been and a gunman who was now fast losing his ratings. The two men got friendly, and a short time later they arrived in San Antonio with the intention of painting the town red. King Fisher didn't know it, but Ben had some mighty powerful enemies in San Antone, and when these enemies chopped Ben down as he and Fisher were doing the rounds, thirteen slugs that had been meant for Ben missed their target and inadvertently put an end to the tiger-chap'd terror of Eagle Pass. John King Fisher's rather tattered remains were returned to his ranch, and here they were buried—tiger chaps an' all. Fisher left a widow—a girl named Sarah Vivion, whom he had married on April 6, 1876—and two young daughters. (See THOMPSON, BEN.)

FISHER, KATE   Kate Elder is occasionally, and incorrectly, given this name. (See ELDER, KATE.)

FITZGERALD, EDWARD   Better known under his stage name of Eddie Foy. (See FOY, EDDIE.)

FIVE CIVILIZED TRIBES Blanket term that embraces the Cherokee, Creek, Seminole, Choctaw, and Chickasaw Indians. The Five Civilized Tribes must not be confused with the Five Nations, a confederacy of five eastern tribes: Seneca, Cayuga, Oneida, Onondaga, and Mohawk. Any of these last five tribes may be described as "Iroquois Indians." (See CHEROKEE STRIP.)

FLAGELLANTS Fanatics who, in the name of religion, indulge in self-chastisement or allow others to administer punishment in an effort to atone for real or imaginary breaches of faith. The Penitentes of New Mexico were rather good at this type of thing. (See PENITENTES.)

FLATBOAT A crude, keelless craft that was propelled by oars or poles, occasionally aided by a makeshift sail. Flatboats were little more than large rafts of timber on which rough shelters for passengers and cargo had been built. Only suitable for slow inland waterway travel, these boats frequently made only one journey, being broken up and sold as lumber on reaching their destination.

FLATHEAD INDIANS Descriptive term applied to the Chinook Indians. (See CHINOOK INDIANS.)

FLOATING HOG RANCH Any craft—flatboat, keelboat, or whatever—that served as a floating brothel. These crafts plied their trade along any navigable river where waterfront towns made whoring profitable.

FLORES, JUAN A small-time rustler and horse thief who broke into the big time after escaping from San Quentin Prison (where he was serving a stretch for horse theft) in the fall of 1856. The escape of Flores and a gang of lesser-known villains is probably unique, inasmuch as they forcibly commandeered a provision ship that had been tied up at the prison wharf and sailed erratically away, landing further down the coast that same day. After this spot of piracy, Flores joined up with another ex-jailbird named Andres Fontes, and within a matter of weeks they had recruited a gang of more than fifty guns and established headquarters in the hills outside San Juan Capistrano, a small town in Southern California that lies about sixty miles south of Los Angeles. This area was to be terrorized for months. Stores in the town were looted, coaches and freight vehicles were robbed in the hills, and travelers were kidnaped and held for ransom.[8]

By January of 1857 complaints and requests for help were reaching the county sheriff's office at Los Angeles, and on the evening of January 22 Sheriff James R. Barton swore in five deputies, hired a guide who knew the plagued region, and rode South for a clean-up. Barton was bucking enormous odds, but when a gang of twenty mounted bandits attacked him and his men on the afternoon of the twenty-third, the posse held its ground. Two deputies were killed in the first volley and then lawmen and outlaws clashed head-on, a powder haze in which Sheriff Barton was shot dead by Andres Fontes[9] and a further deputy was riddled into eternity before the two

[8] One kidnap victim, a German settler who wouldn't, or possibly couldn't, raise Flores' ransom demand, was taken into the plaza at San Juan Capistrano and brazenly shot to death.
[9] A bandit who had been arrested by Sheriff Barton some years previously, an arrest that had resulted in Fontes' doing a stretch in prison. When the gang was finally broken up, Fontes escaped to Baja California (that part of California that is Mexican territory) where, shortly after his arrival, he was shot to death in a gunfight.

surviving lawmen and their guide wheeled their horses and managed to make their escape.

When news of the killings reached Los Angeles, citizen posses were formed: more than fifty Spanish Americans armed with lances and under the command of Don Andres Pico, and some forty gringo Americanos who were led by a certain Doc Gentry. These two formidable posses scattered the gang within days, arresting many of the bandits in the process, but it was not until Sunday, February 1, that Juan Flores was arrested, an arrest that occurred after a near bloodless gun-duel (a posseman was wounded) between Flores and the Doc Gentry posse. The bandit leader was taken to the ranch of Don Teodocio Yorba and placed under heavy guard. Even so, he managed to escape, but he only remained at liberty a bare forty-eight hours before being recaptured and lodged in the Los Angeles jail. The Angelenos put Flores' fate to the vote, and the ballot returns were unanimous in their verdict: hanging, and no buts about it. So be it, and so was it, the hanging taking place on Saturday, February 14, 1857. Flores is reported to have been about twenty-two years old at the time of his death.

FLUME   An artificial watercourse that can either be at ground level—as is the case when the course of a river is altered (by damming) so that gold mining can be carried out in the original riverbed—or that can be a pylon-supported chute used to channel water to any private or industrial operation.

FLYING SAUCERS   Authenticated instances of saucer- or shield-shaped[10]

objects that are on record as having been sighted in the skies west of the Mississippi during the latter half of the nineteenth century.

1873   Fort Riley, Kansas. Cavalry horses[11] bolted when a shining object roared over the parade ground.

1873   Bonham, Texas. Shining object zooms and counterzooms over a party of field workers. One man killed in the panic.

1897   Benton, Texas. Searchlight reported shining from this saucer.

1897   Kansas City, Kansas and Missouri. Disk-shaped object bearing colored lights.

1899   El Paso, Texas. An illuminated disk at a terrific height.

1899   Prescott, Arizona. Similar to the El Paso sighting.

Some credence may be attached to these sightings, for they occurred well before planes and pieces of man-made scrap iron had begun to litter the heavens.

FOLSOM MAN   An identification tag that has been applied to those aborigines who are known to have settled in the Southwest some twelve thousand to fifteen thousand years ago. Remains of such men were first discovered in 1926 near Folsom, New Mexico; hence the name.

FONTES, ANDRES   A native Californian who became a bandit shortly after the territory had been ceded to the United States in 1848. (See FLORES, JUAN.)

FORD, ROBERT   The "dirty rotten coward who shot Mr. Howard" of west-

---

[10] Cigar-shaped, serpent-shaped, and Raquel Welch-shaped objects are, in deference to the heading, ignored in this entry.

[11] Hannibal's elephants are reported to have done much the same thing when similar flying objects made Hannibal and his men turn pale more than two thousand years ago.

rn ballad history; a man whose name was deemed unfit for inclusion on Jesse James' tombstone; and a man whom present-day historians of the West would have us believe was shunned by all. Hardly a character reference that Mr. Ford would have been keen on possessing, yet it is all something and nothing. The ballad, which was hastily sung together by some anonymous troubadour, can be excused on the grounds that "coward" rhymes with "Howard" (Jesse's alias at the time of his long-overdue removal); the inscription chiseled on Jesse's tombstone "Murdered by a coward whose name is not worthy to appear here" was carried out at the James family's request, and although childish—for why should Ford's name be expected on the marker?—this is understandable; less understandable or excusable are the reports that Ford was shunned by all after he had shot Jesse James, for these reports are evidently based on ballad-and-marker surmise -who'd-love-a-dirty-rotten-coward line of reasoning, rather than on facts; the facts being that after that fateful morning of April 3, 1882, Ford seems to have done quite well for himself in enterprises that relied on the goodwill of his contemporaries.

Let us take a look at Robert, bringing him into focus from around seven-thirty on that Monday morning of April 3, 1882. Robert and his brother Charley are walking toward a single-storied frame house that stands on a small hill on the outskirts of St. Louis, Missouri. The Fords are cousins of the Jameses, but there have been strained relations between the two families for some time, although on this morning the Ford brothers have been invited to the house by Jesse, who wishes them to join up with him for a raid that he has planned for that evening on a Platte City bank. Sometime earlier Charley had been negotiating with Governor Thomas T. Crittenden regarding a ten-thousand-dollar "dead or alive" offer that hangs over Jesse's head, and the governor has agreed that should either Robert or Charley be forced into killing Jesse while attempting his capture, he, the governor, would see to it that the killer would be pardoned after going through the formalities of a trial, which may have turned into a "thumbs down" affair.

So Robert and Charley were out to get Jesse when the opportunity presented itself, and at a little after eight o'clock on that Monday morning, Jesse got himself into a position that appeared to make the setup perfect. After finishing his breakfast, Jesse walked into the parlor to speak with the Ford brothers, unbuckling his gun harness and tossing it aside[12] as he moved into the room, where, for some unknown reason, he decided that picture straightening (or dusting?) should be given priority over holdup arrangements and forthwith climbed onto a chair to carry out this minor domestic chore. Robert, who was standing with his back to the open front door and had

[12] An odd theatrical gesture which, by inference, suggests that Jesse deemed it more dangerous to be unarmed at the breakfast table—unless, of course, he used his guns to blow the tops off his eggs—than when meeting relatives whom he knew bore him a grudge. If one accepts the fact that Jesse wore his guns at breakfast, why did he remove them in Robert Ford's presence? This ostentatious gesture could have been done to give Bob the impression that he was unarmed. If so, Jesse's picture-straightening-dusting routine begins to have some significance; could he not have used this device to observe Robert's reactions via the reflection, confident that a hideaway gun and the speed of his draw would save him in the event of Ford making a hostile move? Farfetched? Not really; not half as farfetched as the assumption that Jesse James would toss his guns aside and, while unarmed, turn his back to a man he did not trust.

Charley crowding behind him, saw his chance, and as Jesse turned his back to straighten or dust the glazed picture, Bob raised a single-action Colt .44[13] and thumbed back the hammer; a slight yet often heard sound that made Jesse turn around. Ford's gun roared, and when Jesse's wife ran from the kitchen, her husband was already dead. Robert spoke in a stunned voice, "It went off accidentally," to which Zerelda James replied, "I guess it must have."

Charley had already left the scene and was on his way to the nearest telegraph office to wire the governor. Robert surrendered to the law and was tried and convicted (that he was convicted seems odd, for Jesse was outside the law and was wanted either dead or alive), but he was immediately pardoned by the governor. After collecting the reward, Robert and Charley toured the music halls with an act called "Outlaws of Missouri." This well-paying enterprise continued until May 6, 1884, on which date Charley was found dead in his hotel room at Richmond, Missouri. The coroner's verdict was suicide, and people who had never met Charley immediately surmised that he had done the deed in a fit of remorse—a highly dramatic yet most unlikely theory, which remains current to this day.

Shortly after this sad event, Robert started living in either holy wedlock or simmering sin with a chorus girl named Nellie Waterson, a lass who engaged in the twin professions of hoofing and whoring, and who was known as Dottie both on the boards and between the sheets. With Dottie in tow Robert joined the Barnum freak show, but within a few years he had given up this show-biz existence and was running a saloon *cum* gambling establishment at Walsenburg, Colorado. This business prospered, and when a mining boom occurred in the southwestern section of the state in the late 1880s, Robert and Dottie had sufficient funds to move their equipment to these golden pastures and open up in larger premises at the newly established mining camp of Creede. This was a two-story structure that Robert named The Creede Exchange. Robert ran the bar and gambling side of the business, which was located on the ground floor, and Dottie sergeant-majored a string of girls who helped rugged miners air the beds in the upstairs rooms. At Creede, Robert established a reputation for fair dealing and generosity and became well liked. He employed Poker Alice to give tone to his gambling, his whiskey is reputed to have been the best for miles around, and—although there are no testimonials available—it may be assumed that Dottie's doxies were of a similarly high standard. At this time running such an establishment was not frowned upon—for this was an era of broadmindedness in the most liberal sense—and when Robert and Dottie were run out of town in the fall of 1891 it was merely the aftermath of too much exuberance on the part of Robert: He'd gotten drunk and shot a few of the town's lights out.

The Fords moved to Pueblo, Colorado, but by the opening months of 1892 the Creede council had relented, and Bob and Dottie were back in town and their place was doing "business as usual." A short time after their return to Creede a fire swept through the town and The Creede Exchange was burned to

---

[13] Robert said he used such a gun, and there seems no reason for his lying over such a small detail, yet there is a .44 single-action Smith and Wesson going the rounds that is engraved with the words, "Bob Ford killed Jesse James with this revolver." Photographs of Robert show him posing with a Colt revolver, so his statement is most likely correct.

the ground. Bob, however, managed to salvage their baby grand from the holocaust, and within forty-eight hours they were back in business, Bob's part of the enterprise being carried out in a large tent, while Dottie and her girls carried on in a nearby boarding house. Robert Ford was now thirty-two years old, and he was to remain this age for all eternity. On the afternoon of June 8, 1892, a woman called at the tent saloon to raise funds for the burial of a local girl who had committed suicide, and Robert gave her ten dollars. This was his last earthly act, for as the collector left, a man who had brushed past her in the entrance raised a double-barreled shotgun and let Robert have both charges. The murderer, a man named Edward O'Kelly, was arrested by a deputy sheriff within minutes. Robert Ford was buried at Creede,[14] and a great number of mourners were present at his funeral. (See CUMMINS, JIM; HITE, WOOD; JAMES, JESSE WOODSON; and O'KELLY, EDWARD.)

FORK The raised forepart of a saddle; otherwise known as the pommel.

FORTS In the American West, forts could be either civilian or military establishments. Whether they possessed a defensive stockade (or wall) or had no such protection depended on their location and date of erection, walled structures becoming less frequent as the Indian problem was resolved. Construction usually depended on the availability of materials; therefore, if we allow for a few exceptions, timber forts were to be found in the North, while adobe forts were usually confined to the arid regions of the Southwest. Many of these so-called forts were little more than barracks, while a few were merely supply camps. Crumbling ruins mark the sites of a number of these old forts, but of the majority no tangible trace exists. A fairly comprehensive directory of forts, both civil and military, that were erected west of the Mississippi during the 1800s is given below. Locations (verified from maps or approximated from old records) and status are given in each instance, basic information to which additional details have been added when the importance of the post or clarification of an entry outweighs the dictates of space-saving brevity. Unless otherwise stated, all these posts may be assumed to be things of the past.

Abercrombie. Military post. Dakota Territory.

Abraham Lincoln. Military post. Near Bismarck, South Dakota. Established 1872. Extensive barracks and social quarters enclosed in a fenced triangle. Blockhouse at each corner. Originally named Fort McKeen, being renamed in November 1872. Site is now marked out.

Alamo. Mission used as a fort. (See ALAMO, THE.)

Alexander. Military post. Montana; on the north bank of the Yellowstone directly across from the mouth of the Rosebud. Established 1843.

Anderson. Civilian trading post. Texas; the site being near the present-day town of Ralls. Usually referred to as Anderson's Fort.

Apache. Military post. San Carlos Indian Reservation, Arizona.

[14] But Creede wasn't in Bob's home state of Missouri, so Dottie saved up her nickels and dimes, and two years later she had Robert's remains disinterred and taken to Missouri for reburial.

Arbuckle. Military post. Oklahoma. Established 1851. Abandoned, and all transportable material moved to Fort Sill in 1861. Site near present-day town of Davis.

Astoria. Civilian fur-trading post. Oregon. Site at present-day city of Astoria.

Atkinson. Military post. Northwestern Iowa. Established 1840. Abandoned 1849, after which date the name was applied to an Army post in southern Kansas.

Aubrey. Military post. Kansas; in the extreme west of the state on the north bank of the Arkansas.

Baker. Civilian post. Central Texas.

Bascomb. Military post. New Mexico; on the south bank of the Canadian. Site near present-day town of Logan.

Baxter. Civil War federal military post. Baxter Springs, Kansas.

Bayard. Military post. New Mexico; about ten miles northwest of Silver City.

Beach. Military supply depot. Established 1874. Sometimes referred to as Fort Otter. Ruins on Otter Creek near the present-day town of Tipton, Oklahoma.

Beale. Military post. (See *Piute;* in this entry.)

Belknap. Military post. Texas; on the east bank of the Brazos some fifteen miles north of Clear Fork. Established 1851. Abandoned 1861, and a crumbling ruin some ten years later.

Bent. Civilian post(s). (See BENT'S FORT and BENT, WILLIAM.)

Benton. Civilian post that was later adapted for Army use. Established by the American Fur Company on the north bank of the Yellowstone in Montana in 1846, and originally named Fort Lewis. Sold to Northwest Fur Company in 1847. Taken over by the government and established as an Army post in 1869. The present-day town of Fort Benton now occupies the site.

Berthold. Military post. North Dakota; on the east bank of the Missouri between Forts Burford and Rice, and on the Fort Berthold Indian Reservation.

Bliss. Military post. Texas; a few miles north of El Paso. A replica of the fort now occupies the original site. This replica, which is located in the grounds of the Fort Bliss Guided Missile establishment, houses a museum that is open to the public.

Boise. Military post. Idaho. The site is near the present-day city of Boise.

Bonneyville. Civilian post. Western Wyoming, on the north bank of the Sweetwater. Established 1832. Abandoned 1834.

Bowie. Military post. Established 1862 to guard Apache Pass in Arizona. Abandoned 1896. Ruins now mark the site.

Bragg. Military post. California. The present-day town of Fort Bragg now occupies the site.

Breckenridge. Military post. Eastern Arizona.

Bridger. Civilian post. (See BRIDGER, JIM.)

Bridges. Military post. Southeastern Wyoming.

Brown. Military post. Southern Texas; across the Rio Grande from Matamoras, Mexico. (See CORTINA, JUAN NEPOMUCENA.)

Browning. Military post. Northeastern Montana.

Buchanan. Military post. Southeastern Arizona.

Buford. Military supply base. North Dakota; at the confluence of the Missouri and Yellowstone rivers.

Casper. Military post. Wyoming; on the south bank of the North Platte at the Oregon Trail crossing. A replica of the fort now occupies the site.

Cass. Military post. Montana; on the south bank of the Yellowstone slightly north of the mouth of the Big Horn River.

C. F. Smith. Military post. Southern Montana; on the east bank of the Big Horn River. Established by Colonel Carrington in 1866. Log- and adobe-stockaded structure with blockhouse. Abandoned 1868.

Chadbourne. Military post. Texas. Established about 1855 and abandoned some ten years later. The site is near the present-day town of Winters.

Charles. Civilian post. Montana; on the north bank of the Missouri some ten miles east of the mouth of the Milk River.

Churchill. Military headquarters for Nevada Territory. Established 1860. Very elaborate stone and adobe structure. Abandoned 1869. Ruins partially restored in the 1930s. Now a historical landmark and tourist attraction. Located about twenty miles east of Virginia City, Nevada.

Cibola. Civilian post. Western Texas. Adobe-walled compound. Site is four miles north of the ghost town of Shafter.

Cienega. Civilian post. Western Texas. Adobe-walled compound. Site is seven miles east of the ghost town of Shafter.

Clark. Military post. North Dakota; on the east bank of the Missouri directly across from the mouth of the Knife River.

Clark. Military post. Texas; some sixty miles north of the present-day town of Eagle Pass.

Cobb. Military post and Indian agency. Oklahoma; on the north bank of the Washita near the mouth of Pond Creek. Established 1859. Abandoned by troops in 1861 but continued as an agency. Agency destroyed by Indians in 1862.

Collins. Military post. Northern Colorado.

Colville. Military post. Northeastern Washington; between the Columbia and Pend Oreille rivers.

Concho. Military post. Texas; site at San Angelo.

Connor. Military post. (See *Reno;* in this entry.)

Cooke. Military post, and usually referred to as such. Wyoming; on the south bank of the Missouri about midway between Fort Benton and Cow Island.

Cooper. Civilian post. Montgomery County, Missouri.

Craig. Military post. New Mexico; on the west bank of the Rio Grande. Site is about twenty-five miles south of the present-day town of San Antonio, New Mexico.

Crittenden. Military post. Frequently referred to as Camp Crittenden. Established 1868. Abandoned 1873. Ruins stand midway between the present-day towns of Sonoita and Patagonia, Arizona.

Cummings. Military post. New Mexico. Site located northeast of the present-day town of Deming.

Custer. Military post. Montana; in the "V" that is formed by the junction of the Big Horn and Little Big Horn rivers. Established 1877. Elaborate wooden barracks. Site near present-day town of Hardin.

Dalles. Military post. Oregon; on the south bank of the Columbia near the mouth of the Deshutes River.

D. A. Russell. Military post. Southeastern Wyoming. Site just west of the present-day city of Cheyenne.

Date Creek. Military camp and usually referred to as such. The site is about fifty miles southeast of the present-day town of Prescott, Arizona.

Davis. Military post. Texas. Established 1854. Abandoned during the Civil War years and reactivated in 1867. Finally abandoned in 1891. Elaborate barracks. The site is near the present-day town of Fort Davis. Partially restored.

Davy Crockett. Military post. Northeastern Utah; on the north bank of the Green River and adjacent to the Wyoming border.

Defiance. Military post. Northeastern Arizona; near the Arizona–New Mexico line. The site is ap-

proximately twenty-five miles northwest of the present-day town of Gallup, New Mexico.

Douglas. Military post. Utah. Site about one mile northeast of present-day Salt Lake City.

Drum. Military barracks. Southern California. Site now engulfed by present-day city of Los Angeles.

Elliot. Military post. Northwestern Texas; about twenty miles northwest of the headwaters of the Washita.

Ellis. Military post. Montana; on the Bozeman Trail between the Yellowstone and Gallatin rivers.

Ellsworth. Military post. (See *Harker;* in this entry.)

Fauntleroy. Military post. (See BENT, WILLIAM.)

Fetterman. Military post. Eastern Wyoming. A ninety-degree bend in the North Platte River protected the fort's northern and eastern flanks and separated the post from the Bozeman Trail. The site is a few miles north of the present-day town of Douglas.

Floyd. Military camp, and usually referred to as such. Utah; about twelve miles west of the Great Salt Lake.

Frederick H. Brown. Military post. (See *Washakie;* in this entry.)

Galpin. Military post. Montana; north bank of the Missouri about ten miles northwest of Fort Peck.

Garland. Military post. Southern Colorado. Established 1858. Abandoned 1883. Adobe structure. Ruins have now been restored, and the fort, which houses a museum, is open to the public. Located about fifty miles west of the present-day town of Walsenburg.

Gibson. Military post. Eastern Oklahoma; on the north bank of the Arkansas. Established 1824, at which time it was the most westerly of the Dragoon outposts. Log-stockaded structure. Ruins partially restored in the 1930s.

Grant. Military camp. Southeastern Arizona; on the west bank of the San Pedro.

Griffin. Military post. Texas; on south bank of the Clear Fork of the Brazos at the Western Trail crossing. The hide hunters' town of the same name was nearby.

Gunnybags. (See *Vigilance;* in this entry.)

Hall. Military post. Southern Idaho. Established 1834. The site is near the present-day town of Fort Hall.

Halleck. Military post. Southern Idaho.

Hancock. Military post. Texas; on the east bank of the Rio Grande between Fort Quitman and El Paso.

Harker. Military post. Kansas; on the north bank of the Smokey Hill River near Ellsworth. Sometimes referred to as Fort Ellsworth.

Harney. Military post. Colorado; on the Malheur Indian Reservation.

Hawley. Military post. Montana; on the east bank of the Musselshell a few miles south of its junction with the Missouri.

Hays. Military post. Kansas; on Big Creek. The present-day town of Hays embraces the site, and the guardhouse now houses a museum.

Hempstead. Civilian post. Montgomery County, Missouri.

Henrietta. Military post. Oregon. Established 1855. Abandoned in the 1860s. The site is near the present-day town of Echo.

Henry. Civilian post. Montana; on the eastern bank of the Yellowstone at its junction with the Missouri. Established in 1823 as a fur-trading post. The site is about twelve miles north of the present-day town of Fairview.

Huachuca. Military post. Arizona. Established around 1876. The site is some twenty miles southwest of Tombstone.

Independence. Military post. Western Nevada.

John. Civilian post. (See *Laramie;* in this entry.)

Kearney. Military post. Nebraska. An Oregon Trail fort that is frequently confused with Fort Phil Kearny. The site is near the present-day town of Kearney.

Keogh. Military post. Montana; in the inverted "V" formed by the confluence of the Yellowstone and Tongue rivers. Occasionally spelled Keough.

Kincaid. Civilian post. Montgomery County, Missouri.

Kiowa. Civilian post. South Dakota. Established by French fur traders. Also known as Fort Lookout. The site is about twelve miles north of the present-day town of Chamberlain.

Kipp. Military post. Montana; on the north bank of the Missouri some forty miles west of the Montana–North Dakota border.

Klamath. Military post. Southwestern Oregon; on the Klamath Indian Reservation.

Lancaster. Military post. Texas; on the east bank of the Pecos. Established 1851. Abandoned 1868. Ruins of post are some thirty miles west of the present-day town of Ozona.

Lapwai. Military post. Northern Idaho; on the Nez Percé Indian Reservation. Sometimes spelled—incorrectly —Lapawi.

Laramie. Civilian post that was later adapted for Army use. Established as a fur-trading post by William Sublette and Robert Cameron in 1834. This was a log-stockaded structure named Fort William, which was located in the lazy "V" formed by the junction of the North Platte and Laramie rivers in southeastern Wyoming. Sublette and Cameron sold the post in 1835, and a short time later the new owners sold out to the American Fur Company. In 1841 the log stockade was replaced by an adobe wall, and the post became known as Fort John on the Laramie, a cumbersome title that was soon reduced to Fort Laramie. In 1849 the government purchased the fortress and converted it into an Army post, which in time became very elaborate and extended beyond the walls. Abandoned in 1890, the fort remained derelict until 1939, at which time the remains were classed as a National Monument, and some of the buildings were restored. Fort Laramie is now open all the year 'round as a museum and tourist attraction.

Larned. Military post. Kansas; on the south bank of Pawnee Creek some six miles west of the Arkansas River.

The site is approximately midway between the present-day towns of Ellinwood and Kinsley.

Leaton. Civilian post. Texas; on the north bank of the Rio Grande directly across from the mouth of the Rio Concho. Usually referred to as Leaton's Fort or El Forton. Established about 1848. Very elaborate walled structure. Abandoned about 1880. Ruins still visible.

Leavenworth. Military post. Established 1827. Leavenworth, Kansas, now engulfs the site.

Leche. Civilian post. (See *Pueblo;* in this entry.)

Lemhi. Civilian post. Idaho; in the Lemhi Valley. Log-constructed Mormon stronghold.

Lewis. Civilian post. (See *Benton;* in this entry.)

Lincoln. Military post. Western Kansas.

Logan. Military post. Montana.

Lookout. Civilian post. (See *Kiowa;* in this entry.)

Lowell. Military post. Arizona. Established 1873. Abandoned 1891. Adobe ruins partially reconstructed in 1963. Located near Tucson.

Lupton. Military post. Northwestern Colorado.

Lyon. Military post. Southern Colorado. Sometimes referred to as Fort Lyons. Originally a civilian post built by William Bent.

Maginnis. Military post. Central Montana.

Mann. Military post. Kansas; on the north bank of the Arkansas just west of the Cimarron crossing of the Santa Fe Trail.

Manuel. Civilian post. Iowa. Established by Manuel Lisa in 1819. The site is a few miles north of the present-day city of Council Bluffs.

Mason. Military post. Texas. The site is near the present-day town of San Saba.

Massachusetts. Military post. New Mexico. The site is about twenty-five miles east of the Rio Del Norte River, and about the same distance from the New Mexico–Colorado border.

Maurice. Civilian post. Colorado. Established about 1830 as a fur-trading post. Elaborate log and adobe construction. Sometimes referred to as Crow's Nest, Buzzards Roost, or El Cuervo. Abandoned 1840, and had completely disappeared by 1845. The approximate site is near the present-day town of Florence.

McDermitt. Military post. Nevada; in the extreme north, at the point where the Oregon-Idaho boundary meets the Nevada line.

McDowell. Military camp, and usually referred to as such. Arizona. The site is on the west bank of the Verde River, at a point approximately twenty-five miles northeast of the present-day city of Missoula.

McKavatt. Military post. Texas. Established 1852. Ruins can be located some twenty miles west of the present-day town of Menard.

McKeen. Military post. (See *Abraham Lincoln;* in this entry.)

McKeon. Military post. North Dakota. Established 1872. The partially restored ruins are near the present-day town of Bismarck.

McKinney. Military post. Site near present-day town of Buffalo, Wyoming.

McPherson. Military post. Nebraska; on the south bank of the North Platte and adjacent to the Oregon Trail.

Meade. Military post. South Dakota. The site is approximately twelve miles east of the present-day town of Deadwood.

Miller. Military post and trading post. Fresno County, California. Established 1851. Now houses a county museum.

Missoula. Military post. Northwestern Montana; on the north bank of the Blackfoot River. The site is now engulfed by the present-day city of Missoula.

Mojave. Military post. Western Arizona. The site is near the present-day town of Mojave City.

Moroni. Civilian post. (See *Rickerson;* in this entry.)

Murray. Military post. Texas; near Fort Belknap. Established in 1861 by the Confederate Army and used by their troops until the close of the Civil War.

Muscleshell. Civilian post. Montana; on the west bank of the Musselshell at its junction with the Missouri. It later became known as Downes' Trading Post.

Musselshell. (See *Muscleshell;* in this entry.)

Nisqually. Military post. Washington State. The site is about twenty miles west of the present-day city of Olympia.

Osage. Civilian post. Missouri; on the east bank of the Osage River. The site is a few miles east of the present-day town of Jefferson City.

Otter. Military post. (See *Beach;* in this entry.)

Owen. Civilian post. Montana; on the east bank of the Bitterroot River. Established by Major John Owen as a trading post in 1851. A timbered stockade, which was later replaced by an adobe wall, surrounded the post. Abandoned in the 1870s. Site is about forty miles south of the present-day city of Missoula.

Paiute. Military post. Usually spelled Piute. (See *Piute;* in this entry.)

Parker. Civilian post. Texas; on the Navasota River. Established in 1835 by Daniel Parker and his family. Log-stockaded structure that, during Indian uprisings, was used as a retreat by the Parkers and their immediate neighbors. The reconstructed fort may be visited at Groesbeck, Texas.

Pease. Civilian post. Montana; near the mouth of the Big Horn River. Log-stockaded structure. Established 1875. Abandoned 1876.

Peck. Civilian post. Montana. The present-day town of Fort Peck now occupies the site.

Phantom Hill. Military post. Texas; on Dead Man's Creek. Established 1851. Abandoned 1854. Ruins near the present-day town of Abilene, Texas.

Phil Kearny. Military post. Wyoming; on the Bozeman Trail about eighteen miles north of Clear Creek. Established in 1866 by Colonel Carrington. Timber stockade with blockhouses. Abandoned in 1868 and immediately burned down by Red Cloud's Sioux.

Pierre. Civilian fur-trading post. South Dakota. The site is on the west bank of the Missouri near the present-day city of Pierre.

Pike. Civilian post. Usually referred to as "Pike's Stockade." Established in 1807 by Captain Zebulon Pike. Located a few miles east of the present-day town of La Jara, Colorado. A replica of the fort now occupies the site.

Piute. Military post. California. Solid stone construction. Known as Fort Beale for a short spell. Abandoned around 1868. Ruins are on the California-Nevada border about twenty miles southeast of Nipton, California.

Point. Military post. San Francisco, California.

Provo. Military post. Site is approximately fifty miles south of Salt Lake City, Utah.

Pueblo. Civilian post. Colorado; on the north bank of the Arkansas River some twelve miles west of Fountain Creek. Adobe-walled stronghold that the Mexicans called Fort Leche. Established 1842. Abandoned and destroyed by Indians in 1854.

Quitman. Military post. Texas; in the northwest on the east bank of the Rio Grande. The site is approximately due west of the present-day town of Sierra Blanca.

Radziminski. Military supply camp, and usually referred to as such. Oklahoma. Established 1858. Abandoned by the Army in 1859. Used by the Texas Rangers for twelve months, then finally abandoned. The site is near the present-day town of Tipton.

Rains. Military blockhouse. Oregon; on the west bank of the Columbia

River a few miles south of Mill Creek. Officially the blockhouse was unnamed, but the civilian populace named it "Fort Rains."

Ramirez. Civilian ranch dwelling and fort. Live Oak County, Texas. Established about 1810. A small descriptive marker is erected on the site.

Randall. Military post. Southeastern Montana.

Recovery. Civilian post. South Dakota. Established by the Missouri Fur Company in 1821. Timber-stockaded structure. Abandoned 1824. The present-day town of Chamberlain now covers the site.

Reno. Military post. Wyoming; on the west bank of the Powder River and adjacent to the Bozeman Trail. Originally named Fort Connor. Abandoned 1868.

Reno. Military post. Oklahoma. The site is about five miles west of the present-day town of El Reno.

Rice. Military post. North Dakota. The site is on the west bank of the Missouri some four miles north of the Cannonball River.

Richardson. Military post. Texas. The site is near the present-day town of Jacksboro.

Rickerson. Civilian post. Arizona. Established in 1880 by John W. Young, a son of Brigham Young. This was a stockaded structure named Fort Moroni. Taken over by the Arizona Cattle Company in 1883, after which the stockade was removed and the building became known as Fort Rickerson. Abandoned around 1920. The site is about nine miles north of the present-day town of Flagstaff.

Ridgeley. Military post. Southwestern Minnesota.

Riley. Military post. Kansas; on a plateau between the Republican and Smokey Hill rivers.

Robinson. Military post. Extreme northeast of Nebraska.

Ross. Military post. California; five miles north of the mouth of the Russian River.

Ruby. Military post. Eastern Nevada. Log and adobe barracks. Site on the fortieth parallel near Ruby Lake.

Russell, D. A. Military post. (See *D. A. Russell;* in this entry.)

St. Anthony. Military post. (See *Snelling;* in this entry.)

St. Vrain. Civilian post. Usually referred to as St. Vrain's Fort. Central Colorado; at the headwaters of the North Platte.

Sam Houston. Military post. San Antonio, Texas.

Sanders. Military post. Southeastern Wyoming. The site is approximately forty-five miles northeast of the present-day city of Cheyenne.

Sarpy. Military post. Montana; on the south bank of the Yellowstone about thirty miles east of the mouth of the Big Horn River.

Scott. Military post. Kansas. Established 1843. Abandoned by troops in 1865, after which civilian squatters moved into the barracks and used them as homes. Site near the present-day town of Fort Scott.

Sedgewick. Military post. Nebraska; on the south bank of the Platte and approximately midway between Forts Laramie and McPherson.

Selden. Military post. New Mexico. Established 1865. Abandoned 1892. Ruins some sixteen miles west of the present-day town of Las Cruces.

Shaw. Military post. Montana; on the Sun River some dozen miles west of its junction with the Missouri.

Sill. Military post. Established 1869. Stone, brick, and wood construction. Still operational. Located on the west bank of Cache Creek in southwestern Oklahoma.

Simco. Military post. Washington State. Established 1856. Some of the original buildings are still intact, and others have been restored. The fort is near the present-day city of Yakima.

Sisseton. Military post. (See *Wadsworth;* in this entry.)

Smith. Military post. Arkansas. The present-day city of Fort Smith now occupies the site.

Smith, C. F. Military post. (See *C. F. Smith;* in this entry.)

Snelling. Military post. Minnesota; on the north bank of the Minnesota[15] at its junction with the Mississippi. Established 1820 and originally named Fort St. Anthony. Stone-walled and very elaborate. Site is a few miles southeast of the present-day city of Minneapolis.

Solden. Military post. Site is approximately fifteen miles southeast of the present-day town of Rincon, New Mexico.

Sophienburg. Civilian post. Established 1845. Site near the present-day town of New Braunfels, Texas.

[15] St. Peter's River on old maps.

Stanton. Military post. New Mexico; on the north bank of the Rio Hondo.

Steele. Military post. Wyoming; on the west bank of the North Platte.

Stevenson. Military post. North Dakota. Site near present-day town of Mandan.

Stockton. Military post. The present-day town of Fort Stockton, Texas, now occupies the site.

Sully. Military post. South Dakota; on the west bank of the Missouri. Site is approximately fifteen miles northwest of the present-day city of Pierre.

Sumner. Military post. New Mexico. The remains of the post are near the present-day city of Fort Sumner. (See FORT SUMNER, NEW MEXICO.)

Supply. Military supply camp. Oklahoma; at the junction of the north fork of the Canadian River and Wolf Creek.

Supply. Civilian post. On the Mormon Trail in southwestern Wyoming. Established by the Mormons in 1852. Log-stockaded structure that was used as a supply base by the Mormon wagon trains.

Sutter. Civilian post. Usually referred to as Sutter's Fort. Established 1840 on the site of the present-day city of Sacramento, California.

Tejon. Military post. Southern California; in the Tehachapi Mountains.

Terrett. Military post. Northwestern Texas.

Thomas. Military post. Southeastern Arizona; on the south bank of the Gila River.

Thompson. Military post. South Dakota; at the mouth of the White River.

Thorn. Military post. New Mexico. The site is a few miles west of the present-day town of Rincon.

Tipton. Military post. Central Missouri. Site between the present-day towns of Sedalia and Jefferson City.

Towson. Military post. Eastern Oklahoma; on the east bank of the Kiamichi River.

Tullock. Military post. Montana; on the east bank of the Big Horn at its junction with the Yellowstone.

Turley. Civilian post. New Mexico; in the Sangre de Cristo Mountains. Established by Simeon Turley to protect his "Taos Lightning" distillery from Indian attacks. Site near Taos.

Uinta. Military post. Utah; on the east bank of the Uinta River about twenty miles north of the mouth of the Duchesne River.

Union. Military post. New Mexico. Established 1851. Stone and adobe construction, and one of the largest of the frontier forts. The ruins have been restored, and the post is classed as a National Monument. Located near Wattrous.

Union. Civilian post. North Dakota; on the north bank of the Missouri facing the mouth of the Yellowstone, and on the North Dakota–Montana boundary. Established by the American Fur Company in 1829. Wooden, stockaded structure. Abandoned 1868.

Van Buren. Military post. Montana; on the north bank of the Yellowstone near the mouth of the Tongue River. Abandoned and burned down in 1847. Site is near the present-day town of Miles City.

Vancouver. Civilian post. Oregon. The largest fur-trading post in the Northwest. The site is approximately fifty miles southeast of the present-day city of Astoria.

Vandenburg. Civilian post. Central North Dakota. Established by the Missouri Fur Company in 1822. Abandoned 1823.

Verde. Military camp, and usually referred to as such. Sometimes known as "Little Egypt." Site approximately sixty miles northwest of the present-day city of San Antonio, Texas. (See CAMELS.)

Verde. Military camp, and usually referred to as such. The site is on the west bank of the Verde River, about thirty miles west of the present-day town of Prescott, Arizona.

Vigilance. Civilian post. California. Business premises that were converted into a fortress by San Francisco's Second Vigilance Committee. Occupied by vigilantes from sometime in June 1856 until August 18 of the same year. During this period the building was known locally as "Fort Gunnybags."

Wadsworth. Military post. North Dakota. Established 1864. Abandoned 1889. Originally known as Fort Sisseton. The site is near the present-day town of Ordway.

Wallace. Military post. Kansas; on the north bank of the Smokey Hill River. The site is about thirty miles due east of the present-day town of Sharon Springs.

Walla Walla. Military post. Washington State. The site is near the present-day city of Walla Walla.

Washakie. Military post. Wyoming; on the Wind River Indian Reservation. Originally named Fort Frederick H. Brown, the name being changed in honor of Chief Washakie of the Shoshone.

Washita. Military post. Southern Oklahoma. Established 1842. Abandoned 1861.

Watson. Military post. Northeastern Utah.

Weld. Military post. Northern Colorado.

Whipple. Military post. Arizona. Site near present-day town of Prescott.

Wichita. Military post. Oklahoma; on the Washita River some fifteen miles east of Fort Cobb. Site near present-day town of Carnegie.

William. Civilian post. Site approximately thirty miles west of the present-day city of Portland, Oregon.

William. Civilian post. (See *Laramie;* in this entry.)

Wingate. Military post. Site near the present-day town of Gallup, New Mexico.

Wise. Civilian post. Kansas; on the north bank of the Arkansas River.

Wise. Name given to William Bent's New Fort. (See BENT'S FORT and BENT, WILLIAM.)

Worth. Military post. Site engulfed by present-day city of Fort Worth, Texas.

Yates. Military post. North Dakota; on the west bank of the Missouri some ten miles north of the Dakotas boundary. Site near the present-day town of Fort Yates.

Yuma. Military post. California; on the west bank of the Colorado across from the mouth of the Gila River. Sometimes given as "Fort Yuma, Arizona," although the post was on the California side of the Colorado, a river that separated the fort from Arizona City, Arizona. The site is near the present-day town of Yuma,[16] Arizona. (See GLANTON, JOHN J.)

Zarah. Military post. Kansas; on the east bank of Walnut Creek and adjacent to both the Arkansas River and the Santa Fe Trail. The site is near the present-day town of Great Bend.

FORT SUMNER, NEW MEXICO
A small collection of adobe buildings that grew up around the military post of Fort Sumner. The village is of interest only inasmuch as Billy the Kid met his end here and was buried in the fort's cemetery.[17] The Fort Sumner of Billy the Kid's era has long since disappeared from both the maps and the face of New Mexico, but the site can be located on the east bank of the Pecos River some seven miles from the present-day city of Fort Sumner.

FORTY-NINERS   The gold-hungry folk from all parts of the compass who streamed into California's Mother Lode region in 1849. The first Forty-niners set

[16] Arizona City became Yuma sometime during the 1860s.

[17] A stone marker bearing the words, "Pals—Tom O'Folliard, died Dec. 1880. William H. Bonney [Henry McCarty would have been correct] alias Billy the Kid, died July 14th 1881. Charlie Bowdre, died Dec. 1880," was erected on the approximate site of the Kid's grave in the 1930s. This is more of a historical marker than a grave marker, for the bodies of O'Folliard and Bowdre are located in other areas of the cemetery. The plot is frequently referred to as "hell's half acre."

foot on Californian soil on February 28, 1849. These first arrivals, who came on the steamer *California,* can be classed as charter members of the Forty-niner movement. This influx of folk numbered more than a hundred thousand before the year was out, and included nationals from nearly every country on earth. An example of the intensity of this gold fever is best illustrated by the fact that dozens of ships were left to rot in the harbor[18] of San Francisco after being abandoned by captains and crews who had headed for the gold fields. For some time after their arrival a shortage of women must have necessitated the majority of Forty-niners living a celibate or unmentionable existence, but they evidently made up for this after the arrival of large and lurid numbers of the fair sex[19] who were only too ready to cater to their pent-up pressures; hence the following jingle, which sums the situation up neatly:

> The miners came in forty-nine,
> The whores in fifty-one,
> They rolled upon the barroom floor,
> Then came the Native Son.

FORTY-ROD A descriptive term applied to many of the frontier whiskies, quite a few of which were little more than pure alcohol colored with coffee or burned sugar. After imbibing on any of these brews one could expect to travel about forty rods before paralysis of the central nervous system made further movement impossible. (See TAOS LIGHTNING and WHISKEY.)

FOUNTAIN, ALBERT J.
World traveler, onetime newspaperman, and a successful lawyer who was appointed judge and became special prosecutor for Lincoln County, New Mexico, in the 1890s. Prior to this period, Fountain had served as a lieutenant in the 1st California Volunteer Cavalry during the 1861–64 years of the Civil War; had been a colonel of the 1st Regiment of New Mexico Cavalry during the Geronimo uprising; and had unsuccessfully defended Billy the Kid against a murder charge in 1881. On January 31, 1896, Judge Fountain and his eight-year-old son left Lincoln by buggy to return to their home at Las Cruces, and somewhere in the White Sands area of New Mexico the Fountains and the buggy completely disappeared. The finding of a piece of blood-stained wearing apparel, known to have belonged to the Fountains, made it appear a possible murder case, and sometime later Sheriff Pat Garrett swore out murder warrants against Oliver Lee, William McNew, and James Gililland, but at a subsequent trial all three were acquitted. The case has never been cleared up, and the bodies of the Fountains have not been found to this day.[20] (See GARRETT, PATRICK FLOYD.)

FOY, EDDIE   Real name Edward Fitzgerald, but better known under his stage name as Eddie Foy. Foy, who started his career in the New York halls, arrived on the western scene in the 1870s with a collection of corny gags, some catchy songs, and a winning personality. Dodge City, Kansas, got its first view of Eddie in 1878, a view it didn't appear to appreciate, for a gang of Texans lassoed him during his act and dragged him from the stage. Eddie counted his bumps and cursed inwardly as he smiled outwardly— a wise choice of expression, which won the hearts of the rowdies and established his reputation as a "jolly good fellow."

---

[18] Many were beached and converted into saloons or business premises.
[19] Bearing such delightful names as Frisco Sue, Galloping Cow, Bareback Millie, Waddling Duck, and Crying Squaw.
[20] Rumor has it that folks were searching for the bodies as late as 1960.

From then on Eddie was Dodge's favorite comedian. But life in Dodge was never tranquil. One night Ben Thompson whipped out his .45 with the intention of making Eddie dance to its tune, and an ugly incident was only prevented by the timely arrival of Bat Masterson; Charles Chapin,[21] a Shakespearean actor who was leading man in a touring company that was playing Dodge, took a few pot shots in Eddie's direction after a minor dispute concerning a lady of the town; and on the night of July 26, 1878, Dodge's favorite comedian had to throw himself down on the boards when a salvo of bullets meant for Wyatt Earp came whistling into the Comique Theater. A local girl named Dora Hand occasionally shared the Comique stage with the comedian, and on these occasions, and after a performance that usually ended around midnight, Eddie and Dora would entertain in the local saloons and honky-tonks until Dodge "rolled up the sidewalks" (usually about 4 A.M.). Eddie had about three seasons at Dodge before returning East, where he toured the vaudeville circuit until some thirty-odd years and seven children[22] later, at which time the movie industry became interested in his talents, with the result that in 1915 he was signed up by Triangle Films, and later that same year appeared in a comedy titled *A Favorite Fool*. A book of Foy's reminiscences, *Clowning Through Life*, was published in 1928.

FRANKLIN, EDWARD Member of the Musgrove gang of horse thieves and highwaymen, who occasionally appears in the record under his alias of Charles Myers. The gang operated as independ-

ent units, and in the summer of 1868, Franklin, who was Musgrove's most able lieutenant, made a lone raid on Fort Sanders, Wyoming, and galloped off leading a string of government mules, but a few miles from the fort he was run to earth by a detail of more than a dozen troopers, and after a long-drawn-out gun battle in which he was wounded in the chest, the outlaw was overpowered and returned to the fort, where he was lodged in the guardroom and given medical attention. While convalescing, Franklin received intelligence that Musgrove had been captured and was being held in the Denver, Colorado, jail while awaiting trial. This news spurred Franklin into making an escape from the fort, and a few days later he was heading for Denver with the intention of raising funds to finance a jailbreak. Somewhere along the trail he met up with a certain Sandford S. C. Duggan, a gentleman who, although unconnected with the Musgrove gang, was not averse to a spot of skulduggery.

These two buddies arrived in Denver on the afternoon of Friday, November 20, 1868, and as soon as darkness had set in, they proceeded to carry out a series of stand-and-deliver actions, one of which resulted in Judge Brooks of Denver having his wallet removed at gunpoint. The judge was one of Denver's foremost citizens, a leading light who almost glowed in the dark, and when he lodged his complaint at the city marshal's office, an immediate hue and cry was raised. The posse, which was led by Marshal Dave Cook, tracked the pair of miscreants to Golden—a mining camp a short distance from Denver—and on the Sun-

[21] This was most likely a serious attempt at murder, for some years later Mr. Chapin murdered his wife, for which he got a life sentence in the New York State Penitentiary at Ossining (Sing-Sing).

[22] Five boys and two girls, one of whom—Eddie Foy, Jr.—appeared in numerous movie musicals during the 1940s.

day following the lifting of Brooks' leather, a whiskey-soaked Franklin saw the door of his room in the Overland Hotel crash open and Dave Cook and two of his men spill into the room with their guns and handcuffs at the ready. The outlaw, who had been resting on the bed and was clothed only in a set of faded long johns, grabbed for his pistol. Dave Cook evidently disapproved of either long johns or such hostile acts, for he remonstrated by sending "a ball crashing through his [Franklin's] very heart."[23] (See COOK, DAVID J.; DUGGAN, SANDFORD S. C.; and MUSGROVE, L. H.)

FREDERICI, LOUISA
The St. Louis, Missouri, girl who became the wife of Buffalo Bill Cody. Louisa, a girl of French parentage, met Cody in the spring of 1865, at which time she was about sixteen years of age and still attending school. Cody most likely had a formal introduction to Louisa, although other versions of their first meeting cannot be entirely discredited; after all, he could have gone to her aid after her horse became unmanageable, or he may have rescued her from the attentions of a gang of whiskey-soaked soldiers. Whichever, Louisa married William on March 6, 1866. Louisa was an accomplished seamstress, and over the years she put this asset to good stead by designing and "running up" many of the great showman's theatrical costumes. Louisa Frederici Cody died in 1921,[24] and her remains were buried next to those of her husband's. (See CODY, WILLIAM FREDERICK.)

FREE, MICKEY Sometimes known as Mickey Ward or Mickey Wadsworth. Mickey was born in 1853, the misbegotten son of a Mexican mother and a caddish brave who had effectively interfered with the girl during a short period she had spent as an Apache captive. In 1860 this girl and her half-breed son were living with John Ward,[25] a hard-bitten Irishman who had a small ranch on the Sonoita River some twelve miles from Fort Buchanan in Arizona Territory. In October of that year, Pinal Apaches raided the ranch while Ward was absent and rustled off both all his stock and Mickey Free, leaving a distraught *señora* to acquaint Ward with the facts on his return. On learning that Mickey wasn't free any more, Ward headed for Fort Buchanan, and on hearing his tale, the officer in command of the fort sent out a patrol under the leadership of Lieutenant George N. Bascom, an officer who didn't know a Pinal from a Chiricahua or a Tonto from a Mimbreño. Bascom decided that Cochise and his Chiricahuas had abducted the boy, and during a meeting with Cochise that was held under a flag of truce, the lieutenant had the chief and some of his followers arrested and placed under guard—a rash act that started an Indian war[26] but did nothing to help Mickey Free. The Pinal Apaches did, however, finally release Mickey, and he grew up to be a government scout and interpreter whom Al Sieber has described as "half Irish, half Mexican, and a whole son-of-a-bitch." After reading Sieber's somewhat inaccurate (nationalitywise) character reference, and after

---

[23] Mr. Cook's own words. Note the word "ball"; this was the era of the cap-and-ball revolver, but even after metal cartridges had superseded them, the term "ball" was used in preference to "bullet." Rarely, if ever, were the terms "bullet" and "slug" used in the West.
[24] A year previously a book of Louisa's reminiscences had been published under the title *Memories of Buffalo Bill*.
[25] Sometimes given as Johnnie Ward or John Wadsworth.
[26] Cochise escaped from the tent in which he was being held, rustled up his braves, and went on the warpath.

studying a photograph of Mickey taken during his scouting days, and after his left eye had been gouged out by a deer, one thing is for sure: Had Mickey been kidnaped over this period there wouldn't have been all that fuss about getting him back. He was, however, an excellent scout, and despite his appearance, he was married twice. Both wives died in fever epidemics, and Mickey had outlasted his second spouse by a good number of years when he threw in the towel on December 31, 1913. (See COCHISE.)

FREMONT, JOHN CHARLES
Soldier, explorer, and politician who was born at Savannah, Georgia, in 1813, and who was teaching mathematics by the time he was twenty; a bright youth who was to go far in the most literal sense, and who in later years was to become known as "The Pathfinder." In the late 1830s Fremont joined the Topographical Corps of the U. S. Army, the start of a career in which he was to make his name and rise to the rank of general. During these military years he led five expeditions into the Far West; three of these expeditions were to chart migrant routes and two were railway system surveys. His first expedition in 1842 reached as far west as South Pass, Wyoming, while his second in the following year got him to the mouth of the Columbia River in Washington. On both these expeditions —which were actually one venture—he employed Kit Carson as guide, so there was little likelihood of Fremont's toes ever pointing in the wrong direction.

In 1845 Fremont pushed west once more. There was a James Bondish quality about this mission, for Fremont carried secret orders, and after his arrival in California in January 1846, and at the outset of the Bear Flag[27] Revolution, he put these mysterious instructions into operation and helped the gringo settlers to take over the northern area of the territory. By January 1847 the whole of California was in American hands, and that same year Fremont resigned from the Army after having a spot of trouble with General Stephen W. Kearny, the military governor.

In 1848 the Pacific Railroad Company was employing Fremont's pathfinding talents—or at least his ability to choose good guides—and he was searching for passes for their iron with Bill Williams as his guide, when his party got trapped by a blizzard in the La Garita Mountains of Colorado. For more than a week the party huddled in holes in the snow. Their mules, after turning cannibalistic, perished under a howling mass of snow, and frozen mule flesh became the staple diet of Fremont and his men.[28] After eleven of the party had perished, the blizzard finally abated and the survivors reached California in time to hear of the initial gold strike. Four years after staggering out of the Colorado mountains, Fremont led his fifth and final expedition. This was a railroad survey party, and on completion of this mission Fremont turned his back on exploration, and as a member of the Republican party began to devote his time to politics. John Charles Fremont died in 1890, exactly seven years after completing a five-year term of office as territorial governor of Arizona, the highest political post he ever attained. Fre-

[27] California's state flag, which was first raised in 1846; so named because it contains a drawing of a brown grizzly on a white background. The Bear Flag Movement was a revolt of Anglo-Americans against the tyranny of Mexican rule. There probably never was any tyranny; the gringo settlers, once they felt strong enough, wanted an excuse to steal land that had been under Latin American rule for hundreds of years. "Fust the red-sticks, then the greasers" seems to aptly sum up American policy during the nineteenth century.

[28] These events occurred over the 1848 Christmas period, and this forced camp has gone down in western history as "Camp Desolation."

mont was a little man—a sock thickness over five feet—but at least he was a doer.

FRIEND, JOHN A Kansan and an ex-Civil War veteran and widower who settled in Texas with his five-year-old son Lee shortly after a bullet had invalided John out of the federal forces in 1864. In the spring of 1866, John married a Texas girl named Matilda, and by the following February the Friends were established in a new home that John had built —a timbered cabin nestled in the shadow of Cedar Mountain, about twenty miles north of Fredericksburg. The turkey gobble of Comanche raiders was not unknown in the area, and on the Tuesday of February 5, 1867, a war party came down Cedar Mountain. A raging blizzard streaked their paint and powdered their trade blankets with snow, and a carpet of white muffled the drumming of their ponies' hoofs as they approached the Friends' place. The Comanches were to meet with little opposition, for a short time before their arrival, John Friend and two settlers named Johnson (brothers) had left for Fredericksburg to get supplies, leaving Matilda and Lee to share the cabin with the wives of the Johnsons—a couple of lasses named Rebecca and Samantha (each of whom was nursing an infant child), and two girls who were visiting the Friends (a teenager named Armanda Townsend and an eleven-year-old named Malenda Caudel). Matilda heard the turkey gobble first, and she knew it of old,[29] but before she could bring her husband's muzzle-loader into play the door of the cabin had burst open and war clubs were swinging and arrows were flying.

Hours later, and after a two-mile crawl through the snow, Matilda reached the house of a neighbor. A Comanche shaft speared one of her arms, two more were embedded into her rib cage, and a scalplock had been torn from her head. The neighbors called in a doctor and sent word to Fredericksburg, and a few hours later John Friend and the Johnson brothers returned at the head of a posse. Friend paused long enough to make sure his wife was being cared for, and then the party of horsemen rode out on the trail of the Comanches: a few frozen pony tracks and blood on the snow. They found the Johnson babies first, lying on the snow with their brains bashed out. Armanda's naked form, staked out for rape but now dead from multiple knife wounds, was found on the summit of Cedar Mountain, while a short distance farther along the trail were found the bodies of Rebecca and Samantha, skulls split by hatchet wounds. Sickened beyond thought of revenge, the posse gathered up the corpses and returned to their homes, all hopes of ever seeing Lee Friend and Malenda Caudel again having disappeared as falling snow obliterated all traces of the Comanche tracks.

Slowly, Matilda recovered, and during the last week of February she gave birth to a baby girl. A few weeks after the birth, John Friend moved his family to his hometown of El Dorado, Kansas, and here he settled on a small farm and Cedar Mountain memories began to dim. But not for long. In October 1867, the Comanches released Malenda Caudel, and when Friend heard that the girl had stated that his son was still alive, he climbed into the saddle and went searching for his boy, a search that was to cover thousands of miles and last for four years, a search that ended when a cavalry detail brought Lee into Fort Sill, Okla-

[29] Matilda, a blond, blue-eyed girl who was born in 1847, was twelve years old when her father, the Reverend Jonas Dancer, her only surviving parent, was killed by Comanches. From this time on, until her marriage to John Friend when she was nineteen, Matilda was cared for by relatives.

homa, in the spring of 1872. The boy was now a thirteen-year-old youth who could speak only Comanche, and he died after being reunited with his father for only a few months. Over the years, the Friends had five more children, and although Matilda recovered from her arrow wounds, the wound on her scalp needed treatment until the day she died in the winter of 1909. John Friend died in 1938 at the age of ninety-nine years.

FRISCO SUE A San Francisco gambling hall shill who in 1876, and when she was about twenty-three years old, moved into the Nevada gold fields with the intention of trying her hand at stage holdups. In Nevada Sue shacked up with a small-time owlhoot named Sims Talbot, a gentleman who was to become her accomplice in a short-lived career of crime. Sue and Sims robbed their first coach in August 1876 and got a little more than five hundred dollars for their efforts. Frisco Sue sneered, Ye gods! In her San Francisco days she had been able to con that amount from sugar daddies within minutes, and without resorting to the use of firearms. Sims did some "not to worry" soothing; they'd hold up the same coach on its return trip. Very unwise, for when the stage came clattering along, a double guard was on the boot, and Sims was shot dead before he had time to realize his stupidity. Sue was captured, tried, and given a three-year stretch. After this the girl seems to have disappeared from the records, which is a pity, for Sue is alleged to have been a beautiful lass whose tall figure was a mass of eye-popping curves.

FRONTIER COLT
A .44-caliber single-action revolver. (See COLT FIREARMS, subheading *Frontier*.)

FUNG GOW or FUNG JING JOY A Chinese hatchetman who is usually referred to as "Little Pete," although Fung Gow or Fung Jing Joy may have been his correct name. (See LITTLE PETE.)

FUSIL A lightweight flintlock musket. The Hudson's Bay Company carried this type of gun as a trade piece, and subsequently the musket filtered into the West via the hands of trappers.

G ADSDEN PURCHASE A fifty-five-thousand-square-mile strip of land that the United States Government purchased from Mexico in 1853. It covers roughly that area of Arizona and New Mexico that lies south of the Gila River and that is bounded by the Colorado River in the west and the Rio Grande in the east.

GALLAGHER, JACK One of Sheriff Henry Plummer's deputies and a member of that gentleman's gang of road agents. In November 1863 Gallagher shot and seriously wounded a blacksmith named Jack Temple,[1] and a short time later Gallagher was suspected of the murder and robbery of a Mormon who had suddenly disappeared after flashing a roll in Jack's presence. Vigilantes arrested Jack on January 13, 1864 (they found him hiding in a roll of bedding), and on the afternoon following he was marched to the gallows. Gallagher's last words may be of interest to collectors of such: "I hope forked lightning will strike every strangling . . . of you!" It didn't, and they hanged Jack without further ado. (See PLUMMER, HENRY, and VIGILANTES OF MONTANA.)

GAL LEG SPUR A spur in which the shank is shaped like a girl's leg—bent at the knee and complete with high-heeled shoes and garter. Popular among Texan riders.

GALVANIZED YANKEE Any Confederate prisoner of war who regained his freedom by volunteering to fight the Indians as a soldier of the Union.

GAMBLER'S BELT A body belt on which three small-calibered, six-shot,

[1] This shooting occurred in Coleman and Loeb's saloon at Virginia City, Montana, and after Gallagher had remonstrated with Temple when the latter had started kicking a dog; evidently Gallagher wasn't all bad.

double-action revolvers have been se-
curely mounted. The short-barreled pistols could be fired simultaneously by
squeezing a giant trigger mechanism that
rested against the right side of the wearer's abdomen. Cumbersome, and no
doubt a rupture hazard, but like the
broadside from a battleship when fired.

GARRARD, HECTOR LEWIS
A sickly youth who made a tour of the
West in 1846–47—presumably to put a
bloom in his cheeks—and who has left a
valuable record of his travels for posterity. Hector traveled the Santa Fe Trail,
arriving at Taos, New Mexico, via Fort
William,[2] in April 1847; a few weeks after the Taos insurrection,[3] but in time to
witness the execution of five of the ringleaders. On the return journey Garrard
spent a month at Fort Mann (near Cimarron Crossing in Oklahoma), arriving
back at his home city of Cincinnati, Ohio,
in July 1847. Over the next three years
he wrote *Wah-to-yah*[4] *and the Taos
Trail*, a history of his travels, which was
published in 1850.[5] Garrard, who tried
his hand at medicine and banking and
dabbled in local politics over the remaining years of his life, died at Cincinnati
in 1887 aged fifty-eight years.

GARREAU, PIERRE The half-breed
son of a French-Canadian fur trapper
and a Cree squaw. Pierre, who was born
in the shadow of Turtle Mountain, North
Dakota, in 1798, lived with the Arikara
Indians until he was thirty-four, after
which age, and for reasons unknown, he
left the tribe and joined the white man's
world. In 1837, and after trying his hand

at river freighting and working in a St.
Louis, Missouri, bakery for some three
years, he became a meat hunter for Fort
Clark, North Dakota. On one of these
hunting trips he and a companion were
attacked by about a dozen Assiniboines
led by Chief Red Stone, and after his fellow hunter had been killed, Pierre was
taken prisoner. This, however, was not to
be the end of Pierre, for somewhere out
on the prairie he pulled a hideaway gun,
got the drop on Red Stone, and managed to make his getaway with all of the
war party's mounts. Garreau was completely illiterate and therefore couldn't
keep a diary,[6] so we hear little more of
him until some thirty-eight years and
three sons later. It is now 1876, and the
aged half-breed is living in a cabin at
Fort Berthold, and when more than
eighty Sioux decided to raid the fort,
Garreau walks out to meet them waving
a large knife and with his belt bristling
with pistols and other killing stuff. Waving his knife, the old man told the war
party exactly what type of fool he'd made
out of Red Stone, called them a bunch
of squaws, and challenged each and every
buck to a knife duel. None accepted, and
after listening to this type of tough talk
for more than half an hour, the Indians
climbed onto their ponies and thundered
away, either scared stiff or bored thataway. Garreau's three sons were killed
and scalped by the Sioux a short time
after this loquacious encounter, and in
1881 Pierre perished in a mysterious
blaze that burned down his cabin.

GARRETT, PATRICK FLOYD
One of six children of wealthy plantation

---

[2] One of the Bent brothers' forts; sometimes referred to as the "Old Fort."
[3] A Mexican and Pueblo Indian attempt to overthrow gringo rule in which twenty Americanos—one of whom was Governor Charles Bent—were killed.
[4] Indian name for the Spanish Peaks, twin mountain peaks that are located in southern
Colorado and are part of the Sangre de Cristo range.
[5] The authorship is given as Lewis H. Garrard; this is either a printer's error or an odd
attempt at a pen name.
[6] A great number of pioneers, trappers, etc., did keep diaries.

owner Colonel John L. Garrett. Pat, who was born in Alabama on June 5, 1850, moved West in 1869, a few years after the Civil War had ruined the family fortunes and shortly after the death of his parents. That same year he got a job as a cowhand at Lancaster, Texas, a job he held for six years, after which he became a buffalo hunter, his working area being the South Plains and his base being the small buffalo hunters' town of Fort Griffin. In 1877, and while hide hunting, Pat had a row with a fellow hunter named Glenn. The argument was over the division of hides, and when Glenn grabbed an ax and charged at Pat, the latter leveled a Big Fifty and shot him dead. This was a clear case of self-defense, and Pat wasn't even indicted, but it marked the end of his buffalo-hunting period, and after gambling all his hide-hunting profits away at Tascosa, he moved down into Fort Sumner, New Mexico, in search of a job. Rancher Pete Maxwell ended Pat's search, and it was while Garrett was spending his cowhand pay in the gambling dens of Fort Sumner that he became acquainted[7] with Billy the Kid.

Early in 1879 Pat married Juanita Gutierrez, a Mexican girl who died before the year was out, and on January 4, 1880, Pat remarried, his bride on this occasion being Apolinaria Gutierrez, his dead wife's sister. In the fall of 1879 Pat had left Maxwell's employ and invested his savings, first in a restaurant and then as a partner in Beaver Smith's Saloon, but shortly after his second marriage Pat

was persuaded into becoming a lawman, and in the summer of 1880 he pinned on a badge for the first time after being sworn in as a deputy by Sheriff George Kimbell of Lincoln County. Kimbell's tenure of office expired in November 1880, and a few weeks later Pat Garrett was appointed sheriff after defeating Kimbell by a short head at the polls. Pat's first job as sheriff was to clear the county of Billy the Kid and his gang, a cleanup that was brought to a successful conclusion with Garrett's slaying of the Kid on the night of July 14, 1881.[8]

At the close of his term of office in January 1882 Pat moved South and established a small ranch on the banks of the Rio Hondo, but he failed to settle down, and at the tail end of 1884 he temporarily abandoned this project to accept a captaincy in the Texas Rangers. This job only lasted about six months, but it was not until 1887, and after having worked for a detective agency and then a cattle outfit,[9] that Pat returned to his spread on the Rio Hondo. Two years later he stood for sheriff of Chavez County, but he was defeated in the election, and a somewhat embittered Pat sold his ranch and moved to Ulvalde County, Texas, where he invested in a small horse ranch. This was a fairly successful venture, but in 1897 he returned to New Mexico to accept the appointment of sheriff for Dona Ana County. Pat was re-elected on two consecutive occasions, and much of his time over this period was devoted to solving the mystery of Judge Fountain's disappearance, a riddle

[7] Around this time Billy was known as "Little Casino," so it is not surprising that Garrett, who was 6 feet, 4 inches, came to be nicknamed "Big Casino" during this period of gambling. The Kid was never Pat's best friend, as often stated; he was an acquaintance and nothing more.

[8] After which Garrett and a buddy of his named Ash Upson got together and wrote a book that was published in 1882 under the title, *The Authentic Life of Billy the Kid, the Noted Desperado of the Southwest*, and under the authorship of Pat F. Garrett.

[9] The VV spread, a large and prosperous outfit mainly under the control of Englishman Brandon Kirby. Garrett had the job of ranch manager, and it is possible that he did not get along with Kirby, for Garrett was fired for reasons unknown.

that was a hangover from his predecessor's days. Pat was unsuccessful in this, for although he swore out warrants for the arrest of three men, none of them was ever convicted, and the case was still open when Pat turned in his badge in 1900.

A few months later Pat was appointed collector of taxes at El Paso, Texas. President Theodore Roosevelt, who was a Wild West buff and consequently a fan of the man who shot Billy the Kid, did the appointing, and Pat was only relieved of his post when he fell from presidential favor some five years later. Garrett, cursing his ill luck, returned to New Mexico, where he once again took up ranching, this time in the Organ Mountains near the small town of Mesilla. This was to be Pat's last attempt at establishing himself as a rancher, and as such it was a complete failure.

On the morning of February 29, 1908, Garrett was thirty-five hundred dollars in debt, and he was talking over the sale of his ranch with prospective buyer Carl Adamson as the latter's buckboard carried them along the road to Las Cruces. Somewhere along the road a tenant of Pat's named Wayne Brazel overtook the slow-moving buckboard, and Brazel questioned Garrett's right to sell the ranch while he, Brazel, was still a tenant. Shortly before lunchtime on that same day Brazel and Adamson arrived in Las Cruces, and Brazel surrendered himself to the authorities for the killing of Garrett; he had fired two bullets from his six-gun when the ex-sheriff had reached for a shotgun. At a subsequent trial, Adamson backed up this statement, and Brazel was acquitted on a self-defense verdict—a rather remarkable verdict, con-

sidering that Pat had been shot in the chest and through the back of the head; a spent Winchester shell had been found near the body, and horse droppings and hoofprints at the side of the road suggested that some unknown person had been present at the time of the shooting. Garrett left a widow and five children. (See BOWDRE, CHARLIE; BRAZEL, WAYNE; CHISUM, SALLY; FOUNTAIN, ALBERT J.; MCCARTY, HENRY; MILLER, JIM; O'FOLLIARD, TOM; RUDABAUGH, DAVE; and UPSON, ASH.)

GATLING GUN   A multibarreled, hand-cranked machine gun invented by Richard Jordan Gatling in 1861. The original model had six barrels. Later models could have as many as ten or as few as five. Other variations included belt-, clip-, or drum-fed[10] models, all of which could be either wheel- or tripod-mounted, and the gun could be had in the following calibers; .42, .43, .45, .50, .55, .60, .65, .70, and 1 inch. Rate of fire depended on the man at the crank: A 98-pound weakling would manage 400 rounds a minute, while anyone who wouldn't allow sand to be kicked in his face would easily crank out more than a 1,000 rounds a minute. A few Gatlings were used at the battle of Petersburg during the Civil War, and Custer had four to help out his 7th,[11] but the bulk of the Colt's factory output found its way into Europe, and many of these were used to keep the British Empire's sun from setting. Until the 1950s, the Gatling held its place as the fastest-firing machine gun ever invented.[12]

GERMAIN, JOHN   A Georgia-born ex-Civil War veteran who, accompanied

---

[10] A drum held 400 rounds.

[11] Unfortunately for Custer, he left them behind on his last march.

[12] When powered by an electric motor, a Gatling could pump out 3,000 rounds a minute, but even this rate of fire has now become pretty small beer, for the new American Vulcan machine gun can waste cartridges some 50 per cent quicker.

by his family, was heading for Colorado in the spring of 1874 when his wagon was overtaken by a Cheyenne war party while he was fording the Smokey Hill River in western Kansas. John and his wife and small son were killed by the hostiles, and his four daughters (Catherine, who was sixteen; Sophie, fourteen; and Julia and Adelaide, who were six and four, respectively) were carried away into captivity. This outrage got the Army on the move, and on November 6, 1874, Julia and Adelaide were rescued by a mixed detachment of cavalry and infantry under the command of Lieutenant Frank Baldwin.[13] The two older girls, Catherine and Sophie, were surrendered to the Army when Stone Calf's band of Cheyenne lay down their arms on February 26, 1875.

GERONIMO   Spanish for "Jerome" and the white man's name for Gokliya,[14] a Mimbreño brave who, at the head of a handful of warriors, terrorized the Southwest for more than fifteen years. Geronimo was born in the Janos River area of Mexico in 1834, and although he was not a hereditary chief, he became recognized as a war leader when he was around twenty-four and after his somewhat easygoing nature had been incited to a homicidal pitch by the brutal slayings of his wife and three children. Mexicans were responsible for this spot of infamy, and for the next ten years northern Mexico was to feel the weight of the Apache's wrath. These raids were carried out by the combined forces of Mangas Colorado (copper-mine Mimbreño chief until his death in 1863) and Cochise (Chiricahua chief), but Geronimo was invariably on these raids and, in 1863 and on his own initiative, he and his warriors looted and sacked the town of Crasanas. The American side of the line also suffered raids

during this period, and it was to the U. S. Cavalry that Cochise surrendered in 1871. After this, Geronimo became a renegade who rarely had more than two dozen men under his command, but over the next fifteen years—until his surrender in 1886—Geronimo's small band managed to kill more than twenty-five hundred U.S. citizens.

After accepting Geronimo's olive branch, the government shipped him off to Florida, but by 1894, and after spending some time in Alabama, the old renegade had been moved as far west as Fort Sill, Oklahoma. While at the fort, Geronimo, who had always liked his tizwin, spent most of his weekends in an alcoholic haze, only sobering up on Mondays after the application of many damp towels. Just after the turn of the century he was given leave to tour the country with the Pawnee Bill shows, and had he lived long enough he may have made a fortune out of this, for he did a roaring trade selling photographs of himself at two dollars a time. Geronimo died of pneumonia at Fort Sill on February 17, 1909. (See COCHISE and MANGAS COLORADO.)

GHOST RIDERS   Midwestern term for a sky effect in which wind-whipped clouds with the sun behind them scurry across the field of vision, their semi-silhouette often giving the impression of horsemen or a herd of cattle on the move. Although fairly common in the Midwest, "ghost riders" are considered an ill omen by the superstitious-minded.

GHOST TOWN   An abandoned or near-abandoned town. The American West is littered with these derelict towns, the majority of which have been gold camps in their heyday. Many of these towns, particularly those located in dry areas, are still in a fit enough state of

13 Bat Masterson was scouting for Baldwin at this time.
14 Roughly translated, "he who yawns." Sometimes spelled Goyothlay or Goyathlay.

repair to be used as movie sets after a spot of face-lifting. Treasure hunting among the ruins can be a quite remunerative pastime; stagecoaches and hearses have been found, and old bottles and guns are being dug up daily.

GIANTS Indian legends would have us believe that a race of giants once tromped across the American continent. This appears to be the stuff of nightmares, but as pre-Amerind remains of humans topping the 12-foot mark have been found in California and a mummy of similar size has been dug up in Arizona (in 1833 and 1891), there may be a little substance to these tall tales. The discovery of a human heelprint measuring more than a foot across (no pun intended) is also of interest, for if the person who stamped his foot way back was of a similar build to contemporary man, that person would have a foot measuring 4 feet in length and an overall height of more than 25 feet. If this theoretical height is correct, the remains measuring 12 feet may be those of wee bairns.

GIG A lightweight, two-wheeled vehicle that is designed to be pulled by one horse.

GIGLINE, ART Marshal of Telluride, Colorado, in the late 1890s. Telluride used up marshals pretty quickly, and Art was no exception. Seems Art and a miner named Jesse Munn both fancied a lass who worked at an establishment located in the red-light area. Said girl had been under Munn's wing for some time when Art stepped in, and when the hard-rock man saw the marshal strolling down the street one night with this passion-provoking morsel on his arm, it was too much: four shots from Munn's .45, which, sadly enough, Gigline didn't survive. Munn didn't get the girl; he was ar-

rested, tried, and convicted, and given a life term in the Canon City Penitentiary.

GILA MONSTER A poisonous lizard found in the southwestern United States and in Mexico. Slow-moving and sluggish, the Gila monster is about 20 inches long and of ungainly appearance. Irregularly shaped orange markings cover its black body, and it has a bite as tenacious as a bulldog's. Despite all this, people have made pets of these lizards, and during the 1870s a saloon swamper of Brownswood, Texas, took one wherever he swamped. There is no record of this particular monster ever having bitten anyone, but as it ate saloon scraps and drank saloon dregs, it may have been in an alcoholic stupor most of the time. The Gila monster's bite is not fatal to humans. People have died after being bitten by Gila monsters, but in all the known cases (about thirty), the lizard's bite has only been a contributing factor in the cause of death, heart disease, alcohol, etc., doing 90 per cent of the job.

GILLETT, JAMES BUCHANAN Born at Austin, Texas, on November 4, 1856. When he was fourteen Gillett began work as a cowhand, but after following cows for five years he enlisted in the Texas Rangers as a private. Over the next six years he served in Companies D and A and worked his way up to sergeant. During this Ranger service he shot a small-time owlhoot and killer named Dick Dublin to death while endeavoring to make an arrest; arrested a murderer named Enofre Baca without having to resort to violence; and sent at least one Apache to the Happy Hunting Grounds via Colt's express. Gillett received an honorable discharge from the Rangers on December 26, 1881, and a short time later he was appointed deputy marshal at El Paso. Dallas Stoudenmire was the marshal at the time, but he left the job within a few weeks of Gillett's appointment and the ex-Ranger stepped into his shoes. During his twelve-month stint as marshal, Gillett had little trouble, although some of the toughest characters around were in El Paso at the time. Some say this shows that Gillett kept a tight rein on the town; could be, but the fact that he employed such unpleasant types as "Mysterious" Dave Mather and Billy Thompson as deputies may have had something to do with it. After turning in his badge, Gillett became a rancher, an enterprise he was active in until his death in 1937.

GLANTON, JOHN J.

Tennessee-born thug who, after escaping from the Nashville jail where he had been serving a life sentence for murder, moved West and enlisted in the U.S. forces to fight in the Mexican War of 1846, and who, on being mustered out of the Army in 1848, organized a gang of border scum and went in for the brutal business of scalp hunting.[15] Glanton and his gang delivered their baled-up scalps to the governor of Chihuahua, and they had made close to a hundred thousand dollars before both the Mexican and United States authorities realized that many of the scalps brought in had been taken from the heads of Mexicans and dark-complected Americans whose scalps could be passed off as those of Apaches. Rewards totaling more than eighty thousand dollars were offered for Glanton's capture, and Glanton and his men, realizing that as far as they were concerned the bottom had fallen out of the scalp trade, moved farther West in search of easy pickings.

This was during the days of the Cali-

fornia gold rush, and when they reached the Colorado River[16] they found a ferry that was being run at great profit by a man named Able Lincoln. Glanton, who saw this pot of gold in the middle of February 1850, decided this was the place, and within a short time he had pressured Lincoln into taking him in as a partner, and he and his gang had erected a log stockade in which to take up residence. Yuma Indians under Chief Naked Horse helped the ferry operators during rush periods, and things ran smoothly until March, around which time a tough wagonmaster named Patterson refused to pay Glanton's exorbitant rates, and instead hired Naked Horse and his warriors to help him build rafts to get his train across. After the wagon train had been safely ferried across the Colorado, Naked Horse found himself in possession of a couple of large rafts and a few handfuls of dollars. The Yumas had never had it so good, and they decided to go into business. The old chief hired an ex-Army sergeant named Gallagher and set up a ferry service in opposition to Glanton's.

Compared with Glanton's charges the Yumas operated a half-price ferry, and the onetime scalp hunter soon began to feel the pinch. He and his men retaliated by attacking the Yumas' ferry, killing Gallagher, wrecking the rafts, and carrying a number of nubile Yuma girls back to their stockade. Naked Horse went one better. At noon on the twenty-third of April 1850 he and his warriors overwhelmed their rivals, and all save three, who escaped downriver, were killed within minutes, Naked Horse being personally responsible for hatcheting Glanton to death. Some idiot claimed it was an Indian uprising, and in August a troop

---

[15] The going rate for Apache scalps was: one hundred dollars per male, fifty dollars per female, and twenty-five dollars per child. Glanton and his gang raped all their female captives before killing them and lifting their hair.
[16] The boundary between California and what was then the territory of New Mexico.

of a hundred whatever-kept-them-so-long volunteers arrived to quell the disturbance. The Yumas routed them completely. After that the truth of the Naked Horse–Glanton mess must have risen to the surface, for when an Army post was established near Glanton's old stockade in December 1850, it was named Fort Yuma in honor of the tribe who had rid the area of one of the worst gangs of scum the West had ever seen.

GLASS, HUGH   One of the many mountain men who joined the Major Andrew Henry expedition to the upper Missouri in the spring of 1823. By the summer of that year, and when the party was exploring and trapping in the vicinity of the Grand River,[17] and after Hugh failed to return from a long hunt, members of the expedition went out to search for him. The search party encountered a wounded grizzly near the mouth of the South Fork, and after dispatching it they pressed on and found a severely mauled Hugh lying unconscious on the north bank of the river. He had obviously had a tremendous battle with the grizzly they had killed a short time earlier, and he appeared to be near death. Major Henry decided to press on, and two volunteers were given forty dollars apiece to stay with Hugh till he expired, after which they were to bury him and then catch up with the expedition. The two volunteers, John S. Fitzgerald and nineteen-year-old Jim Bridger,[18] prepared a grave and waited for Hugh to die. The old mountain man failed to oblige, and after waiting a few hours Fitzgerald and Bridger decided they had had enough, and after appropriating

Hugh's rifle and other equipment, they hurried off to catch up with the main body of the expedition, explaining when they did so that old Hugh had died and was now safely under the sod. While in a semicoma Hugh had heard the two volunteer samaritans talking over the division of his kit, and when he finally recovered complete consciousness he swore to himself that he would exact his revenge on the two deadbeats if he had to follow them to the ends of the earth. Thoughts of revenge, plus a diet of wild berries, evidently sustained him, for he managed to more or less crawl to Fort Kiowa, which lay some 150 miles to the southeast of where he had been left to die. Hugh Glass did recover, and he did track down both Bridger and Fitzgerald, but this vendetta trail fizzled out somewhat quietly, for on finding his quarry[19] old Hugh merely gave each man a lecture on their unethical conduct and left it at that. After this little more was heard of Hugh.

GOAD, JOHN   An itinerant Baptist preacher who toured the Nevada gold camps during the 1870s. Goad, who became known as John the Baptist, is remarkable in the fact that he carried a loaded derringer inside a Bible whose pages had been hollowed out to receive same, and that he was not afraid to use the gun when the occasion demanded. One such occasion occurred at Carson City, Nevada, and Mike Fink, a local bullyboy who had been employed by the ungodly element to break up one of John's meetings, received a ball in the chest while trying to give his employers their money's worth.[20] After this impres-

---

[17] In the northwest area of what is now South Dakota.
[18] Not any Jim Bridger, but *the* Jim Bridger.
[19] Bridger was tracked down at Fort Henry on the Yellowstone, and Hugh caught up with Fitzgerald at Council Bluffs, Iowa.
[20] This Mike Fink—who, as far as is known, was no relation to the keelboat man of that name—recovered from his brush with death.

sive sermon the rowdy element steered clear of John's meetings, and he was left to preach in peace until his death in California in 1907.

GODDAMMIES   Term sometimes used by Indians when referring to the over-blasphemous element of the white population.

GODFREY, GUSA   Born at Mendota, Minnesota, in 1839, the only son of a French-Canadian father and a black mother. His parents had him adopted at an early age, and little is known about this period of his life, but we do know that in 1861 he left the home of his foster parents and married a Sioux Indian girl and became a member of her tribe. During the Minnesota Indian uprising of 1862 Godfrey personally butchered nine white settlers and is known to have thrown at least one child into an oven and baked it alive. When the outbreak was finally quelled in October of that year, the mulatto and more than 300 Sioux were taken into custody and charged with crimes ranging from rape to murder. The mass trial concluded in November with Godfrey and 302 Sioux being sentenced to hang. This savored of revenge more than justice, and after reviewing the sentences, President Lincoln decided that only 68 Sioux should mount the scaffold on December 26, 1862. The remainder had their sentences reduced to prison terms. Godfrey escaped with fourteen years, and he came out of the Davenport, Iowa, jail in the middle of 1876. Godfrey's activities and whereabouts over the next twenty years are vague, but by the late 1890s he was firmly established among the Santee Sioux on a reservation in Sarpy County, Nebraska. By 1904 he was running a small farm on the reservation, and in that same year he married a seventeen-year-old Santee girl who evidently knew nothing of his past. Gusa Godfrey, mixed-blood, squaw man, and vicious killer, died on the reservation in 1909.

GOKLIYA   Better known under his Spanish name of Geronimo. (See GERONIMO.)

GOLDFIELD, NEVADA
A gold-mining camp that sprang up in southwestern Nevada after Harry Stimler and Billy Marsh had struck gold in the Rabbit Springs area in 1902. Goldfield prospered for a number of years, but by 1910 the decline had set in, and the town is now a complete ghost.

GOLDSBY, CRAWFORD   Born at Fort Concho, Texas, on February 8, 1876, his parents being George Goldsby, a man of Mexican-Anglo-Sioux extraction who at that time was serving in the 10th Cavalry, and Ellen Beck Goldsby, a mixed-blood girl of black-Anglo-Cherokee strain. The Goldsbys separated in 1883, and young Crawford was sent to live with a black woman at Fort Gibson, Oklahoma. This foster parent is alleged to have indoctrinated Crawford with a large helping of never-let-yourself-be-sat-on wisdom, and in 1894 Crawford, who was then eighteen, put the old lady's advice into practice by shooting a black who had beaten him up at a dance hall. The black didn't die, but Crawford thought it advisable to take to the brush, and a short time later he had taken up the alias of Cherokee Bill and was riding with Bill and Jim Cook, a couple of medium-time outlaws who were a heady mixture of seven-eighths Anglo and a dash of Cherokee bitters. On June 26, 1894, a posse that was out to arrest Jim Cook on a larceny rap caught up with this criminal League of Nations, but the trio escaped after Crawford had shot and killed a posseman named Sequoyah Houston.

This was Crawford's first killing, but it was not to be his last. A short time later, he killed brother-in-law James Brown after a domestic upheaval;[21] Richard Richards became his third notch when he was killed during a railroad depot holdup, and Samuel Collins and Ernest Melton became his fourth and fifth victims respectively; the former being shot down after an argument on a train, and the latter being killed during a store holdup at Lenapah, Oklahoma. After this last killing rewards totaling some thirteen hundred dollars were offered for the capture of Cherokee Bill Goldsby, and by the New Year of 1895 an acquaintance of Goldsby's named Ike Rogers,[22] was figuring how he could get his hands on the money. For some time Ike had been allowing Goldsby and a young lass named Maggie Glass to use his front parlor for activities of a none-of-your-business nature, and by January 29 Ike was ready to make his move. When Goldsby arrived that evening Rogers was entertaining a neighbor named Clint Scales,[23] and of Maggie there was nary a sign. Cherokee Bill became suspicious and sat up all night with a Winchester cradled in his arms, but the following morning he relaxed somewhat, and when he leaned over the fireplace to light a cigarette Rogers clobbered him with a lump of firewood, finally overpowering the outlaw with the help of his pal Scales. Goldsby was tried for the murder of Melton and sentenced to death, but while awaiting execution he somehow came in possession of a gun, and he killed guard Lawrence Keating during attempted jailbreak. A further trial sued, after which he was sentenced hang for the murder of Keating. T was it, and Cherokee Bill Goldsby w hanged at Fort Smith, Arkansas, March 17, 1896. (See COOK, BILL.)

GOLIAD MASSACRE Occurred March 26, 1836, and after Gene Urrea's Mexican forces had taken ab 300 Texan prisoners during an enga ment that had occurred the previ week, an engagement in which 25 Tex had been either killed or wounded. M of these prisoners, together with oth who had been captured earlier, w executed at the Mission La Bahia Goliad in southern Texas. This Mexican territory at this time, so the 4 prisoners who were shot were regar as revolutionaries by the Mexican G ernment rather than as soldiers of hostile nation.

GOODHUE, FRANK   Self-confes alias of Frank Eaton. (See EAT(FRANK.)

GOODNIGHT, CHARLES
Texas cattle baron who was born in Illin in 1836. In 1845 the Goodnight fam moved to Texas, and by 1857, and af trying his hand at freighting for a tir Charles, partnered by a stepbrother, I established a small herd and was sett in the Keechi Valley. By 1860 Ind raids had put an end to this venture, Goodnight joined the Texas Rangers, a as a private he spent the next four ye helping to clear the Comanches from

---

[21] James had been beating up his wife, and Crawford stepped in because said wife h pened to be his sister Maude.

[22] Rogers, who was of Cherokee-black-Anglo extraction, was a deputy U.S. marsh but Goldsby may not have been aware of this. Rogers came to a sticky end in 1897 when was shot dead on the railway platform at Fort Gibson. Goldsby's brother Clarence was s pected of this crime, but he was never apprehended.

[23] Sometimes given as Clint Searles.

range. Within two years of leaving the Rangers, Goodnight had built up a herd of some two thousand longhorns, and in June 1866 he went into partnership with Oliver Loving, and the two cattlemen moved their combined herds from Texas and moved West,[24] selling their beef cattle at Fort Sumner, New Mexico, and afterward establishing a ranch in southern Colorado with their stock cattle. Loving died in 1867, the victim of Comanche arrowheads, and for the next eight years Goodnight ran the Colorado ranch without a partner, only taking time out to travel to Hickman, Kentucky, in 1870 to marry a longtime flame named Mary Ann Dwyer. In 1875 Goodnight moved his herd back into Texas and located in the Palo Duro Canyon, where he built the Old Home Ranch and, some years later, went into partnership with a wealthy Irishman named John Adair. This enterprise operated under the JA brand, and by 1884 the partners owned one hundred thousand head of cattle and more than two thousand square miles of grazing land. Adair died in 1885, and after negotiating with the widow Adair, Goodnight dissolved the partnership on receipt of a fifth of the herd and around 140,000 acres of pasturage, a complete outfit known as the Quitague Ranch. While operating this ranch Goodnight tried crossing buffalo with domestic cattle, but although the resulting cattaloes were immune to most range pests, the experiment was a financial failure. In 1890 Goodnight sold the Quitague Ranch and returned to the Old Home Ranch in Palo Duro Canyon. This was to be his headquarters from then on, for although he owned a secondary ranch near Goodnight, Texas, he confined most of his

activities to the Palo Duro area. In 1926 Mrs. Goodnight died, and after spending a little over three years as a widower, Charles Goodnight was carried off by a heart attack on December 12, 1929. (See LOVING, OLIVER.)

GOOSENECK SPUR A spur in which the shank has been molded into the likeness of the head and neck of a goose.

GOPHER A name that can be applied to the North American land tortoise, although it usually refers to any of the forty species of ground squirrels that are found throughout the West. (See MARMOT and PRAIRIE DOG.)

GORDON, LONNIE Member of Bill Cook's gang of Oklahoma hard cases. Lonnie, who is known to have taken part in at least one bank robbery, was shot down and killed while resisting arrest at Sapulpa, Oklahoma, on August 2, 1894. (See COOK, BILL.)

GORE, GEORGE An Irish knight who left his County Sligo castle in the 1850s for a game-hunting tour of the Wild West. Sir George's party consisted of more than forty men, over a hundred horses, two dozen oxen, and twenty-seven wagons. This titled Irishman made a gory mess out of the West, and after he and his trigger-happy hunters had killed twenty-five hundred buffalo, forty grizzlies, and a few hundred head of smaller game, the United States Government called a halt to the slaughter and bade Sir George "begone." (See BRIDGER, JIM.)

GRAHAM, J. W. The man who took those famous posthumous photographs

[24] For this trail-driving adventure Goodnight had a covered wagon converted into a cookhouse on wheels; this was the first chuckwagon to be used in the West. Some years later this inventive streak surfaced once again, and the Goodnight side saddle for ladies was introduced and was an immediate success.

of Jesse James. Graham, who was born in 1856, had six years of experience as a photographer behind him and was working at the James Porch photographic studios at St. Joseph, Missouri, on the morning of Jesse's death. After hearing of the shooting he succeeded in getting exclusive permission to photograph the body,[25] and he was around at the Siedenfaden Funeral Parlor with his 8-inch-by-10-inch plate camera before Jesse had been given time to cool. Graham exposed two plates, both of which were successful, and for the next few months, orders for the prints poured in.[26] This was the highlight of Graham's career, yet it was far from the end of it. By 1890 he had opened his own studio, and that this was a success is evident from the fact that he was able to retire in the early 1900s.

GRAHAM-TEWKSBURY FEUD
Usually referred to as the Pleasant Valley War. (See PLEASANT VALLEY WAR.)

GRAHAM, WILLIAM B. A man from Missouri who began to lay the foundations of his "Curly Bill" Brocius image on becoming one of the Old Man Clanton's key men in the early months of 1880. Prior to this period the activities of William Brocius Graham are somewhat vague. He had ridden for various Texas cow outfits and he was known in the Kansas trail towns, but whether he had indulged in any rustling enterprises or had killed anyone before his arrival in Arizona Territory has never been established. On October 26, 1880, Curly Bill, accompanied by Pony Deal and

other members of the Clanton gang, ro(into Tombstone from their headquarte at Galeyville. During that same eveni Curly and Pony got likkered up, and twelve-thirty the following morni Curly shot Marshal Fred White when tl latter was attempting to arrest him. (hearing the shot, Wyatt Earp came White's assistance, and after buffaloi Curly, he lodged both him and Pony the local jail. Curly[27] was charged wi the murder of White, but as the dyi marshal had made a deathbed confessi(to the effect that the rustler's gun ha been discharged accidentally, Curly w released.

In July 1881 a number of Curly Bil men attempted to hold up the store (Isaac and William Haslett at Huachit New Mexico, but they were driven o after two of their number, Bill Leona and Harry Head, had been killed by tl Hasletts. Curly objected to this reducti(of his forces, and a few days later and John Ringo rode into Huachita an calmly shot Isaac and William to deatl No arrests were made for this double kil ing, and during that same month, Cur reached a new "high" in his murdero career when he, Ringo, and other men bers of the Clanton gang ambushed Mexican trail herd in the San Luis Pa and killed fourteen *vaqueros* before mo ing off with their cattle.[28]

On December 28, 1881, Brocius pa ticipated in the attempted assassination (Virgil Earp, and a short time lat(he engaged in a couple of sta holdups: the Tombstone-Bisbee sta robbery of January 6, and the Toml stone-Benson stage robbery that o(

---

[25] Graham also got permission to photograph the Ford brothers, who at the time were b ing held in the local jail. These negatives have, unfortunately, now been lost.
[26] Two sizes, which sold for twenty-five and fifty cents apiece.
[27] At the hearing Graham gave his name as William Rosciotis.
[28] Six *vaqueros* were killed with the first volley. The remainder surrendered, only to t tortured to death by Curly Bill and his men.

curred the following day.[29] The robberies got deputy U. S. Marshal Wyatt Earp on the trail of Brocius and company, but the outlaws lay low in the Chiricahua Mountains, and the posse returned to Tombstone without making any arrests. Curly should have stayed in the healthy climate of the mountains, but he returned to Tombstone on March 17 to organize the murder of Morgan Earp— an ambush killing that occurred that same night. After the killing Brocius and his gunnies headed for the timber, but now there was no place to hide, for a posse led by Wyatt was hunting them down with a show of relentlessness that has rarely been equaled. On March 23 the posse caught up with the outlaws at Iron Springs (now Mescal Springs) in the Whetstone Mountains, and William Brocius Graham was killed by a double blast from Earp's shotgun, which had been fired from such close range that the outlaw was nearly blown to pieces. (See BREAKENRIDGE, WILLIAM MILTON; CLANTON GANG; CLANTON, N. H.; EARP, MORGAN; EARP, VIRGIL; EARP, WYATT BERRY STAPP; and RINGGOLD, JOHN.)

GRAND CANYON A giant gorge in northwestern Arizona through which a two-hundred-mile stretch of the Colorado River flows. Roughly speaking the canyon runs in a longitudinal direction and confines that length of the Colorado, which lies between the mouth of the Little Colorado in the east and the eastern extremity of man-made Lake Mead[30] in the west. This natural wonder has a maximum depth of one mile and is twenty miles across at its widest point, and its sides and free-standing pillars reveal varicolored rock layers that go back millions of years in geological history.[31] The first white American to see the gorge was James Pattie, a mountain man who visited the area in 1826. Forty-three years later, Major J. Powell made the first successful boat passage of the gorge. The Grand Canyon is a major tourist attraction.

GRANNAN, RILEY Top western gambler who was born at Paris, Kentucky, in 1868, and who started his working life as a hotel bellboy. Riley was a student of the ponies, and as such he is credited with the invention of modern form-betting, but he is probably best remembered as the only man to have put $275,000 on a horse and won. In 1907 Riley bought a plot of land at Rawhide, Nevada, for $40,000. On this site he planned to erect a palace that would cater to all the lowdown whims of man. What Riley had in mind will unfortunately never be known, for on April 3, 1908, and before his plans had gotten off the ground, poor Riley died. The assets of the deceased toted up to a little over $100— obviously a case of "easy come, easy go."

GRANT, JOE A Texas gunman who was shot dead by Billy the Kid in Bob Hargrove's Saloon at Fort Sumner, New Mexico, in January 1879.[32] This is about all we know of Mr. Grant; a small walk-on, carry-off role in the saga of Billy the Kid. Despite this lack of facts, western historians have, over the years,

---

[29] On the Tombstone-Bisbee robbery, which netted the outlaws more than eight thousand dollars in cash, Graham was accompanied by Frank Stilwell, Pony Deal, Ike Clanton, and Pete Spence. The Tombstone-Benson job netted around twenty-five hundred dollars, but Curly had to share this with Pony only.

[30] The pileup of waters behind Boulder Dam.

[31] According to scientists, one billion years, but maybe we can give or take a year or so.

[32] Invariably given as 1880 in spite of the fact that Billy the Kid confessed to the shooting of Grant before a court of inquiry that was held in 1879.

been giving Joe a buildup, and now he is usually allowed to deliver a few hundred words of tough dialogue before a bullet gets mixed up with his beer. These versions vary inasmuch as the shootouts occur in either Lincoln or Fort Sumner, but otherwise they are basically the same. Joe, who is out to get the Kid and is wearing an engraved or unengraved single- or double-action revolver[33] that has one or two empty cartridge cases in its cylinder, begins to "lean" on Billy when the latter enters the saloon where Joe is getting tanked. The Kid plays it cool and smooth-talks the Texan into letting him examine his engraved or unengraved gun, then Joe snatches it back and takes a pot shot at the Kid: "Click!" Yup! The Kid's spun the cylinder so the hammer has fallen on one of those empty shell cases we mentioned, and before Joe can recover from his surprise the crafty little outlaw has shot him dead. That a tough Texas gunman[34] would hand over his gun and then not notice it was being tampered with takes some swallowing, but if he did, he deserves all he got. (See McCARTY, HENRY.)

GRAPESHOT REVOLVER
This French importation was a nine-shot double-barreled (over and under) percussion pistol from which an additional charge, consisting of twenty-gauge shot, could be fired through the lower barrel. Not very sporting, and its use was no doubt frowned upon by the more conventional type of gunslick.

GRATTAN FIGHT   Occurred when Lieutenant Grattan led thirty men on a punitive expedition[35] against an encampment of Miniconjou and Brule Sioux that was located about ten miles east of Fort Laramie. The lieutenant and his walk-a-heaps had muzzle-loaders and two howitzers to back up their play, while their opponents, some four thousand Sioux under Chief Conquering Bear and Man Afraid of His Horses,[36] had enough arrows to darken the sky. Grattan opened hostilities by firing a couple of rounds from his howitzers into the camp, a badly aimed salute that caused no casualties and, oddly enough, failed to provoke the Indians. This would never do, so the lieutenant had his men open up with their small arms, and this brought results: Conquering Bear fell with the first volley, and Grattan's career was nipped in the bud by the Indians' flinty-headed return volley. The dead lieutenant's command attempted a withdrawal, but it was a slow business on foot, and the Indian cavalry ran them into the ground and killed them to the last man. The fight took place on August 19, 1854, and it is usually, though incorrectly, referred to as a massacre.

GRATTAN MASSACRE   This was a fight, not a massacre. (See GRATTAN FIGHT.)

GRAVES, WILLIAM   Member of Henry Plummer's gang of road agents. William, who usually wore a stylish plug hat and went around under the alias of

[33] Joe is sometimes credited with carrying two revolvers.

[34] Very tough, and his guns are sometimes given a varying number of notches to prove it. These notches also help to give him a vague background, and foster the impression that Joe wasn't exactly a failure before meeting up with the Kid.

[35] The Indians had shot a white man's cow after it had run amok in their encampment and wrecked a couple of lodges. Grattan's command of foot soldiers consisted of a sergeant, a corporal, twenty-five privates, two musicians, and a half-breed interpreter named Lucien Auguste.

[36] The accepted translation, although "They Are Afraid of His Horses" would be more correct.

Whiskey Bill, is known to have taken part[37] in the robbery of the Virginia City–Salt Lake City stage in November 1863. No one was injured during this holdup, and the outlaws got a mere five hundred dollars for their efforts; in other words, it was a pretty small beer. The vigilantes, however, regarded the holdup in a different light, and when they caught up with Whiskey Bill at Fort Owen, Montana, in January 1864, they immediately carried him off into the wilderness and hanged him without further ado. (See INNOCENTS; PLUMMER, HENRY; and VIGILANTES OF MONTANA.)

GRAYBACK   Common term for a louse. Grayback, Texas, once a lice-ridden cow camp, derives its name from the vermin.

GREASY GRASS   Indian name for the Valley of the Little Big Horn; located in Montana and the site of the Custer disaster. (See BATTLE ON THE LITTLE BIG HORN.)

GREAT SALT LAKE   A large body of saline water located in northwestern Utah. Covering an area of 1,500 square miles but having a maximum depth of only 20 feet, the Great Salt Lake is all that remains of a huge prehistoric lake that geologists refer to as Lake Bonneville. Three rivers feed the lake, and as there is no outlet, evaporation has transformed the waters into a 20 per cent saline solution, mainly sodium chloride (i.e., common salt).

GREELEY, HORACE   New York newspaper owner, editor, and reporter who, although known in other spheres, is only of interest here by reason of the fact that he toured the Wild West in the summer of 1859 and left a lively account of his travels for posterity.[38] Greeley, who was born at Amherst, New Hampshire, on February 3, 1811, arrived in New York in 1831 with only a few dollars in his pants, but within eighteen months he had acquired sufficient capital to go into partnership with Francis V. Story and become a cofounder of the Morning Post. This enterprise failed within a matter of weeks, but by 1836, and after various other journalistic ventures, Horace was solvent enough to get married,[39] and some five years later he founded the world-famous New York Tribune. Much of Greeley's later life was devoted to politics, and in May 1872 he was nominated for President, but he was defeated at the polls by Ulysses S. Grant. Horace Greeley died at New York on November 29, 1872, exactly thirty days after the death of his wife. He was survived by two daughters, Gabrielle and Ida.

GREEN, BALDY   Stagecoach whip who drove his six-in-hand along the trails linking the Nevada gold camps in the 1860s. Baldy's route was plagued by highwaymen, but no harm ever came to Green, for he always handed the strongbox over with a great show of politeness —almost as if he were glad to get rid of it, in fact. Wells Fargo is alleged to have fired Baldy while they still had some

[37] Three men took part in this holdup, the other two being George Ives and Bob Zachary.
[38] An Overland Journey from New York to San Francisco in the Summer of 1859. Published by C. M. Saxton, Barker and Company, New York (1860). Republished by Alfred A. Knopf, Inc., New York (1963) and MacDonald and Company, London (1965). Territories and states traversed by Greeley during his tour included Missouri, Kansas, Nebraska, Utah, and California.
[39] The bride being Mary V. Cheney, whom he married on July 5, 1836. Mary gave Horace seven children, but only two survived infancy. Horace had a second love, a girl named Margaret Fuller. This relationship is reputed to have been platonic, and it ended with the death of Margaret (by shipwreck) in 1850.

strongboxes left. They may have, for he did leave their employ, after which he is reported to have become a justice of the peace. The "Ballad of Baldy Green" is a rollicking sendup of Green's stagecoach days.

GREENHORN An inexperienced person, a simpleton; synonymous with "tenderfoot."

GREEN RIVER KNIFE Any knife manufactured at the Green River works of J. Russell and Co. These knives, which were produced from around 1836 onward, vary as to blade shape, but all are on the small side (6-inch blades) and have the wording "J. Russell and Co., Green River Works" stamped on their blades. The latter portion of this wording ended near the wooden handle, hence the mountain man expression "to give him up to Green River"—which meant to sink your blade into a person up to the hilt. By extension "up to Green River" meant to carry out a task thoroughly. English knives imported during the 1820–30 period had "G.R." (George Rex—George IV) stamped on their blades, and the fact that "G.R." can be abbreviation of anything from "Green River" to "get ruptured" has led many a historian into the erroneous belief that these English knives were the original Green River knives.

GRIEGO, FRANCISCO A Mexican who was born in the land of the gringos and who is sometimes credited with wearing a town marshal's badge for a period, while other reports suggest he was a real bad *hombre* whose gun butts were corrugated with notches. He could have been either, neither, or both. In the spring of 1875 Francisco, or Pancho (as he is usually referred to) is alleged to have killed or wounded three U.S. troopers[40] during a brawl that occurred in Hank Lambert's Saloon at Cimarron, New Mexico. Some reports state that Pancho was wearing the Cimarron town marshal badge at the time, and as he was allowed to remain at liberty after the shootout, it appears likely that he may have been. Some months after this fracas a friend of Pancho's named Cruz Vega was lynched by a mob in which Clay Allison was a prominent member, and on hearing of Vega's death, Pancho swore to get Allison. On November 1, 1875, the two men met in Hank Lambert's Saloon but Allison drew first and put one, two or three bullets into the Mexican, and Pancho expired *mucho pronto*. Someone then shot out, or blew out, the lights, and the body of Pancho wasn't found until the following morning; which prompts us to ask, "Had no one gotta match?" (See ALLISON, CLAY, and VEGA, CRUZ.)

GRINGO Contemptuous Mexican name for Anglo Americans. The fact that "Green Grow the Rushes" was a favorite nineteenth-century American song has given rise to the belief that "gringo" is more or less phonetic rendering of "green grow"; this is an ingenious surmise and nothing more.

GRIZZLY BEAR A variety of dish faced bear. (See BEARS.)

GROS VENTRE INDIANS The French name,[41] now universally accepted, for a tribe of nomadic plain plateau dwellers who were ranging the Wyoming-Idaho area in the 1800s, having filtered down from Canada over the

---

[40] Clay Allison is reputed to have done the same thing, in the same place, sometimes at the same time.

[41] Pronounced "Gro Vant," and literally meaning "fat bellies."

previous century. Although belonging to the Algonkin language group, the Gros Ventre mode of life seems to have been adopted from the Mandan and Hidasta tribes. (See MANDAN INDIANS.)

GROUARD, FRANK General George Crook's chief of scouts during the North Plains Indian campaigns of 1876–77. Grouard[42] was born on the island of Ana[43] in 1850, the marital offspring of a French missionary father and his Polynesian bride.[44] In 1852 the Grouards left the South Seas and settled in California, and here Frank was educated and indoctrinated with the American way of life. In the closing years of his teens Frank started work as a mail carrier on the Fort Ellis (Montana)–Fort Hall (Idaho) run, but this job didn't last long, for after making only a few trips he was captured by Sioux Indians, who, in deference to his dark complexion, treated him rather well, so that for the next six years Frank was quite content to remain with the Indians as a more or less voluntary captive. Over this period Grouard became well acquainted with Crazy Horse and Sitting Bull, the latter adopting him as a brother, whom he christened "Sitting with Upraised Hands" (Frank was probably always wanting to leave the tepee). In the early months of 1876, Sitting with Upraised Hands left the Sioux and, as already related, became an Army scout.[45] At the close of the North

Plains campaign Grouard had deteriorated into a poxed-up wreck of a man, and he died some years later.

GROUND HOG Popular name for a marmot. (See MARMOT.)

GROUND SQUIRREL Any member of the forty species of ground squirrels that are well distributed throughout the United States. Gophers,[46] prairie dogs, and chipmunks are all ground squirrels. (See MARMOT and PRAIRIE DOG.)

G-STRING The adjustable string that circles the waist of Indian males. The breechcloth[47] that passed between the legs was supported by this string so that the ends of the clout hung like miniature aprons at both front and rear of the wearer. The string could also be used to support leggings.

GULCH A narrow yet deep ravine that has steep sides and has been formed by the torrential action of water.

GUNBELT Any belt that has been manufactured for the specific purpose of carrying a pistol or has been adapted for that purpose. Holsters could be a permanent fixture, although usually they were merely slotted[48] onto the belt. With the advent of the metal cartridge, cart-

---

[42] At some period of his career Grouard is believed to have used the name of Prazost.

[43] A small island in the Friendly Group.

[44] Now for some variations: Frank is sometimes reputed to have been the bastard offspring of an American sailor and a grass-skirted lass of Hawaii, or alternatively, the illegitimate product of a French trapper named John Brazeau and some unspecified Indian girl.

[45] After this spot of turncoat behavior—at least to the Indian way of reasoning—the Sioux more or less struck Sitting with Upraised Hands from the roll and rechristened Frank "The Grabber." The sketching of a snake's tongue against the latter name would have been quite in order, for it is reliably reported that Frank was a monumental liar.

[46] The twenty-five species of which are classed as true ground squirrels.

[47] A piece of cloth or skin which, on average, measured about 5 feet by 1 foot.

[48] Or occasionally fitted to a stud (or, alternatively, fastened to a rawhide thong), which allowed the holster to swivel.

ridge loops, in varying numbers, became an integral part of most gunbelts. (See BUSCADERO; CARTRIDGE BELT; and HOLSTER.)

GUNFIGHTER A term which, when used correctly, describes a dextrous pistoleer who has a noncriminal past and who is usually a lawman or ex-lawman. In other words, any man whose pistol skill is exceptional and whose gunplay can be legally justified.

GUNFIGHTING Any dispute in which pistols are used can be loosely classed as gunfighting. The term, however, immediately brings to mind visions of the old West where the advent of the six-shooter, coupled with the lack of law enforcement, established an era in which gunfighting became the accepted method of settling an argument, preferably permanently. Between the years 1850 and 1890 around twenty thousand men died in Wild West-type shootouts, so it is not surprising that over this period gunfighting developed into something like a fine art. Methods of carrying a gun (or guns) varied considerably, as did the choice of weapons, although single-action[49] revolvers were usually preferred to double-action models, and an empty chamber was invariably left under the firing pin as a safety precaution. The guns themselves frequently dictated the manner in which they should be worn; Colt's Dragoon and Navy percussion revolvers possessed trigger spurs that were at a ninety-degree angle to the frame, and these guns could be brought into action quicker if they were holstered[50] with

their butts foremost; other pistols, such as Colt's Peacemaker and Frontiers, and Remington's Army and Navy models, whose trigger spurs angled to the rear, could be drawn and cocked faster if worn in the more conventional (butts facing rearward) manner. A man who spent much of his time in the saddle would usually wear his gun, butt foremost, on the left hip; this meant making a crossdraw (which is somewhat slower, for the arm has farther to travel), but it did prevent his pistol from flying out of its holster when he mounted his horse in a hurry. Two guns were rarely worn,[51] but if they were it didn't necessarily mean that their owner was ambidextrous. Such a gunnie would draw his favored gun first, only resorting to bringing his second pistol into play if he'd done little damage with his first five shots; this rarely happened, for if our two-gun man had failed to put his opponent out of action by then, he would most likely be dead before he had squeezed off his sixth shot. Most gunfighting was done at close range, instances being on record in which the victim's clothes have been set on fire by his opponent's gun flash. The first shot to hit its target[52] was usually the clincher, for a .45 slug drives a man backward like a giant fist, and the second shot (if necessary) could be placed at leisure. To sum up: Although essential, a fast draw took second place to a calm mind; such fancy Dan stuff as fanning was a sure-fire way to end up on Boot Hill, and being too quick on the trigger could end up with the shooter being minus a toe (Clay Allison is alleged to have done this on one occasion). (See BUSCADERO; CAR-

---

[49] The opening shots—the crucial ones usually—can be squeezed off faster from a single-action revolver.

[50] If holsters were used. Hickok, who used Navy Colts for the greater part of his career, rarely used holsters, preferring to carry his twin Navy's tucked into a sash or a belt.

[51] Two Colts, plus gunbelt and cartridges, weigh around 8 pounds; this explains the shortage of two-gun men.

[52] Usually the belt buckle. Fancy stuff like shooting between the eyes or blowing off a bloke's earlobes was rarely indulged in.

TRIDGE BELT; FANNING; FAST DRAW; GUNBELT; and LOVING, FRANK.)

GUNMAN Any armed man who will use his gun against armed or unarmed men while he is engaged in activities of a criminal or terrorist nature.

GUNNISON MASSACRE Occurred in Utah's Pahvant Valley when Captain John W. Gunnison and his party[53] of eleven men were overwhelmed by a Paiute war party at dawn on the twenty-sixth of October 1853. Four of the party managed to escape, but the remainder were killed and mutilated.

GUNSIGHT LODE One of the many "lost mines" that are alleged to litter the West. (See LOST MINES.)

[53] The party, which was surveying a route for the Central Pacific Railroad, consisted of Captain Gunnison, R. H. Kern, F. Creuzfeldt, W. Potter, a camp cook, and seven soldiers. All those named, plus the cook and three of the privates, were killed by the Indians.

Hacienda Ranch or large plantation with dwelling. Spanish-American hangover from the days when the southwestern territories were Mexican possessions.

HACKAMORE Corruption of the Spanish *jaquima*, meaning "headstall." A horse-riding halter. (See HALTER.)

HALTER Lead rope for a horse, or riding equipment consisting of headstall, noseband, etc. Can be of rope, but is usually of leather.

HAND, DORA Sometimes known as Fannie Keenan, a name that may have been genuine, although this mystery girl is usually referred to as Dora Hand. Little is known about her prior to her arrival at Dodge City, Kansas, and as this pre-Dodge period accounted for a probable 99 per cent of her lifetime, legend and rumor have tended to fill this vacuum. Dora may have been born in the Beacon Street area of Boston, and she may have been educated in Europe and had a brilliant career singing in grand opera in both Europe and the States, but if the foregoing is correct, one wonders why she ever left this luxurious existence to become the answer to any cowboy's prayer in a rough-and-ready cowtown such as Dodge. We can only step onto solid ground (almost hand-in-hand with Dora) from the time she descended from the coach that brought her to Dodge City in the early spring of 1878. The newcomer to Dodge was some woman; such a beautiful lass that when word-of-mouth stories spread the gossip that ten to twelve men had been killed in disputes over her favors, said stories were readily believed.

In Dodge, Dora led a double life; genteel and kind and helper of the poor and needy during the hours of daylight; saloon and theater singer until they "rolled up the sidewalks"; and then a good stint whoring in her quarters, which were situated south of the railroad tracks.[1] That she sang in saloons, and on occasion trod the boards with Eddie Foy gives credence

[1] To quote one of Dora's contemporaries, ". . . only thing anyone could hold against her was her after-dark profession, and by Godfrey, I allow she elevated that considerably."

to the "grand opera" background, and although she became known as "Queen of the Fairybelles," these frowned-upon after-dark capers did not prevent her from being a regular churchgoer.

At this time the mayor of Dodge was James H. ("Dog") Kelley, and he may have been responsible for Dora's arrival at Dodge, for during this period of her life "Dog" was her closest friend—a friendship that was to prove fatal for Miss Hand. Through the summer of 1878 a feud had been smoldering—possibly over Dora—between Kelley and a cowboy named James Kennedy, and at four o'clock on the Tuesday morning of October 8, 1878, after having become suitably "juiced," Kennedy galloped up to "Dog" Kelley's shack and pumped two .45 slugs in the general direction of where he assumed the mayor would be sleeping. The second of these slugs killed Dora Hand outright, for, unknown to Kennedy, His Honor was sufficiently indisposed to be tucked up in bed at the post hospital at Fort Dodge, and Dora, who during his absence was sharing his crude residence with a doxie named Fannie Garretson, was sleeping in the mayor's bed.[2]

Little detective work was needed, and a coroner's jury named James Kennedy as the killer in quick time, so that Sheriff Bat Masterson built up a posse—a posse whose spine was stiffened by such men as Wyatt Earp, Charlie Bassett, Neal Brown, and Bill Tilghman—and thundered off after the culprit. The fugitive didn't freeze when the lawmen got within long gun range; he should have, for Bat put a bullet in Kennedy's right arm, and

Wyatt brought Kennedy's horse down. When the lawmen gathered around, the shattered Kennedy wanted to know whether he'd "gotten 'Dog' Kelley," and on being told that he'd killed Dora Hand, he made words to the effect that Bat should have shot him dead. This show of remorse, plus top-rate lawyers and a pathetically crippled right arm, helped at his subsequent trial, and he was acquitted.[3] The victim of this tragic error was given one of the grandest funerals in the history of Dodge, the cortege that followed her to her last resting place within the precincts of Prairie Grove Cemetery consisting of the majority of the cow capital's citizens.[4] (See FOY, EDDIE, and KELLEY, JAMES H.)

HANKS, CAMILLA This unpresentable individual, who was born in DeWitt County, Texas, in 1863, is frequently referred to as "Deaf Charley" and occasionally as Charles Jones, the former being a nickname that alluded to a right-ear failure, and the latter being an adopted alias. The Pinkerton files[5] give his legal profession as "cowboy" and his criminal profession as "train robber," the latter activity being engaged in while riding with the Wild Bunch. In the summer of 1892 he was arrested in Teton County, Montana, on suspicion of being concerned in a Northern Pacific train robbery, and that same year he was handed down a ten-year stretch in the Deer Lodge Penitentiary after a jury had decided the suspicion was well founded. On April 30, 1901, the gates opened for Charley, now a barrel-bodied thirty-eight-year-old with his ginger hair in a hog

[2] There are other versions, but as these tend to further tarnish Miss Hand, let us be generous and accept this version.
[3] A rather odd verdict, for it was a cowardly attack that caused the death of Dora Hand.
[4] Most writers state that Dora was buried here—instead of the ignominious "Boot Hill" —because she was held in high esteem, but this is incorrect, for on the completion of Prairie Grove Cemetery, the makeshift Boot Hill was no longer used. (See BOOT HILL.)
[5] In these files his name is given as O. C. Hanks.

bristle cut, and just over two months later he was giving a hand in the robbery of a Great Northern Railway express at Wagner, Montana. The proceeds were good from this caper, and he was still passing the bank notes taken in this robbery when he got mixed up in a saloon brawl in San Antonio, Texas on October 22, 1902. When the local law arrived, Charley flashed a gun, but a piece of lawful lead transferred him into the past tense before he could do any damage. Pink Taylor is the lawman who is usually credited with this example of instant justice. (See WILD BUNCH.)

HARDIN, JANE   The wife of John Wesley Hardin. (See BOWEN, JANE, and HARDIN, JOHN WESLEY.)

HARDIN, JOHN WESLEY   Born on May 26, 1853, at Bonham, Texas, the second son to be born to Rev. James G. Hardin and Mary Elizabeth Hardin. Little did these God-fearing parents know that John Wesley, whom they hoped would follow in his father's footsteps, would become the most sadistic killer ever to come out of the Lone Star State. In his later years Wes blamed a lifetime of homicidal activity on the Civil War and its aftermath; this was when he had around forty killings behind him and at a time when he may have had a desire to see someone else in the mirror.

A black man became his first victim when fifteen-year-old Wes emptied a Colt .44 into the man, our "hero's" justification being that the man "shook a stick" at him. This "justification" didn't set well with the local norms, so Wes became a fugitive, and as Texas was under Yankee military rule at this period, a cavalry detail of three troopers was put on his trail. During his flight Wes had picked up from his older brother Joe a twin-holstered belt and a brace of .44s, and when the troopers overtook him he used this hardware to good effect, killing the trio in exchange for a wound in his left arm.

A short time later, and while still on the run, Wes, aided on this occasion by a cousin of his named Simp Dixon,[6] ambushed and killed two more Yankee soldiers. After this affair he surfaced in Towash, where, on December 25, 1869 (good will to all men!), he killed a gambler named James Bradley; hard words after a poker game were Mr. Bradley's swan song. This shootout exposed Wes' mean streak to a marked degree; Bradley was begging for mercy with two bullets in his body when Hardin squeezed off four more shots.

Over the next eighteen months Wes must have given off a heady aroma of gunpowder fumes, the kill count over this period being four police officers, one redskin (during a trail drive—Wes worked occasionally), and a half-dozen Mexicans (the same trail drive). When this battle-weary trail crew arrived in Abilene, Kansas, on June 1, 1871, its key men, Mannen and Gyp Clements (Wes' cousins), and the eighteen-year-old Wes, were given a hearty welcome by Ben Thompson and Phil Coe, two colorful characters whom Wes had met in Brenham, Texas, while he was taking a breather from being a fugitive. Ben followed up this welcome by attempting to incite Wes into gunning down the town marshal. Wild Bill Hickok was behind the badge at this time, and he and Ben had not been seeing eye to eye for quite a spell, mainly on account of Ben's over-sexed sign that advertised his Bull's Head Tavern, and, to a lesser degree, Ben's shady gambling activities. Hardin turned

[6] Simp, who had a fair price on his head, was later killed by troopers in Limestone County, Texas.

this suggestion down, which may or may not suggest that he considered the odds a trifle risky.[7]

Yet, even though Wes may not have wished to have a serious showdown with Hickok, during Wes' Abilene days he is alleged to have murdered a Mexican, rescued Mannen Clements from jail, and killed an intruder who, intent on mayhem or worse, ventured into a room of the American Hotel that Wes was sharing with cousin Gyp. After this last-mentioned killing Wes and Gyp disappeared into the night, a hasty retreat without pants or boots that Gyp may have accelerated by suggesting that Hickok would be most likely coming around to inquire what all the shooting was about. Whatever the reason, Hardin never showed in Abilene again. Gonzales County, Texas, felt his sanguinary presence next, Wes' death tally in this area being five black policemen who wanted to arrest him, and one Mexican road agent who merely wanted his wallet.

In the spring of 1872 Hardin married Jane Bowen, a girl from Coon Hollow whom he had been courting between powder-burning episodes. Marriage failed to quiet Wes, although it did steady him inasmuch as he built up a horse-trading business so that he would have a steady income on which to support his wife. Around August 1872 he got into an argument over a bowling game with a man named Sublett, and in this instance it was Wes who was carried from the field shot to the point of touch-and-go. While recovering from this incident, but still confined to his bed, he killed a police officer who visited the sickroom flashing a warrant. After this killing he surrendered to Sheriff Dick Reagan, but after second

thoughts on the matter he escaped from custody while en route to the Gonzales jail.[8]

It wasn't long after returning home to Jane that Wes got involved in the Sutton-Taylor feud, and as an indirect result of this, Deputy Sheriff J. B. Morgan and Sheriff Jack Helm became fatal casualties of Hardin's guns, the former at Cuero, Texas, in April 1873, and the latter at Albuquerque, Texas, in the fall of the same year. Some six months later, in May of 1874, and while celebrating both his twenty-first birthday and a big win at the Comanche races, Wes killed Deputy Charles Webb in a Comanche saloon. At long last folk were getting tired of John Wesley, and he was only saved from a neck-stretching session by the timely arrival of Sheriff Karnes who, on sensing the temper of the mob and not wishing to have a lynching on his hands, allowed Wes to escape instead of taking him into custody, as had been his intention.

The sight of an angry lynch mob may have chilled Hardin somewhat, for he put a greater distance between himself and his pursuers than he had ever felt called upon to do before, only settling down with Jane when they reached Gainesville, Florida. Here, under the name of J. H. Swain, he bought a saloon, but this was a short-lived venture, and by the early months of 1875 he was running a cattle business near Jacksonville, Florida. Pollard, Alabama, saw him next in the guise of a timber merchant, but in spite of all these moves and a change of name, the lawmen had not given up their quest for Wes.

Back in Texas, Ranger Captain John Armstrong, a tenacious bloodhound who wanted Hardin for the murder of Deputy

[7] In Wes's biography, published after Hickok's death, this Texas hellion gives a few accounts of how he made Wild Bill back down on more than one occasion. If this bugle talk had much substance, how come he didn't do good old Ben the favor asked?

[8] According to Wes this was in October 1872. Some unnamed individual smuggled a hacksaw to him, and he cut through the bars.

Sheriff Charles Webb, received the intelligence that Neal Bowen (Wes' father-in-law) had been getting mail bearing the Pollard, Alabama, postmark. The outcome of this was that Captain Armstrong and Ranger Jack Duncan arrived at Pollard on August 22, 1877, and within days, Hardin had been tucked safely away behind the walls of the Montgomery, Alabama, jail. There was no hacksaw this time, and after being transferred to Comanche, Texas, to stand trial for the murder of Webb, on October 1, 1877, Wes heard himself being sentenced to twenty-five years in the State Prison at Huntsville.

After more than sixteen years spent mostly at hard labor—punctuated with an occasional abortive attempt at escape, and crimped periods of leisure spent reading law and the Bible—Wes was granted a pardon and released from prison on February 17, 1894. After his release Hardin settled down to study law, and by the winter of 1894 he had become a fully qualified attorney and was displaying his shingle at Gonzales, Texas. Clients, however, steered clear of Wes, and the following year he pulled up stakes and transferred his practice to El Paso, Texas. He got a client here, the type of client who would jack up the eyelids of any male, a luscious, blue-eyed blonde who filled her clothes profusely in all the right areas and who introduced herself as Mrs. Martin McRose. Her husband, wanted for numerous criminal offenses, was hiding out south of the Rio Grande, but, explained Mrs. McRose, he wished to return to home comforts: Would Wes protect him from El Paso's hair-trigger lawmen and look after his interests? Case accepted.

Wes began to see a lot of Mrs. McRose on business, and a lot more of her on no one's business, so that when Martin McRose was shot to death while attempting to cross the Rio Grande, neither client nor mouthpiece regretted his passing. In the first week of August 1895 Wes had to visit Pecos for a couple of days, and during his forty-eight hours' absence the blue-eyed blonde was arrested by policeman John Selman, Jr., for being drunk and disorderly and firing a pistol on the street, a misdemeanor that got her a fifty-dollar fine. Wes was furious that anyone should take such a liberty with his woman, and when he met John Selman's father on the street he berated him for siring such a misbegotten son. This was unwise, for Old Man Selman had ushered around twenty men into funeral parlors, and although pushing sixty, he was still handy with a gun. He was also a cop. At about eleven-fifteen on the night of August 19, 1895, the end came for John Wesley Hardin. It happened in the Acme Saloon on San Antonio Street, and Old John Selman made it happen. Some say Wes was shot in the back, but Selman denied this, and J.W.H. couldn't have cared less. (See BOWEN, JANE; CLEMENTS, EMANUEL; HELM, JACK; HICKOK, JAMES BUTLER; SELMAN, JOHN; SUTTON-TAYLOR FEUD; and THOMPSON, BEN.)

HARMONICA PISTOL   A type of multishot pistol, the magazine of which moved from left to right when the trigger was squeezed. This magazine was a flat metal block that somewhat resembled a harmonica. Mostly manufactured in France and Belgium, but some being produced in the United States from 1862 onward.

HARRIS, FRANK   They decided to call their strike "Bullfrog," for that was roughly the shape, size, and color of the piece of gold-bearing rock that the smaller of the two men had levered from the ground with the tip of his pick. This was in the fall of 1904, and the strike was to develop into one of Shorty Harris' better hits, Bullfrog and rhyolite mushrooming almost overnight in that arid area of Nevada's Armagosa Desert. Shorty went on a bender to celebrate, as was his custom, and on awakening with a king-sized headache, found, to his amazement, that he had sold his share in the bonanza for a mere $25,000.[9] Shorty wasn't too despondent over this, for it was a "play it again Sam" happening, and anyway, he always said he'd "rather find 'em than mine 'em."

Harris, who was born in the vicinity of Providence, Rhode Island, on July 21, 1857, started working his way West in 1871, provisioning himself by taking on any unskilled work that was available, and transporting himself by riding the rods. Frank arrived in California in 1879. He had now reached his full growth, 5 feet, 4 inches tall and weighing a bare 25 ounces to the inch, so from then on he was "Shorty." The following year he made a strike at Leadville, Colorado, but he sold out almost immediately at fractional value and got rid of the take in bordellos and booze joints; this set the pattern for all future operations. Coeur d'Alene, Silver Peak, Tombstone, then back to California, where he could be seen peeling 'taters to earn enough to live. Then a grubstake and a find in the Panamints, after which he sold his share for $7,000. Free drinks all around for a couple of months, and then back to the breadline. Strikes color in Death Valley; asks $15,000 for his share, but a monumental thirst forces him to accept a quick $1,000, and so on, and so on.

In his later years, Shorty settled at Ballarat, or, more correctly, Ballarat settled around Shorty, for this mercantile supply base for Death Valley expeditions was built around his campsite. It was here that Shorty fell in love with the local blacksmith, and, let us hasten to add, there was nothing abnormal about this, for the blacksmith at Ballarat was Miss Bessie Hart. Bessie was a lot of woman, over six feet tall and tipping the scales at around the two-hundred-pound mark, so it is not altogether surprising that when Shorty proposed, this Amazon turned him down. He didn't do any more proposing; he just spent the remainder of his life searching the Death Valley area for the biggest strike of all so that he could go to Paris (France) and get to know some of them mademoiselles he'd heard so much about. He never did find that last big one, but he hadn't given up hope of finding it, for he was still searching at the time of his death in 1934. He is buried beneath a cairn of stones near Hanaupah Canyon, Death Valley, and, owing to an error in both grave and casket measurements, Frank "Shorty" Harris is buried standing up.

HARRIS, SHORTY A little prospector who had his ups and downs. (See HARRIS, FRANK.)

HART, PEARL Born Pearl Taylor at Lindsay, Ontario, Canada, in 1878, but this surname was soon changed to Hart, for at the tender age of sixteen, and while still at boarding school, Pearl eloped with a ne'er-do-well named William Hart. William only worked to support his thirst, so, rather than starve, Pearl left him and moved south of the forty-ninth parallel. Around about her twenty-first birthday Pearl was slinging hash in a Mammoth, Arizona, eatery, and here she met a mineworker named Joe Boot. Joe was no outlaw, but when Pearl needed some quick money (to visit her mother, who was seriously ill), he was

[9] Ed Cross, his partner at that time, sold his share for $125,000.

the one who suggested robbing a stage-coach. Pearl seconded this suggestion, and on May 30, 1899, the Benson-Globe stage was flagged down by this pair of amateurs; Joe was armed with a scatter-gun, and Pearl, clad in male attire, was armed with a tough expression. Pocket-ing the loot, a little over four hundred dollars taken from the passengers, the two holdup artists disappeared into the brush. Boot and Pearl didn't have horses, and when they arrived at their cabin a few days later the lawmen were waiting on the doorstep. Joe Boot got thirty-five years in the territorial prison at Yuma, and after the doors had clanged behind him we hear nothing more about him. This was not the case with Pearl, for al-though sentenced to five years, she was pardoned after serving little more than two years, a short enough spell to have kept her alive in the public memory. Billed as "The Arizona Bandit," she toured the theaters giving a padded-out version of her criminal career.[10] This theatrical stint lasted about a year; then in 1905 we hear of her again. In that year she was arrested in New Mexico on suspicion of participating in a train rob-bery, but later released for lack of evi-dence. The only thing we know about her over the next nineteen years is that she was getting older; then, in 1924, a well-groomed lady walked into the Pima County, Arizona, jail and requested that she be allowed to have a look around; the officials granted this request when she introduced herself as Pearl Hart.[11] After this . . . nothing.

HARTE, FRANCIS BRETT
American writer who was born in New York City in 1836. In his eighteenth year Brett traveled West to California, where he worked as a journalist, and it was here that he began writing stories with Wild West backgrounds. More than two hundred of these stories were pub-lished,[12] the most famous of which was "The Luck of Roaring Camp," a tough weepie published in 1868. He returned to New York in 1870, and eight years later we find him serving as a U.S. consul in Europe, where he spent two years in Germany and five in Scotland. Harte died in 1902.

HASHKNIFE OUTFIT One of the better-known cow outfits. (See AZTEC LAND & CATTLE COMPANY.)

HASLAM, ROBERT Better known as "Pony Bob." Contemporary of Buf-falo Bill Cody, and one of the top riders of the short-lived Pony Express enter-prise. Prior to joining the Pony Express, Haslam had carried mail across 400 miles of hostile Paiute territory without serious incident, but some five years later, and while getting the *mochila* through, a couple of Paiute arrowheads found him, and he slumped from the saddle at the end of his relay—about 100–20 miles —with arm and jaw shattered. On August 14, 1860, Bob, the last in a chain of riders, got honorable mention when he drummed his pony into Fort Churchill, Nevada, carrying the news of Lincoln's election.[13] There is some evidence that he did a little prospecting in later years, and we do know that he spent his last years of active life as advance agent for Buffalo Bill's Wild West Show. (See PONY EXPRESS.)

[10] A photo of Pearl taken during this period depicts her wearing male attire and armed with a rifle and a brace of pistols. One wonders if she knew how to fire this collection of kill-ing stuff.

[11] Some writers describe this visitor as "little white-haired old lady," but Pearl could hardly have merited such a description at the age of forty-six.

[12] Under the name of Bret Harte, a *t* having been dropped from "Brett."

[13] From Churchill the news could be tapped over the wires to California.

HASSAYAMPA A spinner of tall tales; a liar. Derived from the legend that anyone drinking from the waters of western Arizona's Hassayampa River will, from then onward, be unable to speak the truth. Sometimes spelled Hassayamper.

HATCHETMEN   The professional killers employed by the Chinese tongs. (See CHINESE TONGS and LITTLE PETE.)

HAUN'S HILL MASSACRE Occurred on October 30, 1838, in Missouri. On the afternoon of this day Nehemiah Comstock led more than two hundred men in an unprovoked attack against an encampment of Mormons, slaughtering twenty men, women, and children, then, after tossing the corpses down a well, plundering the camp. This sorry affair was committed in the name of religion. (See MOUNTAIN MEADOWS MASSACRE.)

HAVASUPAI INDIANS A minority group of Pueblo Indians who, from the dim past, have lived in northwestern Arizona, their village being situated on the floor of a sheer-walled canyon that is part of the Grand Canyon complex. During the warmer months crops are reared and seeds gathered, but during the late fall and winter, hunting parties work the high plateaus in search of game. As access to their village is limited to a couple of trails that will only accommodate horse traffic, the Havasupai are somewhat insular, but their thatched houses denote a Papago influence. Present-day Havasupai make a living selling tanned deer hides (tanning being a speciality of theirs) and acting as guides in the Grand

Canyon area. Pronounced "Ha-va-SUE-pie."

HAWKEN RIFLE This weapon, one of the most famous long guns of the Old West, was a capstock rifle manufactured by Jake and Sam Hawken at St. Louis, Missouri,[14] from 1822 onward. Hawkens came in a variety of calibers and barrel lengths, calibers ranging from .44 to .53 (a rare exception being as heavy as .66–.68), and the octagonal barrels being anywhere between 34 and 38 inches in length. Most of the locks were of foreign origin, being imported from a London gunsmith named R. Ashmore. The guns originally retailed at around $25, but as demand outgrew supply, the price was jacked up to the $40 mark. In 1862 Sam, the only surviving brother, sold the business to John Gemmer, and the latter continued to manufacture Hawken-type rifles until 1915.

HAYFIELD FIGHT A minor U. S. Army vs. Indians engagement that occurred in a hayfield located within sight of Fort C. F. Smith, Montana Territory. On the morning of August 1, 1867, Second Lieutenant Sigismund Sternberg and eight troopers, accompanied by nine civilians, were attacked by a large war party: a mixed force of Sioux, Cheyenne, and Arapaho. The white men were able to reach the shelter of a makeshift corral, and although the feathered cavalry mounted attacks throughout the day, they failed to dislodge the defenders, and by late afternoon the Indians withdrew, leaving the field littered with their dead. Of the white men, Sternberg, two of his men, and one civilian were the only fatal casualties. This skirmish could be seen and

---

[14] Much of this gun's early success may have been due to the fact that Jake and Sam had located well, St. Louis at that time being the headquarters of the fur-trading and trapping fraternity.

heard from within the fort, yet no relief party was ever ordered out to help the beleaguered men.[15] (See FETTERMAN FIGHT.)

HAYS CITY, KANSAS Located between the Smokey Hill and Big Creek rivers in Ellis County, western Kansas. Riproaring Hays City was founded in 1867, many of its buildings already having seen service in Buffalo Bill's town of Rome. Saloons and brothels were Hays City's backbone, and with more than two thousand soldiers being barracked at Fort Hays, a bare two miles from the townsite, trade in these places was never slack. A more sober type of commerce was also carried out at Hays. As it was situated like a period mark on an offshoot of the Santa Fe Trail, wagon trains used the town as a supply base and as a storage depot for freight that had been hauled in from New Mexico, such freight usually being raw materials whose ultimate destinations were the manufacturing centers of the middle-western and eastern states. By 1872 the Kansas Pacific tracks had reached Hays City, giving it the status of a cattle-shipping center, and in that year the town experienced the usual end-of-track population explosion: a mushroom cloud whose fallout consisted mainly of gamblers, prostitutes, dance-hall girls, saloonkeepers, and other soulless souls who were intent on separating the trail crews from their pay. Over this period, three large dance halls, more than twenty saloons, and countless red-light cribs kept the visiting Texans off the streets but not out of trouble. In 1873 Dodge City became the magnet for both cattlemen and parasites, and Hays City lost its aura of colorful wickedness. Still a thriving town that possesses a museum dedicated to its hectic past. (See ROME, KANSAS.)

HAYS, JACK A famous Texas Ranger captain. (See HAYS, JOHN COFFEE.)

HAYS, JOHN COFFEE Born in Wilson County, Kentucky, on April 26, 1818. John Coffee left home in his early teens, his idea being to head for Texas, but en route he paused to take up employment as a surveyor along the lower reaches of the Mississippi, and it was not until four years later that he finally reached his goal. In the fall of 1840 large Comanche war parties were causing havoc on the South Plains, and this, together with the ever-present threat of Mexican guerrillas making raids across the border, was mainly responsible for bringing the Texas Rangers into being. John Coffee had arrived at the right time, for, with the rank of captain, he was given the task of organizing one of the first Ranger companies.

By the time he was twenty-three Captain Hays had been blooded in numerous skirmishes involving either Mexicans or Comanches, a battle with the latter being won when 120 Rangers routed a force of more than 1,000 of these caliper-legged braves. Then in 1841 came the Battle of Plum Creek. By this time Hays had armed his men with five-shot Paterson Colts of .34 caliber, and with these weapons, his command of 25 men put more than 100 Comanches to flight, a goodly number of the redmen not pausing until they reached the Happy Hunting Grounds. Three years later Hays and his Paterson-armed men whipped a force of nearly 100 Comanches. These white-man victories put a damper on large-scale Indian raids.

In 1846 Hays and his men were roped in to give battle in the Mexican War, he and his veterans taking part in the fighting at Palo Alto and Monterrey. In the

[15] Possibly due to the fact that the Fetterman disaster had only occurred the previous year, and it was still fresh in the minds of fort commanders along the Bozeman Trail.

st-mentioned battle, Hays is reputed to ave challenged a Mexican colonel to a ber duel. This was a somewhat shabby ffair, for while the colonel was stripping or action, John Coffee tossed away his lade, whipped out a concealed pistol, nd shot that Mexican dead; of such odi-us acts are heroes sometimes made. The lexican War took Hays and his com-and as far as Mexico City.

It was not until 1848 that he returned o Texas, where, having chickened out n previous occasions, he finally married usan Calvert, a girl whom he had been ourting since 1841. By 1850 John and usan had settled in San Francisco, and e was appointed sheriff here for a spell. ver the next decade Cap'n Hays dabbled a local politics and real estate, but in 860 he hopped back into the saddle, and earing the rank of colonel led more tan 700 Nevada Volunteers against the aiutes, a few days of glory that culmi-ated on June 2, when the Volunteers nocked hell out of the red varmints at yramid Lake, Nevada. John Coffee lays died in California in 1883.

IAZELL, JESSIE The prairie flower vho has star billing in the controversial lickok-Coe shootout. (See COE, PHIL.)

IEAD, HARRY   Member of the Clanton gang who, after the Benson stage obbery of March 15, 1881, escaped outh of the border just ahead of a posse. Three months later Harry was back in Arizona, and in July 1881 he was shot lead while attempting to rob the store of saac and William Haslett at Huachita, New Mexico. (See BENSON STAGE MUR-ERS; CLANTON GANG; and GRAHAM, WILLIAM B.)

HEADSTALL   A head harness for horses; not including the bit. (See HACK-AMORE.)

HEATH, JOHN   The instigator and mastermind of the robbery that sparked off the infamous Bisbee Massacre. At sundown on the evening of December 8, 1883, five masked men rode into the min-ing town of Bisbee, Arizona Territory, and, after tethering their mounts, tromped through the dust until they reached the store of A. A. Castanada. Magazine rifles and six-shooters appeared from the folds of their heavy overcoats, and two of the men entered the store while the remainder covered the shadowy street with their hardware.

The store was on the point of closing, but a half-dozen customers were still on the premises when the two masked men entered, and one of these customers, Mr. J. C. Tappenier, was shot down and killed when he appeared to be reaching for a gun. This killing shot caused pan-demonium. Citizens rushed from their homes to see what all the shooting was about, and the "minders" stationed out-side the store began raking the street with lead, an indiscriminate display of firepower that brought death to two men and a woman.[16] Three minutes later the five men left the stricken town, disappear-ing into their own dust cloud with around three thousand dollars and various items of jewelry.

The sheriff's office at Tombstone[17] was notified, and Sheriff J. H. Ward (suc-cessor to John Behan) put Deputy Sher-iff William Daniels on the case. Daniels formed a posse and enlisted the services of a volunteer named John Heath to act as tracker. After leading the posse in

16 The victims being D. T. Smith, J. R. Nolly, and Mrs. R. H. Roberts.
17 Tombstone, some twenty miles from Bisbee, being the county seat.

circles, John Heath,[18] for a variety of reasons, came under suspicion, and he was arrested at gunpoint and lodged in the Tombstone jail. Once inside the calaboose Mr. Heath became quite talkative: He had known about the robbery plans but hadn't taken part in the sanguinary mess. That point settled, names rolled off his tongue: Daniel Dowd, Comer Sample, James "Tex" Howard, William Delaney, and Daniel Kelley were the guilty ones. Daniels went in pursuit of the quintet, but as they had fled to all points of the compass, some months elapsed before they were all safely behind bars in the Tombstone jail.

The trial was a speedy affair, and five of the accused were sentenced to hang; Heath was the odd man out, for although he had planned the crime, his turning informer swayed the bench to leniency, and he was given a life sentence. The Bisbeeites were not too happy about Heath's sentence, and on February 22, 1884, an irate mob overwhelmed the jailers at Tombstone, and a short time later John Heath was dangling lifeless from a telegraph pole.[19] Dowd, Sample, Howard, Delaney, and Kelley had leading parts in a multiple hanging that occurred on March 8, 1884. (See DELANEY, WILLIAM E.; DOWD, DANIEL; HOWARD, JAMES; KELLEY, DANIEL; and SAMPLE, COMER.)

HEDGEPATH, MARION Like many before him, Hedgepath, who was born and raised at Prairie Home, Missouri, drifted West in his teens, and by the time he had reached his majority he had the reputation of being a rustler, holdup man, and killer—a dubious character reference, which he had built up while trailing around Montana, Wyoming, and Colorado in the 1880s. By 1890 he had left the Far West and was making a name for himself as the leader of a small gang of holdup men known as "The Hedgepath Four,"[20] St. Louis, Missouri being the city suffering this blight. City life brought out the dandy in Marion and from this period onward he was always immaculately groomed—slicked-down hair (usually hidden under a curly-brimmed bowler hat), well-cut suit and topcoat, and a flashy cravat. Graduating from small-time stickups and muggings, the gang turned to train robbery on November 4, 1890, a Missouri Pacific express in Nebraska that netted them little more than a thousand dollars. Better profits were made the following week when they escaped with more than five thousand dollars after robbing a train on the outskirts of Milwaukee, Wisconsin. Toward the end of November this tight-knit gang made its all-time "hit," tucking around fifty thousand dollars into their saddlebags before fleeing from a Glendale, Missouri, train job. The Pinkertons were now on Marion's trail, and Hedgepath was finally run to earth in San Francisco, where both he and his wife[21] were taken into custody. After a trial in St. Louis, Marion was given a twenty-five-year stretch in the state pen. When he had served only a few years, a number of top-echelon Missourians began a campaign for his release on the grounds that

[18] At this time Heath was running a saloon *cum* dance hall at Bisbee. Prior to this he had owned a saloon at Brewery Gulch, and it is suspected that he led an outlaw band in this area.

[19] His marker can still be seen in Tombstone's burial ground: "John Heath, taken from County Jail and lynched by Bisbee mob in Tombstone, Feb. 22nd, 1884."

[20] Marion plus Albert D. Sly (an alias surely!), James Francis, and Lucius Wilson.

[21] A well-contoured blonde who merited the description already applied to Marion's cravats.

he was "a friend of society,"[22] but it was not until July 1906 that he was finally pardoned, by which time he was riddled with tuberculosis. Fourteen months later this sick ex-con was arrested for robbing a safe at Omaha, Nebraska, a crime for which he served two years. On his release, the outlaw was on his last legs, a physical wreck of a man, but a man who would never learn that "crime doesn't pay." New Year's Eve 1910 saw him leading a gang of hastily recruited deadbeats into a Chicago saloon with the object of robbing the cash drawer and customers. Bells were ringing out the old year and Marion was ringing up "No Sale" when a policeman entered, took in the situation at a glance, and shot Mr. Hedgepath dead.

HEFFRIDGE, BILL Member of the Sam Bass gang. Bill, together with Joel Collins, was shot down and killed by soldiers at Buffalo Station, Kansas, on September 26, 1877. (See BASS, SAM.)

HELM, BOONE A vacant-faced killer who was born at Log Branch, Missouri, about 1824. In September 1851 Boone, who was married and had a daughter by this time, committed his first recorded murder when he stabbed a man named Shoot to death during a drunken argument. Boone fled westward, but he was overtaken and arrested in the Indian Territory and taken back to Missouri. His trial was postponed three times because of a shortage of material witnesses, and Helm was finally set free. Shortly after his release from custody, Boone packed his personal effects and, abandoning his wife and daughter, rode off toward the setting sun. By the spring of 1852 he had reached the Oregon border, and when he heard Elijah Burton asking around for a guide to lead him and his small party across the mountains to Salt Lake City, Boone Helm volunteered for the job. Traveling southeast, snow blanketed the mountains, keeping progress to a snail's pace, and for a variety of reasons[23] members of the party, singly and in groups, began to drop behind, so that eventually Elijah found himself alone with Boone. Belts had been tightened to the limit, for hunger now marched with these men in the van, and when Elijah became stricken with snow blindness, Boone put a bullet through the man's head, butchered the corpse, then settled down to a grisly meal. Soon afterward a well-fed Boone arrived in Salt Lake City, parts of Elijah still in his parfleche. Helm's stay in Salt Lake City was brief, for after his particularly brutal killing of a gambler, he was driven from the city. San Francisco got the odor of Boone shortly thereafter, and here he got into a brothel brawl that ended with him killing his opponent with an overabun-

---

[22] This may seem odd, but while in the St. Louis jail awaiting transfer to the state pen, Marion had, for a short spell, shared a cell with a detainee who went under the name of H. H. Holmes, a man awaiting trial on a swindling charge. During this enforced pad sharing, Marion gave Holmes an introduction to a noted criminal lawyer named J. D. Howe, for which favor Holmes promised to pay five hundred dollars. Holmes got out on bail but failed to keep his part of the bargain. This was most unwise, for while confined with the train robber, Holmes had mentioned swindling an insurance company, a ghoulish ploy that involved insuring a party, identifying a cadaver—purchased from a body snatcher—as the insuree, then collecting from the unsuspecting company. By a roundabout route Hedgepath conveyed this information to the authorities, and this intelligence was partly responsible for the arrest of Holmes (an alias of Herman Webster Mudgett) on a murder warrant; this is evidently the reason why Marion was classed as "a friend of society." Footnote with a footnote: Holmes, who had twenty-seven murders to his credit, was convicted of the murder of Benjamin F. Piezel and hanged on May 7, 1895.

[23] To name but three, fatigue, hunger, and snow blindness.

dance of hatchet- and bowie-knife blows. We next hear of him from Idaho, where he killed a man known as "Dutch Fred." As Fred was unarmed at the time, Boone was arrested, but nothing came of this, and on his release from custody he headed North and crossed the line into Canada. Nothing is heard from him again until 1861, in which year his name appeared on the Mounted Police blotter; seems he'd gone trapping with a man named Angus McPherson but returned to his base without the Scottish Canadian, and Boone was being held on suspicion of murder. No trial resulted from this for no body could be found,[24] but Boone was ordered to leave Canadian soil. In June 1863 Helm arrived at Bannack,[25] a tough mining camp overrun by Henry Plummer's gang of road agents, an outlaw legion that called themselves the "Innocents." Boone became a key man in this criminal organization, enjoying a killing and looting spree in the Bannack area that lasted until the fourteenth of January 1864. On the morning of this day, Helm was arrested by vigilantes, and after lunch he found himself facing a plethora of murder and robbery charges. The charges stuck, and Boone Helm felt a rope being adjusted around his neck before sundown that same day—a fast-moving day for sure for Helm. (See BANNACK, MONTANA; INNOCENTS; and PLUMMER, HENRY.)

HELM, JACK   Captain of the state police and sheriff of DeWitt County, Texas, during the period of the Sutton-Taylor feud. Helm's earlier background is hazy, about the only thing being certain is that he fought for the Confederacy during the Civil War, and, not so certain, that he was such an ardent reb that he shot a black man dead for whistling a Yankee tune. In 1873 Helm, as a state police captain, had more than two hundred men under his command, a considerable force whose weight was solidly behind the Suttons during those bloody feuding days. Unfortunately for Helm, John Wesley Hardin's guns were backing the Taylors. In the April of 1873 Hardin killed Helm's chief deputy, and Jack, who may have seen the writing on the wall, arranged a meeting with Hardin: not to put the cuffs on the killer, but to hand around the peace pipe in the Sutton-Taylor affair. John Wesley didn't trust Helm, and the truce meeting ended with Hardin backing from the room with his guns covering the sheriff. Shortly after this, Helm, at the head of a large posse, went looking for Hardin, but his quarry wasn't home that day, and Helm worked off his spleen by bawling out Mrs. Hardin. Wes didn't cotton to folk who abused his better half, so this may have been the reason why he went searching for Helm. Accompanied by Jim Taylor, Wes' quest took him to Albuquerque, Texas, and here, on a May afternoon of 1873, at a blacksmith's forge,[26] this game of cat 'n' mouse came to a close. Suddenly Helm came into the forge and got the drop on Taylor, but he failed to notice Hardin, and Wes hammered him to the dirt floor with two shots; then, taking careful aim, the Texas killer put three more balls into the dying sheriff.[27] (See HARDIN, JOHN WESLEY, and SUTTON-TAYLOR FEUD.)

[24] Victuals had run short on that trapping trip, so Angus had most likely gone through the same digestive tract as had Elijah.

[25] In Idaho that year; the following year it was Bannack, Montana.

[26] Sometimes described as a saloon.

[27] Alternatively, Wes used a shotgun on Helm, then Taylor finished off the sheriff with handgun lead. Most writers favor the version given in the entry.

HENRY RIFLE Went into production in 1861, having been patented the previous year by B. Tyler Henry, an executive of the New Haven Arms Company. During the Civil War the federal government purchased about two thousand of these .44-caliber, sixteen-shot repeaters, but a far greater number—possibly around nine thousand—were bought privately by northern troops. After the close of the Civil War these lever-action repeaters became common throughout the West, a wide-open region where they won such descriptive praise as "The rifle you load on Sunday and fire all week," and, by the Indians, "The spirit gun of many shots." Henrys, which retailed at around forty-five dollars, were manufactured until 1866, after which time they were superseded by the Winchesters.[28] (See VOLCANIC RIFLE and WINCHESTER RIFLE.)

HERRING, ROBERT Born in Eastland County, Texas, in 1870. In his sixteenth year Bob became a horse thief, a chosen profession that he carried out fairly successfully, inasmuch as he was stealing and selling horses for almost a decade throughout the Southwest without encountering any serious trouble. In 1894 Herring joined the Joe Baker gang, a trio of owlhoots composed of Joe and a couple of misfits known as "Buck" and "Six Toes." This gang didn't last long as a foursome, for before the year was out, and after a gunpoint altercation with Joe, Herring lit out, most of the gang's winnings tucked in his saddlebags. After this spot of treachery Bob Herring was leery of surfacing for quite a spell, but in 1899, having heard that Baker and Six Toes had been killed,[29] he settled in Dallas, Texas, and started to live it up. By a quirk of fate, Buck—last surviving member of the Baker trio, re-member?—encountered Herring in Dallas, and after hard words, cartridges were activated in a most reckless manner, the result of this action being that Mr. "Buck" and two innocent (give them the benefit of the doubt) spectators were beyond recall, and the victorious Bob was marched off to jail. Herring got a thirty-five-year stretch, but he only served thirty of this, for in 1930, and while still in the pen, he died of tuberculosis. Herring's saddlebag loot—about thirty thousand dollars in gold—is reputed to be buried in the Wichita Mountains of Oklahoma. (See BAKER, JOE.)

HICKOK, JAMES BUTLER
The voice of the Colt's Peacemaker drowned the murmur of voices and clinking of coin in Deadwood's Number Ten Saloon, its leaden message plowing through the head of a seated card-player and coming to rest in the arm of the man he had been facing; the time was 4:15 P.M. on Wednesday, August 2, 1876, and the roar of the gun and a grunted "Take that" were possibly the last sounds to reach the consciousness of the man who slid from the stool, for it is almost certain that he was dead by the time he slumped to the floor clutching his last hand of cards, the aces and eights that were to give the term "dead man's hand" to the language. Thus ended the spectacular career of Wild Bill Hickok, the thirty-nine-year-old pistoleer who had been born James Butler Hickok at Troy Grove, Illinois, on March 27, 1837. With the birth of James Butler, his parents, Alonzo and Polly Hickok (formerly Miss Polly Butler), had a brood of four boys, the earlier children being Oliver (born 1830), Lorenzo (born 1832), and Horace (born 1834); by the time Jim was six, two sisters had made the scene:

---

[28] The company changed its name to Winchester Repeating Arms Company and started marketing a "much-improved rifle," to whit, the Winchester.
[29] Six Toes being killed while attempting a jailbreak in 1899.

Celinda in 1840 and Lydia in 1843. In May 1852 Alonzo Hickok died, and Jim, although only fifteen, helped to pull his weight by doing casual work: wagon driving, wolf hunting (for bounty money), and anything else that came along. In the summer of 1855, and while employed as a muleskinner in the building of the Illinois and Michigan canal, Jim had his first taste of violence. After taking much abuse from a fellow driver named Charlie Hudson, young Hickok pushed his tormentor into the canal. A lot of bubbles came to the surface but no Charlie, and Hickok, thinking he had killed the man,[30] clouded up the towpath's dust, the start of a hasty flight to which there was little pause until he reached St. Louis, Missouri. The odyssey had begun. Hickok slowed to a walk in Kansas, a territory kept in constant turmoil by clashes between pro- and anti-slavery factions, and amidst this chaos Jim got himself a job as bodyguard to a prominent abolitionist. While engaged as bodyguard, Hickok found time to carry on an ardent courtship with a Shawnee-Anglo girl named Mary Jane Owen,[31] an affair that may have led to him building a dugout near Monticello township. Around this time he may have had the hazy intention of settling down to a life of homesteading with this girl, but in 1858, for reasons unknown, he became a stage and wagon driver along the Santa Fe Trail, and within a short time he was living it up in Santa Fe, the Mary Jane episode a thing of the past. Somewhere

along the Santa Fe "Jim" had been dropped, and now folk were calling him "Bill,"[32] and it was as Bill Hickok that he had his famous encounter with a grizzly. This occurred toward the end of 1860 when he was driving a wagon through New Mexico's Raton Pass, and although Bill succeeded in bowie-knifing the bear to death, when the next wagon in the convoy arrived on the scene, Bill was found to be very much split at the seams. His employers —Russell, Majors, and Waddell—got Bill patched up then sent him to Kansas City, where he was under medical care until the spring of '61. In March that year Russell, Majors, and Waddell sent the still-convalescing Bill to their relay station at Rock Creek, Nebraska, light duties such as stocktending only being expected of him. It was here, some four months after his arrival, that Hickok shot Dave McCanles to death after an argument that hardly concerned Bill. The Civil War was now raging, and Bill, a true Yankee at heart, moved into the arena to give the Union cause a hand; not as an enlisted man, for Hickok was too much of an individualist for that, but as a civilian volunteer. Serving as Army scout, supply train wagonmaster, and spy, Bill's hair-trigger adventures during the Civil War years are far too numerous to detail in this condensed entry; suffice to say that it was while in Army service that he earned the fearsome title of "Wild Bill."[33] Two months

[30] He hadn't; but Hickok was lost in his own dust by the time Charlie surfaced.

[31] Fairly solid stories of his being married to Mary Jane still circulate, but as no court records exist to prove this marriage, most historians class these stories as pure fiction. This lack of evidence, however, proves little, for many events went unrecorded (e.g., no records of deputy U.S. marshal appointments were kept until many years later), and many tons of official papers were either accidentally burned or lost over the early years of the West.

[32] Could this be an abbreviation of "Duckbill," a nickname inspired by Hickok's king-size nose, or alternatively, his protruding and slightly upturned top lip?

[33] A barkeep pal of Bill's shot a tanked-up troublemaker in the saloon where he was employed, a disciplinary act that got Bill's pal into trouble with a twelve-man lynch mob, and it was only the timely arrival of Hickok with guns at the alert that made the mob disperse. As the unofficial jury slunk away, a woman in the crowd of uncommitted spectators is reputed to have shouted "Good for you, Wild Bill!"

after the close of the war, Bill gave the legend a boost by killing Dave Tutt. It happened at Springfield, Missouri, and one bullet was all that was needed. Early in 1866 Hickok was appointed deputy U.S. marshal at Fort Riley, Kansas. This was a fairly uneventful lawman stint, possibly the most notable happening being Bill's meeting and friendship with H. M. ("Dr. Livingstone, I presume?") Stanley. On handing in his federal badge, Hickok climbed into buckskins, and for the next three years earned his keep as a government employee, with Army scout and mail carrier being but a brace of his activities. A few days before Christmas in 1867, a dusty buckskinned figure, twin guns butt foremost and tongue exploring parched lips, stepped into a shanty bar in Nebraska to siphon up a beer. This was Wild Bill the plainsman. Four beery customers were evidently unaware of this, for they began to cast disparaging remarks about the overall appearance of the newcomer, fighting words that dwelled on Bill's nasal organ, untrimmed ox-yoke mustache, and general state of unkemptness. This was too much for Wild Bill, and he gave one of the men a blow in the face, an act that fanned the quartet into going for their guns. Black powdersmoke made darkness at noon, and when the haze had cleared three of the baiters lay dead and one was minus a part of his jaw. Roll call: Seth Beeker, Frank Dowder, and John Slater all dead, and John Harkness wounded. Wild Bill's souvenir of this action was a slight arm wound, which kept him out of action for a few weeks. In March 1868 Hickok was wounded in the arm during a skirmish with a Cheyenne war party, and he returned to Troy Grove to recuperate,

memories of meetings with Buffalo Bill and the Custers still fresh in his mind.[34] Troy Grove must have appeared appallingly dull, and in June 1868 he returned to the plains to act as guide to Senator Henry Wilson's party, a five-week tour that earned Bill a fee of five hundred dollars and, as an end-of-tour gift, a pair of ivory-handled Colt .36 Navy revolvers. These guns much in evidence, Wild Bill was appointed sheriff of Ellis County, Kansas, in August '69; this was to fill a temporary vacancy until election time. A month after accepting this county badge he was given the job of town marshal at Hays City, Kansas, thus holding two lawman jobs until his tenure of office as sheriff expired with his defeat at the polls in November of that year. While displaying the badge around Hays City, Bill kept a tight grip on the town, a grip that resulted in the local undertaker being called out on three occasions. On October 9, 1869, a notable tough named John Strawan had his last gunfight when he braced Hickok in Tommy Drum's Saloon. Two months later a small but aggressive Irishman pressed his gun muzzle against the marshal's head and then went into a long diatribe as to why and how he was going to put Bill under the turf— a bad case of logorrhea that had fatal results for this son of Erin, for after distracting his attention for a second, Bill shot the bigmouth dead. Bill's third shootout at Hays was on a much grander scale. Much of the trouble around Hays was caused by the men of Custer's 7th Cavalry, stationed at Fort Hays and at their most belligerent when the general was absent. Bill rubbed along smoothly with the general, but Bill had stirred up the hatred of Captain Tom Custer by ar-

[34] All of whom he had met in his travels. Custer, who may have seen his reflection in Hickok, went into narcissistic raptures when writing of Bill: ". . . one of the most perfect examples of physical manhood I ever saw . . . entirely free from bluster and bravado . . . his skill with rifle and pistol was unerring." Women also loved Wild Bill, and Elizabeth Custer uses ecstatic adjectives when describing the plainsman in *Following the Guidon*.

resting him and having him fined for disturbing the peace. Tom Custer brooded, and early in the New Year of 1870—and while in temporary command during one of his brother's absences—he rode into Hays at the head of a three-man detail, the object of this militant exercise being to "get" Wild Bill. The marshal came upon this quartet in a saloon run by Paddy Welch, a hard-bitten Irishman who was a good friend of Hickok's. This was the right place at the right time, for after Bill had been beaten up and disarmed by the troopers, Paddy tossed him a fully loaded shooting iron, and Hickok squeezed off the loads so fast the pieces of lead spewing from the muzzle must have looked like a five-car express. Such speed hardly indicated panic shooting, for when the hammer clicked to rest, one soldier was dead and two lay mortally wounded. Tom Custer lit out for the fort, intent on returning with every trooper who wasn't on furlough, and Bill, realizing there was a good argument for the use of discretion, hopped a fast freight that dropped him at Ellsworth a short time later. Bill's stay at Ellsworth, although brief, was of sufficient length for him to whip up an affair with a pay-to-dance gal named Emma Williams and leave one corpse in his wake, the chilled one being William Thompson (no relation to bullyboy Ben), a gunnie who had tried to shoot Bill dead, the most likely cause being what Emma had available. By March, Bill was living it up in Topeka with his old buddy Will Cody, while the summer of that year saw Bill preparing for the opening of a Wild West show at Niagara Falls. This was the first Wild West show ever to be organized, and it was a dismal failure, Bill ending up his one-day stand by selling his small buffalo herd—captured by Bill and the mainstay of the show—to a local butcher in an attempt to recoup some of his losses. By

the end of April 1871 Bill was back behind the badge, having been appointed marshal of Abilene, Kansas, on April 15. At Abilene trouble came in the formidable shapes of Ben Thompson, Phil Coe, and John Wesley Hardin, but only in the case of Coe did this undercurrent of hostility finally get filed away under "Gunfights." This shooting, which was fatal for Coe, took place outside the Alamo Saloon on October 5, a sorry affair inasmuch as Hickok accidentally killed Deputy Marshal Mike Williams, the latter having gotten into the line of fire by a sheer fluke. It was at Abilene that Hickok started paying court to Mrs. Agnes Lake, the owner of a traveling circus that had paused to play the town. Agnes was available, her husband having become a gun-law victim in 1869, and she was the girl whom Hickok would marry some five years later. This contact with Agnes may also have resurrected Bill's earlier show-biz urge, and in the fall of 1873 we find him treading the boards with Buffalo Bill's "Scouts of the Plains." Wild Bill played himself in this badly written piece of hokum, and he soon became so utterly disgusted with muttering Buntline's inane dialogue—which only the front row could hear—that he filled in most of his onstage time ogling Mademoiselle Morlacchi, a tempting morsel of womanhood who played the part of Dove Eye when the script called for a spot of frontier sex. This Morlacchi lass got star billing in the show and most likely a spot of Wild Billing after the curtain dropped; this is only a theory, but something must have kept Bill hooked to this miserable production for the seven months he was with it. He finally took his departure—after shooting out some of the house lights on a couple of occasions—in March of '74. By the fall of 1874, Cheyenne, Wyoming, was Hickok's location. His sight had been failing for a number of years, and now, on rare occasions, his eyes were lost behind smoked lenses. He had gone to Cheyenne with the intention of working his way into the Black Hills of Dakota, scene of the latest headline-making gold discoveries; but there was no hurry. Cheyenne was bursting with elegant gambling halls, good friends, and, to Bill's way of thinking, even better womenfolk whose virtue wasn't exactly inviolate. Time passed and the spots on the cards grew dimmer, then, in February 1876, Agnes Lake reappeared on the scene, and Bill, possibly having become jaded with beer, bawds, and brawls, married this woman from the past on March 5, 1876. A couple of weeks of married life, then Bill was eager to get to the gold fields; not as a fugitive from domesticity, but in order to prove to Agnes that he could become an instant millionaire; maybe. Up into the Black Hills, accompanied part of the way by Calamity Jane, a onetime prairie playmate during a short buffalo hunting session in 1870. June, in Deadwood, a muddy gulch flanked by shanties. June 28, smoke and moccasin rumors of slaughter on the Big Horn, three-days-old news that may have brought a sardonic twist to the lips of Wild Bill Hickok. Through July, mining gold at the poker tables in Nuttall and Man's Number Ten Saloon; better than hanging around in his tent back down the gulch. The second day of August and

Carl Mann, Cap'n Frank Massey, Charlie Rich, and Wild Bill have been playing cards since around 3 P.M.; the murmur of friendly bantering, the clinking of coin, and the swish of cards whose pips get ever dimmer. The voice of the Colt's Peacemaker . . . Epilogue: after lying in state for a few hours, the remains of James Butler Hickok were given the finest funeral that rough-and-ready mining camp could provide, a fitting last salute to the greatest gunfighter ever to leave his mark in the West.[35] (See CANNARY, MARTHA JANE; COE, PHIL; CRAWFORD, JOHN WALLACE; HARDIN, JOHN WESLEY; McCALL, JACK; MC-CANLES, DAVID C.; THOMPSON, BEN; and TUTT, DAVE.)

HICKOK, JANEY   Calamity's name for Jean Hickok. (See HICKOK, JEAN.)

HICKOK, JEAN   According to the diary of Calamity Jane, this girl was the legal offspring of her marriage to James Butler Hickok. Having first met Hickok on the plains outside Abilene, Kansas, in 1870, Calamity became Mrs. Hickok on September 1 of the following year, the Reverends W. F. Warren and W. K. Sipes conducting this prairie ceremony, which was held "en route to Abilene, Kansas," documentation of this marriage being carried out on the flyleaf of a Bible.[36] Although makeshift, this appears to be a genuine document, complete with names of witnesses, etc. On

---

[35] Hickok was buried in Deadwood's cemetery at Ingleside, and a wooden marker was erected; carved on the marker was, "A BRAVE MAN, THE VICTIM OF AN ASSASSIN; J. B. HICKOK (WILD BILL), AGED 39 YEARS: MURDERED BY JACK McCALL, AUG. 2ND 1876." On August 3, 1879, the coffin was disinterred for transfer to Mount Moriah—Deadwood's new burial place—where it was to be reinterred at the expense of Charlie Utter, a friend of the deceased. While above ground the coffin was opened, and although the burial clothes had started to decompose, there was no sign that any such activity had attacked the corpse; Bill was more or less in mint condition. Some form of petrifaction had evidently taken place, leaving Bill pale and hard but without the least trace of putrefaction. After reburial Charlie Utter paid to have a stone marker erected, and about 1906 this was joined by a life-sized stone effigy of Bill, the whole plot afterward being fenced in.

[36] The Reverend Warren imparted information regarding this marriage to his daughter Ella; confirmation of this was given by Ella in 1941.

September 25, 1873, at Benson's Landing, Montana Territory, Calamity Jane
gave birth to a girl child, naming this
child Janey. (N.B.: When but a few years
old, Janey adopted the name of "Jean,"
and henceforth in this narrative the latter name will be used.) When Jean was
four years old, her mother allowed her
to be legally adopted by Captain James
O'Neil and his wife, Captain O'Neil being an Englishman, a Cunard Line captain who resided at Richmond, Virginia.
Around 1875 Hickok divorced Calamity
to marry Agnes Lake, a Calamity Jane
assertion that cannot be backed up by
legal proof at this time of writing. With
the acquisition of new parents, Jean's life
fell into the pattern of shuttling across
the Atlantic with Captain O'Neil and his
wife, the ship being the *Madagascar* and
its terminal points being Liverpool and
New York. In 1912 Captain O'Neil died,
and with his death Jean came into possession of her mother's diary, marriage
evidence, etc., Calamity having left these
with the captain when he adopted the
child, the mother's express wish being
that they reach Jean after O'Neil's death.
By 1912 Jean was thirty-nine years
old and married; Mrs. Jean Burkhardt,
living at Richmond, Virginia. The possession of these papers was responsible
for the breakup of this marriage, Mr.
Burkhardt divorcing his wife on seeing
evidence that more than indicated that
she was the daughter of such frontier
hell-raisers. In 1918 Jean remarried, the
groom on this occasion being Edward
McCormick, an American fighter pilot,
who shortly after the ceremony was
killed in action. Jean never remarried,
earning her livelihood over the years by
nursing, teaching, and making rodeo appearances. In 1941 Jean Hickok Burkhardt McCormick applied for old-age assistance, using the documents handed
down via O'Neil as proof of her parentage, etc. On September 6, 1941, the U. S.

Department of Public Welfare granted
relief, the documents having satisfied this
government department that Jean was
the legal daughter of Martha Jane Cannary and James Butler Hickok. So be it.
(See CANNARY, MARTHA JANE.)

HIDALGO A Spanish nobleman of
low rank; a Mexican contribution to the
linguistic currency of the Southwest,
where the word is somewhat loosely
used.

HIDATSA INDIANS Pronounced
"Hee-DAT-sa." At the time of the white
man's arrival, this Siouan language tribe
was settled in what is now the state of
North Dakota, living in permanent villages composed of countless dome-
shaped earth lodges and sustaining themselves by crop rearing. To supplement a
mainly vegetarian diet, parties went out
into the Great Plains at the advent of
the buffalo-hunting season, and during
these nomadic excursions, tepees were
used. Pottery making was carried out,
their earthenware suggesting an Iroquois
influence, but being much inferior to
that of the Pueblo tribes of the Southwest. As their villages were scattered
along the Missouri, waterway travel was
essential, bullboats being used for this
purpose. In the 1830s the Hidatsa were
almost eliminated by smallpox, a deci-
mation that prevented their opposing the
coming white invasion. Descendants of
these Hidatsa now live in Montana. (See
BULLBOATS.)

HIGHBINDER Member of a Chinese
highbinder society. Highbinder societies
never achieved tong status, although
they were an offshoot of the latter, and
the tongs employed highbinder hatchetmen when the occasion demanded, during tong wars and to eliminate competition. (See CHINESE TONGS and LITTLE
PETE.)

HILL, TOM Alias of sometime member of the James gang. (See RYAN, WILLIAM.)

HINNY Sterile cross resulting from the mating of a she-ass with a stallion; a hybrid noted for its stamina. Sometimes called a "jinette," and pronounced either "hinny" or "jinny."

HITE, WOOD Friend of Jesse James and member of the latter's gang. Hite, who was born in Logan County, Kentucky, in 1848, rode with the James gang from 1870 until 1881, taking part in many of the gang's holdups. In July 1881 he took part in the Winston train robbery, after which the stooped and narrow-shouldered—and now very jittery —Hite lay low in a succession of hideouts, his father's place in Kentucky and the home of Robert and Charlie Ford being but two. At this time the Ford brothers were living in Ray County, Missouri, and on December 5, 1881, Dick Liddell and Jim Cummings—both of whom were attached to the James gang—and Wood Hite were sheltering at this home. Sometime during the evening of this day the tightly sprung Hite began to suspect that Liddell may have been contemplating selling him (Wood) out to the law, and whether right or wrong in his suspicions, he went for his gun. Dick Liddell was faster, and Wood Hite died in the early hours of the following morning.[37] (See JAMES GANG.)

HOBBLE A pair of rawhide loops, frequently connected by a metal ring, that are used to fasten a horse's forelegs to-gether to prevent it from straying. Hobbles can also be made from a long strip of rawhide, the metal ring being dispensed with by twining the rawhide.

HOBBS, JAMES Born in 1819 in what is now Jackson County, Missouri. In 1835, while guarding a fur-trading caravan between St. Louis, Missouri, and Bent's Old Fort at the mouth of the Purgatoire in southwest Colorado, Hobbs was taken prisoner by the Comanche. Spared the ultimate fate, he was adopted by the tribe, and he stayed with these Indians for the next four years, during which time he became a squaw man by marrying the chief's daughter. After deserting the tribe, and his squaw, in 1839, he roamed the mountains, pastures, and deserts of the Far West—at one time a fur trapper, then a buffalo hunter, and occasionally reaching an all-time low as a scalphunter. In 1847 we find him fighting in the Mexican War with the rank of captain; then some two years later, we pick up his sign heading for California— and gold. En route for the gold fields, he is alleged to have stayed for some time at Yuma Crossing, this pause in his journey being occasioned so that he might help a party of Yuma Indians defeat a degenerate scalphunter named Glanton. If correct, we can only assume that at this time Hobbs was trying to make amends for his own otokan-lifting activities of an earlier date. He finally reached the gold fields, and shortly afterward found himself in jail for claim jumping. Nothing came of this, for Hobbs crashed out one night, heading in a roundabout way back to his squaw and her half-breed son, the latter being a Hobbs-inspired

[37] It has been reported that after the killing of Jesse James, Robert Ford was charged and tried for the murder of Hite, and on being found guilty, pardoned by the state governor. This must have been a real trumped-up charge, for at the trial of Frank James in 1883, testimony that was irrelevant to the James case made it abundantly clear that Dick Liddell was responsible for the killing of Hite. Liddell was never charged with the murder of Hite; immunity for turning state's evidence, perhaps?

product from way back. He stayed until his wife was in a delicate condition and then went back to roaming the wilderness of the Southwest. It was while he was bumming around this expanse of nothingness that an experience occurred, the like of which should happen to every man. Hobbs was huddled in his fireglow one night when a girl dashed into his camp. She was beautiful full frontal and naked, but before any erotic ideas had time to germinate within Hobbs' mind, the girl had gasped out an honor-saving burst: A band of Navahos was hard on her heels. To Hobbs, a man who had fought grizzlies to a standstill, putting the red varmints to flight was but a small matter. He was, however, not to taste the immediate fruit of this victory, for during the battle the girl had completed her story, and after hearing that she was a Mexican general's daughter, a mental montage of *mucho dinero* began to cover her nakedness, a vision of greaser gold that ejected all notions of campfire capers from the victor's thoughts, so that the girl was returned to her parents *mucho intacto*. This was a highlight of Hobbs' career, for he became something of a hero in Mexico, and while the kudos lasted he remained south of the border taking active interest in revolutionary politics and spending much time at the gambling tables. Not having any emotions regarding pro- and anti-slavery arguments, Hobbs steered clear of the war between the states, finally ending his wanderings in Grass Valley, California, where he died in 1879. (See GLANTON, JOHN J., and KIRKER, JAMES.)

HODGES, THOMAS J. Possibly the only medical practitioner ever to ride the owlhoot trail in the Far West. Thomas J. Hodges was born at Rome, Tennessee,

about 1825. In 1846 he moved West with the Tennessee Volunteers to take part in the Mexican War of 1846–48, and it was during this war service that he trained as a physician, so that on being mustered out of the service he was a qualified practitioner. Around 1850 Dr. Thomas J. Hodges, a handsome and robust swashbuckler, arrived in California intent on finding his pot of gold, but of all the holes he dug and streams he panned, none showed color. Disappointed, the doc turned his attention to the card tables, his winnings from gambling being sufficient to allow him to drown his sorrows in the hard stuff. Boozing led to brawls, and in one of these thumpups he got his nose bent so out of true that he could no longer be termed handsome. Shortly after this traumatic incident Thomas started making small-scale robbery his career, and in 1855 he was tossed into Angel Island prison for theft. Within a matter of weeks he had made his escape, being accompanied in this breakout by Bill Gristy, a low-I.Q. roughneck with a record of encyclopedic proportions. These two escapees built up a small gang[38] that must have had the firepower of a battalion, Doc alone going into the field carrying six revolvers and numerous knives of the Bowie type.[39] Graduating from beer-money jobs, on August 12, 1856, Hodges and company attempted the biggest stage holdup of all time. This was the Camptonville-Marysville coach carrying one hundred thousand dollars in gold bullion and, unknown to the gang, a very tough apple named Bill Dobson, who was riding shotgun. When the gang attacked, Dobson cut loose with buckshot, thus sparking off a small-scale battle. The bandits' fire found targets in three of the passengers, killing

---

[38] Edward Connor, Monte Jack Lyon, James Smith, Juan Fernandez, and an Englishman named Robert Carr.

[39] Plus the added weight of a sheet-iron chest protector.

one woman and wounding two men, but the attackers also had lead problems, for Dobson, now wielding Colts, blasted two of them out of their saddles, and this spot of pistoleering prompted Hodges to sound the retreat, whereupon the surviving members of the gang hightailed off, leaving the bullion untouched. After this loused-up effort, legal and illegal posses were always in the outlaws' dust, and toward the end of September Gristy and another member of the gang were arrested while gulping down a hurried meal in a Knight's Ferry eatery. Within twenty-four hours of a cell door clanging behind him Gristy talked, and soon afterward the sheriff of Stockton was leading a posse out to the Hog Ranch on the Nevada City road.[40] When the lathered-up posse arrived, Doc had blown, but on October 4, 1856, the posse finally caught up with the fugitive: It was at the base of a sycamore tree, and the sheriff had to raise his eyes to find Dr. Thomas J. Hodges, for a vigilante posse had gotten to him first and strung him up amidst the leaves. During most of his criminal career Hodges went under the alias of Tom Bell.

HOGAN A hut covered with earth and bark. A Navaho word for their place of dwelling.

HOLE IN THE WALL GANG A rather loose term that described a gang's territorial affiliations and little

more, embracing, as it did, the gangs of Laughing Sam Carey, Black Jack Ketchum, and Butch Cassidy, plus any other smaller group of outlaws who happened to use Hole in the Wall as a retreat. Hole in the Wall, which was located in Wyoming about fifty miles south of Buffalo and due east of the Powder River, was the most northerly of three outlaw rendezvous.[41] From around 1880 horse thieves, holdup men, and gangs of rustlers had used Hole in the Wall, but it was not until after the collapse of the cattle trade in 1884 that the Hole began to experience a small population explosion. Out-of-work range hands, morals beginning to crumble through their inability to find work, wandered into the Hole and gravitated around leaders whom they thought capable of leading them to a fast grubstake. A shanty town of shacks and the odd saloon rose groggily from the wilderness, and it was from this sorry mess of a place that the outlaw bands who were collectively known as the "Hole in the Wall gang" emerged to pillage and murder. Names of members of the three key gangs are given below;[42] an asterisk after a name indicates that the party has a separate entry.

Butch Cassidy gang: Parker, Robert Leroy* (alias Butch Cassidy, George Parker, George Ingerfield); Carver, William* (alias Tod Carver); Hanks, Camilla* (alias Deaf Charley, Charles Jones); Kilpatrick, Ben;* Lay, Elza;* Logan, Harvey* (alias Kid Curry); Logan,

[40] This place was owned by a sizzling redhead named Elizabeth Hood, a woman who dealt in an intangible form of merchandise that only appealed to men. Liz' broadmindedness even extended to allowing her three daughters to live on the premises. The eldest of these girls was about fourteen, and some say that this juvenile temptress was the main reason for Hodges choosing this place as a hideout.

[41] After a 250-mile ride to the southwest Brown's Hole was reached, a fairly inaccessible valley that straggled the junction of Wyoming, Colorado, and Utah. Another 250 miles to the south, in San Juan County, southeastern Utah, a semi-arid scrub region was known as Robber's Roost. These three outlaw stations were connected by renegade-blazed trails that were virtually unknown to honest folk.

[42] These gangs had blurred outlines, members sometimes transferring their allegiance to another leader.

Lonnie; Longbaugh, Harry* (alias The Sundance Kid); Manuse, George* (alias George Curry, Big-nose George, Parrot-nose Curry); McCarty, Tom; McCarty, William; O'Day, Tom;* Rose, Della* (alias Clara Hays, Laura Bullion, Laura Casey); Tracy, Harry.*

Black Jack Ketchum gang: Ketchum, Tom* (alias Black Jack Ketchum); Ketchum, Sam; Atkins, David; Bullin, Edward; Franks, G. W.; McManus, Irving (alias Black Bob McManus); Meeks, George.

Laughing Sam Carey gang: Carey, Samuel (alias Laughing Sam Carey); Wilcox, Harry; Denslow, "Bud"; and a killer named Taylor.

Poker-faced Carey was more or less a founder member of the Hole in the Wall community. The above lists are not exhaustive, for more than 100 long riders and many female camp followers used the Hole as their headquarters. (See WILD BUNCH.)

HOLLADAY, BEN   A Kentuckian who made his first faltering steps westward in 1836 at the age of sixteen, his first stop being St. Louis, Missouri, where, over the next four years, he worked his way up from liquor salesman through saloon keeping to proprietor of a hotel. In 1846, at the start of the Mexican War, he succeeded in getting a contract to supply provisions and transportation to the U. S. Army, a moneymaking enterprise that left him with a solid stake when the war ended in 1848. Twelve months later came the California gold rush, and Holladay, after investing his savings in provisions and other merchandise, freighted his purchases to Salt Lake City, Utah; this was a supply point on the overland route to the gold fields, and Ben made a handsome profit by selling his goods at inflationary prices to underprovisioned

argonauts. In March 1862 Holladay leaped into the coaching and express business by getting control of the Central Overland California and Pike's Peak Express Company, a move that made him the owner of twelve hundred miles of stage routes plus rolling stock. Almost overnight the C.O.C. and P.P. Express Company became the Overland Mail and Express Company, and one of Ben's first moves as a stagecoach nabob was to bring in a fleet of new Concords. The line grew, and by 1866 the route mileage had been doubled by the acquisition of the Butterfield Overland Dispatch. Another shuffle and the line was now the Holladay Overland Mail and Express Company. Around this time Holladay's coaches started to be hit by war parties, and this, together with the far more important fact that the Union Pacific and Central Pacific were pushing steadily toward Promontory, caused Holladay to sell all his holdings to Wells Fargo in that year. He didn't come out of this deal too badly: $1,500,000 in cash and $3,000,000 in Wells Fargo stock. Ben Holladay, King of the Concords, died at Portland, Oregon, on July 8, 1887. (See BUTTERFIELD OVERLAND MAIL COMPANY; CONCORD COACH; OVERLAND STAGE LINE; PONY EXPRESS; UNION PACIFIC RAILROAD; and WELLS FARGO & COMPANY.)

HOLLIDAY, "DOC"   The dental practitioner who became the answer to an undertaker's prayer. (See HOLLIDAY, JOHN HENRY.)

HOLLIDAY, JOHN HENRY   As his patient was shrugging into his jacket the physician answered the query that had just been put to him:

"It is difficult to say in these cases. Galloping consumption does have its vagaries, but if you live a temperate life you may extend your span for another one, or perhaps two years." The young man with the corn-colored hair and sweeping mustache adjusted his cravat. "How temperate, sir?" he asked. "No hard liquor. Drink plenty of milk instead. Wear red flannel next to your skin, and get as much fresh air as possible. It may be a good idea to move your practice farther west, Colorado or Arizona perhaps. But remember, John: While there's life, there's hope."[43] Dr. John Henry Holliday, dental practitioner, who displayed his shingle in Atlanta, Georgia, took little heed of this advice. He did move toward the sunset, but most of his time west of the Mississippi was spent in the smoky atmosphere of saloons and gambling halls, premises wherein his daily intake of whiskey was never allowed to slip below the two-pint level. He may have worn red flannel next to his skin, but there is no evidence to suggest that he ever drank milk. They should have been writing his obituary by 1874 at the latest, but Doc Holliday survived for fifteen years on the frontier, a period of violence during which he was the direct cause of many an obituary being scribed somewhat prematurely—as we shall see.

John Henry Holliday was born at Griffin, Georgia, in 1852, the only son of Major Henry B. Holliday—planter, lawyer, and medium-sized cog in local politics—and Alice Jane Holliday. At the twilight of his teens, John Henry began studying dentistry at a Baltimore, Maryland, college of dental surgery, and by 1872, fully qualified, he set up practice at Atlanta. It was here that the coughing fits started, prompting Holliday to seek medical advice, and shortly afterward, Dallas, Texas, got a new dentist. Unfortunately, the good, and bad, people of Dallas appeared unaware of his services,

and to help fill the financial vacuum caused by this large volume of no business, Holliday began to spend much of his time at the faro tables, a pursuit that made dexterity with firearms an essential. John Henry rapidly acquired a certain amount of wizardry with both revolver and derringer, and armed with one of either weapon, plus a bowie knife for good measure, he became a full-time faro dealer. Sometime in 1874 this gentleman from Georgia, who aspired in all the right places but hung around in all the wrong ones, tested out his arsenal by killing a man in Dallas. This wasn't an obvious case of self-defense, so rather than push his luck before twelve men good and ornery, he clouded out and didn't stop until he had reached Jacksboro, a roughneck settlement some two hundred miles west of Dallas.

Jacksboro, socially and architecturally, was a far cry from Dallas, but as it was a town where an honest man was regarded with suspicion, John Henry, having become a card cheat extraordinary, shrugged off any inelegancies it may have possessed and settled down to skinning the transient table trade. Doc—to give him his frontier moniker—stayed in this malodorous dump for two years. The last five or six months of this period were probably the most stimulating for Doc, for early in 1876 a copper-haired lovely hit town, a lady gambler named Lottie Deno who, so rumor hath it, set John Henry's Adam's apple a-bobbin'. Doc rendezvous-eyed her, but return encouragement from Lottie was lacking. However, as Lottie made other frontier *femmes fatales* appear only fit for branding, it is reasonable to assume that Doc would have prolonged his stay in Jacksboro until his southern charm had worn the redhead down if circumstances had

[43] This dialogue is fictional, but it is authentic inasmuch as it is based on the accepted method of treating consumption (tuberculosis) at this time.

so permitted. Circumstances didn't permit. In June of that year, Doc put a period mark to a gambling brawl by killing a trooper of the 6th U. S. Cavalry, immediately afterward putting a great number of miles between himself and the remainder of nearby Fort Richardson's garrison. Denver, Colorado, was his chosen hideaway, and here he went under the name of Thomas Mackay. This stay was rather brief, for after almost killing a fellow gambler named Bud Ryan with a spot of knifework, Doc left town and thundered South.

Arizona and New Mexico had him for a short spell; then around September 1876 he moved back into Texas and settled at Fort Griffin. Griffin was little more than a dosshouse for herders and hide hunters, a frontier compost heap whose fetid aroma could be detected over a radius of miles; but Lottie Deno was there, having arrived from Jacksboro a short time previously. But there was still no luck with Lottie, and Doc finally settled for Big-nose Kate Elder, a free-lance whore who was working the town and who was as far removed from Miss Deno in both looks and graces as it is possible to imagine. It was at Griffin that Doc made the acquaintance of Wyatt Earp when the latter arrived in the town on the trail of Dave Rudabaugh. Doc may have helped Earp to trace Rudabaugh, but whatever the reason for this first meeting, it was to establish an on-off relationship that extended over the years. Violence erupted once again in December 1877. A disagreement over cards was the prologue, and the bowie-knife disembowelment of one Edward Bailey was the action sequence. Doc was arrested by the town marshal and locked in a hotel room, no jail being available at Griffin. Now, this Ed Bailey had been a popular member of Griffin's evil-smelling community, and after dark, to lynch or not to lynch became a talking point in the

saloons. Big-nose Kate heard these rumblings, and when a mob began to form, she put torch to a shack, thus distracting the combined attention of this threat to her loved one while she rescued Doc and got him clean away.

This oddly matched twosome set up home at Dodge City, Kansas, calling themselves Mr. and Mrs. J. H. Holliday, and here Doc had another shot at dentistry. Kate behaved herself for a couple of months, then went back to whoring, and Doc, equally fed up with respectability, tossed away his business cards and returned to the faro layouts. Over this period, Wyatt Earp was toting a star as a deputy marshal at Dodge, and in September 1878 he may have been thankful that Doc was in town, for in that month the gambler-dentist extricated Wyatt from an ugly situation that involved a number of Texas herders. The following year Doc moved southwest, on into New Mexico, where he had a last fling at legitimacy by opening a dental surgery at Las Vegas. This was a failure, so Doc put up the shutters and bought a saloon. He remained a saloon proprietor until late in the summer of 1879, around which time he had a main-street shootout with a hard case named Mike Gordon, and on the expiration of Mike, Doc became a fugitive once more. He returned to Dodge, most likely in the hope of seeing Wyatt, for on learning that Earp had left for Tombstone, Arizona Territory, Doc did likewise.

At Prescott, en route for Tombstone, Doc paused to sample the gambling tables, and it was here that he was reunited with Big-nose Kate, so that when he arrived at Tombstone in January 1880 this indelicate dish was tagging along. Shortly afterward the Earp-Clanton feud began to simmer, Doc's guns being behind the Earps from the start, and after the Benson stage murders on March 15, 1881, pro-Clanton Sheriff Behan accused Doc of doing the job. There was no direct evidence against Doc, so this outburst from Behan was ignored for some time; then, in July, Doc had a barney with Kate, and Behan saw his chance: The sheriff got Kate liquored up, and while she was under the influence, he got her to sign a document that accused her fancy man of the murders. Doc was lodged in the Tombstone jail, but within hours Wyatt had bailed him out and persuaded brother Virgil—town marshal at the time —to jockey Big-nose into the vacated cell, ostensibly on a D & D rap. This fast move gave Kate time to sober up, and when the blood had gone from her eyes she retracted her confession. Kate may have thought this about-face would reinstate her with Doc, but he had evidently had a sufficiency of Kate, and after giving her a thousand dollars for mad money, he told her to stir up the dust.

On October 26, 1881, the Earp-Clanton sparring erupted into the powder burning at the O. K. Corral, and as an aftermath of this, Doc went to Denver, Colorado, where on May 15, 1882, he was arrested at the request of an Arizona peace officer and charged with the murder of Florentine Cruz.[44] Things looked bad for Doc, but for some unknown reason David C. Cook, a power in Denver law-enforcement circles, backed Holliday, and Governor Pitkin of Colorado refused to return Holliday to Arizona. On his release from custody, Doc wandered to Deadwood, Dakota Territory, staying there until the winter of 1882, then returning to Colorado, where he finally settled at Leadville in the spring of 1883. By the following summer Doc must have reached an all-time low, for he was being dubbed for the return of a five-dollar loan by Police Chief Bill Allen, and in the early days of September he shot Allen when the latter requested his five bucks at gunpoint.[45] In the same month Doc killed A. J. Kelly, an off-duty cop who was out on a bar cruise. At a subsequent hearing, Doc's self-defense plea was accepted, and he was discharged. Doc had won a lot of battles, but he must have known by this time that he was losing the main one, and in May 1887 he entered a sanatorium at Glenwood Springs, Colorado, in a belated attempt to gird his loins against his malady. He survived for six months, dying on November 8, 1887, shortly after having downed a tooth glass full of whiskey. (See BENSON STAGE MURDERS; COOK, DAVID J.; CRUZ, FLORENTINE; DENO, LOTTIE; EARP, WYATT BERRY STAPP; ELDER, KATE; and O. K. CORRAL.)

HOLSTER A leather[46] pouch in which a handgun is carried. Usually referred to as "scabbards" in the Old West, and invariably made so that the leather molded itself around the weapon, albeit somewhat loosely in the early models.[47] Holsters could have gun-retaining flaps or be open, the former type being almost exclusively military. Unlike the trim-fitting, briefly cut holsters used by modern television gunslingers, the majority of old scabbards used up a lot of leather. They could be stitched, riveted, or thonged with rawhide, and were usually open at the toe. This open toe served two purposes: It allowed the holster to accept a variety of barrel lengths, and it also permitted rain water to drain away. In most instances an L-shaped piece of

44 A Clanton man whom Wyatt had killed.
45 It has been reported that he killed Allen and, alternatively, that Allen was only wounded. It may have been but a wound, for Holliday got an acquittal on being charged with the shooting.
46 If we ignore the webbing variety, these being virtually unknown in the early West.
47 Billy the Kid's had ample room for a couple of packets of candy as well as his six-gun.

leather was used in their manufacture, the horizontal bar of the L being cut to the contours of the weapon, then folded over and secured, while from two to six horizontal slits were made in the downstroke of the L. The completed work was then folded so that the vertical stroke of the L became a slotted panel through the slits of which the pouch section could be slotted; the gun belt could then be threaded between panel and pouch so that the fold in the scabbard rested on the top edge of the belt.[48] (See BUSCADERO and GUNBELT.)

HOMBRE
The Spanish term for "man." In fairly common use.

HONDA   A loop. The small loop on a lariat; the loop through which the rope is pulled to tighten the noose.

HONKY-TONKS   Business enterprises of a somewhat depraved nature. Honky-tonks[49] could be either elegant—elegance coming with the owner's prosperity—or iniquitous ventures enclosed within clapboard shacks or leaky tents. Girls were a necessity, and as those who applied for work in such establishments were usually rejects from the bagnios of both the East and the frontier, a bar was an essential, clients having to be somewhat tanked before their lusty imaginations could visualize these demoted harpies as sparking companions. A piano was a luxury, and these were only found in the better-class (?) honky-tonks, the outlay for such an improvement evidently finding justification in the notion that the more cultured type of stud who could be expected to use these places liked to shuffle the doxie of his choice around the floor a couple

of times before whipping her off for a lust-filled session, a light touch of romance thus being added to the wholly mercenary proceedings. Honky-tonks should not be confused with hurdygurdys, the latter being dance halls. (See DANCE HALLS.)

HOOKER JIM   Solemn-faced Modoc Indian who was a leader in the Modoc-U. S. Army war of 1853. (See MODOC WAR.)

HOPI INDIANS   A major pueblo tribe that is the main tribe in the Uto-Aztecan family. The Hopi have been located in the northern Arizona area for centuries, Oraibi, one of their main villages, having been continuously occupied for the past nine hundred years. The Hopi raise crops from their arid surroundings, rear sheep for meat and wool, and are highly skilled in basket and pottery making and the weaving of blankets, the males of the tribe taking active part in all these pursuits. Hunting was never a large-scale occupation, but parties would periodically venture onto the plains in search of buffalo and other game, bows and arrows being used against the larger beasts, while a small boomerang-type stick was used to take rabbits, etc. The Hopi snake ceremony has become the subject of numerous paintings and photographs, and the dance, during which the dancers handle live rattlesnakes, attracts crowds of tourists when it is performed at yearly intervals. The snakes, which have been allowed to retain their poison fangs and glands, are blessed by the priests, then taken out into the desert and released, the object of this exercise being that the snakes—which represent lightning—carry the prayers of the priests to heaven.

[48] Other types dispensed with the slotted panel, the scabbard being attached to the belt with a metal stud or rawhide thong. Shoulder holsters, of course, were not unknown.

[49] It has been suggested that this is perhaps a word originating with blacks, from the ghettoes of the South.

Oddly enough, the Hopis never seem to be bitten by these vipers.

HORN, RICHARD Alias of the man known as Frank M. Canton. (See CANTON, FRANK M.)

HORN, TOM Young Willie Nickells slumped from his horse and twitched into eternity as the double clap of the Winchester stomped its echoes around the valley. When the hoofbeats of Willie's runaway horse had drummed into silence, the crouched figure of a man, Winchester at the trail, emerged from the cover of a cluster of rocks, and, in a shuffling, barefoot gait, covered the three hundred yards that had separated him from his target. Face shadowed out by the wide brim of his black stetson, the killer bent over his blood- and dust-soiled victim, indecision clouding his mind and the vague stirrings of indigestible panic putting the taste of bile on his tongue. He could have sworn he'd had Kels Nickells in his sights, not the bastard's thirteen-year-old son; he'd killed the colt instead of the stallion. Using his free hand, he reached into a jacket pocket and fingered out a couple of round stones, and, clicking them like dice, he began to herd his thoughts back into their corral. The men in Cheyenne would be awaiting news of Kels Nickells' assassination, and as much of the six-hundred-dollar flat fee he had received for the killing had already found its way across the liquor-stained mahogany, it might be wiser to prove responsibility in an error of identity rather than have his employers suspect that he was ducking an assignment.

Tom Horn, the most lethal hired gun to ever stalk the West, gave a slight shrug, and bending forward, prodded the two stones beneath the head of the Nickells boy. His trademark in position, Tom Horn began his grueling, barefooted return journey to his black gelding, ground-hitched a half mile or more away.

During his lifetime Horn had many admirers, and after reading contemporary prose that is tailored around him, it soon becomes evident that even at this late date his fan club is enormous. This pro-Horn following lays stress on his honest appearance (well-chiseled features sporting a tawny, coathanger mustache), his wonderful physique (which comes in a variety of sizes that range from average height to well over six feet), and his outstanding bravery, particularly in the Apache wars of the 1880s and the Spanish-American War of 1898. As there is no record of Tom ever having had a face-to-face gunfight with any man, and anything worthy of mention in dispatches was broadcast by Tom alone,[50] it is hard to understand why Tom still retains an admiring following. Let us take a brief look at what Tom was doing, suspected of doing, and convicted of doing over his judicially allotted span:

1861: Born in Scotland County, Missouri. 1863: Parents and two-year-old Tom moved to Ohio.[51] 1874: Left home, possibly after having row with Horn, Sr. 1874: Reported to have met Billy the Kid in a Las Vegas, New Mexico, saloon. Had a row with Billy and slapped Billy's face. If Tom was born in 1861, this can only be classed as a

[50] If we ignore a glowing character reference read at his trial. This was forwarded by Al Sieber, an Army scout who had known Horn some fifteen years previously; trails and traits can grow dim in almost two decades.

[51] In 1960 Mrs. Eva Whitehead (nee Eva Horn, daughter of a cousin of Tom Horn) wrote that Tom Horn's parents moved from Ohio to Etna, Missouri, in 1853, when Tom was two years old. This would give Tom a birth year of 1851, not 1861. This earlier birth year is worth bearing in mind, for it would mean that Tom was a man and not a fugitive from a classroom when he started his muscle-building frontier chores.

kid's fight, Billy being about fifteen and Tom thirteen at this time. 1877: Driving a six-in-hand coach for the Overland Mail at fifty dollars a month. 1880(?): In California. Met Al Sieber and learned to speak fluent Spanish. 1883–85: Fluent Apache had now been mastered, and Tom was living the life of scout and interpreter attached to various U. S. Army units stationed in Arizona Territory. 1886: Attached to Captain Emmett Crawford's cavalry detail, which moved deep into Mexico on the trail of Geronimo. Trilingual Tom Horn extricated the cavalry out of a sticky situation when they were mistakenly attacked by Mexican forces, but not before Captain Crawford and some of his men had been killed. Tom in at the surrender of Geronimo. 1887: With the Apache wars over, Tom got a job as deputy sheriff of Yavapai County, Arizona, under Sheriff Glen Reynolds. While wearing a star, worked a mine on Arivaipa Canyon. Horn says he killed his first man around this time. 1888: Won steer-roping contest at Globe, Arizona, rodeo. 1890: Sold his mining interests for eight thousand dollars, and, according to his own statement, became a Pinkerton operative. 1891: Left Arizona for good. 1893: Became a range detective for the Swan Land and Cattle Company, doubling in brass as a Pinkerton man at the same time. 1894: Left Pinkerton employment (own statement). While a Pinkerton, Horn arrested a train robber named "Peg-leg" Watson (alias McCoy), probably at some jeopardy to himself. Wandered up into Wyoming. 1895: Suspected of killing a small-time rancher and suspected rustler named Lewis, the victim being shot in the back. 1896: Employed at the Iron

Mountain ranch of John C. Cable. Suspected of killing a rancher named Levi Powell.[52] 1898: Volunteered for the Spanish-American War and served as a mule train supervisor with the U.S. forces in Cuba. Contracted yellow fever and invalided out of the services. 1899: Back at the Iron Mountain ranch. 1900: Prime suspect in two murders that occurred in the Brown's Park area of Wyoming; Matt Rash (or Rush) was killed by rifle fire on July 6, and on October 11 a black man named Isham Dart was killed in a similar manner. Both victims had the type of character reference that could be expected to bring the wrath of a range detective down upon their heads—i.e., they were suspected of throwing a wide loop (rustling).[53] 1901: Still at Cable's Iron Mountain spread.

On July 18, 1901, Willie Nickells, the thirteen-year-old son of a sheepman, was killed by two slugs fired from a Winchester while he was riding along Horse Creek. Kels P. Nickells, the boy's father, was wounded by rifle fire a short time after the death of his son. Deputy U. S. Marshal Joe Lefors took an active interest in the Nickells case, and after first throwing suspicious glances in the direction of a certain Victor Miller, he directed his attention toward Horn after Miller had established an alibi. In January of the following year, Lefors accosted Horn while the latter was pickled with booze, and at this meeting, Horn bragged at great length about his record of kills, laying particular stress on the Nickells job. Lefors arranged a further meeting with this very prime suspect, having a concealed stenographer present on this occasion. Horn, who was well known as a braggart in regard to how many

---

[52] Powell's six-year-old son identified Horn as the slayer of his father, but nothing was done about this.

[53] We have another ectoplasmic suspect in these two murders: a hornery Mexican named Joe Good ("Joe Good" probably being an anglicized rendering of José Bueno).

notches could be credited to him, obliged Lefors by repeating his earlier story, the result being that he found himself sobering up in jail. At his trial Horn was well represented, some five thousand dollars being paid into his defense fund by parties unnamed, but this legal talent failed to save him, and he was found guilty and sentenced to death. On August 6, 1903, while awaiting execution, Horn came into possession of an automatic pistol, and with a fellow prisoner he succeeded in breaking jail. Freedom, however, didn't last long, for an off-duty brothelkeeper recognized him, got the drop on him, and handed him over to a lawman who came up on the double. On November 20, 1903, Tom Horn was hanged at Cheyenne, afterward being interred at Boulder, Colorado.

HORNED TOAD   A girdle-tailed lizard that is a member of the iguana family. Found in the arid lands of western North America and Mexico. Some species lay eggs, while others are viviparous, and although spiky protuberances give this reptile a formidable appearance, they are quite harmless and make good pets. Sizes vary; the Texas variety averages about 6 inches in length.

HORNER, JOE   Alias of the man known as Frank M. Canton. (See CANTON, FRANK M.)

HORSESHOE STATION   Telegraph station based on the Horseshoe Ranch. Located on the Bozeman Trail in southeastern Wyoming, approximately 190 miles south—trailwise—of Fort Phil Kearny, and 25 miles north of Fort Laramie. On March 19, 1868, a Sioux war party under the leadership of Crazy Horse, American Horse, and Little Big Man attacked the station, a minor engagement during which the buildings were fired, but the line wasn't put out of action. (See PHILLIPS, JOHN.)

HORSE-THIEF TRAIL
An unmarked trail that wended its way through Utah, Arizona, New Mexico, and Texas, its terminal points being Salt Lake City in the north and the Mexican border in the south. As it was used for the movement of stolen horses, it naturally steered well clear of the commercial routes.

HOTCHKISS GUN   Name that can be applied to either a machine gun capable of firing four hundred rounds a minute, or an automatic cannon that could fire two-pounder shells at the rate of fifty per minute. Both were the inventions of Benjamin Berkeley Hotchkiss, an American gunsmith (1826–85) who manufactured these weapons at his factory in France. (See WOUNDED KNEE MASSACRE.)

HOUSTON, SAMUEL   The premier adopted son of the Lone Star State. Houston, who was born in Virginia on March 2, 1793, turned to politics after first attempting to make the Army his career. At the age of thirty-four, and after time spent in the U. S. Senate, he was made governor of Tennessee. When the Texans revolted against Mexican rule in 1835, Sam soon found himself back in military finery, and as General Sam Houston he led his troops to victory at San Jacinto in 1836. Houston became the first President of the new Lone Star State. This post lasted until 1845, at which time the state became part of the Union. Over the years 1859–61 he was governor of the state. Sam Houston died on July 26, 1863. (See BATTLE OF SAN JACINTO.)

HOUSTON, TEMPLE LEE
Flamboyant younger son of Sam Houston (see the previous entry). Temple was born at Austin, Texas, in 1860, his initial appearance being in the governor's mansion. Some thirteen years later, Temple— a large, rawboned type with shoulder-length hair—was working as a trailhand, moving cattle as far north as Montana. In 1875, after a spot of fast grooming, he exchanged his cowhand attire for the uniform of a page in the U. S. Senate, and it was here that he began to study law, with the result that by the time he was eighteen he had passed the Texas bar examination and been elected district attorney for a large area of southern Texas. Around this time he is alleged to have had a friendly shooting match with Billy the Kid, said match—which had been promoted by Bat Masterson—taking place at Old Tascosa and being won hands down by Temple. In 1883 he married a girl named Laura Cross, and six years later he and his wife moved to Oklahoma, settling at Woodward, where Temple practiced law—successfully, one might add. It was here that he had a courtroom row with Al Jennings, the aftermath of which was that Temple and a friend shot dead Al's two brothers, Ed and John. This occurred in a Woodward saloon, and as the Jennings brothers had started the fracas, Temple's record remained unsullied. This was Temple Lee Houston, long-haired master of courtroom and barroom rhetoric, wearer of rattlesnake-skin ties, and pistoleer extraordinary. Temple died at Woodward in 1905. (See JENNINGS, AL.)

HOWARD, JAMES One of John Heath's infamous band of Arizona tearaways, a gang which in their early days used Heath's saloon at Brewery Gulch as their meeting point, and were suspected of rustling activities. In December 1883 James "Tex" Howard took part in the Bisbee robbery, which terminated with the Bisbee massacre. After this crime, the gang split up, Howard and a man named Sample heading Northeast until they arrived at Clifton in Graham County. Here Howard and Sample attracted attention to themselves by heavy spending and the reckless distribution of gifts to a couple of girls. Unfortunately for the two fugitives, they had lured one of these girls away from her steady date by this show of generosity, and the slighted suitor talked. It wasn't long after this that Deputy Sheriff Bob Hatch of Graham County had these two gentlemen under lock and key, the arrest having taken place when Howard and Sample were taking their Clifton cuties for a spin in a rented surrey and after Sample had been wounded in the arm. Howard became a key figure in a multiple hanging that took place at Tombstone on March 8, 1884. (See HEATH, JOHN.)

HOYT, GEORGE The waddy from Texas whom Wyatt Earp unhorsed with his Buntline on the night of July 26, 1877, Earp being under the impression that George was intent on murdering him. Hoyt is reported to have been a fugitive from Texas justice at the time of this attempted assassination of Earp, the attempt appearing to have been activated by the promise of a thousand-dollar reward for ushering Wyatt into Boot Hill, plus the additional bonus of having the Texas warrant (unspecified) against Hoyt quashed. A cattleman—possibly Tobe Driskill—may have been the one who made this offer, although Hoyt failed to mention any names in his alleged deathbed confession printed in a local paper. Hoyt died on August 21, almost a month after the shooting, and was buried on Boot Hill. (See EARP, WYATT BERRY STAPP.)

HUCKERT, ALICE Married name of Alice Ivers (alias Poker Alice). (See IVERS, ALICE.)

HUCKSTON, JOHN
Alias Arkansaw Johnson, a name under which he became a tail-end member of the Sam Bass gang, never being fully accepted by Sam, who may have been somewhat revolted by Huckston's brutality. Huckston is reported to have been born in Ireland around 1843, but the date of his arrival in the United States is unknown. We do know, however, that he was of about average height, possessed an unkempt brownish beard, and had a pox-scarred countenance. During the Civil War he served with the northern armies, and on being mustered out in 1865, he turned to a life of crime, housebreaking with murderous accompaniment appearing to have been his speciality in the Arkansas region where he operated. In Arkansas he was responsible for the bludgeon murders of an elderly couple named Wilberforce, the lootin' of their sumptuous home, and the multiple rape of their daughter,[54] a sickening crime that necessitated his leaving Arkansas at great speed. About 1876 we find him in the Kearney, Nebraska, jail, and here he met Henry Underwood, a fellow convict with whom he escaped a short time later. Underwood most likely talked Huckston into the Sam Bass mob in the early months of 1877, for he is known to have participated in the Eagle Ford and Mesquite robberies that occurred in April of that year. Arkansaw Johnson Huckston was finally run to earth by Texas Rangers in Wise County, Texas, on June 12, 1878, and he was

shot to death while resisting arrest. (See BASS, SAM.)

HUFFMAN, LATON ALTON
Frontier photographer who has left in his wake more than a thousand plates that reproduce excellent atmospheric prints of the twilight of the Old West. Huffman, who was born in Iowa in 1854, became interested in photography in his late teens, and by the time he was twenty-one he had opened his own studio at Postville, Iowa. This wasn't a success, and three years later he was working in a photographic supply store in Minnesota. Over the years Kansas, the Dakotas, and Montana all saw Huffman; part of the time as a rancher, much of the time as post photographer at Fort Keogh, and after 1880, as a commercial photographer at Miles City, Montana. Numerous present-day publications can be found that are illustrated, or partially illustrated, by reproductions of Huffman's photographs. Huffman died at Billings, Montana, on December 28, 1931.

HUGHES, JOHN R. The Illinois farmer's son who spent the greater part of his adult life as a Texas Ranger. By the middle 1870s John was working cattle in Indian Territory (Oklahoma), and here he is credited with the killing of Big Nig Goombi, a rustler who was attempting to reduce the herd that Hughes was holding at the time of Goombi's passing. By 1877 Hughes had worked his way to Texas, and twelve months later he had established a small horse-ranch in the state. Sometime after this, rustlers raided his stock, and southpawing his six-gun, Hughes went on their trail, overtaking the gang in the wilds of New Mexico; tally count after the smoke cleared =

[54] This experience is reported to have made a raving lunatic of Miss Wilberforce, the girl dying in an asylum a few years later.

four rustlers dead and two in custody. His stock, however, continued to dwindle, so in 1887, the long-suffering Hughes rode into Georgetown, Texas, and signed up as a Ranger private on the principle that "iffen he had to fight rustlers he might as well git paid fer it." In the written record of Hughes' Ranger service, punctuation marks tend to come from the muzzle of his six-gun, a number of full-period marks on outlaw careers no doubt being the reasons behind his promotion to sergeant in charge of Company D, Frontier Battalion, in 1893. Shortly after this, Captain Frank Jones of Company D was killed by Mexican bandits, and Hughes was promoted to captain to fill the resulting vacancy. The *banditti* whose actions were responsible for this leap in rank were, over the next few months, found fouling up the atmosphere of the Rio Grande country in positions most stiffened and couchant. As a loner, Captain Hughes went on the trail of Juan Perales, a much-feared buscadero type from south of the Rio Grande. Perales was lucky; Hughes brought him in alive. So the years passed, nailing many a tamale-eating tearaway and unknotting such rustler mobs as the Friar, Ybarra, and Massay gangs. Captain John R. Hughes left the Ranger service in 1915, and he died at Austin, Texas, in 1946, aged ninety-one years.

H U N K P A P A   S I O U X   One of the seven divisions of the Teton Sioux. In earlier publications it is usually given as "Uncpapa." (See SIOUX INDIANS and SITTING BULL.)

H U N T ,   Z W I N G   Hunt arrived at Tombstone, Arizona, in the winter of 1880–81, apparently an honest youth, but after a short spell of honest toil— freighting by ox team—Zwing palled on with William Grounds, a youth who liked to be known as "Billy the Kid" and who knew all the worst people. This friendship led Zwing on the owlhoot trail, and over the next few months he and Grounds were suspected of rustling. In the spring of 1881 these two pals were hanging around with the Clanton gang, and in July of that year they almost certainly took part in the Guadalupe Canyon[55] massacre. After this, Hunt and Grounds lay low for a spell. Then, on one evening in March 1882, two masked men made uninvited entrance to the office of the Tombstone Mill & Mining Company; whether robbery was intended, no one can say, but in the ensuing excitement a man named Peel was shot dead by the gate crashers. Hunt and Grounds were prime suspects. Warrants were issued, and Deputy Sheriff W. M. Breakenridge led a posse out in search of the two men. The posse caught up with the fugitives at Chandler's Ranch, and the usual "You're coming with us!"—"We're not!" gunfight took place. When the gun barrels cooled, Billy the Kid Grounds was measuring his length for the last time, Zwing was seriously wounded, and one of the possemen was dead, the latter being a victim of Zwing's .45. Hunt was placed in the local hospital to either die or fatten up for trial, but on April 27 he disappeared, having been smuggled from his sickbed by his brother, Hugh Hunt. The brothers hid out in the Chiricahua Mountains, and here, on May 31, they were attacked by a small band of Apaches. Hugh finally drove the renegades off, but not before Zwing had been killed by the Indians. Zwing Hunt was buried under a juniper tree that flourished at the scene of his passing. Hunt

[55] After this atrocity it became known as Skeleton Canyon.

as twenty-four years old at the time of is death. (See CLANTON GANG.)

IUNTER, RICHARD   Member of the roup of bounty hunters known as the Outlaw Exterminators." (See ALLMAN, OHN, and OUTLAW EXTERMINATORS.)

HURDY-GURDY HOUSE   Western name for a dance hall. Obviously derived from the fact that "hurdy-gurdy" was originally the name of a small wind-instrument, and latterly of a barrel organ. (See DANCE HALLS.)

Iᴄᴇ Bᴏx Bᴇʀɴɪᴇ The somewhat derogatory nickname given to the incompetent safe-cracking member of the Soapy Smith mob. (See Sᴍɪᴛʜ, Jᴇꜰꜰ.)

Iᴅᴀʜᴏ Northwestern state flanked on the east by Montana and Wyoming and on the west by Washington and Oregon, its northern boundary being Canada and its southern boundary, Nevada and Utah. Originally part of the Oregon country, a vast area that was under British and American jurisdiction until 1846, Idaho was admitted into the Union as the forty-third state in 1890. Still has large wilderness areas. Mainly mountainous, and known as the Gem State. Boise is the state capital.

Iɴᴅᴇᴘᴇɴᴅᴇɴᴄᴇ Rᴏᴄᴋ Landmark on the Oregon Trail in central Wyoming. This dome-shaped rock is located on the north bank of the Sweetwater, approximately twenty miles west of its junction with the North Platte. Pioneers used the rock as an autograph book and message pad; the more permanent of these jottings—those carved in the rock—are still visible.

Iɴᴅɪᴀɴ Cʜᴀʀʟɪᴇ One of Wyatt Earp's notches. (See Cʀᴜᴢ, Fʟᴏʀᴇɴᴛɪɴᴇ.)

Iɴᴅɪᴀɴs The people now referred to as Amerinds most likely arrived in North America about twenty thousand years ago, their point of entry being the west coast of Alaska, this being the first landfall that nomadic Asians would reach after crossing the frozen Bering Strait. When Europeans first contacted these people, they dubbed them "Indians," faulty compass and star reading evidently being responsible for this error in nomenclature, as Columbus was confident that he had arrived at the Asian subcontinent of India. It has been estimated that there may have been about one million of these aborigines at the time of the white man's arrival.[1] This neat figure embraced more than three hundred tribes speaking a like number of languages, and is usually divided into seven main cultural areas, five of the latter—Northwest Coast, Plateau, Californian, Plains, and Southwest—being located west of the Mississippi. The "red" adjective that sometimes prefixes "Indian" refers to their use of red (war or ceremonial) paint, and not to their skin coloring, skin pigmentation varying to such a degree that we have Indians who are pale mongoloid yellow, coppery suntan red, and almost negroid black. Hair coloring also varies, for although black is the most common, medium-blond and reddish locks are not unknown, Crazy Horse being of the penultimate class and some Californian Indians being of the latter. Body and facial hair were usually sparse or absent, and any shoot that dared to appear anywhere other than on the head was soon plucked from its seating.[2]

Keeping roughly west of the Mississippi—as was our original intention when compiling this book—we find tribes that were nomadic, these usually living by the hunt; seminomadic peoples who indulged in both hunting and agriculture; pastoral, seed-gathering, and crop-rearing tribes who lived in permanent settlements (notably the pueblo tribes of the Southwest); and essentially fish-harvesting peoples who lived in substantial wooden houses that were elaborately decorated with murals of an ancestor-inspired motif (primarily among the coastal tribes of the Northwest).

The dwellings of these people varied considerably, availability of materials and climatic conditions usually dictating style and the activities of the tribe ruling whether a dwelling be permanent or temporary. The portable hide tepees of the buffalo-hunting nomads of the plains are possibly the most picturesque, while the pueblo apartment houses and mesa cliff-dwellings of the Southwest are the most permanent. Bark wigwams of some northern tribes, and the bird's-nest construction wickeyups of Apacheria are both of an expendable nature. Grass huts were found in areas where vegetation made them possible and the climate made them ideal, while dome-shaped earth lodges were found in a variety of regions where climatic conditions called for a dwelling that was warm in winter and cool in summer. Most villages were open, but some, notably along the Upper Missouri, were pallisaded. Intertribal commerce was well established before the arrival of the white man, dog-travois and waterway transportation being used for this purpose. After the arrival of the Spaniards the horse was to supplant—but not entirely—both the dog travois and the rivercraft, and it is more than likely that the Spaniards also introduced slave trading to the tribes of the Southwest as an additional form of commerce. The Indians did not have that boon to mankind, the wheel; this inventive omission is usually given as proof that these people were extremely backward, but as the South American aborigines knew of the wheel but did not use it for transportation purposes, one wonders if their northern cousins were also aware of it but had little reason to employ it;[3] a wheeled cart in a vast area of no roads is as a pressure cooker to a man without fire.

[1] Their numbers are now reduced to about 900,000.
[2] There were exceptions; some tribes—notably in the Northwest area—allowed mustaches to grow.
[3] They possessed circular shields, and their children played with hoops; not such a great leap to the wheel, surely?

Indians treated war as a game and a pastime, rarely going in for the mass-extermination target of the white man. Consequently, in the beginning, the push westward met with little hostility from the red man, and it was only when their way of life and tribal lands became threatened that they went on the warpath. By then, of course, their enemies had increased a thousandfold, and the outcome of these wars was easily predictable. Night warfare was regarded with distaste, their assumption being that if they were killed during the hours of darkness, their souls would have difficulty finding the right trail to the Happy Hunting Grounds. Pure democracy of the "do thine own thing" type, not just the word type, was the rule among most tribes, and this extended to the battlefield; e.g., if a brave broke off the fight to go hunt an antelope or somesuch, he need have no fear that he would be accused of being a coward on his return to his village. Cannibalism was rarely practiced; an overabundance of game and an underabundance of fellow red men may have had something to do with this.

Tribes found west of the Mississippi who have brief entries in this volume are as follows: Acoma; Apache; Arapaho; Arikara; Bannock; Blackfoot; Caddo; Cayuse; Cherokee; Cheyenne; Chinook; Comanche; Crow; Havasupai; Hidatsa; Hopi; Kiowa; Klamath; Mandan; Navaho; Nez Percé; Osage; Paiute; Papago; Pawnee; Pima; Shoshone; Sioux; Tonkawa; Ute; Wichita; Yakima; Yuma; and Zuni. (See ABALONE; ACOMA, NEW MEXICO; BERDACHE; BRONCHO APACHE; BUCKSKIN; BUFFALO HORSES; BULLBOATS; CALUMET; CANNIBALS; CANOE; COUP; CUT-NOSE SQUAW; DOG SOLDIER; FIVE CIVILIZED TRIBES; FOLSOM MAN; GIANTS; HOGAN; INDIAN TERRITORY; LACROSSE; MANITOU; MEDICINE BUNDLE; MESA VERDE; MESCAL; MOCCASINS; PEMMICAN; PEYOTE; PLAINS INDIANS; PUEBLO INDIANS; RESERVATIONS; ROACH; SCALPING; SHAMAN; SIGN LANGUAGE; SMOKE SIGNALS; STONE BOILING; SUCCOTASH; SUN DANCE; TEPEE; THUNDERBIRD; TOMAHAWK; TORTILLA; TOTEM POLE; TRAVOIS; TUMPLINE; WAMPUM; WAR BONNET; WARPAINT; WICKEYUP; WIGWAM.)

INDIAN SUMMER A period of mild and tranquil weather occurring in the late fall is frequently referred to as an "Indian summer." Originated with the early settlers, who experienced this type of weather in regions that were, at that time, essentially Indian territory.

INDIAN TERRITORY In accordance with a treaty that the Five Civilized Tribes were pressured into signing in 1835, these Indians were moved from their homes in the Carolinas and settled in an area that to all intents and purposes had the same boundaries as present-day Oklahoma.[4] The Creek, Cherokee, Choctaw, and Chickasaw[5] were given allotments of land in the eastern half of this rather arid, flat, and unwanted region, the northwest section being unallotted land, which became known as the Cherokee Strip. Over the years, other tribes, notably the Kiowa, Comanche, Osage, and Apache, but also many others, were rounded up and corraled within the remaining southwestern strip. This was Indian Territory, a region that was administered by tribal councils and patrolled by Indian police. Free from the

[4] The only difference being that Indian Territory did not encompass that narrow strip of present-day Oklahoma that lies north of the Texas Panhandle; in those days this 170-mile-by-40-mile (approximately) piece of land was considered a no man's land.

[5] The Seminole—the "runaways" of the Creek nation—never did arrive; these Indians are still officially at war with the United States.

harassment of punitive expeditions organized by military glory-hunters, these peoples were allowed to remain unmolested until the white men once again turned avaricious eyes in their direction. This came to a head in 1889 when white settlers and speculators, together with honky-tonkers and an assortment of even scurvier deadbeats, were allowed to enter and settle in Indian Territory. After the turn of the century, oil was discovered beneath this land, and by a strange quirk of naturally dispensed justice, some of the displaced Indians became rich overnight. That they were allowed to reap the benefits from this oil bonanza may seem odd after all their years of harassment, but the Wounded Knee Massacre had occurred but a short time previously, and shrapnel from this sorry affair may have pricked the conscience of the folk with the big stick. (See OKLAHOMA and OKLAHOMA LAND RUSH.)

INGALLS, OKLAHOMA   In 1893 Bill Doolin's gang of owlhoots were using the quiet, rural town of Ingalls as an "off-duty" recreational center, bringing their own recreation in the rather immature forms of Cattle Annie and Little Britches,[6] and using the Pierce Hotel to recreate in between bouts of boozing and gambling. Bill Doolin's main interest in the town was a lass named Edith Ellsworth, the minister's daughter, while Bitter Creek George Newcomb is alleged to have been courting Rosa Dunn in these here parts.[7] Lawmen on the trail of the Doolin gang were unaware that their quarry were living and loving openly in Ingalls, and it was not until the night of August 31, 1893, that an informer acquainted the U.S. marshal's office at Guthrie with this fact. The U.S. marshal for Oklahoma Territory, Evett Dumas

Nix, immediately rallied a baker's dozen of his deputy marshals, gave them a quick briefing, and then saw them climb into a couple of canvas-topped wagons and head out for Ingalls, thirty-five miles to the northeast. At high noon on the following day, September 1, 1893, these lawmen were about to meet seven members of the Doolin gang in a fast gun battle that would leave three of the deputies quite dead. The full cast of characters, both the good and the bad, is given as follows so that you may make their acquaintance before the melee gets under way:

Deputy U.S. marshals: Jim Masterson (brother of Bat); William Roberts; Henry Keller; Hi Thompson; George Cox; Hank Janson; Lafe Shadley; Dick Speed; John Hixon; Tom Houston; Steve Burke; Red Lucas; and Ike Steel. *Doolin gang members:* Bill Doolin; Roy "Arkansas Tom" Daugherty; George "Bitter Creek" Newcomb; William Dalton; Dan "Dynamite Dick" Clifton; George "Red Buck" Waightman; and "Tulsa" Jack Blake.

Six of the Doolin mob were drinking and playing cards in Murray's Saloon, loot from the recent double robbery at Wharton no doubt still sagging their pockets, when the wagons rolled into town; the seventh member, Arkansas Tom, was resting up in a room of the Pierce Hotel, having complained of feeling unwell. The deputies had just gotten fanned out when, for reasons best known to himself, "Bitter Creek" Newcomb left the saloon and mounted his horse. This action sparked off the battle, for Deputy Dick Speed saw him and sent a Winchester slug after him. This lead put the outlaw's rifle out of action and wounded him in the leg as the sound of the shot brought Arkansas Tom to the window of his hotel room; Tom took in the situation

6 Two juveniles of sixteen and fifteen respectively.

7 Edith married Bill in 1894, but Bitter Creek didn't get Rosa; this girl married an honest joe some years later.

at a glance, and split seconds later, Speed jackknifed to the dust, dying from three bullet wounds. Other lawmen came on the double and began mushrooming the dust around Bitter Creek, but the five card players were now pouring lead from the interior of Murray's Saloon, and the wounded outlaw made good his escape. Meanwhile, the deputies had taken cover, and their leader, Deputy Hixon, called upon the cornered gunmen to surrender.

The outlaws made a traditional break for their horses, tethered in a nearby stable. Arkansas Tom, being unable to see all this fuss from his window, had by now climbed onto the hotel roof, and from this vantage point he killed Deputy Houston with his next two shots. This diversion allowed Dynamite Dick, Bill Doolin, Tulsa Jack, Red Buck, and Bill Dalton to get to their mounts without hurt, and minutes later they dashed from the stables in a do-or-die effort at escape. Dalton's horse was brought down, but he remounted behind Doolin, and soon the lawmen had only dust to shoot at. During this blast of action, three of Dalton's shots had killed Deputy Shadley.

The remaining deputies now concentrated on Arkansas Tom's improvised fortress, but it was like trying to get a turtle to vacate its shell, and after an hour of trading lead with Tom, Jim Masterson got a couple of sticks of dynamite and threatened to blow the Pierce property and Tom to all hell and back. This brought results, for the outlaw tossed out his hardware and surrendered. That was the end of the Battle of Ingalls, and these were the casualties: dead: Deputies Speed, Shadley, and Houston, and a town youth named Dell Simmons; wounded: Murray and Rawson, joint owners of Murray's Saloon, an innocent bystander named Walker, and Bitter Creek and Arkansas Tom of the Doolin gang. After

this, Ingalls went back to sleep, the sleep getting deeper and deeper, until by the 1930s only the weathered shells of a few of the buildings remained. There may still be a bit of firewood lying around on the prairie about fifty miles west of Tulsa and eleven miles east of Stillwater, and if there is, that is all that is left of Ingalls. (See BLAKE, JACK; CLIFTON, DAN; DALTON, WILLIAM; DAUGHERTY, ROY; DOOLIN, BILL; DOOLIN GANG; DUNN, ROSA; McDOUGAL, ANNIE; NEWCOMB, GEORGE; STEVENS, JENNIE; and WAIGHTMAN, GEORGE.)

INNOCENTS An ironic name given to a veritable legion of outlaws, gunmen, and road agents who were organized into a ruthless and efficient gang by Henry Plummer. These men began to filter into what is now the southwest corner of Montana after gold had been discovered in the Deer Lodge and Grasshopper Creek[8] regions in 1862. Soon the plethora of newly erected towns, villages, and mining camps began to get a generous quota of these gold-hungry vultures, many of whom were experienced thieves and killers who had drifted across the Bitterroot Mountains from the Salmon River diggings of Idaho, leaving this earlier stamping ground after vigilantes had made minor reductions to their ranks. Individual escapades of these work-shy arrivals plagued the honest citizens from the beginning, but it was not until Henry Plummer arrived with a few key men from an earlier gang enterprise in Idaho that any attempt at organization and master planning was attempted. Plummer had sufficient personality and gun ability to keep these rugged characters in line, and when his crime empire was at full peak it became virtually impossible to move a gold shipment between any two

[8] Later known as Beaverhead Diggings.

points that came under the gang's surveillance without it being held up and looted by a detail of Innocents.[9] Undercover members of the gang placed secret markings on all wagons and coaches transporting anything of sufficient value to make a holdup worthwhile, and as Plummer had been elected sheriff, the victims who survived gun disease met with little success when they shuffled into his office with their complaints. The sheer weight of these outlaw depredations was responsible for quite a few towns becoming ghosts or near ghosts as the harassed businessmen and miners located their premises and dwellings elsewhere. This exodus of honest folk failed in its objective, for the gang merely extended its area of operations by moving its headquarters from Bannack to Virginia City.[10] This state of affairs, however, couldn't last, and by the fall of 1863 a powerful undercover force of vigilantes was ready to drop upon the Innocents like the Hammer of God. Four days before Christmas of that year, a leading member of the Innocents named George Ives felt the hemp being adjusted. George was the first of the gang to dangle; others followed in rapid succession, and that was the end of the Innocents. (See BANNACK, MONTANA; BEIDLER, JOHN XAVIER; DOLAN, JOHN; GALLAGHER, JACK; GRAVES, WILLIAM; HELM, BOONE; IVES, GEORGE; KEENE, JOHN; LANE, GEORGE; LYONS, HAZE; MARSHLAND, STEPHEN; PARISH, FRANK; PIZANTHIA, JOE; PLUMMER, HENRY; RAWLEY, R. C.; RAY, NED; SKINNER, CYRUS; STINSON, BUCK; VIGILANTES OF MONTANA; VIRGINIA CITY, MONTANA; WAGNER, JOHN; and ZACHARY, ROBERT.)

INSCRIPTION ROCK A castellated mesa in western New Mexico on which travelers have left their names and marks since the beginning of the seventeenth century.

IOWA Midwestern state bounded by the Mississippi River in the east and the Missouri and Big Sioux rivers in the west, and snuggling between Minnesota and Missouri, which lie to the north and south, respectively. Iowa became the twenty-ninth state in 1846; Des Moines is the state capital. Iowa is referred to as the Hawkeye State. Iowa Indians once roamed this area—hence the name.

IRISH TOM
Member of the Daly gang. (See DALY GANG.)

IRON JACKET Alternative name for Iron Shirt. (See IRON SHIRT.)

IRON SHIRT The white man's name for Pohibitquasho, a renegade Comanche chief who went into battle protected by a suit of Spanish torso armor. On May 12, 1858, Iron Shirt's camp, containing about sixty-five lodges and located on the Canadian in the Texas Panhandle, was subjected to a surprise attack by a mixed force of a hundred Texas Rangers and a like number of reservation Tonkawa Indians. The "iron shirt" had saved the chief's life on many an occasion, but on this day he was killed by a bullet that found its way between the plates of his hip armor. A Tonkawa named Jim Pockmark is credited with firing this shot.

[9] All of whom are reported to have worn red bandanas and used a secret handclasp and the word "innocent" for identification purposes; this was necessary, as the gang may have topped the three-figure mark at the height of its power.
[10] Secondary meeting places for the Innocents were Cyrus Skinner's Saloon at Bannack and Pete Daly's roadhouse, located on the Virginia City–Bannack road. This latter was a two-story building that could be used as a lookout post from which a spotter could keep track of wagon and coach movements. Both these buildings are still standing.

ITALIAN JIM   Member of the John Daly gang. (See DALY GANG.)

IVAN, RED   Of interest inasmuch as he was responsible for gunning down the only psychic gambler who ever worked the Colorado camps. (See ARONDONDO, PEDRO.)

IVERS, ALICE
The gal who worked the gambling halls and saloons of the West and is usually referred to as "Poker Alice." Alice, who was born in Sudbury, England, in 1851, and received a finishing-school-type education in that country, came over to the States with her father when she was in her late teens. The Ivers settled in Colorado, where Mr. Ivers found a position as a schoolteacher, an occupation he had been active in way back in England. Shortly after their arrival, Alice married a mining engineer named Duffield, but this was a short-lived housewife stint, for Duffield was killed in a mine accident before Alice had reached her twenty-first birthday. Alice, probably propelled by boredom, began frequenting gambling saloons. Gambling evidently fascinated this girl, for within a short time she was dealing poker professionally and keeping herself in a fashion to which she had hitherto been unaccustomed. The finishing-school language began to be replaced by such refined remarks as "You cheating bastard" and "I'll shoot you in the puss"; cigars of great length and girth were smoked continuously; and Alice frequently carried a man-sized .45, but even so, "breeding tells," as the old saw saws, and Alice would never gamble on Sundays.

When gold fever took over in South Dakota, Alice pulled up stakes and moved to Deadwood, not returning to Colorado until 1890, when we hear of her being employed as a poker dealer at Bob Ford's saloon and gambling hall at Creede. In the late 1890s Alice returned to Deadwood, and it was here that she regained her marital status, the lucky man being a professional gambler named Tubbs. The newlyweds bought a chicken farm, enjoying a rather odorous yet pastoral existence until 1910, in which year Tubbs made Alice a widow by dying of pneumonia. Alice kept counting eggs for a few years, and then she was back behind the green baize, saving her earnings and winnings until she was able to open a place of her own. Poker Alice's place was located in South Dakota, between Fort Meade and the town of Sturgis, and —possibly because of the proximity of the fort—Alice imported a few lovelies and used the top floor as a brothel, an annex of joy to which soldiers and civilians could withdraw when satiated with liquor and gambling. Traces of a puritanical upbringing were still with Alice, however, and a ban on whatever-you-do-in-a-joyhouse was in operation on Sundays. Over this period of private enterprise, Alice married again, George Huckert of the gambling fraternity being the one who gave her his moniker on this occasion. Prohibition now darkened the land, but the Elliot Nesses of the Dakotas seem to have turned a blind eye to the illegality of Alice's establishment for quite a spell, and George had gone to join his predecessors by the time they put the padlocks on in the late 1920s.[11] Alice was now getting long in the tooth, and the perpetual giant cigar she always had in her face must have been getting heavier with the years, so she retired to a small clapboard house she had had built at Sturgis. Alice Ivers Duffield Tubbs Huckert died at Sturgis in 1930.

[11] It has been reported that Alice killed a drunken soldier in self-defense, and that after her acquittal an irate D.A. closed the place. "She never!" say folk who were around Fort Meade at this time.

IVES, GEORGE One of the leading members of Henry Plummer's band of thieves and road agents. This tall, well-mannered, good-looking, blond-haired hard case was born at Ive's Grove, Racine County, Wisconsin, about 1835. Sometime in the early 1850s he headed West, pausing long enough in his travels to write his mother a letter saying that her poor son George had been killed by Indians; what name he used to sign this lying epistle is unknown, but it was obviously done to sever all family ties. California had George over the years 1857–58, and he was toiling honestly as a miner over this period. In 1859 he had moved North to Oregon and was employed by the U. S. Army as a mule train supervisor working in the Walla Walla region.[12] While in this employment, he stole a number of mules and sold them, his *modus operandi* being to tell the officer in charge that the animal had died. Ives' gray mare brought him to the Beaverhead Diggings of eastern Idaho[13] in 1862, and it was here that he threw in his lot with Plummer, becoming a key man of the Innocents. Before embarking on his crime career, Ives established a stable for draft animals in Alder Gulch, thus giving himself a visible means of support that could be expected to account for any instant wealth that came his way. He is known to have taken part in two mail coach robberies that occurred in October and November 1863, and he was strongly suspected of numerous highway robberies carried out along the Snake River trails, but when he was finally taken into custody, it was for the murder of a young German, whose mutilated body had been discovered in mid-December 1863, some ten days after his disappearance. The victim, Nicholas Tbalt, was well known and well liked, and he had been robbed of gold and mules belonging to his employer. Rumblings ran through the mining camps, and when Ives came under suspicion, a miners' posse of more than two dozen armed men placed him under arrest. This was on December 18, 1863, and on the twenty-first of that month, twenty-three men of a twenty-four man jury voted Ives guilty as charged. George Ives was hanged at Nevada[14] about four hours after he had heard the verdict of the court. (See INNOCENTS; PLUMMER, HENRY; and VIGILANTES OF MONTANA.)

[12] Walla Walla is now located in the state of Washington, but in Ives' time it was in the Oregon country.
[13] Now located in southwestern Montana.
[14] A Beaverhead mining camp, not the state.

FREDERIC REMINGTON

J ACKASS A male ass. Alternative names with a territorial flavor are Arizona nightingale and California canary. At Fairplay, Colorado, a monument to a jackass can be found; it was erected in 1930 to the memory of a hard-working ass called Prunes who died in harness way back in the 1800s. (See BURRO; HINNY; JENNY; and MULE.)

JACKASS MAIL Unofficial name for the San Antonio and San Diego Mail. In June 1857 a government mail contract was awarded to John Burke,[1] and one month later the first coach drawn by six mules left San Antonio to commence its 1,476-mile run. After leaving San Antonio the Jackass Mail swung its way through Ulvalde, Fort Lancaster, Fort Davis, and El Paso in Texas; La Mesilla in New Mexico; and Tucson in Arizona before reaching the terminal point for coaches at Fort Yuma on the Arizona-California line. From here the mail and passengers were transported over the 180-mile stretch to San Diego by mule-deck. A single-passenger trip cost two hundred dollars, and journeys were started from each terminal point on the ninth and twenty-fourth of each month. In 1858 the Butterfield Overland Mail took over the run as the last lap of its journey from Tipton, Missouri, but the Jackass coaches continued to roll over the route until 1861. (See BUTTERFIELD OVERLAND MAIL COMPANY.)

JACKRABBIT A contraction of jackass-rabbit, but a misnomer nonetheless, for these creatures are hares. There are three types of these hares: white-tailed, black-tailed, and white-sided; the first two being common in most areas of the West, while the latter is only found

[1] Late president of the California Stage Company. Shortly after getting the Jackass Mail shuttling between San Antonio and San Diego, Burke was drowned at sea.

in Arizona and New Mexico. All are great jumpers, twenty-foot leaps having been recorded.

JACKSON, FRANK Member of the Sam Bass gang who sometimes went under the aliases of Bill or Bob Downing. Frank was born on June 10, 1856, in Llano County, Texas. His father, Robert Jackson, was the local blacksmith, and both parents were diehard Methodists. Robert Jackson died in 1863, and his wife Phoebe followed him in 1864, leaving Frank, two brothers, and a like number of sisters to be taken care of by an uncle on their mother's side. As this uncle had little money, no prospects, and no ambition, the Jackson brood had a limited start in life, but even so, in 1871 Frank managed to find employment with a Dr. Ross of Denton County, living in the Ross home until one of his sisters married, after which he settled with the newly-weds. Over this period, Frank learned to read and write, and he mastered the tinning trade. He took employment as a tinsmith, and this lasted for some years, but by 1876 he was working at Jim Murphy's Ranch in Denton County. In this year he killed a black man after an argument over a horse, but as he was never charged with this crime, he remained working at the Murphy Ranch until the early months of 1877. On leaving Murphy's employ he returned to live with his sister and brother-in-law, and once more he took up the trade of tinsmith. Nothing more might have been heard of Frank, but toward the end of 1877 he met Sam Bass, and that gentleman persuaded him to join his outlaw band. Frank was active in all the gang's train robberies that occurred in Texas. The last we hear of Frank was on July 21, 1878. On that day he is riding from the disastrous gunfight at Round Rock, one of his arms attempting to keep the dying Bass in the saddle; then the dust becomes opaque, and from that time onward Frank's history is blotted out forever. (See BASS, SAM.)

JAGUAR One of the two great cats—the other being the puma—that are found in the West. Now fairly rare in North America, the range of the jaguar is limited to small areas of Arizona, New Mexico, California, and Texas. They are similar to the leopard of Africa and Asia, but of heavier build[2] and having a black marking in the center of their rosettes, which leopards lack. Localized names for the jaguar are "tiger" and *el tigre*. (See PUMA.)

JAMES, ALEXANDER FRANKLIN Older brother of the more notorious Jesse and the first child born, on January 10, 1844, to Robert and Zerelda James, Kentuckians who had settled in Clay County, Missouri. In the early days of the Civil War, Frank became a soldier of the Confederacy, serving for about four months before being taken prisoner at the Battle of Wilson's Creek on August 10, 1861. The Union was lenient in those early months of the war, and on giving his word not to rejoin the rebel forces, Frank was given his liberty. Still a "Yankee" hater, Frank joined Quantrill's guerrillas, thus retaining a "split hair" type of honesty, but becoming a member of the bloodiest-minded force that ever terrorized the border states. Frank took part in the Lawrence massacre, his behavior on this occasion being "as ferocious and merciless as a hyena."[3] Two months after Lee's surrender at Appomattox, Quantrill died from wounds, and on

---

[2] A fully grown male jaguar may weigh 250 pounds (about 50 pounds more than its leopard counterpart). In spite of this, the jaguar is not as aggressive as the leopard.

[3] Quote of William Elsey Connelley, author of *Quantrill and the Border Wars*.

July 26, 1865, Frank James surrendered. In February of the following year Frank, together with Cole Younger and ten other outlaws, raided the Clay County Savings and Loan Association at Liberty, Missouri, and escaped with fifty-seven thousand dollars. This was the first rung of Frank's outlaw ladder, and it was not until some twenty robberies later, and after the death of Jesse, that Frank surrendered to Governor T. T. Crittenden at Jefferson City, Missouri, on October 5, 1882.[4] In July 1883 he was placed on trial for the murder of Frank McMillan, a passenger who had been killed during the robbery of a Chicago and Rock Island train at Winston, Missouri, in 1881, but after a parade of witnesses that lasted seven days, and two days of legal argument, Frank was acquitted. Over the remaining three decades of his life, Frank tried many jobs: starter at the Springfield race track; a spell of circus life; farming; and on one occasion being employed as a shoe salesman in a St. Louis store. Alexander Franklin died at the old Samuels home at Kearney, Missouri, on February 19, 1915.[5] (See COLE, ZERELDA M.; JAMES GANG; JAMES, JESSE WOODSON; LAWRENCE MASSACRE; and QUANTRILL, WILLIAM CLARKE.)

JAMES, DINGUS Family name for Jesse. (See JAMES, JESSE WOODSON.)

JAMES, FRANK Jesse's older brother. (See JAMES, ALEXANDER FRANKLIN.)

JAMES GANG The gang that evolved around Frank and Jesse James and Cole Younger in the early days of 1866. Over its fifteen years of active life about fourteen riders are known to have ridden with the gang, although the maximum turnout during any given operation was twelve men. The long run of success this gang enjoyed may be partially accounted for by the elaborate espionage work undertaken by Frank and Jesse—escape routes, lawmen in the vicinity, etc.—before embarking on any robbery, but it must also be remembered that the gang was held in high esteem by a great number of Missourians who regarded Jesse and Frank as local Robin Hoods,[6] misguided folk who gave the gang shelter and remained tight-lipped when the lawmen started asking questions. Linen duster coats were usually worn, and those engaged in a robbery would filter into the target area in ones and twos. Frank James and Cole, Bob, and Jim Younger started the ball rolling on February 13, 1866, by robbing the Commercial Bank at Liberty, Missouri, of fifty-seven thousand dollars, killing an innocent bystander in the process. If we omit the attempted robbery[7] of William McLain's bank at Savannah, Missouri, on March 2, 1867, a fairly comprehensive list of profit-making enterprises attributed to the gang is as follows:

Lexington, Missouri: Alexander and Company looted on October 30, 1866; bank at Richmond, Missouri, robbed of about four thousand dollars on May 23,

[4] For gun buffs: Frank handed over a .44 Remington revolver holstered onto a forty-loop cartridge belt.
[5] Leaving a widow, Anna, who died on July 6, 1944, aged ninety-one, and one son, Robert Franklin, who died on November 18, 1959, aged eighty-two.
[6] Ridiculous, of course, for there is no evidence that Frank or Jesse ever gave a cent to anyone. As the total gang take, over fifteen years, amounted to little more than three hundred thousand dollars, and this had to be sliced a number of ways, there couldn't have been much gravy to splash around among the poor. The gang did rob the rich, but this has been the policy of holdup men from time immemorable, as quick profits cannot be realized by robbing the penurious.
[7] The takings were zero, so it can hardly be termed a robbery.

1867; Long and Norton's bank at Russelville, Kentucky, raided on March 20, 1868 (take-home money for the bandits was fourteen thousand dollars, but they missed an additional fifty thousand dollars); Daviess County Savings Bank hit on December 7, 1868, netting the gang a mere five hundred dollars for Christmas gifts; a bank at Corydon, Iowa, had the James boys in July 1871, and was nearly fifty thousand dollars down the drain when the dust cleared; the Deposit Bank at Columbia, Kentucky, must have been near insolvent when the gang called on April 27, 1872, for the boys got little more than beer money; a Chicago, Rock Island, and Pacific express derailed at Adair, Iowa, in July 1873, and the express car was looted of seven thousand dollars; on January 15, 1874, a stagecoach near Hot Springs, Arkansas, swelled the kitty by about four thousand dollars; another train at Gads Hill, Missouri on the last day of January 1874; April 7, 1874, saw a stagecoach robbed between Austin and San Antonio, Texas, but, at best, this must remain a maybe; a train relieved of fifty thousand dollars near Muncie, Kansas, on December 12, 1874; Texas was invaded again on May 12, 1875, when a stagecoach near Austin had its box looted of nearly three thousand dollars; near Ottersville, Missouri, on July 7, 1876, the gang had its greatest success when more than one hundred thousand dollars was taken from a Missouri-Pacific express car. Two months to the day after this jackpot take, the gang was cut to ribbons at Northfield, Minnesota, only Jesse and Frank, of a seven-man detail, escaping after an abortive attempt to rob the First National Bank.

Over the next three years the shattered gang has been accused of not one crime. This, of course, does not mean that they had disappeared into monasteries or were living on charity, for during this period of criminal nonactivity, Jesse, Frank, and the brothers Ford were doing a spot of prospecting around Leadville, Colorado, a region that wasn't entirely devoid of crime during the quartet's stay. Missourians knew the gang was back in the state when a Chicago and Alton train was held up at Glendale on October 7, 1879, and robbed to the tune of ten thousand dollars. Five months later a stagecoach was relieved of around five thousand dollars near Muscle Shoals, Alabama, the gang returning to bank robbery on July 10, 1881, on which day they looted the Davis and Sexton Bank at Riverton, Iowa, of a sum of about five thousand dollars (round figures all the time; these weren't nickel-and-dime boys). Five days later saw another train job when a Chicago and Rock Island train was knocked off at Winston, Missouri; the gang had less than a thousand dollars to divvy up after this effort, a messy job that left a couple of corpses in its wake. On September 7, 1881, the Chicago and Alton Railroad got a return visit from the gang when another of their express cars was robbed at Glendale, Missouri; a pathetic twelve hundred dollars was split after this job, a peanuts swan song, for this was the last robbery of the James gang.

A fairly complete gang roll call—many of whom fell by the wayside—follows: Arch Clements; Robert and Charlie Ford; Cole, Bob, and Jim Younger; Bill Chadwell; Clelland Miller; Dick Liddell; Wood Hite; Jim Cummins; and Charlie Pitts. (See CHADWELL, BILL; CUMMINS, JIM; FORD, ROBERT; HITE, WOOD; JAMES, ALEXANDER FRANKLIN; JAMES, JESSE WOODSON; LIDDELL, DICK; MILLER, CLELLAND; PITTS, CHARLIE; NORTHFIELD, MINNESOTA; and YOUNGER, COLEMAN.)

JAMES, JESSE WOODSON Born in Clay County, Missouri, on September 5, 1847, the third son of Reverend Robert

James, a Baptist minister and graduate of Kentucky's Georgetown College, and Zerelda James (nee Cole). Rumors abound that Jesse was conceived on the wrong side of the blanket, and it has been stated that the lad was born with granulated eyelids, a combination of rumor and fact that elevates Jesse into the novelty class at a tender age, for the eyelids thing is such an extremely rare cross to have to bear it is virtually unheard of,[8] although continuous blinking is the reported symptom. By the time Jesse was eight his mother was married to her third husband, a Dr. Reuben Samuels,[9] who over the years was to provide the James children with two stepbrothers and two stepsisters.

In 1861, after older brother Frank had gone to the wars, Jesse became obsessed with the desire to join the rebel cause, but it was not until 1863 that he managed to find acceptance in Quantrill's band of irregulars; Quantrill didn't want him, for he was a weedy youngster, but "Bloody" Bill Anderson, one of the guerrilla leaders, took Jesse under his blood-drenched wing. Jesse was now affectionately known as "Dingus," and as Dingus he took part in the Centralia massacre in 1864, in which sanguinary exercise he is credited with the brutal killing of a federal officer. During this guerrilla service he is also reputed to have been used as an espionage agent, "Bloody" Bill sending Jesse into enemy territory dressed as a girl. After Lee's surrender, Jesse received his first major wound. Jesse was coming in to surrender under a flag of truce when a ball pierced one of his lungs, the federal rifleman probably having mistaken the flag of truce for the much-disputed rebel banner. Miss Zerelda Mimms, a cousin of Jesse and a girl of

rare beauty, nursed him back to health. But full recovery was slow, and although he, brother Frank, and Cole Younger talked over the idea of forming a gang to commit robberies, in the early days of 1866, when the newly formed gang cracked down on a bank at Liberty in February of that year, Jesse, still being unfit to ride, had to stay home.

It wasn't until October that Jesse's Navy Colts supplemented the gang's artillery, but they most likely didn't throw any lead until March 1867, when the gang attempted to rob a bank at Savannah. On this occasion all the mob's guns blazed in the direction of the bank president, but such was the marksmanship of these putrid pistoleers that only one shot grazed the target. Two months later the collective aim of the gang appears to have improved, for when they rode from the town they left a man and his fifteen-year-old son lying dead in the dust, Jesse sometimes being fingered as the double killer.[10]

This man with the fluttering eyelids may have been the one who suggested that the gang turn its attention to railroad express cars, possibly planning the gang's first known venture into this form of outlawry, for the derailment of a Chicago and Rock Island express near Adair, Iowa, on July 21, 1873—which resulted in the death of the engineer—had the stamp of Jesse's callous brand. Two months after this outrage, Jesse and Frank—t'hell with Cole and the boys on this occasion—looted the cash office of a Kansas City fairground of some ten thousand dollars. Around this time numerous railroad and banking firms engaged the Pinkerton National Detective Agency in an effort to combat the depredations of

[8] Medical books, folklore remedy tomes, and suchlike have failed to reveal any information regarding this malady.

[9] It is difficult to ascertain whether Samuels was a medical doctor, the divine type, or merely a horse doctor.

[10] If so, he was probably shooting at someone else, for his aim was notoriously bad.

the James gang, and when agent J. W. Whicher, who had been sent out to arrest the James brothers, was ambushed and shot dead while en route to Liberty, Missouri, the conviction at Pinkerton headquarters was that Frank and Jesse had committed this murder. This resulted in a large force of operatives being put in the field, and on January 25, 1875, these men lay siege to the Samuels home. The wanted men made their escape,[11] but at the high point of the battle an iron pot of Greek fire[12] had been tossed into the Samuels living room, and when the smoke cleared, Mrs. Zerelda Samuels had lost most of her right arm, and nine-year-old Archie Samuels lay dead.

In April of this unfortunate year, Jesse entered holy wedlock by marrying cousin Zerelda, the lass who had nursed him way back, and over the years the marriage was to result in two children—Jesse and Mary. The following year at Northfield, Minnesota, honest citizens who would not be intimidated decimated the James gang, only Jesse and Frank escaping from this holocaust of flying lead. This show of public outrage scared the James brothers into lying low for slightly more than three years, a period of gang inactivity during which Jesse used the name of Howard and kept on moving around Tennessee, California, and Colorado, the latter state seeing him working a strike in California Gulch with brother Frank and the Ford brothers. Back into harness with a newly recruited gang in October 1879, a Chicago and Alton train being the target on this occasion. Four more robberies of an assorted nature in 1881, the last occurring at Glendale, Missouri, on the seventh of September. After this date, the James gang wasn't heard from again, and Jesse had but seven months to live.

A bullet from Bob Ford's .45 put a fitting close to Jesse's murderous career on April 3, 1882. After the death of the outlaw, his gunbelt and guns were auctioned off for fifteen dollars. These guns were a .45 Colt Peacemaker and a .45 Smith and Wesson Schofield, Jesse evidently having dispensed with his out-of-date Navy revolvers, possibly in the late 1870s. Even so, for many years afterward, Jesse's mother sold guns that she guaranteed to be the genuine possessions of her late son; these, of course, were old relics she had bought by the dozen to sell at greatly inflated prices.

Reports still circulate that Jesse James was not the victim of Ford's bullet; that the real Jesse James was a well-known citizen of Guthrie, Oklahoma, as late as 1948, and that he died at Granbury, Texas, are but two of these stories. To give these stories substance, Bob's bullet is said to have terminated the career of a small-time crook named Bigelow, the inference being that Bigelow was living with Jesse's wife and children under the name of Thomas Howard without them being aware of this impersonation. This "old outlaws never die" philosophy, which encompasses the names of a plethora of baddies who are known to have been made very dead, still finds acceptance in many parts of the world. Postmortem photos of Jesse are an extremely good likeness if compared with earlier photos of the man. (See ANDERSON, "BLOODY" BILL; COLE, ZERELDA M.; CUMMINS, JIM; FORD, ROBERT; GRAHAM, J. W.; JAMES, ALEXANDER FRANKLIN; JAMES GANG; NORTHFIELD, MINNESOTA; QUANTRILL, WILLIAM CLARKE; and YOUNGER, COLEMAN.)

JAMES, ZERELDA Can refer to either Jesse's and Frank's mother or to

---

[11] If they were there at the time; opinions differ.

[12] Some reports state that this was a bomb, but it was most likely a nineteenth-century version of a Molotov cocktail.

Jesse's wife. (See COLE, ZERELDA M., and JAMES, JESSE WOODSON.)

JAYHAWKER Term used to describe any member of the irregular bands that fought on either side during the years of the Civil War. The term lost much of its scope at some later date, when it became synonymous with a native of Kansas. It has also been used to describe any Forty-niner who survived the crossing of California's Death Valley.

JEFFORDS, THOMAS JONATHAN Jeffords, who was born at Chautauqua, New York State, in 1832, spent the early part of his adult life working on the steam packets plying the Great Lakes, a nautical career that culminated with him becoming a riverboat captain on the Mississippi. Sometime during his late twenties he left the waterways behind him and moved West, possibly spending time in Kansas and Colorado before moving into Arizona Territory in 1870. Here, at Tucson, Captain Tom Jeffords became superintendent of the Overland Mail Depot. This was at a time when Cochise's Chiricahuas were pincushioning mail riders with monotonous regularity,[13] victims of an Apache campaign that had been rampaging through the territory for almost a decade. Jeffords, possibly guilt-ridden by a feeling of sending men out to their deaths, decided to do something about this state of affairs.

At great risk to himself, and employing only one Apache friendly to lead him to Cochise, Captain Jeffords rode out toward the Chiricahua's stronghold in the Dragoon Mountains. Smoke talk was exchanged between Jeffords's guide and the renegades as they pushed on through the canyons, but the guide, not wishing to meet his wilder brethren, left Jeffords to

go it alone before immediate contact with the Chiricahuas had been made. This could have been the last anyone was to hear of Tom, but the aging chief must have liked what he saw in this big, red-bearded white-eye, for a friendship developed between these two men that was to remain unsullied for all time. The first visit failed to stop the Apache raids, but sometime later Jeffords mingled blood with Cochise, and when Jeffords escorted General O. O. Howard—*sans* cavalry detail—to the stronghold in the fall of 1871, and acted as interpreter at the meeting of Howard and Cochise, a lasting peace with the Chiricahuas was established. But for Jeffords this would never have come to pass, for one of Cochise's stipulations was that his friend be made Indian agent, and although Tom didn't relish the job, he accepted it to please the chief.

This friendship lasted until 1876, the last meeting between these men being at Cochise's deathbed. Their final talks lasted for hours, and to read their words is to take flight in a happier dimension. Cochise was troubled as to whether they would ever meet again, and after saying that he would die two hours before high noon the following day, he asked Jeffords whether he thought there was any chance of a reunion. Jeffords, who had persuaded the chief to have medical aid and was impatient to bring a doctor from Fort Bowie, returned the ball into Cochise's court. "You say you do not know," answered Cochise, "and my thoughts are not clear on this thing. I have this feeling, a feeling that fills my heart, that somewhere up there"—pointing feebly to the smokehole of his wickeyup—"we will meet again, my friend." Jeffords hurried from the wickeyup, but when he returned with a doctor around noon the following day,

[13] Twenty riders killed in one month! Yet others still applied for a job that paid but $125 a month.

Cochise had already passed beyond earthly aid, two hours before high noon being the time of the old chief's passing.

In January 1877 the military took over the administration of the Chiricahua reservation and initiated a policy of allowing ranchers and prospectors to invade the Indian lands. Jeffords, sick at heart at this treachery, resigned, spurning any form of government employment until 1886, when he acted as an Army scout in the closing phases of the Geronimo campaign. After this he tried his hand at a variety of jobs before settling in a deserted ranch building and taking employment as a mine caretaker. He was still living in this shack, surrounded by a cactus-dotted wilderness, at the time of his death in 1914. His grave and marker—the latter being erected by the Daughters of the American Colonists in 1964—can be found in a Tucson cemetery. (See COCHISE.)

JEHU Name applied to the men who held the reins of the four- or six-in-hand coaches used on the overland mail and passenger routes. Taken from the biblical reference ". . . like the driving of Jehu . . . for he driveth furiously." (2 K. 9:20)

JENNINGS, AL One of the four lawyer sons of Judge Jennings. Al, who was born in 1864, may have led his three brothers in minor enterprises of an off-color nature in the early 1880s,[14] but as we only have Al's word for this, and as all the Jennings boys passed their bar examinations and became practicing lawyers, stories of these early capers must be regarded with suspicion. We do know that on October 7, 1894, two of Al's brothers got into a gunfight with a flam-boyant mouthpiece named Temple Houston, and that Temple must have been the better shot, for Ed Jennings was killed, and brother John was seriously wounded and died soon afterward. Stories abound that this shootout was responsible for Al and Frank taking to the outlaw trail, but as the only crime laid at this duo's door was the robbery of a Rock Island train on October 1, 1897, these "justification" stories seem rather wild. Al and Frank netted about three hundred dollars and a turnip-size pocket watch from this operation.[15] They were caught shortly afterward, and the interest charged on this peanuts loot worked out at five years hard for Al, and seven for Frank.

On his release, Al was readmitted to the bar, and he became a highly respected member of his profession, with a practice in Oklahoma City. In later life Al moved to California, where he multiplied his activities by becoming an author and film producer. Highly intelligent and voluble, Al, looking twenty years younger than the records proved him to be, was still sprightly and giving interviews until shortly before his death on December 26, 1961. (See HOUSTON, TEMPLE LEE.)

JENNINGS GANG
One robbery, and that was it. (See JENNINGS, AL.)

JENNY A female burro. (See BURRO; HINNY; JACKASS; and MULE.)

JEROME Sometime name for Geronimo. (See GERONIMO.)

JERSEY LILLY Lily Langtry was given this name. (See BEAN, ROY, and LANGTRY, LILY.)

[14] Like posing as deputy U.S. marshals and charging trail crews so much a head for escorting their herds through "dangerous" Indian country.
[15] As the brothers had recruited three deadbeats to give the gang bulk, this minor jackpot had to be split five ways.

JICARILLA APACHE A division of the Apache nation that located in the northeast corner of New Mexico. The Jicarilla had a mixed culture, their tepees,[16] beadwork, and braiding of hair reflecting a strong plains influence. (See APACHE INDIANS.)

JIM CROW A term originally used to denote a renegade or a turncoat. Derived from the blacks' song and dance of that name, a line of the song being "Wheel about and turn about." Now used to denote discrimination, particularly against the Negro in the South.

JINGLEBOB OUTFIT John S. Chisum's spread. (See CHISUM, JOHN S.)

JINGLER A horse wrangler; the rider who takes charge of the *remuda*.

JOHN THE BAPTIST A frontier hellfire and damnationer. (See GOAD, JOHN.)

JOHNNY BEHIND THE DEUCE A small-time gambler. (See O'ROURKE, JOHN.)

JOHNSON, "ARKANSAW" A regional nickname. (See HUCKSTON, JOHN.)

JOHNSON COUNTY WAR In January 1887 a three-day blizzard hit the cattle ranges of the Northwest with a fury hitherto unsurpassed. Riders died frozen in their saddles as they tried to rescue their charges from drifts, and cattle barons became paupers as the vast herds of Wyoming were decimated overnight. By the spring, the chinook-softened ranges were a bone orchard, and bone gathering was the only form of employment to be found in this empty land. After all these bones had been shipped East for fertilizer, unemployed cowboys threw up small shacks or squatted in deserted line camps and fenced-off small plots of ground. Homesteaders followed, establishing themselves on land from which range detectives had once deterred all but the most hardy, their dwellings and sodbusting activities pockmarking the range from the Big Horns to the Powder River. These were the seeds from which the cattlemen-homesteader skirmishes blossomed, for when the cattlemen who had survived the disaster began to restock their ranges, they found that Johnson County had become a stronghold of homesteaders, a stubborn breed who were bound together by a deep mistrust of cattlemen.[17]

The cattlemen—most of whom were absentee owners residing at Cheyenne—were all members of the Wyoming Stock Growers' Association, so when news began to filter in from their spreads that cattle were being rustled,[18] the association began the large-scale hiring of range

[16] All the other Apache tribes had wickeyups.

[17] A distrust of homesteaders was also inherent in the cattlemen, and to some extent one can find reasons for sympathy with the latter. They were the ones who had pushed into the land at the beginning, a time when the reception committees were armed with tomahawks and scalping knives, and, rightly or wrongly, they considered the territory to be theirs and theirs alone.

[18] This never got above the 3 per cent mark, but in an aggregate of two million head, this was still a sizable number—sixty thousand. In many cases of absentee ownership, the ranch foreman would do a little rustling to build up a small herd; he would then blame "outside" rustlers for any shortages.

detectives.[19] There is no reason to doubt that rustlers were active in the Powder River country; cowboys who had become settlers established small herds by "mavericking," and when victuals ran short and game was in short supply, homesteaders would go in for a spot of slow elk hunting, but the methods used to combat this form of pilfering are open to criticism. Numerous nesters who came under suspicion were buried without marker, but as this form of retribution left the victim's whereabouts open to question—the party may have left the area under his own dust cloud—it thereby failed in its objective, and the lynching of suspects became the order of the day, a method of elimination after which exercise "justice" could be seen to have been done. Occasionally, suspected rustlers, who had not been summarily dealt with, were handed over to the Johnson County authorities, but the end results of these rather more friendly overtures were invariably the same: The suspect, however obvious his guilt, would be freed by a jury of homesteaders.

With such stubborn cusses on either side, it is not surprising that the hangings and shootings continued. But the nesters were getting stronger all the time, and when hard-eyed Frank Canton came under suspicion of having organized a few of the lynchings, he had to flee the state when a well-armed posse of nesters got on his trail. The Wyoming Stock Growers' Association must have realized that even though the acting state governor was behind them, time was not on their side, so in the early months of 1892, after raising a fighting fund of one hundred thousand dollars, the men in Cheyenne sent out the word: Major Frank Wolcott, cattleman and ex-Army officer, rode South through Colorado with a Texas-born range detective named Tom Smith,[20] being joined somewhere along their route by Frank Canton, and these three men rode on into Texas to recruit hired guns. Twenty-six Texans accepted the five dollars a day and expenses, plus a fifty-dollar bonus for each kill, that was offered, and on April 5 this cavalcade of rabble reached Cheyenne; the latter part of the journey—from Denver, Colorado, onward—was via a privately hired Union Pacific train. At Cheyenne recruits from the northern ranges, plus a physician and two news reporters, swelled the ranks of this force to more than fifty men, and at 6 P.M. on April 5 this small but well-equipped and well-mounted army[21] was shipped to Casper by rail, the ultimate destination being Buffalo in Johnson County. The object of this invasion was the extermination of Sheriff "Red" Angus and his deputies and the token slaying of some thirty homesteading Buffaloites. After these hangings —for such was the method favored, possibly because it would give an air of legality to the proceeding—puppet lawmen of the Stock Growers' Association were to take over the law enforcement of Johnson County—a grandiose scheme suggestive of military strategy, and, by extension, the brainchild of Major Wolcott.

On reaching Casper, the party left the railroad cars and headed North, Canton having in a pocket of his topcoat a "dead" list that featured seventy names.

[19] Thin-lipped characters such as Canton and Horn. These men did little detecting, but anyone whom they suspected of rustling met with a hard time. Occasionally, if witnesses were present, a suspect would be handed over to the law, but usually any such party would be removed from the surface of the range with the aid of firearms and a posthole spade.

[20] Not the Tom Smith of Abilene fame.

[21] Each man had two handguns and a rifle, and all mounts had been hand-picked, these latter having been stamped with an unidentifiable brand before the move into Johnson County began.

During the hundred-mile ride North, word reached the invasion force that two "rustlers," Nate Champion and Nick Ray, were living in an old K. C. Ranch building, and after checking, and finding that their names were on Canton's list, Wolcott ordered a detour for a mopping-up operation. The outcome of this proved fatal for Ray and Champion,[22] but at the same time the shootout delayed the march on Buffalo, and although the telegraph wires had been cut, word-of-mouth news of the invasion had reached Sheriff William H. "Red" Angus, and the holdup gave him the necessary extra time in which to organize a force of homesteaders. "Red" Angus' superposse consisted of well over two hundred men, forty of whom were men of the cloth under the leadership of the Reverend M. A. Rader, and all of whom were heavy with lead-throwing hardware. Angus also attempted to enlist the aid of troops stationed at Fort McKinney, but this request was turned down, and the posse rode South without further ado.

Wolcott, the military genius whose battle plans were souring, heard of this force's movements long before contact was established, and he fell back on the deserted buildings of the T. A. Ranch, ordering his men to throw up log breastworks and then retire to the main ranch building to withstand a siege, which appeared imminent. When the army of homesteaders arrived, its ranks had been swelled to more than three hundred men, and throughout the night of April 11 these men dug rifle pits and threw up barricades around the T. A. buildings, so that by sunup there was little chance of the defenders making a breakout. The invaders were trapped, but it was a stalemate, for although spasmodic firing was indulged in throughout the following day, it soon became obvious to the homesteaders that no

amount of small arms would ever flush out their enemies.

Lead slinging was switched to low key by the nesters, and during this more tranquil period the gray matter of an ex-Indian fighter named Arapaho Brown came up with the idea of a gigantic mobile bomb. This infernal machine, which has gone into the books under the names of "Go Devil" and "Ark of Safety," was more or less two wagon chassis lashed to each end of a barricade of logs. The idea was to push this movable breastworks—suitably loaded with sufficient dynamite to blow the invaders to "where've they gone?"—up against the side of the ranch building, and then . . .

On the morning of the thirteenth the ark was lumbered into position, and Arapaho may have been on the point of dragging a lucifer across the seat of his pants when the notes of a cavalry trumpet caused all participants to freeze into non-aggressive poses. Metal flashed in the early-morning sunlight and guidons rode a dust cloud that approached from the direction of Fort McKinney, and a short time later Troops C, D, and H of the 6th Cavalry lathered to a halt in the arena of conflict. Sheriff Angus requested that the invaders should be put in his custody, but Colonel J. J. Van Horn, not wishing to have more than fifty hangings on his conscience, took the crestfallen gunfighters under his wing and escorted them back to Cheyenne. And that was the end of the Johnson County War, for after much legal wind had swept Wyoming, no one was ever charged with any offense. (See AVERILL, JAMES; AVERILL, TOM; CANTON, FRANK M.; CHAMPION, NATHAN D.; HORN, TOM; MAVERICKING; RUSTLER; and WATSON, ELLA.)

JOHNSON, GEORGE   Hanged by mistake, he was; it says just that on his

---

[22] Sickened by these cold-blooded murders, the physician and one of the reporters left the expedition.

small marker in the cemetery that is on the town limits of Tombstone, Arizona. The known saga of Mr. Johnson has all the earmarks of black comedy, but as this man died with a smile on his lips after soliloquizing to his audience, there is little reason for dewing the type with tears. George was a grandstander without much talent, a thin gent of middle years with a condescending laugh who used ten-dollar words, and who wanted his moment of glory. George, with his wife Nancy Independence and a brood of undernourished kids, must have been one of the first settlers in Tombstone, and although the Earp brothers never mention him in their memoirs, they must have noticed him often enough as he staggered to and fro betwixt home and the Crystal Palace Saloon. As early as 1880 he was having appearances in court on drunk-and-disorderly charges. During these alcoholic sprees he had visions of hurrah-ing the town, so it must have been a let-down to find out—upon sobering up—that he had done nothing of note during his blackout.

We see him toughening up a little over the years. There are reports of him buy-ing new guns as often as his limited re-sources would permit; probably more often, for on at least one occasion he was up before the court for nonsupport. He entered the Crystal Palace one day, straddle-legged and slightly weaving, and tested a new piece of hardware. The .45 slug wrecked the cash register, and George was clobbered into insensibility by the irate barman, who then carried the unconscious gunman to the local lockup. Fined the next day, and advised by the bench to get work so that he could support Nancy Independence and com-pany, George went in search of a job. He got one. The local depot of the Tombstone-Bisbee stage required a well-armed gunslick to act as watchman, and our man got the job.

On a bright day in October 1882, Mr. and Mrs. M. E. Kellogg climbed into a Concord at Bisbee, evidently the only two people who wanted to undertake the twenty-mile journey to Tombstone on that run, and, as nothing of value was in the boot, no shotgun messenger rode the box. Even the driver left his gun be-hind, evidently under the impression that the absence of a messenger would make any would-be highwayman realize that the four-in-hand wasn't worth stopping. A few miles south of Tombstone a lone rider, the lower part of his face masked by a bandana, jockeyed his mount be-tween the giant spurlike saguaros flank-ing the trail, and waving a fistful of argument, called upon the driver to halt. A shot was fired as the coach swayed to a stop, and Mrs. Kellogg felt her husband collapse by her side, whereupon the lady screamed, causing the holdup man's horse to bolt and unseat its rider. The stagecoach driver, upon seeing the ban-dit fall to the dust and lose his gun, pounced from the box and grappled with the man, but the masked one was python-hipped and agile, and he made good his escape on foot. The stage driver then cut a couple of his team from their traces and mounted Mrs. Kellogg onto the back of one of them with the instructions that she ride for Tombstone and the sheriff; he then mounted the second horse and thundered in pursuit of the would-be highwayman.

A couple of hours later a buzzard cir-cled up from the coach as the sheriff of Cochise County and a small posse ap-proached the scene. Two of the posse, a doctor and an undertaker, entered the coach, the former to make a legalized check as to whether the presence of the latter was necessary.

At about this time Tombstone was in a gala mood; the coach driver had brought in the highwayman—who had been instantly recognized as George— and now, having heard the driver's tale, the citizens were preparing to suspend George from a telegraph pole before the old fusspot of a sheriff returned. The prisoner was at his most voluble. He had always been aware of the price he might be called upon to pay for his leading such a brazen life of crime, but he had no regrets, and he would meet his fate like a man. Nancy Independence had been called to witness what can only be described as her husband's finest hour.

When the posse returned with the coach containing the remains of Mr. Kellogg, George had left this sordid scene; he was hanging some ten feet above ground level with an expression of frozen contentment on his face. The sheriff cussed, and then asked the townies why they'd gone and done what they'd did. The lynch mob, who had now become mere spectators, explained: just deserts, dirty rotten killer, and suchlike stuff. Then the sheriff explained, and a cloud passed over the mining camp: Poor Mr. Kellogg, a man who had sold guns and other hardware all his life, had expired from a heart attack on hearing the sound of the highwayman's shot; George hadn't killed or robbed anyone. Guilt-ridden, folk shuffled their feet and then dispersed, those with money disappearing into saloons and brothels, while those without went home; but conscience pricked, and later that day the citizens had a collection, the eight hundred dollars raised being handed over to Nancy I. Johnson to compensate for her having lost the family breadwinner(?).

JOHNSON, JOHN This is the liver-eating character. He is usually found under this name, although his correct moniker was Johnston. (See JOHNSTON, JOHN.)

JOHNSON, JULIA Emmett Dalton's light of love. (See DALTON, EMMETT.)

JOHNSTON, JOHN Usually referred to as "Liver-eating" Johnson, the *t* having been mislaid somewhere down the trail. This large, rawboned man of Scottish descent, with the red beard and vacant eyes, who, according to most authorities, was born in 1826,[23] started working the eastern slopes of the Shining Mountains as a trapper about 1843, and he was to trap, trade, and wage a one-man vendetta against the Crow Indians in this region of the Northwest for almost twenty years. In 1847 Johnston was living with a Chinook Indian girl in a cabin near the Canadian line and was shadowed by the mountains at sundown. This cabin was also on Crow Indian territory, and in May 1847, during one of Johnston's absences, a Crow war party killed "Mrs." Johnston, who, at this time, is reported to have been "heavy with child." This experience is reputed to have started Johnston on his liver-eating vengeance trail. At the end of this gory trail, some three hundred Crow livers—plus a few Sioux and Assiniboine—had been credited with passing through Johnston's gizzard. It was not until twenty-two years after the murder of his "wife" that the "Liver Eating" sobriquet began to prefix this cannibal's name; after a minor engagement

[23] In New Jersey, it is said, but the birth year is open to doubt. John Xavier Beidler—who knew Johnston slightly—stated in 1866 that Johnston had been working the Rockies and Bitterroot Mountains as a trapper, trader, and wolver for thirty years; if this is correct, it would appear that Liver Eater must have been born before 1826, as it is unlikely that he would have been leading the life of a mountain man at the tender age of ten years. Beidler is also on record as stating that Johnston found his way into the Rockies from the Oregon country, his starting point being the western seaboard, where he had been employed as a sailor (or cabin boy?).

with Indians at the mouth of the Mussel-shell River in Montana, a fellow mountain man is supposed to have dubbed him thusly after seeing Johnston stuffing his gut with the liver of a late adversary. Whether Johnston attached any symbolism to this liver eating, merely possessed epicurean taste buds, or found it a good substitute for haggis, has gone unrecorded. He did not, however, confine his cannibalism to viscera alone, as we shall see.

In 1861 he was in the Bitterroot Mountains leading a couple of pack horses loaded with forty gallons of rotgut whiskey. His intention was to trade this load of mischief with the friendly Chinooks for plews or whatever, but before he could reach his destination, he was pounced on by a party of Blackfoot Indians, who, on recognizing him as Absaroka Dapiek (Crow Killer), took him prisoner with the intention of trading him to the Crows. This would have been a fitting end to the Johnston story, but unfortunately the Blackfoot got tanked up on the captured whiskey, and their prisoner was able to take advantage of this. Confined to a tepee with but one inebriated guard, Johnston managed to kick the man unconscious, after which he severed one of the Indian's legs at the thigh, slung the dripping limb across one of his shoulders, and escaped. This severed leg provisioned him until he got back to base.

As much of Crow Killer's story has all the authentic ring of a tenth-rate dime novel written in the Bronx, there seems little reason to report every ghastly exploit of the man over the years. Suffice to say that on the Christmas Eve of 1866,

he and John Xavier Beidler are supposed to have helped Portugee Phillips on the last lap of his memorable ride;[24] 1876 saw Crow Killer on the North Plains scouting for the U. S. Army, and he is alleged to have killed a black man named Sam Grant with a tomahawk[25] around this time; sometime later Johnston was throwing his weight around in Leadville, Colorado; then in the early 1880s we hear of him as a deputy sheriff in Wyoming; in the late 1880s a spot more roaming around the mountains; and then he was getting too old to cause any more excitement. Over the above briefly noted period, Johnston made friends with his old enemies, the Crows—a judicial move, for if he had remained at war with these Indians they may have taken his liver now that he was getting slow. His last job was as town marshal of Red Lodge, Montana. He was elected to this post in 1888, and as his most dangerous activities consisted of chasing children or giving them backhanders, he survived this post for a number of years. Finally the Crow Killer's health cracked up, and he was shipped off to a veterans' hospital in California, where he died on January 21, 1900.

JONES, CHARLEY Alias of Camilla Hanks. (See HANKS, CAMILLA.)

JONES, FRANK A hard-boiled Texas Ranger who was born at Austin, Texas, in 1856. In 1873, at the age of seventeen, Frank Jones joined Company A of the Texas Rangers, but it was not until after a year of initial training and a transfer to Company D that his Ranger service began to provide him with some action. One of his first assignments was

[24] Over the Christmas period of 1866 Beidler is known to have been at Helena, Montana —some five hundred miles to the northwest of Fort Laramie—so someone appears to be glory-hunting here.

[25] Tomahawk? Yup! Hawken rifle, revolvers, scalping knives, bowie-type cutlery, and tomahawks; Crow Killer carried dead-making tools by the ton.

the capture of a gang of Mexican horse thieves, a tracking job undertaken with two other Rangers. The Rangers were ambushed by their quarry, and when his two companions had been rendered inactive by flying lead, Frank carried on the fight alone, killing two of the bandits and taking a third man back to base as his prisoner.

This action started him on the ladder of promotion, first to a corporal, then, a short time later, to sergeant. As a sergeant, Jones took a posse of seven men and went out hunting for a large gang of Mexican rustlers, only to run into the second ambush of his short career; three of his men were killed outright, and Jones and the remainder were taken prisoner. It would have been better for the greasers if they had shot Frank on the spot, for while they were congratulating themselves on having the edge over the gringos, the Ranger sergeant wrenched a Winchester from one of the guards, and, levering cartridges into the breech and working the trigger like a Morse key, he shot every man of the gang into eternity. Promotion followed quickly, Jones being made captain of Company D in June 1877. Almost three years of obliterating rustlers followed, and then came a slight change in the action: Captain Jones dusted off an old murder warrant made out for the arrest of Scott Cooley and went in search of the fugitive. He didn't find Cooley, but during his search three desperadoes blasted Jones from the saddle and left him for dead. Jones regained consciousness to find himself with a bad chest wound, but with sufficient strength to stagger from the area, and later that night he came upon the camp of the trio who were responsible for his condition. The Ranger waited until the men were asleep and then gained possession of one of their rifles, so that when the men stirred at sunup he had gotten the edge.

One of the men didn't see it that way and got shot dead for his lack of acumen, but the other two hard cases—rustlers by the names of Frank Munger and Lafe Worley—surrendered and were later given stretches for horse theft.

In 1881 Jones killed an Indian who was suspected of cattle rustling in a stand-up gunfight, and two years later a gunnie known as Tex Murietta allowed himself to be arrested only after he'd damn near lost his all in a saloon gunfight with Jones. Captain Frank Jones won a few more shootouts after this, but the odds were getting shorter all the time, and in June 1893 he went out on what was to be his last mission. On June 29, the captain, at the head of a detail of four Rangers, set out to arrest Jesus Maria Olguin and his son Severio, both of whom were wanted for stock theft, and the following day saw the Olguin dwelling besieged by the Rangers. A bitter gun duel ensued, during which Captain Frank Jones was cut to pieces, dying almost immediately. This fight occurred on an island in the Rio Grande, and although only a short distance from San Elizario, Texas, it was actually across the Mexican line, so the Rangers really had no authority in the area. (See COOLEY, SCOTT, and MASON COUNTY WAR.)

JONES, TOM An alias used by both Wild Bill Longley and Roy Daugherty. (See DAUGHERTY, ROY, and LONGLEY, WILLIAM P.)

JORNADO A journey or a chore that can be completed in one day, or an arid strip of desert country. Mexican-Spanish term confined to the Southwest.

JORNADO DEL MUERTO A long strip of desert in New Mexico, lying from north to south and flanked by the Caballo Mountains to the west and the San Anreas Mountains to the east. Approximately ninety miles in length, a long day's journey, but not to be undertaken unless sufficient water be carried, for this journey of Death is studded by markers of folk who underestimated their requirements of this essential liquid. (See TORNADO.)

JOSEPH   The white man's name for a Nez Percé chief whose Indian name, roughly translated, was Thunder Traveling over the Mountains. Joseph, who had been partially educated at one of the missionary schools, became chief of a band of Nez Percé living in the Wallowa Valley of Oregon sometime in 1861. The Nez Percé had always been disposed in a friendly way toward the white invaders, but by 1863 settlers were pushing into the Valley of Winding Waters, and the government was applying diplomatic pressure to Joseph and his tribe in an attempt to persuade them to move from their valley and settle on the Lapwai Reservation. Joseph listened politely to the Indian commissioner's gobbledegook but refused to sign any treaty. This stalemate lasted until 1873, when, in June of that year, President U. S. Grant issued an order prohibiting white settlers from moving into Joseph's territory.

Joseph must have been delighted at this turn of events, but the white settlers were sufficiently incensed to make wild threats about their intentions of wiping out the Wallowa Valley Nez Percé, and the chief, realizing that any laurel branch he might wave would be metaphorically shot from his grasp, began preparing for war. The tough talk of the settlers was, however, never backed by any action, and a state of armed alertness existed in the valley until 1875. In this year the President countermanded his earlier order, and Joseph and his tribe were ordered to move to Lapwai so that his land might

be stolen in a peaceful manner. Joseph stayed put, and it was not until April 1877 that he was given notice that the Army would be sent to move against him if he did not immediately move his tribe to the reservation. This was taken as the last straw by some of the younger braves of the tribe who, against Joseph's instructions, went on a minor killing spree, which resulted in 18 settlers losing their lives and their hair.

On June 16, 1877, Colonel David Perry, at the head of a force of 90 men of the 1st Cavalry and ten civilian scouts, left Lapwai to give battle to Joseph's Nez Percé. Joseph attacked the column in White Bird Canyon at dawn on the seventeenth, and after a violent engagement, Perry was forced to retreat, leaving a third of his command dead in the canyon. Joseph at no time had more than 250 fighting men, yet, with this small force, in July he repulsed an attack of more than 400 troopers as the tribe made their way northward, toward Canada and safety. More than 2,000 troops were now in the field against Joseph, and the 7th Cavalry was moving from Fort Keogh to block the escape route to the north. In the second week of August a force under General Gibbon attacked the Indian encampment during the night, but when an easy white victory appeared imminent, Joseph regrouped his forces, drove Gibbon off, and captured one of the howitzers that had been supporting the troops.

But Joseph was unable to draw on a vast reservoir of manpower, and when General Nelson A. Miles attacked the Indians in the Bear Paw Mountains on September 30, it was the beginning of the end. A blizzard that numbed the senses swept the battleground, but Joseph held out against impossible odds until October 5, on which date he surrendered to the combined forces of Generals Miles and Howard. Raising an arm to indicate the coppery disk that hung in a sky the color of soiled linen, Chief Joseph concluded his surrender speech with the words, "Hear me, my chiefs. I am tired. My heart is sick and sad. From where the sun now stands I will fight no more forever." At the time of his surrender Joseph's force had been reduced to about 90 fighting men, and these, together with the squaws, children, and old people, were transported to Fort Leavenworth in Kansas prior to being settled in Indian Territory at a later date. In 1885 Joseph was transferred to the Colville Reservation in Washington, and he died here in 1904 at the age of sixty-four years. (See NEZ PERCÉ INDIANS.)

JOSEPHITES   Mormon malcontents who, after dissenting with the Mormon Church authorities, left Salt Lake City and traveled North to establish a small colony on the headwaters of the Salmon River in Idaho. The nucleus of this settlement was a log fort named Fort Lemhi. (See MORMONS.)

JOSHUA TREE
A large treelike member of the yucca family that can grow to a height of forty feet. In the United States it is confined to the Southwest.

JOY HOUSE   An apt and melodious name for a brothel, and far more imaginative than the latter name. (See BROTHELS.)

JUANITA
An allegedly beautiful Mexican gal who was hanged at Downieville, California, on July 5, 1851. On the Fourth of July, Juanita had a brush with a miner named Cannon, a hefty Scot who had fallen through her front door while under the influence, but although he was berated something shocking by the *señorita* no weapons were brandished by Juanita on that day of rejoicing. It was on the following morning that violence flared After a night's sleep, Cannon, somewhat hung over, went around to apologize,[26] but Juanita must have found his apology unacceptable, for as a climax to a tirade of Spanish invective she introduced a large knife into Cannon's anatomy, which killed him on the spot. An unpleasant crowd gathered around the killer and her victim, and lynch talk was being bandied around before those at the back knew what had happened. That this ugly mood stemmed from hangovers rather than a sense of civic duty is obvious, for when a certain Dr. Aitken spoke up on Juanita's behalf he was more or less given to understand that he had better shut up or be strung up. A more legally minded spectator suggested they give her a fair trial, then hang her. This dubious lead, which amounted to little more than a reprieve for the lass, set well with the crowd, and Juanita was not hanged until after she had been allowed a brief but voluble appearance before a hastily convened kangaroo court.

JUDSON, EDWARD Z. C.
Edward[27] Zane Carroll Judson, a small ginger-haired bundle of energy who is better known under his pen name of Ned Buntline, was born at Stamford, New York, in 1823, the son of a virtually unknown author named Levi C. Judson. In 1833, after a row with his father, young Ed ran away from home and signed up on a freighter as a cabin boy, the start of a nautical career that lasted until 1842 On returning to the life of a landlubber

[26] He may have had other motives if the description of Juanita is reliable, for it is unlikely that he would have been stabbed if he'd merely gone around to pay for the front door.
[27] Sometimes given as Elmo.

he began to establish himself as a writer, adopting Ned Buntline[28] as his professional name. His stories were highly forgettable, but his output was immense, an unbelievable—in more senses than one—six hundred pages of fine longhand being completed in under three days of frenzied activity on one occasion. The sexual side of Ned's life was almost as wild as his fiction, for during his lifetime he is known to have married at least eight women, known two women who claimed him as their husband, and breached his promises to quite a few aspirants to the title of Mrs. Judson; and this is a mere sampling of the menu of dainties that kept Ned's carnal appetites in check.

In 1843, Buntline, riding high as the publisher of a scurrilous tattle sheet entitled *Ned Buntline's Own*, was living in Nashville, Tennessee, and having a torrid affair with a young married woman. The girl's husband, a certain Robert Porterfield, on hearing of this, went after Ned with a loaded revolver, but the writer was as fast with a gun as he was with his prose, and Mrs. Porterfield was quickly made a widow. The next twenty-four hours was a fast-moving period for Buntline. After allowing himself to be taken into custody, he was given a magistrate's hearing, but these sober surroundings became the setting for further violence when Porterfield's brother opened fire on Ned while he was on the witness stand. Ned got three bullet burns, but otherwise the outburst turned to his advantage, for the magistrate, no doubt swayed by this vendettalike action, released the defendant, and Ned was allowed to return to his hotel. Although the cuckolder had shot the cuckold in self-defense, an irate mob was after Ned's blood, and he had to make a fifty-foot leap from a third-floor room of the City Hotel to save his hide,[29] after which he was lodged in the local jail. He should have been safe for a spell, but after darkness fell the mob stormed the place, dragged this womanizing killer to the nearest upright that would suffice as a gibbet, and lynched him forthwith. Luckily for Ned, this wasn't the end; unknown friends cut him down, and he was returned to the turmoil of his daily existence.

In 1849 he was sentenced to a year's imprisonment on Blackwell's Island for playing a major part in an anti-British riot in which thirty-four New Yorkers were killed, and on his release he wrote a book about this ill-spent year, a doubletitled effort named *The Convict's Return or Innocence Vindicated*. During the Civil War he joined the Union armies, and although never in a forward area, he made the rank of sergeant. Incessant boozing led to him unpicking his stripes before the close of the war, but on his return to civilian life he made up for this by promoting himself to Colonel Ned Buntline. After women, liquor appears to have been the second major hobby of Ned's, yet, even though he was known as a hard tippler, this didn't prevent him from giving temperance lectures. Whether these were given tongue in cheek, or whether he had a genuine desire to save the uninitiated from the evils of the demon rum, has never been ascertained.

In 1869, Buntline, who was then earning more than twenty thousand dollars a year from his writings, partook himself westward in search of fresh material, a move that was instrumental in bringing Buffalo Bill Cody and Wild Bill Hickok into the limelight. His first dime novel Western, *Buffalo Bill, King of the Border Men*, was so successful that he paid Cody to keep him supplied with incidents, sto-

[28] A name inspired by his sailing days, a buntline being a rope that is used in the hauling of a square sail.
[29] After this episode he had a permanent limp.

ries, and tall tales, all of which, inflated to the bursting point, found their way into subsequent epics. Theatrical enterprises followed, *Scouts of the Plains*, starring Buffalo Bill in person, being Ned's first venture into this medium.[30] This show, during which Buntline interrupted his nothing plot by giving a lecture on the perils of alcohol, was the all-time turkey of American show biz; it was so bad it had the audience laughing when tears should have flowed; but, by golly, they loved it. Any improvement would have elevated it to the merely lousy, so Ned wisely left it as it was and found he had a success on his hands. After Cody branched out on his own, Buntline tried his hand at further shows, but none of these brought in the dollars like his first effort had. Buntline continued churning out pneumatic prose until the end; he most likely had to, what with alimony, child maintenance, divorce fees. . . . Edward Zane Carroll Judson, surely the fastest writer ever known, died on July 16, 1886. (See BUNTLINE SPECIAL; CODY, WILLIAM FREDERICK; DIME NOVELS; and HICKOK, JAMES BUTLER.)

JULES, SIMONE   A French girl[31] who arrived in California at the height of the 1849 gold rush stampede. Although only nineteen at the time of her arrival in the West, by the following year she was firmly established as the leading roulette croupier at San Francisco's Bella Union, a position she hung onto until she had accumulated sufficient capital to open a place of her own. By the time she left the Bella Union in 1853, rumors abounded (and were later substantiated) that San Francisco was going to illegalize gambling, so Simone moved 150 miles to the northeast and settled in wide-open

Nevada City. Here she adopted the name of Eleanor Dumont, and within a fortnight of her arrival the Dumont Palace gambling saloon was open for business. So successful was this undertaking that within a short time Mme. Dumont was looking around for a junior partner, a position that was soon taken by a gentleman named Dave Tobin on the understanding that he receive a fixed salary, a thin slice of the profits, and a large slice of Madame.

At this time Simone Jules Dumont was a beautiful girl, the faint hairy endowment on her top lip not yet having blossomed into a full-fledged mustache, and this arrangement with Dave worked out fine until the lad asked for a bigger wedge of the cake, whereupon his boss, possibly somewhat incensed that a stud to whom she had been giving her all should still be thinking in terms of cash, paid him off and showed him the door. The lady gambler may have afterward regretted this move, for after Dave's departure she began hitting the bottle, and a short time later she pulled up stakes and moved to Pioche, Nevada. Mining camps boomed and dozed, and at the first sign of the sandman, Simone moved to livelier pastures.

In the early 1860s she was running a gambling saloon *cum* joyhouse at Bannack, and it was in this sin spot of Montana that she is reputed to have instructed Calamity Jane in the art of dealing the pasteboards. The mustache must have been in full bloom by this time, for it was at Bannack that an inebriated miner dubbed her "Madame Mustache," an indelible brand that appears in the record with far greater frequency than either the genteel Jules or the more robust Dumont. In the early 1870s Madame sold out her

---

[30] Some reporters, on hearing Ned boast that writing the play had only taken four hours, were curious to know why it had taken him so long.

[31] Whether direct from France, or whether she was a Creole from the Mississippi Delta region, is uncertain.

gambling interests and invested her capital in a sizable cattle spread that was located near Carson City, Nevada. This should have made retirement from the tables easy, but a certain con man named Carruthers, having sized up her assets, talked her into marriage, and after giving her his name and having her sign everything over to him for safekeeping, he quietly sold out and decamped. This left Madame Mustache with little more than her jewelry, but Carruthers didn't exactly come out the winner, for when his deserted better half caught up with him, a double blast from her scattergun ushered him through the Pearlies.[32]

The widow Carruthers moved on to Bodie, California, and settled down to dealing once more, and it was here that she killed her second man: Attacked by two footpads one night while returning to her lodgings with the day's takings, she whipped out a muff cannon, killed one of the baddies, and put the second man to flight. Madame Mustache was now forty-eight; much of her charm had gone, and her luck appears to have been going with it, for on the night of September 6, 1879, after being cleaned out by a couple of sharks, she went to her room and ended it all with a dose of hydrocyanic acid.

JULESBURG, COLORADO   A small town that grew up around the trading post of Jules Beni, a rugged French-Canadian who had located near the mouth of Lodge Pole Creek in the extreme northeastern corner of Colorado.[33] In 1859, nine years after Beni had first reached the area, Russell, Majors, and Waddell built a stage station adjacent to the trading post, and as this was an important station equipped with a telegraph office, folksy folk and non-

folksy folk soon began to settle in the vicinity, traders, settlers, buffalo hunters, saloonkeepers, gamblers, and honky-tonkers throwing up a few wagonloads of prefabricated buildings and putting a new town on the map within a matter of weeks. Someone named this instant settlement Julesburg in honor of old Beni, and the name stuck. Beni's trading post had been no Boy Scout meeting place, so it is hardly surprising that the town became known as the "wickedest city on the plains." In 1865 the Indians purged this sin spot by burning it to the ground, but the citizens, undaunted and en masse, moved a few miles to the southwest and relocated on the banks of the South Platte. This was Stage 2 in the saga of Julesburg. When the Union Pacific track layers came pushing into Colorado in 1867 and failed to give the new town railroad status by avoiding it like the plague, Julesburg once again pulled on its boots, moving lock, stock, and a plethora of barrels, and dumping itself astraddle the tracks. This was its last move, and it is still there to this day.[34] (See BENI, JULES, and JULESBURG FIGHT.)

JULESBURG FIGHT   The citizens of Julesburg, Colorado, noticed there were Indians in the vicinity on the morning of January 7, 1865, but as sixty troopers were permanently stationed at nearby Fort Sedgwick, there appeared little cause for panic. The Indians showed themselves only in small numbers, and later that day the garrison commander, unaware that nearly a thousand Sioux and Cheyenne were in the area, led his men out to put the red varmints to flight. Sixty cavalrymen and four civilian volunteers skidded to a halt and reversed into

[32] This shooting would have remained unsolved if Madame Mustache hadn't admitted the deed a short time before her death.

[33] Beni's place was more or less on the Colorado-Nebraska Line.

[34] Nowadays it is a quiet, clean little town with a population of about twenty-five thousand.

hasty retreat when the main body of Indians appeared, but even with this quick thinking, fourteen troopers and the four volunteers had been killed before the remainder reached the safety of the fort. The fort's howitzer soon drove the Indians to a safe distance, and during this lull the citizens of Julesburg flocked to the safety of the post's stockaded walls. This was the beginning of an extremely frustrating period for the occupants of the fort, for they had a grandstand view as that overwhelming force of Indians wrecked and looted the deserted town. On the nineteenth, when the town was completely bereft of victuals, liquor, and all forms of merchandise, Red Cloud and Crazy Horse had torches put to the empty buildings, and when the beleaguered citizens and soldiery ventured forth the following day, only smoldering ashes remained.[35] (See JULESBURG, COLORADO.)

JULY, MAOMI   Member of the notorious Buck gang. (See BUCK GANG.)

[35] This was the only town that could be said to have been completely removed from the map as the direct result of an Indian action; others may have become ghosts because of Amerind troubles, but Julesburg was sure enough "taken out."

CHARLES M. RUSSELL

KANSAS

Lying almost exactly in the center of the conterminous United States, Kansas is bounded by Nebraska in the north, Missouri in the east, and Oklahoma and Colorado in the south and west, respectively. As it consists mainly of undulating prairie it is topographically boring, but as such trail towns as Abilene, Caldwell, Dodge City, Newton, and Wichita are all confined to the Kansas territory, it is not without historical interest. Derives its name from the Kansa Indians who once roamed the area, and is known as the Sunflower State. Kansas was admitted to the Union as the thirty-fourth state in 1861. Topeka is the state capital. Kansans are sometimes referred to as "jayhawkers." (See JAYHAWKER.)

KEATING, LAWRENCE
One of Cherokee Bill's notches. (See GOLDSBY, CRAWFORD.)

KEELBOAT A rather crude craft that shared the navigable waterways of the West with the contemporaneous flatboat until superseded by the steam-driven riverboats. Having a heavy wooden keel, these craft could be steered by a man on the rudder bar while the crew propelled the boat with sweeps which could be up to twenty feet long—a decided advantage over the flatboat, which relied on the river current for propulsion. The larger type of keelboat could be a hundred feet or more in length and have around fifty sweeps which required double that number of crewmen to handle them. Passenger accommodation consisted of separate compartments, which were sufficiently large to allow folk moving house to travel with all their domestic appliances; heating—usually in the form of a wood-burning stove—was provided in each compartment. (See FLATBOAT.)

KEENAN, FANNIE Name sometimes used by Dora Hand. (See HAND, DORA.)

KEENE, JOHN A hanger-on of the Innocents who managed to take hasty leave of Virginia City—where he had been employed as a barkeep—before the vigilantes got around to looking into his affairs. This exodus was in the spring of 1865, and Keene traveled more than a hundred miles to the northwest and settled at Helena. Other fugitives from vigilante hemp were in Helena at this time, and one of these, a gambler named Harry Slater, was a gentleman whom Keene had once had trouble with in Salt Lake City—a state of affairs that was bound to erupt into violence. Shortly after his arrival at Helena, Keene spotted Slater dozing off a few jugs outside Sam Greer's saloon, and Keene, realizing that opportunity was knocking hard, whipped out a pistol and shot his enemy dead before anyone realized what was happening. Keene was arrested by John Xavier Beidler and handed over to the sheriff almost before the smoke had cleared, and in no time at all the killer found himself trying to justify his action before an impromptu court of hard-faced miners. The justification, "He hit me in Salt Lake City," didn't go down too well, and it was decided that Keene should hang. On hearing this grim verdict, the prisoner said he had no money to pay for the trial, but his mind was quickly put at rest on being informed that both the hearing and the hanging wouldn't cost him a cent. After this he was given an hour's grace to prepare for his passing before he was strung from the limb of a giant pine and left to dangle like some grisly mobile.

Not wishing to jeopardize Keene's chance of a fair trial, some of his earlier escapades have hitherto been ignored; but now they can be told. In pre-Civil War days Keene had worked in Memphis, Tennessee, but with the outbreak of hostilities he joined the Confederate Navy as a crewman on a ram. He was little help to the southern cause, for shortly after his enlistment he hammered his captain insensible with a marlinespike

and had to be put in irons to await court-martial. Somehow he managed to escape and make his way back to Memphis, which, by this time, had been occupied by federal troops. At Memphis, Keene killed a man named James Dolan, and after this he fled the city and adopted the name of Bob Black, under which name he organized a gang of cutthroats who went in for highway robbery on a grand scale. Keene, alias Bob Black, was finally arrested by the military, but he escaped from the guardroom and worked his way north to St. Paul, Minnesota. Here he used some of his ill-gotten gains to open a saloon, an honest business that was little more than a cloak for illegal operations carried out along the highways around the city. Things finally got too hot for Keene, and he headed west for Montana; and that is where we left him dangling. (See BEIDLER, JOHN XAVIER, and INNOCENTS.)

KELLEY, DANIEL   Member of the gang that was responsible for the Bisbee massacre of 1883. After this sanguinary affair, the gang split up, Kelley heading East into New Mexico, allowing his whiskers to grow and generally fouling up his appearance en route in the hope that he would pass as a tramp. Rewards of fifteen hundred dollars per head had been posted for these men, a princely sum that gave the lawmen of Arizona's Cochise County a tenacity of purpose, and Deputy Sheriff William Daniels succeeded in tracking Kelley as far as Deming, New Mexico. Kelley, unaware that Daniels was in the vicinity, and possibly believing that he had lost his pursuers, visited a local barber shop as Stage 1 in the shedding of his tramp image. This was most unwise, for the barber, one Augustin Salas, on removing Kelley's facial underbrush, immediately recognized his customer as one of the wanted men, and holding a razor across the shaved one's Adam's apple, he sent a messenger to search out Daniels. And that's about it; Kelley was returned to Tombstone as the first stage of his trip to the gallows. (See HEATH, JOHN.)

KELLEY, "DOG"   A dog-loving Dodge City character. (See KELLEY, JAMES H.)

KELLEY, JAMES H. A senior citizen of Dodge City and a leading businessman of the town. Kelley, who was an early arrival at Dodge, was a retired sergeant of cavalry who had served the last years of his Army career as Custer's orderly in the 7th Cavalry. One of his duties as orderly was to care for his CO's hounds, a chore from which he derived the nickname of "Hound" Kelley, a name that clung to him when he settled at Hays City after leaving the forces. Here he bred dogs for coursing and racing, his original hounds having been a gift from Custer.[1] To better the strain, he imported greyhounds from England, so that in time Kelley's hounds were known the length and breadth of Kansas. With the decline of Hays City's prosperity, the ex-sergeant transported himself and his dogs to Hays' successor: Dodge City, lying eighty-four miles to the southwest. Kelley, a tough Irishman with a possible touch of larceny in his soul, prospered at Dodge as never before,[2] becoming part owner of the Alhambra Saloon, Dodge City Opera House, a restaurant, a dance hall, and numerous bordellos within but a short time of his arrival. Political ambitions followed, and in spite of his being a brothelkeeper—or maybe because of this—he was elected

mayor in 1877, thus becoming mugwump of one of the toughest towns in the state.[3] The following year saw him reelected, and in the spring of that year a Miss Dora Hand[4] appears to have become the unofficial mayoress. This wasn't a very lasting relationship, for Dora was murdered some months later, the crime occurring while His Honor was being treated for some unspecified complaint in Fort Dodge's dispensary. This bereavement marked a turning point in "Dog's" fortunes, for he was defeated at the polls in the next election, and after this little more was heard of him. (See HAND, DORA.)

KELLEY, JEM   In July 1864 the stage en route from Virginia City, Montana, to Salt Lake City, Utah, was held up and robbed by highwaymen, much gold dust being the holdup men's loot. When news of this outrage reached the gold camp of Nevada, Montana, ex-Innocents Jem Kelley and "Hard Hat" John Dolan immediately became prime suspects, and a posse of more than twenty vigilantes rode out in search of these two baddies. After a long, wet ride South, the posse met up with a party of ten buckskinned prospectors in the vicinity of Fort Hall, Idaho, and they were pleased to note that this group of wanderers had gotten a badly beaten up Kelley as their prisoner. The prospectors explained: They had found their captive hiding in a haystack a short time after their discovery of a shot-up corpse, and they figgered they'd gotten the killer. After that it didn't matter whether Jem had helped in the stage job or not. They let him smoke a pipeful of 'baccy, say a

[1] Point of interest: Custer must have had a high regard for Kelley for before setting off on what was to be his last march he left his hounds in the care of his ex-orderly.

[2] At Dodge most folk referred to our hero as "Dog" Kelley.

[3] Mayors weren't merely figureheads in those days; they were the almighty top of the heap.

[4] Some scurrilous knaves have suggested that Kelley brought Dora to Dodge to manage his red-light undertakings.

few words—"Iffen I'd never drunk any whiskey I'da bin a better man," and then they hanged him from a balm of Gilead tree.[5] (See DOLAN, JOHN, and INNOCENTS.)

KELLOGG, MARK   The only reporter who was with Custer on his last march. Very little is known about Kellogg apart from the skeleton facts that he had worked on newspaper staffs in Council Bluffs, Iowa, and St. Paul, Minnesota, before becoming chief reporter for the Bismarck, North Dakota, *Tribune* from its inception in July 1873. Kellogg was reporting affairs of the 7th Cavalry from 1874 onward and became a great friend of the Custers, so it is hardly surprising that he was the only accredited correspondent accompanying Custer's command when it marched to its death on June 25, 1876. Kellogg, who died with the rest of the command, was about thirty-five years old at the time of his death. No relations of this man were ever traced. (See BATTLE ON THE LITTLE BIG HORN.)

KELLY, A. J.   A Leadville, Colorado, cop who went looking for Doc Holliday with a chip on his shoulder, and got shot dead by Doc. (See HOLLIDAY, JOHN HENRY.)

KELLY, BILL   A Creek-black horse wrangler who, while working at the Reagan Brothers Ranch in southwestern Texas, found gold-bearing quartz in what is now Reagan's Canyon.[6] A few days after his find, Kelly hopped a freight to San Antonio and left his samples with an old friend named Lock Campbell, the latter promising to have them assayed. Sometime later a letter arrived for Kelly, but as the half-breed couldn't

read, it was read by others; the quartz samples assayed at more than seventy thousand dollars to the ton.[7] Other folk now knew of Nigger Bill's find, and the morning after the arrival of the letter, the half-breed wasn't around for breakfast. The Reagans stated that he had stolen a horse and decamped, but sometime later the partially decomposed body of a black man who was to remain officially unidentified was dragged from the Rio Grande. The defunct one could have been Nigger Bill, for since that evening in 1887 there is no proof that he was ever seen again. The Lost Nigger Mine is reported to have been found on more than one occasion, but at the time of going to press, it is back in the "lost" category.

KELLY, JEM   Sometimes spelled with the extra *e*, and that's our way. (See KELLEY, JEM.)

KELLY, JOSEPH   Usually referred to as "Bunco" Kelly, a name dubbed upon him by the Portland, Oregon, Police Department around 1860, and a name that stuck to him throughout his lifetime. Kelly, who was born at Liverpool, England, in 1838 and educated in that country, started his working life as a seaman while in his early teens, and he had traveled over much of the world before he arrived on America's western seaboard in 1879. At this time Kelly was a dark-haired, hard-eyed lad who possessed elegant sideburns and a nicely trimmed mustache plus a firm jaw and a stocky, well-muscled build. Handsome, and with a taste for the doxies, Kelly must have suddenly realized that he was wasting his time at sea, for he left the ship and became a landlubber at Portland.

To frequent the bordellos and booze

[5] Makes a change from the old cottonwood.
[6] Can be located in the National Big Bend Park.
[7] An assay of two hundred dollars to the ton is considered worth the effort of mining.

joints of Portland required cash, and of this Kelly had little, so he went into a line of business that required no initial capital. It was at one time known as press-ganging and latterly as shanghaiing, but it was all the same to the down-and-out bums whom Kelly got paralytic before delivering them, at so much a head, to tough, seagoing skippers who couldn't get crewmen in any other manner. This enterprise prospered, and Kelly opened a run-down fleapit of a boarding house so that he could always have a few deadbeats on "ice." The largest order undertaken by this mass kidnaper was for the supplying of twenty-four able-bodied seamen to Captain White of the *Flying Prince*, $720 being the price promised for such a package of humanity. This rush order came through in October 1880, and as his doss house could supply nothing like that number, Kelly set out after dark to comb the sleaziest depths of Portland. He found his merchandise in one neat package: twenty-four down-and-outs who had broken into the cellar of an undertaker's and gotten rigid through an overindulgence in embalming fluid. After renting a couple of wagons, Kelly delivered his freight and was paid off, but sometime after his departure, it was noticed that *rigor mortis* was establishing itself in fourteen of the able-bodied seamen he had supplied, and that only energetic stomach pumping would be likely to save the remainder. The outcome of this was that Bunco found himself having a lot of explaining to do, but luck was with him, and he wasn't prosecuted.

Of great help to Kelly over the years he was shanghaiing the boozed-up drifters of Portland, was a young duck named Esmeralda and a saloonowner known as Liverpool Liz. Esmeralda, who was Bunco's constant companion, acted as a tangible lure when her master invited some bum to accompany him to some secluded spot for a duck supper, while the gal from Scousetown sent word to her compatriot when any of her customers became too stiff to make further orders. Bunco Kelly's name became known far and wide, and although Liverpool may have regarded him as just another local boy who had made good, so many reluctant crewmen were being scattered around the globe that Maritime of London offered £100 reward for the delivery of Bunco's ears to their head office. Quite a few hard boys who had been shipped out of Portland in an alcoholic daze had a try for this bounty on their return to their stamping ground, but Kelly always managed to retain both his ears and his life, either by keeping out of sight or running like hell.

Esmeralda disappeared one day, and Bunco's luck seems to have changed, for a short time later, Kelly, plus a smoking gun, was found in the home of the late George Sayer. As George was lying on the floor, having been just made "late," it was an open-and-shut affair, and Joseph "Bunco" Kelly was given a long stretch in the Oregon pen. What happened to Kelly after his release is controversial, inasmuch as some folk say he was given lead slugs in exchange for his life on his return to Portland, while others state he died in South America at the ripe old age of ninety-six.

KELLY, LUTHER SAGE
Better known as "Yellowstone" Kelly, as this was the area in which he became best known. Kelly arrived on the scene too late to be classed as a mountain man, for these gentlemen were past their heyday at the time of Kelly's birth at Geneva, New York, on July 27, 1849; but as an Army scout he had no peers. Luther spent much of his younker period horsing around with neighboring Iroquois tribesmen, these eastern redsticks giving him his first lessons in Indian lore

276

Wild and Woolly

and an enduring passion for a life beyond the fringe of civilization. In 1863, although only in his fourteenth year and small of stature, Kelly managed to enlist in the Union forces, and as a private in the 10th United States Infantry he served until well after the close of the Civil War, being given his honorable discharge at Fort Wadsworth in Dakota Territory in 1868.

Deciding that now was the time to see the big country to the west, Kelly vaulted onto a pony and moved west and northwest, his most northerly point on this trip being Fort Garry across the Canadian line. In Canada our wanderer encountered a party of métis who were traveling south to the buffalo country of the North Plains on one of their annual trading expeditions. Kelly stayed with these people until they made their return journey to the north, a six-month period over which he absorbed a good working knowledge of many Indian languages and dialects, plus further insight into their social behavior. In 1873 Kelly had a dwelling on the west bank of the Missouri, from which stand he was selling cordwood to the riverboat captains, and in the spring of this year, Captain Grant Marsh tethered the Far West almost outside the front door of Kelly's shack and hailed the frontiersman into the open to introduce him to General G. H. Forsyth, a gentleman who required the services of a scout to lead a survey expedition up the Yellowstone. Kelly got the job, and from then onward he was known as "Yellowstone" Kelly.

Although most of Kelly's lifetime was spent in the service of the U. S. Army as a scout and mail carrier, there were periods when, jaded by military routine, he would wander off for a season of buffalo hunting and wolfing. During these stints as a loner, he had many encounters with Indians, both hostile and otherwise, and although it is difficult to estimate

how many scalps he collected during his frontier years, a shootout with two braves as re-enacted before the camera of photographer Stanley Morrow at least allows us extant earthlings into the secret of how to dispatch a brace of redskins in a few spectacular movements. In 1876, after Custer's defeat, General Nelson A. Miles promoted Kelly to chief of scouts in his command, a position that Kelly held until the surrender of Sitting Bull brought a termination to the North Plains Indian wars. Kelly was still on the Army payroll, but as scouts were by this time a drug on the market, his activities were confined to general duties, and it wasn't until 1898 that he got the opportunity of leading any more expeditions. This, and a similar venture in the following year, were comparatively tame trips, both being of an exploratory nature into the chill wilds of Alaska.

While Kelly was away up North the Spanish-American War had been fought and won, and as an aftermath of this— and upon receiving lightning promotion —Captain Luther Sage Kelly spent a couple of years in the Philippines with the American forces of occupation. On his return to the States, President "Teddy" Roosevelt appointed him agent on the San Carlos Reservation in southeastern Arizona, and he held this position until 1908. Kelly was pushing sixty by this time, but he spent a few years prospecting in Nevada's "color" regions before finally retiring to a small ranch in California in 1915. After his death some years later, the remains of "Yellowstone" Kelly were buried on a high point of a mountain (now named in his honor) that overshadows Billings, Montana. (See FAR WEST and MÉTIS.)

KELLY, MARY A young migrant girl who was killed, scalped, and mutilated by an Oglala war party in July 1864. The wagon train carrying Mary, accompanied by her parents and younger brother Andy, left Geneva, Kansas, on the fifteenth of May 1864, the train consisting of six wagons, which were transporting a total of eleven souls into the Northwest via the Oregon Trail. In the middle of July, and while slowly winding their way through the foothills of Wyoming's Laramie Range, the wagons were overtaken by a war party of more than two hundred Oglala Sioux, and although the Indians made no hostile moves at this stage, their very presence, riding herd on the wagons, tautened the nerves of the migrants to fiddle-string pitch. Kelly, Sr., who had been voted wagonmaster, wishing to avoid trouble, parleyed with the redmen and invited them to share a meal with the party. Whether Kelly provided intoxicants with this meal is unknown, but while in the midst of wolfing through the white folks' supplies, the Indians suddenly erupted into violence, killing three of the party's menfolk and wounding two others before the stricken ones could retaliate.[8]

Kelly grabbed Andy and managed to escape into the brush, but Mrs. Kelly and Mary, together with a Mrs. Larimer and her infant son, were taken prisoner. After nightfall Mrs. Kelly succeeded in leaving Mary by the side of the trail, hoping that the girl would find her way into safekeeping, a hope that no doubt allowed the mother to go into captivity with a lighter heart. The following morning, Mary was sighted by a small detail of cavalry, but a band of Indians put the soldiers to flight before they had a chance of reaching the girl and lifting her into a saddle. Later that same day, Mr. Kelly and Andy met up with the routed cavalrymen, and after much persuading, Mr. Kelly had them return with him to the spot where Mary had been sighted. The girl was still there, but now she was embedded with Sioux arrow shafts, and she had been scalped and mutilated.[9] Of the prisoners, Mrs. Larimer and her child escaped soon after their capture, but Mrs. Kelly had to endure five months of captivity before the Indians surrendered her to the soldiers at Fort Sully.

KELLY, NIGGER BILL He found a gold mine and lost it; or maybe he just lost his life. (See KELLY, BILL.)

KELLY, "YELLOWSTONE" A small man with a big reputation. (See KELLY, LUTHER SAGE.)

KENNEDY, JAMES Son of Mifflin Kennedy of the King Ranch, but mainly of note as being the killer of Dodge City's Dora Hand. (See HAND, DORA.)

KENO A lottery game in which a player has a numbered card or a section of a numbered table, plus a stack of chips, the latter being used to cover the player's numbers should they be called by the game's operator, who draws said numbers from a keno "goose."[10] The player who gets his allotted numbers covered first is the winner. Akin to bingo, tombola, and Housey-Housey, and a favorite pastime in the cowtowns and mining camps of the West. Sometimes spelled "keeno."

KENTUCKY RIFLE Manufactured mainly by independent German gunsmiths who were firmly established in Pennsylvania by the first quarter of the

---

[8] Those killed being Messrs. Taylor and Sharp, and a black servant named Franklin. Seriously wounded were Messrs. Larimer and Wakefield.

[9] Mary's grave, a cairn with a small marker, can still be seen by the side of the Old Oregon Trail.

[10] Somewhat like an old-type tea urn, but supported on brackets so that it could be tilted to allow numbered chips to drop out into the caller's palm.

eighteenth century. Rifles that were to become known as the Kentucky type were copied from the old Jaeger rifles of Germany, although the guns manufactured by the American "Dutchmen" were longer barreled, lighter in weight, and of a much more streamlined appearance. By 1845 these backwoods gunsmiths were issuing a more or less standardized model. This was a rifled-barreled flintlock with an over-all length of from 56 to 58 inches. Barrels were octagonal, stocks usually extended the full length of the piece, and all had a brass-lidded compartment in the butt wherein greased linen patches could be carried. The most popular calibers were .36 to .45, but guns could be had in calibers ranging up to .80. After the Revolution (1775–83) the brass furniture on these guns became somewhat more elaborate, and crescent-shaped butts became popular, but "Kentucky" rifles otherwise remained basically unaltered until they dwindled into obsolescence in the mid-nineteenth century. As more than six hundred gunsmiths were making these weapons by hand, no two are exactly alike. These guns are usually referred to as "American" rifles in Europe.

KETCHUM, AMI   One of Print Olive's victims. (See OLIVE, I. PRENTICE.)

KETCHUM, "BLACK JACK" Leader of a Hole in the Wall gang. (See KETCHUM, TOM.)

KETCHUM, SAM   Older brother, and partner in crime, of the more notorious "Black Jack" Tom Ketchum. (See KETCHUM, TOM.)

KETCHUM, TOM Thomas E. Ketchum, leader of a gang recruited from the legion of outlaws who infested such rendezvous as Hole in the Wall, Brown's Hole, and Robber's Roost, was hanged at Clayton, New Mexico, on April 26, 1901, the crime that brought him to the gallows being "attempted train robbery," an offense which, at that time and place, carried the supreme penalty. The hanging was a messy affair. Owing to an error in judgment in the length of the drop, Tom's head was snapped off. Shudder a mite, but don't drain the tear ducts, for it was a fitting end to a man who, at the head of a gang, had looted and killed across seven states during a ten-year career of crime.

In 1887 Tom, who was then twenty-five years of age, was working as a cowhand with his brother Sam on various ranches in the Panhandle, these two sons of a physician having odd-jobbed north from their birthplace near San Angelo, Texas.[11] Tom, a black-haired lad with an epidermis that tanned like an Indian's may have gotten his "Black Jack" handle around this time, for he was known by this name when he and Sam were trail-herding between Roswell and Clayton, New Mexico, in 1890. Tom, who appears to have had a brain that was subject to meteorological-like pressures, attracted a certain amount of attention to himself by hanging around the railroad depot and puffing lead shot at train engineers from the muzzle of a peashooter tube.[12]

---

[11] A third brother, Berry Ketchum, took no part in the outlaw activities of Tom and Sam, and this brother became a prosperous cattleman in the Panhandle.

[12] At Clayton, Tom received a note from a cutie named Cora that made him aware of the fact that he had been spurned, the gal's affections having been transferred to a waddie designated merely as "Slim." After absorbing this message, Tom clobbered himself about the head with the butt of his six-shooter, an odd habit he indulged in when storms whistled betwixt the canyons of his mind. Whether this rejection slip from Cora sparked off the orgy of pellet puffing mentioned in the entry is unknown, but it does give an insight into the type of lad we're spotlighting.

After this episode, he and Sam turned their backs on gainful, honest employment and entered a life of far more gainful dishonest endeavor, their curtain raiser being the murder of Levi Herzstein, a post office- *cum* storeowner of Tucumcari, New Mexico, who was trailing the boys after they had robbed his place of business. The brothers Ketchum were next heard from in Wyoming's Hole in the Wall country. A gang of long riders were now eating the brothers' dust, some of these new recruits being Wild Bunch regulars who only followed Tom when Butch Cassidy was resting between jobs.

Over the next eight years Tom and Sam led varying numbers of men on store, train, bank, and payroll robberies, the area of these depredations ranging from Wyoming in the north to the Rio Grande in the south. Over these years, the Ketchum gang has been credited with at least twelve murders and the stealing of currency and bullion to the estimated total of $250,000. Black Jack, whose gun had been responsible for at least two killings over this spell,[13] now had a reward of $10,000 hanging over his head, and both he and Sam were running out of crime time. They were now back in New Mexico, and here, near Twin Mountains, they committed a trio of train robberies in rapid succession. After this things soured between the brothers, and after an argument over the division of booty, Sam took off in a huff and formed his own gang.

On July 11, 1899, Black Jack and a couple of men named Franks and Lay made a fourth attack on a train in the region of Twin Mountains, but on this occasion they failed to shake the posse that was hot on their trail, and shortly after a gunfight in which Sheriffs E. Farr and W. H. Love were killed and Ketchum was wounded, the most wanted man in the Southwest was arrested. Tom was placed in a hospital in Trinidad, Colorado, and while he was recovering from an arm wound he most likely received word that brother Sam had been wounded while attempting a fifth train job at Twin Mountains; and later, that Sam had died of gangrene on July 24, 1899.[14] Tom got a "guilty" verdict handed down at his trial at Santa Fe, New Mexico, but various appeals postponed the carrying out of the sentence until the date given at the beginning of this entry. (See HOLE IN THE WALL GANG; KILPATRICK, BEN; LAY, ELZA; LOGAN, HARVEY; PARKER, ROBERT LEROY; and WILD BUNCH.)

KID CURRY An alias of Harvey Logan. (See LOGAN, HARVEY.)

KIDDER MASSACRE Name given to a fight that occurred on Beaver Creek in northwestern Kansas in July 1867. Detailed to carry important dispatches to field headquarters of the 7th Cavalry, whose exact whereabouts were unknown, Lieutenant Lyman S. Kidder of the 2nd U. S. Cavalry, with an escort of ten troopers and a Sioux Indian guide named Red Bead, were attacked by an overwhelming force of Sioux under the leadership of Pawnee Killer while they were camped on Beaver Creek. Pawnee Killer had three hundred warriors behind him, and Kidder and his command,[15] together with Red Bead, were quickly obliterated by the flint-tipped missiles of the enemy. The bodies were stripped, mutilated, and partially burned before the Indians withdrew. The bodies were discovered by the 7th Cavalry as they made their way from the South Platte, en route for Fort Wal-

[13] A deputy sheriff named Angelo Carley in Colorado, and a storeowner in Arizona.
[14] Sam was about forty-five years old at the time of his passing.
[15] These were green troops whose first Indian engagement happened to be their last.

lace, and Custer had the bodies buried where they had fallen.

KIENTPOOS A Modoc Indian chief who usually appears in print under the name of Captain Jack. (See MODOC WAR.)

KILLEEN, MIKE D. The victim of one of those triangle dramas that can occur at any time in any place, but as this occurred at Tombstone, Arizona, in 1880, and has left a controversial mess of print in its wake, it is not without interest. In the early days of June 1880, Mary Killeen, a beautiful girl who was married to Mike, left her husband's board and moved into lodgings. Mike, a fairly tough character who at this time was employed as a bouncer at the Crystal Palace Saloon, took this somewhat calmly until it was brought to his attention that blue-eyed Mary was being squired about in public and sparked about in private by a blond pistoleer by the name of "Buckskin" Frank Leslie.

On the night of June 22, Mike loaded his shooter and wandered the town in search of his wife and "Buckskin," and when he spied them on the porch of the Cosmopolitan Hotel accompanied by a friend of Leslie's named George Perine, the cuckolded one pulled his piece and went into action. Perine was heard to shout "Look out, Frank!," but the warned one had already swapped shots with Mike, and both men having missed, Frank was now trying to prevent his antagonist from beating his brains out, for Mike, who had a bouncer's grip on the other's pistol, was using his own weapon about his head with dizzying effect. Perine had now opened fire and

Mike felt the bullets strike, whereupon he left the near-unconscious Leslie, advanced on Perine, and treated the latter as he had Frank, after which he collapsed. Killeen survived long enough to make a deathbed statement, and the foregoing portion of this narrative has been adapted from this. Now comes the mess. Both Leslie and Perine were placed in the cooler by the town marshal, Fred White, and once inside, Leslie admitted to the shooting of Killeen.[16]

After the death of Mike, the prisoners were given a hearing, the result of which was that Leslie was released without restraint and Perine on one thousand dollars' bond. Shortly afterward, Deputy Sheriff Wyatt Earp rearrested Perine, a murder warrant having been sworn out by a citizen named W. T. Lowry, said warrant naming Perine as the killer of Mike Killeen. This time Perine's examination lasted some days. Frank Leslie, appearing for the defense, once again claimed credit for the killing, while a second defense witness, Mary Killeen, who by this time was Mrs. Frank Leslie, claimed that she hadn't seen Perine on the night of the action. This kind of testimony would have fogged Solomon, so it's not surprising that the jury gave Perine a clean bill of health. And that is how "Buckskin" Frank got Mary Killeen and a phony kill credit, and the real villain beat the rap. (See LESLIE, FRANK.)

KILPATRICK, BEN As Ben was about 6 feet, 4 inches in height, he is frequently referred to as the Tall Texan. Kilpatrick became known around the three main outlaw "club" hideouts—Hole in the Wall, Brown's Hole, and Robber's Roost—from about 1890 after riding in

[16] There could be quite a few reasons for his doing this: As Killeen had fired the first shot, it was a clear case of self-defense if Frank had been the one to fire the fatal shot (if this is the reason for his admission, it was obviously done to help Perine); a man of "Buckskin's" type wouldn't like it to get around that he had missed his target; after having his marbles loosened by Mike, the admission could have been born of desire.

from the Southwest with fellow Texans Tom and Sam Ketchum. Over the next decade Ben rode the owlhoot trail with either "Black Jack" Ketchum's mob or Butch Cassidy's Wild Bunch, although Ben is usually recognized as being a Cassidy man, as he spent most of his time with this gang. Both of these gangs were highly successful, so much of Ben's spare time could be spent visiting the fleshpots of the West and Middle West. This liking for city life was eventually to bring about the tall one's downfall.

After taking part in a Wild Bunch train robbery at Wagner, Montana, on July 3, 1901, Ben collected his share of the loot, and with a "camp" follower named Della Rose (a girl who had been living with "Buncher" Will Carver until the latter's demise from gunshot wounds), headed for the noise and glitter of St. Louis, Missouri. Here, under the names of Mr. and Mrs. Benjamin Arnold, the couple rented rooms and began to live it up, spending Bank of Helena (Montana) currency—which was uncommon in Missouri—with reckless abandon. The St. Louis Police and the Pinkertons followed this trail of hot money, and Ben and Della were arrested on November 5, 1901. The cops third-degreed a confession out of Ben, and this, plus the currency evidence, got him a fifteen-year stretch in the Federal Penitentiary at Atlanta, Georgia.

After serving eleven years he was released on the eleventh of June 1911, whereupon he returned to the West and settled in southwestern Texas, in an area that was the Lone Star State's equivalent of Robber's Roost. There were no big-name outlaw leaders around by this time whom Ben could follow, so he teamed up with an older ex-con named Ed Welch,[17] and they made pocket money as best they could. On March 13,

1912, these two, posing as Union Pacific detectives, succeeded in halting the Sunset Limited of the Southern Pacific at Dryden, Texas. And that was as far as they got. A Wells Fargo messenger named David Truesdale killed Ben when the holdup man's attention strayed; then, picking up the outlaw's fallen Winchester, Dave blasted Ed past all hope of recovery. As was the custom of the time, Ben and Ed's bodies were held erect for the camera just as soon as a photographer could reach the spot. Note: Dave Truesdale received his reward for this double hit in 1930—that's right, 1930, eighteen years after the attempted robbery and just eighteen years before Dave's death from natural causes. (See CARVER, WILLIAM; HOLE IN THE WALL GANG; KETCHUM, TOM; PARKER, ROBERT LEROY; ROSE, DELLA; and WILD BUNCH.)

KING, LUTHER   Small-time member of the Clanton and Curly Bill gangs whom little is known about. Luther's only serious crime appears to have been when he participated in the Benson Stage robbery of March 15, 1881. Wyatt Earp, at the head of a posse, took King into custody on March 19, an arrest that was made without any show of violence from King, although he had two revolvers and a Winchester and twenty boxes of cartridges about his person. After stating that "he only held the hosses," the prisoner made a full confession and named his accomplices, after which he was handed over to Sheriff John Behan for transfer to the Tombstone jail. Behan, perhaps intentionally, allowed King to escape from the jail office, and although King had a price on his head and the search for him wasn't abandoned for some time, after riding away from the Tombstone jail he seems

[17] Also known as H. O. Beck and Ole Hobeck.

to have disappeared completely. He may have remained a goodie from that time onward. (See BENSON STAGE MURDERS.)

KING, MELVIN   A Civil War veteran who, after the close of hostilities, made the Army his career, and who was known as a hell raiser in most of the cowtowns of Kansas, wherein he spent most of his furlough time. In 1875, by the time he was twenty-eight years of age, King had reached the rank of sergeant in the 4th Cavalry. Having some free time in July 1875, he made for Wichita, Kansas, a trail town where he could meet some of his cowboy pals. On arrival at Wichita, and after hearing that the town had appointed a new marshal since his previous visit, Melvin sank a few drams and proceeded to tell anyone who would listen exactly what he was going to do to this new tin-badge named Earp. Town Marshal Wyatt Earp, on hearing of these boasts, approached the military troublemaker, and the latter drew his Cavalry model in preparation for a shootout, but Earp, by not drawing his gun, caused confusion 'neath the campaign hat of King, and he was disarmed, thumped about the head, and arrested. The outcome of this was that Melvin was fined $100 and had his leave ruined.

This was to be a bad month for Sergeant King. After a brooding 280-mile return trip to Fort Elliott, Texas, barracks room scuttlebutt informed him that a lass whom he considered to be carrying his brand was having an affair with a civilian named Bat Masterson. The girl, Molly Brennan, who was employed as a dance-hall girl at the Lady Gay gambling saloon and dance hall in nearby Sweet-

water,[18] had been seen disappearing into the Lady Gay after hours with Bat in tow, wee-hours trysts that gave rise to bawdy speculation. On the payday following this depressing news, King rode into Sweetwater with blood in his eyes and pushed his way through the batwings of the Lady Gay on trouble bent. When the sergeant roared in, Bat and Molly unclinched from their dancing and turned to meet the threat as King unshipped his pistol and fired. Molly, who had moved to shield Bat, fell to the floor with a ball in her abdomen[19] as King's second shot spun Bat to the sawdust with a shattered pelvis. The third explosion came from Bat's .45, and Sergeant Melvin King crashed to the floor as dead as could be. (See MASTERSON, WILLIAM BARCLAY.)

KING RANCH   Established in 1854 by Colonel Richard King, a onetime captain of a Rio Grande steamboat. Located in southern Texas on the San Catrudos River, a river which, with its tributaries, watered King's 84,000 acres and gave the spread its original name of Santa Catrudos Ranch. At a later date King took in Mifflin Kennedy[20] as a copartner, and although Santa Catrudos profits slumped extensively over the years 1860–74 owing to the activities of Juan Cortina's legion of rustlers, by 1880 around 65,000 cattle, 10,000 horses, 7,000 sheep, 8,000 goats, plus a *remuda* of 1,000 saddle horses, were keeping a force of more than 300 Mexican *vaqueros* in full-time employment. Over the years the Santa Catrudos became known as the King Ranch, and at the present time this spread is acknowledged as being the largest in the world, its

[18] Later to be renamed Mobeetie.
[19] Miss Molly Brennan died shortly afterward.
[20] Father of the James Kennedy who killed Dora Hand; James gets a mention in the entry on Miss Hand.

dominion now extending over 1,000,000 acres on which graze more than 150,000 head of livestock. All livestock bear the Running W brand.[21] (See CORTINA,

JUAN NEPOMUCENA.)

KIOWA-APACHE INDIANS
A minority tribe that may be referred to as the plains division of the Apache nation. In 1650 they were located in what is now Montana, but in the middle of the eighteenth century they settled in the Southwest, having traveled from the North with their allies the Kiowa. These Indians were typical tepee-dwelling plains nomads, being linked with the other Apache tribes by language only. Being few in number, they rode with the Kiowa and Comanche when making raiding sorties. Pronounced Kie-o-way a-pach-ee. From 1865 they became reservation Indians.

KIOWA INDIANS The Kiowa, being of the Uto-Aztecan language group, are linked linguistically with the pueblo tribes of the Southwest, yet, for some undiscovered reason, these Indians were living in what is now Montana in the middle of the seventeenth century, and it was not until a hundred years later, as fully mounted nomads, that they moved South and settled in the area that embraces the Staked Plains and southeastern Oklahoma. From this time onward these tepee-dwelling plains Indians, who lived by the hunt, were neighbors and allies of the Comanche, and combined war parties from these tribes became the scourge of the South Plains, sometimes extending their operations deep into Mexico. Kiowa war parties also worked independently, but on these occasions they usually confined their raids to the territory north of the Wichita Mountains.[22] In 1849 Asian cholera swept the plains of the Southwest, and when the epidemic had burned itself out, the combined total of the Kiowa and the Comanche had been reduced to around three thousand souls. After this the Kiowa may be classed as a minority group, yet even so, they and their Comanche allies succeeded in causing the white settlers a lot of grief for a further twenty-six years until they were finally settled on a reservation in southeastern Oklahoma in 1875. Pronounced Kie-o-way. (See SATANTA.)

KIPP, JOSEPH Born at Fort Union on the North Dakota–Montana line in 1847, the son of James Kipp[23] and his Mandan Indian bride. At the age of eighteen Joseph took employment with the American Fur Company[24] at Fort Benton, Montana, and after he had shown initiative beyond the call of duty by recovering a stolen stallion from a Blackfoot encampment, his grateful employers put up the money to give Joe a period of schooling at a mission school at St. Joseph, Missouri. This was a somewhat cursory education, which lasted a bare twelve months, after which Joe moved up into Canada to try his luck at prospecting. This was unsuccessful, and in 1869 he returned to Montana and became an interpreter for the 13th

21 Alternatively known as the Little Snake Brand.
22 Kiowa raiding parties, however, are known to have traveled farther from their bases than any other Amerind group, there being some evidence that they may have struck as far south as Honduras.
23 James Kipp, who was born in Scotland in 1798, arrived in the United States in 1822, and he was quite a big wheel in the American Fur Company by 1830.
24 At this time under the proprietorship of George Steel and Matt Carroll.

Infantry, a position he held for about a year.

In January 1870 a trapper named Malcolm Clarke was murdered by a party of Blackfoot, and when Colonel E. M. Baker's command moved out from Fort Ellis to punish the Indians, Joe went along as guide. He did not, however, take any active part in the infamous Baker Massacre of January 23, 1870, for his CO, being fully aware that Kipp's sympathies were with the Indians, had, before the slaughter commenced, detailed two troopers with the duty of preventing the scout from taking any part in the action.[25] After this sanguinary affair, Joe resigned his Army position, and a short time later he went into partnership with a man named Charlie Thomas.

The Kipp-Thomas enterprise consisted of trading whiskey to the Indians in exchange for pelts, and as this was an illegal venture, they prudently established their log trading post on the Canadian boundary, thus making it difficult for any U.S. marshal who wished to put them out of business, and after one such abortive attempt by the law the post became known as "Fort Standoff." Joe and Charlie prospered as never before, and by investing their "fullproof" profits into the opening of whiskeyless posts they had, some ten years later, established centers on the Musselshell, Birch Creek, and Marias rivers.

In later life, Kipp settled at Browning, Montana, a small town in which he owned a hotel, general store, and sawmill. By this time any enmity the Blackfoot may have harbored against him for his being with Baker on that day in 1870 had long since abated, and from 1890 and over the following decade, he is reputed to have been the unofficial head of the Blackfoot nation. Joseph

Kipp died at Browning on December 12, 1913. (See BAKER MASSACRE and CLARKE, MALCOLM.)

KIRKER, JAMES
A fully buckskinned, heavy-bearded hard case of the Southwest who, after his parents had been killed by Apaches while he was still in his teens, had declared war on the whole nation of those desert raiders, only sweeping his hatred under the cactus after he had indulged in a decade of killing and hair lifting, and after having realized that the vengeance trail can be a time-consuming and near-profitless venture. In 1837 more than 400 Mimbreno Apaches were lured into the plaza of the village of Santa Rita del Cobre by an English scalp hunter named James Johnson, ostensibly for a fiesta, but after being fed and suitably liquored they were slaughtered, and Kirker, who took no part in the massacre seized the opportunity of establishing friendly relations with his onetime enemies by freighting medical supplies, weapons, and rotgut to the mauled Mimbreños. The tribesmen were sufficiently grateful to allow bygones to remain that way, and some five years later, and after having led numerous war parties in attacks on wagon trains, Kirker was more or less accepted as an honorary chief of the tribe.

In the spring of 1842 Kirker, at the head of a raiding party, captured a wagon train boss[26] named James Hobbs as the initial move in an attack on the latter's charges. Hobbs, however, persuaded the white renegade to allow train safe passage by suggesting that far greater profits could be obtained if scalp hunting were indulged in on the grand scale, the idea being that Hobbs, who had been born in the Shawnee country of Missouri and was on

[25] The number of Blackfoot slain in this massacre is usually given as 170, but Kipp claimed to have counted the bodies of 217 men, women, and children.
[26] Wagonmasters usually rode well ahead of their charges in those early years.

extremely good terms with that tribe, would rustle up a party of these aboriginal Missourians, join forces with Kirker, and their combined forces would ride through the Indian nations lifting hair by the wagonload, all of which could be sold to the Mexican Government, who, in an effort to resolve the Indian problem for all time, paid *mucho dinero* for the scalps of these nomads. After a handshake of partnership and an agreement that the two forces should meet at Pinos Altos, Kirker left, and Hobbs returned to his convoy. Kirker most likely intended to keep the Pinos Altos appointment, but around this time Mangas Colorado, chief of the Copper Mine tribe, returned from a highly successful raid on Sonora, Mexico, and Kirker was kept busy disposing of the loot—most of which was traded to the Comancheros—over the period when he should have rendezvoused with Hobbs. After correlating information about this raid, and learning that the gringo Kirker had supplied the Apaches with rifles, the governors of Sonora and Chihuahua put a joint reward of 10,000 gold pesos on Kirker's nit-infested head, and when smoke and moccasin headlines spread this news around, Kirker left the Mimbreno region, evidently not wishing to be disconnected from such a valuable property.

It is some months before we hear from him again, roaming the country north of the Rio Grande at the head of a gang of nine cutthroats of dubious parentage. In this region he became reunited with Hobbs, who was leading more than a hundred Shawnees, and after resolving differences arising from Kirker's failure to appear at Pinos Altos, the two commands combined and went in for scalp hunting as originally intended. Navahos and Apaches were slaughtered and

scalped in large numbers, together with the odd Mexican or suitably maned Americano[27] in a campaign that reached its peak when more than 300 scalps were taken from one Apache village. The sum total of scalps taken by the Kirker-Hobbs legion had now reached such a number that Kirker decided it was time to freight them into Mexico and collect an estimated 22,000 gold pesos. Before moving South, Kirker removed his beard and exchanged his bloodied buckskins for a velvet suit; then, identity hidden beneath this bluejawed Fauntleroy image, he and Hobbs led their merry men across the Rio Grande and hastened to Chihuahua to collect their reward. The Chihuahua authorities totaled the bounty payout at 23,300 gold pesos, a princely sum, which was more than ten times greater than the treasury possessed, so Kirker collected 2,000 gold pesos in cash and Hobbs accepted a "promise to pay" chit for the balance. A few days later Kirker disappeared with his saddlebags loaded, and Hobbs never saw him again. After this Kirker kept north of the border, finally settling in a log cabin on the slopes of California's Mount Diablo. This choice of location may have been prompted by the notion that "The Devil looks after his own," but on this occasion the Lord of the Flies failed to live up to his billing, and Kirker died here of alcoholic poisoning in 1852. (See HOBBS, JAMES, and MANGAS COLORADO.)

KLAMATH INDIANS

Tribe belonging to the Penutian language family who have resided in the southern Oregon-California border region since at least 1650. Despite their location, the Klamath are classed as Californian Indians, as they are culturally akin to this

[27] This unholy pair wouldn't have flinched from lifting their own daddios' top knots if the latter had been available.

group. Their villages were usually to be found on the banks of lakes or rivers, clusters of dwellings that were either of the wigwam or dome-shaped variety, both types being composed of rushes sheathing a sapling framework. Although possessing horses, water travel was essential, and dugout canoes that were propelled by long poles were used for this purpose. Being of the seed-gathering group, these Indians were mainly vegetarian, but small game was hunted to supplement this diet. In 1864 the Klamath became reservation Indians, sharing their land with the Modoc Indians for a short time. This made virtually no difference to their way of life, for the land allotted to them had been Klamath territory for as long as the tribe could remember.

KUSZ, CHARLES   A New Yorker who moved West in 1875 at the age of twenty-six. On reaching Colorado, Kusz put down temporary roots, pausing long enough to realize $150,000 from mining operations before leaving the state in 1880 and moving down into New Mexico Territory. Here, at Manzano,[28] he set up house and invested some of his fortune in publishing a newspaper. The sheet produced by Kusz had the offbeat title *The Gringo and the Greaser*, was printed throughout in italics, and its entire contents were written by the editor and publisher—to whit, Kusz. This rag was ag'in' Roman Catholics, rustlers, the whole educational system of the region, and anything else that had the temerity to disturb Mr. Kusz' digestive tract, so it came as slight surprise to the citizens of Manzano when Kusz was murdered. Two rifle bullets smashed through the window of an upstairs room of his home on the night of March 26, 1884, killing Kusz as he was sharing his evening meal with a friend. No one was ever arrested for this murder, but in the considered opinion of this writer, the killer was most likely a gringo, a greaser, a Roman Catholic, a rustler, or a schoolteacher; elementary.

[28] A thriving cattle and mining community located almost in the center of the territory.

FREDERIC REMINGTON

LACROSSE   A ball game that at some unknown date originated among the Amerinds who were resident in what is now the eastern United States.[1] By the early years of the eighteenth century the game had spread west of the Mississippi, where by mid-century it had become accepted as a major sport by numerous tribes. Lacrosse sticks employed in these games varied, some tribes favoring a crooked stick with a large area of webbing, while others preferred a stick that had a small webbed hoop at one end. Friendly tribes would engage in matches that lasted from about 9 A.M. until sundown, colossal shin-fracturing contests in which up to a thousand players would be scooping and slinging the ball toward their opposite numbers' goal posts.

LAFITTE, JEAN   A multilingual gentleman who ruled over a community of more than four hundred freebooters for more than a decade. Lafitte, an un-disputed Frenchman, is reputed to have been born at Bordeaux in 1780, the son of either a wandering seadog or a blue-blooded aristocrat, the latter guess finding some support in the rumor that both his parents had appointments with the guillotine during the French Revolution. Jean and a man who was introduced as "my brother Pierre" arrived in New Orleans in 1806, possibly after spending a few years preying upon the merchantmen that frequented the Indian Ocean.[2] Shortly after their arrival, Jean and Pierre opened a smithy and a mercantile establishment, both places of business being used as outlets for smuggled goods.

---

1 The Iroquois of the northeastern woodlands may have been the actual originators.
2 They could have been pimps in Paris, for this lad's early years are lost in mist.

This was a well-known "secret" that was hardly frowned upon, for over this period the majority of New Orleans merchants were buying their stocks from a horde of privateers, who, between acts of piracy in the gulf, landlubbered at Barataria, a bayou hideout some forty-five miles south of the city. This colony of freebooters, composed mainly of the crews of Dominique You, "Cut-nose" Chighizola, Vincent Gambi, and Rene Beluche, sailed under the flag of the Republic of Cartagena and carried letters of marque supplied by that republic, said letters of marque giving paper-thin legality to any attacks that may have been made against Spanish merchantmen while Cartagena was in revolt against Spain. Such was the gang of mother-loving throat slitters whom Lafitte was to command from 1808 onward. In that year the importing of slaves into the United States became illegal, a governmental act that inflated the price of blacks overnight and that gave anyone whose interests lay in smuggling a dollar-propelled impetus to include "Black Ivory" in his catalogue of illicit imports. Lafitte, who was aware that a slave bought in Cuba for three hundred dollars could be sold for treble that amount at a U.S. auction, felt this impetus most strongly, and he made his way to Barataria, intent on gaining command of the hydra-headed mob that called it "home." By employing a line of smooth talk that promised an end to their lethal bickerings and far greater prosperity, Lafitte won their confidence, and those hard-bitten wolves of the sea allowed him to remain to organize their raids and negotiate with their outlets. Under Lafitte's guidance the freebooter community blossomed as never before. Thatched-roofed houses, saloons, gambling halls, and brothels were erected, together with giant store-houses and a massive compound for the black slaves. What the sanitation was like

is anyone's guess, but in the center of this village, Lafitte had himself built a stone-and-brick mansion of magnificent proportions, and by the time he had finished these civic improvements the population had increased to well over the thousand mark, a fifth of whom were the somewhat soiled doves who kept the brothels operational. Slaves were brought in from Cuba, although the majority were taken from seagoing slavers, but even so, the looting of merchantmen was far from neglected during the years of Lafitte's success. Businessmen visited Barataria in droves, to either bid for such items as silks and satins or the more vigorous type of merchandise that was on offer at the weekly slave auctions. Purchases, both alert and inert, were smuggled into New Orleans via the bayous, a chore that Lafitte would take care of for an additional fee. In 1813 the governor of Louisiana turned a jaundiced eye on the Lafitte monopoly and made the rather pathetic gesture of offering a five-hundred-dollar reward for the capture of Jean. No one bothered to go looking for Jean, but Pierre, who had been left in charge of the New Orleans premises, was picked up and charged with "aiding and abetting," an offense which got him a light sentence in the local jail. By the following year more powerful men than the state governor were becoming concerned about the Baratarian legion, and in September of that year a U.S. naval force destroyed the settlement and captured nine vessels and more than a hundred of the freebooters. This was during the final stages of the British-American War of 1812–14, and the Lafittes, who had escaped from the Baratarian disaster, on receiving intelligence that the British were about to attack New Orleans, offered their services to the U. S. Army on the condition that they and their men be afterward pardoned for past indiscretions.

After much haggling, this was agreed to. The imprisoned freebooters were released, and in the subsequent Battle of New Orleans the British were decimated into deciding to get back to their ships. The brothers Lafitte, their captains, and all their motley crews received their pardons, and Jean bought a fresh fleet of ships.[3] Barataria having been razed, the Lafitte squadron sailed in search of new headquarters. They tried Hispaniola but were given twenty-four hours to get under sail, and it wasn't until 1816 that they settled for a small island that was adjacent to the coast of Texas. Lafitte named this small strip of land Galveztown,[4] and in a short time it possessed all the amenities of their original headquarters. In September 1816, while cruising Matagorda Bay, one of Lafitte's ships captured the *Santa Rosa,* a Spanish merchantman from which two million dollars in silver was taken. This colossal take marked an end to Lafitte's attacks on merchant ships, and after this the Galveztown colony confined its activities to the raiding of slave ships. By 1820 the U. S. Government was taking an interest in the vermin that infested its southern hemline, and early the following year the U. S. Navy delivered an ultimatum to the pirate chief: Evacuate the island within three months or the community will be wiped out. Lafitte got the message, and after putting the torch to the buildings, the freebooters sailed away. Lafitte's fortunes were now on the decline. The

fleet consisted of three ships when Galveztown fell astern, but two of these deserted him within a short time, and by the time he finally established a base on an island off the Yucatan coast, all the steam had gone out of Jean. No grand dwellings were erected here, just a few rickety shacks, and nary a saloon or bordello. From this shantytown Lafitte raided coastal craft until 1826. In that year he made a trip to the Yucatan mainland, was struck down by some unspecified fever, and died shortly afterward. (See DAWSON, ROBERT.)

LAKE, AGNES Born Agnes Mersman at Alsace[5] in 1826, the Mersman family arriving in the United States in 1829 and settling at Cincinnati, Ohio. In 1842 Agnes, who was then sixteen years of age, met a circus clown named William Lake,[6] and a short time later she eloped with him and they were married in Louisiana. The young bride traveled with her husband, and such was the active interest she took in circus life that within a short time she was being billed as a wire-walking act. The Lakes were attached to the Spalding and Rogers Circus[7] for more than a decade; then in 1863, William founded his own circus, the William Lake Circus. Sometime after this Agnes originated her Mazeppa act, a tough role in which she was strapped to the back of a supposedly runaway stallion,[8] and when the circus toured Europe in the winter of 1863–

[3] Actually his own ships; the government auctioned off the vessels taken at Barataria, and Lafitte bought them.
[4] Now Galveston, Texas.
[5] German territory at that time.
[6] Actually William Lake Thatcher, the "Thatcher" having been dropped for show-biz simplicity.
[7] This was a floating circus. Erected on a gigantic barge, it was towed to the waterfront towns by riverboat.
[8] This girl-in-pink-tights-on-a-stallion act was quite popular out West, and many of Agnes' contemporaries rode their way to riches during the act's boom years. When Adah Isaacs Menken played Mazeppa at Virginia City, Nevada, the miners who made up her audience, upon recovering their collective breath, showed their appreciation by taking up a collection, the result being that Adah got a two-thousand-dollar bonus in silver. The act owes

64, this rather sexy act was the highlight of the show. A daughter had been born to the couple in 1855, a child who was later to follow in her parents' footsteps, and whom they named Emma. When Emma was fourteen, William Lake was shot dead by a troublemaking rube—a crime that took place at Granby, Missouri, and for which the killer served a few years in prison. After this Agnes took over the management of the show, and it was while the circus was touring Kansas that the widow Lake met Wild Bill Hickok, the renowned pistoleer. This chance meeting was sufficient to impress their respective auras, and some five years later, on March 5, 1876, Agnes became Mrs. Hickok. This marriage lasted five months, Agnes being rewidowed by a piece of explosively propelled lead on August 2, 1876. After paying a hail-and-farewell visit to Wild Bill's grave, Agnes joined her daughter, Emma now being twenty-one years of age and employed as an equestrienne with Barnum's Circus, and mother and daughter toured the country with this, and other shows, until 1883, after which time Agnes more or less retired and settled at Jersey City, New Jersey. Agnes Lake Thatcher Hickok died on August 21, 1907. (See HICKOK, JAMES BUTLER.)

LAKOTA INDIANS   The Dakota or Sioux Indians, Lakota being a dialect rendering of Dakota.

LA MESILLA, NEW MEXICO   A small town in southern New Mexico

that came under United States rule as part of the Gadsden Purchase, the treaty being formally ratified in a ceremony that took place in the town's plaza on Independence Day 1854.[9] Kit Carson, Lew Wallace (of *Ben Hur* fame), and other noteworthy characters spent time in the town, and Billy the Kid spent time in the jail. The majority of the buildings are adobe structures. A nice little town that is still on the map, and if you ever pay it a visit, you can bend your elbow in the Billy the Kid Bar.[10] (See GADSDEN PURCHASE.)

LANDUSKY, PIKE   An extremely hard case who became a victim of Kid Curry's gun. Pike started his career in the West as a trapper, his working area being central Montana, and it was during this period that a Blackfoot arrowhead removed part of his jaw and many of his teeth, a wound that did little to improve his appearance and that troubled him for the remainder of his days. Landusky then tried his hand at prospecting, and after making a lucky strike in the Little Rocky Mountains of north-central Montana, he had his moment of glory when the folk who had raised a gold-mining camp near the spot, named the place Landusky. Pike settled here, married, and helped raise four stepdaughters, one of whom, Elfie,[11] on reaching nubile status, was to be the unwitting cause of Landusky's premature demise. By the time Elfie was "fully growed" she was the best bit of wolfbait in Landusky, a pulchritudinous piece of mountain music whom Harvey

---

its inspiration and stallion activity—and little else—to the writings of Byron, and the female thespians of the frontier who used this routine must have given a far more well-rounded performance than did the original Mazeppa, the latter being Ivan Stephanovitch Mazeppa (1644–1709), a tough, blue-blooded Cossack trader who got his enforced ride as punishment for interfering with a bit of marshmallow named Theresia, a lass who happened to be a Polish nobleman's wife.

[9] The community had been established about eight years at this time.

[10] Housed in what was the old courthouse; a building wherein the Kid made an appearance.

[11] Sometimes given as Elvie.

Logan—among other riders from outlying spreads—began to notice. Harvey, who is better known as "Kid Curry," made the grade but good with Elfie, and when the results of his sparking became readily apparent in the silhouette of his beloved, Pike Landusky, who was sporting a deputy sheriff's badge at this time, went in search of the libertine.[12] Harvey could not be found, and it was not until Christmas Eve 1894 that the deputy encountered the man who had left his mark on Elfie. Pike was tossing them down in Jew Jake's Saloon[13] when Harvey sallied in for a spot of seasonal cheer. Fighting words were exchanged, and a fist fight developed. Landusky, whose fists were of watermelon proportions, had pummeled his opponent panda-eyed before a lucky blow from Harvey sent him to the floor. Being floored caused Pike to lose his perspective, and he clawed for his shoulder gun, but a bullet from Harvey's .45 slammed him back to the sawdust, dead. Landusky was fifty-five years old at the time of his passing. (See LOGAN, HARVEY.)

LANE, GEORGE   Member of Henry Plummer's gang of "Innocents" who was hanged by the vigilantes of Montana. George—sometimes known as "Club Foot"—had spent time as a horse thief and,—oddly enough, as a sheriff, before he arrived in the Alder Gulch region of Montana in 1863. Although known to be a member of the Innocents, there seems to have been little concrete evidence to endorse George's hanging, but on the evening of January 13, 1864, the executive committee of the vigilante movement, which strongly suspected him of having taken part in a stagecoach robbery and other crimes, voted that he should be arrested and hanged. This resolution was put into effect the following day, when George, having been given little chance to plead his cause, was hanged at Virginia City. (See INNOCENTS.)

LANGTRY, LILLY   The Christian name is usually spelled "Lily." (See LANGTRY, LILY.)

LANGTRY, LILY   Married name of Lily Le Breton, an English actress who was born in Jersey, Channel Isles, on October 13, 1852, the daughter of the Reverend W. C. Le Breton. At the age of twenty-two Lily married Edward Langtry and shortly afterward she made her stage debut under the name of Lily Langtry, later becoming known as "The Jersey Lilly." Extremely popular over a great number of years—possibly because of her beauty rather than her acting ability— Lily appeared at her best in lightweight roles, although gloomy Shakespearean roles were not beyond her powers. At the pinnacle of her success she toured South Africa and the United States, and in 1903, while on her third tour of the States, she visited Langtry, Texas, a whistle-stop that Judge Roy Bean was reputed to have named in her honor. The townsfolk of Langtry gave Lily the deceased Bean's pet bear and ancient revolver, and although the bear wandered off into the wilderness Lily kept the revolver in a place of honor in her English home until her death on February 12, 1929. (See BEAN, ROY.)

LARAMIE, WYOMING   Located on the Laramie River some three miles northeast of old Fort Laramie. Being adjacent to the Oregon Trail, it was firmly established by 1868, and it now has a

---

[12] Some writers suggest that the bad blood between these two men may have arisen from Landusky arresting Harvey for some minor offense. This doesn't negate the reason given in the entry if viewed as a twin, rather than as an alternative reason.

[13] A primitive saloon and general store, of which there were a trio in Landusky.

population of over twenty thousand. Named after Jacques La Ramie,[14] a gentleman who was killed by Indians while working the area as a trapper in the early 1820s. (See FORTS, subheading *Laramie.*)

LAREDO, TEXAS   Originally established by the Spanish in 1751, this town, which is located on the Rio Grande in the southwest of the state, became part of the United States in 1846 when it was liberated from Mexican rule by a large force of Texas Rangers. Universally known as the site of "The Dying Cowboy,"[15] Laredo is now a prosperous town of almost seventy thousand souls and possesses an excellent tourist trade.

LARIAT   Anglicized rendering of *la reata,* the latter being the Spanish term for "the rope." Lariats, which vary in length between twenty and sixty feet, can be manufactured from rawhide, silk manila, braided cotton, hair, etc. Rawhide[16] lariats are superior to other types, but being expensive and of a short working life, they are the least popular. The honda of a lariat—the loop through which the noose is tightened—is frequently built around a metal ring or half ring. In the cow country a lariat is referred to as a "catch rope," never as a "lasso."

LARRABEE, NELLIE   One of the half-breed daughters of Joseph Larrabee, a trader and Army scout based at the Red Cloud Agency. Nellie acted as interpreter at the agency, and it was here, in the spring of 1877, that Crazy Horse became acquainted with the girl. The Oglala chief, who was married to the tubercular Black Shawl, was smitten with the eighteen-year-old Nellie, paying court with the ultimate goal of having her share his tepee as a cowife to Black Shawl. Joe Larrabee didn't relish the prospect of one of his daughters becoming a bride of Custer's nemesis, but the agency officials approved—they being of the opinion that such a union might persuade the war chief into a more tolerant attitude toward the white men. Official pressure prevailed and the couple were married, but the marriage was of short duration, Crazy Horse being killed a few months after the ceremony. At some later date, Nellie Larrabee remarried and moved to the Pine Ridge Reservation with the man of her choice, a Sioux brave named Greasy Head. After marrying the widow of Crazy Horse, Greasy Head adopted the name of her first husband,[17] calling himself Crazy Horse for the remainder of his life. Nellie's second husband died in the early 1900s, leaving her with one son. Over the years numerous families named Crazy Horse lived at Pine Ridge, a fact that makes it difficult to ascertain exactly when Nellie Larrabee died. Nellie is sometimes referred to as the Larrabee Woman, and although "Nellie" has been

[14] Sometimes given as La Ramee.

[15] This waddie, who has been cocooned in white linen for more than a century, has been identified as the "Unfortunate Rake" of the British ballad of that name, the resurrected rake of the American variation of the ballad having been stetsoned and spurred, given a better set of morals, and allowed to die from the effects of a malady common to the region wherein he was reincarnated, a gunshot wound being the cause of the demise of the lad from Laredo.

[16] Termed a *reata* by the working cowhand. Usually braided, although some earlier types were made from one long strip of leather, the lariat length being cut spirally from a single hide.

[17] A not uncommon custom, and perhaps a wise one; should the bride, while sleeping, breathe the name of her first husband, that worthy's successor need have no reasons for misgivings. This voluntary choice of name has, however, led to some confusion; photographs of Greasy Head having been sold as true likenesses of the Oglala war chief.

accepted by such eminent authorities as Mari Sandoz, Helen Larrabee—our heroine's sister—always spoke of her as Cheechela. Note: In 1948 a U. S. Army private named Crazy Horse was killed in the Pacific theater of operations, and one gets to wondering if this youth may have been a grandchild of Nellie Larrabee. (See CRAZY HORSE.)

LASSEN, PETER A native of Copenhagen who was born in 1793. Lassen arrived in the United States in 1822, settling in Boston, Massachusetts, for a short spell before commencing a westerly migration that brought him to California—via Missouri, Kansas, and Oregon—in 1841. Here Lassen worked at his original trade of blacksmith for some years, during which time—having visions of becoming a ranchowner—he made various applications for a land grant. In 1844 Governor Micheltorena acceded to Lassen's request for a twenty-six-thousand-acre land grant in the Sacramento Valley, and in that same year the Dane established a ranch on Deer Creek. Three years later he erected mercantile buildings and dwellings on his land, the nucleus of a town that he named Benton, but shortly after he had attracted a number of inhabitants, the gold strike of 1849 denuded the place, and Lassen was left with but a healthy-looking ghost. Somewhat dispirited, Lassen abandoned his ranch and moved North, settling at Shasta, California, in 1850. At Shasta he became friendly with Isaac Roop, the local postmaster, and when Shasta was razed to the ground by a fire that swept through the town in 1853, the two men moved South and located in an area that was, at that time, astride the California-Utah border. In 1856 Lassen and Roop, having

become disenchanted with the governors of California and Utah and the whole federal government, organized a group of settlers and laid claim to thirty-three thousand square miles of territory, which they had named Nataqua.[18] No bloody battles resulted from this act of secession, and in 1857, after reorganization within the Lassen-Roop movement, Nataqua was abandoned in favor of the territory of Sierra Nevada, Roop becoming the first territorial governor. The Sierra Nevadans had a little local trouble over nonpayment of taxes, but of major problems they had none.[19] In 1859 Pete Lassen shelved his territorial claims and went prospecting in the California-Oregon border country, and he was killed in this area by renegade Indians on April 26, 1859. Mount Lassen, Lassen Volcanic National Park, and Lassen County—all of which are in California—are named after this rebel Dane.

LASSO Derived from the Spanish *lazo* —a snare or noose. The dudes' name for a lariat. (See LARIAT.)

LATIGO A strap used to tighten the cinch of a saddle. Latigo leather is supple, oil-tanned hide.

LAWRENCE MASSACRE Occurred in 1863 at Lawrence, Kansas, a town of some 2,000 inhabitants located on the Kansas River in the extreme east of the state. On the evening of August 20, William Clarke Quantrill, leading a force of some 450[20] mounted guerrillas, invaded the town from the southeast. This command of border scum met little opposition from the small force of Union troops

18 Roughly encompassing a third of present-day Nevada.
19 The Sierra Nevadans' claim was never officially recognized, and the movement became a thing of the past when the territory of Nevada was established in 1861.
20 Some accounts almost double this figure.

stationed in the town,[21] and when darkness fell Lawrence was a Dante's Inferno of blazing buildings soundtracked by the rebel yell and the screams of its inhabitants. There was little chance of escape, for prior to the attack Quantrill had thrown a cordon around the town, and it is quite possible that every male in Lawrence would have died that night had not a sentry brought Quantrill the news of a strong Union force that was approaching from the east. This intelligence reached Quantrill about 9 P.M., and a short time later the guerrillas—many of whom were drunk—had been regrouped and left the town, leaving only a small rear guard, which retreated with the coming of the dawn. In their wake they left little more than a disaster area. The town had almost been wiped from the map. More than 200 of its inhabitants —one of whom was the mayor—had been murdered; 182 buildings had been totally destroyed; two banks had been looted; and only one hotel remained functional. The damage done during that murderous attack was later estimated at around the $2,000,000 mark. (See QUANTRILL, WILLIAM CLARKE.)

LAY, ELZA   Texas-born cowhand who became a member of the Hole in the Wall outlaw community in the early 1890s, having, immediately prior to settling in the Hole, worked on the Calvert Ranch near Baggs, Wyoming. The Pinkerton files list "Elza Lay" as being an alias of William H. McGinnis, although in most circles the reverse is generally accepted as being correct.[22] Lay, who possessed the type of dazzling smile that

only a mouthful of gold teeth can provide, rode the outlaw trail as a member of both the Black Jack Ketchum gang and Butch Cassidy's Wild Bunch; Butch usually referring to Elza as "the educated member of the Wild Bunch." Lay must have won the complete trust of Cassidy for in April 1897, during an interval between train and bank robberies, he and Lay, as a two-man unit, staged a successful mine payroll robbery at Castle Rock, Utah. Lay's last job with the Wild Bunch was most likely the Union Pacific train robbery at Wilcox, Wyoming, on June 2, 1899. After this he was on the scene during two or three of the Ketchum gang's train jobs in New Mexico. On July 16, 1899, Lay, as a rider of the Ketchum gang, took part in the robbery of the *Texas Flyer* at Twin Mountains, New Mexico. Within hours after committing this robbery, the gang was being pursued by a heavily armed posse led by Sheriff Ed Farr, and some thirty-five miles from the scene of the holdup[23] a pitched battle ensued between lawmen and outlaws. After this engagement—during which Sheriff Farr was killed—the gang splintered, Lay and a gunnie named Black Bob McManus pairing off and traveling South. These two disappeared for a few months, but on August 17 1899, they were spotted near Carlsbad New Mexico, and after an exchange of lead with a posse, Lay was captured Tried on the charges of murdering Sheriff Farr and interfering with the United States mails, Lay was convicted and given a life stretch in the penitentiary at Santa Fe, New Mexico. (See HOLE IN THE

[21] Consisting of 26 recruits from the 14th Kansas Regiment, and about 20 men of the 2nd Colored Regiment; 17 of the former group were killed, but most of the black troopers escaped. There was no question of cowardice involved in the 2nd's light losses, for these lads had neither uniforms nor weapons.

[22] The Pinkerton files are not infallible, but it is of interest that they list Lay-McGinnis with a secondary alias of "Johnson." Lay's Christian name is frequently given as Eliza or Ezra.

[23] This fight occurred in Turkey Creek Canyon, New Mexico.

WALL GANG; KETCHUM, TOM; PARKER, ROBERT LEROY; and WILD BUNCH.)

LEDUC, MAURICE
Native of France who arrived in the United States in 1818, settling in Wisconsin for a short spell before pushing West and establishing himself as a trapper and trader in Colorado. Maurice located within a few miles of the Bent brothers' first fort, and here, by employing Mexican labor, he erected a fur-trading post that became known as Fort Maurice. While at this post, Leduc became something of a squaw man, at various periods over the years boudoiring a Ute, a Sioux, and a Blackfoot girl, a passion-appeasing trio who, collectively, introduced three masculine "bundles of joy" into the Leduc ménage. Maurice Leduc traded here until a sagging pelt market and competition from the Bents persuaded him to abandon the post in 1840. Sometime after this, our squaw man moved South into New Mexico and married a Spanish girl named Mendoza, a marriage which, over the years, gave Leduc two more sons. In 1858 Maurice became a widower, whereupon he returned to his earlier Colorado stamping ground and built himself a crude shack—an inelegant dwelling that he was soon sharing with a teen-age *señorita*. This arrangement lasted some years. The girl tended their vegetable patch while Maurice went steak hunting or did a spot of fur trapping. Sometime in the mid-1870s, Leduc returned to New Mexico and settled with friends at Cimarron, and he died here in 1880. (See BENT'S FORT and FORTS, subheading *Maurice*.)

LEE, NELSON Born at Brownsville, New York, in 1807, Nelson Lee began his itineracy of the West when he was twenty-four years of age, spending some time in Missouri and Louisiana prior to his arrival in Texas in 1840. If we accept his writings,[24] Lee had a far from uneventful life. The major part of his life over the period 1840–55 was spent with the Texas Rangers, serving in the commands of Jack Hays and Sam Walker. Lee was there blazing away when the Rangers defeated the Comanches at Plum Creek, and he was well in the van of Hays' Regiment during the Mexican War of 1846–48. Minor skirmishes with Indians were vacation stuff, and swimming the Rio Grande was simpler than taking a bath. Tranquil pursuits—such as horse trading—were only indulged in by Lee for short intervals, peaceful spells that lasted until he had recovered his wind. In 1855, after hearing of the fabulous profits to be made from the sale of mules in gold-crazy California, Lee went into partnership with a man named William Aitkens, and after buying sufficient units of mule-flesh to make up a herd they headed West, being accompanied on their journey by twenty-five like-minded adventurers. On the evening of March 31 the party night-camped in the Sacramento Mountains. Twenty-three of the party never awakened on April Fool's Day. Comanches hit the camp at 3 A.M. Luckily for Lee he possessed a turnip of a watch that had a built-in alarm, and when this gimmick suddenly became vocal, the Indians forgot their killing spree and took Lee, Aitkens, and two other survivors prisoner; a case of heap big medicine savem toupee. The unnamed pair were dispatched by tortuous methods shortly after their arrival at the Comanche village, but the man with the medicine watch and his partner were spared, the latter possibly for only a short period, for after having words together one eve-

24 A ghost-written book entitled *Three Years Among the Comanches*. Originally published by the Baker Taylor Company of Albany, New York, in 1859, a new edition being produced by the University of Oklahoma Press in 1957.

ning, Aitkens left their tepee prison with an armed guard, and Lee never saw him again. Nelson Lee spent three years as a Comanche captive, during which time he married one of the young girls of the tribe.[25] After three years Comanche vigilance was more or less nonexistent, and on finding himself alone with a somewhat drunken chief in the summer of 1858, Lee dispatched the Indian with the latter's own tomahawk, and two months later he got back to civilization.[26] In November 1858 Nelson Lee returned to his native state, rich in experience but lacking produce of the U. S. Mint, and in an attempt to fill his empty pockets, he sold the story of his life to a New York publisher. His pockets were still little more than hideouts for moths when he died some years later, but as his book lives on, he can be considered to have left more in his wake than many an extinct millionaire.

LEGADERO   A stirrup strap. Spanish-American term used in the Southwest.

LEONARD, BILL   A jeweler whose expertise in the assessing of gold and silver made him a valuable member of the Clanton gang. Leonard, a gentleman who, previous to his arrival in the Tombstone area and his joining the Clanton gang, had operated a successful jewelry business in Las Vegas, New Mexico,[27] took part in the Benson stage robbery of March 15, 1881. With a posse in his dust and a Wells Fargo reward of two thousand dollars hanging over his head, Leonard rode South and escaped across the international line. Three unshaven

nightingales, Ike Clanton and the brothers McLaury, conspired to get this reward, promising Wyatt Earp they would keep him informed of Leonard's whereabouts if and when Leonard returned to American soil. A couple of months later, Bill came back across the line, but the trio of turncoats never did get their hands on the bounty, the valuable Mr. Leonard getting himself shot dead while attempting to rob the Haslett brothers' store at Huachita, New Mexico, in July 1881. (See BENSON STAGE MURDERS; CLANTON GANG; and GRAHAM, WILLIAM B.)

LEROY, BILL   Rocky Mountain road agent who usually operated in Colorado. In 1879 Leroy teamed up with veteran Bill Miner, and as a twosome they staged a few successful train and stagecoach robberies, but in 1880 vigilantes got on their trail, and Leroy was captured and summarily executed by hanging. (See MINER, BILL.)

LE ROY, KITTY   A fine example of the type of life led by the demimonde of the frontier. Texas-born Kitty started her career as a Jig dancer at a Dallas theater at the tender age of ten years, nubility and a lively disposition establishing her as the toast of Dallas a few years later. At some later date, Kitty abandoned her theatrical ambitions and became an accomplished faro dealer, a choice of occupation that led to her becoming something of a pistol expert and perambulating arsenal. Folks say that around this time Kitty possessed twelve bowie knives and seven revolvers; they also say that she married her first husband because he was

[25] A girl named To-ma-no-a-ku-no (The Sleek Otter). Lee describes this spouse as an expert swimmer who was, oddly enough, rather dirty.

[26] He was a long way from civilization, the years of his captivity most likely having been spent in the wilds of Sonora and Chihuahua (Mexico).

[27] At Las Vegas he became acquainted with Doc Holliday when the latter opened a dental surgery in the same building.

the only male around who had sufficient guts to allow her to shoot apples off the top of his head while riding past at a fast gallop. In 1876, at the age of twenty-six and with four husbands[28] and numerous gold camps behind her, Kitty arrived at Deadwood, Dakota Territory. Here, flamboyantly attired in Romany raiment, our lady gambler opened the Mint Gambling Saloon, a successful money-trap that was no doubt patronized by such frontier headliners as Wild Bill Hickok, Calamity Jane, and Sam Bass. Kitty prospered here for about two years, unaware that the Dakota mining camp was going to be her "end of track," for in 1878 she was murdered by husband V—a gentleman who afterward shot himself. This couple, who evidently couldn't live together, were buried together.

LESLIE, FRANK   He dusted into Tombstone, Arizona, in the early months of 1880, and had Custer not perished some four years earlier, the residents of the mining camp may have suspected that the general was paying them an unscheduled visit, for the stranger with the long, blond locks and drooping mustache was clad in a jacket of fringed buckskins, yellow-braided cavalry pants, and a wide-brimmed sombrero—splendid raiment to which a fully laden twin-gun harness added a lethal touch, and all of which was carried around on two-inch heels.[29] This was "Buckskin" Frank Leslie, a man with a past as nebulous as a fading smoke signal but dressed in a manner that suggested a backtrail of violence. Rumors abounded. Frank was credited with from ten to fourteen notches[30] and a past full of hectic adventure: prospecting in the Comstock, scouting for General Miles during the North Plains campaigns and, prior to his arrival at Tombstone, attached to Al Sieber's band of scouts during the Apache wars—heady stuff that cannot be proved or otherwise. Shortly after his arrival in turbulent Tombstone, Frank got himself a job measuring out three fingers and sloshing schooners of suds across the bar at the Oriental Saloon. This choice of vocation kept him in the public eye, so over his years in the camp we have a good idea of his activities. Soon after his taking employment at the Oriental, Frank started shacking up with a certain Mike Killeen's wife, a lass named Mary who became Mrs. Frank Leslie within a few weeks of her husband's sudden demise, the latter having been propelled into the unknown by a powdersmoke salute that Leslie is usually, yet erroneously, credited with. This marriage that had been arranged by Colt's firearms didn't last. Seems that Frank, prior to any show of eroticism, stimulated his whatever by having a terrified Mary freeze against their bedroom wall while he outlined her statistics in the plaster with the craters of bullet holes,[31] a somewhat kinky practice that the court figgered was sufficient grounds for granting Mary a rapid divorce. Between putting a head on beer and bouncing the unruly, Frank, naturally, had time off,

[28] A comparatively wealthy German is reputed to have been a member of this quartet, Kitty having driven him from the nest when his funds ran out. Another of these marriages was of extremely short duration: After mortally wounding one of her many admirers, Kitty, showing ambivalence to a marked degree, married the victim of her attack a few hours before he expired.

[29] One occasionally wonders if hidden elevators were built into these boots, for Frank is variously described as being small, medium, or large. Official statistics have him stretching to 5 feet, 7 inches, weighing in at 133 pounds, and trotting around in size 5 shoes.

[30] A ridiculous figure, for the shootouts mentioned in this entry are the only ones he ever witnessed or took part in.

[31] This exhibition of pistoleered pinups was much admired for many years.

and although much of this free time was spent over at Bisbee, where he knew a lot of Cousin Jacks (Cornish miners), as he was also acquainted with members of the Clanton gang, he may have participated in an occasional stagecoach robbery. Reports of Frank's gang activities are, however, invariably based on the quicksand of rumor and suspicion. On November 14, 1882, Frank left his bar unattended for a few minutes, returning after he had shot an inebriated troublemaker named Billy Claiborne to death, an incident that became an open-and-closed affair over the short period of time required by Frank to puff through a cylinder of Bull Durham. A Niagara of suds was to cross the bar of the Oriental before Frank hit the headlines once more. Heavy drinking had, by 1889, begun to take its toll on our still-buckskinned hero, and in July of that year he was "drying out" at a ranch in the Horseshoe Valley of the Swisshelm Mountains, accompanied on this enforced vacation by a nifty blonde named Molly Williams.[32] On the evening of July 10 hard words were exchanged between Molly and Frank. The buckskinned one, who was unpleasantly drunk, may have become jealous of Molly's behavior toward a hired hand named James Neal, but whatever the cause, the climax to this slanging match came when Frank shot the girl dead and put two bullets into Neal's anatomy. Believing he had killed them both, Frank staggered away, his fogged mind possibly working out ways in which he could lay the crime at some unknown's door, but he was arrested before he had time to sober up, and at his subsequent trial, during which Neal appeared for the prosecution, Frank was given a twenty-five-year stretch in the Yuma Penitentiary. Within a few weeks of his entering the prison Leslie was assigned to pharmacy duties,[33] an easy chore that kept him occupied until 1893 when, for some unaccountable reason, he was given a pardon. Over the next four years, Leslie's trail is clouded, but on December 1, 1897, a man who gave his name as Nashville F. Leslie married Belle Stowell at Stockton, California,[34] and it has been established that the groom was our man from Tombstone. The remainder of Leslie's life may only be reconstructed by linking a minimum of fact with a maximum of assumption. After the turn of the century he may have spent some time with the Buffalo Bill shows, for although his name does not appear on any of the shows' programs—which were highly detailed—he did have in his possession an elaborate silver-buckled belt that was engraved with both his and Cody's name. Around 1911 Frank was working as a saloon swamper at Oakland, California, and over the years 1913–22 he was managing a pool room at Sausalito, California. Toward the end of 1922 he moved to San Francisco, where he got a job managing a pool and billiards hall, and he was employed here until 1924, in which year the owner of the establishment reported Frank's disappearance to the police, together with the information that the missing man had stolen an old revolver, and he gave the serial number of the revolver. Three years later, the skeleton of an aged male was discovered in a canyon on the outskirts of Martinez, California. The

[32] Miss Williams, although occasionally listed as an attraction at the Birdcage Theater, was much in demand by the army of uncultured slobs who patronized the red-light district wherein she spent most of her time.

[33] A soft berth, which Frank may have been eased into by John Behan, a onetime lawman of Tombstone who, at that time, was a Yuma turnkey.

[34] Whether Leslie was christened "Nashville" or whether he assumed this name to fog his past cannot be ascertained.

bones were never officially identified, but a rusty revolver found near the remains bore the same serial number as the gun that had been stolen in 1924. So was this the end of "Buckskin" Frank Leslie? No one knows for sure—for the gun may have changed hands after being stolen—but if Frank did become a suicide shortly after stealing the gun, he would have been about eighty-two years of age at the time of his death. (See CLAIBORNE, BILLY; KILLEEN, MIKE D.; and RING-GOLD, JOHN.)

LEVI'S   Invented—possibly by accident[35]—in 1848 by a San Francisco tailor named Levi Straus. Levi's, which are copper-riveted at stress points, were originally regarded as overalls rather than as trousers. They are still being manufactured by the Levi Straus Company.

LEVY, JIM   A bit player in the saga of the West whose moment of glory occurred in 1877, when he emerged victorious from one of those typical Main Street shootouts. The auditorium was Cheyenne, Wyoming, and the prologue to this affair was set in Bowlby's Gambling Saloon, where an argument developed between Levy and a gunnie named Charlie Harrison. Both men were unarmed at the time, but when tempers reached killing pitch they hurried off to collect their hardware, thus allowing a short interval before the main event during which their audience could place bets on the outcome. Levy was a new arrival from Deadwood, and as little was known about his pistol prowess, Harrison was the favored one.[36] The interval over, the street cleared, and Levy and Harrison played out their deadly game against a backdrop of the Dyer House. Charlie shuttled his trigger to shake out all his loads in a magnificent display of firepower, while Jim took his time and sent one piece of lead at his rival. That single bullet disappeared into Charlie's smoke screen and killed him instantly. Charlie was carried into the local undertaker's, and thus ended one of the classic gun duels of the West. An aura of glory was still hanging around Levy when he was shot dead by Dave Neagle in Arizona Territory some years later.

LEWIS AND CLARK EXPEDITION   A survey expedition that was sponsored by Thomas Jefferson and that got under way in the spring of 1804 when Meriwether Lewis and William Clark led a party of twenty-seven men out of St. Louis, Missouri, on a trail-blazing trip across the uncharted West. These pioneers moved across what is now Nebraska, the Dakotas, Montana, and Washington, a journey that took eighteen months and during which they established friendly relations with numerous Indian tribes and made copious notes regarding terrain, etc. The expedition arrived back in St. Louis in September 1806, and although it can only be classed as a moderately successful geographical survey, it was of major importance inasmuch as it sparked a nation's imagination and stimulated westerly migration. (See SACAGAWEA.)

LEWIS, MERIWETHER   Prior to his becoming nationally known as the leader of the Lewis and Clark Expedition, Lewis, who was born in Virginia in 1774,

---

[35] The story being that Straus used copper rivets to repair the denim pants of an old prospector, and the client's enthusiasm for the riveting job persuaded Levi to use copper rivets from then on.

[36] The folk of Cheyenne were obviously unaware that Mr. Levy had killed a man named Mike Casey in Pioche, Nevada, some years earlier.

had served in the American infantry and spent some time as the private secretary of President Thomas Jefferson. As a tribute to his success as leader of the 1804–6 survey expedition, on his return Lewis was appointed governor of Louisiana Territory, a position he was holding at the time of his death in 1809.[37] (See LEWIS AND CLARK EXPEDITION.)

LIDDELL, DICK Born in Jackson County, Missouri, in 1852, Dick started his working life as a laborer on the Hudspeth brothers' farm near Independence, Missouri,[38] and it was here that he met the James brothers in the fall of 1879 and became an on-and-off member of their gang. Liddell hasn't left many tracks, but it is known that he spent much of 1880 in Tennessee with the James boys; took part in the Winston train robbery of July 15, 1881; shot Wood Hite to death in December 1881; did an eight-month stretch in an Alabama jail from September 1882 to April 1883; and was a state witness at the trial of Frank James in July 1883. Some years later we catch a glimpse of Dick in Las Vegas, New Mexico, where he is running a saloon in partnership with Bob Ford. After this his trail disappeared. (See HITE, WOOD, and JAMES GANG.)

LILLIE, GORDON W. A small, stocky individual who became one of the big names of American show business in the latter years of the nineteenth century. Gordon, however, was anything but a dude. Born at Bloomington, Illinois, in 1860, he left home at an early age, spending most of his teen years with the buffalo hunters of the North Plains, years during which he developed a latent linguistic ability to the full, being fluent in Pawnee and other Indian tongues when the twilight of the hide trade persuaded him to seek his fortune elsewhere. In 1882 he was working as a cowhand on the Zimmerman Ranch in Oklahoma, but as his fame as an interpreter spread, he became much in demand as an aide to the U. S. Government in its relations with the Indians, and life on the range was reduced to a minimum. Over this period as an interpreter he was made an honorary chief of the Pawnees, after which he is usually referred to as "Pawnee Bill," a name that made for good billing when Mr. Lillie broke into show business in the spring of 1888.

Pawnee, whose only connection with show biz prior to this time had been in the supplying of a quota of genuine red Indians to the Buffalo Bill shows, opened his Frontier Exhibition in Philadelphia, but a snowstorm of freightage bills from the railroads soon began to flatten the show into the ground, and a timely merger with a rival show that had the names of Annie Oakley and Frank Butler on its broadsheets was the only thing that kept Lillie solvent. Years later, and free of partners, the Pawnee Bill Far East show toured Europe, giving performances before the crowned and uncrowned heads of the Continent, as Cody had done in earlier years. By 1910 Pawnee Bill's most serious rival, the Buffalo Bill tenting empire, was wallowing in debt, and on being made aware of this,

[37] This occurred in October of the year when Lewis was traveling through Tennessee. Two pistol shots were heard shortly after the governor had retired to the sleeping quarters of his lodgings, and the following morning he was found dead from gunshot wounds. Whether Meriwether was a suicide or a murder victim has never been resolved, for although lack of both money and jewelry pointed to his being an armed-robbery casualty, there remains the possibility that some unknown party may have been attracted by the shots and, upon investigating their source, have stripped the corpse of valuables.

[38] Around 1874–76 this employment was interrupted while Dick served two years and seven months in the penitentiary for some unascertainable offense.

Lillie, who had a great admiration for the older man, threw Cody a lifebelt: The two shows merged, and Lillie paid off the outstanding debts. The Buffalo Bill Wild West and Pawnee Bill Far East Show went on the road in 1911, and it is hardly surprising that an enterprise with such schizophrenic billing should only survive until 1913; an avalanche of debts forced the two Bills into bankruptcy, and the whole show was auctioned off to help settle up with the bill wavers. In later years, Lillie and his wife[39] settled on a ranch they had established near Pawnee, Oklahoma, during the boom years, and Pawnee Bill died here on February 3, 1942. (See CODY, WILLIAM FREDERICK, and OAKLEY, ANNIE.)

LINCOLN COUNTY WAR A war that had its origins in a clash of commercial interests. On one side were Major L. G. Murphy and James J. Dolan, partners in a monopolistic banking and mercantile operation; two gentlemen who were backed by U. S. Attorney Thomas B. Catron; had the county sheriff, William Brady, in their combined pockets; and were not averse to buying stolen cattle.[40] These neopolitical big wheels, together with an assortment of hired guns who were usually referred to as "possemen," were the men in the black hats. On the other side of the fence were an Englishman named John Henry Tunstall; John S. Chisum, a rancher whose herds were being thinned out to keep the baddies in cheap beef; and Alexander A. McSween, Tunstall's partner in an attempt to break the

Murphy-Dolan stranglehold. These were the men in the light sombreros.

In 1877 Tunstall and McSween, with the backing of Chisum, opened the combined Lincoln County Bank and General Store. This was located in Lincoln, New Mexico, and was directly across the street from the Murphy-Dolan premises. The new enterprise, which didn't resort to the sharp practice of the pioneer establishment across the street, prospered at the expense of its rival, and Murphy and Dolan got their minds working to find a solution to the problem. In February 1878 Murphy pressured Sheriff Brady to arrest Tunstall on a trumped-up charge of horse theft, and on February 18 the Englishman was murdered by a posse of hastily deputized gunmen. This started a powdersmoke haze that was to hang over Lincoln County for many months to come.

Billy the Kid, a fast lad with a gun and a rustler who had been trail herding large numbers of Chisum's stock into the Murphy-Dolan corral, had become deeply attached to the Englishman,[41] and on learning of the latter's murder, he speedily switched sombreros, rounded up a few of his buddies, and went searching for targets. Sheriff Brady and a few of his "deputies" died with their boots on, and the occasional self-professed neutral such as Buckshot Roberts fared no better.[42] These guerrilla tactics continued until July 1878, when the last "battle" of the war was waged from within and around the McSween home. Here Billy the Kid, a dozen of his buddies, and Mr. and Mrs. McSween held out for three days against an army of lawmen and gunmen, the

---

[39] A girl named Mae, whom Gordon had married in 1886. Shortly after celebrating their golden wedding anniversary in 1936, Mae was killed in an automobile crash.

[40] These were needed to fulfill government contracts to supply reservation Indians with beef cattle.

[41] This was mutual, for Tunstall had a high regard for Billy.

[42] It was safer to back one or the other of the warring factions, for both sides appear to have shot at neutrals.

services of the U. S. Army being required
to bring about a cease-fire. As far as this
entry is concerned the siege of the Mc-
Sween home can be considered to mark
an end to the Lincoln County War, but
as some twoscore men died over this
period of violence, debris from this affair
may be found in a number of entries.
(See ANDREWS, JESSE; BAKER, FRANK;
BARBER, SUSAN MCSWEEN; BECKWITH,
ROBERT; BRADY, WILLIAM; BREWER,
DICK; DOLAN, JAMES J.; MCCARTY,
HENRY; MCNAB, FRANK; MCSWEEN,
ALEXANDER A.; and TUNSTALL, JOHN
HENRY.)

LINN, CHARLES N. "BUCK"
Friend of flamboyant gunnie Bill Rayner.
(See RAYNER, BILL.)

LISA, MANUEL   A Spaniard from
New Orleans who established a fur-
trading and river-freightage empire. In
1800 Lisa founded the Missouri Fur
Company, and but a few years later,
trading posts had been established in Missouri, Arkansas, and the Southwest. After the successful return of the Lewis and
Clark Expedition in 1806, the enterprising Latin was stimulated into extending
his area of operations, and in 1807 he
pushed into the Northwest and erected
a trading fort on the Yellowstone.[43]
Some five years later, during the British-
American War of 1812, Lisa, although
regarded as a "furriner" and incapable
of pronouncing but a few words of English, helped the American cause by instigating intertribal clashes between the
plains tribes at a time when the British
were attempting to unite the Indians and
align them to the British cause. Even so,

Meriwether Lewis regarded him as a
"scoundrel and a puppy," while others
considered him to be full of "rascality"
and "villainy." Whatever folks' opinions,
Lisa continued to use his fleet of rivercraft to shuttle trade goods or pelts between his outposts and his St. Louis, Missouri, headquarters, and in 1819 he
opened a further post in Nebraska.[44]
This was to be the limit of the Lisa empire, for Manuel died on August 12,
1820, at the age of forty-nine years. Manuel Lisa contracted three marriages during his lifetime, the brides of his choice
being two white girls and a Mandan
Indian girl.

LITTLE BRITCHES   As this teen-
age lass—together with Cattle Annie—resisted arrest with both tooth and claw,
one wonders if this nickname is but an
incorrect rendering of an arresting
officer's exclamation. (See STEVENS,
JENNIE.)

LITTLE CASINO   A nickname
affixed to Billy the Kid by the gambling
fraternity of Fort Sumner, New Mexico.
Pat Garrett—all 6 feet, 4 inches of him—
who was acquainted with the Kid and
frequented the same dives, was Big
Casino.

LITTLE PETE   One of the many
hatchetmen who accepted skull-splitting
contracts from the various Chinese tongs
that operated along the Pacific Coast
from around 1860 until the 1920s. Little
Pete—his Chinese names sound like the
roll call of a Cantonese chorus line[45]—
had been born in China in 1864, but as
he was brought to San Francisco at an

[43] This post was located near the present-day town of Custer, Montana.
[44] Usually accepted as being in Iowa, but as it was located some ten miles NNW of where
the present-day town of Council Bluffs is situated, the post may have been on the west bank
of the Missouri, in which case a Nebraska location is correct.
[45] Fung Gow alias Fung Jing Toy, or vice versa.

early age, by the time he reached adulthood he was a completely Westernized "heathen." By 1885 Pete was the owner of a shoe factory on Washington Street, a legitimate enterprise initially financed by monies accrued from our little villain's less honorable pursuits: "poppy" peddling, dealing in female slaves for the concubine market, dispatching by hatcheting, kidnaping, and the rigging of lotteries being just a few of the fascinating yet off-color endeavors he is known to have busied himself with.

How many of the split-personalities found lying around in the alleys of the local Chinatown were the handiwork of Little Pete has never been ascertained, but as a member of the Gin Sin Seer highbinder society, he is known to have accepted a number of "kill contracts." On one occasion, Pete chopped a high-ranking member of the Suey On tong into the morgue, whereupon the Suey Ons immediately employed rival hatchetmen to equate matters out. These killers —three in number—caught up with Little Pete in a suitably dark alley, but when one of them swung his hatchet down upon its skullcap target, there was a metallic "clang" instead of the more accustomary "thunk," while torso blows being administered by the other members of the trio were merely producing "clinking" sounds. Pete now went into action, and two of his attackers were dispatched by his chopper while their fingers still tingled. The third man escaped, it thus becoming known that Little Pete owed his immunity to a chain-mail shirt and headgear made of steel. Armed with this knowledge, two more killers went on the

trail of Little Pete. These men dispensed with their hatchets, and they were armed with revolvers of .45 caliber when they descended upon Pete on the evening of January 23, 1897. The Terror of Chinatown was sitting in a barber's chair[46] when two men entered the tonsorial parlor and put two bullets into his uncapped head. Pete was pretty well used up by then, but the gunmen were perfectionists: The muzzle of a .45 was inserted beneath the chain-mail shirt, and it was only after a series of muffled explosions had ensured a more even distribution of lead that the executioners left the premises. (See CHINESE TONGS.)

LITTLE WOLF A warrior chief of the northern Cheyenne who had waged war against the U. S. Army in the Montana-Wyoming region for more than a decade prior to his surrendering in 1877.[47] Shortly after laying down their arms, more than 900 northern Cheyenne —among whom was Little Wolf—were moved South, arriving at the Darlington Agency in Indian Territory (Oklahoma) on August 5, 1877. The reservation was a featureless expanse, possessing a poverty of game and water and having but few trees to shade its arid acreage. Here the Cheyenne were plagued by flies and smitten with both corporal and spiritual sickness, and on September 9, 1878, Chiefs Little Wolf and Dull Knife left the agency accompanied by 335 followers.[48] Talking wires spread the news, and bugles got the dust stirring in numerous forts and barracks, but the Cheyenne had moved a hundred miles to the north and crossed into Kansas before

[46] As Pete was a typical pigtailed Chinese of the period, he was most likely having a head shave and a queue cut.

[47] It was Little Wolf's band—working under the direction of Chief Red Cloud—that burned Fort Phil Kearny to the ground in 1868. This warrior chief was also prominent at the Battle on the Little Big Horn in 1876.

[48] There were only 89 men—many of whom could hardly be classed as prime fighting stock —in this group.

the yellow-stripes found them. The Indians had few guns, but after a minor
engagement in which three troopers were
killed, the soldiers retired, and Little
Wolf led his followers due West, pausing
briefly south of the Arkansas to loot a
hide-hunters' camp of much-needed rifles
and ammunition before swinging North
once more.

On September 23 the Cheyenne
crossed the Arkansas and the Santa Fe
tracks east of Dodge City, then pushed
on in a northwesterly direction. More
troops were now in the field, and clashes
between fugitives and soldiers became
more frequent, but after three engagements in western Kansas and a further
one in southeastern Nebraska, the Cheyenne were still pushing North. Military
technicians, who now had more than
12,000 troops at their disposal, reasoned
that the Indians would have to cross the
Union Pacific's iron somewhere between
the North Platte and Sidney, Nebraska,
and trains loaded with troops were stationed along this 200 miles of track in an
attempt to halt the renegades' march to
their homeland in Montana. Army reasoning was sound, but their barrier was
ineffective. The Indians, in small groups
and under the cover of darkness, ghosted
their ponies between gaps in the perfora-
tions of light streaming from the railroad
cars, and by first light, pony and moccasin tracks were the only evidence of
their passing.

Some forty miles north of where they
had breached the barrier,[49] Dull Knife
and Little Wolf parted company, the
former chief leading about 150 followers
into the sand hills to the northwest with
the intention of reaching the old Red

Cloud Agency, while Little Wolf and the
remainder continued on a true northerly
course. Most of Dull Knife's Cheyenne
found death in northwestern Nebraska,
but Little Wolf's band succeeded in
reaching their homeland on the Powder
River in Montana in March 1879. Here
they surrendered and were moved to Fort
Keogh, but this was little more than a
show of official muscle, and a short time
later they were allowed to return to their
tepees. Never again were they ever harassed or molested; the 1,000-mile trek
from Oklahoma had been very worthwhile. Little Wolf died in 1904 at the age
of 83 years, and his remains were interred on the Tongue River Reservation.
(See DULL KNIFE.)

"LIVER-EATING" JOHNSON
A cannibalistic character who usually appears under this name but whose correct
name was Johnston. (See JOHNSTON,
JOHN.)

LLANO ESTACADO
The Staked Plains of western Texas
and eastern New Mexico. (See STAKED
PLAINS.)

LOCO WEED A weed that grows in
most areas of the West,[50] scarlet loco
weed being the most common variety. As
this weed possesses great moisture-
holding properties, it remains a bright
chlorophyll green during periods of
drought, attractions that may be the reason for its being sought by range stock,
horses, cattle, and sheep evidently being
unmindful of the fact that after an intake
of such greenery they become subject to
fits of crazy behavior.[51] Horses in particular become quite addicted to the

---

[49] The track crossing was made within sight of the town of Oglala.

[50] Loco, Texas, is reputed to have been named after this botanical bomb.

[51] As most grazing animals avoid any plant whose adverse effects they have learned
from experience, it could well be they enjoy being "hooked." If one accepts the foregoing
assumption, it would appear that the hoofed members of the animal kingdom may have a
drug problem to contend with at some future date.

weed. Sometimes referred to as "crazy weed."

LOCUST   Any member of the seven genera of short-horned grasshoppers that are classed as locusts. When migrating, a cloud of these grasshoppers may be half a mile in depth and blot out the sun over an area of more than 2,000 square miles, and when such a flight descends to feed, an area far in excess of the cloud will be stripped of all vegetation and anything else the insects find palatable. The Rocky Mountain locust—which is usually referred to as the "American grasshopper"—is about 2 inches in length, possesses a reddish-colored body, and has wings that are speckled with black and white markings. From the early days of settlement in the West reports of localized plagues of locusts have found their way into the press, stories of the Salt Lake City incident of May 1848 possibly having reached a greater audience than any other of these settlers vs. insects news items.[52] The year 1874 saw a full-scale invasion of the insects. From Oregon to Minnesota and down into Texas, airborne armies rained from the skies in countless millions, each separate cloud establishing complete dominion over areas of as much as 150,000 square miles by sheer weight of numbers. They stripped the land clean. Crops vanished overnight and trees took on the appearance of driftwood, and when all greenery had been removed from the land, leather harnesses, clothing, and soft wood were chomped through for dessert. Railroad trains skidded to a standstill on tracks made impassable by the bodies of the invaders' "glorious dead," and the state treasury of Minnesota became bankrupt through paying out a bounty of $.50 a bushel on the bloated corpses of the enemy. When there was nothing left to forage, the armies of insects disappeared, leaving in their wake thousands of impoverished settlers, many of whom had, quite literally, been victimized down to their underpants. Thus it was that 1874 became known as the "Year of the Grasshopper."

LOGAN, HARVEY   Harvey and his three brothers—Louis, Johnny, and Henry —all of whom were Virginia-born, descended upon some kinfolk at Dodson, Missouri, in 1875, a quartet of Anglo-Amerind mixed-bloods who were seeking free board and lodgings after their paw had become dead and their maw had become missing. At this time Harvey was ten years old and the senior member and undisputed leader of the Logan brood, and it was he who, some eight years later, persuaded brothers Louis and Johnny[53] to dust from Missouri and head West, allegedly stolen mounts being used for this purpose. Over the next few years the Logans are reputed to have worked on various ranches in Wyoming and to have rustled stock when the occasion permitted; could well be, for by the late 1880s they were excellent gun handlers, somewhat bowed of leg from much saddle polishing, and all using the alias of "Curry"[54] when they considered it expedient to do so.

Sometime in 1888 Harvey and his brothers, together with a flat-faced kinsman named Bob Lee, either bought

---

[52] A plague from which the Mormon settlement of Salt Lake City emerged victorious, all "praise bes" going to a gigantic flock of seagulls that allied themselves to the saints' cause by feeding upon the invading force before irreparable damage could be done. A monument to this "miracle"—the Seagull Monument—is located in Salt Lake City's Temple Square.

[53] Henry always remained a "home boy" and never got into any trouble with the law.

[54] They most likely adopted this name because one of the all-time "greats" of the rustling fraternity—George Manuse—used the alias of George Curry. One does read of the Logans having ridden with the Manuse gang, but this is unlikely, as George was strung up in 1881.

or leased a broken-down ranch located near Landusky, Montana, stocking this spread with cattle most likely stolen from the Powder River country of Wyoming and periodically making trips to nearby Landusky for supplies and entertainment. Harvey was now a twenty-three-year-old veteran of the range, a man of medium height with dark brown hair who cultivated a waterfall mustache which, by masking his lips, endowed him with the deadpan expression of the dedicated gunman. This was the "Kid Curry" the folk of Landusky were to know over the next six years—a hard-eyed lad who spent most of his leisure hours in the local saloons but who also became involved with a gal named Elfie, a free-roaming chicken who was a stepdaughter of Pike Landusky, founder and No. 1 citizen of the settlement. Harvey may have meant well by Elfie, for through 1889 he undertook honest employment as a cowhand on the Diamond Ranch, but by 1894 Elfie, although still unwed, was showing ominous signs of having been effectively "Curried," and after a dispute with Pike involving the pregnant one's honor, Harvey shot Landusky to death and fled the state accompanied by Louis and Johnny.[55]

The Logans didn't allow their dust to settle until they reached the outlaw hideout of Hole in the Wall in Wyoming, a natural stronghold from which numerous bands of owlhoots operated. Here the Logan brothers were to become fully qualified buscaderos, most likely gaining experience in all forms of outlawry as members of Black Jack Ketchum's gang. In the fall of 1895, Harvey heard news that a rancher named James Winters, who lived near Landusky, had been "informing on the Curry brothers," and in

January 1896 the Logans rode back into Montana with the express intention of making a stiffened example of the bigmouth. Winters, however, was a good man with a scattergun, and after Johnny Logan had been blasted into a pine box, Harvey and Louis returned to Wyoming, their mission unaccomplished. Shortly after their return to the Hole, and after taking part in a Ketchum gang train job, Harvey quarreled with Black Jack, and from then on the Logans may be classed as members of Butch Cassidy's Wild Bunch, Cassidy being a rather good-natured slob who had arrived in the Hole during the Logans' absence.

On June 27 of the following year Harvey Logan, together with the Sundance Kid and two other Wild Bunch gunnies, was arrested and lodged in the Deadwood, South Dakota, jail after an attempted bank robbery at nearby Belle Fourche, but Harvey spent little time behind bars, for he and Sundance succeeded in escaping, and they were back with Cassidy in November. The surviving Logans' next big job with the Wild Bunch was the Union Pacific train robbery at Wilcox, Wyoming, on June 2, 1899, Harvey being responsible for the killing of Sheriff Joseph Hazen during a gunfight with a posse of lawmen who were still in their dust some seventy-two hours after the robbery. After this affair, the Logan brothers parted company, Harvey fleeing South with Cassidy, Sundance Kid, Ben Kilpatrick, and Bill Carver, while Louis lit out for their foster parents' home at Dodson, Missouri. The five who had ridden South went to ground at Fort Worth, Texas, where, dressed as city dudes and domiciled within the luxurious surroundings of Fannie Porter's bagnio, they remained for some time. Louis Logan wasn't this

---

[55] After this episode Elfie referred to herself as "Elfie Curry," and there is little doubt that she kept in touch with Harvey Logan for many years after this.

lucky: Law-enforcement agencies got a line on his whereabouts, and at eight o'clock on the morning of February 28, 1900, lawmen visited the farm at Dodson. Louis met them with blazing guns, an inhospitable act that resulted in him being puppeted about by slugs until he was dead.

Meanwhile, Cassidy, Harvey, and company had left Fannie's place, and they were now hanging around their Robber's Roost headquarters in southeastern Utah, and it was here that they received news that a fellow "Buncher" who was a pal of Harvey's had been killed by the lawmen of Moab County, Utah. On hearing this, Harvey, as was his wont, traveled North to equalize matters, and on May 16, at Moab, he killed Sheriff John Tyler and Deputy Sheriff Sam Jenkins in a street shootout. One month later, he is reputed to have killed two brothers named Norman, and on August 29 he was giving the Wild Bunch a hand when they robbed a Union Pacific train at Table Rock, near Tipton, Wyoming; then another trip to Fannie's place to spend some of his loot and become reacquainted with a member of the fleshpot's staff,[56] a passionate interlude that carried Logan well into the spring of 1901.

On July 3, 1901, he was back on the treadmill of dishonest endeavor, helping Cassidy rob a Great Northern train at Wagner, Montana; three weeks later Harvey headed for Landusky, where, on July 26, he settled an old score by emptying a full cylinder of lead into James Winters. After ensuring that Winters was dead, Harvey fled South with his pockets full of currency, and we don't hear much from him again until the close of the year. On December 13, 1901, a head-splitting fandango in a Knoxville, Tennessee, poolroom brought three cops to the scene, and it was only after two of the cops had been wounded that a derby-hatted, cue- and pistol-waving drunk was subdued. The drunk was finally recognized as Harvey "Kid Curry" Logan, and on November 2, 1902, he was given a twenty-year stretch for his fit of bad temper. Accustomed to the wide-open spaces and the joys of Madame Porter's, Logan liked jail far less than any city boy, and on June 27, 1903, he overpowered a guard, came into possession of a brace of revolvers, and made his escape at gunpoint. After shaking off pursuit, Logan is known to have become obsessed with the idea of joining Cassidy and Sundance in South America, the latter two having left the country shortly after the Wagner train robbery. There is some evidence[57]

[56] A tall, good-looking strumpet named Annie Rogers. Annie was photographed with Harvey—possibly on more than one occasion—and she remained his favorite for about three years.

[57] (1) Toward the end of 1903 the various police forces of Bolivia, Chile, and Peru were complaining to the U. S. State Department about three North American outlaws who were committing bank and train robberies in their territories. The South American authorities named the three men as being Butch Cassidy, Harvey Logan, and the Sundance Kid. (2) The manuscripts of the late Lieutenant Colonel P. H. Fawcett—as edited by Brian Fawcett and published by Hutchinson's of London in 1953 under the title *Exploration Fawcett*—devote some thirty-four lines of text to a Texan gunman named Harvey whom Fawcett met at Rurenabaque, Bolivia, on three occasions over the years 1907–13. This Harvey is described as being very fast with a handgun, and as having large rewards hanging over his head back in the States; also mentioned is the fact Harvey wasn't much of a talker until he'd had quite a few drinks. The latter points are worth noting, for Logan's Stateside file mentions a "reserved manner" and "heavy drinking habits." (3) There are other reports of Harvey Logan being sighted in Bolivia, so the gunman of Rurenabaque may have been Kid Curry. The fact that Fawcett describes "Harvey" as a "Texan gunman" means little, for to every non-American an outlaw from the States is usually regarded as a Texan gunman.

that Logan reached Bolivia and joined his fellow "Bunchers," although the Pinkertons would have us believe otherwise, closing their "Kid Curry" file after the following chain of incidents.

A bare ten days after Logan's escape, three outlaws held up and robbed a train near Parachute, Colorado. Posses were soon on their trail, and on July 9 a gun battle ensued near Glenwood Springs. When the smoke cleared, two of the gang had managed to escape, but the third man was found lying dead from a self-inflicted head wound. The body was brought into Glenwood Springs, where many of the locals readily identified it as being the remains of Tap Duncan, a Texas cowhand who had been working in the area. On hearing of this, the Pinkertons insisted that the corpse be photographed to aid identification, and although the resultant camera work shows us a haggard-faced individual with an extremely pointed nose who is wearing a battered hat and a moth-eaten cardigan, a top-echelon Pink and some of the Knoxville jail guards insisted that Tap Duncan was in reality Harvey "Kid Curry" Logan. If the Pinks are correct, Harvey must have been a remarkable lad; in the twelve days that elapsed between his escape and his death, he had covered some fourteen hundred miles of territory (as the crow flies), established himself as a ranchhand with a completely new identity, organized a small gang, committed a train robbery, and spent two days on the run. (See HOLE IN THE WALL GANG; KETCHUM, TOM; LANDUSKY, PIKE; PARKER, ROBERT LEROY; and WILD BUNCH.)

LOGAN, JOHNNY One of the in-

famous Logan (alias Curry) brothers. (See LOGAN, HARVEY.)

LOGAN, LONNY Family nickname applied to Louis, youngest of the three Logan brothers who became outlaws. (See LOGAN, HARVEY.)

LOGAN, LOUIS Usually referred to as "Lonny" or "Lonnie." (See LOGAN, HARVEY.)

LONGBAUGH, HARRY
Better known as the Sundance Kid, although this musical-sounding name was but one of a string of aliases—(Kid Longbaugh, Harry Alonzo, Harry Place, and John Arnold[58])—that Longbaugh used to cloud his whereabouts over his outlaw years. Longbaugh is reputed to have been born at Plainfield, New Jersey, in 1866, but whether he had the "God-fearing, industrious" parents that almost every other outlaw with a vague background is reported to have been either blessed or saddled with is unknown. Harry must have left home at a tender age, for his Pinkerton press releases aware us to the fact that he served eighteen months in the jail at Sundance, Wyoming, for horse theft "when a boy." From this time onward he was the Sundance Kid, a young man with an Indian cast to his features who developed into a "highwayman, bank burglar, cattle and horse thief," and the fastest gun in the Wild Bunch. Upon his release from the Wyoming jail, Sundance worked as a cowhand, possibly remaining honest until the blizzard of 1887 left but few cattle to chaperone—a natural calamity that rendered thousands of waddies redundant.

From about 1888 until 1892, Sundance most likely rode with any, or

---

[58] "John Arnold" must only be regarded as a possibility, the inclusion of this alias being prompted by the fact that a photographic print that is alleged to be of Arnold has obviously been reproduced from the same plate as that which has given us a likeness of Harry Longbaugh.

many, of the various bands of rustlers who plagued the Powder River country of Wyoming, for his first definitive act of train robbery didn't occur until shortly after the cattlemen's invasion of Wyoming –the Johnson County War–had dispersed the rustlers from the area. In December 1892 Sundance, aided by two jobless cowhands named Bill Madden and Harry Bass, held up and robbed a train near Malta, Montana.[59] This was big-time stuff from which there was no turning back, and for many years afterward the outlaw hideouts of Hole in the Wall (Wyoming), Brown's Hole (located where the boundaries of Wyoming, Colorado, and Utah meet), and Robber's Roost (in southeastern Utah) were to see much of Sundance. In 1896 he became acquainted –or re-acquainted–with Butch Cassidy, and from then on Sundance's destiny was to be inextricably linked with that of Cassidy's. (See LOGAN, HARVEY; PARKER, ROBERT LEROY; and WILD BUNCH.)

LONGHORNS   The wild progeny of Andalusian cattle that had been allowed to lose their domestic status some three centuries earlier. (See CATTLE.)

LONGLEY, WILLIAM P. Reputed to have killed thirty-two men, most of whom are unnamed, but all of whom may be classed as murder victims. By resorting to the familiar practices of blackening the characters of his victims, dropping veiled hints of their six-gun abilities, or having them sneer their way into a stomachful of lead, many misguided souls have elevated William Preston Longley into the gunfighter category.

Nothing could be farther from the truth. This beanpole of a man with the oxbow mustache and billy-goat beard used his gun as a first-degree murder tool rather than as a defensive weapon. William was born on August 6, 1851, in Austin County, Texas, of parents who are usually rubber-stamped "God-fearing and hard-working," fears and attributes which can hardly have been passed on to William, as he was hanged for murder on October 11, 1878. Between the date of his birth and the date of his being "returned to sender," this Texas gunman left little more than a pile of dead men whom folk have been trying to pigeonhole ever since, so let us follow in the wake of his horse droppings, ticking off and burying his reputed victims as we come to them.

It is now 1866 and Longley, aged fifteen, is fleeing Houston, Texas, after shooting a black state policeman to death, the latter having talked himself into an early grave by asking Bill–in an "arrogant manner"–to identify himself. On to Lexington, Texas, where, but a short time after qualifying for his first notch, Bill kills two black men who happen to be dancing (arrogantly?) in the street.[60] The white folk were now calling him "Wild Bill" and "Nigger Killer," while the heavily pigmented section of the community was accurately referring to him as "white trash," so, possibly loath to vacate the spotlight, Wild Bill continued to keep his public happy. In the summer of 1868 he shot up a circus after being refused free admission, fun stuff that was followed up by his killing another black man in the fall and his termination of a U. S. Army sergeant's lease on life on Christmas Day.

[59] The Sundance Kid managed to avoid arrest for this caper, but Bill Madden and Harry Bass (no relation to Sam) weren't that lucky: They were quickly picked up, subsequently tried, and given ten and fourteen years, respectively.

[60] Some reports state that he was wearing a KKK-type hood while engaged in this homicidal activity.

After this he joined Cullen Baker's band of farm looters, and it is during this period that Longley is reputed to have had his famous hairsbreadth escape from death at the hands of vigilantes,[61] an incredible incident that tends to overshadow the stories of him having gunned seven men into a like number of cemeteries over the same period. When Baker collided with a few long-overdue pieces of lead in 1869, Bill reverted to his loner status, killing eight black men in and around Evergreen, Texas, without any fear of having to share the kudos for the acts.

We next meet up with Bill when he is engaged in a spot of honest toil. A cattleman named James Rector is moving beeves through Kansas, en route from Texas to Utah, and Bill is trail herding with the outfit; like Wild Bill, Rector has some tame relatives up in Utah and he is working his passage thataway to pay them a visit. From Texas to Utah is quite a piece to travel[62] without gunplay, so somewhere in Kansas, Bill killed the "overbearing" Rector, putting five bullets into his victim.[63] By the time they were replacing the turf over Rector, Wild Bill was having a beer in nearby Abilene— one for the road before visiting his kin and killing a soldier in Salt Lake City. The Army got him for this offense, transported him back to Kansas, and threw him in the Fort Leavenworth stockade. Some reports state he escaped from Leavenworth, while others have him doing a two-year stretch for the killing, so to play it safe we'll not get him back in

the saddle until some two years later, around which time another killing occurs that sounds vaguely familiar: Wild Bill makes an "unscrupulous" sergeant very dead and is tossed into the Leavenworth stockade, only to escape after a brisk trial and but a short time before he was to be shot at dawn. The ouija board will neither confirm nor deny the incidents and alternative incidents relating to Bill's clashes with the military.

By 1874 Bill was still floating around, killing a "card cheat" in Kansas around this time, then moving back into Texas, where he killed an unarmed "bully" whom he had also accused of "stacking the deck." During the years 1875 and 1876, his trail masked by such aliases as James Webb, William Black, Tom Jones, and Jim Patterson, Longley was busy making corpses in Texas: a brace of Mexicans who may have been armed, and an unarmed man named Wilson Anderson, this trio being quickly followed to the grave by another of those "arrogant" black men, a certain Reverend W. R. Lay, and a man named Cooper.[64] By the middle of 1876, Texas Rangers were looking under rocks for Wild Bill Longley, so our subject rode across the line into Louisiana with the object of laying low, a move that kept him at liberty until May 13, 1877, on which day—a Sunday—he was arrested and whisked back to Texas. Two days later, at Giddings, Texas, Wild Bill found himself being charged with the murder of Wilson Anderson. Bill made no more escapes. After a two-day trial in September, he

---

[61] This instant-justice team strung Bill up high for horse theft. They then rode away, displaying their jubilation with much firing of guns as they disappeared into the yonder, the whole mob remaining blissfully unaware of the fact that one of their bullets had severed Bill's rope before he'd time to gurgle his way into eternity.

[62] Especially if one makes such an oxbow detour as Rector appears to have been making.

[63] A brilliant display of ultrafast pistolwork? Could be; on the other hand, Rector may have been a very slow-moving individual who took his own sweet time in bedding down.

[64] Bill may have had a genuine grievance here, for it is suspected that Cooper may have been arranging to trade Bill in for a two-thousand-dollar reward.

was found "guilty as charged" and sentenced to death, a much-deserved sentence that was carried out on October 11, 1877. Rumors abound that Longley was cut down before he expired and hustled south of the border with little more than a stiff neck, but such stories can only be classed as utter rubbish; after Bill had been cut down, some four thousand spectators were witness to the fact that his head could be rotated until his billy-goat beard was resting between his shoulder blades. (See BAKER, CULLEN M.)

LOST MINES Throughout the gold- and silver-bearing regions of the West, and in many areas where geological formations make credible the suggestion of hidden wealth, stories of "lost mines" abound. Their approximate locations are sprinkled like confetti on the map, small X's that are frequently "questioned" by the metal detectors of contemporary bonanza hunters. Some of these mines, river deposits, and outcroppings of precious metals that have "gone missing" most certainly exist, and it is reasonable to suppose that many a desert rat, if lucky enough to locate such a prize, would allow it to remain in the "lost" category while he quietly amassed a tax-free fortune. The reasons for a find becoming lost are many and varied: A badly orientated prospector may lose his bearings after a flash flood has given a new look to the terrain; minor earth tremors can readjust rock formations, thus altering their appearance; and Indians would frequently remove all trace of an area having been worked after they had disposed of the workers. Brief details relating to the better known of these legendary jackpots may be found below, a list that is far from extensive, owing to the limitations of space.

Lost Adams. Discovered in 1864 by a party of prospectors led by a man known only as Adams, the white men having been led to the gold-bearing dry wash by an Apache half-breed. A short time after their having made the find, Apaches killed a number of the party and put the survivors to flight, and for the next decade war parties made the area untenable for white men. The "mine" can be considered lost from then on, for after the Apache problem had been resolved, some ten years later, Adams returned to the area but was unable to relocate the canyon wherein lay the gold. Located in one of the many canyons that lie south of the Little Colorado River in northeast-central Arizona, a canyon reputed to have been named Sno-ta-hay by the Apaches. Usually referred to as the "Lost Adams Diggings." The film *Mackenna's Gold*[65] was based on the facts and legends surrounding the Lost Adams.

Lost Blue Bucket. In 1846 some pioneers from a wagon train camped near the middle fork of the Malheur River in eastern Oregon are reported to have filled a blue papier-mâché bucket with "stones" from a nearby creekbed, their find only being identified as gold at some later date. A few hardy souls attempted to retrace their steps but evidently failed to do so, for the "mine" is still considered to be lost.

Lost Bonanza. A gold-bearing ledge discovered by John Esterly, a Mormon who was traveling across Nevada in the 1860s accompanied by his three teen-age brides. After making his

[65] From the novel by Will Henry.

discovery, Esterly worked some of the ore loose and took it to Carson City—some 500 miles to the south-west—to have it assayed; $150,000 to the ton was the assay office verdict. John was going to be rich enough to buy Texas and support a few more wives with a strike like that; trouble is, he never found the gold-bearing ledge again. It is quite possible that it may be relocated at some date, for it most certainly lies somewhere within the triangle formed by the towns of Lee, Wells, and Currie in northeastern Nevada.

Lost Breyfogle. Details of this find may be found a few hundred pages back. (See BREYFOGLE, JACOB.)

Lost Cabin. Rich river deposits of gold found by Allen Hulbert while working the southwestern Montana region in 1863 with two fellow prospectors. The trio erected a stockaded cabin, but they had hardly started to pan when a Sioux war party struck, and Hulbert, the only survivor, fled South to save his scalp. Hulbert spread news of his find, which was most unwise, for his complete disappearance shortly afterward tends one to the belief that he may have become a murder victim. In 1865 a shifty character named Henry Comstock, and others, went searching for the Hulbert cabin deposits, but their search was in vain, it later being assumed that the Sioux must have destroyed the cabin and all traces of the prospectors' workings. Could be located somewhere in the vicinity of the junction of the Yellowstone and Big Horn rivers, near the present-day town of Custer, Montana.

Lost Cement. A ledge of almost pure gold that is reported to have been discovered in northern California in 1857. The flake gold with its bonding of red earth had the appearance of brightly colored cement; the discovery was thus named "Cement." The prefix "Lost" was added to both the find and the two men who had discovered same about five years later, and shortly after one of the men had sold a certain Dr. Randall a map that detailed the area of their discovery. The doc hunted but never found, so if this highly valuable cement ever existed, there may still be some lying around about forty miles south of Lassen Peak.

Lost Crazy Woman. A mine worked by Ira Tucker and his young wife during the summer of 1860, Ira having discovered gold-bearing quartz in the area in the spring of that year. When the leaves turned brown the couple left the workings with the intention of heading for Denver to pass the winter. They never arrived in the Colorado capital, but Dora Tucker, evidently having suffered much privation and obviously hazy of mind, did arrive at Golden, Colorado, explaining that she had become lost from her husband somewhere in the mountains. At some later date Mrs. Tucker changed her story, telling friends about the mine and admitting that she had killed Ira with a shot from a muzzle-loading rifle while he was sleeping, her motive being her husband's constant abuse. As Dora was now showing signs of being completely demented, her confession to murder was kept from the authorities, but later events would suggest that she had been telling the truth. In 1896 two old-timers, prospecting an area of southern Gunnison County, Colorado, came upon the skeletal remains of a man who had been shot in the head. A weather-corroded muzzle-loading rifle and three pieces of gold ore lying nearby tentatively identified the remains as those of Ira Tucker. The pieces of ore assayed at twenty-seven hundred dollars to the ton, a heavy gold content that has kept people searching for the mine ever since. Using Placita, Colorado, as a base, the Crazy Woman may be within a forty-mile radius of the town.

Lost Dutchman. Probably the most widely known of the genre. Numerous films have been made around the legends of the Dutchman, and an even greater number of men have found death 'stead of gold while searching for this bonanza. Details may be found under separate entries. (See SUPERSTITION MOUNTAINS and WALZER, JACOB.)

Lost Dutch Oven. Probably originally discovered and worked sometime in the 1850s or later, an Indian massacre of these early prospectors being the most likely reason for the mine becoming lost. In 1894 a Southern Pacific Railway employee named Thomas Scofield, water prospecting in the Clipper Mountains of Southern California, found traces of a long-deserted camp and mine workings. The skeletons of seven mules were in the vicinity, together with the corroded remains of mining equipment and cooking utensils, among the latter group of which Thomas found a Dutch oven full of gold nuggets. Loaded with gold, he lit out for San Francisco, converted his find into cash, and had a razzmatazz of a time until the money was gone. Easy come, easy go. Back for more gold

went Thomas, but, sad to relate, he never found the mine again. Could be in some canyon of the Clipper Mountains about midway between the towns of Danby and Nipton.

Lost Frenchman's. Details relating to this may be found elsewhere. (See BELFILS, LOUIS E.)

Lost Gunsight. A reef heavily laden with silver located in California's Death Valley. So named because the man who discovered it—one of a party of Mormon migrants—fashioned a front sight for his rifle from silver taken from the reef. Reports of the reef having been found, then lost, then found, have filtered out of Death Valley for decades, shifting sands probably being the reason for these on-off reports.

Lost Jim Bowie. Can also be referred to as the "Lost San Saba" or the "Lost Los Almagre," although it is quite possible that "Lost Bull Droppings" would be more apt. The Comanche and Lipan tribes are reputed to have known the location of the old Spanish Los Almagre workings, and Bowie is supposed to have been given the location of one of these shafts after mingling his juice with that of a Lipan chief. This was in the 1830s, and from then on blood brother Bowie had always gotten plenty of silver bullion lying around. Proof of the mine's existence? Hardly, for a lad like Bowie could have gotten the bullion elsewhere. This mine is alleged to be situated some seventy miles southeast of San Angelo, Texas; probably a few miles north of the San Saba River, and roughly midway between Salery and Buck creeks. (See BOWIE, JAMES.)

Lost Klickitat. Mine alleged to have been worked by the Klickitat Indians of the Pacific Northwest. The location of this fabulous mine is reputed to have been known to but one Indian at a time. If this is correct, one is prompted to ask two questions: (1) Did the knowledgeable one immediately expire after passing on the information regarding the mine's whereabouts? (2) How did they manage to work the mine and transport its yield? If the mine exists, it is probably in some canyon lying between the Big and Little Klickitat rivers.

Lost Padre. Originally an Indian mine, which was later taken over by Spanish missionaries. Some years after the California gold strike of 1849, the Southwest had an influx of gold-hungry adventurers, and the padres, fearful of their mine being discovered, sealed off the workings. All the Indian and Mexican laborers employed in the mine are reputed to have been killed and left within the gold-lined passages as an added security measure. Said to have been found and lost quite a few times over the next century, many of the finders having been made violently dead shortly after their discovery of the prize. Lies somewhere within the 113,809 square miles that make up the state of Arizona, so it is going to be quite a job to find. Another Lost Padre Mine is reported to be attracting searchers to the Eagle Pass area of southern Texas.

Lost Rhoades. Gold- and silver-bearing ledge that is most certainly located in the Uintah Mountains of northeastern Utah. Mormon-owned and guarded with strict secrecy, the exact location of the ledge was probably known only to Brigham Young, a few elders of the Mormon Church, and two members of the Rhoades family who were entrusted with the transporting of the metals from the Uintahs to Salt Lake City. Thomas Rhoades was entrusted with the mission sometime in the 1850s, and on his death in 1869 his son Caleb stepped into his shoes, the latter continuing to make journeys into the mountains until 1877, in which year the Indians placed a ban on his visits to the ledge, a ban that had to be taken seriously, for the metal-bearing rocks lay within the precincts of the Uintah Reservation. By the turn of the century, Caleb was the only person living who knew the whereabouts of the onetime Mormon "bank," and on his death in 1905 the "mine" was well and truly lost. It must be noted that Caleb did leave a crude map of the area— Rock Creek and Moon Lake being the only landmarks indicated—but this has been of little help to searchers up to the time of writing (1975).

Lost San Saba. Alternative name for the Lost Jim Bowie Mine. (See *Lost Jim Bowie* in this entry.)

Lost Sheepherder. Rich float discovered in the vicinity of Jarbridge[66] sometime in the 1870s by a prospector named Ross. At some later date Ross shared his secret with a sheepherder named Ishman, and when the prospector failed to return to Jarbridge after a particularly hard winter, Ishman went in search of his friend. At some point—now unknown—Ishman found the skeleton

66 Now a ghost town in the extreme northeast of Nevada.

of a man and some rusty mining tools. Using this as a macabre base, Ishman began to search the area, and a few weeks later he found the rich fissures of gold that Ross had told him about. Elevated, Ishman returned to the ranch, whereupon he took his employer into his confidence, and the following spring both men started out for the strike. Unfortunately, Ishman was smitten by a stroke en route, and he died without regaining consciousness; and that is how the Lost Sheepherder got that way.

The above sixteen pointers to possible wealth are but a handful from the hundreds of fairly well-documented reports of lost mines that circulate in the West. Arizona alone has more than twenty possible sites, and although some of these "lost mine" stories must be regarded with suspicion, the occasional discovery that results in a strike being removed from the "missing" list seems sufficient proof that not all these stories are myths. In 1959 some long-lost Spanish mines were discovered in the Burro Mountains some twenty-five miles northwest of Lordsburg, New Mexico, and a mine previously referred to as the "Lost Coconimo" was relocated in Arizona's Sycamore Canyon in 1965.

LOUISIANA   Gulf Coast state and the smallest of the states west of the Mississippi. Bounded on the north by Arkansas, on the west by Texas, and on the east by the state of Mississippi. Originally a French possession and named after Louis XIV, many of its towns and geographical features have Gallic names, while the still extant "Cajun" language[67] is a hangover from the early days of French —and Spanish—settlement. The southeast of the state is Mississippi River Delta country, an area of swamps and bayous from which moss-hung cypresses rise and wherein wading birds, bullfrogs, and alligators abound. Became a United States possession in 1803 as part of the Louisiana Purchase, and achieved statehood in 1812. Baton Rouge is the state capital, and Pelican State is its unofficial title. (See LOUISIANA PURCHASE.)

LOUISIANA PURCHASE   A colossal real-estate deal in which President Thomas Jefferson secured the 828,000 acres of French territory that lay to the west of the Mississippi River for the modest sum of fifteen million dollars, the seller being Napoleon Bonaparte and the date of turnover being April 1803. This was one of the best bargains in history, for the whole—or larger parts thereof—of thirteen western states now occupy this outsize building lot, which accounts for almost one third of the land mass of the continental United States.[68] As the French had failed to develop their territory outside the borders of Louisiana, only the state bears ample evidence of their once having sovereignty in the region.

LOVE, HARRY   Texas-born deputy sheriff of Los Angeles County, California, who had his brief moment of glory as the captain of a party of California Rangers who went out after the head of Murieta and returned with a head in a bottle. Murieta's? More likely John Doe's. (See MURIETA, JOAQUIN.)

LOVING, FRANK   Onetime cowhand turned faro dealer who participated in a

[67] Or Creole language—"Creole," in this instance, signifying a person of French or Spanish parentage who is Louisiana-born.
[68] If we ignore the state of Alaska.

much-discussed passage of arms that occurred at Dodge City, Kansas, on the Saturday evening of April 5, 1879. At the time of the affray, Frank, a twenty-five-year-old man whose pupils sought togetherness to such a marked degree that he had been dubbed "Cockeyed Frank," possessed a steady nerve but no known kill credits, while his opponent, a hide hunter and freighter named Levi Richardson, was known to be a fast man with a gun whose dexterity with same had already put three[69] of his foes 'neath prairie sod, and who had been honing up his gun-fanning technique in and around Dodge for some weeks prior to the Saturday in question.

We'll now go buy a beer in the Long Branch Saloon and watch the action. A grumble of argument from the table where Loving and Richardson are seated, then we hear "Cockeye" growl "Son of a bitch!," and both men erupt to their feet, Levi clawing out his Colt .45 as Frank unships a Remington .44. Levi's left hand blurs across the top strap of his gun, and five pieces of lead are trying to find Frank before he's thumbed back the hammer. The five pieces of lead miss Frank, and Levi is damned near lost in his own powdersmoke when Cockeye begins to squeeze off with cool deliberation: The first shot hits Levi, the second makes him a little nearer dead, and the third confirms his exodus. This fracas was carried out at such close range that poor Levi—having learned that fanning the hammer is an easy way to lose a gunfight—disappeared behind a nearby billiards table with his clothes trailing smoke. A few days afterward a coroner's jury handed down a self-defense verdict, and Frank was free to hang around the bars

telling how he cooled Levi. He was probably still explaining how a cool head could beat a fast fanner when he was shot dead at Trinidad, Colorado, some years later.[70]

LOVING, OLIVER   Born in Kentucky in 1812 and married at twenty-one, Oliver Loving didn't move West until 1845, settling in Collin County, Texas, in 1846, and homesteading here with his wife and eight children for the next nine years. In 1855 he pulled up stakes and established both a home for his family and a general store on the east bank of the Brazos River in the vicinity of Fort Belknap, but a static life failed to appeal to Oliver, and the following year he was involved in the cattle industry, performing the hitherto unheard-of feat of moving a herd of beef cattle from Texas to Illinois that same year. During the Civil War years (1861–65), Loving held a contract to supply cattle to the Confederate armies, after which he went into partnership with Charles Goodnight. This was to be but a brief business association, for in June 1867, while heading for Santa Fe in quest of beef contracts and accompanied only by a cowhand named Wilson, Loving became a victim of Comanche bullets and arrowheads, and although the two men finally reached safety, Oliver Loving died of gangrene at Fort Sumner on September 25 of that year. (See GOODNIGHT, CHARLES.)

LOWE, JOSEPH   Better known as "Rowdy Joe." This portly gent in a bow tie and beaver hat may almost be classed as the Lucky Luciano of the trail towns, for during the lush years of the 1870s

[69] Kill credits were usually inflated by 50 per cent, but as Levi could hardly have killed 1½ men, we'll allow him 2 certs.
[70] By a man named Jack Allen, who copped a self-defense plea for removing "Cockeyed" Frank Loving, said Allen having been a Dodge City lawman back in 1876.

his Kansas honky-tonks were regarded as the swiftest joints in the state. Joe, with his wife "Rowdy Kate," established honky-tonks[71] in Texas, Kansas, and Colorado, expanding their dance hall-bagnio enterprises into the trail towns of Kansas from their original headquarters at San Antonio, Texas, as the cowboy stamping grounds blossomed and got hair on their backs. In 1871 the Lowes had a place in Newton, Kansas, and during this same year Joe killed a rival fleshpot operator named Sweet while engaged in a free-for-all that occurred in the Lowes' place. Dodge City had the couple for a short spell around 1872–73, while 1874 saw the Lowes' place at Wichita luring lonesome trail hands through its portals. The Wichita establishment was located directly opposite a like venture operated by a hard case named John "Red" Redfern, a propinquity of rival interests that led to "Red" being shotgunned to death by Lowe when Redfern invaded the latter's place on a wrecking spree. This was a clear case of self-defense, and Joe never had to face trial, but the following year town lawman Wyatt Earp put the padlocks on the Lowes' sin spot and the couple moved elsewhere, finally locating near Denver, Colorado, where some years later, "Rowdy" Joe Lowe was shot dead in a saloon brawl.[72] (See HONKY-TONKS.)

LUCAS, ELMER Onetime Oklahoma cowhand who rode with the Bill Cook gang of outlaws in the early 1890s. Elmer—nicknamed "Chicken"—was arrested after being wounded in a gunfight that occurred immediately after the gang had robbed the Lincoln County Bank at Chandler, Oklahoma, on July 31, 1894, and shortly afterward he was given a fifteen-year stretch in the Michigan State Penitentiary. (See COOK, BILL.)

LYNCHING Name applied to the death penalty when carried out by vigilantes or other adherents to the principles of mob-law justice. While death by hanging was the most common method of disposing of an alleged malefactor, any form of violent death occasioned by the verdict of a body of private citizens may be classed as "lynching." The term[73] is strictly American in origin, probably being first heard in the early years of the nineteenth century.

LYONS, HAZE Member of Sheriff Henry Plummer's gang of road agents who, assisted by two other gunnies, murdered Plummer's chief deputy—a man named Dillingham, whose only "crime" was his being incorruptible—in the fall of 1863. Haze was arrested for his participation in the killing, and after a hearing before a people's court he was sentenced to hang, a verdict that was reversed immediately prior to the sentence being carried out; this about-face occurred after someone had read aloud the prisoner's "last" letter to his mother, a sentimental piece of prose that was responsible for the hard-bitten miners' cry of "Give him a [censored] horse and let him return to his [censored] mother!" and Haze being given his freedom. Lyons, in his own interests, should have

---

[71] Joe preferred to call them "dance halls."

[72] Other reports of his death state he was killed while attempting to stage a Union Pacific train robbery near Big Springs, Nebraska, but such reports are incorrect.

[73] Reputed to have derived its name from (1) James Lynch Fitz-Stephen, a sixteenth-century Irishman who, while engaged as the warden of Galway Jail, is alleged to have hanged his own son for murder; (2) a Virginia farmer named Joseph Lynch, who hanged black men with reckless abandon in the 1780s.

returned to his mom, for thoughts of his being at liberty didn't set well with the local vigilante movement, and on the morning of January 14, 1864, he was taken into custody by this band of hard-faced men and hanged that same afternoon. (See INNOCENTS and PLUMMER, HENRY.)

MACKAY, THOMAS Sometime alias of Doc Holliday. (See HOLLIDAY, JOHN HENRY.)

MACKINAW BOAT Type of craft used on the Missouri and Yellowstone rivers from about 1800 until 1880. Flat-bottomed, but otherwise free of the dictates of design, all possessed stern rudder-sweeps; sizes could be anywhere between 15 and 90 feet in length, with beams varying from 6 to 20 feet; all were propelled by sweeps, although many possessed a mast from which a makeshift sail could be hung, and the larger craft frequently had superstructure accommodation for passengers or crew. Originally used by the fur traders, the boat's numbers increased in relation to the influx of settlers, the boom years of the commercial mackinaws probably being over the years 1863–68, during which period hundreds of these boats ferried thousands of gold seekers into Montana Territory.

MADAME MUSTACHE A somewhat derogatory nickname bestowed upon Simone Jules (alias Eleanor Dumont) by a tactless prospector. (See JULES, SIMONE.)

MADAME VESTAL Professional name adopted by Belle Siddons after she became a lady gambler. (See SIDDONS, BELLE.)

MADSEN, CHRIS A man from Denmark who became one of the big names in western law enforcement. Madsen, who was born at Copenhagen in 1851, had served in the Danish Army and spent some four years in the French Foreign Legion when he arrived in the United States in 1876, so it is hardly surprising that his first act upon stepping onto American soil was to inquire as to the way to the nearest recruiting center. The 5th Cavalry got him, and over the next few years Madsen saw service at Forts Hays, Reno, Russell, and Riley, and although he took part in few Indian engagements, he did see Buffalo Bill Cody kill Chief Yellow Hand at War Bonnet Creek.[1] While still in the Army Madsen married a gal named Margaret Morris; sired two little Madsens; and barely managed to survive on a miserable thirty bucks a month. Chris left the Army in the late 1880s and tried ranching for a short time without much success; then in the early days of 1891 he became a deputy U.S. marshal, his boss being Marshal William Grimes of Oklahoma Territory, and a couple of his co-deputies being Heck Thomas and Bill Tilghman.

Whiskey peddlers, rustlers, common or

---

[1] He is on record as having stated that he saw Cody kill and scalp Yellow Hand.

garden murderers, and an assortment of downright no-good deadbeats frequented Oklahoma Territory, the crude raw material from which the U.S. deputies were expected to manufacture both jail and cemetery tenants, and Chris did his best to live up to federal expectations; "By jiminy!" he did. Acting either as a loner, or riding at the head of a posse, Deputy U. S. Marshal Madsen harassed the ungodly of the territory for the next six years, arresting dozens of whiskey peddlers, train robber Henry Silva, and triple killers "Kid" Lewis and Foster Crawford, and being in at the kill of Doolin mobsters "Tulsa Jack" Blake and "Red Buck" Waightman at various dates during these hard-riding years. Early in 1898 Chris handed in his badge, and in May of that year his wife died. The Spanish-American War was now in progress, and Chris enlisted in Teddy Roosevelt's Rough Riders, serving as a quartermaster sergeant in Cuba until a dose of yellow jack reduced him to a pale shadow of his former self.[2] A short time after his return from Army service Chris once more became a lawman, drawing a deputy U.S. marshal's pay until Oklahoma became a state in 1907 and such men as he became redundant. Later years saw the ex-lawman settled at Guthrie, Oklahoma, and he died here—in a local hospital from the after effects of a fall—on January 9, 1944.[3] (See DOOLIN GANG.)

MAD STONE Name that may be applied to almost any porous pebble that can be used as a medicinal drawing agent on wounds suspected of being infected, although most "mad stones" (the bestest, for sure) are obtained from the viscera of grazing animals, these latter usually being composed of hairs solidified within calcium. Used mainly as a sure-fire prevention from contracting rabies after being bitten by any animal whose mad behavior has suggested it may be carrying the virus. The stone, after being soaked in milk,[4] was applied to the wound, where it is reputed to have stuck until it had absorbed all toxic substances. If the stone fell off the wound on application, the victim was presumed to have a clean bill of health. If we accept—as has been stated—that the science of today is the folklore of tomorrow and assume the reverse to be equally valid, the mad stones of the West may have been effective.

MAGRUDER, LLOYD A veteran of the Mexican War (1846–48) who, after being somewhat successful as a prospector in the Salmon River region, established himself as a merchant at Elk City, Idaho. After the discovery of gold in the Grasshopper Creek area of what is now Montana in 1862, Magruder, an enterprising man withal, organized pack trains to freight merchandise into the rapidly blossoming gold camps that lay some two hundred miles to the east. Thus it came about that in the fall of 1863 Magruder was in Virginia City, Montana, where, having sold the twenty-four thousand dollars' worth of goods he had transported into the Territory by a sixty-strong mule train, he was hiring teamsters and guards to accompany him, his money, and his lightened animals back through the Bitterroot Mountains to his home base. Lloyd's hired help consisted of three guards—transient gunmen named How-

---

[2] This probably wasn't a bad thing, for in his prime Madsen bore a strong resemblance to that "Captain" character of the Katzenjammer Kids strip: moon-faced, overlarded, and heavily mustached.

[3] This date is most likely accurate, although Hunter and Rose's *Album of Gunfighters* gives the year as 1948.

[4] When available.

ard, Lowry, and Romaine[5]—and five teamsters (a couple of brothers known only as Chalmers, a muleteer named Bill Page, and a couple of prospectors named Charlie Allen and Will Phillips). There were three bad apples among this motley crew, as we shall see. Sometime during the first week of October 1863 the returning Magruder mule train night-camped in the Bitterroots, and around ten o'clock that night the bad apples went into action: Magruder and the Chalmers brothers were dispatched with an ax, while Phillips and Allen were respectively bowie-knifed and shotgunned to death, this spot of infamy being carried out by the three "guards." Page was spared and allowed to become an unwilling accomplice, he probably being the only one capable of leading them out of the snow-blanketed range with their ill-gotten gold. About this time, way back in Lewiston (a town a few miles north of Elk City), a friend of Magruder's named Hill Beachy awakened from a nightmare in which he had seen the Elk City merchant being axed to death, a psychic touch that resulted in Beachy going in search of the killers before the bodies had been found.[6] (See BEACHY, HILL.)

MAJORS, ALEXANDER   One of the big names in western transportation circles. Majors, who was born in Kentucky in 1814 of wealthy parents, began moving West at the age of five when his parents abandoned their native state and moved to Missouri. Here, the Majors bought a large farm, and Alex's early working years were spent in the employ of his father. At the age of thirty-four and with fourteen years of married life be-

hind him, Alex undertook his first independent venture. This was a freight run between Independence, Missouri, and Santa Fe, New Mexico. Half a dozen ox-drawn wagons were employed on the service, and the boss expected his employees to forsake cussin', likker, and loose livin' while they were in his employ. In 1854 Majors went into partnership with William H. Russell and W. B. Waddell, a triumvirate who organized the freighting and staging firm of Russell, Majors, and Waddell some four years later, and the legendary Pony Express of 1860. A great success for a number of years was Alex, but by the 1900s he had been reduced to accepting handouts from one of his early-day employees.[7] (See RUSSELL, MAJORS, AND WADDELL.)

MALEDON, GEORGE   Judge Isaac C. Parker's neck-stretching sidekick over the judge's Fort Smith years, a twenty-one-year period during which George staged more than eighty hangings, some of which were six-trap no-waiting multiple affairs. George, who was sired and produced by German immigrants in the industrial grime of Detroit, had worked at many jobs before he and Parker formed their rather unholy alliance in 1875. Around 1859 Maledon was functioning as a city cop in the employ of the Fort Smith Police Department; the years 1861–65 saw him in the uniform of the Union Army; while over the next decade he was engaged in lawman duties, initially as a deputy sheriff and later as a deputy U.S. marshal working out of Fort Smith.

This thin little man with the high-domed forehead and sunken eyes, whose

[5] A trio who had most certainly seen service with Sheriff Henry Plummer's gang of road agents, Howard being a known acquaintance of a Plummer gunnie named Bob Zachary.
[6] The skeletons of the victims were not recovered until April 1864. Magruder's battered skull was given to his widow, and she kept it until her death in 1900, after which it was interred with her remains.
[7] Substantial rumors name Buffalo Bill Cody as the donor.

straggly mustache and beard obliterated every feature south of his nostrils (and much of his tie), jockeyed himself into becoming a full-time executioner in easy stages by volunteering for any such grisly chore while wearing his federal badge. After "Hanging" Judge Parker came along, life must have become a bed of roses for George. Between hangings all of George's spare time was spent oiling his ropes and fiddling around with his infernal machine, macabre remarks such as "I never hanged a man who come back to have the job done ag'in" occasionally spilling from his lips like drippings from a garbage pail. For some time after Parker's death Maledon continued to work his lethal lever, but when the supply of raw material upon which his calling relied began to dry up he gave in his notice, afterward touring the country for some years displaying his equipment and giving lectures of a "Crime does not pay" nature. At some later date he tried his hand at farming, but as he had barely sufficient strength to pull up a weed, this wasn't a success. George Maledon died at Johnson City, Tennessee, on May 6, 1911. (See PARKER, ISAAC C.)

MANDAN INDIANS A tribe of the Siouan language group[8] whose origins have yet to be satisfactorily established. In the first decade of the seventeenth century, Mandan towns—whose inhabitants were described as being pale-skinned, blue-eyed, and fair of hair—were located over an area that is now part of Minnesota and the Dakotas. More than a hundred years later, in 1738, a clini-

cally minded Frenchman visited the Mandans' domain, afterward reporting that the Indians had been delighted to meet other "white men," that the women were beautiful, and that 20 per cent of the nation possessed light hair. George Catlin, after visiting the tribe in the 1830s, returned with similar reports, the only Catlin addition being the fact that various shades of hair were in evidence among the Mandans. Villages were composed of hundreds of earth lodges[9] surrounded by a log stockade, the land outside the stockade being utilized for the growing of melons, beans, tobacco, etc. Although essentially farmers, buffalo and small game were hunted as a dietary supplement and for the raw materials from which clothing was manufactured: fringed buckskin shirts (which were occasionally fur-trimmed), leggings, moccasins, etc. In affairs militant the Mandan were extremely skilled in the use of a primitive-type mace; this was a large stone fastened to a rawhide thong, which was much favored in warfare, although bows and spears were also used. Settlers and homesteaders were making their appearance on Mandan territory during the period when Catlin was creating portraits of these tribesmen, and within a few years of his departure the Mandan were preparing to clear these "other white men" from their range. This, however, they were never to accomplish, for before they had taken to the warpath a smallpox epidemic[10] decimated the tribe, and when the epidemic had burned itself out, there were only 128 survivors out of an estimated original total of about 1,800. This was the end of the Mandan nation,

---

[8] This, of course, does not mean that they spoke any of the Dakota (Sioux) dialects, travelers having added a touch of mystery by reporting that Welsh and Scandinavian words could be heard in their speech.

[9] Log-built houses divided into separate compartments, a covering of earth giving them the appearance of inverted basins.

[10] A disease that was unknown on the North American continent until the arrival of the Europeans.

for the pockmarked few who still lived were quickly absorbed within other tribes. (See BULLBOATS and CATLIN, GEORGE.)

MANGAS COLORADO The Spanish name[11] for Dasoda Hae, a 6-foot, 6-inch Mimbreno Apache who became chief of the Copper Mine tribe after chief Juan José and many of his followers had been murdered in the town plaza of Santa Rita del Cobre.[12] At the time of the above-mentioned slaughter the Copper Mine tribe had been at peace with the Mexican and Anglo Pinda-lik-o-yi (white-eyes) for some fifteen years, but after this sorry event, coexistence was a thing of the past, and the dead in the plaza had been avenged a hundredfold before Mangas Colorado reached the end of his wartrail in 1863. Mangas Colorado, with a pool of around four hundred fighting men at his disposal, was exacting retribution from both gringo and greaser within weeks of Juan José's death. A party of twenty-two gringo trappers was annihilated while in camp on the Gila River, and the inhabitants of Santa Rita del Cobre were reduced to near famine after a couple of supply columns, which had been freighting food and goods from bases in Sonora and Chihuahua, were destroyed in a narrow pass a few miles south of the town. Nothing could get either in or out of Santa Rita. Work in the copper mines came to a halt, and finally, in desperation, the whole community of approximately four hundred men, women, and children evac-uated the town and headed for Janos, a Mexican town that lay a hundred miles to the south in the district of Chihuahua. Few of them reached their destination. After three days of sun-scorched desert travel, and about midway in their journey, Mangas Colorado attacked. Bullets and arrows decimated the fleeing Santa Ritans until only a bare half dozen survived, these few being allowed to continue their journey in the knowledge that they would spread the news of the power of Mangas Colorado.

Over the next nine years the Copper Mine Apaches raided deep into Mexico, and at the outbreak of the Mexican War in 1846 the chief and his followers allied themselves to the Americano cause, supplying the gringos with horses and mules and aiding them in their fight against the greasers. Friendly relations between Mangas Colorado and the Americanos continued until 1851, in which year the chief buried the olive branch after he had been bound to a post and whipped by a party of prospectors. Over the next decade Arizona, Texas, and New Mexico felt the wrath of Mangas Colorado, an era of violence that culminated at the Battle at Apache Pass in 1862. The Copper Mine chief was wounded in this engagement, and he was taken to Janos for medical treatment, Geronimo acting as talk man on their arrival at the town by making the definitive demand, "Make well. If he die, so does everyone in Janos." This straight-from-the-shoulder stuff spurred the local surgeon into putting his all into the saving of Mangas Colorado, and the

---

[11] The English rendering of which is "Red Sleeves."

[12] Occurred in 1837. The Apaches were invited to a great feast in the town plaza, the object of the invitation being to get the Indians within a small area where they could be easily massacred when they had become somnolent with food and liquor. The scheme originated in the mind of an English scalphunter named James Johnson shortly after the Mexican authorities had posted the offer of one hundred dollars for an adult male scalp, fifty dollars for a squaw's, and twenty-five dollars for a child's; a couple of howitzers, small arms, and bowie knives were used for the slaughter. An estimated four hundred Indians perished in the massacre, and Mangas Colorado was one of the few survivors.

aging chief slowly recovered after the removal of a bullet.

Toward the end of 1862, Mangas
Colorado must have realized that the
white-eyes were getting too numerous to
fight, and on January 17 of the following
year, after being apprised of the fact
that the soldiers were prepared to talk
peace, the chief and fifteen of his warriors contacted troops at an Army camp
located near Fort McLean. The boys in
blue were sufficiently cordial to persuade
Mangas Colorado to order his escort to
return to camp while he remained to
await the arrival of Colonel J. R. West
from Fort McLean. The colonel, arriving well after dark, found the old
Mimbreno chief sleeping by a campfire,
an opportune moment to pronounce an
obviously worded death sentence on the
Apache before retiring to his tent to allow his men to act upon his instructions.
Shortly afterward Mangas Colorado was
bayoneted and shot until he was dead.
(See BATTLE AT APACHE PASS.)

MANHATTAN REVOLVER
A five-shot percussion revolver manufactured by the Manhattan Firearms
Company of Newark, New Jersey, from
1851 onward. These guns are blatant
copies of Colt's 1851 Navy revolver, being virtually indistinguishable from the
latter. Belle Starr carried an 1864 .36-
caliber Manhattan revolver during the
early years of her outlaw career. (See
COLT FIREARMS, subheading Navy.)

MANITOU   The great unseen force
that can influence the lives of the American Indians. An Algonkin word that can
refer to the Spirit of either Good or Evil.

MANUSE, GEORGE   Reputed leader
of a gang of rustlers who plagued the
Powder River region of Wyoming in the
late 1870s. George, whose aliases include "George Curry," "George Parrott," and "Flat-nosed George," is over-
frequently confused with Harvey Logan,
a gentleman who hid behind the alias of
"Kid Curry" and who began frequenting
the Hole in the Wall hideout that Manuse
had favored for years toward the end of
the latter's earthly span. In 1878 Manuse
led a gang in an attempted train robbery.
A length of Union Pacific track was removed near Carbon, Wyoming, but the
train was well behind schedule and the
gang dispersed when their handiwork was
discovered by a track inspection crew.
The UP employees carried news of the
vandalism to the nearest sheriff's office,
and shortly afterward a posse of lawmen
led by Bob Widdowfield and Tip Vincent
engaged the outlaws in a running gunfight, the pursued only escaping after
Manuse had killed Vincent and an unidentified gunnie had blasted Widdowfield into eternity.

If we wish to avoid falling into the trap
of confusing Manuse with the aforementioned "Kid Curry," we must lose Manuse for a couple of years until he makes
a definitive appearance in a Miles City,
Montana, saloon in July 1880. Here, after blowing off too much froth, George
started belching forth remarks about his
killing of Deputy Sheriff Widdowfield,
the aftermath of this bragging being that
within a matter of days George found
himself behind bars in the jail at Rawlins. Tried in November of that year,
Manuse was sentenced to death, the date
on which the sentence was to be carried
out being April 2, 1881. George was destined never to meet the public hangman.
On the night of March 22, 1881, a mob
stormed the Rawlins jail, and George was
liberated so that he might be strung
from a nearby telegraph pole. This was
not the end of the saga of Manuse. A
couple of surgeons toyed around with his
remains, the good doctors manufactur-

ing a pair of moccasins and a tobacco pouch from his suitably tanned hide before they dropped the rest of him into a barrel of alcohol and dumped the whole mess behind their premises and forgot about him completely. George was rediscovered in 1950. The barrel was bone dry, and George was little more than dried bones. You may still view evidence of Manuse's existence, tanned skin being exhibited at a museum at Rawlins, while the skull may be seen in a museum at Omaha. (See LOGAN, HARVEY.)

MARIAS MASSACRE   Alternative name for the Baker Massacre. (See BAKER MASSACRE.)

MARMOT   A large-sized ground squirrel with a comparatively short tail that is usually referred to as a "woodchuck" or a "ground hog." Three species of marmot inhabit the United States, but only two of these—the yellow-bellied and the hoary marmot—are found west of the Mississippi. The yellow-bellied variety, a reddish-brown rodent that derives its name from the yellowish fur of its underside, can be found in most western states, the range of this species extending from Washington to the Dakotas and as far south as New Mexico and California. The hoary marmot, so named because its fur is tipped with white, is the rarer of the species, its habitat being confined to the Northwest. All marmots are vegetarian, and the two western representatives of the family are community dwellers.[13] Hoary marmots may reach a length of about 30 inches, this being some 5 inches longer than the yellow-bellied variety.

MARSHAL   A law-officer appointment that can be prefixed by either "town" or "United States." (See TOWN MARSHAL and UNITED STATES MARSHAL.)

MARSHLAND, STEPHEN   Member of Henry Plummer's gang of "Innocents." Marshland, a charming young man and a college graduate, was probably the least violent of any of the thieves and road agents who were operational in the Montana gold fields in 1863. In the fall of 1863 Plummer detailed Steve and "Dutch John" Wagner with the chore of robbing a gold-shipping caravan, but the pair of "Innocents" were forced to retreat without laying hands on any of the gold, and Marshland had to lay low with a ball in his chest. On the evening of January 15, 1864, vigilantes traced Steve to a ranch at Big Hole, and that was the end of the line for the lad, the unhealed bullet wound in his chest being deemed sufficient evidence to justify his immediate dispatch by hanging. Marshland, as far as is known, had never been guilty of murder. (See INNOCENTS.)

MASON COUNTY WAR   In September 1875 a cattleman named Timothy Williamson was shot to death by an irate mob while he was being escorted to jail by John Worley, a deputy sheriff of Mason County, Texas. This incident sparked off the fuse that exploded into the so-called Mason County War, a tit-for-tat war of attrition that left the debris of some dozen losers littering the county before the Texas Rangers called a halt to the shooting match. The dead cattleman had friends, the foremost of these being an ex-Texas Ranger named Scott Cooley, who had known Williamson in the Kansas trail towns. Cooley, obsessed with the notion that Worley was more or less an accessory before the fact in his friend's death, rode to the lawman's home and shot the man dead, after which he let it be known that he intended to have the hides of all others who shared complicity in Williamson's death. This fighting talk

[13] The woodchuck is a loner that hibernates for six months of the year.

attracted friends of the deceased cattleman to Cooley's banner, and when
Cooley rode into Mason, Texas, to kill
Daniel Hoerster, whom he suspected of
being involved in Williamson's death,
John Ringgold, George Gladden, brothers John and Moses Beard, and brothers
Peter and Elijah Backus were all giving
Cooley a hand when Daniel was made
dead and heavy. Other deaths followed in
rapid succession. Mob-law practitioners
Peter Bader and Luther Wiggins were
ushered out by Colt salutes; the Backus
boys died dangling from a tree; and
lead termites put Moses Beard under the
sod. Three or four more participants had
been permanently removed from this
arena of nail-biting suspense before a
company of Texas Rangers arrived on
the scene and put an end to the killing
without firing a shot. The majority of the
troublemakers disappeared back into
their holes, only Ringgold and Gladden
having to spend some time behind bars
to atone for their crimes. (See COOLEY,
SCOTT; JONES, FRANK; and RINGGOLD,
JOHN.)

MASTERSON, BAT   Nickname of
frontier lawman William Barclay Masterson. (See MASTERSON, WILLIAM BAR-
CLAY.)

MASTERSON, EDWARD J. Eldest
of the Masterson brothers. Born in Illinois in 1852, Ed had worked at many
jobs before he was appointed assistant
city marshal of Dodge City, Kansas, in
June 1877. Five months after this appointment he was wounded in the chest
while arresting a Texas troublemaker
named Robert Shaw in the Lone Star
Dance Hall, but Ed had sufficiently recovered from this wound to take over the
duties of marshal when his predecessor
—Marshal Larry Deger—was removed

from office on December 4 of that same
year. Four months later—the late evening
of April 9, 1878—Marshal Masterson left
his office to investigate some promiscuous
shooting in the Lady Gay Dance Hall.
This was to be Ed's last official act. A
drunken cowhand named Jack Wagner
pushed the muzzle of his pistol into the
marshal's abdomen and pulled the trigger, igniting the lawman's clothing and
causing a fist-sized wound from which Ed
died a half hour after the shooting. (See
MASTERSON, WILLIAM BARCLAY.)

MASTERSON, JIM   Born in Illinois
in 1856. James moved West with older
brothers Ed and "Bat" while still in his
teens, working with a railroad-grading
crew for some time before starting a lawman career as a deputy under the assistant city marshal Wyatt Earp, at Dodge
City, Kansas, in the summer of 1876.
This badge-toting period was to last for
some time, Jim working as either a
Dodge City lawman or a Ford County
deputy sheriff until 1879 when he turned
in his star and moved up into Canada for
a short time. If the Dodge City census of
1881 does not err, Jim had returned from
the north country by this time and had
been appointed city marshal. The following year Marshal Masterson went into
partnership with a man named Peacock
in an enterprise that has been alternatively described as either a dance hall or
a saloon, so it was most likely a honky-
tonk.

A few weeks after joining forces with
Peacock, bad blood developed between
Masterson and their head barman, a man
named Al Updegraff who happened to
be Peacock's brother-in-law; Jim wanted
Al fired, and Peacock said "nay." Jim,
evidently thinking that this stupid argument might lead to his being dry-gulched,
sent a telegram[14] to brother Bat at

[14] It may only be presumed that Jim sent the telegram, for no forwarder's name appeared at the foot of the message.

Tombstone, apprising Bat of the fact that a death in the family appeared likely. Bat arrived at Dodge City on April 16, and within a matter of hours, bullets had ricocheted around the plaza, Al Updegraff had been severely wounded by a piece of Bat's lead, Jim had turned in his badge and sold his business interests, and the brothers Masterson were heading for Colorado. Over the years Jim wore a deputy U.S. marshal's badge for varying periods of time, being a federal lawman while taking part in the Cimarron County Seat War of 1889[15] and the Battle of Ingalls in 1893. After this last engagement little more was heard of Jim. (See CIMARRON COUNTY SEAT WAR; INGALLS, OKLAHOMA; and MASTERSON, WILLIAM BARCLAY.)

MASTERSON, TOM The youngest of the four Masterson brothers. Thomas, who was born in Illinois about 1858, migrated westward with the family some twelve months after the close of the Civil War, his parents settling on a farm in Missouri for a few years before finally establishing themselves as farmers and landowners about twenty miles north of Wichita, Kansas. Tom's surname jockeyed him into this volume, for he remained a homesteader for the greater part of his lifetime, only stepping into the reflected glow of his older brothers for a short time during their years as peace officers in and around Dodge City, and, many years later, getting a further squib of publicity after his taking part in the affair at Cimarron. (See CIMARRON COUNTY SEAT WAR and MASTERSON, WILLIAM BARCLAY.)

MASTERSON, WILLIAM BARCLAY Better known as Bat Masterson, a name which, given the right inflection, conjures up the vision of a dauntless town-tamer whose gun butts are saw-edged by more than a score of notches. This, however, is a somewhat overblown vision, for although it cannot be argued that Bat was anything but dauntless, the records show that had he been stupid enough to mutilate his guns he would have been entitled to carve but three notches on their walnut butts. Illusions shattered, we will now get him born, de-diapered, and be-gunned as the prologue to his debut in the western arena.

He was born in Illinois in 1855, the second son[16] of Thomas and Catherine Masterson, natives of New York State who were moving West in easy stages. In 1866 the family crossed the Mississippi and settled in Missouri, remaining here for a few years before moving into Kansas and laying permanent roots by establishing a farm that was located about midway between Newton and Wichita. In 1872 Bat and elder brother Ed left home and moved 150 miles west to Dodge City, a collection of dugouts and soddies whose inhabitants blended well with the architecture. Dodge, however, was on the threshold of expanding into one of the foremost sin spots of the frontier, for that sure guarantee of a population explosion, the railroad—pushing ever westward— was nearing the outskirts of town at about the same time as the Mastersons were getting their first close-up whiff of the aroma of hide hunters. While the AT and SF terrier crews were in the Dodge area, Bat and Ed hired themselves out to grade a small stretch of right-of-way west

[15] Bat was in Denver, Colorado, at this time, but some writers have him throwing lead in this battle while Jim is home in bed or someplace; this is no doubt done to give a lift to Bat's saga during one of its many dull periods.
[16] Thomas and Kate produced a total of six offspring: Edward (1852), Minnie (1853), Nellie (1854), William Barclay (1855), James (1856), and Thomas (1858?).

of Dodge, a muscle-twanging stint that got them three hundred dollars. Ed returned home after this, but Bat got himself a buffalo gun and joined a party of hide men who were heading for the Staked Plains.

Bat's buffler-killin', whiskey-swillin', Comanche-dodgin' spree lasted until the 1874 Battle at Adobe Walls persuaded Bat and company to return to the settlements while they were still in possession of their scalps. Within a matter of weeks Bat had found employment as a scout attached to the Army, a position he held until the much-feared Sergeant King punctured him in a gunfight that occurred at Sweetwater in July 1875. The pelvic wound Bat sustained in this fracas removed him from the powdersmoke circuit for a while, but sometime in the summer of 1876 he appeared in Dodge City, limping around with the aid of a walking stick and looking for a job. Dodge was the right place at the right time. A buffalo-hunting acquaintance named Wyatt Earp was assistant city marshal at Dodge, and Bat was quickly deputized to become one of a trio of lawmen[17] who backed Earp's play during the 1876 cattle season. The pay was seventy-five dollars a month, and it was the start of Bat's rather short career as a lawman.

In the fall of the following year, 1877, we see him elected as sheriff of Ford County for a two-year term, an appointment that kept him anchored at Dodge, for the cowtown was the county seat, and the sheriff's office was located there. Bat's most traumatic experience was to occur during this tour of duty. On the night of April 9, 1878, he was summoned from his office by the news that his brother—the city marshal, Ed Masterson—was being hurrahed by cowhands outside the

Lady Gay Dance Hall. Bat was still some twenty paces from the scene of the disturbance when he heard the roar of a shot and saw Ed stagger away from a gun-wielding duo named Jack Wagner and Alf Walker, a mind-distorting scene to which Bat reacted instantaneously, his gun glare washing him into relief as he thumb-busted lead into Alf and Jack. The mortally wounded targets staggered into Peacock's Saloon, Wagner clutching a belly wound and Walker trailing blood from a punctured lung and a shattered arm. Ed Masterson died within thirty minutes of the shooting and Wagner died twenty-four hours later, while Walker became the third fatality of that sanguinary Tuesday evening when he succumbed from his lung wound a month after the shootout.

During the remainder of his term of office Bat met such frontier notables as Doc Holliday, Ben Thompson, comedian Eddie Foy, and the James brothers,[18] put the collar on notorious baddie Dave Rudabaugh, and spent most of his free time pursuing a fortune in the local gambling halls. In November 1879 the residents of Ford County voted Bat out of office by a near two-to-one majority, and Bat, who was far from a good loser, departed for Colorado after casting a few disparaging remarks relating to rigged elections. Early in 1881 he appeared in Tombstone, Arizona, but although the Earps were more or less resident lawmen, Bat showed little inclination to join them, and it was a rare occasion if he absented himself from the gambling tables to join an Earp posse. Arizona had Bat for only a short time, for upon receipt of a telegram a couple of months after his arrival, he hastened to Dodge City to help brother Jim extri-

---

[17] The other deputies being Bat's brother Jim and a man named Joseph Mason.

[18] Frank and Jesse were living in peaceful coexistence with the law at this period, being engaged in the pastoral pursuit of trailing cattle. Bat got on well with Frank, and he kept in touch with him until the latter's death in 1915.

cate himself from a business predicament. After an explosive four hours at Dodge, Bat and Jim hightailed for Colorado, where, within a matter of weeks, Bat was sporting a Los Animas County deputy sheriff's badge.

For many years after this appointment Bat's life was a transient affair: He ran gambling concessions at Creede, Colorado; made frequent return visits to Dodge;[19] was in Fort Worth, Texas, when his buddy Luke Short devitalized Courtright; and established himself as something of a man-about-town at Denver, Colorado. It was at Denver that Bat took over the management of a troupe of lovelies who had been poured into pink tights, a leg-show burlesque act that no doubt stimulated Bat into getting married to a variety-show lass named Emma Walters in the fall of 1891. The newlyweds moved to Creede, where Bat had been offered the post as manager of a saloon and gambling hall, but Bat survived this post for only a short time, owing to his somewhat erratic behavior patterns: The onetime hard drinker who had become an ardent prohibitionist in 1876 once more returned to the juice, his manner became pugnacious, and he was wont to swagger around in a gunbelt heavy with Colt .45 in open defiance of a city ordinance that forbade the carrying of sidearms. It was decided that Bat had to go. Our man was tippling a high-noon whiskey when a gun barrel tickled his kidneys and a voice requested he leave Denver by the 4 P.M. train. Bat went. The West was getting tame.

In the summer of 1902 Bat arrived in New York City and took up residence.

The New Yorkers regarded Bat as a living legend rather than as a troublemaker, and within a few years of his arrival, President Theodore Roosevelt appointed him United States marshal of the southern district of New York State. This was a nine-to-five desk job with a steady salary and little chance of ever encountering powder smoke, but Bat was getting older and he didn't appear to miss the action and pungent aromas of the plains towns of his youth.

In 1907 he resigned from the marshal's post and made a rather startling leap into journalism by accepting the position of sports editor on the *Morning Telegraph*. Bat had little formal education and no literary background, but as a column of hard-hitting tripe is much appreciated by sports fans, he held this position until the end of his days. It was while so employed that Bat got into the habit of supplying notched guns to his legion of awe-stricken admirers. Bat bought these guns at hock shops and junk stores and carved twenty or more notches into their butts before handing them out, so it is quite conceivable that dozens of "this was Masterson's" sixguns are still going the rounds. William Barclay Masterson died at his desk on October 25, 1921, while in the midst of writing his column.[20] (See BATTLE AT ADOBE WALLS; BUNTLINE SPECIAL; CIMARRON COUNTY SEAT WAR; GERMAIN, JOHN; KING, MELVIN; MASTERSON, EDWARD J.; and MASTERSON, JIM.)

MATADOR OUTFIT Established by a Texan named Henry Harrison Campbell in 1878. Campbell, with an

---

[19] In 1884 he established the *Vox Populi* at Dodge City. This was a weekly newssheet—leastways, it was planned that way—that dropped dead after its first issue.

[20] An oft-reported and deeply philosophical piece, a slightly abridged extract of which follows: "Some folk argue that we all get the same breaks in this world. I suppose they reason that because we all get the same amount of ice, the rich getting it in the summertime and the poor getting it in the wintertime, things break out even for all. Maybe so, but I don't see it that way."

estimated initial capital of $50,000, located south of the Prairie Dog River in the Texas Panhandle, his herds having been purchased from New Mexico cattle king John Chisum and his original headquarters being little more than a timber and sod dugout. The enterprise flourished, and Scottish backers financed an expansion program that soon had the Matador occupying most of the Panhandle and owning rangeland in Montana and the Dakotas. In 1951 the amalgam of ranches known as the Matador Outfit was the second largest spread in the United States, its only rival being the King Ranch of south Texas. In the spring of 1951 American interests made an offer of $18,960,000 for the Matador ranches, and at a shareholders' meeting held at the home office in Dundee, Scotland, on April 15 of that year it was agreed to sell the Matador holdings. With ratification of the sale the Matador ranches passed into the hands of the Pease River Cattle Corporation and the Turtle Hole Cattle Corporation. The Matador operated under the Flying V brand.

MATHER, DAVE   This gent is the "Mysterious" Dave Mather who, considering that little is known about him, wanders on and off the western stage with irritating frequency. Reputed to be a native of Massachusetts and a direct descendant of Cotton Mather,[21] Dave appeared in Dodge City around 1878 with a reputation of having killed more men than any of his contemporaries, some reports crediting him with processing seven men into corpses in a single shootout. For varying periods during his Dodge years Dave served as assistant city marshal, city marshal, and deputy sheriff of Ford County, while on one of his rare absences from Dodge—spring 1881 to spring 1882—he served as an El Paso (Texas) deputy marshal under Marshal James Gillett. In the early days of 1884 we find Dave wearing a Ford County deputy sheriff's badge and jacking up his lawman's pay as senior partner in Mather and Black's Dance Hall, which was located at Dodge. Sometime after this, Assistant City Marshal Tom Nixon closed the dance hall for undisclosed reasons, a tactless move that lit the fuse of a powder keg that exploded Nixon out of office a few months later. On the evening of the eighteenth of July, after an argument between these two men, Nixon fired a round at Dave then headed for the timber. The bullet didn't even part Dave's hair, but it did get his mad up. The following Monday night four shots from Dave's .45 created an immediate vacancy in the city marshal's office. The incident occurred outside the Dodge City Opera House, and the deputy sheriff surrendered to the law before the smoke had cleared. In December of that same year Mather was tried for the offense and acquitted, after which he moved up into Nebraska and settled at Long Pine. His activities in this area appear to have been confined to hunting and prospecting, and it has been reported that he got on well with the locals. Dave, however, was not the type to remain in one place for too long, and he pulled up stakes one evening and headed for . . .

MAUST, CHARLES
Alias of small-time Cherokee Strip outlaw Ben Cravens. (See CRAVENS, BEN.)

MAVERICK   An unbranded calf. The term "maverick" is reputed to have been coined by neighbors of Samuel Maverick, a lawyer and signatory of the

[21] An undiluted Puritan preacher and writer who lived at Boston, Massachusetts, for the whole period of his lifetime (1663–1728).

Texas Declaration of Independence who entered the cattle industry just prior to the Civil War after he had accepted a small herd in payment of a debt. Maverick branded these with the MK brand, but having little time for his role as cattleman he failed to brand the progeny of his original herd, an omission that prompted neighbors into referring to any unbranded stock as being "one of Maverick's." It is worth noting that in the early years of the cattle industry the appropriation of any unbranded calf that was not following its mother was not classed as rustling. In the post-Civil War era in Texas there was an over-abundance of wild free-roving longhorns and probably more unbranded than branded stock.

MAVERICKING   The appropriation of branded or unbranded cattle, whether they be calves or otherwise, an art that is more commonly referred to as "rustling." "Mavericking" is a verbalized adaptation of "maverick" and a term that came into the linguistic currency of the West many years after "maverick" had lost much of its original meaning. (See MAVERICK.)

MAXWELL, DELUVINA
The Navaho Indian girl who is frequently regarded as being one of Billy the Kid's sweethearts. Deluvina, who was born in the Cañon de Chelly area in 1847, was taken captive by the Apaches while still a child, the Indians trading her to Lucien B. Maxwell for a number of horses at some later date—hence the name "Maxwell." Deluvina always classed her relationship with the Kid as

platonic rather than carnal, and the fact that she kept the Kid's grave well supplied with flowers for many years after his death doesn't necessarily prove that modesty prevented her from telling the truth.[22] Deluvina died at Albuquerque, New Mexico, in 1927. (See MAXWELL, LUCIEN BONAPARTE, and MC-CARTY, HENRY.)

MAXWELL, KATE   Name sometimes used by Ella Watson, the "Cattle Kate" of Wyoming's wild and woolly past. (See WATSON, ELLA.)

MAXWELL LAND GRANT   A large piece of southwestern real estate owned by Lucien B. Maxwell. Don Guadalupe Miranda and a French-Canadian named Beaubien were the original owners of this land, the 1,777,000-acre tract[23] having come into their possession as a gift from the Mexican Government as a reward for their pioneering activities in the Mexican province of New Mexico. At some later date a financial deal resulted in Beaubien becoming sole owner of the land grant, and after Beaubien's death in 1864 Maxwell stepped into the picture and purchased the land from the heirs to the estate. (See MAXWELL, LUCIEN BONAPARTE.)

MAXWELL, LUCIEN BONAPARTE
Lucien's tombstone, which lies within spitting distance of Billy the Kid's, gives the facts of Lucien's life in a nutshell: "A native of Kaskaskia, Illinois. A fur trader and trapper who by industry, good fortune, and trading became sole owner in 1864 of the largest single tract

---

[22] Deluvina was thirty-four years of age at the time of the Kid's death, a point that is worth bearing in mind, for many of the Kid's biographers tend to describe her as a wrinkled old hag at the time of his passing.
[23] Approximately five sixths of which is in northern New Mexico, while the remainder lies in southeastern Colorado.

of land owned by any one individual in the United States. Maxwell founded the First National Bank of Santa Fe, New Mexico, and invested $250,000 to help build the Texas Pacific Railroad. Dynamic, charitable, lavish. One of the great builders of the American West. Died in quiet retirement, July 25, 1875, at Fort Sumner, New Mexico. Born September 14, 1818." Pretty good, huh? But chiseling in a tombstone makes for economy of effort, and much has been omitted. After coming into possession of the land grant mentioned on his marker, Lucien was regarded as being the richest man in the region, living like a feudal lord in a mansion he had built at Cimarron (New Mexico), supping his bubbly from goblets of gold, and carving his T-bones on platters of silver. He employed an army of servants, possessed vast herds of sheep and cattle, married the aristocratic Señorita Luz Beaubien,[24] and sired a half-dozen offspring.[25] In later life tycoon Maxwell began to lose his Midas touch. The fortune poured into the Texas Pacific venture was like money down the drain, and financial pressures forced him into selling his banking interests and his vast holdings of land; the latter transaction bringing him a mere $750,000, a price that worked out at slightly over $.40 an acre.[26] As his fortune diminished, Lucien left the grandeur of Cimarron and moved his family to the town of Fort Sumner, where he established a home in the old officers' quarters of the fort. (See MAXWELL LAND GRANT.)

MAXWELL, PETE   The name by which Pedro Maxwell, only son of Lu-

cien B. Maxwell, is usually known. Pete, who had spent his childhood in luxurious surroundings, lived for the greater part of his life at Fort Sumner, New Mexico, becoming, in later life, one of the most prosperous sheepmen in the region. Mainly of interest because of his association with Billy the Kid. (See MAXWELL, LUCIEN BONAPARTE, and McCARTY, HENRY.)

MCCALL, JACK   The cross-eyed killer of Wild Bill Hickok. McCall was born at Louisville, Kentucky, in 1851, and he remained in this area until 1871, in which year he left home and drifted westward. The following year saw him hunting buffalo in Colorado, and a year later he was suspected of hunting other folks' range stock in Hitchcock County, Nebraska. During his stay in Nebraska he is reputed to have been known as "Curly Jack," and as Curly Jack he became involved in a vendetta with a prospective sheriff of the county, a man named Baldwin, who nailed Jack into the ground with a piece of timber of railroad-tie proportions when the latter came searching for him with a couple of .45s at the alert. This pile-driver blow ruined Curly's headgear, rendered him comatose for twenty-four hours, and was probably responsible for the cross-eyes and dual personality that later acquaintances were to comment upon.

Jack McCall arrived at Deadwood sometime in the spring of 1876. Here he used the name of Bill Sutherland, earned his coin from accepting any laboring jobs that came along, and spent same while leaning against liquor-sodden bartops. Wild Bill Hickok drifted into the

---

[24] Daughter of the French-Canadian from whose heirs Maxwell purchased the land grant.
[25] These being Pedro (usually known as Pete), Odila, Amilia, Virginia, Sophia, and Paulita.
[26] The purchasers subsequently sold out to an English combine for approximately double the amount they had paid Maxwell.

gold camp about a month after Jack's arrival, and as Bill spent much of his time in the saloons, he was—over the next few weeks—to become slightly acquainted with the man who was going to blow his brains out. Shortly after 4 P.M. on August 2, McCall entered Nuttall and Mann's Number Ten Saloon, where Hickok was engaged in a game of cards, and ordered a shot of the hard stuff; then, after the drink had fired his viscera, he sidled up behind Wild Bill and put a bullet through the onetime lawman's head.[27] Hickok died instantly, and McCall was arrested shortly afterward. The following day McCall appeared before a miner's court to establish whether he was guilty of murder or otherwise, a "trial" that one would have expected to result in a "legal" lynching, but Jack spun a yarn about how Hickok had killed his brother—a completely nonexistent person—on some unspecified date, and he was acquitted after the jury had brought in a "not guilty" verdict.

Shortly after his acquittal, McCall moved to Laramie, Wyoming, and here he began to frequent saloons and do much grandstanding about his shooting of Hickok and his phony defense. A deputy U.S. marshal, after listening to much of this loose talk, put the collar on Jack, and on November 27 Jack found himself in the federal court at Yankton, Dakota Territory, charged with first-degree murder. This trial resulted in a "guilty" verdict, and Jack McCall was hanged at Yankton on March 1, 1877.

The evening before his execution McCall wrote the "full and truthful account" of his motivation for the killing of Hickok, but he destroyed this document before anyone had the opportunity of reading it.[28] (See HICKOK, JAMES BUTLER.)

MCCANLES, DAVID C. Born in 1821 in North Carolina, where, on reaching adulthood, he married and raised a family and served as sheriff of Watauga County for some time. By 1859 married life was beginning to pall, so Dave, in an effort to reinject a little romance into his life, headed West with a twenty-six-year-old filly named Sarah Shull. The couple established themselves on the Oregon Trail at Rock Creek, Nebraska, and here McCanles prospered, but within a short time he was having misgivings about his family and he had them join him at Rock Creek. Early in 1861 Russell, Majors, and Waddell made an initial payment for the purchase of McCanles' Rock Creek property, and he moved his family onto a ranch a few miles distant.

A man named Horace Wellman was placed in charge of the Rock Creek station, being assisted in his task by fellow employees of the company Bill Hickok and Joseph Baker. The nubile Sarah now steps back into the picture. When the McCanleses moved from Rock Creek, Sarah remained behind to live in one of the outbuildings. The pad marks of big Dave McCanles were never given time to disappear from her path, yet for much of

[27] Jack's luck was in that day, for all the other cartridges in the cylinder of his gun were defective.
[28] There are dozens of speculative reasons to account for McCall's killing of Hickok. Jack McCall was an only son (he did have three sisters), so his expressed reason for the killing at his first "trial" may be disposed of as a pack of lies. A far more likely reason is that the assassination may have stemmed from an argument that Hickok is alleged to have had with a man named John Varnes, an incident that took place in July and revolved around a card game. After this, Varnes was heard to mutter threats against Hickok, and it is assumed he may have paid McCall to assassinate Wild Bill. The United States marshal's office appears to have attached some credence to this theory, for it sent lawmen looking for Varnes. He was, however, never arrested.

the time she was alone, and Hickok was in the vicinity. Whether Bill ever took advantage of this girl who is reputed to have been ever desirous of being taken advantage of will never be known, but Dave, who had a contract to supply fodder for the Rock Creek livestock and was a frequent visitor, may have suspected that Bill was sowing his oats in what Dave regarded as McCanles' pasture; the latter assumption being based on the fact that Dave began passing insulting remarks that were targeted at Bill's rather prominent nasal organ, and he requested the younger man to more or less confine his activities to shoveling whatever one shovels in a stableyard.

Sometime in June this ill will against Hickok was diluted when Dave turned his wrath against Wellman; Russell, Majors, and Waddell were behind with their station payments and fodder bills, and Dave—somewhat irrationally—blamed Wellman for this. On the 11th of July Wellman visited his employers in an attempt to get the money to pay Dave, but he was unsuccessful in this and he had to return to the station empty-handed. On hearing of this, McCanles decided to clean up the mob at Rock Creek, and on the afternoon of the twelfth he buckled on his precision-made killing tools and headed for the stage depot accompanied by his twelve-year-old son Monroe, cousin James Woods, and a hired hand named James Gordon.

By the time the McCanles faction reached the station yard, the Rock Creek personnel—Wellman and his common-law wife, Hickok, Baker, and the latter's step-daughter—were forted-up in the main building. McCanles thundered his demands from the yard: "Hand over the station or else!"; "Send Wellman out or we'll come in and get him!," and suchlike stuff. When his demands went unheeded, Dave pushed his way through the front door and was immediately shot dead by Hickok. The shot brought Woods and Gordon hotfooting to the house, but after being winged by Hickok they turned tail and tried to escape, with Wellman and Baker hard on their heels. They didn't get far: Wellman killed Woods with a garden hoe, and Baker dispatched Gordon with a blast from a shotgun. And that is the end of the affair at Rock Creek, for although Wellman, Hickok, and Baker were arrested shortly after the incident, they were never brought to trial. Note: There is no evidence that either Woods or Gordon fired a gun that day, so they were most likely unarmed. (See HICKOK, JAMES BUTLER.)

McCARTY, CATHERINE

The married name of an immigrant girl who was born Catherine Devine in Ireland in 1840. Catherine was about sixteen or seventeen years of age when she married Patrick McCarty and she bore him two sons: Joseph (most likely in 1858) and Patrick Henry (in 1859).[29] Catherine became a widow sometime in the 1860s, and in 1873 she married William H. Antrim. For almost a century writers have been saddling Catherine with a third husband, a phrase-and-fable character whom Kate had most likely never heard of, but a gentleman who has been given the name of William H. Bonney.[30] (See ANTRIM, CATHERINE; ANTRIM, WILLIAM H.; BONNEY, WILLIAM H.; and McCARTY, HENRY.)

[29] This is the lad who grew up to be the notorious "Billy the Kid."

[30] Just a passing thought: The only way we can put a little flesh on this "Bonney's" bones is to be presumptuous enough to suggest that Antrim may have used the alias of Bonney at some time. There is no evidence to support this, but the "William H." may be the link that will tie Antrim to the shadow at some future date.

MCCARTY HENRY The second son of Patrick and Catherine McCarty. Born on September 17, 1859, in New York City and christened Patrick Henry McCarty eleven days later at the Roman Catholic Church of St. Peter on Barclay Street. Sometime in the 1860s, either in New York or while heading West, Patrick, Sr. must have died,[31] for when Catherine and her two sons appeared in New Mexico in the early 1870s, Catherine was classing herself as a widow. In 1873 Catherine married William H. Antrim at Santa Fe, New Mexico, witnesses to the ceremony being her two sons, the younger of whom was now signing himself "Henry McCarty," Patrick evidently having been abandoned at some earlier date. Shortly after the marriage the family moved to Silver City in the southwestern corner of the territory, and here the newlyweds established a somewhat seamy boardinghouse which Catherine managed while her husband worked in the local silver mines.

On September 16, 1874, Catherine McCarty died, and young Henry, who wasn't on the best of terms with his stepfather, moved into the Star Hotel, an establishment owned by friendly neighbors and a place where Henry received free board and lodgings in return for helping out with the chores. Making beds and washing greasy dishes kept young McCarty busy for about twelve months; then he came under the influence of a sinful lad known only as "Sombrero Jack," an association that led to Henry being arrested on September 23, 1875, for stealing clothes from a couple of Chinese laundrymen. Two days later Henry escaped from the local lockup via the chimney and hightailed across the

Arizona line, settling in the region of Camp Grant, where he managed to find employment as a cowhand. In the summer of 1877 Henry, who was now known as Kid Antrim, was working for the J. W. Smith Ranch, and it was while he was thus employed that he shot a blacksmith named Frank P. Cahill to death. The shooting occurred in Adkins' Saloon at Fort Grant on the seventeenth of August, the "Kid" belly-gunning Cahill to death after the latter had called him a ". . . pimp!" Shortly after being arrested by Sheriff M. L. Wood, Henry made his second escape from a jail and headed back to Silver City.

At around this time southwestern New Mexico was being plagued by a gang of horse and cattle thieves led by Jesse Evans, a boyhood friend of Henry's during his early Silver City years, and a rustler whom Henry may have worked with prior to the killing of Cahill. Whether Henry was actively engaged as a rustler in 1876 cannot be confirmed, but after his escape from Camp Grant he is known to have teamed up with Evans and operated as a horse thief and stage robber, the stage job being a profitless bit of skulduggery that took place near Fort Cummings, New Mexico, in October 1877. A month after the abortive stage robbery, Kid Antrim appeared at George Coe's small ranch on the Ruidoso. George and his cousin Frank liked the bucktoothed little youth, and they allowed him to stay for most of the winter. This friendship with the Coes led to the Kid being introduced to John H. Tunstall, a wealthy English rancher whose spread was on the Rio Feliz, some thirty miles south of the town of Lincoln, New Mexico.[32] Tunstall evidently shared the

31 To have him die ties things up neatly, but although it is sometimes reported that he may have died of cholera in Kansas, there is always the possibility that Catherine called herself a widow to cover up the fact that her husband had left her.

32 One wonders if McCarty found this interview with Tunstall embarrassing, for he was well aware that he and Evans had rustled the Englishman's stock.

Coes' sentiments with regard to the little rider, for in January 1878 the Kid joined the Tunstall outfit, and a warm friendship developed between the tweedy gentleman from Middlesex and his new employee. (At this period Henry McCarty was using a plethora of names—Kid Antrim, Kid Billy, William H. Bonney,[33] and Billy the Kid—so to avoid confusion from here on, he will be referred to as "Billy the Kid," "the Kid," or just plain "Billy."

At this time Lincoln County was divided into two camps, its settlers either backing the Murphy-Dolan combination or supporting the Tunstall-McSween faction. The former group may be regarded as the shifty-eyed mob, while the latter group may be regarded as being on the side of the angels. Self-professed nonpartisans were regarded with suspicion by both sides. This state of affairs was to allow Billy but a short period of friendship with Tunstall, for Billy had hardly gotten around to smoking the boss' cheroots when the Englishman was murdered. This crime, which occurred on February 18, 1878, sparked off the shooting match known as the Lincoln County War, a period of murder and mayhem that was to keep the Kid's guns warm over the months to come. On March 9, Frank Baker and William Morton—active participants in the murder of Tunstall—fell before the guns of a posse of Tunstall hands that was led by Dick Brewer and Billy the Kid. On the first day of April, Sheriff William Brady and Deputy George Hindman were gunned down by the Kid and five of his henchmen,[34] and three days later a man named Jesse Andrews died after a grim shootout with Dick Brewer and Billy the Kid and a few of their gunnies. Jesse Andrews had not gone out unaccom-

panied. The fiery little man who had bee known as "Buckshot Roberts" had take Dick Brewer with him, and from th time on, Billy the Kid may be regarded ɛ the talk man for the Tunstall avenger Over the next few weeks two McSwee supporters were found dead in a ditcl and on May 1 Billy lost a top gunhan when Frank McNab died in an ambus killing.

Throughout this explosive period tl pockets of the Murphy-Dolan setup co tained a number of lawmen and polit cians whose shadows were anything b straight, and after encountering a nun ber of legal setbacks, McSween and h followers began to suspect that their con plete elimination was the object of the rivals. These suspicions led to some fort men and three women forting themselv behind the adobe walls of three of tl McSween properties on Monday, July 1: 1878. The three buildings, which wei located in Lincoln, consisted of the M Sween home, the adjacent Tunstall Stor and an adobe and stone tower know as the Torreon. The McSween home wa occupied by Mr. and Mrs. McSween; tl latter's sister; Billy the Kid; Jim Frencl Doc Scurlock; Harvey Morris; To O'Folliard; five Mexicans named Zamor Romero, Chavez, Gonzales, and Salaza and a certain Mrs. Ealy. Next do George Coe, Charlie Bowdre, an Hendry Brown peered out from behin the store's glazing, while Don Marti Chavez was in charge of a furth twenty-five gunnies who occupied tl Torreon.

Shortly after the McSween faction ha readied themselves to withstand a sieg newly appointed Sheriff George Pepp and Deputy Sheriff Marion Turn dusted into Lincoln at the head of a pos of forty guns. Peppin had a fistful c

---

[33] Spelled "Bonny" in the wanted fliers of a later date.
[34] James French, Frank McNab, Charlie Bowdre, Tom O'Folliard, and Fred Wayte.

murder warrants, and he demanded the immediate surrender of the besieged. Billy the Kid sneered, and shots began to buzz across the main street of Lincoln. There was plenty of noise over the next forty-eight hours of the action, but a minimum of casualties: Charles Crawford, a Peppin posseman, was the only participant who was unfortunate enough to stop lead during this period.[35] Sheriff Peppin requested help from Fort Stanton, which lay a few miles to the west of Lincoln, and Colonel N. A. M. Dudley, accompanied by a detachment of cavalry, two Gatling guns, and a piece of heavy ordnance, arrived at Lincoln on Thursday the eighteenth. This show of military muscle created little impression, and the status quo in Lincoln remained unchanged until early Friday morning, when Dudley arranged a truce to allow the womenfolk to leave the bullet-riddled McSween home. Mrs. Ealy and Mrs. McSween's sister took advantage of the lull and left the premises, but Mrs. McSween decided to stay with her husband.

In the early evening the rear of the McSween home was fired by Bob Beckwith and others in an attempt to smoke the inmates out. The fire took hold, and one can but imagine the situation that Billy the Kid faced; Mrs. McSween was playing the piano, her husband was chanting psalms, and although a bucket brigade was doing its damnedest, the flames were gaining control. At twilight Billy arranged a brief truce to allow Mrs. McSween to leave the inferno, a move that silenced the dangblasted piano and thus allowed his mind to function. To the rear of the premises the Rio Ruidoso flowed—if they could hold out until darkness, they might just make it. . . . Flames were dancing against a backdrop of indigo darkness when the Kid led the breakout, and all hell broke out. Gun flashes probed the night, and McSween died on his feet seconds before Beckwith was killed by a shot through the head; Romero and Zamora dropped and were still soaking up lead minutes after their deaths; Harvey Morris was killed as he reached the back-fence gate, and Salazar[36] dropped near the body of McSween. Billy the Kid and the remainder were lucky, fording the Ruidoso and reaching safety under cover of the darkness.

The death of McSween terminated the Lincoln County War, for although McSween had been backed by powerful cattle-baron John S. Chisum, the latter was in no mood to continue the feud after the death of his front man. Chisum funds, which had been paying the wages of Billy the Kid and company, were no longer available for this purpose, and the Kid went back to stock theft to keep himself off the bread line. On August 5, 1878, the Kid's gang raided the Mescalero Agency in southwestern New Mexico and rode off with a number of horses after killing agency clerk Morris J. Bernstein; this being but one incident in a string of operations that were carried out between the Panhandle and the Arizona line and that were mainly confined to whittling away at the Chisum herds. Much of the Kid's off time was spent in Fort Sumner, and here he became well known at the home of Pete Maxwell and even better known by the local *señoritas,* while his recreational pursuit of gambling was responsible for his becoming acquainted with Pat Garrett.

Meanwhile, the trouble in Lincoln County had not gone unnoticed by the White House, and in September 1878 President Rutherford B. Hayes relieved S. B. Axtell of his duties as territorial

[35] A large piece from a Sharps Big Fifty, which resulted in his death two days later.

[36] Although severely wounded, Salazar recovered, dying at Lincoln in 1936 at the age of seventy-three.

governor of New Mexico and appointed General Lew Wallace to the vacancy in the hope that Wallace would be able to heal the wounds that the feud had left in its wake. One of the new governor's first acts was to issue a proclamation that granted amnesty to all who had been engaged in the Lincoln County gunplay, provided such persons lay down their arms and were not—at the time of the amnesty—under indictment. As warrants for the Kid were awaiting execution at this time, the amnesty could hardly have been applicable to the little killer, but on March 17, 1879, the Kid and the governor met in secret at the home of Squire Wilson at Lincoln and made an attempt at coming to terms.[37] What transpired at this meeting is unknown, but it may be assumed that Wallace promised the Kid his support if the Kid would surrender to the law and stand trial for the various killings that were laid at his door; this assumption being based on the fact that Billy and Tom O'Folliard surrendered themselves to the authorities four days after the meeting.

Whether the governor attempted to help the Kid is open to dispute, but if he did, it was of little avail, for on April 15, Billy was indicted for the murders of Sheriff Brady and Deputy Hindman and placed under confinement to await trial. The jail was anything but escape-proof, and on June 17 Billy and O'Folliard vacated the premises and rode out of Lincoln. Shortly afterward the Kid was undisputed leader of a gang of rustlers that included O'Folliard, such past acquaintances as Doc Scurlock, Charlie Bowdre, and Hendry Brown, and newcomers Fred Wayte and Jack Middleton.

When the Dave Rudabaugh gang of rustlers joined up with the Kid at some later date, the united gangs can more or less be regarded as having monopolistic control of all rustling activities in the territory. Numerous reports have it that Billy the Kid killed a man named Joe Grant at Fort Sumner during this period, but as Billy was referring to Grant in the past tense some twelve months prior to this time, the shooting must have occurred at some earlier date.

In the spring of 1880 Pat Garrett was elected sheriff of Lincoln County, and the Kid's days were numbered. Although the Kid is reputed to have been well liked in the territory, after his killing of posseman James Carlyle at the Greathouse Ranch near Coyote Springs in November 1880, tips poured in to Garrett regarding the outlaw's whereabouts,[38] and on Christmas Eve 1880 Garrett—heeding one of these canaries—was lying in wait with a posse on the outskirts of Fort Sumner when Billy and four of his long-riders appeared out of the blizzard that was raging at the time. Guns flamed in the poor visibility and O'Folliard got a death wound in the first volley, but the other four riders disappeared into the gloom and were not overtaken. Two days later some of the Kid's luck ran out. Garrett got a tipoff that the Kid and four of his associates were holed-up in a derelict adobe hut at Stinking Springs, and Garrett got a cordon of possemen strung out around the building in the early hours of the twenty-seventh. The end result of this was that Charlie Bowdre was killed and Billy the Kid, Dave Rudabaugh, Tom Pickett, and Billy Wilson were taken into custody.

[37] A meeting that is reputed to have been arranged by Mrs. McSween.

[38] One of these, written and posted by a certain Zaferino Saenz at Arabela, New Mexico, on June 25, 1881, was somewhat tardy in arriving, being a deep-freeze hot tip when it was delivered to Garrett's heirs—Parvis P. Garrett and Paulina Garrett—in 1966 (eighty-five years too late).

Indicted under his alias of William H. Bonney for the murder of Sheriff Brady, the Kid was brought to trial in the federal district court at Mesilla, New Mexico, in the first week of April and, after being found guilty, he was sentenced to be hanged at Lincoln on May 13, 1881. The Kid was transferred to Lincoln and lodged in a top-floor room of the Lincoln County Courthouse, sheriff's deputies Bob Ollinger and James Bell being entrusted with the duties of guards. Handcuffs braceleted the prisoner's thin wrists, and leg irons controlled his movements, but on the twenty-eighth of April the Kid succeeded in cheating the hangman. At lunchtime on the day in question Ollinger left Bell in charge of the prisoner while Ollinger went across the street for his midday meal.

What transpired in the upstairs room of the courthouse after Ollinger's departure will never be ascertained, but we do know that Ollinger came running back to the courthouse after hearing the sounds of shots and that Billy the Kid killed him with a double blast from a shotgun whose twin muzzles protruded from an upstairs window of the courthouse. Shortly afterward, *sans* fetters and unopposed, Billy rode out of Lincoln, and a few minutes after he had disappeared the body of Deputy Sheriff Bell was found at the foot of the courthouse stairs, a bullet from a Colt .45 having accounted for his death. The Kid, who could have easily crossed the line into Mexico, returned to Fort Sumner. Legend has it that nubile hips and pneumatic breasts were the lure that attracted Billy back to his old stamping ground: Deluvina Maxwell, the newly widowed Manuela Bowdre, or the flashing-eyed Celsa Gutierrez? *¿Quien sabe?*

Early in July, Garrett received news that the escapee was in the Fort Sumner area, and on the night of July 13, 1881, accompanied by deputies Tip McKinney and John W. Poe, Garrett began making the rounds of the town in an all-out search for the Kid. Sometime after midnight Garrett entered the home of Pete Maxwell after detailing his deputies to remain on the porch. The sheriff entered Maxwell's bedroom and shook Pete awake to ask him if he knew the Kid's whereabouts at the same moment as Billy moved onto the porch and bumped into the deputies. Garrett heard the Kid querying the deputies' reason for being there, and Garrett ducked down beside Pete's bed as the deputies—who had failed to recognize the small silhouette—satisfied the new arrival that they meant no harm. Seconds later the Kid entered the gloom of Maxwell's bedroom and asked in rapid Spanish, "Who are those men outside, Pete?" The Kid was standing against the moonlit rectangle of the doorway with a double-action Colt dangling from his right hand. Garrett had the advantage. He clicked back the hammer of his Colt, and gun lightning illuminated the scene as the double-action was being raised. By the time a lamp had been lit, the Kid was dead; Garrett's bullet had pierced his heart. The bloody trail of Patrick Henry McCarty was ended. Point of interest: There are three—perhaps four—photographs of the Kid still extant; the full-length portrait, which is usually printed in reverse and gives the impression of the Kid being left-handed (which he was not) is more frequently used than the others. (See ANDREWS, JESSE; ANTRIM, CATHERINE; ANTRIM, WILLIAM H.; BAKER, FRANK; BARBER, SUSAN McSWEEN; BONNEY, WILLIAM H.; BRADY, WILLIAM; BROWN, HENDRY; CHISUM, JOHN S.; CHISUM, SALLY; EVANS, JESSE; GARRETT, PATRICK FLOYD; GRANT, JOE; LINCOLN COUNTY WAR; MAXWELL, DELUVINA; MAXWELL, PETE; McCARTY, CATHERINE; TUNSTALL, JOHN HENRY; and WILSON, BILLY.)

MCDOUGAL, ANNIE
A little wench whose brief association with the Doolin gang has led to her going down in the books as "Cattle Annie." Annie, born near Pawnee in the Osage nation[39] in 1876 of penurious parents, left home with a teen-age lass named Jennie Stevens when she was sixteen and became a camp follower of the Doolin gang who, at that time, were using Ingalls, Oklahoma, as their recreational center. While supplying the Doolin band with carnal comforts, Annie is reputed to have taken part in a few minor rustling raids and to have engaged in the peddling of illicit whiskey, minor crimes that can be regarded as little more than childish pranks. Annie and Jennie were finally arrested by Deputy U. S. Marshals Bill Tilghman and Steve Burke after being traced to an old farmhouse at Pawnee. Annie put up a tooth-and-claw resistance that denuded Burke of much of his hair, but a short time later she found herself behind bars at Perry, and within a matter of weeks she was starting a two-year stretch at Farmington, Massachusetts. Shortly after her release in 1896, Annie got herself married and settled down in her old hometown, honest domestic obscurity being her lot from then on. (See STEVENS, JENNIE.)

MCDOWELL, JOHN   Member of the Daly quartet of hard cases. (See DALY GANG.)

MCGINNIS, ELZA LAY   Possibly an alias, although there is some doubt about this. (See LAY, ELZA.)

MCGLUE, LUKE   A nonexistent character who ghosted around Dodge City, Kansas, during its boom years. The creation of Dodge's in-set, the unsub-

[39] In northeastern Oklahoma.

stantial Luke was blamed when any visiting greenhorn complained of being the victim of a practical joke or petty theft. Luke McGlue can therefore be regarded as a fictitious patsy and nothing more.

MCINTYRE, CHARLES   Native of Pennsylvania who was lynched by the 301 Vigilante Movement at Belmont, Nevada, on June 2, 1874. The fact that Charlie had never killed or robbed anyone and was only sixteen years old at the time of his death makes his lynching somewhat unique. McIntyre and an acquaintance named John Walker were arrested after the latter had wounded a man named Sutherland in a gunfight, although Charlie had been little more than a spectator at the time. On May 31—eleven days after the shooting—the two youths broke jail, but within forty-eight hours they had been traced to a disused mineshaft and rearrested by Sheriff J. Caldwell. Sometime around midnight of the day of their arrest a mob stormed the local jail, and McIntyre and Walker were hanged from a ceiling beam of their underground cell. The motivation for this mob action appears flimsy, but if we take heed to the rumors that the two young men had been trying to organize the mine workers in the area, it could well be that mining interests were behind the vigilante action.

MCINTYRE, JAMES   Texas gunman whom Jim Courtright employed as an aide during the latter's squatter-busting activities. After being involved in the murder of two Frenchmen, McIntyre was arrested by the Texas Rangers, but before he could be brought to trial he escaped from jail and fled to South America. Some years later—when old crimes had become pretty old-hat—Jim recrossed the international line and settled down at Woodward, Oklahoma. What he did in South America is anyone's guess, but after his return to the States we do know that he hung up his guns, and that at some later date he became a one-shot author after publication of a book he had written about his experiences in the Panhandle and points west. (See COURTRIGHT, JIM.)

McKINNEY, JAMES A buttocks-and breast-mutilating sadist who was born in Illinois in 1861, moving into California's San Joaquin Valley with his parents at some later date. McKinney killed his first man at Leadville, Colorado in 1879, afterward shooting off one of the nipples of his victim's girlfriend as a closure to the incident; the maimed girl's lack of interest in James having been the cause of the dispute. Over the next few years James gave a cancan dancer fun-stuff wounds in her rump, placed lead in a barman's backside, whittled a piece from one of a schoolteacher's ears, and knifed a couple of lawmen; a lot of stupid assin' about that finally got him a seven-year stretch in San Quentin.

After his release, friends of McKinney's[40] brought him up to date by giving him a brief rundown as to what had occurred during the time he had spent behind walls. One such piece of information, relating how a man named Sears had sparked McKinney's flame for a solid fourteen days while the girl had been a prisoner of the said debaucher, brought a mad gleam to James' baby-blue eyes, and on December 13, 1901, he shot Sears to death. Within seconds of the shooting James is reputed to have put bullet-sculptured canyons into the bare butt of a lawman who appeared

from within a nearby privy to see what all the fuss was about, the typical "McKinney touch" thus becoming an epilogue to the episode. McKinney, oddly enough, was acquitted of this killing and maiming affray, but by the following year folk were getting fed up with wearing cast-iron pants when James was around, and they let it be known that his presence was no longer desired around his home base of Porterfield, California. Badman McKinney didn't wish to leave, but after wounding two lawmen and a citizen and killing a man named William Linn, he fled the state with a posse following his surrey tracks.

The fugitive clouded the dust across Arizona, with Tucson and Tombstone noting his passing as he headed for the border. James crossed the line into Sonora in the vicinity of Aqua Prieta, then, for some unaccountable reason, he reversed direction and dusted back toward California, shotgunning two prospectors to death near Kingman, Arizona, before the territory saw the last of him. By the second week of April 1903 McKinney had let it be known that he had gone to earth within an opium den at Bakersfield, California, and was awaiting a showdown with the lawmen. On the night of April 18, City Marshal Jeff Packard and five deputies kicked open the front door of McKinney's retreat, and gunfire rocked the town. The marshal and Deputy Marshal William Tibbett[41] were killed within seconds of entering the opium den, but James McKinney died from a large intake of Winchester and shotgun lead before he could do any further damage.

McLAUGHLIN, PATRICK One of a pair of highly insolvent Irish pros-

40 Seems kinda strange that he should have any.
41 Of passing interest: Deputy Marshal Tibbett was the father of Lawrence Tibbett, the Metropolitan Opera star who appeared in a few movies during the 1930s.

pectors who discovered the fabulous Comstock Lode. (See COMSTOCK LODE.)

MCLAURY, FRANK Onetime cow-hand[42] who, in partnership with his brother, had established a small spread a few miles south of Tombstone, Arizona, by the late 1870s. As both Frank and Tom had the reputation of being stock thieves, they may have established themselves as ranchers in this manner. Although hard-working ranchers, the brothers were also members of Old Man Clanton's gang, and Frank most likely did his share of killing in the Guadalupe Canyon massacre. Frank was shot to death during the gunfight outside the O. K. Corral at Tombstone in 1881. The name is frequently spelled "Mc-Lowery," but this is incorrect.[43] (See CLAIBORNE, BILLY; CLANTON GANG; and O. K. CORRAL.)

MCLAURY, TOM Younger brother of Frank McLaury and the latter's almost constant companion in affairs both legal and illegal. Although a Clanton man, there is no record of Tom ever having killed anyone, for he wasn't in attendance at the bloody affair in Guadalupe Canyon. Thomas was dropped in his tracks by much lead at the O. K. Corral in 1881. (See CLAIBORNE, BILLY; CLANTON GANG; MCLAURY, FRANK; and O. K. CORRAL.)

MCNAB, FRANK Friend of Billy the Kid and active participant in the Lincoln County War. Frank was an accessory in the murders of Sheriff William Brady and Deputy Sheriff George Hindman, and he was a member of the Dick Brewer posse that escorted prisoners Morton and Baker to their rendezvous with death.[44] On May 1, 1878, Frank McNab became the victim of an ambush killing. (See BAKER, FRANK; BRADY, WILLIAM; LINCOLN COUNTY WAR; and McCARTY, HENRY.)

MCNELLY, LEE H. In 1874 Lee McNelly, a frail and consumptive Southerner who had been a captain in the armies of the Confederacy, was appointed commandant of the Special Battalion of Texas Rangers, a force that had been organized to combat international smuggling and rustling rings that operated in the U.S.-Mexican border region. Despite the professed duties of the battalion, one of McNelly's first actions was to suppress the Sutton-Taylor feud, an entirely domestic affair that had been taking its toll of the inhabitants of De-Witt County. After this McNelly moved down to Brownsville, and in June 1875 he and a detail of his men were engaged in a running gunfight with a band of Juan Cortina's rustlers who had been herding more than two hundred head of King Ranch stock toward the border. As the end result of this skirmish, twelve Mexican rustlers lay dead on foreign soil, McNelly had lost a "soldier," and the stolen beeves were heading back North. At some later date, obsessed with the desire of smashing Cortina's empire, McNelly crossed the Rio Grande with some three dozen of his "soldiers" and shot it out with Cortinastas whenever they came upon them, on one occasion

[42] Both brothers had worked at a number of ranches in the Arizona and New Mexico territories, one of these being the John S. Chisum Jinglebob outfit.

[43] A third brother, who had a law practice at Fort Worth, Texas, wrote numerous letters after the affair at the O. K. Corral condemning the Earps' actions, and in all of these he signed himself "W. R. McLaury."

[44] Seconds before the killing of Morton and Baker, McNab shot fellow posseman Thomas McCloskey to death after an argument that revolved around the possible fate of the prisoners.

routing more than three hundred outlaws in a single engagement. McNelly's invasion, which was somewhat illegal, reduced the Latin Americans' desire to cross the boundary, and large-scale rustling sorties into Texas were soon a thing of the past. Early in 1877 McNelly resigned from the Rangers for reasons of ill health, and he died on September 4 of that year from tuberculosis at the age of thirty-three years. (See CORTINA, JUAN NEPOMUCENA, and SUTTON-TAYLOR FEUD.)

MCSWEEN, ALEXANDER A.
Born in Prince Edward Island, Canada, of Scottish parents who molded their son into their own strict Presbyterian image. On reaching adulthood, McSween took up residence in the United States, and here he studied law, setting up a practice at Eureka, Kansas, after graduating from Washington University in St. Louis. In the early 1870s he moved his practice to Atchison, Kansas, where, in 1874, he married a Pennsylvania girl named Susan Hummer. In 1875, possibly for reasons relating to McSween's health, the couple moved West, settling at Lincoln, New Mexico, where McSween resumed his interrupted practice. Local mugwump Major Lawrence G. Murphy became one of the new resident's first clients when he retained McSween to defend a number of rustlers who were accused of reducing John S. Chisum's herds, but McSween's Presbyterian conscience persuaded him to retire from the case upon his becoming convinced of Murphy's collusion with the accused. Crossing Murphy led to McSween becoming associated with John S. Chisum and a transplanted Englishman named John H. Tunstall, and in 1877, partnered by Tunstall, McSween became joint proprietor of the Lincoln County Bank and General Store. These enterprises, which were in direct opposition to similar concerns backed by Murphy and his partner James J. Dolan, were to lead to a clash of business interests that was to break out into open warfare with the killing of Tunstall in February 1878. The fact that McSween never fired any shots—although he may have poured many from a bottle—during the bloody affray that was to become known as the Lincoln County War is pretty well established, but this lack of active participation didn't prevent him being shot to death during the night of July 18–19, 1878. (See BARBER, SUSAN MCSWEEN; CHISUM, JOHN S.; DOLAN, JAMES J.; LINCOLN COUNTY WAR; MCCARTY, HENRY; MURPHY, LAWRENCE G.; and TUNSTALL, JOHN HENRY.)

MCSWEEN, SUSAN A red-headed gal from Gettysburg, Pennsylvania, who had to duck much flying lead during the latter part of her marriage to the ill-fated Alexander McSween. At some later date Susan remarried, an event that has led to her having a somewhat larger entry under the name of "Barber." (See BARBER, SUSAN MCSWEEN; LINCOLN COUNTY WAR; MCCARTY, HENRY; and MCSWEEN, ALEXANDER A.)

MEDICINE BUNDLE Name given to a bundle of objects that were considered sacred by their Amerind owner or owners. A medicine bundle could be either communally or privately owned; in the former case the custodian of the bundle would be the medicine man, while a privately owned bundle could be passed down from father to son or—in some instances—buried with its owner. An assortment of almost anything of animal, mineral, or vegetable origin, or small man-made objects, could make up the contents of a bundle, an object being deemed "sacred" after its owner had been made aware of its value by its appearance in a dream or vision. Wrappings could be of cloth, buckskin, fur, or the complete skin of some small animal, and a rawhide loop would be attached for carrying purposes. Bundles were assumed to have healing and protective qualities and were of aid when attempting to establish contact with the Great Spirit. An assortment of sacred objects carried in a small bag and worn hanging from a neck cord is usually referred to as a "medicine bag."

MEDICINES AND REMEDIES

Although frontier medical doctors were usually highly talented, didn't drop dead of shock if they were called out at 2 A.M. but readily hastened to the patient's side even if it involved a fifty-mile ride by muledeck, and were tardy in sending out padded accounts, they were few in number. This shortage—which led to large areas being out of reach of a diplomaed man's services—together with many an early settler's lack of faith in anyone who appeared so unsure of his own ability that death certificates outnumbered the bills in his wallet—made a cursory knowledge of folk medicine a must for residents of the wilderness. A few of the crosses of a medical nature that prairie and backwoods folk had to contend with, and some of the remedies that were used in their efforts to avoid the erection of crosses of a more substantial nature, are given below.

Aches and Pains. Laudanum or morphine. These drugs could be readily obtained from mail-order houses in the 1900s. They may not have cured anything, but they made the patient feel ruddy good.

Boils. Soap and sugar; two parts of soap to one of sugar, heated and used as a poultice.

Bruises. See *Inflammation and sprains* in this entry.

Cuts. Soot or cobwebs used to stop the flow of blood.

Ear Abscess. A few drops of urine in the affected ear.

Inflammation and sprains. Comfrey leaves boiled in water. The mass of hot greenery is applied to the affected area, a bandage being used to keep the medicant in position. Comfrey is frequently referred to as "knitbone." This is a very effective remedy.[45]

Kidney complaints. Watermelon seeds boiled in water, the liquid being drunk after it had been strained.

Mad-dog bite. Application of a mad stone to the wound.

Rabies. If bitten by any creature suspected of being in a rabid condition, a mad stone was used to draw the wound.

Rheumatism. Rattlesnake oil, bear oil, or goose grease rubbed into the affected area. Alternatively, flick the offending area with a switch of nettles.

Septic wounds. Pack salt pork around the wound. Reputed to have been highly effective.

Snake bite. Open the wound with a knife and suck like mad. Mad stones were occasionally used.

Stomach ache. Oil of peppermint or mustard in hot water.

Ulcerated mouth. Mouthwash brewed from red oak bark.

Whooping cough. Treated with an unholy stew of sheep tallow, turpentine, beeswax, and coal oil. A rag that had been soaked in the mess was worn on the chest.

[45] Sure is! This writer has used the concoction on numerous occasions.

During the famine of M.D.s—and for many decades afterward—medicine shows toured the West, and although most of these were run by confidence tricksters who sold "cure-alls" that invariably had a high content of morphine or alcohol, they no doubt brought much solace to the nonjunkies and teetotalers who liked to get high in a genteel manner. Mystic healers (faith healers) and practitioners of the art of powwowing[46] also had their following. (See MAD STONE.)

MEDICINE WHEEL The name that has been given to a giant man-made landmark that is located on a high mesa in Wyoming's Big Horn Mountains. The rim, hub, and spokes[47] of this monumental effort are composed of slabs of limestone, and as these lie on rather flat ground, the "wheel" may only be viewed as such from the air. This mysterious marker—or whatever it was intended to be—is about 250 feet in diameter. Assumed to be of prehistoric origin, an unoriginal line of thought that will have to stand until something better comes along.

MEEKER MASSACRE An incident that occurred in northwestern Colorado during the Ute War of 1879. In September of that year a Ute war party under the leadership of a subchief named José Ignacio swept down upon the White River Ute Agency and murdered Agent Nathan C. Meeker and all his male staff. Mrs. Arvilla Meeker, her daughter Josephine, and a sixteen-year-old girl named Flora Price were taken captive, but they were released within thirty days after Chief Ouray had intervened on their behalf. (See MEEKER, NATHAN C., and OURAY.)

MEEKER, NATHAN C. Member of the editorial staff of Horace Greeley's New York *Tribune* who moved West in the spring of 1869 to establish a colony on the White River in northwestern Colorado. Nathan was fifty-two years of age at this time, had been married some twenty-five years,[48] and possessed a brood of five children, and he was a strict teetotaler who was somewhat short of U.S. currency. He was, however, not short of energy. The temperance colony of Greeley became a place on the map, and such was Nathan's fanatical hatred of both free-roaming beeves and whiskey-soaked bums that he had a barbed-wire fence erected around the town to prevent its hallowed precincts being plagued by either menace. In 1878 the near-penurious Meeker was lucky enough to be appointed agent on the White River Ute Reservation. Meeker, a well-meaning idiot who most likely had a "There's no fun like work" motto hanging over his bed, immediately attempted to herd his wards into the civilized rat-race by insisting that an Indian who didn't work wouldn't eat. By adopting this policy, the new agent trod on a large number of moccasin-covered corns, and in the year following his appointment a war party of Utes impaled poor Nathan to the ground of his own backyard. Agent Meeker left a widow and four children.[49] (See GREELEY, HORACE, and MEEKER MASSACRE.)

[46] The art of commanding the complaint to "Begone!," "Get lost!," or whatever. Practiced mainly by folk of Teutonic stock, and not altogether successful, for although the complaint usually heeded the command, it not infrequently took the patient with it.

[47] There are twenty-eight of these.

[48] A Connecticut girl named Arvilla Delight Smith having become his bride in April 1844.

[49] Widow Arvilla died in 1905 at the age of eighty years.

MELDRUM, ROBERT A small, unpleasant individual who is on record as having been born in New York, New York, in 1865, reputedly the son of a British Army officer. Meldrum has left such a blurred negative of his passing that only a patchy print of his early whereabouts and activities may be obtained, and it is not until he was thirty-four years of age that we hear from him again. The year is 1899 and Meldrum is working as a saddle- and harnessmaker in a store at Baggs, Wyoming, and here folk avoided him as a troublemaker when the rumors got around that he had a few killings behind him. The following year, possibly in view of his rumored past, he was appointed town marshal of Dixon, Wyoming, and in the spring of 1901, while thus employed, he killed a man named Noah Wilkinson, the latter being a Texas gunman with a price on his head. Shortly after this shootout Meldrum moved to Telluride, Colorado, to take up employment as a guard with the strike-hit Smuggler Union Mine, but although a few strikers were made very dead over the next couple of years, we may only speculate as to whether Bob had a hand in any of these killings.[50]

On April 1, 1904, another definitive notch was added to Meldrum's tally when he killed Olaf Thisall, a miner who was smuggling whiskey into the workings in defiance of company orders. Four years later Meldrum was arrested for the killing of miner David Lambert, but on April 15, 1908, a jury handed down a "not guilty" verdict, and Bob was released. Shortly after this brush with the law Meldrum returned to Baggs accompanied by a girl who may, or may not,

have been his wife, and within a matter of weeks of his arrival he is reputed to have been authorized to wear a deputy sheriff's badge.

In the summer of 1910 John "Chick" Bowen—a happy, extrovert half-breed from Oklahoma—got a fatal dose of lead from Meldrum's pistol after he had come under suspicion of casting randy glances in the direction of "Mrs." Meldrum. Bob was arrested for this "green-eyed" killing, but after being granted bail[51] at his preliminary hearing, he fled the state[52] and he didn't return to stand trial until six years had elapsed, and it was not until June 28, 1916, that he was convicted of manslaughter and given a five-to-seven-year stretch in Wyoming's State Penitentiary. The jailbird spent about three months behind bars, and then he was released on parole into the custody of a Carbon County rancher named Will Daley. At the termination of his parole in 1923 Meldrum settled at Walcott and opened a saddler's business, but this enterprise was doomed by Bob's fits of uncontrollable rage, and when the place was burned to the ground in 1929 few tears were shed for its passing. What became of Meldrum after this must remain a mystery, although he is reported to have been seen, or have died, in California, Colorado, or New York at later dates. (See HORN, TOM.)

MERRICK, DICK
Convicted, together with a man named Jebb Sharp, of the robbery-murder of John Bascum, a Missouri horse trader. The crime occurred in Jackson County, Missouri, in 1864, and preparations for the sendoff of the killers, via the local hanging

---

[50] Sometime around this period he is known to have been acquainted with Tom Horn, and he may have helped Tom with a few of his killing chores.

[51] Local ranchowners raised the eighteen-thousand-dollar bail, a generous gesture that leads one to suspect that Bob may have been an accessory of Horn's (see previous footnote).

[52] He probably went in search of his woman, for the lass had skipped out immediately after his arrest.

tree, had been completed within twenty-four hours of the jury having reached a verdict. The hanging went off according to schedule, but on returning to the jail, Deputy Sheriff Clifford Stewart found Merrick and Sharp safe and well inside their cell; someone had blundered. Hours later an explanation was forthcoming: Two drunks who had been tossed into the tank the previous night to sleep off their orgy had been taken from their cell and hanged in error while still in an unprotesting hungover state. The passing of these boozed-up innocents imparted a silver lining to the clouds that clustered around the heads of Dick and Jebb, for the presiding judge, on being notified that they had not been hanged at the time stated in his sentence, ordered their immediate release. This little story should go down very well at any temperance meeting.

MERWIN HULBERT REVOLVER Six-shot metal-cartridge revolvers that were manufactured for Merwin Hulbert and Company by the gun-making firm of Hopkins and Allen, the pistols thus being named after their distributor rather than their manufacturer. The revolvers came in a variety of calibers and barrel lengths, in models with or without top straps, and were similar in appearance to the contemporaneous Smith and Wessons. The guns were distributed throughout the West during the 1870s by Fred Merwin, who acted as selling agent for the company, and within a short time of his being killed by Indians in the late 1870s, Merwin and Hulbert sidearms became a thing of the past.

MESA A high, flat plateau with precipitous slopes on all sides that is frequently found in the vicinity of a river valley. The word is Spanish for "table."

MESA VERDE Located in southwestern Colorado, this high plateau was the home of various aboriginal cultures that flourished in the area from the beginning of the first century A.D. to around A.D. 1300. The site contains hundreds of ruined villages (many of which have still to be excavated) and well-preserved pueblo buildings and cliff dwellings. The Mesa Verde National Park, an area of 80 square miles that contains all these archaeological treasures, was established in 1906, and it is now one of Colorado's foremost tourist attractions.

MESCAL An intoxicating and hallucinatory drink that is prepared by the distillation of the fermented juices of the American aloe or maguey plants.

MESCALERO APACHES Tribal division of the Apache nation whose domestic habitat was the southeastern area of New Mexico but whose range extended as far west as the Rio Grande and south into Mexico.

MESTEÑA, JUANA The Mexican name for Sarah Jane Newman or Sally Skulle. (See NEWMAN, SARAH JANE.)

MÉTIS Name applied to a race of plains traders whose origins and activities were born out of the North American fur trade. Although domiciled in Canada, the métis[53] made annual pilgrimages across the United States border to trade with the plains tribes; lumbering

---

[53] The French term for one of mixed blood, and very apt in this instance, for a heady mixture of English, Scotch, French, and Amerind blood flowed in their veins; none of the métis was racially pure.

wooden carts,[54] which could be drawn by either horses or oxen, were used for these journeys. These traders from the north country were fluent in the languages of the tribes they dealt with and were well versed in Indian lore, joint accomplishments that led to them being well received over the whole area of their operations. Boise brulé[55] is an alternative name for the métis.

MILLER, CHARLIE Born in a covered wagon that was moving toward the sunset in the shadow of Mount Shasta (northern California), its ultimate destination being Sacramento. At the age of eleven, Charlie was riding pony on the express route between Sacramento and Carson City, Nevada, a short-lived chore that got him an arrowhead wound before the Pony Express came to an end in the fall of 1861. After this Charlie had many jobs, broncho busting—which earned him the sobriquet of "Broncho Charlie"—and stagecoach driving being but two of these. In 1867 Charlie's parents had their lives and their hair taken by a party of hostiles, and over the next few years the orphaned youth served as an Army scout and dispatch rider as a retaliatory gesture against the red varmints. In later life "Broncho Charlie" joined the Buffalo Bill Wild West show,[56] and England had him for a spell in 1887 when Cody's show was touring Europe. In 1918, although sixty-eight years of age, Charlie managed to enlist in the 18th Hussars by cutting more than twenty years off his age, and he served in the British Army for eight months during the latter stages of World War I. Charlie Miller died in New York City on January 15, 1955. Shortly before his death Charlie laid claim to being the last of the Pony Express riders, and as he was 105 years old at the time he checked out, his claim could well be justified.

MILLER, CLELLAND A swarthy-complected, curly-haired youth who became a member of the James gang in the early 1870s and who is sometimes reported—quite incorrectly—as having adopted the alias of William Stiles.[57] After serving little more than an outlaw apprenticeship by taking part in a few of the gang's robberies and holdups, Clel was shot to death during the Northfield disaster in 1876. A young medical student named H. M. Wheeler was responsible for Clel's demise and, as such, he claimed his "trophy" and had the curly-haired remains rendered down to skeleton status so that his victim might aid him in his studies. Skeletons were hard to come by in those days, so Clel must have been worth his weight in lead to Wheeler, and when the latter became a fully qualified practitioner he showed his appreciation by giving Miller's framework free lodgings in a cabinet in his office. (See JAMES GANG and NORTHFIELD, MINNESOTA.)

MILLER, HORN Old-time mountain man who was born at St. Louis, Missouri, in 1825. By the time he reached his teens, bare-knuckle boxing was the favorite sport of the Mississippi waterfront towns, and it wasn't long before Horn, who possessed fists like cast-iron pineapples, was wearing the cherished red belt of a cham-

[54] Axles and all running gear were also made of wood; no metal whatsoever was used in the construction of these carts.
[55] Canuck-French for "burned wood," but a term that may also be applied to a half-breed.
[56] Charlie Miller is listed in the official program as an "eight-horse driver."
[57] Bill Chadwell, another ill-starred follower of Jesse James, used this alias, and this might have given rise to the confusion.

pion. Sometime during the 1840s Miller moved into Montana Territory and took up trapping for a livelihood, an occupation he was active in until 1862, in which year he was bitten by the prospector bug after hearing stories of the gold strikes being made along Grasshopper Creek. From this time on[58] Horn became completely obsessed with locating a bonanza, but although he found sufficient yellow metal to keep him in necessities and tobacco, he never succeeded in making the Big Strike. In 1872 Miller staked three claims—Stump, Shoo Fly, and Josephine —in southern Montana,[59] and he was still engaged in the working of these claims when he died in 1913. Montana's Miller Mountain and Miller Creek are named after this onetime fisticuff champion of the Mississippi Valley.

MILLER, JIM A dapper little man who never cussed, was quiet of speech and mild of manner, yet a man who is reputed to have been a hired killer whose gun butts could have been justifiably corrugated with notches had he been of a whittling turn of mind. It is difficult to ascertain whether this reputation of homicidal activity is justified, for most of his alleged victims are nameless men who died on dateless days and are buried in unmarked graves. We do know that Miller was born in McCulloch County, Texas, and that he achieved a certain amount of notoriety through marital ties that linked him with the loudmouthed Mannen Clements and John Wesley Hardin, and that much of his adult life was spent in the legitimacy of the hotel business; it is a fairly well-established fact that he killed his brother-in-law, and it is

a well-recorded fact that in April 1895 he was wounded in a gunfight with a gent named Frazier.[60]

During the month of February 1908 well-substantiated reports place Miller at Las Cruces, New Mexico, where he was posing as a wealthy Oklahoma rancher, although there is no evidence that he ever possessed such a spread. Over this period a man using the name of Carl Adamson was negotiating with Pat Garrett over the sale of the latter's ranch, and Adamson told Garrett that "rancher" Jim Miller was putting up some of the money. This deal was never accomplished, for Garrett was shot dead on the morning of February 29, and a man named Brazel surrendered to the authorities for the killing. Despite Brazel's confession, Miller has long been suspected of the slaying of Garrett, and there is a vague possibility that Miller and Adamson may have been one and the same man, Miller having used this name and the pose of a prospective buyer in order to win Pat's confidence so that Miller could accomplish a contract murder at little risk to himself. If this assumption is correct, we have to accept as a fact the theory that Brazel was paid to accept responsibility for this "self-defense" killing and that parties unknown footed the bill for the murder. The question "Who killed Garrett?" will never be resolved to everyone's satisfaction, for Miller didn't live long enough to write his memoirs.

Early in April 1909 Jim killed City Marshal "Gus" Bobbitt at Ada, Oklahoma. This was a contract murder executed from ambush, but it wasn't entirely successful, for Bobbitt named his killer before he died, and Miller and his em-

[58] If we ignore a short spell spent as an Army scout during the Nez Percé outbreak of 1877.
[59] Located between the town of Gardiner, Montana, and the Montana-Wyoming boundary.
[60] The fight occurred at Pecos City, Texas, and although some reports state that Miller was wearing a local lawman's badge at this time (city marshal or deputy sheriff of the county), there appears little to support these stories.

ployers—three men named Allen, Burwell, and West—were arrested and lodged in the local jail. Bobbitt, who in private life had been a moderately wealthy cattleman, had been an extremely popular resident of Ada, and in the early hours of April 19 an irate mob cut down the town's power lines and stormed the jail. The early-morning sunlight, filtering into the cool interior of a local disused barn, illuminated the dangling forms of Jim "Killer" Miller and his three employers, all of whom had been launched into eternity from the back of a white horse that was unconcernedly searching for fodder when a photographer arrived on the scene to preserve the grisly group for posterity.[61] (See GARRETT, PATRICK FLOYD.)

MILNER, MOSES A vague figure whose "California Joe" sobriquet is frequently come across when reading of "saber vs. tomahawk" encounters. Little is known of "Joe's" early life, and although it is generally accepted that his actual name was Moses Milner, such alternatives as Joseph Milmer and Joseph Hawkins cannot be disregarded as being just a "load of bullrushes." As an Army scout, Moses was evidently in demand, for he was earning his baccy and booze money in this capacity for almost two decades, being Custer's chief of scouts during the Washita campaign and during the Black Hills expedition of 1875. Moses was still engaged as an Army employee when his string ran out, this terminal point in his earthling role being brought about by a gent named Tom Newcomb, who shot California Joe dead at Fort Robinson, Nebraska, on October 29, 1876. Although Tom had shot Moses in the back, he was never brought to trial

for the crime, for at that time civilian law had yet to reach the region.

MILTON, JEFFERSON Jefferson Davis Milton, who was born in Marianna County, Florida, on November 7, 1851, and started his working life as a store clerk, moved West in 1867 to live with relatives, a move that was instrumental in channeling Jeff's activities into the lawman's role he was to be engaged in for the greater part of his lifetime. After working for a couple of years as a ranchhand, Milton joined the Texas Rangers in 1880, completing a three-year tour of duty with this paramilitary force before accepting a job as deputy sheriff of Val Verde County, Texas. In 1885 Jeff moved West into New Mexico and pinned on a deputy sheriff's badge at Socorro, and two years later he was serving in a similar capacity under Sheriff Perry Owens of Apache County, Arizona. Jeff wore this latter badge for but a few weeks before he moved back into Texas to take up the duties of a border patrolman, and anti-smuggling activities kept him occupied until 1889.

The following year saw him as a Pinal County deputy sheriff in Arizona, and after handing in this badge he tried for a heavier paycheck by taking up employment with a railroad company, but by 1894 he was completely jaded with both fireman and conductor duties, and when he was offered the appointment of chief of police at El Paso, Texas, he eagerly accepted. It was while he was wearing the El Paso badge that Jeff had his run-in with "Texas killer" John Wesley Hardin, a bulletless encounter that occurred in 1895, and shortly after Jeff and his boys had killed outlaw Martin McRose. John Wesley, who at this time was shacking up

---

[61] Dapper Jim Miller hangs on the left of this photograph, and although the rope has jerked his head far backward, his derby hat still remains in position; it must have been a helluva tight fit.

with Mrs. McRose, spread the gossip that his money had bribed the cops into blasting McRose, but when Milton braced him with spreading this scandal, the Texas killer backed down and admitted he was a liar. On leaving El Paso, Jeff became a Wells Fargo express guard, and on February 20, 1900, at Fairbanks, Arizona, he received a slight bullet wound while guarding a rail shipment, a skirmish that ended with one of the gunmen dead and four others in custody. Later years saw Milton employed with the Immigration Service as a border patrolman, duties that consisted of patrolling the Rio Grande on the lookout for Chinese and Mexicans who were attempting to enter the United States illegally. Jefferson Davis Milton died in 1947, after spending his years of retirement in southern Arizona. (See HARDIN, JOHN WESLEY.)

MIMBREÑO APACHES   Tribal branch of the Apaches who located between the Rio Grande and the Mogollon Mountains in southwestern New Mexico. Mangas Colorado of the Copper Mine band was one of the better-known Mimbreño chiefs. (See MANGAS COLORADO.)

MINER, BILL   A rather unique character who spent about fifty years of his life clocking up crime time and is reputed to have been the originator of the "Hands up!" curtain raiser that usually precedes any robbery. William, who was born at Bowling Green, Kentucky, in 1847, drifted West around 1860 to try his luck in the California gold fields, but Bill was evidently a miner in name only, for where he panned, one would have needed the Midas touch to produce color, so in 1863 he gave up searching and took up employment as an Army dispatch rider,

a short-lived spell on sweating mounts from which he accrued sufficient capital to set him up in a one-man mail-carrying business. This mail run, which was based on San Diego, California, and had a delivery service that extended as far east as the Gila River in Arizona, kept Bill supplied with funds until his tastes outgrew his income, and toward the end of 1868 the monkey on Bill's back had become so heavy that he was forced into bankruptcy to pay off his creditors.

This business failure, bad companions, or both, may have been responsible for Bill's straying from the straight and narrow, for in 1869, by committing his first stage robbery, he joined the legion of "bad actors"[62] who infested the California gold fields and whose mining equipment consisted of little more than cap-and-ball pistols. This effort was staged near Sonora, the loot was of famine proportions, and Bill was arrested shortly afterward and given a fifteen-year stretch in San Quentin on being convicted. Safely behind the walls, Bill became interested in religion, and after serving but two thirds of his sentence he was radiating such a saintly glow that he was released for good behavior, possibly in the hope that he would spread the word. He didn't. Bill moved into Colorado and teamed up with a hard case named Bill Leroy. This two-gun twosome notched up a string of stage and train jobs before a hard-riding posse dissolved the partnership, for although Miner escaped, Leroy was captured and given an on-the-spot suspended sentence that left him quite lifeless and limp. After this brush with hemp Bill left the States and toured the Old World, passing through pre-Jack the Ripper London and pre-Common Market Europe in a journey that took him as far east as Turkey.

[62] Used in the sense of "badmen" or "outlaws"; if taken literally, California may still be said to have an overabundance of same.

Some of the ingredients that are a must for a best-seller costume novel colored Bill's life while he vacuumed up the breezes from the Bosphorus, for he became acquainted with an olive-oil-faced slave trader who persuaded him into the lucrative pursuit of abducting nubile pieces of Turkish delight and selling them off as harem equipment. It is somewhat of a mystery—to this writer at least—why Bill ever left this Garden of Allah existence to return to the States, but return he did, and in November 1880 he held up a stagecoach at Sonora and escaped into the yonder with some three thousand dollars tucked into his saddlebags. In March of the following year Bill, accompliced by a gent with the out-of-character moniker of Stanton T. Jones, held up and robbed the Del Norte Stage, a crime that got a tenacious posse on their trail whose interest only flagged after "Never Kill a Man" Miner had winged three of them out of their saddles.

By the fall of 1881 Miner was associating with an owlhoot named Jimmy Crum, and on November 7 these two loose-livers pulled off a stagecoach job at Sonora that resulted in them both being arrested shortly afterward, and Miner was soon back in San Quentin with the prospect of sitting out twenty-five years. Good behavior and making like a missionary once more sliced quite a piece of Bill's time, and he was released in 1901. Around the time of his release Bill was a benign-looking gent whose face was furnished with a white mustache and whose headgear consisted of a Baden-Powell-type hat, his overall appearance thus giving the impression of a kindly Scoutmaster whose only interest in life is centered around leading patrols into the woods in search of their merit, or demerit, badges. But appearances can lie. On September 23, 1903, aided by two other gunnies, Miner held up and robbed an Oregon and Washington train near Corbett, Oregon, after which he drifted up into Canada, where he posed as a wealthy Californian while spending the fruits of his labors. When the loot ran out, Bill turned his attention to the Canadian railways, and he succeeded in holding up and robbing a couple of Canadian Pacific trains and giving himself a five-figure loot balance before the Northwest Mounted Police put the collar on him in 1906 and one of His Britannic Majesty's judges gave him a lifetime behind bars; he hoped.

Canada had now lost much of its attraction, so Bill escaped in the summer of 1907 and slipped back into the States, where he pulled a couple of jobs over the next four years: a Portland, Oregon, bank in 1909, and a Southern Railway Express car in Georgia two years later. Pinkertons grabbed Old Bill after this last job, and upon conviction he was given another life term, which he was expected to spend in Milledgeville, Georgia, Penitentiary. To expect Miner to settle down at his time of life was a bit much, and no one was very surprised when he escaped in the fall of 1911, but he was now getting a little old to be pulling such capers, and he hadn't given the dogs much of a run before he was recaptured. The following year saw Bill doing two more cross-country runs with bloodhounds at his heels, twenty-minute breaks that make one wonder if Bill was being allowed these periodic crashouts to keep the dogs in trim. William "Old Bill" Miner died in his cell in 1913, the cause of death possibly being a gastric ulcer.

MINICONJOU SIOUX   One of the seven bands that make up the Teton division of the Sioux nation.

MINING CAMPS   May usually be regarded as the diaper stage in the life of a mining town. (See MINING TOWNS.)

MINING TOWNS These communities, which blossomed in the gold- and silver-bearing regions in large numbers, had a far greater mortality rate than mercantile, trail, or company towns,[63] many of the mining communities returning to the wilderness without achieving anything more than camp status, while even the more substantial settlements could become "ghosts" in less than a decade. Mining towns (or camps, for many retained their temporary-sounding title after becoming well established) had a far greater incidence of violent crime than had the trail towns, and the complete absence of law or the fact that town marshals were being used up at an alarming rate was responsible for the formation, in many areas, of the vigilance committees that were almost exclusively products of the mining centers. Many of these places had a fair sprinkling of Cornish miners who were usually referred to as "Cousin Jacks" and whose expertise was in great demand, while California locations got a rich quota of Chinese, who, much to their peril, engaged in menial tasks or initiated bored mining types into the intricacies of opium smoking. The names given to these settlements were rarely stodgy, descriptive titles, "hair on the chest" nomenclature being much favored by the pan, pick, and riffle-box brigade. Many of these towns still survive, but a far greater number have long since been abandoned, California, Idaho, Montana, and Nevada being particularly rich in the skeletal remains of many of the latter class. (See ALDER GULCH; ALLENTOWN, OREGON; ANGELS CAMP; AURORA, NEVADA; AUSTIN, NEVADA; BANNACK, MONTANA; BODIE, CALIFORNIA; CANDELARIA, NEVADA; COMSTOCK LODE; DEADWOOD, SOUTH DAKOTA; ESMERALDA; FORTY-NINERS; GHOST TOWN; GOLDFIELD, NEVADA; PANAMINT; RHYOLITE; ROUGH AND READY; TIN CUP, COLORADO; TOMBSTONE, ARIZONA; and VIRGINIA CITY, MONTANA.)

MINNESOTA North-central state that lies to the west of Wisconsin and Lake Superior and has the Canadian line as its northern boundary, with the Dakotas to the west and Iowa to the south. Popularly known as the Lake or Gopher State, Minnesota became the thirty-second state in 1858 after having spent nine years as a territory. More than ten thousand lakes lie within its boundaries, one of these, Lake Minnetonka, being the one where I "first made love to you." St. Paul is the state capital.

MIRAGE An optical illusion that may be experienced when the refraction of light—through distortion—causes unseen objects to be projected within one's field of vision. On the Great Plains a mirage may take the form of a tree-surrounded lake, while in the deserts of the Southwest the dim silhouette of some apparently distant city may be little more than the fragmented reflection of some mountain peaks that are beyond visible range.

MISSISSIPPI RIVER The most important and the second-longest river in the United States. From its headwaters in northern Minnesota the Mississippi flows south like a sidewinder until it empties into the Gulf of Mexico some 2,350 miles from its source, draining in the process that vast area of land that lies between the Rocky Mountains and the Appalachians. The terminal point for oceangoing liners and freighters is Baton Rouge, about 200 miles from the Gulf, but the river is navigable for flat-bottomed craft for the greater part of its length. Approx-

[63] An example of a company town may be found under the entry dealing with DE MORES, MARQUIS.

imately 20 miles north of St. Louis it is joined by the Missouri River,[64] the latter being the chief tributary of the former and the longest river in the United States (2,700 miles). The Mississippi is sometimes referred to as "The Father of Waters."

MISSOURI   A midwestern state that is bordered on the east by the Mississippi River; has Iowa and Arkansas to the north and south, respectively; and has Kansas and Nebraska on its western flank. The territory became part of the United States on completion of the Louisiana Purchase in 1803, and it was admitted to the Union as the twenty-fourth state in 1821. Jefferson City is the state capital, and Missouri may be referred to as the Bullion State. A certain amount of fussin' an' feudin' is sometimes indulged in in the backward Ozark region of the state, and Missouri-bred mules are generally accepted as being the best in the whole doggurned country.

MISSOURI RIVER   Originating with the joining of the Gallatin, Jefferson, and Madison rivers in southwestern Montana, the Missouri meanders through Montana and the Dakotas, becomes the state boundary between Nebraska and Iowa, and bisects Missouri before emptying into the Mississippi about 20 miles north of St. Louis, a 2,700-mile journey that makes it the longest river in the United States. Sometimes known as the "Big Muddy." (See MISSISSIPPI RIVER.)

MOB PISTOL   A four-barrel flintlock pistol that was manufactured during the first half of the nineteenth century and was intended, as the name suggests, for the quelling of mob violence. All barrels fired simultaneously, and as they were arranged like the splayed fingers of a hand,[65] someone was sure to get in the way of a ball. As these guns were popular with seagoing skippers, quite a few of them may have found their way into the West when whole crews abandoned their ships to go in search of California's gold.

MOCCASINS   Algonkin name for a type of footwear originated by the American Indians and worn by the majority of tribes. Moccasins are close-fitting, rarely reach above the ankle, and possess a drawstring to keep them in position. Buckskin or other supple leather is used in their manufacture, and although some tribes favored a rather austere model, the plains tribes used additional materials such as beads and porcupine quills to decorate their footwear.

MOCHILA   A type of saddlebag that was devised and manufactured for Pony Express use. Manufactured from leather and roughly saddle-shaped, a mochila was more or less a false saddle with two mail pouches on each side that could be dropped into position across a regular saddle, two slits in the former allowing the fork and cantle of the latter to protrude and thereby hold the mochila in position. This was a time-saving invention, as it dispensed with saddle changing at way stations, the mochila being whipped from the saddle of a horse that was at the end of its run and tossed across the saddle of a remount within seconds. Named after an early type of saddle covering that was fashioned on similar lines. Pronounced "Mo-chee-la." (See PONY EXPRESS.)

[64] The Lower Mississippi (from the mouth of the Missouri to the Gulf of Mexico) and the Missouri are sometimes classed as one river, the Mississippi-Missouri, and if this is accepted, this 3,760-mile length of waterway becomes the third-longest river in the world.
[65] Or a duck's foot, for this piece was sometimes referred to as a "duck's foot" pistol.

MODOC WAR Name given to a series of skirmishes between Modoc Indians and United States troops that occurred over a period extending from November 1872 until June of the following year. The fuse leading to the explosive had been ignited some eight years previously when the Modocs had been moved from their homes in the Tule Lake region of the California-Oregon border and placed on the Klamath Reservation in southern Oregon. The Klamath, who had always been on the worst of terms with the Modoc, refused to allow the new arrivals to hunt game on what they considered to be Klamath territory, and after more than six years of wind-filled bellies, Modoc chief Captain Jack[66] and a subchief by the name of Hooker Jim left the reservation and led their people back to Tule Lake.

White settlers, who by this time were firmly established in the area, didn't take kindly to the Modocs' arrival, and complaints were lodged with the authorities, but it was not until the night of November 29, 1872, when Major James Jackson led a thirty-six-strong cavalry detail into the Modoc camp, that the shooting started. When the smoke cleared, eight troopers lay dead and seventeen Modocs were on their way to the Happy Hunting Grounds. After disengaging, Captain Jack led his people into the lava-bed formations that lay south of Tule Lake, and here he became reunited with Hooker Jim's band, the latter group having been busy eliminating a few settlers while Jack's band was swapping lead with the soldiers. The barren region created by some long-dead volcano was an ideal stronghold and it wasn't until the following January that a mixed army of cavalry, infantry, and civilian volunteers moved into the lava beds to flush out the Modocs. This force of around four hundred men, which was equipped with howitzers, made contact with Jack's six dozen braves on the morning of January 17. Thick fog blanketed the battleground throughout the engagement, but when the shooting stopped, sixteen soldiers had been killed, although Jack had lost nary a man, an inequality of casualties that leads one to suspect that the Modocs may have had X-ray vision.

Further troops were drafted into the area, and General Canby at the head of a thousand men was striving to establish contact with the Modocs when Washington ordered a cease-fire to allow peace talks to get under way. A blood relation of Captain Jack's, a rather overfat squaw named Toby Riddle,[67] volunteered to act as intermediary between the opposing forces, and after two fruitless sessions of talk a third meeting, which was to take place in the lava beds, was arranged for the morning of April 11. Grouped around an Army-surplus tent, erected amid the grim, gray rock formations of solidified lava, red man and white man met on this day to resolve their differences. Captain Jack, Schonchin John, Boston Charlie, and Hooker Jim, with such unpleasant-sounding types as Scarface Charley, Shacknasty Jim, and Steamboat Frank, and other braves lending hard-eyed support from the wings, represented the Modoc contingent: Peace Commissioner Alfred B. Meacham, General Canby, and the Reverend Eleazer Thomas represented Washington's talk men; and Toby Riddle and her husband, sensing the Indians were in an evil mood, represented a very worried couple.

With such a cast against such a forbidding background it is little wonder that the meeting was a complete failure. The Modocs had spent too many nights

---

[66] The white man's name; his Indian name was Keintpoos.

[67] Originally Princess Winema, the princess evidently having decided to become a "commoner" upon her marriage to a Kentuckian named Frank Riddle.

mattressed on lava, and Meacham and Canby had little to offer but words and a few cigars, and Captain Jack and Boston Charlie, after tossing away their butts, drew handguns and killed Canby and Thomas, and only the timely intervention of Mrs. Riddle enabled the remainder of the Peace Commission to escape a like fate. The Army now pulled out all the stops. Colonel J. C. Davis took over command and subjected the lava-bed retreat of the Modocs to an artillery barrage that would have made Rommel lose his tan. Hooker Jim, Scarface Charley, and a few other tribesmen soon waved bits of rag and changed sides to become Army scouts, and on May 31 the war came to an end when Captain Jack was taken into custody. Captain Jack, Boston Charlie, Schonchin John, and a bit player named Black Jim were hanged in October 1873, the body of Captain Jack afterward being preserved so that he could be put on view at $.10 a peek.

MOJAVE DESERT An arid region that encompasses an area of 15,000 square miles of Southern California. South of the Sierra Nevada and extending from the southern extremities of Death Valley in the east to the Coast Range in the west. The Mojave River, which runs underground for the greater part of its length, roughly bisects the area from north to south. Vegetation is mainly yucca. Sometimes spelled as pronounced —i.e., "Mohave."

MONK, HANK Wells Fargo six-in-hand driver who sped his Concord across the Sierras between Sacramento, California, and Virginia City, Nevada. Henry has got into the record mainly through his brief association with Horace "Go West, young man" Greeley, Mr. Monk being the driver who transported Greeley from Carson City, Nevada, to Placerville,

California, via a rib-cracking ride that occurred in 1859 and that left Greeley too bruised and shaken upon arrival to give a scheduled lecture. As Horace's head is reputed to have gone through the top of the coach on numerous occasions while he was in transit, this is not too surprising. Hank got 'em set up for years while folk listened to his padded-out versions of this ride, but there came a time when everyone had heard it more than somewhat, and Hank had to resort to buying his own. Brandy was his favorite tipple, and it was remarked upon his death in 1883 that the thoroughbraces of his coach—which bore the scars of countless near disasters—were sodden with distillations of the grape. (See GREELEY, HORACE.)

MONSTERS   From about 1860 onward camels, which had been allowed to run wild, were responsible for many "monster" sightings, yet if we ignore these there are still reports of unclassified "things" roaming the West that have never been explained away. Brief reports on four nightmare species follow:

California. A gigantic creature of whale proportions that possessed membranous wings and three pair of legs, and was equally at home on land, sea, or in the air. Made its home in Lake Elizabeth from about 1830 (first sighting) until its disappearance in the 1880s.

Pacific seaboard. Giant ape-men known as Sasquatch. Reputed to have been about 7 feet tall and up to half a ton in weight. A young male is reported to have been captured in 1884 and put on show. This specimen only weighed 140 pounds.

Arizona. Monster flying reptile sighted by two waddies in the spring of 1890. This creature had a 25-foot wingspan, leathery skin, eyes like dinner plates, and legs like an elephant. Said waddies shot at it but appeared to make no impression. Report of sighting given big spread in the Tombstone *Epitaph.*

Nevada. Reports of a massive marine creature foaming up the waters of Lake Walker have been bandied around since men first panned for gold. This specimen is reputed to be still around, so maybe the Syndicate has it under contract as a tourist attraction.

All creatures of the bottle, or do they in fact exist? (See CAMELS and GIANTS.)

MONTANA Northwestern state with Canada as its northern boundary. Montana has 147,000 square miles of land, the western two fifths of which contain ranges of the Rocky Mountains, while the remainder is almost level plain. Became United States territory in 1803 as part of the Louisiana Purchase and was admitted to the Union as the forty-first state in 1889. Helena is the capital. Tourist attractions are the Custer Battleground National Monument; Big Hole National Monument, which occupies the site of a major engagement between Chief Joseph and the United States Army; Glacier National Park, with its scenic wonders and tribes of Blackfoot Indians; and Virginia City, a more or less reactivated ghost town that in the 1860s was the stamping ground of the Plummer gang and the vigilante movement that put an end to their stamping. May be referred to as the Mountain or Treasure State.

MONTEZ, LOLA The professional name adopted by Rosanna Gilbert, an Irish girl who was born in 1818 and who rose to prominence in her chosen theatrical career in the 1840s by touring Europe with her Dance of the Tarantula, a bouncing and navel-exploiting exhibition that had all the belly fetishists of the Continent fighting for her favors, King Ludwig of Bavaria being reputed to have fought a trio of duels and to have ordered a spot of beheading while steamed up over the eye-popping curves of Lola. In 1851 Lola hit New York with her act, and a short time later she arrived at San Francisco to play a much-extended season at the Jenny Lind Theater. While appearing at the Jenny Lind, Lola became much enamored to a gentleman named Patrick Hull, a onetime charter member of the Forty-niner movement who was assistant editor of the San Francisco *Courier.* Dalliance with Pat, however, didn't prevent Lola from spreading happiness among her legion of admirers, and during his turbulent years with the tarantula dancer Hull had to make a couple of unnamed individuals very dead to ensure his position in the scheme of things.

When audience ratings began to dwindle at the Jenny Lind, Pat and Lola moved to Grass Valley, and here they had a sumptuous residence erected, the decor of this establishment[68] being of such a sensual nature that rugged miners may have been stimulated into breathless eroticism had there been no female within miles. At Grass Valley Pat and Lola became legally knotted, and here Pat dug for gold while love-hungry prospectors dug into their pokes to take advantage of his spouse's favors and mastiffs and pet bears kept the queue in line. This state of affairs wasn't exactly what Pat had had in mind when the cou-

---

[68] This residence may still be viewed at Grass Valley, California. The furnishings—procured at great expense by Lola—are still intact, although the red-velvet drape that covers the Montez king-size divan bears witness to either the passage of time or a plethora of brief encounters.

ple settled at Grass Valley, but when he protested Lola flashed an "honor-saving" dagger (no kidding!) from her garter and threatened violence, so he was no doubt somewhat relieved when she terminated his nagging by obtaining a divorce.

As a free roamer Lola returned to Europe with the intention of recapturing the admiration of the crowned-head deadbeats who had thundered upon her door in days of yore. But this was not to be, for by this time other and better midriffs were vibrating across the stages of Europe, and the tour was a flop. Our embittered tarantula dancer returned to the States and settled in New York, and she died here—in Brooklyn—on January 17, 1861.

MONUMENT VALLEY Located in northeastern Arizona adjacent to the Utah border and in the northern section of the Navaho Reservation. The valley is a flat desert whose floor is studded with an impressive collection of towering buttes and small mesas, many of which are named. This region has been used as a location for many of John Ford's Western movies, the Valley making its first appearance on the silver screen as a backdrop to his memorable *Stagecoach*.

MOOAR, J. W. The initials "J.W." could be used by either John Wesley Mooar or John Wright Mooar, Vermont-born brothers who established a buffalo-hunting and business partnership in 1872, their operational headquarters being located near Fort Dodge, Kansas. John Wright did most of the killing, while John Wesley took care of transportation problems—shipping buffalo robes east, etc. In 1874 Indian raiding parties persuaded the Mooar brothers to relocate, and they moved down into the Texas Panhandle and established a

base on the Canadian. Some two years later, when the buffalo herds along the Canadian had been reduced to noncommercial proportions, the brothers moved deeper into Texas, where they decimated the buffalo throughout Mitchell County until little more than bleached bones were scattered over the landscape. When the buffalo had been hunted to the point of extermination, J.W. and J.W. began collecting the skeletal remains of long-dead beasts and shipping them east for fertilizer, a business that had a high profit margin but didn't survive for very long. In their later years John Wright operated an agency for the Hynes Carriage Company, and John Wesley went into the ranching business. J. Wright died at the turn of the century, and J. Wesley died in 1918 at the age of seventy years.

MOORE, EDWIN JUSTIN Born at Bolton, in the county of Lancashire, England, in 1822, the third son of well-known local surgeon John Moore and his wife, Clare Maria. News of Sutter's gold strike lured men from far places, and Justin was but one of many who made their way to California in 1850. Justin was one of the unlucky ones, for he was killed by "Digger" Indians on October 16, 1850. His parents had the body shipped back to England, and it was interred in the parish churchyard. The grave marker, upon which are chiseled the facts of his death, may still be visited. Pssssst! Justin was allowed into this volume by the author's desire to drag a fellow Boltonian into the limelight.

MOORE, EUGENIA May be classed as a Dalton gang irregular. Eugenia, who probably became attached to the gang on becoming acquainted with Robert Dalton in 1889, frequently acted as advance scout for the outlaws, posing as a newswriter to obtain information regarding ank layouts and rail shipments. Miss Moore died of an unspecified internal complaint in September 1892, a loss to the Dalton ranks that may have been partially responsible for the gang being cut to ribbons in the badly organized raid that occurred at Coffeyville, Kansas, shortly after her death. (See COFFEY-VILLE, KANSAS.)

MOORE, LESTER The capitalized wording on the plank headboard of railway tie proportions reads: *Here lies Lester Moore, four slugs from a .44, no Les no more.* Almost everyone must be acquainted with this poetic obituary, which transforms a grim marker in Tombstone's burial ground into a fun thing, yet this writer is of the opinion that no one has ever fertilized the arid patch upon which the marker stands, for despite unconfirmed rumors that a Wells Fargo guard gave Les his fatal dose of lead, the aroma of the prankster emanates from this plot of ground; no date of death accompanies the verse, and had the latter originated during Tombstone's lead-swapping period, *"four balls from a 44"* would have been apt for the times.

MOOSE The largest member of the deer family, a fully grown male weighing about three quarters of a ton, having a length of 10 feet and a shoulder height of up to 90 inches. Their habitat in the West is confined to the Rocky Mountains of the Northwest,[69] where they are usually found in the vicinity of lakes, water plants being one of their favorite delicacies. A drooping muzzle, short neck, and a flap of skin hanging from beneath the throat identify the moose, while massive antlers, shaped like serrated leaves and spreading from the heads of the males, help separate the girls from the boys. The

mating season occurs over the last weeks of September into early October, and the young (usually one) are born in the following May. The overall color is dark brown, gradating to a lighter shade on the legs and muzzle.

MORGAN, BILL Alias reputed to have been used by Bill Miner. (See MINER, BILL.)

MORMONS A religious sect that had its origins in the *Book of Mormon,* a work alleged to have been written by a youth named Joseph Smith while under heavenly guidance. The book was published in 1830, and in that same year the first Mormon service was held in a small church at Fayette, New York. Smith published a second volume of revelations, and congregations grew, but the Mormon practice of polygamy,[70] their adoption of the title "Chosen People," plus a tendency to advocate community ownership of property led to them being harassed into frequent changes of location. By 1843 these self-styled Latter-Day Saints had been driven as far west as Nauvoo, Illinois. The following year Smith was murdered by an irate mob, and the leadership of the sect was placed into the hands of Brigham Young. In 1847, to escape constant oppression, Brigham Young led the Mormons on their monumental exodus toward the setting sun, a fifteen-hundred-mile journey that terminated with their leader exclaiming "This is the place!," the "place" being the shores of the Great Salt Lake of Utah, or, in the phraseology of the saints, "Deseret, Land of the Honey Bee." Here, in the wilderness, the sect met with little opposition, and Salt Lake City was established as a Mormon stronghold, a position it holds to the present day. Nowa-

---

[69] Confining this entry to the American West; moose are also found in the northeastern states, Canada, and Alaska. In Europe the moose is known as the "elk."

[70] No use rushing to join the "colors," lads; this practice was discontinued in 1890.

days Mormon missionaries tour the globe spreading the word and looking for converts. (See BRIDGER, JIM; DANITES; HAUN'S HILL MASSACRE; LOCUST; LOST MINES, subheading *Lost Rhoades;* MOUNTAIN MEADOWS MASSACRE; SMITH, JOSEPH; and YOUNG, BRIGHAM.)

MORMON TRAIL   Blazed by Mormon migrants in the late 1840s, this seventy-mile stretch of trail[71] left the Oregon-California route at Fort Bridger, Wyoming, and weaved in a southwesterly direction, passing through Echo Canyon in the Wasatch Mountains as it journeyed to its terminal point at Salt Lake City, Utah. In 1860 the Pony Express utilized the trail as part of its route.

MORROW, DAVE   Better known as "Prairie Dog" Dave, a sobriquet he earned in the 1870s when he was hunting these burrowing varmints in the area of Dodge City and selling them as pets at five bucks a pair. Prior to this period Dave, who is reputed to have been born somewhere east of the Mississippi in 1837, had spent time in California searching for color, ridden with the 1st California Cavalry in expeditions against both Indians and Johnny Rebs, and done a few years as a buffalo hunter headquartered in Hays City. When the bottom fell out of the prairie-dog market Dave returned to getting buffalo in his sights, chalking up a notable "first" when he killed an albino bull and sold the hide to a Dodge City buyer for a thousand dollars. Although Dave became acquainted with all the big-name characters who spent time at Dodge[72] and did frequent stints behind a lawman's badge (either as a Ford County deputy sheriff or a deputy marshal at Dodge),

there are no reports of him ever having killed a man, Dave's only known shoot out resulting in him being tried and acquitted for the wounding of a man named Lawrence.[73] In later life "Prairie Dog" left Dodge and took up farming in Oklahoma, but by 1883 he was back in Kansas as a resident of the State Soldiers Home quartered at Fort Dodge, and he died here on October 18, 1893.

MORSE, HARRY N.   Appeared in California as a teen-age youth about 1850, his antecedents being unknown and unqueried. Morse settled at Oakland working for a number of years at various jobs before establishing himself as a lawman by being elected sheriff of Alameda County in 1862. The folk of Alameda had voted for the right man at the right time, and over the next few years Harry was tossing outlaws into the calaboose or blasting them out of their chaparreras in a clean-up campaign that appears to have been mainly directed against the godless of Mexican extraction. Narrate Ponce, killer, stock thief, and part-time pimp, was blasted into eternity when he was overtaken by one of Morse's rifle bullets during a chase through Pinole Canyon; reputed multikiller Jesus Tejada surrendered to Morse without a shot being fired; a *bandido* named Narciso Borjoques, whose favorite ploy was to hammer a stake through the head of each of his victims, was shot dead in a saloon brawl shortly after he had been wounded by Harry and while the lawman was still hot on his trail; these being but a trio of the Grade-B movie-type villains who clashed with Sheriff Morse during his first eight years of office.

Late in 1870 the depredations of Juan Soto were brought to the attention of the

[71] As the crow flies; as the saints slogged, it was more than a hundred miles.
[72] Wyatt Earp, Bat Masterson, Luke Short, etc.
[73] An incident that occurred at Dodge City in the summer of 1874.

sheriff of Alameda County. Soto, a Mexican-Indian half-breed of fearsome visage and gigantic proportions who was an associate of the even more sinister Tiburcio Vasquez, committed his most infamous atrocity in the early days of January 1871 while a posse headed by Morse was searching for his sign, two inhabitants of the village of Sunol being murdered by Soto while he and three of his men were looting the general store. Shortly after the Sunol Massacre (the somewhat grandiose name for Juan's double hit), Morse and his boys cornered the outlaws within a dilapidated adobe hut in the Sausalito Valley, and as the climax to a long-drawn-out gun duel between Harry and Juan, the latter dropped dead with a bullet in his brain. In 1876 Harry N. Morse turned in his Alameda badge in favor of becoming a Wells Fargo special agent, and he was employed in this capacity until the end of his crime-busting career.

MOSES, ANNIE Better known under her professional name of Annie Oakley, the little "Miss Sure Shot" of the Buffalo Bill Wild West shows. (See OAKLEY, ANNIE.)

MOSSMAN, BURTON C. Best known in his role of captain of the Arizona Rangers, a body of men whose inception owed much to Burton C. Mossman. Born on April 30, 1867, near Aurora, Illinois, and raised on a farm in Minnesota to which his parents had moved a few years after his birth, Mossman left home in his middle teens and moved to New Mexico, where he spent some time in the Sacramento Mountains working with a survey crew. Shortly after his seventeenth birthday, Burton entered the cattle business in the lowly role of cowhand, but within a few years he

had worked his way up to becoming a ranch manager, and reports of his efficiency in this capacity led to him being offered the post of manager of the Aztec Land and Cattle Company's spread[74] in north-central Arizona. Burton's first task on taking up this appointment in the early days of 1898 was to crack down on rustlers, and he was personally responsible for tucking one small gang behind bars before he'd gotten around to inspecting the bunkhouse.

Within two years Mossman had cleared the Aztec range of rustlers, but in spite of his efforts the company folded in 1900 and he had to cast around for another job. For the next few months the ex-cattleman operated a butcher's shop with a man named Tovrea, a chore that Mossman left with but few regrets after an interview with the state governor on crime prevention had resulted in the formation of the Arizona Rangers and his being offered the captaincy of the twelve-man force, an offer that Burton accepted, taking over the duties of Ranger captain in the spring of 1901. While in this service Mossman killed payroll robber and killer Juan Saliveras in a stand-up gunfight from which he received a slight wound; had his force reduced to ten when Rangers Tefio and Maxwell were killed by outlaw guns; and spent much of his time searching for Augustine Chacon. Mossman's search for Chacon became something of an obsession, and Mossman only succeeded in putting the collar on this elusive *bandido* within days of his resigning from the Rangers in the summer of 1902, a change in state administration having prompted him into this decision.

Three years after leaving the Ranger service, Mossman married a girl named Grace Coburn and settled down to the life of a rancher in New Mexico, where,

[74] Somewhat better known under its popular name of the Hashknife outfit.

over the years, Grace bore him two children—Burton, Jr., in 1907, and Mary in 1909. Shortly after the birth of their second child, Mrs. Mossman died, and Burton remained a widower until 1925, in which year a Miss Ruth Shrader became the second Mrs. Burton C. Mossman. In 1943 Burton Mossman, Jr., was killed in aerial combat over Europe while holding the rank of major in the USAAF, a melancholy event that may have prompted his grieving father into selling his ranch and retiring from active life the year following the tragedy. The last years of Mossman's life were spent in a wheelchair, and he died at Roswell, New Mexico, on September 5, 1956. (See ARIZONA RANGERS and CHACON, AUGUSTINE.)

MOTHER CAREY'S CHICKENS
A term which, when used correctly, refers to birds in the petrel class. In the West, however, "Mother Carey's[75] Chickens" was far more likely to refer to that flightless species of "bird" whose nesting places were usually to be found behind a red lamp. This classification did not embrace free-lance strumpets; to be a "Mother Carey's" chicken a gal had to be one whose working day was organized by a madame.

MOTHER LODE   Name applied to the golden magnet that attracted thousands of would-be prospectors into north-central California after gold had been discovered in the area in 1849. (See FORTY-NINERS.)

MOTHER LODE COUNTRY
The area embracing all the mining towns and gold camps of east-central California. The country lies to the east of the Sacramento River and may be said to

have its approximate northern and southern limits confined by the fortieth and thirty-seventh parallels, respectively.

MOUNTAIN MEADOWS
MASSACRE
A lamentable incident that occurred on September 7, 1857, in the Mountain Meadows Valley of southern Utah. In August of that year a wagon train of some 140 migrants, led by Captain Charles Fancher and en route to California, paused at the Mormon stronghold of Salt Lake City to revictual, but as they were received with but little cordiality, the party left rather hurriedly, Fancher leading the cavalcade to the southwest and attempting—unsuccessfully—to reprovision at the various Mormon settlements that straddled the trail between Salt Lake City and the Arizona line. While pausing at these settlements Fancher had been overheard making numerous loud remarks relating to what he had in mind to do with the Mormons once he had got shot of the wagon train and had time to muster a small army with which to invade Utah, understandable yet tactless mouthings that may have accounted for the open hostility that the saints were displaying by the time the Fancher party camped in Mountain Meadows[76] on September 5.

At sunup on the seventh Indians attacked the camp, a hair-lifting fracas that resulted in the deaths of about twenty migrants and that may, or may not, have been Mormon-inspired. After the Indians had decamped with the train's cloven-hoofed stock, Fancher appealed to the Mormons for aid, and Mormon elder John D. Lee, accompanied by a regiment of the sect's militia and Indian auxiliaries, agreed to escort the migrants to Cedar City. Somewhat relieved, the Fancher

[75] Corruption of *mata cara* (dear mother).
[76] Located about fifty miles due west of Cedar City, Utah.

party prepared to leave, but they had traversed little more than a few hundred yards when the militia and their Indian allies fell upon them in an orgy of shooting and throat-slitting. Hair was lifted and stomachs eviscerated with little regard to the victim's age or sex, only seventeen very young children being allowed to survive the massacre; mercy being extended to the latter on the grounds that they were much too young to be of any use as witnesses should the perpetrators of the deed ever be called upon to answer for the crime. Seventeen years after this infamous event the Mormon leaders appeased both their consciences and the unbelievers by tossing John D. Lee to the wolves, and after being found guilty at a trial that occurred in July 1875, he was finally executed by rifle fire at the site of the massacre on March 23, 1877. (See HAUN'S HILL MASSACRE.)

MOUNTAIN MEN The buckskinned loners who resembled the Indians they moved among rather than their Caucasian forbears; the rugged individualists who exploited the fur-bearing fauna of the Shining Mountains[77] from the forty-ninth parallel to the Wasatch Mountains in the south, pelts being traded in at the outposts of the American Fur Company, Rocky Mountain Fur Company, Hudson's Bay Company, or the Northwest Fur Company for either coin or supplies. Flintlock rifles, skinning knives, and tomahawks were the tools of the mountain man, and the tanned hides of his victims were the source of his wardrobe. He came down the Big Muddy for supplies that could be only obtained at St. Louis, but he didn't stay for long; a low ceiling of community smog, and horizons

obliterated by buildings had little attraction to a man who had savored the joys of untouchable skies and gazed into distances that could never be reached.

Over the years various rendezvous points in Wyoming saw gatherings of these "ha'f hoss, ha'f alligator" types, get-togethers whereat they became smitten with that form of logorrhea that frequently follows a spell of loneliness, fictional yarns of extreme extravagance being exchanged to prevent any lapse in the conversation. Mountain-man talk was most readily understood only by others of that breed,[78] and if it were possible for it to tomahawk its way into the ears of a present-day listener it would probably make little more sense than the mutterings of a Sioux Indian.

They explored the West—and knew it like the back of their hand—well before any survey parties had taken their first faltering steps west of the Mississippi. They were both kind and vicious to the extreme, and many found their way into unmarked graves. These were the mountain men, men whose destiny was linked with that of the fur trade to such an extent that they followed the dodo into the mists of time with the collapse of the fur trade in 1846; the species having had a lifetime of about forty years. (See TRAPPERS.)

MUD WAGON Popular name for the celerity wagon. (See CELERITY WAGON.)

MUFF PISTOL Name given to various makes of miniature pistols that were popular during the latter half of the nineteenth century. Usually no more than 3 inches in length and of .22 caliber, these guns derived their name from the

---

[77] The Rocky Mountains.
[78] "Well, hos! I'll dock off buffler, and then if thar's any meat that runs that can take the shine outen dog, you can slide." This sample of mountain-man talk has been translated by A. B. Guthrie, Jr., into the following: "Well, friend, I'll except buffalo, and then if there's any meat afoot that surpasses dog, you're crazy."

fact that they were extremely popular with the fair sex, as they could be easily concealed within the muffs of the period.

MUGWUMP
An Amerind word meaning "an important man" that has found its way into the lexicon of the white man. On being transplanted to American English the word more or less retained its original meaning, being synonymous with "tycoon," etc., but some years later it was being used to describe such types as independent voters and fence-sitting politicians, and by the time it had crossed the Atlantic to England it was being used as a Siamese twin of "stupid," "idiot," "halfwit," and the like.

MULADA
Spanish term for a drove of mules. Used mainly in the Southwest.

MULE
A hybrid species that is produced by mating a male donkey with a female horse, mules being unable to multiply. Being better foragers than horses, they were—and are—in great demand throughout the West, and during the nineteenth-century period of western expansion, constant demand for these sure-footed pack animals for both civilian and military use elevated them into becoming the most expensive animals on the plains. Mules from Missouri have the reputation of being the finest in the country. (See HINNY.)

MULE DEER
A fairly common species of deer whose range extends from the Mississippi River to the Rocky Mountains and from the Canadian line to Texas. Mule deer are of somewhat stocky build and, on average, stand about 3 feet at the shoulder and weigh about 300 pounds. Reddish-brown during the winter months, their coat changes to a fawn color for the summer and fall seasons. Easily identified by a black tuft at the end of their tails.

MULVENON, WILLIAM
Sheriff of Yavapai County, Arizona, during the Pleasant Valley War, an affray that gave him his moments of harassment and glory. On two occasions while the feud was in progress, Mulvenon led posses into the valley in attempts to quell the powder-burning, but although two of the participants—John Graham and Charles Blevins—were killed by the lawmen and others were arrested, Mulvenon failed to stamp out the fighting. (See PLEASANT VALLEY WAR.)

MURIETA, JOAQUIN
In 1848 California was ceded to the United States as one of the plums of victory of the recently fought war with Mexico, the territory having been a Mexican possession over the preceding twenty-six years. Almost overnight the original settlers became second-class citizens, but as these Spanish Americans spent much of their siesta time dreaming up ways by which they could put off until tomorrow that which should have been done yesterday and preferred an existence of sit-up-and-sup rather than one of git-up-and-go, the conquerors experienced little open hostility until shortly after the discovery of California's golden wealth. A state law of 1850, which virtually prohibited natives of Mexican ancestry from mining for gold, finally spurred many an *hombre* into a career of pistoleering prospecting, which resulted in hundreds of first-class citizens being made into first-class corpses as the gringos were relieved of their gold by gangs of Mexican *bandidos*. Foremost of these gangs were those led by Joaquin Bottilier, Joaquin Carrillo,

Joaquin Murieta, Joaquin Ocomorena, and Joaquin Valenzuela; reports of their atrocities poured in from Murphy's Diggings, Angel's Camp, Chinese Camp, and almost every other settlement in the Mother Lode. Somewhat understandably, the peon without a shirt to his back applauded these bands as being the Robin Hoods of the Mother Lode, while the gringo whose pockets were bulging with nuggets regarded them as robbing hoodlums whose activities had to be suppressed.

In May 1853 a bearded Texan named Harry Love was authorized to recruit a force of twenty Rangers whose assignment was the capture of all, or any, of the legion of Joaquins who infested the Mother Lode. The California Rangers were given three months to do their duty, ninety days in which they had the opportunity of collecting the one-thousand-dollar reward that Governor Bigler had posted for the "dead or alive" capture of an unspecified surnamed Joaquin. A thousand dollars was *mucho dinero* in those days, so it can be assumed that Captain Harry Love and his boys left no stone unturned in their search for a greaser desperado who fitted the governor's requirements. The fact that descriptions of the Joaquins were unobtainable may have led to frustrations, yet it was this facelessness of their quarry that was to attribute much to the success of the mission.

On July 25, in the region of Tulare Lake, the Rangers came upon a group of six suspicious-looking types who could have been of either Latin or Indian extraction. Guns were fired with much gusto and when the Rangers holstered their hardware two of the suspects lay dead, two were in custody, and a couple were disappearing into the distance. A digit missing from a hand of one of the deceased immediately identified the corpse as having belonged to Manuel "Three-fingered Jack" Garcia.[79] The other body, although that of a complete stranger, was quickly "identified" as being the remains of "Joaquin," but as there was no evidence to support this identification and the Rangers' term of enlistment was on the point of expiring, one tends to the assumption that Harry dubbed the corpse thus so that he and his men would be in a position to claim the reward.

The mutilated hand of Garcia and the decapitated head of "Joaquin" were placed into jars of preserving fluid and transported to San Francisco, where Captain Love proclaimed the identities of the men from whom the curios had been taken; no "buts" or "ifs" being part of said proclamation. Local newshawks scorned the claim, but Governor Bigler was sufficiently impressed to pay out the reward, and on August 12, 1853, "The head of the renowned bandit Joaquin!" and "The hand of Three-fingered Jack, the notorious robber and murderer!" began an exhibitionary tour of the country. The head of whoever it was who was posthumously forced into adopting the identity of "Joaquin" leered from behind the walls of its glass prison until it was destroyed in the San Francisco earthquake and fire of 1906.

That is about all that is known relating to the life, and possible death, of Joaquin, yet on these foundations of quicksand has the legend of Joaquin Murieta been firmly established. John Rollin Ridge, an Anglo-Cherokee half-

---

[79] Garcia is reputed to have been a real bad *hombre* whose favorite nonprofit-making pursuit consisted of tying numbers of Chinese into outward-facing groups by using their pigtails as binding material, upon completion of which task Three-fingered Jack would wander around the perimeter of the group slicing throats en route.

breed[80] and a writer of no mean talent, got the legend well off the ground with the publication of his *The Life and Adventures of Joaquin Murieta, the Celebrated California Bandit* in 1854. Why Ridge chose Murieta as his "hero" may never be ascertained, but that he gave this mysterious *bandido* the substance of a Californian Jesse James and a place in "history" that is ill-deserved, cannot be denied.

According to Ridge's monumental fiction, Murieta was born in Sonora, Mexico, the son of the usual respectable parents that baddies always appear to have. In 1850, at the age of eighteen, Ridge's Joaquin arrives in California accompanied by a beautiful Sonoran girl, a gentle, brown-eyed lad who was to be derailed from the tracks of righteousness by a series of horrid happenings; gringo miners forcing carnal connection upon his beauteous mistress, lynching his half brother, and publicly beating the tar out of Joaquin's hide being but a trio of such happenings that persuaded Murieta into becoming a vengeance-ridden *bandido*. On and on, shootings and lootings and dalliance with damsels keeping the reader breathing asthmatically until Captain Harry Love and his cohorts clash with Murieta and his men on the Monday morning of July 25, 1853. Many an alleged possession of Joaquin Murieta's may still be viewed in various parts of California, but none of these can be authenticated.

MURPHY, JIM   One of the two sons of Henderson Murphy, a rancher of Denton County, Texas. The Murphys were friends of Sam Bass, Jim being a particular buddy of the latter, but within a short time of the family being arrested on May 1, 1878, and charged with the

harboring of Bass and of being accessories after the fact in the outlaw's robberies of the United States mails, Jim procured their release upon promising to supply the authorities with any information that may come into his possession regarding Bass' intentions and whereabouts. On June 15 of that same year Jim contacted Bass and joined his gang, and a month later, upon being informed of the gang's plans to rob the bank at Round Rock, he mailed this intelligence to the authorities. When the Bass gang entered Round Rock on July 21, Murphy excused himself a few blocks from the bank, remaining in the wings while his pals walked into an ambush. Jim Murphy died in June 1879 after swallowing the contents of a bottle of highly poisonous eye lotion. (See BASS, SAM.)

MURPHY, LAWRENCE G.   One of the leading figures in New Mexico's Lincoln County War, Murphy, an Irish immigrant who preferred Army life to service in the Church for which he had been trained in his early years, arrived in the Southwest during the Civil War as a major in the California column. On being mustered out of the service at Fort Stanton, New Mexico, in the late 1860s, Murphy went into partnership with Colonel Emil Fritz, a German immigrant who had been demobilized at the same time and place as Murphy. Under the name of L. G. Murphy and Company they established a trading post on the Fort Stanton Military Reservation, a contract to supply beef to the Army being the mainstay of the business. In 1873, after an employee named Dolan had fired a gun in the direction of an officer and the post had been described in official correspondence

[80] John Rollin Ridge, whose Cherokee name was "Yellow Bird," entered the Mother Lode region in 1850 at the age of twenty-three, and here he became well known as a writer of magazine and newspaper articles. Georgia-born Ridge died in California in 1869.

as "a den of iniquity," the concession was withdrawn, and the Murphy-Fritz business interests were transferred to Lincoln, a sleepy town lying some nine miles to the east of the fort. Here, backed by the shadowy "Santa Fe ring,"[81] L. G. Murphy and Company experienced a period of expansion that resulted in their ownership of such diverse enterprises as a cattle ranch, flour mill, saloon, hotel, general store, and gambling club—a diversity of interests that led to their assuming monopolistic control of the economy of the town and county of Lincoln. In 1875 the death of Emil Fritz gave Murphy complete control, and from this time until the Chisum-backed Tunstall-McSween faction set up rival interests in 1877, the ex-major was at the height of his powers. Lawrence G. Murphy died of pneumonia at Santa Fe, New Mexico, in the fall of 1878. (See DOLAN, JAMES J., and LINCOLN COUNTY WAR.)

MUSGROVE, L. H. Leader of a notorious gang of murderous highwaymen and stock thieves who operated in the Colorado region during the years 1867–68. Musgrove left his hometown of Como, Mississippi, in the 1850s and moved West to California, where he settled in Napa Valley. In 1863 Musgrove, an ardent Confederate sympathizer, killed a valley resident whose allegiance lay elsewhere, a crime that led to his fleeing the state and moving East into Nevada. The following year (after his killing of two men had precipitated his departure from Nevada Territory) saw Musgrove operating as an Indian trader in the vicinity of Fort Halleck, Idaho, an area from which he left hurriedly after he had placed a ball into the head of a half-breed. Shortly after this latter killing Musgrove found his way through the Rockies into Wyoming, and it was here that he organized a gang of outlaws whose range extended into the plains of Kansas and Texas.

By 1867 the outlaw chief was using Denver, Colorado, as his headquarters. This was a sad choice of location, for by the spring of the following year the redoubtable Dave Cook, who was city marshal at this time, was whittling away at the perimeters of the gang and tossing the shavings into the Denver jail. Musgrove was finally run to earth and captured in Wyoming in the fall of 1868, and the Denver jail became his home until November 23, 1868, on which day a mob stormed the pokey, frogmarched the unconvicted one to a nearby bridge, and left him swinging from the parapet. At the time of his death Mrs. Musgrove and a plethora of kids were living a precarious existence as residents of Napa Valley. (See COOK, DAVID J., and FRANKLIN, EDWARD.)

MUSTANG The progeny of horses that had escaped—or been allowed to run wild—by the Spanish invaders of the sixteenth century. These semi-wild horses lack the stamina that is required in a cow pony, but many are broken in for less arduous tasks. Mustangs travel about in troops.

MYERS, CHARLES Alias of a member of the Musgrove gang. (See FRANKLIN, EDWARD.)

[81] A commercial-political group whose members are alleged to have hidden their identities by the use of code names; Murphy is reputed to have borne the organization label of "Chief."

FREDERIC REMINGTON

N ACHEZ A variation of Natchez.
(See NATCHEZ.)

NANA A Mimbreño Apache chief.
Born in 1801, Nana spent the greater
part of his life following such leaders as
Mangas Colorado and Victorio, only being accepted as a chief after he had
gathered a following from the splinter
groups of Apaches who had become
scattered throughout Chihuahua after
the defeat and death of Victorio in 1880.
By this time Nana was crippled by rheumatism, but in July 1881 he led a mixed
band of Mimbreños and Mescaleros
North into New Mexico and engaged in
a four-week period of guerrilla warfare
during which nearly a hundred Americans were killed. More than fifteen hundred U.S. troops were put into the field
against Nana's small force of less than
forty warriors, yet in August 1881 Nana
and his band escaped back into Mexico
after a series of bloody engagements with
the 9th Cavalry. For the next two years
Nana headquartered in the northern ex-

tremities of the Sierra Madre, where he
considered himself safe from Americano
reprisals. In 1883 the signing of a treaty
between the United States and Mexico
permitted the troops of either nation to
cross the international line in pursuit of
hostiles, and the Apaches, remaining unaware of this sudden threat to their well-
being, were caught unprepared when
General Crook descended upon them in
the May of that year, Nana being one of
a large number of Indians who surrendered into captivity and were returned
North to become wards of the San Carlos
Agency in Arizona. Life at San Carlos
must have had little attraction, for on
May 17, 1885, Nana left the reservation
and returned to the Sierra Madre. No
one bothered to go looking for the old
renegade any more and Nana spent the
rest of his days in peace. (See MANGAS
COLORADO and VICTORIO.)

NATCHEZ Natchez,[1] a Chiricahua
Apache and the second son of Cochise, became a recognized Chiricahua

---

[1] An alternative spelling being "Nachez."

leader in 1879, when, rather than submit to being transferred to the arid land of the San Carlos Agency, he left the Chiricahua Reservation with a number of followers and fled into Mexico. Headquartered in the Sierra Madre, Natchez led his band on raids into New Mexico until 1883, in which year, after much harassment by the cavalry command of Captain Emmet Crawford, he surrendered to General Crook on May 25. The next two years of Natchez' life were spent on the San Carlos Reservation; then, on May 17, 1885, accompanied by Geronimo and others, he jumped the reservation and returned to Mexico. Skirmishes with Mexican and U.S. troops and the killing of many Mexicans kept Natchez' band occupied until General Nelson A. Miles—successor to Crook—finally forced them into surrendering, the bands of Natchez and Geronimo placing themselves into the custody of lieutenant Charles B. Gatewood (General Miles' emissary) on August 25, 1886. The prisoners were originally exiled to Florida, but at a later date public pressure resulted in them being transferred to Oklahoma Territory, and here, as a reservation Indian, Natchez spent the rest of his days. (See CHATO; COCHISE; and GERONIMO.)

NATHOY, POLLIE Born in Kwangtung Province of China in 1852 and sold to a slave trader by her poverty-racked parents when she was seventeen, this little saffron-tinted maiden whom the slaver christened "Pollie Nathoy" was smuggled into San Francisco in 1870, a twenty-five-hundred-dollar price tag bearing mute testimony to her cheongsamed charms. No one haggled over Pollie's price. She was quickly snapped up by a well-heeled Chinese by the name of

Hong King so that Pollie might add an oriental luster to a gambling casino *cum* dance hall he owned at Warrens, Idaho. Shortly after her arrival at Warrens, Pollie became acquainted with a saloon-owner named Charlie Bemis, a man who was four years her senior and who passed much of his leisure hours playing poker with Hong King, a combination of circumstances that led to a change of ownership for Pollie, Hong King—who was as old as Confucius and well past the concubine stage—having tossed Pollie into the pot on an evening when Bemis was destined to be the winner. Bemis, who had scooped up Pollie with a twinkle in his eye, was to reap rich dividends from his poker-faced little prize, Pollie accomplishing the king-sized chore of nursing him back to health after a gunshot wound had been diagnosed as fatal by the nearest available medic. In 1894 Charlie and Pollie were legally united by a justice of the peace so that in the event of Charlie's death—which did not occur until 1922—Pollie would experience no difficulty in establishing claim to their small homestead on the banks of the Salmon River. Pollie died at Grangeville, Idaho, in December 1933. (See BEMIS, CHARLES A.)

NATION, CARRY A.
A bar-wrecking, bottle-smashing tornado who swept through Kansas over the decade 1900–10. Mrs. Carry A. Nation, Kentucky-born, twice married,[2] and president of the Women's Christian Temperance Union (whose militant marching song was "A Saloonless Nation in 1920"), made the initial moves of her bar-wrecking bender on May 31, 1900, vandalizing on this day (a Black Thursday for sure!) the half-dozen thirst clinics that operated within the precincts

[2] The fact that Carry's first spouse could have walked away with the "gold medal" at any boozers' Olympiad may have been instrumental in Carry taking up arms against the Demon Rum.

of Kiowa, Kansas. Carry had attacked the booze peddlers of Kiowa's premises with a billiards cue, a fragile weapon that was to be replaced by a hatchet when she led her WCTU "soldiers" in forays against saloons throughout the length and breadth of Kansas. The sound of breaking glass was finally stilled by Carry's death in 1911, but her misguided zest had not been in vain, for in January 1919 the Eighteenth Amendment laid the blight of Prohibition across the land.[3]

NAVAHO INDIANS Major tribe of the Athabascan language group. Located in northeastern Arizona and northwestern New Mexico, an area in which they have lived for more than three hundred years. Clothing has been much influenced by their Pueblo neighbors, buckskins being discarded at an early date in favor of clothes made from tightly woven material whose manufacture they had learned from the Pueblos. The Navahos were such excellent pupils that their weaving soon became superior to that of their teachers, the multicolored blankets of the Navaho being so tautly woven that they easily shed water. Silver is used for decorative purposes, numerous buttons of this metal usually being found on their moccasins and the trousers of the men, while silver and turquoise necklaces and pectorals are worn by both sexes. Conical-shaped earth lodges, complete with vestibules and known as "hogans," are used as dwelling places. Inherently warlike, the Navaho were finally subdued in 1868, their homeland becoming the Navaho Reservation some four years later. Economy is geared to the great sheep herds that they possess. In World War II Navaho telecommunication operators were employed in the Pacific theater of operations, for by confining all their messages to their native tongue they employed a code that the Japanese found unbreakable. (See PUEBLO INDIANS.)

NEBRASKA Northwest-central state. Bordered on the north and south by South Dakota and Kansas, respectively, and stretching from the Missouri River in the east to Wyoming in the west, with Colorado as its neighbor in the southwest. Iowa is to the east, and Missouri is to the southeast. Nebraska became a U.S. possession in 1803 as part of the Louisiana Purchase and was admitted to the Union as the thirty-seventh state in 1867. Popularly known as the "Cornhusker" State. Lincoln is the state capital.

NELSON, JOHN YOUNG The sight of more than two thousand tepees of the Brule Sioux casting their late-afternoon shadows across the Nebraskan prairie beckoned seventeen-year-old John Nelson from the wagon train he was traveling with, faltering steps that led him from the white man's world and into acceptance of the Indian mode of life which he was never entirely to abandon. The year was 1843, and when the wagon train snaked from camp, John, who had been migrating westward from his hometown of Charleston, Virginia, for the past five years, remained behind as a voluntary member of Chief Spotted Tail's band.

For the next four years—during which he had lost what remained of his innocence by becoming a squaw man—Nelson saw few white men, and when Mormon migrants paused to trade with Spotted Tail's band in 1847, this deficiency of Caucasian comrades may have led John into offering to guide

---

[3] A state of affairs which was abolished in 1933 by the Twenty-first Amendment, although some states remained "dry" until later dates.

Brigham Young and his saints to wherever they were going, "West!" being all that Brigham had in mind at the time. Intrepid guide Nelson was finally paid off for his services on the shores of the Great Salt Lake of Utah, Brigham having decided that this region was to be the "Deseret" of the sect. Nelson retraced his steps in the company of a party of trappers, the only incident of note on this return trip being his lifting of the scalp of a Ute who had been one of a band that had had the temerity to attack the party while they had been traversing the Green River area of Wyoming.

Over the years this bearded "Indian" was to share his blanket with a succession of squaws, only terminating his tally count in 1864, the year in which he persuaded a much-used Indian woman into sharing his pad and his pemmican as the ninth "Mrs." Nelson. Throughout the 1860s much of Nelson's time was spent as an Army scout based at Fort McPherson, Nebraska, a choice of occupation that may have been frowned upon by the Sioux but that had no visible effect upon the squaw man's relations with the Indians. Over the following decade our hero engaged in various pursuits of a rugged nature, spending time searching for color as a prospector or earning his coin as a wagon-train guide, mule skinner, or bull-train commander; the volcanic vocabulary that is essential to success in the penultimate and ultimate of these professions being responsible for his becoming known as "the most profane man on the plains."

In the early 1880s he became reacquainted with William Cody, a former scout whom John had met during his Fort McPherson years, and this reunion led to John Nelson becoming a member of the cast of the Buffalo Bill outdoor shows from 1883 onward. For more than ten years Nelson thundered around the arena on the Deadwood Stage, either as driver or shotgun messenger of said diligence, years during which Buffalo Bill publicly acclaimed him thus: "By general honesty and energy he has gained fame and respect among whites and Indians," and privately declaimed him thus: "As a liar he has but few equals and no superiors." Around 1895 John left the B.B. enterprise, and shortly afterward he retired to the Pine Ridge Reservation in South Dakota, dying here on January 6, 1903.

NESTER   Term used to describe a homesteader or sodbuster who established a permanent home on open range. These land claimants were given a hard time by the cattlemen until the ever-increasing numbers of the former resulted in the boot being transferred to the collective foot of the nesters. On the northern range these invaders were usually referred to as "Grangers." (See JOHNSON COUNTY WAR.)

NEVADA   Western state that has Oregon and Idaho on its northern boundary, California along its western and southwestern extremities, Utah on its eastern flank, and Arizona to the southeast. Ceded to the United States by Mexico in 1848 as part of the spoils of the recently fought war, and known as western Utah until becoming a separate territory in 1861, Nevada was admitted to the Union as the thirty-sixth state in 1864. Carson City is the capital of this mainly arid state. Numerous "ghost" towns may be located in the north and west of the state, bleached ruins that date from the discovery of the fabulous Comstock Lode in 1859. If in the state, a trip to Virginia City is a major "must" for any present-day student of western Americana. Popularly known as the Silver or Sagebrush State. (See VIRGINIA CITY, NEVADA.)

NEWCOMB, GEORGE   Born and
raised in Oklahoma's Cherokee Strip,
"Bitter Creek" George Newcomb[4]
started his outlaw career in 1891 as a
member of the Dalton gang, committing
his first robbery as a member of the gang
when the Santa Fe Limited was held up
and looted on May 9 of that year at
Wharton in the Cherokee Strip. Newcomb didn't accompany the gang when
they rode to disaster at Coffeyville, and
when Bill Doolin organized a gang in the
fall of 1892, Newcomb became a charter
member of the newly formed mob.
Handsome and extravagantly mustached,
George is reputed to have been the lover
of the hard-to-trace "Rose of Cimarron,"
and legend would have us believe that
this phantomlike lass rescued him after
he had been wounded at the Battle of
Ingalls; 'twasn't so, more's the pity.
Wounded he was, but he escaped from
the town without the aid of this filly. After recovering from a leg wound, "Bitter
Creek" was to take part in a further five
raids of the Doolin gang before the sand
in his timer ran out. In July 1895, while
traversing the range of the Dunn Brothers' Ranch in Oklahoma, he and co-
outlaw Charley Pierce were recognized
by a couple of rangehands, and after a
harrowing exchange of gunfire, both
Newcomb and Pierce had taken their
leaves of this vale of tears. (See COF-
FEYVILLE, KANSAS; DALTON GANG;
DOOLIN GANG; DUNN, ROSA; INGALLS,
OKLAHOMA; and ROSE OF CIMARRON.)

NEWMAN, SARAH JANE   Born in
Pennsylvania in 1813, the youngest of a
baker's dozen of offspring who were
transported into the Southwest by their
parents to settle in the Mexican province
of Texas in 1821. Here, in the southeast-

ern corner of the province, Sarah—whose
attention was usually attracted by the hollerin' of "Sally!"—was to become a somewhat legendary figure; over the years
establishing a reputation as a pistol-
poppin' horse trader and a female man-
trap who black-widowed at least one of
her spouses into a state of permanent
repose.

This blond-haired "Bluebeard" with a
bosom fair married her first husband in
1826, a man who must go down in the
record as "John Doe," for within a few
years of bedding his beloved he disappeared without his true identity ever having been established; Sally said he'd gone
to fight Indians, but he may have gone
'neath Texas sod. A man named Jesse
Robinson stuck his neck out by marrying
Sally in 1838. Jesse listened to his wife's
sulphurous vocabulary until blistered ear-
drums forced him into obtaining a divorce on the grounds of her being "a
termagant and a common scold" in 1843.
Shortly after being deprived of bed and
board, Sally married a horse trader
named George Skull,[5] and the newlyweds settled on a ranch near Goliad.
Over the next few years Sally engaged in
her husband's business with a surprising
show of gusto, and her name became
known throughout southern Texas. Each
comely hip sported a cap-'n'-ball five-
shooter, a rifle hung in her saddle scabbard, and she could flick flies from the
ears of her charges with a dextrous flip
of her bullwhip. Sometime in the late
1840s George disappeared from the record, it being a matter of some conjecture
whether he accomplished this voluntarily
and vertical or perforated most prone.

In October 1852 Sally became Mrs.
John Doyle, and her new husband joined
her in the horse-trading business. While

[4] Sometimes spelled "Newcombe."
[5] This rather macabre-sounding name, which is frequently spelled "Skulle" or "Scull," is
reputed to have been an alias.

wearing Doyle's brand, Sally is reputed to have had a brush with the famed Mexican bandit Juan Cortina, a brief encounter during which the *bandido* chieftain christened her "Juana Mestena," and this "Mustang Jane" tag was to remain attached to Sally for the remainder of her days. Shortly before the opening shots of the Civil War, John Doyle fell into the Nueces River and failed to surface; presumed drowned, a watery fate that may have led to the circulation of stories that have Sally drowning Doyle in a barrel of whiskey. While cannon thundered in the East, Sally notched up her fifth conquest by marrying a gent known only as Watkins, an enigmatic character who had been scratched from the cast before Lee's surrender, the site of his passing being a hotel room at Corpus Christi. Upon rousing his spouse from slumber one morning, the disturbed one shot him dead, a type of reflex action which rarely results in anything more serious than a shattered alarm clock.

In 1867 a man named William Harsdoff[6] took Sally as his bride, and shortly after the ceremony the couple rode off in the direction of Mexico on a horse-buying trip. That's the definitive end of Sally's saga, for although a mail rider discovered the decomposed body of a woman while dusting along the route the Harsdoffs had taken some months previously, the body was never officially identified as being the remains of Sarah Jane Newman-"Doe"-Robinson-Skull-Doyle-Watkins-Harsdoff. In the 1930s a small marker was erected to the memory of the subject of this entry, "Sally Scull" and "Sally Skulle" being used somewhat recklessly in the inscription thereon.

NEW MEXICO Southwestern state with Mexico and Texas as its southern boundary, Arizona on its western flank, Colorado as its northern neighbor, and Oklahoma and Texas on its eastern flank. Ceded to the United States after the Mexican War of 1846–48, and admitted to the Union as the forty-seventh state in 1912. The capital is Santa Fe—established by the Spaniards about 1609—and the state may be referred to as the Sunshine State. For the tourist in New Mexico, dull moments are rare, the restored remains of Fort Union, Billy the Kid's stamping ground, the fantastic Carlsbad Caverns, and the pueblos of Taos being but a quartet of attractions that may be found in the state.

NEWTON, KANSAS Arose from the prairie in 1871, the arrival of terrier crews of the Atchison, Topeka, and Santa Fe Railroad in the area being sufficient reason to start throwing up false fronts in the hope that the new town would become Abilene's successor as the cattle-shipping center of Kansas. Built on the bawdy pattern of its predecessors, Newton was ready to accept Texans to its bosom, bars, and bordellos at the start of the 1872 droving season. All dance halls, booze joints, and whoring establishments were located south of the railroad tracks, and these formed a diminutive suburb that was known as "Hide Park." Despite these attractions, Newton only experienced a one-season stand as a cowtown, a season during which cartridges were expended almost continuously and a "General Massacre" in Tuttle's Saloon left nine dead and wounded boozers prone upon the sawdust-covered floor. Newton is located in the southeast-central area of the state, about sixty-five miles south of Abilene and twenty-five miles north of Wichita.

[6] A name that comes in a variety of spellings, although all are more or less phonetically the same and retain the initial *H*—a retention that is mandatory in the interests of good taste.

NEZ PERCÉ INDIANS A tribe of plains-plateau Indians belonging to the Penutian language family who were—and are—located in northwestern Oregon and northern Idaho. The Nez Percé[7] possessed a high level of culture, were noted as horse traders and breeders, and were skilled in basketwork. Sustenance was gained by fishing for salmon, collecting berries, and the hunting of buffalo on the North Plains. Raiment consisted of decorated and fringed buckskins, beaded moccasins, blanket coats, and the usual trade-beads accessories, while war bonnets were worn by the meritorious minority; contact with the plains tribes while on hunting expeditions being responsible for the Nez Percé adopting some of these items at various stages of their development. Tepees were used as dwelling places. (See APPALOOSA and JOSEPH.)

NIGHT HAWK Name applied to the rangehand who is in charge of the *remuda* during the hours of darkness.

NO MAN'S LAND Name that embraced that area of Oklahoma which lies north of the Texas Panhandle. This finger of land—approximately 50 miles wide and 160 miles long—lay like an air pocket trapped among the boundaries of Kansas, Colorado, New Mexico, and Texas, and the one-hundredth meridian, which marked the western territorial limit of the Indian-assigned lands of Oklahoma; a state of affairs that led to the no man's land becoming a much-favored retreat of outlaw bands, as it was outside the jurisdiction of either red or white administration. The no man's land was in-

corporated within Oklahoma Territory in 1890. (See CHEROKEE STRIP.)

NORTH DAKOTA Northern state lying on the Canadian border, with Minnesota and Montana lying respectively on its eastern and western flanks, and having South Dakota as its neighbor to the south. Originally the northern half of Dakota Territory, which was organized in 1861, North Dakota was admitted to the Union as a separate state in 1889. Nomadic fur traders worked the area over the first half of the nineteenth century, the first permanent settlement only being established in 1851. Popularly known as the Flickertail State. Bismarck is the state capital.

NORTH, FRANK Best remembered as Major Frank North, intrepid leader of the Pawnee Battalion. Born in New York in 1840, Frank was brought West by his parents while still a small child, the family spending some years in Ohio before finally locating near the Pawnee Reservation in eastern Nebraska in 1858. Here, by associating with the reservation Indians, Frank was soon speaking fluent Pawnee, an accomplishment that led to his taking up employment on the reservation as a clerk and interpreter around the time of his twenty-first birthday. Three years later, Captain J. McFadden persuaded Frank to leave his desk and accept the commission of first lieutenant in a newly formed company of Pawnee scouts that had been organized to carry out sorties against bands of hostiles who had been raiding the reservation for years. By the fall of 1864 Frank's success in dealing with a command that had little

[7] The tribe was given this name in the early 1800s by French-Canadian fur trappers who, on noting that a number of the tribe had shell ornaments inserted into their noses, dubbed them "Nez Percés" (Pierced Noses). The Sioux also knew the tribe as "The People with Pierced Noses" (Pogehodoka), although the "Nez Percé" referred to themselves as "Numepu" (We People).

use for discipline had resulted in him being promoted to captain, and for the next
eighteen months he led a hundred Pawnees in raids against Cheyenne and Arapaho encampments.

The scouts were disbanded in the
spring of 1866, but twelve months later
North was back in the saddle enjoying
the rank of major in command of the
newly minted Pawnee Battalion, a two-
hundred-strong force whose duties were
mainly confined to protecting the track-
laying crews and right-of-way of
the Union Pacific Railroad, duties that
led to the battalion having skirmishes
with Red Cloud's Sioux and a running
battle with a large war party of Turkey
Leg's Cheyenne after the latter band had
derailed and looted a UP train near Plum
Creek.[8] Over the years the battalion was
disbanded and reorganized numerous
times, yet Major Frank North retained
command of each reactivated battalion
until the Pawnee Battalion was finally disbanded in April 1877.

In 1877 North, together with brothers
James and Luther, went into partnership
with Buffalo Bill Cody[9] and bought a
ranch on Dismal River in western Nebraska, an association that was to result
in Frank becoming a major attraction of
Cody's outdoor shows, North being billed
as "The White Chief of the Pawnees"
when the "Wild West, Rocky Mountain,
and Prairie Exhibition" opened at
Omaha on May 17, 1883. By the following year the title of the show had been
reduced to "Buffalo Bill's Wild West
Show," and North was being billed as
"The Pilot of the Prairies," a show-biz

title he possessed when he fell from his
horse while thundering around the arena
at Hartford, Connecticut, in the summer
of 1884. Badly trampled by a horse that
had been following his, North retired to
the family home at Columbus, Nebraska,
to recuperate, which he never did, for he
died here in March 1885 from the after-
effects of his trampling.

NORTHER A cold wind that sometimes sweeps across the southern United
States. A norther may reach a velocity
of Gale Force 10[10] and cause a sudden
20-degree Centigrade drop in temperature.

NORTHERN PACIFIC RAILROAD
Chartered by Congress in 1864, the
Northern Pacific only started pushing
West from Duluth, Minnesota, in 1870.
Over the first three years of track-laying
the financial ribbons were in the hands
of Philadelphia banker Jay Cooke, but
when the company went bankrupt in
1873 with a bare 450 miles of track to
its credit, a German immigrant named
Henry Villard took over control, the latter building up a fresh head of financial
steam that got the terrier crews once
more puffing toward the Pacific. The
tracks crawled across Dakota and into
Montana, along the valley of the Yellowstone and through Butte, then snaked
northward until they reached a point
midway between Garrison and Gold
Creek, Montana, where, on September
8, 1883, they were joined to a length of
track that had been probing east from
Wallula, Washington, since October

---

[8] This incident—the only occasion when Indians successfully derailed a train—occurred in
August 1867.
[9] Buffalo Bill and North had met on previous occasions during the years of the Pawnee
Battalion. Cody was scouting for the 5th Cavalry when they and the Pawnee Battalion attacked Chief Tall Bull's village in northeastern Colorado on July 11, 1869, an attack that
resulted in the complete destruction of this Cheyenne encampment and the death of Tall
Bull, the latter's demise being variously credited to either Cody, North, or a cavalry lieutenant named Hays.
[10] Anything from 55 to 63 miles an hour.

1879.[11] The last length of track, which stretched between Wallula and Tacoma on the Puget Sound, was completed in 1887.

NORTHERN TRAIL Cattle trail that branched from the Western Trail in northwestern Oklahoma, blazed its way west across No man's land, then traveled north across eastern Colorado and western Nebraska, where, on reaching the Dakota line, it angled to the northwest to slice across the southwest corner of Dakota and the northeast tip of Wyoming, fording the Little Powder as it entered Montana. After pushing into Montana it followed the courses of numerous waterways, traveling along the western banks of the Little Powder, Pumpkin Creek, and the Tongue River before crossing the Yellowstone to the west of Milestown,[12] after which the trail traced along the west bank of North Sunday Creek, diagonaled cross-country to move west along the south bank of Little Dry Creek, then continued west until reaching its destination on the east bank of the Musselshell River.[13] Also known as the Texas Trail.

NORTHFIELD, MINNESOTA
Mercantile town that straddles the Cannon River in southern Minnesota. A solid town of bricks and stone and quiet activity whose peaceful existence was so badly shattered by a visit from the James gang on the afternoon of September 7, 1876, that from then on the name "Northfield" would conjure up visions of chaos and gunsmoke wherein horses are frantically pawing the dust and flapping white duster coats blossom with peonies of carmine. The James gang numbered eight this day—Jesse and Frank James; the brothers Cole, Jim, and Bob Younger; Clell Miller; Charlie Pitts; and nineteen-year-old Bill Chadwell. White duster coats concealed their armament and they clattered across the wooden bridge that spanned the Cannon and led them into Bridge Square in the early afternoon with the intention of robbing the First National Bank.[14]

In the square, overlooked by the premises of H. Scriver and of Lee and Hitchcock, which were located in the Scriver block, the gang split into two groups: Jesse, Jim Younger, and Bill Chadwell remained behind to guard their planned line of retreat across the bridge, while the other five members of the gang continued on across the square, rounded the corner of the Lee and Hitchcock store, and made the twenty-yard trip down Division Street to hitch their horses outside the bank. Frank, Bob Younger, and Charlie Pitts pushed into the bank, presenting arms and shaking open grain sacks as they approached cashier J. L. Heywood and teller A. B. Bunker, an opening action that was sharing split-screen time with Cole Younger and Clell Miller, who had remained outside to scan the street and were slit-eying an out-of-focus figure who was ambling toward them. Seconds later, after almost ambling up the muzzle of Miller's six-gun, an inquisitive hardware merchant named J. S. Allen had backed off and ducked down a

[11] This length of track pushed northeast from Wallula, through Spokane, and on into Idaho, curved around the northern extremity of the Bitterroot Mountains, then arrowed southeast into Montana, its construction crews pushing through Missoula before rendezvousing with their counterparts some 50 miles southeast of the town.
[12] Miles City from about 1880 onward.
[13] Although this region was more or less the terminal point of the Northern Trail, other "northern trails" allowed cattle to be moved well into the northwest of Montana.
[14] The gang had traveled north to rob the First National Bank at Mankato, but street-repair activity outside the bank had persuaded them into a last-minute change of plans.

side turning, and now he was souring the caper by calling the citizens to arms.

Cole cussed and fired a round into the air to alert the bridge contingent—a harmless shot that jerked Frank into putting a killing piece of lead into the head of cashier J. L. Heywood, panicked Pitts into wounding teller A. B. Bunker, and harassed the trio in the square into raking the street with a hail of lead that left innocent bystander Nicholas Gustafson lying dead in the dust. In the meantime, shotguns and rifles had been zeroing onto various members of the outlaw band . . . Pitts' horse crashed to the ground, and Charlie squirmed free and vaulted himself across the rump of Miller's mount . . . pellet rash bloodied Miller's face but failed to loosen him from the saddle . . . Chadwell was slammed to his death by rifle fire . . . the marksmanship of a young medical student plummeted a dying Miller from his horse—allowing Pitts to fork the vacated leather as its last tenant died 'midst the horse droppings . . . Jim and Bob Younger were muscled around by wounding lead, and Bob's gelding folded and threw him to the ground . . . Cole hoisted Bob up behind him and a disorderly retreat got under way.

Their planned bridge route abandoned, the surviving outlaws got their mounts into a dust-stirring gallop and headed south in the direction of Mankato. Behind them Morse keys chattered like machine guns, and soon hastily recruited posses were sweeping across southern Minnesota searching for sign. Somewhere north of Mankato the original James gang split up for the last time: Frank and Jesse swung to the west, while Pitts and the Youngers continued south. On the outskirts of Mankato the four who were heading for the Iowa border abandoned their horses and attempted to throw off their pursuers by slogging across country on foot. Swampy ground sucked at their high-heeled boots, and on September 21 Sheriff James Glispin and a six-man posse ran them to earth near Madelia. Guns thundered as the lawmen moved in on the outlaws, and when Pitts dropped dead in the mud with a ball in his chest, the badly wounded Youngers surrendered.[15]

Asphalt now covers the streets of Northfield, but the town still commemorates the defeat of the James gang on its annual "Jesse James Day," and the Scriver block still stands; the onetime premises of Lee and Hitchcock now being occupied by the Jesse James Cafe. (See JAMES, FRANK; JAMES GANG; JAMES, JESSE WOODSON; MILLER, CLELLAND; PITTS, CHARLIE; YOUNGER, COLEMAN; YOUNGER, JIM; and YOUNGER, ROBERT.)

NORTON, JOSHUA His photograph depicts him thus: well fleshed and bearded and wearing pants that concertina onto his boots, a brass-buttoned military jacket with epaulets large as toilet brushes and a beaver hat cockaded with feathers; the pose is militant, Josh being in the act of drawing a cast-off cavalry saber that dangles from his belt. This was self-styled Norton I, Emperor of the United States and Protector of Mexico, a panhandler of charm and no mean ability who endeared himself to the hearts of the citizens of San Francisco during its halcyon years. Mr. Norton arrived in California in 1850 at the age of thirty-one years, an ex-resident of South Africa who, upon settling in San Francisco, engaged in various enterprises of a speculative nature until, some eight years after his arrival, he found himself bewildered and bankrupt and with little to do except

[15] The brothers were heavy with lead: Cole had eleven wounds, Jim had five, and Bob had four.

speculate upon his chances of survival while domiciled within a sleazy bed-sitter.

In the late summer of 1859 a proclamation made the citizens of San Francisco fully aware that Emperor Norton was about to take over their welfare. The commoners' first reaction was one of puzzlement, but this was soon to give way to one of mirth, which was finally replaced by a desire to "go along" with this giant among crackpots. His Royal Majesty's scrip, which printers churned out free of charge, was honored by all bar the most churlish:[16] The Emperor freeloaded of nonalcoholic beverages at any saloon he chose to visit and stoked up on the best of food without fear of any restaurateur slipping him a tab; the city transport authorities never had the temerity to ask him for a fare, and it was a sad store that lacked the patronage of His Majesty when "By Appointment to His Majesty Norton I" status was being enjoyed by the many. Banks gave the Emperor loans without hope of redemption when he was short of the "real stuff"—which was frequent, and no settlement was ever required for the hundreds of telegrams His Majesty had forwarded to his ministers and his overseas contemporaries.[17]

At this late date one can only wonder whether Josh had really lost his marbles or whether he was crazy like a fox, but we do know that the citizenry of San Francisco humored him for more than twenty years and that when he died in 1880 he was held in such high esteem that more than ten thousand mourners lined the route of his last journey.

NOTCHES   The corrugations that talented gunhands are reputed to have whittled on the butts of their hardware, although it is extremely unlikely that any but the most fragile-minded ever indulged in this practice. Many an old-time shooter does have notches sliced into its butt plates, but these have usually been carved at some later date to give a boost to some long dead gunslick's reputation. This writer has seen a Colt .45 with "W.B." (presumably William Bonney) and twenty-one notches carved upon its grips, but—sad to relate—they were as phony as a Coney Island Martian. (See MASTERSON, WILLIAM BARCLAY.)

[16] A Chinese laundryman is reputed to have refused the royal scrip as payment for washing His Majesty's "smalls."

[17] These communications were addressed to such unlikely characters in far-off places that international incidents were only avoided by the fact that they were never forwarded; the kindly operators of the Morse keys made up for this intentional omission by always ensuring that the Emperor received satisfactory replies.

EDWARD BOREIN

O
AKLEY, ANNIE
Name adopted by Phoebe Annie Oakley
Moses[1] on her becoming a professional
sharpshooter. Born in Darke County,
Ohio, on August 13, 1860,[2] of Quaker parents, Annie developed a no-doubt latent
skill with firearms at an early age, and
when her father died in 1870, leaving a
legacy of financial famine, the ten-year-
old girl helped relieve the situation by
shooting grouse and quail in such profusion that there was always "something for
the pot" and an abundance of bullet-
riddled corpses to sell to the neighbors.
Over these years the family[3] diet may have
lacked variety, but a trembling wolf
was kept from the door by fear of
winding up in the Moses' stew. News of
Annie's prowess spread, and in 1879 she
was persuaded to compete against Frank
Butler, a professional marksman who was
throwing out challenges to the locals
from the boards of Cincinnati's Coliseum

Theater. The match ended with Frank
florid of face and Annie a hundred dollars to the good. Butler, rather than have
Miss Moses following him from town to
town reducing his stock of "C" notes,
took Annie under his wing, and the career of Annie Oakley, possibly the greatest shooting star the world has ever seen,
got under way.

In 1880 Butler married Annie, and
they toured the halls as "Butler and Oakley" for the next four years, after which
Frank retired from the act to become his
wife's manager on her acceptance of a
contract with the Sells Brothers' Circus.
In the spring of 1885 Annie Oakley and
her manager joined "Buffalo Bill's Wild
West Show," an association with Cody
that was to last seventeen years—years
during which the Butlers toured the
United States, Canada, England, France,
Germany, Spain, and Italy with the show,
and "Annie Oakley" became a house-

[1] Annie always spelled and pronounced this name as "Mozee."
[2] Some writers give the year as 1864, while others settle for 1866.
[3] Consisting of Mrs. Susan Moses, sisters Elizabeth, Hulda, Lyda, and Sarah, and brother
John.

hold name.[4] A list of the highlights of Annie's life over this period of kudos and good living would include her being adopted into the Sioux nation in 1885 by Chief Sitting Bull, who christened her "Little Miss Sure Shot"; her being presented to Queen Victoria in 1887; and the occasion in 1889, when, upon Royal request, she shot a cigarette from between the imperial lips of Crown Prince Wilhelm of Germany—*Wunderbar!*

In the early hours of October 29, 1901, the specially chartered Buffalo Bill train, howling through the North Carolina darkness, crashed into a freight train near Lexington, and Little Miss Sure Shot was one of the few who were injured. Months of hospitalization followed, and the Butlers were forced to sever connection with the Buffalo Bill enterprises; but the end of the road had not yet been reached, and in the fall of 1902 Annie was playing the lead in a melodrama entitled *The Western Girl*. The toll of the years failed to diminish Annie's shooting skill: In 1912 she was back with the Buffalo Bill Show for Cody's farewell tour; the years 1915–17 saw her engaged as a trap-shooting instructress; and in 1918 she was giving demonstrations of rifle shooting for U.S. troops. Annie Oakley finally retired from the public arena in 1922, and the Butlers settled at Leesburg, Florida, but some three years later Annie felt a desire to return to Darke County, and in the spring of 1926 they returned to Ohio and took up residence at Dayton. Little Miss Sure Shot died at Dayton on November 2, 1926. (See BUTLER, FRANK, and CODY, WILLIAM FREDERICK.)

O'DAY, TOM Small-time member of the Wild Bunch. O'Day, an Irish immigrant who is listed in the Pinkerton files as having the occupation of cowboy and the criminal occupation of bank robber was arrested on June 27, 1897—together with the Sundance Kid, Harvey Logan and another member of the Wild Bunch —after the attempted robbery of a Belle Fourche, South Dakota, bank. By the time Tom regained his liberty, the Wild Bunch had been scattered beyond hope of regrouping, and Tom was forced to re-enter the crime lists as a loner—unsuccessfully, for he was arrested on November 23, 1903, for being in possession of a herd of stolen hayburners. Wyoming the state in which this last transgression was committed, became Tom's compulsory residence while he served a comparatively short sentence. Better for Tom he should have been given life, for on his release he moved to Texas, where he got himself shot dead.

O'FOLLIARD, TOM Born at Uvalde, Texas, in 1859, the only son of an Irish immigrant and his Texas bride. While Tom was still an infant, the O'Folliards moved to Monclova in northern Mexico. This was a tragic choice of location, for in 1860 Mr. and Mrs. O'Folliard died—victims of a smallpox epidemic—and their orphaned child passed through a succession of foster homes until he was finally settled with an uncle on his mother's side. In the fall of 1877, Tom—who was now a gangling beanpole of a youth—left home and wandered off in a northwesterly direction, through San Angelo and on into New Mexico. On April 2, 1878, in New Mexico's Ruidoso Valley, the wanderer had a chance encounter with Billy the Kid, and from then on the Kid's saga was to embrace O'Folliard until the latter met his death before the guns of a Garrett posse on Christmas Eve 1880. Tom O'Folliard lies buried at Old Fort Sum-

---

[4] And so it remains; in the lexicon of American slang an "Annie Oakley" is a much-punched free pass.

ner, flanked by the remains of Billy the Kid and Charlie Bowdre, and topped by a granite marker that is inscribed with the names of the trio and the dates of their passing. (See ANDREWS, JESSE, and McCARTY, HENRY.)

OGLALA SIOUX   One of the seven bands that make up the Teton division of the Sioux nation. Sometimes spelled "Oglalla" and occasionally "Ogallala," but the shorter version given in this entry is correct.

O. K. CORRAL   A not uncommon name for a corral and livery stable, yet ever since that Wednesday afternoon of October 26, 1881, when thirty seconds of small-arms fire spooked the horses in a corral at Tombstone, Arizona Territory, the name has enjoyed the reputation of being the setting for the Earp-Clanton showdown rather than as a hostelry for tired mounts; this is somewhat surprising, for this epic gunfight didn't occur within the precincts of the O. K. Corral but on a vacant lot flanked by an assay office and the twin enterprises of Mr. Camillus S. Fly. The action on that October day was confined to the northwest section of that Tombstone business block, which was, and is, bounded by Fremont Street on the north, Allen Street on the south, and Third and Fourth streets on the west and east respectively. Much of the center of this square was occupied by the stables and sheds of the O. K. Corral, built to the rear of the firm's offices, which fronted on Allen Street, and access to these stables could be obtained by crossing vacant lots, which left gaps between the business premises facing onto the surrounding streets.

Having established the setting, we can now get on with the action. It is shortly after 2 P.M. on October 26, 1881, and dapper John Behan, sheriff of Cochise County, is pushing through the batwings of Hafford's Saloon. The saloon is located on the southwest corner of the block lying east of Fourth Street, and it is in these boozy surroundings that Behan acquaints the Earp brothers with the news that certain nonadmirers of theirs —Ike and Billy Clanton, Tom and Frank McLaury, Billy Claiborne, and Wes Fuller—are hanging around Fremont Street making talk about a showdown. The brothers Earp—Wyatt, Morgan, and Virgil—were not altogether surprised at this turn of events, for earlier that day Ike had been fined twenty-five dollars for carrying deadly weapons after having been buffaloed silly and hauled before the bench by Wyatt. Behan doesn't stay long in Hafford's: After being told by Town Marshal Virgil Earp that he and his brothers will go to arrest the loudmouths, Behan spills onto the street and hurries north up Fourth to keep Ike abreast of the unrehearsed script.

Minutes after Behan had turned left to cross a vacant lot, which would allow him to pass behind the stables of the O. K. Corral, the Earps left Hafford's —three black-garbed and black-stetsoned figures wearing neat bowties, drooping mustaches, and an assortment of deadly weapons. The sun is past its zenith, and the buildings along the west side of Fourth Street are casting short neutral tinted shadows onto the parched thoroughfare as the Earps move north toward Fremont, their sun-drenched reflections having passed across the shadowed glazing of the Can-Can Restaurant and an adjacent coffee shop, when they are overtaken by the emaciated figure of Doc Holliday. Doc, a sartorial replica of the Earps and a late riser who has just left his bed, is carrying a shotgun and is eager to get in on the act. Four pairs of feet scuffing the dust as buildings slide by on their left—a tinsmith's, an assay office, a furniture store;

then a sun-parched vacant lot, from which, seconds before, Wes Fuller has been keeping an eye on their movements; across the street from the lot, sun glints on metal in the window of Spangenberg's gun shop, and from within the shop an idly curious owner may allow his gaze to follow the stiff-legged walk of the drab quartet until they swing left around the corner of the Capitol Saloon, removing themselves from his line of vision as they move west along Fremont.

By this time the Clanton party is occupying a vacant lot that is slotted between an adobe-walled assay office and Fly's lodginghouse and—in the rear of the latter—Fly's Photographic Gallery. Tom McLaury has his back against the adobe wall of the assay office, and he is looking east along Fremont as the four who have taken up Ike's gauntlet come steadily toward him; the McLaury mounts are tethered in the shade of the building against which Tom leans, and brother Frank, Billy and Ike Clanton, and Billy Claiborne are strung out in a line of skirmish to his right. Wes Fuller is conspicuously absent, Wes having drawn the line at taking part in anything more deadly than snooping. The four mustached figures, drab-plumaged as vultures and dragging shadows of indigo gauze, are now strung out across Fremont, moving purposefully forward between the sunlit offices of the Tombstone *Epitaph* and a shadowed lot that is the proposed site of City Hall.

Tom McLaury ducks back into the shade of the assay office as Sheriff Behan halts the four who are coming to give battle in the shade of Bauer's Meat Market. Behan tells Virgil he has disarmed the Clanton party and there is no necessity for gunplay, but Virgil insists that Ike and company should be arrested, and the sheriff of Cochise County is brushed aside so that the Earps and Holliday may complete their business. On reaching Fly's lodginghouse the line pivoted on Holliday and faced onto the vacant lot for a confrontation with their enemies, said enemies' positions and armament being as follows: Tom and Frank McLaury, each armed with a six-gun, are backed against the wall of the assay office, then, fanning out counterclockwise, come young Billy Clanton, followed by elder brother Ike, both of whom are armed with a six-gun then, last in line, Billy Claiborne, farthest removed from the four men in black, yet resplendent in twin-holstered gunbelt. "Give up your arms or throw up your arms!" Virgil's somewhat ambiguous command started the ball and got Mrs. Addie Bourland peering through the window of her millinery enterprise which was sandwiched between the offices of a doctor and a stageline just across the street from the scene of the disturbance. Addie watched fascinated as fists blossomed with Colt .45s and the shooting got under way.

It is difficult to ascertain who put lead in whom during this thirty-second fracas, but it is pretty well established that Wyatt gave Frank McLaury the belly wound that killed him and that a blast from Doc's shotgun finished Tom McLaury. Ike didn't want any part of the fight, and after shouting this fact and imploring the Earps not to kill him, he disappeared through the open doorway of Fly's Photographic Gallery, the door having been opened beckoningly by Sheriff Behan and Camillus Fly. Morgan fell to the ground with a shoulder wound, and Billy Clanton, dying from chest and stomach wounds, was still attempting to squeeze off a shot when Camillus ran from the cover of his studio and removed the gun from his weakened grasp. Two-gun Claiborne threw a few shots in the general direction of Fremont Street then followed Ike's path to safety. The ball was over as suddenly as it had begun, leaving hree men lying dead in the dust and hree members of the Earp party suffering wounds.[5] Sheriff Behan attempted to arest the victors before the powdersmoke cleared, but they walked away, scuffing up the dust as they journeyed into hisory. (See CLAIBORNE, BILLY; CLANTON, JOSEPH ISAAC; CLANTON, WILLIAM; EARP, MORGAN; EARP, VIRGIL; EARP, WYATT BERRY STAPP; HOLLIDAY, JOHN HENRY; and TOMBSTONE, ARIZONA.)

O'KELLY, EDWARD
Edward O'Kelly[6] is the man who shot the man who shot Jesse James. Ed, a native of Harrisonville, Missouri, and possessor of marital links with the infamous Youngers, is reputed to have clashed with Robert Ford on two occasions[7] prior to his shooting Bob dead at Creede, Colorado, on June 8, 1892. O'Kelly was arrested within minutes of the killing, and on July 2 of that same year he was found guilty of Ford's murder and given a twenty-year stretch in the Colorado State Penitentiary. This was to be one of the shortest life stretches in history, for after having his sentence commuted to eighteen years, he was released with a pardon in 1894. At some later date he moved to Oklahoma and settled at Oklahoma City, and he was killed here—by a well-aimed shot from the gun of a cop named Burdett—on January 13, 1904. (See FORD, ROBERT.)

OKLAHOMA   State in south-central United States. Bounded on the north by Colorado and Kansas, with Arkansas to the east and Missouri to the northeast,

Texas to the south and southwest, and having New Mexico to the west of that strip of Oklahoma that lies north of the Texas Panhandle. The territory came into the possession of the United States in 1803 as part of the Louisiana Purchase, and from 1835 until the last quarter of the nineteenth century most of the area of what is now present-day Oklahoma was classed as Indian Territory. In 1890 the territory of Oklahoma was established, and in 1907 it was admitted to the Union as the forty-sixth state. The state still has a higher proportion of Amerind residents[8] than any other state, and certain areas—particularly the Osage Reservation in the northwest—are still recognized as tribal lands. Oklahoma City is the state capital. Popularly known as the Sooner State. (See CHEROKEE STRIP; INDIAN TERRITORY; NO MAN'S LAND; and OKLAHOMA LAND RUSH.)

OKLAHOMA LAND RUSH   Name that may be applied to any of the land rushes that followed the opening of various tribal lands to white settlement. The first of these "rushes" occurred at high noon on April 22, 1889, when a pistol shot signaled the start of a wild stampede of some 10,000 prospective land-grabbers into the Unassigned Lands[9] in the north-central region of the territory. Each grabber was allowed to stake a 160-acre claim for a $15 filing fee. United States troops had been stationed in the area for many days prior to the official "opening time" in an attempt to deter anyone from "jumping the gun," but in spite of this, many a crafty character managed to

---

[5] Morgan, as related in entry; Virgil, with a leg wound; and Holliday, grazed on the left hip.

[6] Sometimes given as Edward Kelly or Edward O. Kelly.

[7] Ford is reputed to have accused O'Kelly of stealing a diamond ring (or stickpin) while the latter was sharing a room with Bob at Pueblo, Colorado, in 1892. This led to O'Kelly visiting Ford's saloon armed with a bowie-type knife and intent on violence, but Bob disarmed him, cracked him across the noggin with a pistol barrel, and tossed him from the premises.

[8] Around the seventy-thousand mark.

[9] Indian Territory that was unassigned tribally.

sneak into the Unassigned Lands and stake a claim while the more noble-minded were still picnicking on the perimeter. These types became known as "Sooners," a name that was later to be applied to the state. Other land rushes that were arranged on similar lines were as follows: The Sac and Fox, Iowa, and Potawatomie-Shawnee lands in central Oklahoma were opened to white settlers on September 22, 1891; the Cheyenne and Arapaho territory in western Oklahoma on April 16, 1892; the Cherokee Strip in northwestern Oklahoma on September 16, 1893; and the Kickapoo land in the center of the territory on May 23, 1895. (See CHEROKEE STRIP and INDIAN TERRITORY.)

OLD BEDLAM   Name by which the Officers' Club at Fort Laramie was known. The building that once housed Old Bedlam[10] may still be visited at the Fort Laramie National Monument in Wyoming.

OLD BLUE   Name given to a longhorn that was used as a lead steer[11] on the Texas-Kansas trails for almost a decade during the great trail-herding days.

OLD SOLITAIRE   Name by which Old Bill Williams was known. (See WILLIAMS, BILL.)

O'LEARY, ROSE   At a somewhat late date this name has crept into print as being the identity of the mysterious "Rose of Cimarron." Could be—anything's possible; but as this Cimarron lass is difficult enough to trace without having an additional contender to the title, let's just say that Rose O'Leary is equal likely to have been the name of Mr O'Leary's cow. Mrs. O'Leary's cow Yup!—that milk-producing ruminant tha is reputed to have caused the Great Ch cago Fire of 1871. (See DUNN, ROS, and ROSE OF CIMARRON.)

OLIVE, I. PRENTICE   Usually r ferred to as "Print Olive." Print an brother Bob,[12] Texas-born and orner bastards both, abandoned their ranch i Williamson County, Texas, in 1876, th region having become too hot for th pair of sadists, who were known to hav whipped and shot a sixteen-year-ol youth to death and were suspected of th murders of various white men and blac men. Traveling north, the brothers relc cated on the south bank of the Disma River in western Nebraska for a sho period, but by 1878 they had move some eighty miles to the southeast an had established a ranch on the Sout Loop, and it was here that Print was commit his crowning infamy. On the ex treme northeast of the Olive range squa ted the small holding of one Luthe Mitchell, an aging hard case with a wif two daughters, and a stepdaughter, th latter being the comely bait that kept neighboring homesteader named An Ketchum in almost constant attendanc at the Mitchell home.

By the fall of 1878 the brothers Oliv who possessed a phobia that led them regard all homesteaders as "slow elk hunters, began to suspect that some c their stock was finding its way onto th menus of both Mitchell and Ketchun and on November 27, 1878, Sheriff An derson of Buffalo County, with a hasti deputized Bob Olive and accompanied b

[10] Although "Bedlam" is usually applied to a lunatic asylum, it is actually a corruptio of "Bethlehem."

[11] A bovine that has a natural-born desire to lead its fellows, whether to fresh pastures o to the packing plants. A bell was sometimes attached to such a critter.

[12] A gentleman who sometimes went under the alias of Bob Stevans.

two others, rode out to the Mitchell place with a warrant for the arrest of Mitchell on a cattle-rustling charge, complainant Print Olive being the instigator of this mission. Ami Ketchum was in the yard when the posse thundered up, and after Bob had let off a round in his direction, Ketchum ducked under a wagon and started to return the fire. Hearing the commotion, Old Man Mitchell came out to put an end to the fussin' with his Winchester. And he did just that. The posse retired with a dying Bob Olive.

The two homesteaders were arrested for the killing, but on the morning of December 10, while being escorted to the scene of a preliminary hearing, the two manacled prisoners were handed into the tender custody of Print Olive in exchange for a large roll of spending stuff. Print and a few of his hands took the purchases back to the ranch and hanged them from a tree, after which the bodies were burned and buried. But not deep enough. The charred remains were dug up, and Print found himself under arrest on a double murder charge. But Print had money, and after spending a quarter of a million dollars in lawyers' fees and being brought before the court on two occasions, he was discharged on December 17, 1880, on the ground that "no complaining witnesses could be found." After his release, Print moved to Trail City, Colorado, where, in the late summer of 1886, he made the error of starting a gun argument with a cool cowhand named Joseph Sparrow; the setting was a local saloon, and a bullet from Joe's .45 made Olive permanently "out of print."

OLLINGER, ROBERT   Ohio-born Robert Ameridth Ollinger[13] arrived in the Seven Rivers country of southeastern New Mexico in 1876 to join older brother Wallace, the latter having established himself as a cattleman after his moving into the territory some years earlier. Shortly after his arrival, Bob took up employment as ranch foreman on the Hugh Beckwith spread, a choice of occupation that was to lead to his developing a friendship with young Robert Beckwith and to Ollinger's becoming involved in the Lincoln County War. During this bloody fracas—details of which may be found elsewhere in this volume— Bob was with the party that lay siege to the McSween home, and he may have been involved in the slaying of Frank McNab.

In August 1878, when the feud had more or less burned itself out, Ollinger accepted the appointment of United States deputy marshal, and later that same year he killed an outlaw named Tom Hill when the latter resisted arrest. About eighteen months later another notch was credited to the deputy marshal. During an argument with a hard case named John Jones, who was strongly suspected of having killed John Beckwith[14] in the Seven Rivers area in 1879, Ollinger killed Jones after the latter had opened fire on him with a Winchester. In the spring of 1881 Bob became acquainted with Sheriff Pat Garrett, an unfortunate meeting that led to Ollinger meeting his death at the hands of Billy the Kid; deputized to guard this convicted killer, Robert Ameridth Ollinger was shot dead by the Kid during a successful jailbreak that occurred on April 28, 1881. Admirers of the Kid usually portray Ollinger as a sadistic jailer who well deserved the double load of buckshot that encompassed his passing,

[13] There is some controversy over the spelling of "Ollinger"; "Olinger" is sometimes given as correct.
[14] Youngest son of Hugh Beckwith, Ollinger's onetime employer.

but the girl he left behind him[15] had naught but good to say about this long-haired lawman, and she regarded his gun, gauntlets, and binoculars as much-cherished heirlooms until her death in the 1930s. (See LINCOLN COUNTY WAR and McCARTY, HENRY.)

O'NEILL, WILLIAM O. Although not a particularly big name in gunfighting circles, William "Buckie" O'Neill is somewhat unique in that he held a law degree and that he was a pistoleering lawman who never killed a man in a gunfight. Before his twenty-first birthday he was editing the Phoenix *Herald,* and from these beginnings he was to remain connected with publishing for the greater part of his life—publishing a stock growers' paper entitled *Hoofs and Horns* at Prescott, Arizona, during the middle 1880s and writing short stories for magazine publication in much of his spare time. O'Neill had his first introduction to gunplay during his early Arizona years. One afternoon a dozen Texas riders "treed" Phoenix with much threatening language and a display of indiscriminate shooting, and the city marshal, Henry Garfias, deputized William to help him cool the troublemakers, the Texans being routed after Garfias had removed two of them from the reach of mortal justice and O'Neill had incapacitated a further couple with marksmanship of a nonfatal nature.

Spending his leisure time "bucking the tiger" at the faro tables led to O'Neill being dubbed "Buckie," and it was as Buckie O'Neill that he was elected sheriff of Yavapai County, Arizona, in 1889. Buckie's most notable exploit during his year of office was the tracking down of a trio[16] of ex-Hashknife cowboys who held up and robbed the Atlantic and Pacific Express near Flagstaff on the night of March 20, 1889, the men being arrested after a six-hundred-mile chase and a nonfatal shootout. In 1897 O'Neill was voted mayor of Prescott, but before his term of office expired the Spanish-American War of 1898 broke out and Buckie shed his political robes to don the uniform of a captain in Teddy Roosevelt's Rough Riders. Captain O'Neill reached Cuba safely, but on July 1, 1898, and just prior to the Rough Riders' attack on San Juan Hill, he was shot dead by a sniper. Captain William Owen "Buckie" O'Neill was thirty-eight years old at the time of his death.

OPOSSUM   Although there are numerous species of opossum, only two species have the West as their habitat. These are the Virginia opossum, which is found over a large area west of the Mississippi, and the Texas opossum, whose range is confined to the valley of the Rio Grande. The opossum, which on reaching adulthood is about the size of a large domestic cat, has a pointed muzzle, rat-like tail and ears, and feet adapted for grasping. Long silver-and-black hairs sprouting from a dense undercoat of creamy-white fur give the opossum a grizzled appearance, only the undersides and face remaining free of this topcoat. The female gives birth to about eighteen young, all of which live in their mother's fur-lined pouch until they are three months old. All opossums are omnivorous eaters and possess a built-in mechanism that automatically renders them into a state of trance when frightened—hence the expression "playing 'possum."

[15] A Miss Lily Casey. At some later date Lily married a man named Klasner.
[16] Four men—Halford, Harvick, Stiren, and Smith—engaged in the robbery, but Smith wasn't arrested until a much later date.

ORCHARD, SADIE A small yet big-busted belle whose Cockney vocabulary of high-voltage obscenities had been heard around Wapping Old Stairs in London well before she arrived in the United States to settle in southwestern New Mexico in 1886. Sadie, who was dragging a sad sack of a husband around at this period, located in the mining town of Hillsboro,[17] and here she established a two-coach stageline and a many-doxied brothel. Madame Orchard's birds were always impeccably dressed when they paraded their charms within their plush-lined aviary. At some later date Sadie opened a restaurant in nearby Kingston, but although this was a huge success, her heart was in the bawdyhouse, an enterprise that survived well into the present century. Madame Sadie Orchard died in the early 1940s, mourned by all who had ever tasted of her crumpets and her strumpets.

OREGON Northwestern state on the Pacific coast, having Washington to the north, Idaho on its eastern flank, and California and Nevada to the south. Organized as a territory in 1848, and admitted to the Union as the thirty-third state in 1859, Oregon has the small town of Salem as its state capital and is popularly known as the Beaver State. (See OREGON COUNTRY.)

OREGON BOOT Popular name for the Gardner Shackle,[18] a sadistic device that prisoners confined within the Oregon State Penitentiary were forced to wear for the whole period of their sentence. The boot consisted of a heavy iron band that was locked around the leg just above the ankle and was supported by a steel ring that had a pair of braces to connect it to the heel of the wearer's boot. As the average weight of these iron bands was about fifteen pounds, walking became a difficult chore for anyone wearing an Oregon Boot. These shackles were made in the prison workshop, and the Oregon State Penitentiary was the only place where they were ever used. By the late 1870s only top-security prisoners were forced to wear the device, but it is difficult to ascertain when the practice was completely abandoned.

OREGON COUNTRY A vast area of land that encompassed the present-day states of Idaho, Washington, and Oregon, and extended into what is now southwestern Canada. Controversy regarding ownership of this region resulted in it being held under the joint dominion of Britain and the United States from 1818 until 1846. On June 15, 1846, an agreement was signed between the co-owners of this land, and all that part of the Oregon country that lay south of the forty-ninth parallel came into the possession of the United States.

OREGON TRAIL The accepted route to the Northwest from the latter half of the 1840s on. Migrants who wished to follow this line of march gathered either at Westport Landing,[19] Missouri, or at Kanesville,[20] which lay a farther two hundred miles up the Missouri River and was located in Iowa. If the latter settlement be chosen as the starting point, a ferry trip across the Missouri got the journey under way. After about twenty-five miles of prairie travel, the Platte

[17] Now a ghost town or near-ghost town.
[18] Invented by J. C. Gardner while enjoying the position of warden of the Oregon State Penitentiary, and patented by him on July 3, 1866.
[19] Later to become known as Kansas City, Missouri.
[20] Now known as Council Bluffs, Iowa.

came into view, and the trail followed the north bank of the river as it wound its way through Nebraska. At Grand Island,[21] migrant wagons that had started from Westport Landing rolled in from the southeast to cross the Platte and join the main trail.

Keeping to the valley of the Platte, the migrants snaked past Fort Kearney[22] and pushed on toward the Northwest. The river flowing slowly east on their left flank became the North Platte, and rough wooden markers, at too-short intervals alongside the trail, made the migrants painfully aware that cholera had not long since passed this way: T. Green, Mildred Moss—aged 25; J. Smith—aged 24; Jonathan Hoover—aged 12, and others and yet others. Who were these people? Other markers that have stood from the beginning of time appeared on the horizon, and soon the wagons were groaning past the twin buttes of Courthouse Rock and Jail Rock, then the stone finger of Chimney Rock, and later, the massive pile of Scotts Bluff. The Wyoming line was crossed, and after a further twenty miles of travel up the valley of the North Platte the trail passed Fort Laramie. At Casper the trail left the North Platte and pushed across country to cross the Sweetwater in the shadow of the domed mass of Independence Rock, then, traveling southwest, on through South Pass, across a barren wilderness to reach and ford the Green River, and then another thirty miles to Fort Bridger. After leaving the fort behind, the trail arrowed northwest, passing up the Bear River Valley to reach Fort Hall in southeastern Idaho.[23]

At Fort Hall the migrants crossed the Snake then followed the north bank of the river until they reached Old Fort

Boise on the Idaho-Oregon border. Here the river swung directly north, and it had to be crossed once more to follow the trail into Oregon. In Oregon the trail led due north for about fifty miles, with the Snake a few miles to the east, after which the trail swung to the northwest, then directly west along the south bank of the Columbia, the Des Chutes being the final river the migrants had to cross before arriving at The Dalles, this being more or less the terminal point of the Oregon Trail proper. Optional cutoffs, which rendered the journey slightly different than as given above, occurred in southwestern Wyoming and Idaho, the former being but a minor variation, while the latter cutoff left the main trail before Fort Hall was reached and followed the south bank of the Snake, rejoining the main trail again at Old Fort Boise.

O'ROURKE, JOHN Better known as "Johnny Behind the Deuce," a nickname that has led to his being referred to as "John," even though his original Christian name is reputed to have been Michael. Where O'Rourke hailed from is anyone's guess, but we do know that he was sixteen years old when he arrived at Tucson, Arizona Territory, in the spring of 1878 and accepted employment as a porter at the Palace Hotel. In the summer or early fall of the following year he moved to Tombstone, and although little is known of this period of his life, it may be assumed that he worked as a miner; that he spent much of his leisure hours at the faro tables is almost certain, for when he moved to Charleston, Arizona, sometime in 1880, he was known by the gambling pseudonym of "Johnny Behind the Deuce." Whether O'Rourke engaged

---

[21] A narrow island which divides the flow of the Platte, which, at this point, is a mile wide.

[22] If the fort was passed after 1850; previous to this time it was known as Fort Childs.

[23] After leaving Fort Hall, migrants could leave the Oregon Trail and follow the California Trail into the Southwest.

in a spot of burglary while at Charleston is open to doubt, but in January 1881 a mining engineer named Henry Schneider was letting it be known that he strongly suspected "Johnny" of having robbed his shack. Shortly after the lunch hour on January 14, 1881, the accused and his accuser had words outside Smith's Restaurant, and Schneider is reputed to have pulled a knife just before O'Rourke shot him dead. The town marshal, George McKelvey, put the collar on the killer without incident and transported his captive to Tombstone, where he was handed into the custody of Marshal Ben Sippy, Sheriff John Behan, and ex-Marshal Virgil Earp and his brother Wyatt. A mob of nothing-to-dos watched as O'Rourke was being handed over, and when they began to bubble with lynch talk, Wyatt is reputed to have held them at bay with a shotgun until the prisoner could be spirited away to Tucson.

"Johnny Behind the Deuce" was confined in the Tucson jail to await trial, but he escaped during the night of April 13–14, and although Sheriff Charlie Shibell of Pima County followed his trail as far as the San Pedro Valley, O'Rourke was never rearrested. From this time on, O'Rourke's fate remains conjectural; some reports suggest he may have killed John Ringo in the summer of 1882 and that he was shot dead by Pony Deal near Sulphur Springs in the fall of that year; others are of the opinion that "Johnny Behind the Deuce" settled in Mexico after his escape and that he never reappeared north of the border. (See RINGGOLD, JOHN.)

OSAGE INDIANS Tribe belonging to the Siouan language family whose vil-

lages were at one time scattered across southern Missouri and northern Arkansas. Their rectangular or oval-shaped dwellings had domed roofs, were covered with hides, and were somewhat similar to the Iroquois long houses of the East.[24] This eastern influence was also apparent in their appearance; leggings and moccasins, with a blanket usually wrapped around the hips, and shaved and roached heads. After they had been forcibly removed to Indian Territory[25] in the middle 1800s, the Osage lost much of their tribal identity by adopting many items of the white man's apparel and allowing their hair to grow long. In 1905 oil deposits were discovered beneath the Osage lands and many an impoverished tribesman became wealthy overnight.

OURAY Chief of the Uncompahgre Utes during the latter half of the nineteenth century. Ouray the Arrow was a trilingual (Ute, Spanish, and English), peace-loving Amerind who accepted much of the white man's way of life and the Methodist version of the Christian faith. Ouray, whose fighting spirit is reputed to have abated after his only son had been killed in a battle with the Sioux in 1860, was employed by the government as an interpreter on the Los Pinos Reservation in Colorado, and he helped to keep the less peaceful members of his tribe from straying beyond the limits of their allotted ground. In 1872 Ouray signed away much of the Utes' land in return for a plump pension of one thousand dollars per annum, a pleasant dwelling, and a prosperous farm, but by affixing his "John Hancock" to this agreement he caused resentment among many of his people, and in 1879 the U. S. Army had a Ute uprising to deal with. In the

---

[24] The average dimensions of the Osage houses were: length, 65 feet, width, 17 feet, height, 10 feet.

[25] The Osage were located to the west of the Cherokee nation in the northeastern section of Indian Territory.

spring of 1880, accompanied by his wife Queen Chipeta,[26] Ouray journeyed to Washington, D.C., to sign a further detrimental treaty. Ouray the Arrow died at his farm in 1880, shortly after returning from the aforementioned trip. (See MEEKER MASSACRE; MEEKER, NATHAN C.; and UTE INDIANS.)

OUTLAW, BASS Bass Outlaw may have been an alias, for this pale-eyed little man is reputed to have dropped hints about his prowess as a killer after his arrival in Texas in the middle 1880s, probably as a fugitive from his native Georgia. Alias[27] or no, the initials may be considered apt. Outlaw enlisted in the Texas Rangers in 1885, was promoted to the rank of corporal in 1890, and was enjoying the rank of sergeant in Captain Frank Jones' Company D some two years later.

In the spring of 1893, Sergeant Outlaw rode into Alpine in western Texas and entered the Buckthorn Saloon, where —in defiance of regulations—he proceeded to get likkered up while supposedly on duty. Sullen when sober, Outlaw became a "man on the prod" when drunk, and after getting involved in a dangerous argument with an ex-Ranger named Abraham Anglin during a game of cards, Bass was run out of town by Sheriff James Gillett.[28] When Captain Jones heard of this blot on the record, he forced Outlaw into handing in his resignation, and for the next few months Bass is reputed to have little better to do than follow up will-o'-the-wisp clues that he hoped might lead him to a cache of outlaw loot supposedly buried somewhere south of Alpine. This quest—if ever undertaken—was evidently unsuccessful, and in the early days of 1894 Bass got himself appointed deputy under United States Marshal Richard Ware.[29]

On April 4, 1894, Outlaw was prowling around El Paso with a chip on his shoulder, which had been placed there by the suspicion that Ware was showing favoritism to other deputies, and shortly before 5 P.M.—possibly in an attempt to work off his attack of spleen—Bass entered Tillie Howard's brothel in search of his favorite lay. The girl was evidently someone else's favorite, and when Bass was informed that she was otherwise engaged and asked whether he would care to see something else, he stamped out the back door and commenced to fire a few rounds at the sky. This commotion, plus the shrill blast of Tillie's police whistle, brought a trio of lawmen to the scene within a matter of minutes, town constables Selman and Chavez and Ranger McKidrick imagining that they had little more than a drunk to deal with. But it was much more. Outlaw opened the ball by killing McKidrick with two well-placed shots before the latter had time to unship his gun, and veteran mankiller Selman got two bullets in his right leg as his gun was blurring from its holster, but fifty-eight-year-old Selman had nearly twenty such encounters behind him, and, remaining erect, he squeezed off a shot that damped Outlaw's boiler for good. The gunman was carried into Barnum's Saloon with a ball in his chest, and he died some four hours later. (See SELMAN, JOHN.)

[26] Chipeta survived her husband by forty-four years, dying in 1924 at the age of eighty.

[27] If an alias, one wonders if this man's surname may have been Bass, the "outlaw Bass" having been reversed into Bass Outlaw.

[28] An ex-Ranger who was, at this time, sheriff of Jeff Davis County.

[29] Ex-Rangers appear to have had law enforcement in Texas pretty well sewn up at this period, for Ware was an ex-Ranger who is sometimes given the credit for the shooting of Sam Bass.

OUTLAW EXTERMINATORS
A party of five bounty hunters who operated in Arizona Territory during the 1870s and early 1880s and who were dubbed "Outlaw Exterminators, Inc." by the press of the period. The group consisted of Deputy Sheriffs Clay Calhoun and Floyd Davis, cattlemen Richard Hunter and Ben Slack, and a barman named Fred Beeber, the last three named only leaving their regular employment when an outlaw appeared on the scene whom they considered worthy of their combined interest. About ten outlaws who had forked their ponies ahead of these so-called "exterminators" were returned to the settlements curved around their mounts, long past seeing the trail unwind beneath them. The group's most notable feat was the tracking down of multiple killer John Allman in the fall of 1877. (See ALLMAN, JOHN.)

OVERLAND STAGE LINE   Organized by Ben Holladay in 1862 after he had come into possession of the equipment and route mileage of the bankrupt Central Overland, California, and Pike's Peak Express Company, an enterprise that had been in the hands of Russell, Majors, and Waddell. The extent of the Overland route may be best appreciated by quoting from a company poster: "Daily coaches from Atchison, Omaha, and Nebraska City via Denver City; connecting at Denver with its daily coaches for Central City, Gregory, and Clear Creek Mining Districts; also with triweekly coaches for Taos, Santa Fe, and other principal points in New Mexico. At Salt Lake City, connecting with its triweekly line of coaches for Virginia City and Helena, Boise City, Walla Walla, The Dalles, and Portland, Oregon; also connecting with the daily coaches of The Overland Mail Company, for Austin, Virginia City,

Nevada, Sacramento and San Francisco, California." This was the Overland Stage Line, which was to last until 1866, for after Holladay had taken over the Butterfield Overland Mail Company in February 1866, the Overland Stage Line became the Holladay Overland Mail and Express Company.[30] (See BUTTERFIELD OVERLAND MAIL COMPANY; HOLLADAY, BEN; and JACKASS MAIL.)

OWENS, COMMODORE PERRY
A more flamboyant character than Commodore Perry Owens probably never tapped and tinkled his way along a boardwalk. With blond locks reaching almost to waist level, wide-brimmed fawn sombrero, fringed and hand-tooled chaps, slim hips circled by a gunbelt more than four inches in width and ribbed with a double row of ammunition, and with a long-barreled Colt .45 dangling butt foremost against his left hip, Owens would have made Wild Bill Hickok appear commonplace. Born in Tennessee on July 29, 1852, and christened Commodore Perry in honor of an American naval hero named Commodore Oliver H. Perry, Owens moved West in his teens and took up cattle working in Texas. In his early twenties he began pushing farther west, buffalo hunting on the Staked Plains to supply meat for the railroad construction crews for some years, then leapfrogging his way across New Mexico in a succession of ranching jobs to arrive in Apache County, Arizona Territory, in the early 1880s. Here he became employed as the manager of a horse ranch located at Navajo Springs in north-central Arizona, and over the years he built up a reputation as a fast gunslinger who had blasted many a rustler into celestial pastures.

In November 1886 Owens was elected sheriff of Apache County, his twelve-month tour of duty to commence on

[30] This last company had 2,670 miles of route at its disposal when Holladay sold out to Wells Fargo in November 1866.

January 1, 1887. This was to prove a busy year for Owens, as we shall see. A posse led by the new sheriff killed Ike Clanton at his base on the Blue River, and shortly afterward Owens arrested Finn Clanton without having to resort to gunplay. In July a local rustler named Mart Blevins disappeared, and although he is reputed to have been killed by Navahos, some folk are of the opinion that Owens may have cut him down during a gunfight that the sheriff omitted to put on his report sheet. Although there is some doubt as to whether Owens killed Mart Blevins, there is no questioning the fact that he killed two of the Old Man's sons in a spectacular stand-up shootout.

On September 4, 1887, Sheriff Owens rode into Holbrook with the express intention of arresting Andy Blevins—alias Andy Cooper—on a horse-theft charge. Arriving around 4 P.M., Owens left his horse at Brown and Kinder's Livery Stable and strode toward the Blevins' clapboard cottage armed with a Winchester and a six-gun, well aware that Andy—while knocking 'em back in Holbrook's Bucket of Blood Saloon—had been heard to boast of having killed sheepmen John Tewksbury and William Jacobs but two days earlier. Andy opened the door in answer to the sheriff's knock, but on being told he was under arrest, he slammed the door and reached for his iron, firing one shot through a door panel before a wagon train of lead splintered the woodwork and threw him across the room. After firing through the door, Owens leaped from the porch as John Blevins appeared around the side of the cottage and began throwing lead

in his direction. The sheriff snapped off a shot that tossed John back against the building and then pivoted to put a killing shot through the head of Moses Roberts[31] as the latter charged from the front doorway with a blazing six-gun. Seconds after Roberts had slumped against the doorjamb, sixteen-year-old Sam Houston Blevins dashed from the cottage with a six-gun lined up on Owens but the sheriff shot him dead before he could squeeze off a shot. That was the end of one of the bloodiest shootouts in Arizona's history; Roberts and two of the Blevins brothers lay dead, and John was seriously wounded.[32]

Before his term of office expired, Owens became involved in the Pleasant Valley War, and during this sanguinary period he is usually credited with the killing of Charlie Blevins. After turning in his badge on December 31, 1888, Owens worked at various jobs before settling down at Seligman, Arizona, in 1900. Here he invested his savings in a general store and became acquainted with a girl named Elizabeth Barrett, whom he married in 1902. Commodore Perry Owens died at Seligman on May 10, 1919. (See BLEVINS, ANDY; BLEVINS, MART; CLANTON, JOSEPH ISAAC; CLANTON, PHINEAS; and PLEASANT VALLEY WAR.)

OWLHOOT TRAIL   Any rider who left the straight and narrow to indulge in enterprises of a criminal nature was said to have taken the "owlhoot trail," the expression being synonymous with "outlaw trail." Outlaws were frequently referred to as "owlhoots."

---

[31] A brother-in-law of the Blevinses.
[32] John recovered and was given a five-year stretch in the Yuma Penitentiary.

PACIFIC UNION EXPRESS
Organized in 1867 by Darius Ogden Mills
and Lloyd Tevis as a subsidiary of the
Central Pacific Railroad Company. The
newly formed express company began
operating in June 1868, enjoying the exclusive rights to the shipment of express
over the entire Central Pacific system and
the right to ship over the Union Pacific
system between Ogden, Utah, and
Council Bluffs, Iowa. The company—as
was intended—robbed Wells Fargo of
much of its business, and the latter company, shaken to its roots, was pressured
into buying out Pacific Union Express for
an exorbitant figure in the fall of 1869.
Shortly after this the affairs of Pacific
Union were wound up, and the company
ceased to exist.

PACK **R**AT   Popular name for a woodrat. (See WOODRATS.)

PACKER, **A**LFRED   A prospector
who made his first recorded appearance
on the western scene in southwestern
Colorado when he was about twenty-
five years of age. This was in the fall of
1883, and Packer had been prevailed
upon to lead a party of five men—Bell,
Humphreys, Miller, Moon, and Swan—

across the San Juan Range and into New
Mexico. Sometime in early January huge
snowdrifts slowed the party's trek to a
crawl, and they made camp near
Powderhorn Creek, located on a small
plateau with the towering mass of
Uncompahgre Peak visible to the north.
Rations began to dwindle, and within days
of their arrival on the plateau gunfire
echoed around the wilderness.

A couple of months later, Packer came
out of the mountains alone and settled at
Saguache, evidently well supplied with
funds. With the arrival of summer and
no word having been received from
Miller, Bell, Swan, Moon, or Humphreys,
relatives of some of the missing men
prompted the law into making a few inquiries. The town marshal of Saguache
interviewed Packer and received a few
shifty-eyed looks and the information
that four of the party had traveled south
and that Moon had died of exposure. Not
altogether satisfied with Packer's story,
the lawman organized a posse and went
into the mountains, and shortly afterward the bodies of the missing quintet
were found on the bank of Powderhorn
Creek. The bodies had been neatly butchered, and it was obvious that someone
had been living high off the hog.

Confronted with this grisly evidence, Packer changed his story. On returning to camp after a luckless search for game, Packer had found Bell dropping pieces of odd-looking meat into the stewpot, and before Packer had time to ask where the victuals had come from, Bell had attacked him with a blood-stained ax—well, like, Packer had killed Bell in self-defense, and it was only then that he had noticed the bodies of Humphreys, Swan, Miller, and Moon, and the fact that the latter had been shorn of some of his flesh. To a man with an empty belly, the mess in that stewpot had smelled powerful nourishing; "It tasted pretty good too iffen yer didn't dwell on what yer were chewin'." The marshal nearly threw up as Packer explained how he had lived off the remains until spring thaws had allowed him to leave the mountains, and of how he had robbed the dead as "they had no use fer the money."

When the marshal recovered his tan he put the arm on Packer and tossed him into the Lake City jail to await trial for murder, but before Packer could be brought before the bench he escaped, and it wasn't until 1893 that he was run to earth in Wyoming, where he had been living under the name of Swartz. This time Packer didn't escape; he was tried, found guilty of murder, and sentenced to death. His lawyers, however, succeeded in getting him a new trial, and on being retried he was handed a forty-year stretch in the Canon City Penitentiary. Few men are kept behind bars for such a length of time, and in 1910, at the age of fifty-two, Packer was released. Alfred "Cannibal" Packer died in 1915. Although Packer may have been telling the truth when he stated he had only killed in self-defense, he can hardly be described as "cuddly."

PADDLE WHEEL A gambling game consisting of a large wheel marked off with a hundred numbered wedges and a large board with a hundred squares likewise numbered. Players placed their bets on their choice of number on the board, the wheel was spun, and the number that stopped near an indicator was the winner.

PAINTER
Regional name for the puma; a corruption of panther. (See PUMA.)

PAIUTE INDIANS
Great Basin tribe belonging to the Uto-Aztecan language family. The Paiute[1] were roaming the area that was later to become the states of Nevada and Utah from early in the seventeenth century until their removal to the Malheur Reservation in eastern Oregon in the early 1860s. The barren land on which they lived supported little animal and vegetable life, consequently these Indians led a nomadic existence, as most of their time was spent searching for sustenance. This permanent state of near famine led to an omnivorous diet, which included roots and berries, grasshoppers and other insects, mice, rabbits, and an occasional pronghorn; and to the Paiutes being classed as "digger Indians" by the white men. Crude wickeyups were used as dwelling places, these being covered by either tule rushes or whatever bird's-nest-type materials were available. Hair was worn long and unbraided, and until the middle of the nineteenth century, dress was extremely primitive, clothing being made from grass, rabbit skins, shredded bark, and tanned skins, with little ornamentation being added; after this time, buckskins bearing a strong plains influence, items of Navaho attire, and the trade blankets and clothes of the white man were all part of the Paiute wardrobe. Al-

1 Pronounced "PIE-ute." Occasionally may be found spelled as Piute or Par-Ute.

though they had little time for cultural activities and were regarded in the manner of "poor relations" by the plains tribes, the Paiute were much skilled in the art of basketwork.

PALOMINO   A saddle horse of a creamy gold color that has been known since well before the Christian era. These golden horses with the almost white manes and tails were much prized by the Spaniards, and when California was ceded to the United States in 1848 at the close of the Mexican War, palominos[2] became popular in North America. The mating of palomino with palomino has an 80 per cent chance of producing a similar-colored offspring, while palominos may also result from the coupling of light-colored horses (light chestnut, etc.) of any of the saddle breeds. Palominos average 15½ hands[3] in height and 1,100 pounds in weight.

PANAMINT   As this settlement located in the Panamint Mountains to the west of California's Death Valley was described as "a suburb of hell," it was obviously a typical mining town of its period. Panamint City—to give its full and rather grand title—was born in the spring of 1873, the discovery of a rich silver-bearing reef in the area in the fall of 1872 being the only reason for its existence. When news of the find leaked out, an assortment of honest, dishonest, and downright disgusting types were attracted to the site in such numbers that their united efforts in erecting dwellings and business premises had the mile-long

street known as Panamint scratching its mark on the map almost overnight. Many honorable businesses thrived in the town—Lloyd's Stage Office, Clovis and Rhine's General Store, a United States post office, James Cohn's Gun Shop, various eateries, and a Chinese laundry being but a few of these—yet the scales were heavily weighted in favor of the more robust and violent type of enterprise, more than forty saloons[4] and a like number of gambling halls, plus Madame Martha Camp's plush-lined bordello[5] and the numerous cribs of free-roaming doxies bearing ample proof of this.

Panamint was located at the top end of Surprise Canyon, and the fact that this was a box canyon meant that a harrowing journey between towering walls of rock had to be made to reach or leave the town. As this path was little more than six feet wide in some places, the canyon became the answer to many an owlhoot's prayer, and stages and silver shipments were ambushed with such frequency that Wells Fargo—which can hardly be classed as a sissy outfit—refused to have anything to do with Panamint's freighting problems. Finally, in desperation, the silver was cast into such gigantic balls that only an Atlas may have moved them, and the baddies, fearing rupture or worse had they tried to lift these metal spheres, left the shipments strictly alone. By the fall of 1875 the silver boom was drawing to a close, but, even so, Panamint was to survive for almost three more years, a flash flood of near biblical proportions swilling it down

[2] Derived from *palomina*, Mexican-Spanish for a light- or cream-colored horse.
[3] A "hand" is a measure of 4 inches.
[4] Two of these saloons, the adjacent Oriental and Dexter, had a wall of sheet iron slotted between their premises. This prevented explosively propelled pieces of lead from vacating either saloon to do damage to the decor or clientele of its neighbor.
[5] Scene of at least one fatal shootout. William McAllister, owner of the Snug Saloon, put three lethal bullets into a night watchman named Barstow as the clincher to an argument regarding who should first have temporary possession of one of Madame's trollops.

Surprise Canyon and into oblivion in the spring of 1878.

PANCHO VILLA   Mexican revolutionary who made a minor excursion onto United States territory. (See ARAMBULA, JOSÉ FRANCISCO VILLA.)

PANHANDLE   Any strip of territory that belongs to one state and extends between two other states, obvious examples being the High Plains region of northwestern Texas and the northwestern portions of Oklahoma.

PANKHURST, CHARLIE
Frequently given, in error, as being the name of a stagecoach driver whose correct name was Parkhurst. (See PARKHURST, CHARLIE.)

PANTHER
Popular name for the puma. (See PUMA.)

PAPAGO INDIANS   Tribe of the Uto-Aztecan language family who have inhabited what is now southeastern Arizona since at least 1650. Although resident in a barren land, the Papago managed to raise crops,[6] the fruits of this husbandry, supplemented by any small game that might be taken, being their chief form of sustenance. Houses were constructed of adobe reinforced with cactus rods, and the houses frequently possessed a patio. Clothing, which was kept to the minimum, was usually made from the woven fibers of wild cotton, and hair was worn in a long bob. Potterymaking and basketwork were the Papagos' chief accomplishments. The present-day representatives of

the tribe still live on the land of their forefathers.

PARFLECHE   A Canuck-French word[7] that means "rawhide" (especially buffalo hide) or any article made from this, although the word is more frequently used to describe the skin holdalls used by the mountain men and the Rocky Mountain and plains Indians. These holdalls were little more than a rectangle of dressed hide in which food[8] and clothing were wrapped, the parfleche being folded in much the same manner as one would fold an envelope, the butting edges then being laced together with rawhide thongs. Indian parfleches were elaborately decorated and occasionally fringed.

PARISH, FRANK   Small-time member of the Innocents who was hanged by a Montana vigilance committee on January 14, 1884. In the fall of 1883 Parish took part in a stagecoach robbery that netted the gang twenty-five hundred dollars, and he also engaged in an occasional spot of horse theft. The decision to arrest and hang Parish—together with five other miscreants—was made but twenty-four hours before the multiple hangings were accomplished, and as the vigilantes were unaware of Frank's hold-up venture and had little proof of his being a stock thief at this time,[9] it had evidently been decided that Mr. Parish should hang as an example rather than as a convicted criminal. (See INNOCENTS and VIGILANTES OF MONTANA.)

PARKER, CYNTHIA ANN   Born in Illinois in 1827, Cynthia Ann was taken into the Southwest by her parents

[6] Mainly beans.
[7] Reputed to have Amerind origins. The word has been in use since about 1700.
[8] Usually pemmican.
[9] The vigilantes may have suspected Parish of minor crimes, but they were unaware of his stock thefts and his complicity in the stage robbery until his post-arrest confession increased their knowledge in this respect.

in 1833, the Parker family settling near the headwaters of the Navasota River in northern Texas, where, in 1835, they erected a stockaded civilian fort known as Fort Parker. This was the land of the Kiowa and Comanche, and on May 19, 1836, a mixed war-party of more than three hundred of these tribesmen succeeded in entering the fort and killing more than forty of its inhabitants,[10] Cynthia and her eleven-year-old brother John being taken into captivity as the only survivors of the Parker family. Cynthia was to spend almost a quarter of a century as a Comanche captive— years during which she bore the chief of the Nokonis band three children and lost most of her command of English—before she was returned to her own people by a battalion of Texas Rangers who, in 1860, routed the band she was traveling with and realized her identity after Cynthia and an infant[11] she was nursing had been taken prisoner. On re-entering the white man's world, Cynthia and her child went to live with relatives, but she had little time to re-establish herself as an Americano, for she died in 1865 at the age of thirty-eight years. (See QUANAH PARKER.)

PARKER, ISAAC C. England had Judge Jeffreys, and some three hundred years later, America had Judge Parker —two gentlemen who were separated by both time and distance but whose harmony of thought has resulted in them being classed as "hanging judges" of macabre proportions. Isaac Charles Parker, Ohio-born and of English ancestry, was admitted to the Ohio bar in 1859, and that same year he moved to St. Joseph, Missouri, and set up practice. Here he met a girl who was to become the legal Mrs. Parker on December 12, 1861. In 1868 Isaac became a circuit judge, a position he held until he was elected to Congress some two years later. Congressman Parker retired from politics in 1875, and before the year was out, he had been appointed federal judge for the Western District of Arkansas.

Headquartered on the federal court at Fort Smith and having jurisdiction over Indian Territory (Oklahoma), which lay to the west, Judge Parker girded his loins to join battle with the legion of owlhoots who infested the Indian-held lands: United States Marshal James F. Fagan was authorized to appoint two hundred deputies with which to rake in the rabble; His Honor prepared to shake it through the sieve; and a sinister-looking little man named George Maledon stood by his gibbet eager to dispose of what got caught in the mesh. Killers and rapists were whisked from the territory and through Parker's court, and on September 3, 1875, the hangings got under way when an economy-size package of six villains[12] made a united exit through one giant trap; to the onlookers, justice could be seen to have been done, the sextet undoubtedly felt it being done, and Maledon knew he'd done it.

During Parker's twenty-one years at Fort Smith more than 160 men heard themselves sentenced to death, but commutations, retrials, etc., resulted in only 79 of these passing through Maledon's

[10] Not all were Parkers, of course; other families settled within sight of the stockade, and they were welcome to take refuge behind its log walls when Indian attacks appeared imminent.

[11] A girl named "Prairie Flower."

[12] Edward Campbell, a black man convicted of a double passion-killing; Daniel Evans, a Caucasian convicted of murder and robbery; Samuel Fooy, a Cherokee convicted of murder and robbery; Smoker Mankiller, a Cherokee convicted of murder; James Moore, a Caucasian convicted of multiple murder; and William Whittington, a Caucasian convicted of murder and robbery.

hands. That most of these men deserved little sympathy cannot be denied,[13] yet on many occasions some of Parker's speeches on sentencing a killer showed a latent form of sadism that a few of those brought before him may have been embarrassed in possessing. Judge Isaac C. Parker died while still in office, passing into history from a combination of dropsy and heart trouble on November 17, 1896, at the age of fifty-eight years and five weeks. (See MALEDON, GEORGE.)

PARKER, ROBERT LEROY Better known as "Butch Cassidy," the happy-go-lucky leader of the Wild Bunch. Robert Leroy was born at Beaver, Utah, in 1866, the first of seven children resulting from the union of Englishman Maximilian Parker[14] and his Scottish bride. Young Robert spent his childhood and early youth learning the arts of riding, roping, and shooting on his father's horse ranch, and it was during these formative years that he became the constant companion of Mike Cassidy, a man who was employed by Max, although much of Cassidy's spare time was spent rustling other folks' stock. There is little doubt that Robert joined Cassidy in many

of his off-color ventures, for Robert adopted the older man's name as an alias to prevent his parents from hearing of these activities.

In 1883 this counterfeit "Cassidy" was arrested for stealing a saddle, but he escaped from custody before he could be brought into court, and shortly afterward he was riding with a gang of owlhoots led by brothers Tom and Bill McCarty and Williard Christiansen—the latter being somewhat better known under his alias of Matt Warner. This mob operated in Colorado, and "Cassidy" is known to have been present when they pulled three of their local jobs: the holdup of a Denver and Rio Grande express near Grand Junction in the fall of 1887; the robbery of the First National Bank at Denver on March 30, 1889; and the robbery of the San Miguel Bank at Telluride on June 24 of that same year. After this last bank job the twenty-three-year-old Robert Leroy is reputed to have worked as a cowhand on various Wyoming ranches until taking a job in a butcher's shop at Rock Springs in 1892. From this time on "Butch Cassidy" was to be the favorite alias of our subject.[15]

Sometime in 1893 Cassidy left Rock Springs and teamed up with a small-time

[13] The names alone of some of these may have convinced many of their guilt: Smoker Mankiller, hanged for murder; Sinker Wilson, hanged for murder; Jack Woman Killer, hanged for killing a man named Nathaniel Hyatt (Jack evidently having stepped out of character); Gus Bogles, hanged for murder; Bood Crumpton, hanged for murder; Matt Music, sentenced to death for rape but later pardoned; Blue Duck, sentenced to death for murder but had sentence commuted to life imprisonment.

[14] Born at Preston, Lancashire, in 1844, Maximilian immigrated to the United States with his parents in 1855. Max's father—Robert Parker—was a founder-member of a small Mormon congregation that had established itself in Preston, and on arrival in the States the family joined the Mormon handcart migration that finally got them to Utah during the winter of 1856–57, although not wholly intact: The head of the family died during the trek West. In 1865 Maximilian married Ann Campbell, a Scottish lass who was to become the mother of Robert Leroy Parker. Note: As most American writers class the Preston of the 1850s as being a small settlement of impoverished farmers, and describe Robert Parker as being the product of such a community, it may be worth noting that by 1850 this town on the Ribble was one of the main centers of the Lancashire cotton industry, a fact that may allow us to imagine Parker Sr., as being an impoverished cotton spinner rather than an impoverished manure spreader.

[15] Other aliases of Parker's include Jim Ryan, George Cassidy, George Ingerfield, Jim Maxwell, and Santiago Maxwell.

stock thief named Al Rainier, a partnership that was dissolved by Sheriff J. Ward when he arrested them in Uintah County, Wyoming, for being in possession of a herd of stolen horses. The arrest occurred in the spring of 1894, and in July of that year Butch was lodged in the State Penitentiary at Laramie to sit out a two-year stretch. In January 1896, after serving some eighteen months, he was released, and he drifted northwest to enter the outlaw hideout of Hole in the Wall, and here, within a short time of his arrival, he became undisputed leader of a loosely knit gang that is usually referred to as the "Wild Bunch."[16] Some of the leading lights in this gang were such big-time outlaws as Harry Longbaugh, Elza Lay, William Carver, Camilla Hanks, Harvey Logan, and Harry Tracy, and of these, Harry Longbaugh—alias the "Sundance Kid"—was to become Cassidy's inseparable companion.

Over the next six years Union Pacific trains crossing Wyoming encountered the Wild Bunch on quite a few occasions, the safes in their express cars being blown by powder of such quality[17] that on one occasion the whole car was shattered, and the gang had to spend much wasted—and dangerous—time picking up some thirty thousand dollars' worth of bills that had been scattered over the range. These militant excursions against the Union Pacific were punctuated by bank robberies and other long-riding activities that could be expected to earn a fast buck, but that also got the Pinkertons and other law-enforcement agencies crowding the Bunch so hard that after knocking off a Great Northern train at Malta, Montana, on July 3, 1901, Butch and Sundance decided to quit the States. After this robbery Butch and Sundance, Bill Carver, Kid Curry, and Ben Kil-

patrick headed for Fannie Porter's brothel at Fort Worth, Texas, their favorite resort when heavy with outlaw loot.

Cassidy and Sundance, accompanied by Etta Place, headed for New York in the early days of 1902. Shortly after their arrival at New York the trio boarded the SS *Soldier Prince* bound for South America, and by the following year Butch and Sundance had established themselves as ranchers in Argentina. These efforts at becoming socially acceptable were ruined when Sundance winged a rancher whose wife he much coveted, and the newly arrived Americanos were forced into moving their headquarters to La Paz, Bolivia, to avoid the Kid being arrested. Soured by this setback, the transplanted members of the Wild Bunch went back into the business in which they were most skilled, and over the next few years these *"bandidos* Yankee" staged numerous robberies in Argentina, Bolivia, and Peru, a period of wild activity during which Sundance shot and killed the manager of the Compania National Store in Argentina while engaged in robbing the place.

In 1907 Sundance accompanied Etta to the States, returning alone shortly afterward to rejoin Cassidy and take up employment with the Concordia Tin Mines which was located in the Santa Vela Mountains of Bolivia. Butch and Sundance were each paid $150 a month for tending the Company's livestock, and had they remained at this task little more may have been heard from them, but in 1909 they fell back into their old ways by stealing some $10,000 in gold coin at Eucalyptus Station and, later, robbing a mule train that was carrying the payroll for a mine at Alpoca. Two or three hours after committing the last-mentioned rob-

[16] Sometimes classed as the "Hole in the Wall gang."
[17] The Kepauno Chemical Company's "Giant" Powder evidently having been recommended to the boys for such chores as this.

bery Cassidy and the Kid rode into the village of San Vincente and booked into the local hotel, little knowing that a silver-gray mule they had left outside was well known to the populace as being the property of the Alpoca mine superintendent and that while they were eating supper this intelligence was being relayed to an Army barracks at La Paz.

At twilight a detachment of Bolivian cavalry rode into San Vincente and dismounted outside the hotel, but their arrival had not gone unnoticed, and when the captain stepped onto the porch to call upon the outlaws to surrender, Butch and Sundance opened fire and killed him and one of his men. The soldiery immediately took cover behind an adobe wall and began pouring rifle lead in the direction of the patio, and, as the twilight deepened, fires were lighted to prevent the outlaws escaping under cover of darkness. By late evening the besieged were running short of ammunition, and the Kid dashed from cover in a bid to reach some extra bandoliers they had left on their mounts tethered in the hotel yard. Imagine him . . . washed by the orange glow of many fires . . . rivulets of sweat deltaing down a face begrimed by powder smoke . . . Harry Longbaugh— alias the Sundance Kid—probably never heard the barrage of rifle fire that killed him.

The crackle of small-arms fire continued throughout the night, and it wasn't until the cold light of dawn had killed the flickering shadows that the troops—under the cover of a withering barrage of lead—closed in on the patio. Cassidy saw them coming, but now there was only one unexploded cartridge in the cylinder of his Colt .45, and there was

little he could do. The soldiers heard the muffled thud of a heavy handgun, and when they reached the patio they found Robert Leroy Parker lying dead with a bullet wound in his right temple. That Butch and Sundance died in Bolivia there is little doubt, but there were—and are— folk who would dispute this.[18] (See CARVER, WILLIAM; HANKS, CAMILLA; HOLE IN THE WALL GANG; KILPATRICK, BEN; LAY, ELZA; LOGAN, HARVEY; LONGBAUGH, HARRY; PLACE, ETTA; ROSE, DELLA; TRACY, HARRY; and WILD BUNCH.)

PARKHURST, CHARLIE   One of the better-known six-in-hand drivers who negotiated their Concords over the rough trails of California's Sierra Nevadas during the latter half of the nineteenth century. Charlie, who is reputed to have been a New Englander by birth, probably arrived in the Mother Lode country around 1850, and for the next twenty years this somewhat mysterious character who rarely mixed with the other drivers and preferred to sleep in the stables was holding the "ribbons" as an employee of various California stage lines. Cigar-smoking, tobacco-chewing, and dram-drinking Charlie retired from driving in 1870 and finally settled on a small holding near Watsonville in Santa Cruz County. On December 29, 1879, visiting friends found Charlie lying in bed. Charlie was dead, and the visitors were amazed to discover that the little gray-haired figure whom they had known as "Charlie" had undoubtedly been a woman. A hastily summoned doctor established that the cause of death was cancer and the fact that the deceased had been a mother at some time. Surprised?

[18] Like Robert Leroy's younger sister, Lula, who was living in Utah as late as 1974. According to Lula a couple of "John Does" bit the dust in Bolivia, and Butch and Sundance, officially dead, returned to the States with new identities and lived out their lives as solid citizens, Cassidy dying at Spokane, Washington, in 1937, and Sundance breathing his last at Casper, Wyoming, in 1957. Ah, well . . . er—on to the next entry.

Or did the lack of masculine pronouns give you a clue?

PARKMAN, FRANCIS   American author. Born at Boston, Massachusetts, on September 26, 1823. In 1846, having come into possession of a legacy of some $150,000, Parkman invested some of the money in a tour of the Oregon Trail, financing a two-man expedition that was to take him and fellow Bostonian Quincy A. Shaw as far west as Fort Laramie[19] and was to result in Parkman establishing himself as an author with the publication of *The Oregon Trail* in 1849. Although Parkman suffered chronic ill health and was half blind from an early age, his literary output was prolific,[20] and he continued writing until his death on November 8, 1893.

PATTERSON, JIM   One of the many aliases used by Wild Bill Longley. (See LONGLEY, WILLIAM P.)

PATERSON REVOLVER
The first of Sam Colt's pistols. (See COLT FIREARMS, subheading *Paterson*.)

PAULINA   Indian renegade who operated in Oregon and northern California during the 1860s. Paulina's tribal affiliations are rather vague, the odds being in favor of either Snake or Paiute lineage, although he may have had a trace of Modoc blood. Thieving and skull-busting activities bearing the stamp of Paulina and his mixed band of Snake, Paiute, and Modoc ne'er-do-wells started around

1862, and over the next five years most of the stock thefts, stage holdups, and ranch raids committed in eastern Oregon and northern California were attributed to this small group which robbed both Indians and whites alike.

During Paulina's hard-riding years more than five hundred white civilians living in the Oregon country were killed by Indians, and although Paulina never achieved a hair-lifting monopoly in this region, we may readily assume that he and his gang were responsible for many of these killings. In the spring of 1864 Paulina had the gall to settle on the Klamath Reservation for a spell, and here he had his photograph taken, little knowing that posterity would be disappointed with his likeness; Paulina having more the appearance of a coal miner from Kentucky than a red man past redemption.

In the summer of 1866 Paulina's band raided the ranch of Howard Maupin in Antelope Valley and made off with a herd of cattle and other stock. Better if Paulina had stayed home that day, for Maupin was one of those to-the-ends-of-the-earth characters who cannot rest until the perpetrator of an unlawful bygone has been rendered into a state of permanent has-been. Maupin was also an excellent shot with a Henry repeater. In the last week of April 1877, near Little Trout Creek in northern Oregon, Maupin got within Henry range of Paulina's band and his first shot crippled their leader. Paulina, knowing he was unable to escape, ordered his half-dozen braves

[19] Parkman and Shaw started from Westport Landing (later to be known as Kansas City, Missouri) on April 28, 1846, journeyed up the Platte and North Platte rivers to Laramie, then struck south to reach Pueblo on the Arkansas before returning east—much of their return journey to Westport being accomplished by following the course of the easterly-flowing Arkansas.

[20] His works include *History of the Conspiracy of Pontiac* (1851); *Vassall Morton*, his only fictional work (1852); *Pioneers of France in the New World* (1865); *The Jesuits of North America* (1861); *Discovery of the Great West* (1869); *The Old Regime in Canada* (1874); *Count Frontenac and New France under Louis XIV* (1877); *Montcalm and Wolfe* (1884); and *A Half Century of Conflict* (1892).

to escape, and as the hoofbeats of their ponies became dying echoes, four more bullets found targets in his torso. Paulina was squirming in agony when the rancher reached his side, but he lay still for a moment when he saw Maupin raise his pistol; they shoot horses, don't they?

PAWNEE BILL The well-earned sobriquet of Gordon W. Lillie. (See LILLIE, GORDON W.)

PAWNEE INDIANS A plains-plateau tribe belonging to the Caddoan language group. By the middle of the seventeenth century the Pawnee[21] were firmly established on the central plains,[22] probably having migrated from the lower Mississippi area at some earlier date. As much of their sustenance was derived from agriculture, the Pawnee lived in settled communities where they could grow their corn, beans, pumpkins, squashes, etc. These villages consisted of a number of dome-shaped earth lodges that had large vestibules and an outer covering of grass and leaves, hide-covered tepees only being used during the hot summer months and while engaged in the hunting of the buffalo. Dress was typical of the plains tribes, fringed buckskins only giving way to garments manufactured from the woven materials of the white man in the latter half of the nineteenth century. A roach of hair on a shaven head was not uncommon among the braves of the tribe, although hair worn long and braided was the usual style.

Human sacrifice, rare among the North American tribes, was practiced by the Skidi-Pawnee branch of this tribe until 1817. Each spring a beautiful maiden of the tribe would be lashed to a scaffold and stripped naked so that half of her body—from forehead to ankle—might be painted black and the remainder red; then, suitably prepared, the girl would be pincushioned with arrows as the climax to a rite that was supposed to make the earth fertile. In 1817 the ceremony was completely ruined when a young brave named Petalesharo, inspired by either passion or chivalry, galloped up to the harlequined maiden, cut her bonds, and thundered from the camp with his prize under his arm. Petalesharo's one-man rebellion put an end to this wastage of talent, for the tribal elders were so impressed by this heroic action—whatever its motive—that they abandoned this sacrificial custom forthwith. In the 1850s the Pawnee were settled on a reservation in eastern Nebraska, and they remained here until their removal to northern Oklahoma in 1874. Traditional enemies of the Sioux, hundreds of Pawnees became scouts for the U. S. Army during the North Plains campaigns. (See NORTH, FRANK.)

PEACEMAKER REVOLVER Name given to the Colt .45-caliber six-gun of 1873. (See COLT FIREARMS, subheading *Peacemaker.*)

PEACE PIPE Usually referred to as a calumet. (See CALUMET.)

PECCARY A small piglike mammal that is confined to the New World. Two species occur, the collared[23] and the white-lipped peccary, but of these only the former has a limited range in the

---

[21] Meaning "wolves"; as the tribe was much skilled in the stalking of game—and enemies —while covered in whole wolf skins, their name may have resulted from this practice. Originally spelled "Pani."

[22] The present-day states of Kansas and Nebraska.

[23] So called because a collar of yellowish-colored hair encircles its neck.

United States, roaming bands of these grayish-colored beasts being found in the border country of Arizona, New Mexico, and Texas. Collared peccary are about three feet in length—a third of which is taken up with head—and have an average weight of about 50 pounds. Diet consists of vegetable matter, small animals, rattlesnakes and other reptiles, and carrion. Frequently called javelines.

PECOS May refer to the Pecos River Valley region of southwestern Texas or to a town of that name that is located in the valley some thirty-five miles south of the New Mexico line.

PECOS BILL A legendary cowboy figure of herculean proportions. Dozens of mythical adventures are credited to this early-day "Superman," who is reputed to have started on his odyssey by falling from his parents' wagon while crossing Texas. Said parents failed to notice their loss, and young Bill was discovered by a band of coyotes, which raised him into something a little larger than life-size. One of his better-known exploits concerns itself with Bill saddling a tornado that he failed to "gentle" until northwestern Arizona was reached; here the tornado gave up trying to buck him and wept so much water that the Grand Canyon was formed by the deluge.

PECOS TRAIL Cattle trail that started in southwestern Texas and wound its way up the Pecos Valley into New Mexico, continued to follow the watercourse until its headwaters were reached, then pushed north and northwest into Colorado and Wyoming.

PEMMICAN Ground or pounded meat mixed with fat; berries or sugar were occasionally added to give extra flavor. The Indians produced pemmican by grinding lean air-dried meat[24] between stones, then mixing this with a slightly less quantity of melted fat. This mixture was packed into hide bags, where it cooled and hardened into a compact mass. Pemmican, which would keep indefinitely, ensured an adequate food supply during the winter months, and it could also be used as "iron rations" when on the move.

PENITENTES A religious sect that flourished in New Mexico, Arizona, Colorado, and Utah during the nineteenth century, and is still active in New Mexico at the time of writing. Penitentes believe that earthly punishment is the only way in which one may be cleansed of real or imaginary transgressions, and self-flagellation is practiced to accomplish this end; *Disciplinas*—whips made from cactus roots—being used for this purpose. Members of this brotherhood may also have punishment visited upon them by other members of the congregation if found guilty of misconduct, the guilty one in this instance being strapped to an upright cross with wet rawhide thongs which may cause excruciating pain as they shrink with drying out. Similar treatment is also experienced by a chosen "Christ" after he has carried his cross from the church to "Calvary"[25] in a microscopic Passion play that is staged each Good Friday.[26] The Penitentes are an exclusive and mysterious sect—only Amerinds and Mexican Norte Americanos being admitted into the brotherhood—and masks are worn during all official activities.

[24] Usually buffalo meat, but some of the Northwest tribes used other flesh (elk, deer, etc.) and occasionally salmon.
[25] Any suitable hill or mesa.
[26] It is suspected that a number of these "Christos" have expired on their crosses.

PENNSYLVANIA RIFLE Alternative name for a Kentucky rifle. (See KENTUCKY RIFLE.)

PEPPERBOX REVOLVER Name given to multibarreled pistols that may be grouped into two distinct types: (1) those having a number of stationary barrels and a rotating firing pin, and (2) those having a cluster of barrels that revolved to bring their charges under the firing pin, the rotating action of the barrels being activated by either the hand or pressure on the trigger. The former group were four-shot pistols, while the latter group—by far the most popular—could be had in models which fired from four to ten shots. Calibers varied from .22 to .36, and although these guns had little accuracy and were rather cumbersome, they enjoyed a great measure of popularity over the middle decades of the nineteenth century.

PEYOTE A small spineless cactus that protrudes little above ground, the exposed portion being gray-green in color and having the appearance of a bunch of carrot tops. These tops, or "buttons," are peeled and chewed to produce a trancelike state in which visions of a usually pleasant nature and of an extraordinary range of color are experienced. The root, which is far more potent, is not recommended for chewing, but a tea made from these roots may be used as a remedy for a variety of afflictions. The plant has been used for the purposes described since the days of the Aztecs, and it was, and is, extensively used by many of the North American tribes. Members of some of these tribes made unorganized use of the plant—individuals chewing their way into another, possibly happier dimension when so inclined, while others accepted the Peyote cult—a semireligious organization that had the plant as its "grail." In the United States uncultivated peyote[27] is probably confined to the lower Rio Grande Valley in southern Texas.

PHILLIPS, JOHN At 11 P.M. on December 21, 1866, a small man riding a big gray thoroughbred left Fort Phil Kearny and began drumming his way south through a wilderness of frozen snow that swarmed with the fighting men of the whole Sioux nation. Fetterman's entire command had been wiped out that morning, and the small man had volunteered to carry a message to Fort Laramie, 230 miles down the Bozeman Trail, and the trail was crawling with Sioux.

Phillips, a Portuguese national who was born in the Azores in 1832, arrived in the United States around 1850, entering via California, probably with the idea of prospecting for gold. Over the first thirteen years of Phillips' residence in the States his activities cannot be truly ascertained, but when he arrived in Wyoming in 1864 to do a little prospecting, the fact that he had a wife and two children in tow seems sufficient proof that he had not been entirely idle over these missing years.

Early in 1866 the man known as "Portugee" was prospecting in the Powder River country, but by early fall, smoke talk in the hills had persuaded him to seek refuge with his family within the stockaded walls of newly erected Fort Phil Kearny. Here he was given employment as a teamster and stock handler as well as a cabin in which he and his family might live. By mid-December the worst winter for half a century was laying its grip on the land, an icy landscape

[27] Let's get technical: Peyote = *Lophophora williamsii*, and may be grown by cacti enthusiasts anywhere. Occasionally spelled "peyotl."

on which Sioux war parties began to make their appearance, and on the morning of the twenty-first, eighty men rode from the fort to scatter the warriors of Red Cloud. They never returned. The Sioux had destroyed them to the last man, and they were lying dead and frozen somewhere beyond the crest of Lodge Trail Ridge. Colonel Henry B. Carrington, officer in command of the fort, aware that the situation was desperate, called for a volunteer to carry a message to Laramie.

How the little bearded man in the buffalo coat ever got through will never be known. Hiding much of the daylight hours and holding his horse's nostrils when Indian riders came within whinnying distance of his mount, Portugee pushed on. Dawn of the twenty-third saw Pumpkin Buttes on his left flank, and by full light a war party was weaving toward him from the east. Portugee quirted the big gray that Carrington had loaned him, and the Indian ponies were soon outclassed, the war party having been lost by the time courier Phillips crossed Antelope Creek. At daybreak on the twenty-fourth the man in the buffalo coat stiff-legged into the telegraph office at Horseshoe Station; a pole might be down, but they would try to get a message through to Laramie. But they couldn't raise Laramie. Portugee climbed back into the saddle; another forty miles, and both horse and rider were almost finished. At eleven-thirty that night Portugee slid from his mount outside the entertainment hall at Fort Laramie. A Christmas Eve party was in progress—crinolines and dress uniforms, the strains of "Oh, Susanna"; Phillips, suffering from frostbite and leaden of leg, staggered in among the revelers, blurted out his story, and collapsed. Outside, on the snow, in the glow from Old Bedlam, the horse that Carrington had loaned him lay dead.

On Christmas Day a long blue centipede of troops snaked out of Laramie and headed up the Bozeman. Early in the New Year Phillips was back in the saddle, and he continued to serve the Army until the Treaty of 1868 established an uneasy truce between Red Cloud and the whites and it became moderately safe to establish a home in Wyoming. By the early 1870s Portugee had accrued sufficient capital from a variety of freighting jobs to establish a small ranch on the Chugwater River in southeastern Wyoming. This venture prospered, expanding until it embraced a stage station, restaurant, hotel, livery stable, and post office. Originally known as the Chugwater Ranch, and later as the Chugwater Hotel, Phillips sold out in 1879 and retired to Cheyenne. John "Portugee" Phillips died at Cheyenne on November 18, 1883, seemingly a forgotten man, but in 1899 his name was disinterred from the records, and the government gave his widow five thousand dollars as posthumous recognition of her husband's heroic journey in the winter of 1866. (See BOZEMAN TRAIL and FETTERMAN FIGHT.)

PICKETT, TOM A two-gun lad who started leaving hit-and-miss tracks on the record from the fall of 1877, at which time he was hanging around Dodge City with the Dave Rudabaugh gang of owlhoots. Tom was still with Rudabaugh when the latter amalgamated with Billy the Kid's gang of rustlers in the fall of 1880, and Tom is known to have been with the Kid on the night O'Folliard died, and he was arrested with the Kid—and others—at Stinking Springs on December 27, 1880 (but as no warrants were out for Tom at this time, he was released). At some later date Pickett moved into Arizona Territory where, in 1885, he took up employment with the newly organized Hashknife outfit.[28] In 1886 he married a girl named Katherine Kelly at Holbrook, and the following year he sided with the Graham faction during the Pleasant Valley War. Just after the turn of the century, Pickett was running a gambling hall at Goldfield, Nevada, and during the four-year period of World War I he served as a deputy United States marshal. In 1925 an old wound in his right leg[29] became gangrenous and the limb had to be amputated. Four years later Pickett returned to Arizona and settled at Winslow, and he died here on May 14, 1934. (See McCARTY, HENRY, and RUDABAUGH, DAVE.)

PICKETWIRE RIVER
Popular name for the Purgatoire River of southeastern Colorado.

PIERCE, ABEL HEAD One of the Lone Star State's pioneer cattlemen. Born at Little Compton, Rhode Island, on June 29, 1834, Abel Head left home when he was twenty and took the sea route to southern Texas, where, shortly after his arrival, he was given employment by W. B. Grimes, a prosperous rancher whose cattle roamed the lower reaches of the Colorado River. Working his way up from odd-job man through horse wrangler to trail boss, Pierce trailed Grimes' cattle as far east as New Orleans. This 6-foot, 5-inch bearded giant's habit of strutting around wearing spurs with rowels the size of windmills led someone to remark that he "looked like a Shanghai rooster," and from then on he was known as "Shanghai" Pierce.

At the outbreak of the Civil War, Shanghai enlisted in the 1st Texas Cavalry, serving as regimental butcher until

he was mustered out at the close of hostilities. Returning to Texas, he went into the cattle business by rounding up strays and putting his brand on them, and from these small beginnings was established the Rancho Grande in Matagorda County, the Pierce slaughterhouse, and the Pierce cattle-shipping wharf, which fingered out into Matagorda Bay. By 1900 Shanghai's range stock were roaming over more than a million acres of his land, and experiments were being made in the crossing of Brahma cattle with domestic breeds.[30] Shanghai died on December 26, 1900.

PIERCE, CHARLEY
A cowboy from Paint Rock, Texas, who became a full-time member of the Dalton gang and, later, the Doolin mob, Charley's "front" while engaged in these criminal activities being that of a successful racehorse owner of Pawnee, Oklahoma. In June 1895 Pierce took part in an express office holdup at Woodward, after which he and fellow outlaw George Newcomb hid out at the Dunn brothers' ranch. At this time the two fugitives had a combined total of ten thousand dollars in rewards hanging over their mustached heads, so when they were shot dead after being discovered by two ranchers in July, both may be said to have been reduced into little more than billfold fodder. (See DALTON GANG; DOOLIN GANG; and INGALLS, OKLAHOMA.)

PIERCE, SHANGHAI
Sobriquet attached to Abel Head Pierce. (See PIERCE, ABEL HEAD.)

PIERRE'S HOLE Located in southeastern Idaho at the western end of the

---

[28] Popular name for the Aztec Land and Cattle Company.
[29] A bullet wound; reputed to have been received while riding with Billy the Kid.
[30] A relative of Pierce's continued along these lines after Shanghai's death, the fruits of these activities being the Texas Brahmas of the present day.

Teton Pass.[31] Mountain men used the Hole as a rendezvous during the first half of the nineteenth century.

PIKE'S PEAK   Mountain peak[32] (14,109 feet) in east-central Colorado that lent its name to the Colorado gold rush of 1859 that brought the "Pike's Peak or Bust" brigade hurrying to reach such "instant" mining camps as California Gulch,[33] Fairplay, and Tarryall, all being located to the northwest of the peak.

PIMA INDIANS   Tribe of the Uto-Aztecan language family who have been located in what is now south-central Arizona since long before the arrival of the Spaniards. The Pima, like their prehistoric forebears the Hohokams, are agriculturists and are skilled in the making of pottery and basketwork, and were —at one time—accustomed to wearing a minimum of clothing, which had usually been woven from wild cotton. Dwelling places were either dome-shaped and thatched or rectangular, flat-roofed affairs with walls of adobe, the latter type of house frequently having a patio. Hair was worn long by both sexes, and the women indulged in a certain amount of facial tattooing. The Pima are closely related to the Papago, the term "Piman" embracing both tribes.

PINKERTON NATIONAL DE-TECTIVE AGENCY   Private National Detective Agency established in 1850 by Allan Pinkerton, a thirty-one-year-old Scot who had arrived in the United States in 1843. The firm's original offices were located at 89 Washington Street,[34] Chicago, Illinois, and the staff numbered nine, but the enterprise was so successful that by the 1890s the agency had additional offices in New York, Boston, Philadelphia, St. Paul, Kansas City, and Denver, and by the time the firm had reached its hundredth anniversary, more than three thousand employees were on the payroll. The Pinkertons, unlike the sleazy lone operators and small firms of fact and fiction, will not undertake the surveillance of women who are suspected of infidelity, nor will they accept commissions to investigate the activities of political figures or public or trade-union officials. The firm's trademark, an open eye underlined with the slogan "We never sleep," is responsible for the term "private eye" creeping into the language. Descendants of the founder are still in charge of the business.

PINTO   A Spanish word meaning "painted" that is applied to black-and-white, bay-and-white, and brown-and-white horses. This type of horse, which is frequently blue-eyed, was much favored by the red Indians. Black-and-white types may be referred to as piebald, and brown-and-white types as skewbald.

PIRATES   With the exception of Jean Lafitte and his motley crowd of Baratarian based sea rovers the only pirates who may justifiably be included within this volume are the landlubber types who confined their operations to the inland waterways; the gangs of thieves who

---

[31] Works its way through the southern end of the Teton Mountains. The eastern end of the pass was, and is, known as Jackson's Hole.

[32] Named after Zebulon Montgomery Pike. Pike led an exploratory expedition of some seventy-four men as far west as the source of the Arkansas River—during which he attempted to scale the peak—in 1806.

[33] The present-day town of Leadville.

[34] These offices were later moved to 191–93 Fifth Avenue.

sailed from their riverbank hideouts in skiffs and canoes to attack the slow-moving flatboats and keelboats that frequented the Mississippi[35] and the lower reaches of some of its tributaries. Many of these piratical attacks were beaten off, for as these river lice had the reputation of sparing neither crew nor passengers the parties attacked could be expected to put up some steel and powdersmoke opposition, which frequently resulted in many a budding "Blackbeard" wishing he'd learned to swim as he went down for the last time. When captured by their intended victims pirates were usually dealt with on the spot, on one memorable occasion some twenty of such prisoners being forced to "walk the plank"[36] so they could be picked off by sharpshooters as they threshed about in the water—a little massacre that failed to check piracy on the Mississippi but that most certainly made the day for the 'gators in the delta. The "Grand Age of Piracy"—Wild West style—occurred during the first few decades of the nineteenth century, reached its peak around 1826, and declined into history as the slow-moving rivercraft were superseded by the speedier "smokepots." (See FLATBOAT; KEELBOAT; and LAFITTE, JEAN.)

PITTS, CHARLIE Born and raised at Independence, Missouri, this villainous-looking member of the James gang has gone down in western history as Charlie Pitts in spite of the fact that his actual name was Samuel Wells. Charlie, who was more or less a charter member of the gang and took part in most of their "outings," was posing as a Texas cattleman in the summer of 1876; well-dressed, well-mounted, and well-heeled from his

share of the Ottersville robbery of July 7 Charlie cut such an impressive figure tha a new acquaintance of his named Bil Chadwell, who up to that time had bee innocently milking his pa's cows rathe than other folks' tills, eagerly sought ac ceptance within the ranks. Charlie fixe it. Better he hadn't, for it was Chadwel who suggested the Northfield job, whicl was to be the end of the line for botl him and Charlie—Bill being killed durin, the robbery, and Charlie getting his S Peter's ticket while on the run some four teen days later.

September 21, 1876, may have marke the end to Charlie's temporal existence yet oddly enough his body and bone have been marching on ever since, th travels and campsites of his remains be ing far easier to trace than any of hi earlier movements. On no one claimin, the body, a certain Dr. Murphy took i upon himself to preserve Charlie intact i a barrel of saline solution—and so Pitt remained, occasionally being dragged t the surface as a talking point (or statu symbol) when Murphy wanted to injec a little life into one of his periodic get togethers. At some later date Murphy fed up with topping-up Charlie's barrel gave the remains to a young medical stu dent who was in need of a skeleton, an Pitts found himself in a holed box at th bottom of Lake Como, Minnesota, shed ding poundage so that what was lef might take on that hygienic plastic ap pearance that all the best skeleton possess. Before the student could retur to collect his bones they were found b a fisherman, with the result that Charli once more passed through the coroner' office before being reclaimed by Dr. Mur phy who, in due course, handed over th

[35] The Ohio was infested to an even greater degree, but the depredations of that river' pirates are outside the scope of this work.

[36] The flatboat and keelboat men probably considered this poetic justice, romantic fictio possibly having led them into the erroneous belief that the oceangoing pirates of an earlie era indulged in this practice.

skeleton to a fellow physician so that the latter might use it to lend tone to his Chicago office. How long Pitts hung around Chicago is unknown, but we do know that sometime after World War II the skeleton came into possession of Mr. Ozzie Klavestad, and that at the time of writing, the framework of Charlie Pitts may be viewed at the Klavestad Stagecoach Museum, Shakopee, Minnesota. (See JAMES GANG and NORTHFIELD, MINNESOTA.)

PIUTE INDIANS The Paiute or Pah-Ute Indians, "Piute" being but a simplified spelling. (See PAIUTE INDIANS.)

PIZANTHIA, JOE Member of Henry Plummer's gang of Innocents who was usually referred to as "The Greaser." Joe's crimes while an Innocent remain unspecified, but he had the reputation of being a murderer and a thief long before he arrived on the Montana scene, and on the Monday morning of January 11, 1864—just twenty-four hours after the hanging of Plummer—the Vigilantes of Montana decided that the time had come for Joe to answer for his past, and, with tread most resolute, they marched up to his cabin and ordered him to "Come forth!" Well aware of the vigilantes' treatment of Plummer, Joe had no desire to come third, fourth, or fifth. He was staying domiciled, and his first shot—which killed vigilante George Copley—was proof of this intention. The Greaser was now a killer—that was for sure. The vigilantes brought up a howitzer and started to demolish Joe's dwelling, and when it was somewhat reduced, they stormed the place. A collapsing front door had knocked Joe silly, so he probably felt little more than gooseflesh when the loads from a few guns were shaken into him. Heavy with lead, and offering little opposition, Joe was dragged into the open, hanged from a pole, and bounced around by more than a hundred handgun missiles. And that wasn't all: The late Mr. Pizanthia's shack was fired, and his remains were tossed onto the flames. The following morning the cooling ashes were sieved in the hope that Joe may have had coins of gold, or fillings of same, in his possession at the time of his passing, but naught but lead was retrieved from the site. Sickening, wasn't it? Who was the baddie that day? (See INNOCENTS.)

PLACE, ETTA An extremely beautiful and fashionably dressed young lady who began to appear in the company of Butch Cassidy and the Sundance Kid around 1899, owing legal allegiance to neither man but sharing, and returning, the love and admiration of both. Etta, who was probably born at or near Denver, Colorado, about 1880, is reputed to have been employed as a schoolteacher at Denver prior to her becoming infatuated with two of the most wanted men in the West; this could well be, for experience in dealing with small boys would have made her an ideal companion to such overgrown kids as Butch and Sundance. Etta tagged along when the boys paid their periodic visits to Annie Porter's fleshpot at Fort Worth, Texas,[37] and her voice remained well modulated and she retained her trust in her boys even when it was learned that Sundance had "caught a cold" while exercising with a lass who would have failed a medical checkup. By the winter of 1901 the two top men of the Wild Bunch had decided to quit the country while they were ahead of the game, and on February 1, 1902, Butch, Sundance, Etta Place, and a valise containing thirty thousand dollars in ill-gotten "mad" money arrived

[37] Such a display of broadmindedness was not uncommon in that time and place.

in New York City as the first step in their journey to South America. The party booked accommodation at a boarding-house on West Twelfth Street[38] and spent the next few days doing the town—like visiting Tiffany's, where Etta was treated to a gold fob-watch costing sixty dollars, and she and Sundance posing for a photograph at De Young's Studio on Broadway, etc.—before boarding the SS *Soldier Prince* and sailing for South America. For the next five years of her life Etta kept house for the transplanted bunchers and rode with them on most of their outlaw operations, the pinafore of the former tasks being replaced by im-maculate riding habit, sombrero, and Colt .45 while engaged in the latter. Sometime in 1907 Etta is reputed to have been stricken with "acute appendicitis,"[39] and Sundance accompanied her back to the States so that she might check in at a Denver hospital for treatment. The Kid left her at the reception desk, and noth-ing more has ever been heard of the girl named Etta Place.[40] (See LONGBAUGH, HARRY; PARKER, ROBERT LEROY; and WILD BUNCH.)

PLAINS INDIANS Those tribes that occupied that area of the United States that has the Mississippi as its eastern boundary and the foothills of the Rocky Mountains as its western limits, and stretches from the forty-ninth parallel in the north to south-central Texas in the south.[41] Originally this region was sparsely inhabited by a few tribes of agri-culturalists who didn't rely on the buffalo for sustenance, and it was only after the horse culture had established itself among the tribes living beyond the pe-rimeter of this area in the last decade of the eighteenth century that these non-plains dwellers began to move into the area already described and take up per-manent residence. These new arrivals, most of whom had been farming peoples, would, at some later date, be classed as "plains Indians"—mainly tepee-dwelling nomads who made the buffalo their com-missariat and did little, if any, farming. (See ARAPAHO INDIANS; ARIKARA IN-DIANS; ASSINIBOINE INDIANS; BLACKFOOT INDIANS; CHEYENNE INDIANS; COMAN-CHE INDIANS; CROW INDIANS; KIOWA-APACHE INDIANS; KIOWA INDIANS; PAW-NEE INDIANS; Plains Caddo [see CADDO INDIANS]; and SIOUX INDIANS.)

PLATTE RIVER A shallow waterway that is formed by the union of the North and South Platte rivers in southwest-central Nebraska. Slightly more than three hundred miles in length, the river flows in an easterly direction to join the Missouri River some fifteen miles south of Omaha, Nebraska. The Oregon Trail followed the course of the Platte and the North Platte for much of the first half of its journey. (See OREGON TRAIL.)

[38] Sundance and Etta booking in under the names of Mr. and Mrs. Harry D. Place, while Butch used the alias of Jim Ryan.

[39] To undertake a long sea voyage while suffering "acute appendicitis" may seem strange until one realizes that the term was frequently used—until well into the 1930s—to excuse a girl's absence while giving birth to an illegitimate child; if this was the case with Miss Place, a joint offspring of the two outlaws may still be getting Social Security checks.

[40] Assuming that all hospitals keep records, it seems rather odd that no further trace of Etta has ever come to light. Questions to irritate the epidermis: Did she recover from her alleged affliction? Did she ever marry? Did she change her name? Is she still alive as a little old lady in her nineties? (in 1975). Some Denverite may still give us the answers, although it may be kinder to Etta—or her memory—to allow her to slip into limbo while still young and beautiful, way back in 1907.

[41] Roughly defined limits—e.g., in some areas one would have had to travel some 150 miles west of the Mississippi before encountering any plains Indians.

PLEASANT VALLEY WAR Along the southern flank of the Mogollon Mountains in central Arizona lies Pleasant Valley, a well-watered region that by the middle 1880s had become the rangeland of many legitimate ranchers and a like number of enterprising settlers who had established themselves as small-time ranchers by throwing a wide loop. Of the latter class the Graham and Tewksbury families were leading examples, the three Anglo-Amerind sons[42] of John D. Tewksbury joining forces with Samuel Graham's trio of male offspring in an operation that consisted of building up a herd with a running iron rather than from the services of a bull. These cattle, most of which had started life as Stinson Ranch stock, were allowed to graze on Graham range on the understanding that the Tewksburys could cut out their share whenever convenient. This arrangement may have worked out with "honest rustlers," but—unknown to the Tewksburys—the Graham boys had registered the new brand under their name, and when their co-operators called to claim their beeves, they were boisterously informed that they had no legal right to any of the cattle, "gentlemen's agreement be blowed!" The Graham-Tewksbury feud had started to simmer.

Until this time the Tewksburys had shared the Pleasant Valley cattlemen's hatred of woollies and had regarded the Mogollons as the border line for sheepmen who grazed their herds to the north of the mountains, but now that the Tewksburys could no longer be classed as cattlemen, they developed an earnest desire to ruin the range for such folk as the Grahams, and in the fall of 1886 they invited the Daggs brothers to bring their woollies across the rim of the Mogollons so that the sheep might munch their way across the cattle range of the valley and leave the grass too short for bovine intake. Tewksbury guns would, if necessary, be used to protect the Daggs brothers' stock. The Graham-Tewksbury feud had now escalated into a cattleman-sheepman confrontation, and residents of the valley—and beyond—flocked to the banner of their choice: the Blevins family of suspected rustlers; Hashknife cowboys George Smith, Tom Pickett, Tom Tucker, John Paine, Buck Lancaster, Bob Glasspie, and George McNeal; and others who had an illegal or legal interest in cattle rallied to the Graham cause, while an assortment of small-holders and folk who never did have any time for cattlemen backed the Tewksburys.

Night-riding cattlemen stampeded sheep over cliffs and slaughtered them with handgun and rifle fire, and in February 1887 a Navaho sheepherder was killed by a sniper's[43] bullet as he tended his flock, thus becoming the first victim of the Pleasant Valley or Tonto Basin War. In July 1887 Mart Blevins disappeared in mysterious circumstances, and on August 10 Hampton Blevins and John Paine were killed and Tom Tucker, Bob Glasspie, and Bob Charrington were wounded when they clashed with the Tewksbury brothers at the Middleton Ranch. One week later, William Graham—eighteen years old and the youngest of the Graham brothers—was killed in a horseback shootout with James Houck, a sheepman who, at that time, was wearing an Apache County deputy sheriff's badge. The Grahams were quick to retaliate.

On the morning of September 2, Tom and John Graham, accompanied by Andy, Charles, and John Blevins and others, attacked the Tewksbury home-

---

[42] Their mother was a full-blooded Indian.

[43] A man named Tom Horn was in the region at this time; this is worth bearing in mind, for Tom was a lad with a gun for hire, and he is known to have been associated with the Tewksburys.

stead and killed John Tewksbury and a partisan named William Jacobs. Two days after this shootout the Graham cause lost four followers when some fast Winchester work by Sheriff C. P. Owens killed Andy and Sam Houston Blevins and Mose Roberts and seriously wounded John Blevins. September 17 saw the Grahams making another raid on the Tewksbury premises, but they were driven off after a cowboy named Harry Middleton had been killed and a follower named Joe Underwood had been severely wounded.

Prior to this last clash of arms, the law had been preparing to take a hand in the matter, and on September 21 Sheriff William Mulvenon of Yavapai County and Sheriff C. P. Owens of Apache County led a sixteen-strong posse into the valley and before the day was out John Graham and Charlie Blevins had been killed while clashing with the lawmen and many members of both sides had been taken into custody. This show of force by the authorities cooled the situation for almost twelve months but failed to bring an end to the hostilities.

On August 13, 1888, a prospector named Billy Wilson, together with a couple of cowhands named James Scott and Jimmy Stott, were hanged by a mob of Tewksbury supporters, although all three can be classed as little more than innocent bystanders; on November 1 Graham partisan Al Rose died in an ambush killing;[44] Tewksbury man George A. Newton disappeared in September 1891; and the last man to die, Thomas H. Graham, was killed from ambush on August 2, 1892. Total casualties of the "war": nineteen men dead, five wounded, and two missing. Edward Tewksbury spent about thirty months behind bars before all charges against him

were dismissed. (See BLEVINS, ANDY; BLEVINS, MART; HORN, TOM; and OWENS, COMMODORE PERRY.)

PLEW   A beaver pelt; term used by the mountain men.

PLUMMER GANG
Sheriff Henry Plummer's legion of thieves and road agents; usually referred to as the "Innocents." (See INNOCENTS.)

PLUMMER, HENRY   One of the all-time "greats" in the roster of western badmen. Henry Plummer was fifteen years old when he left his Connecticut home in 1852 and migrated to California via the Cape Horn route; the Mother Lode country was his goal, and in that same year he settled at Nevada City,[45] where, some twelve months later, he went into partnership with a man named Henry Hyer, and they opened the Empire Bakery. Plummer evidently established a reputation for honesty over the next three years, for in 1856 he was elected city marshal for a twelve-month tour of duty. Plummer was now a well-mannered and quietly spoken youth whose slim figure was always elegantly clothed, yet despite this dandified image, he kept a tight lid on the town while wearing a badge, and it is more than likely that he would have been elected for a second term had not his copulative activities led to his blotting his record.

In September 1857 a miner named John Vedder returned to his timbered dwelling to find City Marshal Plummer sowing his oats in pastures forbidden, and when Vedder protested, Henry whipped out his cap 'n' ball and shot the cuckolded one dead. The ex-marshal received a ten-year prison sentence for this offense, yet he only served a few months of this term,

----

[44] Tom Horn again? See the preceding footnote.
[45] In Nevada County, California.

for friends petitioned for his release on the grounds that he was a consumptive, and in the late summer of 1858 he was back in Nevada City after having received a pardon from the governor.

His image little tarnished, Plummer once more went into business with Hyer, and within a short time the Lafayette Bakery was open for business, but Henry's celibate spell behind bars had evidently given him a desire to make up for lost time, and he began spending most of his waking hours in the brothels rather than in the bakery, an expensive choice of habitat that forced our subject into selling his interest in the bakery and becoming amenable to taking part in any venture—however infamous—that might be expected to show a quick profit. Plummer's first sinful step of a mercenary nature occurred near Washoe, just across the Nevada line, when he and other likeminded types made an abortive attempt to rob a Wells Fargo bullion express[46]—a botched job that led to Plummer's arrest, although he was released shortly afterward for lack of evidence.

After his release he returned to his more or less permanent pad in a Nevada City bawdyhouse, and within these unhallowed walls in the spring of 1859 he shot a man named James Ryder to death as the clincher to an argument that revolved around the establishment's wares. Plummer was once more thrown into the Nevada County jail, but before he could be brought to trial, he paid a jailer to allow him to escape, and once clear of Nevada City, he headed north for Oregon. While moving north the fugitive became acquainted with a desperate character named Jim Mayfield, who was wanted for the murder of a sheriff, a chance association that inspired Plummer into sending dispatches to the California newspapers that contained the misinformation that both he and Mayfield had been hanged in Washington Territory. This ploy may have resulted in all track of Plummer being lost, but his failure to adopt an alias and his penchant for establishing his whereabouts with unorthodox behavior soon had him spotlighted as the seducer of a married woman at Walla Walla, Washington, and the killer of a dance-hall proprietor at Orofino, Idaho.

We next hear of Plummer at Lewiston, Idaho. It is the spring of 1861 and he has found employment in a gambling hall, although much of his spare time is being spent organizing a gang of road agents who, within a few months of his arrival, will have made it virtually impossible to move a gold or money shipment in or out of Lewiston without fear of it being waylaid. For the next eighteen months northwestern Idaho and southeastern Washington were terrorized by Plummer's legion of owlhoots, but by the fall of 1862, rumors of impending vigilante action got Plummer on the move again. Moving east with fellow outlaw Jack Cleveland and two pack mules loaded with loot, Plummer crossed the Bitterroot Mountains and headed for Fort Benton on the upper Missouri with the intention of boarding a riverboat to take him back East. This intention wasn't to be realized, for by the time they arrived, the winter freeze-up had closed the river to traffic, forcing two disappointed outlaws to backtrack to the government farm and Indian agency on the Sun River, where they might sit out the winter.

A forced choice this may have been, yet it had its compensations, for the sister-in-law of the farm's superintendent,

---

[46] Plummer had the worst of outlaw luck on this occasion: When he leveled his pistol at the jehu, the barrel fell off and the coach was disappearing into the distance while the bandits were still blushing.

a beautiful girl by the name of Electra Bryan, was staying at the settlement, and before the winter was out, Plummer had become engaged to the girl. Sometime during their stay at Sun River, Henry began to note that Cleveland—who was an uncouth cad of a lad at best—was leering heavily at Electra and casting avaricious eyes in the direction of the loot, and fearing that Jack might kill him for possession of the spoils, both active and inert, the worried one buried the profits of their outlawry during one of Cleveland's absences, the assumption being that Cleveland would be unlikely to dispose of him while he alone knew the whereabouts of the cache. If Plummer's suspicions had been correct, his unique form of insurance worked, for early in January 1863 both men left the agency and headed for the six-month-old mining camp of Bannack, trust corroded to naught by mutual suspicions but uneasily linked by knowledge of past crimes and the shared desire for easy pickings.

Plummer and Cleveland were financially strapped when they arrived at Bannack, but early in February they were setting them up in Goodrich's Saloon, paying for the drinks with a legacy that had come into their possession after Cleveland had put a bullet into a man named George Evans, whose body had been discovered some eight miles beyond town limits. Cleveland, whose tongue traveled far and wide when he was in his cups, began to drop veiled hints relating to his and Plummer's Lewiston activities, and Henry, having failed to stop the flow with frowns, resorted to sterner measures, which resulted in the exchange of some unbelievable dialogue being punctuated by the sounds of exploding cartridges: "You damned son-of-a-bitch!" snarled Plummer, clearing leather, "I am tired of

this!" (Henry's first shot lodges in a ceiling beam, but his second piece of lead gets Cleveland near the belt buckle as the latter is drawing his gun, and Cleveland falls to his knees.) "Plummer, you wouldn't shoot me when I'm down?" hopefully from Cleveland. "No, you damned son-of-a-bitch!" roared Henry, "Get up!" (Jack does as he is told and gets a ball in the chest and one in the head for his pains, after which the stricken one collapses to the sawdust with his problems and the victor leaves the saloon.) And that is an eyewitness account, believe it or not.[47]

Before the smoke had cleared, Cleveland had been removed to the home of a local butcher named Hank Crawford, but he was beyond surgery, and he died within a few hours. Shortly afterward Plummer accosted Crawford, wishing to know if the dying man had made any statements before he expired, and Hank noted that the questioner appeared much relieved when he received a negative reply. Plummer was arrested and tried for the killing of Cleveland and won an acquittal, but some weeks later Crawford was elected sheriff, and Henry became plagued by doubts regarding Crawford's statement that Cleveland had died without speaking of his past or his associates. These doubts became obsessive, and Plummer went after the new sheriff with a shotgun, but as Plummer was leveling down on his victim, a friend of Hank's threw lead in Plummer's direction and Henry retired from the field with a shattered right arm. Henry now had to learn to use his left hand for gunwork, but Crawford, evidently unwilling to wait around to see if he was successful in this, tossed in his badge and headed back for his hometown in Wisconsin—a chicken move that was to leave the way open for

[47] The fact that the saloon barber was giving a patron a shave throughout this violent episode and he never even nicked his customer speaks volumes of that time and place.

Plummer becoming sheriff later that year.

While recovering from his wound, and between southpawing sessions with his hardware, Plummer was far from idle, organizing the local crooks and holdup artists into a formidable gang that had as its nucleus a number of stalwarts who had been associated with Henry during his Lewiston days and had followed him across the mountains. By early spring of 1863 the wound had healed around the ball of lead that had lodged in his wrist, and he was fairly dextrous in the use of his right hand. His battalion of do-badders now numbered more than a hundred, a secret handclasp was being used for identification purposes, and they were calling themselves "Innocents"; their catalogue of crimes was beginning to drive fearful residents to other settlements, and such was their power that they could nominate, and elect—on May 24—Henry Plummer as sheriff.

In June Plummer made a quick trip to Sun River and returned to Bannack with Electra as his bride but with little intention of settling down. Key gang members served as Sheriff Plummer's deputies, and when the crime wave of his "Innocents" had reduced Bannack to a near ghost town, he moved his headquarters to Virginia City, some forty miles to the east. By the late fall of 1863 the honest residents of the various camps whose lines of communications were being harassed by the "Innocents"—Virginia City, Bannack, Alder Gulch, Nevada City, etc.—decided that they had had enough, and on December 23, 1863, a movement known as the Vigilantes of Montana came into being.

A leading member of the "Innocents" named George Ives had been dealt hempen justice by a miners' posse a bare forty-eight hours before the vigilantes were established, but this had failed to disturb Plummer, and he still remained in the Virginia City–Bannack area after other members of his band had been given the long drop.[48] If Plummer had been of a mind to head for the timber, he left too late, for he was taken into custody and hanged at Bannack on January 10, 1864. Henry is reputed to have killed 15 men during his short career, and 102 murders are known to have been committed by his "Innocents." (See BANNACK, MONTANA, and INNOCENTS.)

POINT MEN The pair of cowhands who flank the spearhead of a herd that is on the move.

POINT OF ROCKS A rock bluff which—from around 1830—became a landmark on the Cimarron cutoff of the Santa Fe Trail. Located in extreme southwestern Kansas one mile west of the Middle Spring of the Cimarron River. (See SANTA FE TRAIL.)

POKER ALICE An English girl of tender upbringing who became quite a character after her arrival out West. (See IVERS, ALICE.)

POLECAT Member of the weasel family of carnivores. The black-footed ferret that inhabits the prairies from Montana to Texas is a polecat, and although skunks are frequently referred to as "polecats" in the West, this incorrect nomenclature does not make them so. (See SKUNK and WEASEL.)

POMPEY'S PILLAR A natural tower of rock that rises from a comparatively level plain on the south bank of the Yellowstone River some thirty-five

[48] Rumors abound that Plummer had made a deal with the vigilantes: a share of the outlaw loot in exchange for immunity; this could account for his keeping his "cool," but if he ever made such a deal, he was obviously double-crossed.

miles southwest of Custer, Montana. Named "Pompy's Tower"[49] by William Clark of the Lewis and Clark Expedition on July 25, 1806, and described by him as being "two hundred feet high and four hundred paces in circumference." Clark's signature, which he chiseled on the rock, is still legible. (See LEWIS AND CLARK EXPEDITION.)

PONY EXPRESS A short-lived but spectacular undertaking that began operation on April 3, 1860, a bare sixty days after the decision to organize a fast mail service between St. Joseph, Missouri, and Sacramento, California, had been taken by Russell, Majors, and Waddell, and their chartering of the Central Overland, California, and Pike's Peak Express Company to administer the project. Starting from the eastern terminal of St. Joseph, a rider was ferried across the Missouri to reach the Kansas shore, and then it was hoofbeats west on a journey that took relays of riders through Kansas, Nebraska, northeastern Colorado, Wyoming, northern Utah, Nevada, and California. Some of the remount stations and landmarks on the route, in order of appearance, are: Elwood; Seneca; Marysville; Hollenburg; Fort Kearney; Midway; Julesburg;[50] Chimney Rock; Forts Mitchell, Laramie, and Fetterman; Casper; Red Butte; Independence Rock; Sweetwater; South Pass; Rock Ridge; Fort Bridger; Salt Lake City; Fort Crittenden; Willow Springs; Camp Station; Castle Rock; Fort Churchill; Virginia City; Carson City;

Genoa; Placerville; and the western terminal of Sacramento. Along this 1,600-mile route were dotted 190 relay stations, each of which was staffed by a minimum of two employees who kept at least two remounts available for the 80 riders who were constantly shuttling between stations.

Originally the journey took twelve days, but this was later trimmed to nine, a speedup that was partially responsible for reducing the mail rate from $5.00 per half ounce to $2.00 per half ounce.[51] Special lightweight saddles, and mochila mail pouches—which allowed a rider to switch mail to a remount in under two minutes—were used by the company, and lightweight youths were usually chosen as riders at an average pay of $125 a month. Thirty to seventy miles a day was expected of these mail carriers, although rides of more than double the maximum of these distances had to be undertaken when station staff—and stations—had been wiped out by Indian attacks. Raiding Paiutes made Nevada the most dangerous stretch of the route, yet despite the fact that numerous stations were wiped out and their staffs murdered, only one mail rider was killed by Indians during the Pony Express' nineteen months of existence; many, of course, were wounded, but they survived.

By the fall of 1861 the transcontinental telegraph had linked East with West, and in October of that year the Pony Express was discontinued. Of passing interest: Before being accepted as a Pony Express rider, an applicant had to

[49] Jean Baptiste, the son of Touissant Charbonneau and Sacagawea, was nicknamed "Pomp" (Shoshone for "Chief") by Clark, and he named the rock in honor of this child. Subsequent editing of the journals of the expedition has, however, led to the butte being renamed "Pompey's Pillar," evidently in the belief that Clark had intended to name the rock after the original Pompey's Pillar in Egypt but had failed to spell the name correctly.

[50] At Julesburg an alternative route could be taken, a detour that swung to the southwest to call at Denver, Colorado, before rejoining the main trail at Fort Bridger.

[51] A reduction that took place after Wells Fargo had taken over the operation in April 1861. As 20 pounds was the maximum weight carried, this reduction meant that $1,920 had been lopped off the cost of transporting this amount of mail between terminal points.

sign the following declaration: "I hereby swear before the great and living God that during my engagement and while I am an employee of Russell, Majors, and Waddell, I will under no circumstances use profane language; that I will not quarrel or fight with other employees of the firm, and that I will conduct myself honestly, be faithful to my duties, and so direct my acts as to win the confidence of my employers, so help me God." Many of the applicants must have kept their fingers crossed while signing this document. (See BENI, JULES; CODY, WILLIAM FREDERICK; HASLAM, ROBERT; JULESBURG, COLORADO; McCANLES, DAVID C.; MILLER, CHARLIE, MOCHILA; and SLADE, JOSEPH A.)

PORCUPINE A large rodent whose long hair is interspersed with spines or quills. The North American porcupine, which is found in the Rocky Mountain region, has a length of about 40 inches, some 6 inches of which is stumpy tail; its quills may reach a length of 2 feet, and they form a crest across the back where they reach their greatest length. These spines are easily removed, and as they are barbed, they have a tendency to work into a wound when lodged in an enemy. Porcupines cannot "shoot" their quills, as sometimes believed, but they usually vibrate them with a rattling sound when anticipating attack. The spined tail is used to ward off small adversaries, but when attacked by a large predator, the porcupine will back toward its enemy. Burrow-dwelling and expert tree climbers, they remain active throughout the winter, living on a diet of roots, barks, berries, etc. The North American Indians used porcupine quills for decorative purposes and—as an alternative to bone beads—when manufacturing breastplates.

PORTUGEE PHILLIPS A little man who made one of the most heroic rides in the West. (See PHILLIPS, JOHN.)

POURIER, BAPTISTE Born at St. Charles, Missouri, in 1840 of French parentage, Baptiste moved into Nebraska Territory in 1854, and in that same year he became the adopted son of Chief Red Cloud of the Oglala Sioux. Two years later, while employed as a freighter, he helped build the foundations for the Denver Trading Post, thus becoming—unknowingly and unintentionally—one of the founders of Denver, Colorado.[52] Despite his friendship with the Sioux, or possibly because of it (he could speak five Indian tongues and was adept at sign talk), he served as a U. S. Army scout under General Crook during the North Plains campaigns, Baptiste's lean, 6-foot, 2-inch frame being responsible for Crook referring to him as "Big Bat." On retiring from scouting, Pourier established a small ranch on Wounded Knee Creek in South Dakota, and here, in the early days of December 1890, he is reputed to have held off a party of more than fifty hostile Sioux without firing a shot; much tough talk and an offer to victual-up the Indians (Bat must have had one helluva big larder) persuading the braves to behave themselves until the Frenchman saw, and grasped, the opportunity of hot-footing out through the back door and escaping up the creek. "Big Bat" Pourier died in 1924.

POWERS, BILL An Oklahoma cowboy who, together with Dick Broadwell and Charlie Bryant, left his employment with the Oscar Halsell Ranch to follow the owlhoot trail. Powers may have been one of those responsible for the looting

[52] At the time of Baptiste's activity, Denver—or more correctly "that which was to become Denver"—was in Kansas Territory.

of an El Reno bank of more than ten thousand dollars in July 1892, although this robbery is usually credited to the Daltons. Late in September 1892 Bill followed the earlier example of Dick Broadwell—and the defunct Charlie Bryant—and joined the Daltons; better he hadn't, for he was killed at Coffeyville on October 5 while engaged in his first sortie with the gang. This heavily mustached gunnie is reputed to have been in his early twenties at the time of his demise. (See COFFEYVILLE, KANSAS, and DALTON GANG.)

POWWOW   American Indian word for a tribal debate or council meeting; a talk to resolve problems or to give counsel.

PRAIRIE CHICKEN   A species of North American grouse that has a range extending from the lower Mississippi to the Canadian line. Alternative names are pinnated grouse and prairie hen.

PRAIRIE DOG   A small marmotlike rodent whose "towns" pockmark the prairies from the Canadian line to Texas and Arizona in the south. Stockily built, with small ears, chubby faces, and a short, white-tipped tail, these smooth-coated little animals live in large communities, the entrances to their burrows frequently covering an area of a few hundred square miles.[53] Reddish-brown with cream undersides and living on a staple diet of grass, prairie dogs produce up to eight young each spring, and although they give high-pitched whistles when danger is anticipated, they remain sufficiently curious to keep an eye on any interloper from the safety of their retreat holes.

PRAIRIE OYSTERS   Term used originally to describe buffalo testicles that had been prepared for consumption by frying in fat. With the near extinction of the buffalo and the arrival of the cattle industry, the organs from castrated calves were—and are—used to prepare this delicacy. Sometimes referred to as "mountain oysters."

PRAIRIE RATTLESNAKE   One of the many species of rattlesnakes that occur in the West. (See RATTLESNAKES.)

PRAIRIE SCHOONER   The covered wagon of the plains, specifically the Conestoga wagon, although the term is somewhat loosely used to describe covered wagons that are not of this type. (See CONESTOGA WAGON.)

PRAIRIE WOLF   Alternative name that may be used to describe the coyote. (See COYOTE.)

PRETTYMAN, WILLIAM S. Frontier photographer. Born in Maryland on November 12, 1858, of English ancestry, William moved West in 1879, finally settling at Arkansas City, Kansas, where he became an apprentice photographer at Bonsall's Studio. Within a short time he had accrued sufficient knowledge and capital to open his own gallery, and for the next twenty-five years he was to expose hundreds of plates that cannot be overrated historically or—in many cases —artistically. Much of Prettyman's work features the Amerinds of Indian Territory (Oklahoma), the land rushes which opened the territory to white settlement, and the establishing of such western towns as Guthrie and Oklahoma City. Outlaws Bob Dalton and Dick Yeager "watched the birdie" voluntarily, and Dynamite Dick, Bill Powers, Dick Broadwell, Grat Dalton, and the aforemen-

[53] There is evidence that "towns" may have covered up to twenty-five thousand square miles at one time.

tioned Bob Dalton were photographed after much lead had reduced them to little more than static props. In 1905, for reasons known only to himself, Prettyman gave up photography, sold all his equipment, and moved to California, where, over the years, he established himself as a wholesale druggist and later as a citrus fruit grower. William S. Prettyman died in 1932.

PRICKLY PEAR Popular name for cacti of the genera *Opuntia,* which have flat oval-shaped stems bearing numerous spines and produce red, yellow, or purple flowers. Common in the arid and semi-arid regions of the Southwest.

PROMONTORY POINT A point established by the United States Government at Promontory, Utah, for the linking of the tracks of the Central Pacific and Union Pacific railroads, the historic "golden spike"[54] ceremony taking place on May 10, 1869. Promontory is near the present-day town of Ogden. (See CENTRAL PACIFIC RAILROAD and UNION PACIFIC RAILROAD.)

PRONGHORN An antelope-like creature that roams the plains and deserts of the West from Canada in the north to Texas in the south, and Southern California in the west. Pronghorns stand some 3 feet tall at the shoulder and weigh about 125 pounds. Their overall color is medium brown, which is relieved by a short, dark-brown mane, and rump and undersides of white. Both sexes sport two-pronged horns, which are shed annually and are composed of tightly bunched hairs. Diet consists of almost any type of vegetation. Frequently called an "antelope," although the pronghorn—which is confined to the New World—is not a true antelope, but is in a class of its own.[55]

PUEBLO Spanish word denoting an Amerind or Mexican village, especially an aborigine apartment-house community whose dwellings as made of stone or adobe. There are many of these villages in the Southwest, the pueblo at Taos, New Mexico, being the best-known example. (See ADOBE and PUEBLO INDIANS.)

PUEBLO INDIANS The apartment-dwelling tribes of the Southwest who are descendants of an Indian civilization that flourished from A.D. 1000 to A.D. 1200. The Spaniards were the first Europeans to make contact with these peoples, and they named them "Pueblos"—meaning "town" or "village"—because of their characteristic use of large multistoried buildings as community dwelling places.[56] True farmers and skilled in irrigation and the making of pottery and basketwork, the Pueblos were not aggressive, although when attacked by their hereditary enemies the Apache and Navaho, they fought well, and in 1847 they staged a brief—and abortive—insurrection against Americano dominance. New Mexico is particularly rich in Pueblo villages, many of which—Taos, San Juan, Santa Clara, San Indefonso, Cochiti, Santo Domingo, San Felipe, etc.—are confined to the valley of the Rio Grande.

54 This gold spike was quickly removed to prevent theft.
55 The *Antilocapridae,* or *Antilocapra americana.*
56 Base measurements of these buildings varied between 150 and 450 yards, and they were frequently 6 stories high, each story having a smaller area than its predecessor so that each succeeding level possessed a terrace that could be used as a work or play area. Entrance was obtained by ladders that reached to the second story; these ladders were withdrawn into the building when Apache or Navaho forces were in the neighborhood. Note: After the white man had tranquilized the area by force of arms and weight of numbers, the Pueblos modified their buildings by cutting doorways in the ground floors.

(See ACOMA INDIANS; HOPI INDIANS; PUEBLO; SANTA FE, NEW MEXICO; SEVEN CITIES OF CIBOLA; TAOS, NEW MEXICO; and ZUNI INDIANS.)

PUMA One of the two great cats that inhabit the West. The puma may reach a length of 8 feet from nose to tail end and weigh around 220–40 pounds. Coloring can vary from grayish-brown, through yellowish-brown, to reddish-brown, with lighter-toned undersides and muzzle. The head is fairly round and not unpleasant, but is rather small in relation to the rest of the animal. For such a large carnivore, diet is varied, anything from a mouse to a deer, or a locust to a lizard being accepted as prey. The scream of the puma is a terrifying sound, but otherwise they are timid creatures, and there are no reliable records of an adult human ever being attacked by one of these cats.[57] (See JAGUAR.)

PURDY, SAM A native of Kentucky who plumbed the depths of infamy as a white slaver who dealt in any-colored merchandise during the early years of the nineteenth century. Purdy's procurers— Messrs. John Gaines, Joe Bontura, James Feeney, Tom McMurren, "Blackie" Coe, and Lou Evans—"stole" girls from riverbank towns on the Mississippi in Missouri, Illinois, Arkansas, Tennessee, Louisiana, and Mississippi, octoroons and darker-complected lasses usually being sold "up the river" and white girls "down

the river."[58] Purdy's auctions, which were attended by dozens of brothelkeepers and "floating hogpen" operators, were usually held at Natchez, the girls being sold from the deck of a flatboat tied alongside the riverbank. Brothelkeepers paid—on average—$200 to purchase one of Purdy's girls, although some exchanged beds for as little as $60, and an all-time high was reached when a nubile eighteen-year-old from Missouri named Marie Field was knocked down at a price of $1,650.

Purdy's sexpot service began to totter early in 1805—thanks mainly to a gentleman named Carlos White—and in the summer of that year the boss of the enterprise was found stabbed to death in his own bed. After Sam's death, five of his procurers were to be dispatched by parties unknown at frequent intervals: Joe Bontura was shot dead from ambush; Tom McMurren and John Gaines met a like fate on July 5, 1805, while sharing the same bed (shame on them!); Lou Evans was blasted into eternity as the climax to a poker game a few weeks later; and "Blackie" Coe met a fate similar to Bontura's before the month was out. Feeney, the last survivor and a grizzled veteran of some sixty-odd ill-spent summers, was hauled into court in December of that same year and given a ten-year jail sentence for abducting Marie Field (the lass with the $1,650 measurements —remember?) and two other girls. (See BECKETT, ROSE, and WHITE, CARLOS.)

[57] Hunters—who frequently refer to the puma as a cougar, mountain lion, painter, or panther—are responsible for the many tall tales of humans being attacked by these cats; tales that are no doubt manufactured to promote the illusion that great courage is required to pump lead into the rear end of some retreating, or treed, animal.
[58] Hence the expression "sold down the river."

Q UANAH PARKER   Born in 1852 in a Comanche camp somewhere in the Texas Panhandle, the half-breed son of Chief Peta Nokona of the Nokonis band and white captive Cynthia Ann Parker. In December 1860, when Quanah was eight years old, the Nokonis village was attacked by a large force of Texas Rangers led by Captain Sul Ross, and although Quanah and his father[1] escaped, his mother was returned to the white man's world—a parental loss that was followed by the death of Nokona some two years later, the subsequent dispersal of the leaderless band, and the ten-year-old "orphan" being adopted by the Cohoite Comanche.

We next hear of Quanah in 1871 when he was chosen as chief of the Kwahadis,[2] and in 1874, when, as Chief Quanah Parker, he led a mixed band of Comanche and Kiowa, with a sprinkling of Southern Cheyenne, in an abortive attack on a party of buffalo hunters who were forted at Adobe Walls. On June 2, 1875, dispirited by his failure at Adobe Walls, Quanah led his band into Fort Sill, Oklahoma, to surrender, and shortly afterward the Kwahadis were allotted land in the southwestern corner of Indian Territory. Here Quanah settled down, and in the middle 1880s Texas cattlemen, possibly guilt-ridden at having rented Comanche-allotted land as additional pasturage for a miserly $1.25 an acre, built the chief a many-roomed and many-

[1] The Texas Rangers reported they had killed Chief Peta Nokona, but it is far more likely that their victim was one of Cynthia's servants, for Quanah Parker stated that his father did not die until some two years later.

[2] A division of the tribe that roamed the Staked Plains. Alternatively spelled "Quehadi."

gabled mansion on West Cache Creek in southwestern Oklahoma.

In 1905 President Theodore Roosevelt[3] visited the Comanche lands to take part in a rather brutal wolf hunt, and during his stay he grasped the politically inspired opportunity to address a speech to Quanah's Comanches, a tough man-to-man diatribe of the you're-welcome-to my-tepee-if-you-don't-step-out-of-line variety that was larded with smiles and punctuated by wild yells of *"ki-yi!"* from the tribesmen. Pleased by this rousing ovation, yet puzzled as to its meaning, Roosevelt asked Quanah what *"ki-yi!"* meant, to be reluctantly informed that "load of bullshit!" was the nearest English equivalent.

In his later years Quanah shared his mansion with a harem of nubile young Indian girls, the chief being of the opinion that although any woman might be good for a young brave, only young girls were good for an older man. Quanah Parker died at his home in February 1911, having been, for some years prior to his death, recognized as the "Talk Man" for both the Comanche and Kiowa tribes. (See BATTLE AT ADOBE WALLS and PARKER, CYNTHIA ANN.)

QUANTRILL, WILLIAM CLARKE A bloody-minded guerrilla leader who used the Confederate cause as an excuse to pillage, burn, torture, and murder during the Civil War years. Born at Canal Dover, Ohio, on July 31, 1837, the first born of the marriage of Thomas Henry Quantrill[4] and Carolyn Cornelia Clarke, William is reputed to have possessed a sadistic streak from an early age—nail-

ing live snakes to trees being but one pointer to his having a sick mind. In 1853, at the tender age of sixteen, this little horror took up employment with the Canal Dover Union School, further supplementing his income by selling copies of *A Tinker's Guide*—a publication that had been written and published by his father. Late in 1855 William left Illinois,[5] and over the next few years he pushed farther West, Kansas and Utah having him for a spell before he moved into the Pike's Peak area of Colorado in the early days of 1859 to try his luck at prospecting.

Digging for gold brought naught but disillusionment, and in June 1859 Quantrill moved back into Kansas and settled at Lawrence. Lawrence had him for a sordid seven months during which the crime rate soared. Violently abolitionist in speech at this period, Quantrill stole black slaves and returned them for stipulated rewards (a form of early-day kidnaping), and indulged in burglary, arson, horse theft, and larceny, all these crimes being committed while he was using the alias of "Charley Hart." "Charley" left Lawrence in January 1861, having to flee the area to avoid the clutches of a United States marshal who was waving a fistful of warrants, the fugitive only pausing during his exodus to assassinate a couple of his associates who may be assumed to have "known too much."

When Confederate forces opened fire on Fort Sumter on April 12, 1861, in the opening move of the Civil War, Quantrill, who was living in the Cherokee nation at this time, attached himself to a band of Cherokees who followed the Rebel

---

[3] A bespectacled Easterner who liked to project the image of being a rugged Westerner, despite the fact that when garbed in full western regalia he looked like a "Keystone Cop" cowboy. "Teddy" Roosevelt did, however, organize and lead the "Rough Riders" during the 1898 trouble with Spain.

[4] Thomas—who was of English ancestry, a tinker, a tinner, and something of a writer—appears to have led a blameless life, but two of his kinsmen—a brother and an uncle—died in prison, the former having been a highwayman and the latter a seagoing pirate.

[5] Rumors abound that he left the state after killing a man at Mendota.

banner of General Ben McCulloch, and as a member of this undisciplined mob he took part in the Battle of Wilson's Creek on August 10, 1861. One month later Quantrill is known to have been with Confederate forces who were attacked by Colonel Moonlight's Union men near Drywood, after which Quantrill appears to have become disenchanted with Army discipline, for a short time later he was engaged in civilian pursuits in Jackson County, Missouri. Here, Quantrill laid the foundations for his guerrilla band, having by December 1861 gathered some seven followers who were willing to plunder and kill for personal profit while paying lip service to the Confederate cause. This force had increased to 20 when Quantrill raided Independence, Missouri, on February 22, 1862, and when he sacked the village of Aubrey, Kansas, on March 7, more than 40 men were following his leadership.

Sometime during this period Quantrill kidnaped a girl named Kate King[6] who, not unwillingly, became his mistress—a hiding in the brush and "living under the brush" existence she was to share with this misfit until the end of his days. By midsummer more than 150 men were riding behind Quantrill, and on August 15, this force was mustered into Confederate service with their leader receiving the instant commission of captain. Five days after the Confederacy had accepted responsibility for his depredations, Captain Quantrill reached the peak of his infamy, leading nearly 500 of his raiders in an attack on Lawrence, Kansas, that was to leave more than 200 civilians dead in its wake.

By September Quantrill was carrying the rank of colonel, but his command was beginning to splinter. "Bloody" Bill Anderson, one of his most able and obnoxious lieutenants, left him; his force had been "outlawed" by the Union; and his activities were beginning to leave an aroma that embarrassed the Confederacy. In March 1864, after leading his depleted band in a few raids into Texas, Quantrill was placed under arrest by Confederate General Henry M. McCulloch,[7] but before Quantrill could face a court-martial he escaped, and a few months later he appeared in Missouri—a colonel leading but 16 men! His activities in Missouri were mostly of a negative nature, and in the fall of the year he led what remained of his men East, the command posing as "Captain Clarke and a detail of the 4th Missouri Cavalry" when any Union forces were encountered.

On New Year's Day 1865 the raiders crossed into Kentucky, Quantrill being desirous of going to Washington, D.C., so that he might assassinate President Lincoln. This desire was never to be realized, for Lincoln got his death wound on April 14 while Quantrill was still busy committing pillage and murder in the towns and hamlets of Kentucky. On May 10, 1865, Quantrill was severely wounded when his guerrillas had a brush with federal troops under the command of Captain Edward Terrill, and unable to resist, Quantrill was taken into custody and confined within the military prison at Louisville. Here he was given treatment, although there was little hope of recovery. Quantrill obviously knew he was dying, for of the four thousand dollars he had in his possession when arrested, he gave half to a priest—possibly in the hope that he might bribe his way past St. Peter—while he willed the remainder to Kate King.[8] Wil-

---

[6] William Elsey Connelley (No. 1 historian of Quantrill) gives the name as "Kate Clarke," but author Homer Croy states that her name was definitely "King."

[7] Brother of the Ben McCulloch whom Quantrill had originally followed into action.

[8] Miss King is to be commended for not squandering this windfall; she used it to open a brothel in St. Louis, Missouri.

liam Clarke Quantrill died at 4 P.M. on June 6, 1865. Of interest: Quantrill's raiders held annual reunions from 1888 until 1920, and a few of the bones of their leader are still in the possession of the Kansas State Historical Society. (See ANDERSON, "BLOODY" BILL, and LAWRENCE MASSACRE.)

QUARTER HORSE   An American breed of horse that has its origins in the stallion activity of an English thorough- bred racehorse named "Janus." Established as a breed since the middle of the eighteenth century, and originally bred to race over quarter-mile distances, the horse has long been favored by cattlemen for the working of cattle, its short bursts of speed and its ability to "turn on a dime" making it ideal for this type of work. The quarter horse is stocky of build and well muscled, and stallions average 15 hands (5 feet) and weigh about 1,200 pounds.

CHARLES M. RUSSELL

RACCOON Medium-sized carnivorous mammal that has a black mask and a tail ringed with black bands. Well distributed throughout the West—and the eastern states—raccoons can live almost anywhere, although a marked preference for well-watered or marshy areas is shown. They will eat rodents, crayfish, amphibians, fruit, insects, and occasionally carrion, all of which will be washed before eating when water is available. They are heavy of build yet agile, being excellent climbers, skilled swimmers, and very adept in the use of their "hands." A fully grown male is about 30 inches in length (a third of which is tail), and may weigh up to 30 pounds, although half this weight is the usual average. Apart from having a white muzzle and "eyebrows," and the black areas already mentioned, their overall coloring is yellowish-gray liberally sprinkled with dark brown hairs. Nests are usually made in hollow tree trunks, and in the northern limits of their range most of the winter months will be spent in these retreats in a state of semihibernation. Very young raccoons may be domesticated, in which instance they make excellent pets.

RAIDLER, BILL A well-educated Pennsylvanian who rode with the Daltons and Bill Doolin during the first half of the 1890s. Bill, like many other members of the Dalton and Doolin mobs, had worked at Oscar D. Halsell's HX Ranch on the Cimarron[1] before turning outlaw, and although Bill took part in a number of bank robberies and the looting of an express office at Woodward, Oklahoma, during his long-riding days, he was absent at the Coffeyville disaster, and his name is not to be found on the roster of those who took part in the Battle of Ingalls. In October 1896 Deputy U. S. Marshal Bill Tilghman trailed Raidler to Sam Moore's ranch on Mission Creek in Osage territory, and after a two-shot gunfight he was taken into custody when a charge from Tilghman's shotgun had rendered

[1] This ranch was located about a dozen miles northeast of the present-day town of Guthrie, Oklahoma.

him more dead than alive. Thanks to Tilghman's early attention to his wounds, Raidler recovered to stand trial and receive a ten-year prison sentence. Upon his release Raidler turned his back on crime, employing no doubt latent abilities to establish himself as a fairly well-known author. (See DALTON GANG and DOOLIN GANG.)

RAMONA The name of a rather obese Indian woman who was living near San Jacinto, California, in the 1880s as the squaw of a Coahuilla[2] Indian known as Juan Diego. On March 23, 1883, Juan, who was a horse thief of no mean ability and a drunk of similar proportions, was shot dead by a man named Samuel Temple for stealing a black stallion. The fact that Juan had tried to knife Sam seconds before the latter had triggered his shotgun led to the acquittal of Temple when he was tried for the offense on March 26. Sometime during the summer following these incidents a child of Ramona's died from smallpox, and this may have been the last we were to hear of Ramona had not a lady novelist named Helen Hunt Jackson resurrected the widow from obscurity by making her the willowy heroine of *Ramona,* a noble-red-man opus first published in 1884 and appearing in tear-jerking print ever since. The typeset Ramona is beautiful;[3] the rum-pot Juan becomes the blameless Allessandro; and poor Sam becomes the evil Indian-hating Jim Farrar, who is held responsible for the deaths of both Ramona's husband and child. Elevated almost to the Hall of Fame by publication of this best seller, the youngish but uncomely Ramona posed for shutterbugs who had the desire to "snap" eye-

blistering photographs at the going rate of half a buck a shot. When this lucrative business dried up, Ramona moved to San Diego and became a prostitute and, despite her appearance, she was kept fully operational in this capacity until at least 1912. After this time little more was heard of her.

RANCH Derived from the Spanish *rancho,* translated roughly into "persons feeding in company." Sometimes spelled "ranche," and originally used in the West to denote "business premises." Later usage was to embrace any livestock farm (cattle, horses, sheep, pigs, etc.), the former use becoming obsolete.

RANCHERIA Literally the Spanish term for a dwelling place of a *ranchero,* but used to denote a stock tender's hut or collection of same, or an Amerind village, especially the Apache *rancherias* of the Southwest.

RANCHERO A stock tender or a ranch owner. Spanish term used in the Southwest.

RANCHO Term that may be used to describe a stock tender's hut, a line camp, or a ranch. (See RANCH.)

RATON PASS Passage through the Raton Mountains that links southeastern Colorado with northeastern New Mexico. Used by caravans taking the Bent's Fort detour of the Santa Fe Trail, and—at one time—roughly graded by Dick Wootten, who erected a toll gate in the pass. In 1876 the pass echoed to the sound of

[2] A seed-gathering tribe that inhabited the Coahuilla Valley of Southern California. Pronounced "Ko-wee-yah."

[3] This is understandable, for few folk want a heroine with a face like a badly kneaded putty-rubber.

small arms fire when the Atchison, Topeka & Santa Fe Railroad and the Denver & Rio Grande became locked in combat over which company should have right of way through the pass, a night-riding, powder-burning episode from which the A.T. & S.F. emerged the victor. U. S. Highway 85 now runs through the pass. (See SANTA FE TRAIL and WOOTTEN, RICHARD.)

RATTLESNAKE DICK   Nickname applied to an unscrupulous Englishman named Dick Barter. (See BARTER, DICK.)

RATTLESNAKE JAKE   Nickname applied to a somewhat ornery Texan. (See FALLON, CHARLES.)

RATTLESNAKES Venomous snakes of the Pit viper[4] subfamily that are only found in the Americas and may be easily distinguished from other snakes by their unique tail-end "rattle," a series of horny interlocking segments that give off a buzzing sound when the tail is agitated. Rattlesnakes produce this sound—which may be heard at a distance of fifteen to twenty yards—as a "stay clear" warning rather than as evidence of their intention to attack, for a snake will remain silent when making a venomous attack on its prey. At birth a snake possesses only one of these segments, an additional segment being added with each sloughing of skin. The popular fallacy that each segment represents a year of the snake's life has no basis in fact, for as a snake may shed its skin several times a year and terminal segments can wear away or break off, the "rattle" can only give a very rough guide to a snake's age. All rattlesnakes are ground dwellers, rather sluggish, and

rarely attack unless provoked,[5] and although they rarely take to water, they are —like all snakes—excellent swimmers. In the northern areas of their range, rattlesnakes congregate in great numbers—in caves, etc.—to hibernate the winter away.

Twelve to fifteen species occur in the United States, three of the most common species to be found west of the Mississippi being: *Western diamondback.* Found in the deserts and prairies throughout the West and easily identified by its diamond-shaped markings, which are outlined by black-and-white scales. Average length is about 4½ feet, although specimens of 7 feet have been recorded. *Prairie rattlesnake.* Found in the areas that its name suggests. Never attains more than 5 feet in length. Uses the burrows of various small mammals as a retreat. *Sidewinder.* Found only in the deserts of the Southwest. Average length is 18 inches, although specimens of almost double this length have been recorded. Living on shifting sands has developed in this snake a unique form of movement, a "side-winding" jerk of the body that leaves disconnected reversed-J-shaped tracks, which are entirely unlike the continuous-ripple tracks left by other snakes. Easily identified by horny growths that protrude above—and shade—each eye.

RAWHIDE   Untanned leather; also used to denote a whip made from such leather.

RAWLEY, R. C.   A chronic booze-hound whose predilection for strong liquids made it impossible for him to hold down an honest job for any length of time, Rawley[6] moved into the Alder

---

[4] Vipers that have pits—or vents—located on each side of the head between eye and nostril. These pits contain a heat-detecting organism that aids the snake in locating its prey; e.g., a rat in a burrow will give off sufficient body heat to inform the snake of its whereabouts.

[5] Most bites, which may prove fatal if early treatment is not available, occur after a snake has been unintentionally provoked, i.e., accidentally kicked or trodden on.

[6] Suspected of being an assumed name.

Gulch area of Montana in the fall of 1863 with a vague background of having been an honest merchant at one time. Throughout the winter of 1863–64 this handsome, well-educated rumpot was suspected of being a spy for Henry Plummer's band of "Innocents," and these suspicions hardened when he took hasty leave of the region shortly after the hanging of Plummer. In September 1864 the suspected "fugitive" returned to Bannack, evidently believing that the vigilantes would allow bygones to remain has-beens, and for the next two months he was allowed to leave his dregs in Bannack and Virginia City saloons unmolested. During these drinking sessions, however, he was frequently heard making tactless remarks regarding the "Strangling . . . !" who had hanged Plummer, and by November the vigilantes were becoming irritated by this "gas." Very irritated. One dark night in November Rawley was arrested at New Jerusalem, escorted to Bannack, and hanged from the same gibbet whereupon had dangled Plummer. Rough justice, which is hereby recommended for present-day muggers and those participating in gang rape. (See INNOCENTS.)

RAY, NED Leading member of Henry Plummer's "Innocents." Plummer appointed Ray as one of his deputies on being elected sheriff of Bannack district on May 24, 1863, and as such Ray was in a strong position to lean on anyone who was toying with the idea of giving evidence against an "Innocent"—"Shut up or be shot up" being the technique used. Deputy Ray shacked up with a soiled dove known as Madam Hall, and although he rarely acted as a road agent, he is known to have participated in the robbery of a man named Henry Tilden between Bannack and Horse Prairie in November 1863. This crime was evidently sufficient to get his name on the Vigilantes

of Montana's "dead list" when that august body was organized in the December of that same year, and on the night of January 9, 1864, he was arrested by this clean-up brigade, who hanged him—together with Plummer and fellow owlhoot Buck Stinson—the following day. (See INNOCENTS.)

RAYNER, BILL A gilded rooster of a man who wore only the best: splendid black sombrero and a matching Prince Albert, gray pants tucked into burnished black boots, white silk shirt, and a hand-tooled gun harness supporting a pair of ivory-handled Colts. This was William P. Rayner, Virginia-born and as southern as fried chicken. By the time he arrived at El Paso, Texas, in 1883 he was reputed to have sent about eight men to permanent rest 'neath "little green tents," while his constant companion, an unkempt crum named Charles N. "Buck" Linn, also wore the "killer" brand. Bill and Buck killed nary a soul in El Paso, but they tried. Rayner went hunting for targets by slapping likely-looking "pigeons" across the face with a pair of silver-gray gloves he invariably carried, but with so many stiffs littering Bill's backtrail, it is hardly surprising that the men of El Paso failed to provoke.

Comes April 14, 1884, and Rayner is working his way along a line of unshaven mushes whose owners are waiting for shaves in a tonsorial parlor. Slap! "Ouch!" Slap! "Ouch!" Slap! "Ouch!" . . . pause, and Rayner queries: "Your name is Earp, I believe?" The tall, slim man with the drooping mustache who is dressed rather in the manner of an undertaker replies: "Yes, Wyatt Earp." Rayner, unaware that Wyatt is unarmed, but realizing he had almost been on the point of dropping an important part of his person, lards things over by inviting Earp to join him in a drink, and the two men walk over to the Gem Saloon and belly up to the bar for a glass of the grape.

Drinks consumed, Rayner wanders into an adjacent gambling room and tries to shake the weight of chips from his shoulder by annoying a faro player named Robert Rennick, who, after he had suffered his hat being pushed over his eyes a few times, more or less requests his tormentor to "agitate the sawdust," "make the spurs tinkle," or "get lost." This, of course, begins to make Bill's day. After warning Rennick that he will return for a showdown just as soon as he has had another drink, Rayner tromps from the room.

As soon as Rayner had removed his presence, Rennick grabbed a six-gun from the dealer's drawer, left his seat, and took up position in a corner of the room, where he steadied his hardware and waited. Minutes later Bill Rayner returned through the doorway, guns blazing, four of his shots splintering the chair in which he had expected Rennick to be sitting before he realized he had erred; the realization being confirmed when two of Rennick's bullets caught him in the abdomen and chest. Rayner dropped his guns, wobble-legged through the batwings and dropped dead in the dust, fouling up all that aforementioned fine raiment but not caring a damn.

When Bill bit the dust, Buck Linn was soaking up the stock of the Ranch Saloon, but within minutes fast-traveling bad news had informed him of the disaster that had overtaken his pistoleering partner and Buck was pushing his way into the sunlight intent on evening the score by killing Bob Cahill, Buck having been misinformed as to who had shot Rayner. Meanwhile the fast-moving courier of calamity had returned to the Gem Saloon and warned Cahill of his impending doom, and Bob, who has never shot anything more deadly than craps,

can think of naught to do but lose his tan.

Luckily, friends are at hand. Dan Tipton slaps a loaded .45 into Bob's sweaty hand and Wyatt Earp instructs him with a spot of quick know-how, "Keep calm—take your time—get him in the belly button" stuff, which is expected to transform Cahill into an instant Hickok. Oddly enough, it worked. Linn crashed into the gambling room and cut loose, firing four ill-aimed shots while Cahill was remembering his instructions and carefully drawing a bead on the gunny's unpolished belt buckle. Cahill's first shot plowed through Buck's last meal and shattered his spinal column, and the second lodged in his heart, so Linn was probably quite dead when he hit the sawdust. The El Paso *Herald*—jaded by such happenings—gave a short report on this clash of armed men, the careers of Rayner and Linn being written off thus: "The victims had no one to blame but themselves. Their train of life collided with loaded revolvers and they have gone down forever in the smash-up. Thus endeth the first chapter of our spring fights."

REATA A lariat made from rawhide. (See LARIAT.)

REAVIS, JAMES ADDISON
A man from Missouri whose extraordinary accomplishments as a forger enabled him to rake in an income of about three hundred thousand dollars per annum for more than fourteen years. Details of Reavis' early life are vague, but he is known to have deserted from the Confederate forces during the Civil War upon hearing that he was about to be arrested for forging his CO's signature, and during the late 1860s he worked his way through many jobs while settled at St. Louis, Missouri—streetcar conductor, store clerk, and dabbler in real estate being but three of these. Sometime in the

middle 1870s he moved to New Mexico and managed to find employment in the Public Record Office at Santa Fe—a position that entailed the handling of numerous ancient documents, many of which related to old Spanish land grants.

This was an opportunity not to be wasted. Reavis taught himself the unbastardized Spanish of the early eighteenth century and somehow found the time and money to visit Mexico, Spain, and Portugal so that he might study old parchments and family crests that would enable him to forge a land title giving him undisputed possession of more than 10½ million acres of the Arizona and New Mexico territories. Reavis lodged his claim at Phoenix, Arizona, on May 9, 1881, the documents in his possession making it abundantly clear that he was the undisputed owner of a land grant that had been awarded to Miguel Silva de Peralta de la Cordoba by the King of Spain in 1758 in recognition of Miguel's services as a soldier in the New World— said Miguel being elevated to Baron de Arizonaca and Caballero de los Colorados by this document.

Lawyers studied the Reavis claim, confirmed that it was genuine, and recommended that ranchers, railroads, or humble squatters who were enjoying occupancy of Reavis-owned land should pay their new landlord any monies he might ask as payment for the land. The Southern Pacific Railroad started the ball rolling by paying Reavis fifty thousand dollars, and for the next fourteen years the "Baron of Arizona" was waist deep in *dinero*. While Reavis was spending the profits resultant from his penmanship, various suspicious-minded bodies were delving through piles of mildewed documents in a search for anything that could be expected to prove Reavis a fraud and scallywag of the lowest type.

By 1895, Reavis' enemies had enough material to get him indicted for land fraud: Seems that no such family as the Peralta clan mentioned in the land grant had ever existed, and the Carmelita Peralta whom Addison Reavis had married was equally phony.[7] Sentenced to six years in the territorial prison at Santa Fe, Reavis was released after serving little more than two years, after which he is reputed to have drifted—broke and bewildered—into that safe hiding place known as obscurity.[8] And that makes a nice moral ending to the story of Mr. Reavis.

RED BUCK   Nickname attached to an indiscriminate trigger flicker named Waightman. (See WAIGHTMAN, GEORGE.)

RED CLOUD   The white man's name for Mock-peah-lu-tah, a chief of the Oglala division of the Teton Sioux, who rose to prominence as a warrior leader during the Indian–U. S. Army skirmishes that occurred along the Bozeman Trail during the 1860s. After being transfixed by a Crow arrow shaft in 1865 Red Cloud

[7] Carmelita was actually the daughter of impoverished Latin American peasants who were natives of California. Orphaned at an early age, Carmelita was "discovered" by Reavis when she was working as a serving girl at a ranch in northern California, a fourteen-year-old girl with no family connections who was to be groomed to "star" in one of the greatest swindles of all time. Money invested in her schooling, etc., resulted in her possessing all the airs and graces of a Castilian of class by the time Reavis had gotten his scheme off the ground and married her.

[8] Protesting his innocence to the end; which makes one wonder. Where did the ex-streetcar conductor get the funds to finance his trips abroad and the remolding of Carmelita? Did parties who may have financed the scheme throw him to the wolves when the bubble burst? Were all the documents that were used as evidence against Reavis scrutinized for indications of possible forgery? (Some unknown party—or parties—who had been victimized financially by Reavis may have fought fire with fire.)

usually confined himself to directing military engagements rather than taking part in same, choosing such notable warriors as Crazy Horse, Little Big Man, Man-Afraid - of - His - Horses,[9] Little Wolf,[10] etc., to lead a number of planned raids against troops and civilians in the vicinity of the Bozeman Trail over the years 1865–67; about 150 civilians and a like number of soldiers being killed over this period of warfare. If we discount the disastrous Wagon-box Fight, Red Cloud's depredations along the Bozeman were a success, for they led to the Treaty of 1868 being ratified at Fort Laramie in April of that year and the abandoning of Forts Reno, C. F. Smith, and Phil Kearny by the U. S. Army some four months later.[11] After this victory Red Cloud buried the hatchet and settled with his people in the Powder River country, and in 1871 he offered only oral resistance when he and his tribe were "persuaded" to move onto the newly established Red Cloud Agency a few miles east of Fort Laramie. From then on Red Cloud was to remain a reservation free-handouts-no-freedom Indian, although he still had sufficient steam to make frequent trips to Washington in attempts to get a better deal for his people. The aging chief lent a touch of color to the World's Columbian Exposition at Chicago in 1893, but by the early years of the twentieth century he was beginning to go blind, and he died in December 1909 at the ripe old age of eighty-seven years. (See CRAZY

HORSE; FETTERMAN FIGHT; HAYFIELD FIGHT; JULESBURG FIGHT; LITTLE WOLF; and WAGON-BOX FIGHT.)

RED-LIGHT DISTRICT That area of any broadminded settlement, town, or city wherein brothels and the premises of free-lance prostitutes are allowed to operate without interference. In the early days these districts usually confined themselves to the poorer half of a town, the railroad tracks frequently becoming a kind of boundary line that separated the rich and righteous element from those folk "living on the other side of the tracks." Needless to say, crosstrack traffic got kinda busy after dark. In one western settlement a bridge spanning a river served as the boundary line. This was an unfortunate choice, for on one occasion when the bridge was destroyed by a flash flood, many a respected male member of the community found himself stranded on the wrong side of the river when daylight dawned. The linking of red lights with brothels originated in Dodge City, Kansas, in the 1870s. Nowadays a red-light district is frequently called a "tenderloin district." (See BROTHELS and DODGE CITY, KANSAS.)

RED RIVER
A one-thousand-mile-long tributary of the Mississippi that has its headwaters on the Staked Plains of northwestern Texas and flows in a generally easterly direction, forming the Texas-Oklahoma

---

[9] Facetiously rendered as "Man-Afraid-of-His-Mother-in-Law" by a reporter who was covering the World's Columbian Exposition at Chicago in 1893.

[10] Chief of a band of Northern Cheyenne.

[11] The abandoning of the forts being part of Red Cloud's terms when agreeing that "From this day forward all war between the parties to this agreement shall forever cease." The Great White Father—who no Indian wanted as their paternal guide—in turn agreed that all the country north of the North Platte River and east of the Big Horn Mountains should be classed as Indian Territory, and that no white person or persons would be permitted to settle or pass through said territory without first obtaining consent from the Indians. This treaty should have settled the North Plains Indian problem "forever," but it didn't; the word of the Great White load of "oonk-Chay" was as shoddy as a fifty-cent shirt, and within a few years the Indians would be defending their lands once more.

boundary for much of its length, then turning south to pass through southwestern Arkansas, southeast to bisect Louisiana, and joining the Mississippi on approximately the thirty-first parallel.

RED SASH GANG   The Pinkertons gave this name to a most likely nonexistent gang that they alleged was led by a chappie named Champion. (See CHAMPION, NATHAN D.)

RED STICKS   Name applied to the native inhabitants of North America by the backwoodsmen of the eastern states: specifically, the Creek Indians, but, by extension, any Indians. Crockett used the term when in Texas.

REE INDIANS   Popular abbreviation of Arikara Indians. (See ARIKARA INDIANS.)

REED, JAMES FRAZIER   Co-leader of the ill-fated Donner party. (See DONNER PARTY.)

REED, JIM   A native of Vernon County, Missouri, who, as an outlaw of no mean renown, shacked up with the notorious Belle Starr. (See STARR, BELLE.)

REED, NATHANIEL   A long-haired owlhoot who was born near St. Paul, Arkansas, in 1862, left his home state at the age of twenty-one, and started his career of big-time crime in 1885 after spending two years of his life as an Oklahoma cowboy. Using the romantic-sounding alias of "Texas Jack," Nat, and others, robbed a Santa Fe express at La

Junta, Colorado, in the summer of 188: some $6,000 finding its way into Nat pants as his share of the loot. Thre years later and Nat is taking part in bank robbery at Riverside, Texas, and i the following year the same bunch c long-riders hold up a stagecoach in Co orado. Arizona got the bunch next, train robbery near Phoenix in 1889 bein a memento of their passing. "Texas Jack Reed and company traveled far down th Rio Grande for their next job, a bank i Brownsville in southern Texas bein robbed by them in 1891. Early in 189 they held up a stagecoach near San A tonio as a farewell gesture before leavin Texas and heading for California wher later that year, they are reputed to hav robbed a gold bullion shipment.

On the Tuesday night of November 1: 1894, "Texas Jack," accompanied b Buss Luckey, Tom Root, Bill Smith, an a few others, held up a Missouri Pacif train near Muskogee in the Cherokee n; tion (western Oklahoma), having bee informed that around sixty thousand do lars was being shipped in the express ca The gang's informant had erred—b good. Deputy U. S. Marshal "Bud" Le better and a trio of his fast-shooting a sociates were in the express car, ar when the gang was driven off "Tex; Jack" was suffering from a heavy intal of Ledbetter's lead. Evidently aware th home is "The place where, when yc have to go there, they have to take yc in,"[12] Nathaniel "T. J." Reed took h shot-up carcass back to Arkansas and h out with relatives.

While Nat was heading for his hom state, Luckey and Root loused things u to a further degree by killing Depu U. S. Marshal Newton LaForce in a "r sisting arrest" gun fracas, and whe Luckey and Reed[13] finally found then

[12] Quote of Robert Frost (1874–1963).
[13] Reed, suffering from a dozen buckshot wounds, surrendered to the authorities c March 18, 1895.

selves within the law's embrace, things didn't look too good, for Root had decided to turn state's evidence, and "Hanging Judge" Parker was wielding the gavel. Things, however, took a turn for the better, for although Luckey was sentenced to hang for the murder of La-Force, the sentence was reversed before he could keep his appointment with long-drop specialist George Maledon,[14] and Reed, after a long-drawn-out series of trials, was finally released on parole in 1897. "Texas Jack" saw the light after his release. He preached "good living"— in the religious rather than the booze-gluttony-satyriatic sense; appeared in a show entitled *Texas Jack, Train Robber;* wrote a little book featuring his version of the story of his life, and for the next fifty-odd years jacked up his resources by selling more than seventy thousand copies of this effort, *The Life of Texas Jack,* at twenty-five cents a copy. Nathaniel "Texas Jack" Reed died at Tulsa, Oklahoma, on January 7, 1950. (See MALE-DON, GEORGE, and PARKER, ISAAC C.)

REMINGTON FIREARMS

Firearms manufactured by E. Remington and Sons[15] at their armory at Ilion, New York. Remington handguns were equal, if not superior, to many of the contemporary Colt models, and the Remington rifles were probably the most popular long guns on the plains during the early 1870s, being used in great numbers to decimate both the buffalo and the Indian.[16] Brief details relating to a few of the firearms produced by E. Remington and Sons are as follows:

Navy model. Six-shot single-action percussion revolver of .36 caliber. Weighed about 2½ pounds, had a 6½-inch octagonal barrel, and an overall length of 13½ inches. Similar to the early Colt revolvers, but having a top strap that gave greater rigidity to the frame, and a web that extended the full length of the ejector rod. The first of the Remington handguns, being patented on September 15, 1858, and manufactured from then on. Retailed at about $12.50.

Army model. Six-shot single-action percussion revolver of .44 caliber. Weighed 2 pounds, 14 ounces; had an 8-inch octagonal barrel, and an overall length of 14 inches. Top strap and web as the Navy model, but otherwise similar to the Colts of the period. Went into production in 1861 and retailed at $12.50.

Army model No. 3. Six-shot single-action metal cartridge revolver of .44 caliber. Weighed 2 pounds, 12 ounces; had a 7½-inch round barrel, and an overall length of 13 inches. Remington's retention of the web under the ejector made the 1875 model readily identifiable from the contemporary Colts. Produced from 1875 on and retailed at around $18.

In addition to the popular models mentioned above, from around 1865 onward, Remington produced a variety of pocket pistols and revolvers with a maximum weight of around 10½ ounces; .32-caliber magazine pistols that could fire

---

[14] Convicted of the murder of LaForce on August 24, 1895, and sentenced to death by Parker fourteen days later, Luckey managed to secure a new trial, which ended with the sentence being reversed, Buss being acquitted of the murder in January 1896. This didn't mean that Luckey could walk out of the court a free man, for he was given a fifteen-year stretch for participating in the train job. His name is sometimes given as "Buzz" Luckey.

[15] Remington also manufactured sewing machines, typewriters, and farming equipment.

[16] Custer had a rolling block sporting rifle at the Little Big Horn—a .50–.70-caliber rifle for which he had paid $91.50.

five shots, and double-barreled "Derringers" that came in a wide choice of calibers being in the former group, and five-shot revolvers with stud triggers and birdshead stocks in the latter. These small revolvers came in a wide range of calibers and barrel lengths, and they retailed at an average price of $10. Most of the Remington handguns were nickel-plated, and many of their Navy and Army models had a butt swivel to which a lanyard could be attached.

Rolling block sporting rifle. Single-shot rifle that came onto the market in 1886 and was—with slight modifications—in continuous production until 1933. Originally chambered to accept .50–.70-caliber center-fire cartridges, but from 1872 onward they were manufactured in a variety of calibers. This gun, although single-shot, could be fired very rapidly, and it was a firm favorite with buffalo hunters and sharpshooters over the 1866–80 period.

Keene magazine rifle. Bolt-action rifle with a tubular magazine beneath the barrel that could hold 8 rounds. Weighed about 9 pounds, had an overall length of 48½ inches, and could be obtained in a variety of calibers. Manufactured from 1880 until 1883.

Many other models of rifles were also manufactured over the frontier years, and a large slice of the shotgun market was held by Remington products. (See COLT FIREARMS and DERINGER.)

REMINGTON, FREDERIC
American artist who was actively engaged in depicting the characters and in-

cidents of the fast-vanishing frontier scene from around 1886 until his death in 1909 at the age of forty-seven. The fact that Remington toured the West, spent time as a cowboy in Montana, Wyoming, Arizona, and the Dakotas, and could ride and shoot with all but the best of his contemporaries, resulted in most of his work having an authenticity of touch that is lacking in the majority of the artwork of the period that features similar subject matter. Remington at his best cannot be overrated, but as he turned out nearly twenty-eight hundred two-dimensional works (pen-and-ink sketches, watercolor drawings, and oil paintings) and twenty-five pieces of sculpture, it is hardly surprising that within the embrace of this monumental output may be found a number of works that can only be classed as "poor."[17] Remington works featuring the United States cavalry, dust-billowing wagons and stagecoaches, and attacking Indians, somewhat somber-hued in many instances but usually sweating with action, have inspired the composition and coloring of many a Western movie sequence. Over the years a few of this artist's works have "gone missing," "Cavalry Charge"—a magnificent action job that is one of this author's all-time favorites—probably being the best of those that have thundered into the AWOL category. A number of Remington works feature a buffalo skull lying in the foreground, an artistic ploy that many a lesser artist[18] has since employed. Should this entry give the impression that Remington was the only artist of quality to confine his attention to the West, it must be stated that the paintings of Charles M. Russell—a contemporary of Remington's—are considered by many to be of equal merit.

[17] To name but two: "Indian Scouts on Geronimo's Trail" and a bomb entitled "The Apaches Are Coming!"
[18] Including this writer; having become somewhat "hooked" on the West by illustrating Buffalo Bill annuals that featured so many buffalo skulls that the books rattled when shaken.

REMUDA A herd of saddle horses, whether held as ranch stock or accompanying a cattle drive or roundup as remounts. Pronounced as spelled by most folk, but "remoother" is favored in the cattle country of the Southwest. In some regions a remuda may be referred to as either a "caballado" or a "saddle band."

RENO GANG A gang of about a dozen strong who leaped to prominence in 1866 by committing the first train robbery in North America. Led by the four Reno brothers—John, Frank, Simeon, and William[19]—the gang had hitherto confined their united attention to saloon holdups, burglary, highway robbery, and the circulating of the artwork of Peter McCartney, an unoriginal yet excellent penman whose engraved copies of produce of the United States Treasury were damn near undetectable. Success in these pursuits led to an escalation of ambition that found outlet in the holdup of an Ohio and Mississippi train near Seymour, Indiana, on October 6, 1866, and the looting of the Adams Express car to the tune of ten thousand dollars.[20] Six months later the Renos crossed the Mississippi[21] and rode into northwestern Missouri to rob the Daviess County treasurer's office at Gallatin of twenty-two thousand dollars. Shortly after this offense John Reno was arrested by the Pinkertons, convicted at a subsequent trial, and given forty years in which to ponder what he could have done with his share of the loot.

This stiff sentence failed to deter the remaining brothers, and in March 1868 Frank Reno led the gang across Iowa to raid the Harrison County Bank at Magnolia, a medium-sized caper that showed a pistol-point profit of around fourteen thousand dollars. Insulated by wads of currency, the gang traveled South, only to be netted intact by the Pinkertons at Council Bluffs and tossed into the local jail. In the early hours of April 1 the gang checked out of these inhospitable surroundings by exiting through a hastily made hole in the wall, and a couple of weeks later they were back in Indiana planning a raid which, unknown to the Renos at that time, would present them with the biggest take-home pay of their criminal careers. On the night of May 22, 1868, the Renos put their plan into operation, boarding a train of the Jefferson, Missouri, and Indianapolis Railroad when it paused to take on water at the whistle stop of Marshfield in southeastern Indiana, and shortly afterward making a clean getaway with paper and gold to the value of ninety-six thousand dollars tucked in their saddlebags.

This marked the end of the gang's lucky streak, for when they made a repeat attack on an Ohio and Mississippi train near Seymour in the summer of 1868 they found the express car filled with armed guards instead of the one hundred thousand dollars they had expected, and after a brisk gunfight all the gang were driven off empty-handed, with gangster Volney Elliott nursing a severe leg wound. Hounded by the Pinks, the three Reno brothers and a mobster named Carl Anderson reached Canada and temporary safety, but gunnies Volney Elliott, Lefty Clinton, and Charlie

[19] A fifth brother named Clinton remained either honest or undetected.

[20] Attendant publicity inspired two misguided youths named Walter Hammond and Mike Colleran to stage a replay of the robbery—the same railroad, the same site, and most likely the same express car. The Renos took a "dog in the manger" attitude on hearing of this holdup, expressing this spoilsport view by beating up the copycats and turning them over to the law.

[21] And thereby becoming eligible for an entry in this volume.

Rosenbaum[22] were not so lucky, for they were arrested by the Pinkertons at Brownstown, and while they were being transported to Seymour by rail to stand trial masked vigilantes flagged down the train, removed the three miscreants, and before you could say "Bums away!" had left them dangling from a stalwart branch of a convenient trackside tree.

Five days after Elliott and company had made their exits, a Reno gangster named James Moore was discovered swinging stiff and extinct from the same branch, and by mid-July Frank, Simeon, and William Reno, together with Carl Anderson, had been slotted behind bars— Anderson and Frank Reno having been successfully extradited from Canada, and William and Simeon Reno having been picked up in Indianapolis by a Pinkerton gumshoe named Will Stoggart. The prisoners were held in the Jackson County jail to await trial, but after the preliminary hearing the quartet was removed to the more substantial Floyd County jail at New Albany in an effort to prevent the Southern Indiana Vigilance Committee from taking justice into their own hands. The vigilantes, however, were not to be thwarted by this move. On the night of December 11, 1868—"The Night of Blood"—well over a hundred red-masked vigilantes virtually took over the town of New Albany and successfully stormed the jail, after which Anderson and the Reno brothers were dragged from their respective cells and hanged from an iron ceiling beam without further ado.

RESERVATIONS Areas of land set aside for the exclusive use of the displaced Indian tribes but within the borders of which they were, to all intents and purposes, confined. Originally "all land west of the crest of the Alleghenies" was

22 Sometimes given as Charles Roseberry.

reserved for the use of the Indians; this grand gesture of allowing the red man to keep land he already owned was, of course, made in the 1760s, before anyone had any desire to move westward. During the following century the Indian-held lands contracted in direct ratio to the white man's desire for western expansion, although as late as 1868 Red Cloud's Sioux were presented with "all the country north of the North Platte and east of the Big Horn Mountains," and Indian Territory, which occupied most of what is now Oklahoma, was not contracted into a fraction of its former acreage until it was nibbled away by the land rushes that occurred over the 1889–95 period.

Indian-held lands were, and are, exempt from taxation—as is any income derived from same—and they are outside the jurisdiction of either state or county law-enforcement officials; prosperous tribes usually relying on tribal police and tribal courts to deal with any crimes of a domestic and minor nature, while federal lawmen—formerly U.S. marshals and deputy U.S. marshals, and later the FBI —are involved when major crimes or crimes of a duoracial nature are committed, federal laws are infringed, or when a tribe is too impoverished to support its own legal structure.

Nowadays, of the old Indian Territory of Oklahoma, only the Osage Reservation remains, yet even so, more than fifty million acres, most of which is west of the Mississippi, are still classed as "Indian country," such land being held in trust by the Commissioner of Indian Affairs, whose department comes within the province of the Secretary of the Interior. The largest of these allotments is the Navaho Reservation, which lies mainly in northwestern New Mexico and northeastern Arizona, and the Navaho will probably be allowed to remain here until the white man runs out of sand to mix with his cement. Other large reservations are Pine Ridge (South Dakota); Standing Rock (South Dakota extending into North Dakota); Wind River (Wyoming); Blackfoot, Crow, and Fort Peck (Montana); and San Carlos and Papago (Arizona). All the states west of the Mississippi, with the exceptions of Arkansas and Louisiana, have reservations within their boundaries. Nowadays there is no such offense as "jumping the reservation," for there are no restrictions on the movements of Indians.[23] (See INDIAN TERRITORY and OKLAHOMA LAND RUSH.)

REVOLVING RIFLE   A multishot rifle with a cylindrical magazine similar to those featured in revolvers. These rifles were manufactured by many firms and came in a variety of calibers and magazine capacities, but all have the overall appearance of an extra-long-barreled revolver to which a wooden shoulder stock has been added. (See COLT FIREARMS, subheading *Revolving rifles*.)

REYNOLDS, CHARLEY   An Army scout, buffalo hunter, and trapper whose preference for his own company, although causing little damage to his popularity, resulted in his usually being referred to as "Lonesome Charley." Born in Illinois in 1844, but having spent much of his childhood in northeastern Kansas,[24] Charley left the family hearth in 1859 and joined a wagon train that was heading into the Northwest. On reaching Fort Kearney, Charley left the safety of the train to team up with an aging mountain man, and for the next couple of years Charley was hunting and trapping in Colorado and southern Wyoming, with this buckskinned veteran as his

mentor. Shortly after the outbreak of the Civil War young Reynolds joined the Union forces, and it was not until the fall of 1865 that he returned to the plains, where, over the years, he established himself as a buffalo hunter and Army scout.

In 1873 "Lonesome Charley" was employed as a scout by General D. S. Stanley, who was leading a survey expedition into the Black Hills of Dakota Territory —an exploratory trip during which Charley became well acquainted with George A. Custer, commanding officer of the 7th Cavalry, which was on escort duty with the expedition. This association of extrovert cavalry officer and introvert scout was to continue. Duties with the expedition concluded, Reynolds became Custer's chief of scouts, a position that entailed delivering messages between Army posts for much of the time. But not all of the time.

On June 25, 1876, the 7th Cavalry rode into the Valley of the Little Big Horn with Charley riding point, but when Custer split his command shortly after high noon, Charley found himself attached to A, M, and G troops under the command of Major Reno, and when the three troops spurred down the valley and crossed Ash Creek in pursuit of a band of Oglalas, "Lonesome" was well in the van. Suddenly, like snow-capped mountains in the sunlight, tepees. Hundreds of tepees. Sioux, Cheyenne, Arapaho— stretching like dragons' teeth as far as the eye could see. And the Indians weren't running any more. Trumpet calls brought the battalion to a dust-clouding halt, and A, M, and G troops swung around and followed their guidons into the shelter of a stand of timber, but this position soon became untenable, and Reno gave the order to sound retreat. Horses and riders exploded from the timber and lathered

---

[23] With the exception of the Papago Reservation, where tribal permission must first be obtained before an Indian may leave the area.

[24] Reynolds, Sr., had relocated in Kansas after becoming a widower in the 1850s.

for Ash Creek, with Reno in the lead and G Troop and Charley straggling in the rear—straggling in the path of a large force of fast-mounted Sioux and Cheyenne. Most of G Troop didn't make it. Neither did Charley. Survivors reported seeing his horse go down before the dust of retreat hid him from view, so it is quite likely that he had been transfixed by arrow shafts and was past all feeling when the unshod hoofs of the Indian cavalry began tearing into his flesh. (See BATTLE ON THE LITTLE BIG HORN.)

REYNOLDS, GLENN Sheriff of Gila County, Arizona, in the late 1880s. Mainly remembered as being one of the Apache Kid's victims. (See APACHE KID.)

REYNOLDS, JAMES Leader of a gang of Colorado highwaymen who terrorized the South Park area in 1864. Texas-born James, together with brother John, had arrived in Colorado to search for gold during the early days of the "Pike's Peak or Bust" scramble, and both brothers had worked as miners in California Gulch[25] until the early days of the Civil War had exposed their Confederate sympathies and had got them thrown into a Union internment compound at Denver. At some later date they escaped from custody and returned to Texas, intent on organizing a band of Confederate irregulars who would make guerrilla raids into Colorado. Colonel McKee of the Confederate Army—who happened to be an admirer of Quantrill—listened attentively to the Reynolds brothers' plans, then scribbled out a pass to get their newly recruited force of twenty-two men through the Confederate lines.

The Reynolds band rode North, and in the spring of 1864 they attacked and looted a wagon train that had been "schoonering" along the Santa Fe Trail north of the Raton Pass. More than forty thousand dollars to the good from this exploit, the gang moved west toward the Spanish Peaks,[26] many of the gang evidently expecting a cut of the take, for when "Captain" Jim Reynolds appropriated the booty in the name of the Confederacy, a dozen of his "troopers" deserted. After burying the plunder in the shadow of the twin peaks, the brothers Reynolds rode North with their depleted force, shortly afterward robbing a coach that had been traversing South Park of around ten thousand dollars in gold dust. To avoid further desertions, Jim divided a percentage of this loot among his men before returning to the Spanish Peaks and burying the remainder.

Before any of the gang's pokes could be reduced by high living, they had a clash with a miners' posse that resulted in one member of the gang being killed,[27] and, ultimately, Jim Reynolds and five of his men being taken into custody.[28] In June 1864 Reynolds and his accomplices were tried at Denver and each given a life sentence. Throughout July and much of August the convicted ones were held in the Denver jail, but on August 19, the authorities, fearing that Confederate sympathizers might free the prisoners, handed them into the custody of Colonel John M. Chivington's 3rd Colorado Cavalry for transfer to Fort Lyon.

[25] Later to be renamed Leadville.

[26] Twin mountains in southern Colorado that were known as "Wah-to-yah" by the Indians.

[27] And decapitated; the luckless one's head—suitably preserved in alcohol—being on display at Fairplay for many years.

[28] John Reynolds and a man named Stowe being the only members of the gang to escape. After staging further robberies, John was finally shot down, reputedly having given the location of the Spanish Peaks' cache to an outlaw named Brown before he expired. P.S.: Brown never found the hidden loot, so it's probably still there.

The prisoners never reached Fort Lyon. On the third day out, as the cavalry moved along Cherry Creek, Captain Cree of Company A gave the order for them to be shot, and they were executed by a firing squad.[29] (See CHIVINGTON, JOHN M.)

RHYOLITE One of the last mining towns to appear in the West. Rhyolite began rising from the arid floor of the Amargosa Desert in southern Nevada in 1904, the steel, concrete, stone, and brick used in its construction making it entirely unlike its earlier counterparts in California, Montana, and Colorado. At its peak in 1908 the town had some fourteen thousand residents; two railroads serviced the town—the Rhyolite railroad depot probably being the most solid structure of its type in the West; the *Bulletin* and *Herald* reported both epic events and boring trivialities; and—of major importance to its hard-living citizens—ice-cold beer was to be had in many of the saloons. The slump set in during 1909, and almost overnight the population figure had dropped by half, the beginning of an exodus that was to leave Rhyolite deserted and on the road to ruin before another decade had elapsed. The remains of Rhyolite, which are fairly substantial, may be located a few miles west of Beatty, Nevada. (See HARRIS, FRANK.)

RICHARDSON, LEVI A hard-bitten buffalo hunter who ended his days as gunfight debris. (See LOVING, FRANK.)

RICKAREE INDIANS Somewhat obsolete name for the Arikara Indians. (See ARIKARA INDIANS.)

RIM-FIRE RIG Term used on the northern ranges to describe the double rigging used on some saddles.

RINGGOLD, JOHN A rather mysterious character whose life story is such a now-you-see-him-now-you-don't affair that it is reasonable to suspect that at various times and places he may have used an alias—or aliases—far different from the obvious abbreviation of "John Ringo." Born in Missouri in 1844, reputedly kin of the Youngers and the equally notorious John Wesley Hardin, Ringo began to weave his way into the tapestry of the West in the early 1870s; a drifting cowhand whom a college education had endowed with the ability to tell folk to "Frig off!" in either Latin or Greek being such a rare bloom in the cowtowns of Kansas that his presence was remarked upon. Somewhere along the way the maturing Ringo must have decided that boring folk with lead was more in keeping with the spirit of the West than boring them with the classics, for in 1876 he was arrested by Texas Rangers for murderous participation in the Mason County War.

This arrest led to his spending some time behind bars, but at some later date he escaped, after which he evidently kept his saddle warm until he had put New Mexico 'twixt him and Texas, for he next appears in southeastern Arizona as a member of the Clanton gang. Although more or less domiciled in the Clanton stronghold of Galeyville during this period, Ringo spent many an explosive hour at Tombstone when gang activities were at a low ebb; one such highlight being his killing of a man named Louis Hancock in an Allen Street saloon, Hancock being gunned down for having the temerity to order a schooner of suds seconds

[29] A somewhat shocking send-off, for the gang had never been known to kill anyone, their robberies being carried out with a display of Old World courtesy that a display of New World ordnance but slightly marred.

after Ringo had requested he drink whiskey. The Tombstone authorities evidently regarded this shooting as little more than a whiskey promotional stunt that had misfired, for there appears to be no record of Ringo having been arrested for terminating Hancock's career. Pistol-point robbery of poker games was, however, frowned upon, and Ringo was arrested[30] by Deputy Sheriff Billy Breakenridge shortly after Ringo had employed this *modus operandi* to clean out a poker playing session that was being held in a Galeyville saloon; charges only being dismissed when it was learned that the man on trial had returned the loot.

Ringo's gang activities were many and varied: He took part in the Guadalupe Canyon massacre; rode with Curly Bill Brocius to wipe out the Haslett brothers; was one of a quartet who attempted to assassinate Virgil Earp; acted as lookout on the night of Morgan Earp's murder; and was only prevented from having a gun argument with Doc Holliday by the timely arrival of the local lawmen.[31] The last act in the saga of John Ringgold is worthy of the attention of any Ellery Queen who may be reading this entry, for many interpretations have been made of the following facts.

On the morning of July 12, 1882, Ringo rode out of Tombstone, and some two hours later, with nine miles of cactus and sand behind him, he was knocking them back in Jake McCann's Saloon at Antelope Springs. Twenty-four hours later, having ridden through the Dragoon Mountains, Ringo is concentrating on getting re-stoned in a saloon at Sulphur Springs, Tombstone now being some thirty-odd miles to the southwest. Later

that same day he sloshed from his saddle in Turkey Creek, a hamlet in the foothills of the Chiricahua Mountains, and here, from a certain Mrs. Smith's grocery *cum* liquor store, he purchased as much of the hard stuff as he could carry away, passed some remark about "returning to Galeyville," and then rode off in the direction of Turkey Creek Canyon. The following morning teamster John Yoas, possibly accompanied by Pony Deal, discovered the body of Ringo.

Ringo's body was sitting against a gnarled oak at the western end of Turkey Creek Canyon, the cause of death obviously being a .45 slug that had entered the right temple and exited high on the left of the skull. No tattooing surrounded the entrance wound, but Ringo's .45, with one cartridge detonated, was clutched in his right fist. Ringo's pocket watch was still keeping time, and two cartridge belts encircled his waist. One of these belts had been buckled on upside down and cartridges that had slipped from their loops littered the ground, the lead in many of these bearing evidence of having been chewed.[32] The corpse was bootless, but the feet had been mummy-wrapped with strips of the victim's undershirt, the "soles" of this improvised footwear proving that Ringo had not walked far in this condition. Ringo's horse and missing boots were discovered later that same day, the former having the latter attached to its saddle when it was picked up on the range of the Chiricahua Cattle Company. Despite the lack of powder burn around the entrance wound, a coroner's jury returned a verdict of "suicide," and the body of John Ringgold was buried beneath a cairn of

[30] Ringo surrendered to the man with the warrant, as he considered "Breck" a friend.

[31] Occurred at Tombstone in December 1881. This could have been the end of the track for Ringo, for Doc would most certainly have killed him.

[32] Some writers regard this as evidence that Ringo had chewed at the lead to increase his saliva when dying of thirst; this is ridiculous, for a creek was but a short distance away, and a profusion of succulent greenery surrounded the oak against which the body was found.

stones at the base of the oak he had last used as a backrest.

Did Ringo die a suicide, or was he taken by one of the following? Wyatt Earp is reputed to have confessed to the slaying of Ringo shortly before his death in 1929, documentary proof—supplied by Earp—backing up this confession, although most writers place Earp in Gunnison, Colorado, at the time of Ringo's demise.[33] Another claimant, Frank Leslie, cannot be overlooked; he was probably under the influence when he said he'd done it, but no one has ever proved he was anywhere else at the time of Ringo's passing. Another candidate is "Johnny Behind the Deuce," strongly suspected by many because he had little love for the deceased and he is known to have been in the area—avoiding a sheriff's posse—at the time. Yet again, an unnamed employee of the Chiricahua Cattle Company may have been the killer, this Mr. X having done the deed as the climax to a horse-trading argument regarding Ringo's mount—it was found on Chiricahua Cattle Company range, remember? (See BREAKENRIDGE, WILLIAM MILTON; CLANTON GANG; DEAL, PONY; EARP, MORGAN; EARP, VIRGIL; EARP, WYATT BERRY STAPP; GRAHAM, WILLIAM B.; HOLLIDAY, JOHN HENRY; LESLIE, FRANK; MASON COUNTY WAR; and O'ROURKE, JOHN.)

RINGO, JOHN This name is regarded by most writers as being the alias of John Ringgold; so be it. (See RINGGOLD, JOHN.)

RIO BRAVO The Latin American name for the Rio Grande. (See RIO GRANDE.)

RIO GRANDE Some 1,880 miles of shallow waterway that rises in the San Juan Mountains of Colorado and meanders in a mainly southerly direction through New Mexico before taking a generally southeasterly course to empty into the Gulf of Mexico near Brownsville, Texas. Since 1848 the last 1,300 miles of the Rio Grande's journey have been recognized as the international boundary between the United States and Mexico.

RIVERBOAT Any craft that has been built for service on inland waterways as a passenger- and/or freight-carrying vessel. During the nineteenth century, flatboats, keelboats, mackinaw boats, and the steam-driven side-wheelers and stern-wheelers all played their part in opening the West via such natural arteries as the Ohio, Mississippi, and Missouri rivers; flat, keel, and mackinaw boats—all of which were propelled by either current, sweeps or sails, or a combination of same —drifting slowly into history as the steam-driven "smokepots" began to dominate the rivers. (See FAR WEST; FINK, MIKE; FLATBOAT; KEELBOAT; MACKINAW BOAT; and RIVER STEAMER.)

RIVER OF NO RETURN Popular name for the fast-flowing Salmon River of Idaho. (See SALMON RIVER.)

RIVER STEAMER
Any large steam-powered craft that is propelled by screw, stern paddle, or port or starboard paddles, and has provision for the carrying of passengers and/or freight, may be classed as a river steamer. This entry, however, will confine itself to the stern-wheelers and side-wheelers that became the dominant form of river traffic on the Ohio, Mississippi, and Missouri, and to a lesser degree the Rio Grande and many of the navigable rivers that had outlets on the Pacific Coast, during the nineteenth

---

[33] As Wyatt's stay in Colorado is not documented on a day-to-day or week-to-week basis, at least one theorist of repute is of the opinion that this claim may be valid on the grounds that the round trip from Gunnison to southeastern Arizona could have been made in a week.

century. From somewhat crude beginnings around 1812, these vessels reached their peak in numbers, size, and elegance of design in the decade preceding the Civil War, yet as late as 1876, magnificent steamers such as the *Grand Republic* were being built, and mutations of similar yet more austere silhouette are still being put into service.

As only the sketchiest of plans were rarely, if ever, consulted during the building of these paddle steamers no two were alike, although all shared port and starboard smokestacks, one or two engine exhausts, a multiwindowed pilothouse[34] located on the top, or hurricane, deck, and twin derricks on the foredeck, which raised or lowered the ship-to-shore gangways. Most of these craft had four decks,[35] a grand staircase that led from the foredeck up into the main saloon, possessed an abundance of rococo work, and, unfortunately, had few if any lifeboats. The saloons, or lounges, usually possessed the best of carpeting, many elaborate clusters of oil-filled lamps hanging from their ceilings, numerous tables and coffee urns, and one or more grand pianos; they were insulated from the elements by passenger cabins whose doorways flanked the saloon on both port and starboard sides and were heated by potbellied stoves.

Amidst these luxurious surroundings nomadic "Mississippi" gamblers fleeced the unwary and were occasionally reduced to ruin by some up-and-coming newcomer to their ranks;[36] religious services were conducted on Sundays; singalongs were held almost anytime, and mint juleps acted as humidifiers. Elegant surroundings beget elegant manners; lady passengers were invariably treated to a show of swashbuckling courtesy,[37] and although pasteboard bankruptcies left an occasional suicide to be disposed of, few, if any, shootouts occurred on these river packets. River travel, however, was not without risks. Few river steamers went into graceful retirement, with collisions, conflagrations, boiler explosions, and common or garden sinkings accounting for the majority of them well before they reached the end of their working days. The skeletons of these disaster-prone "queens of the Mississippi" littered the shallows of the major navigable rivers of the West for many decades, and as late as 1971 there was a report of one such wreck being salvaged from the mud. (See FAR WEST.)

R O A C H   Term used to describe an Amerind hairstyle in which the head is shaved until only a crest of hair stretching from the frontal hairline to almost the base of the skull remains. This was the basic roach to which tufts of deer hair, horse hair, etc., were frequently attached. Many of the plains tribes wore artificial roaches, crests of dyed horse hair or other suitable materials being attached to a head harness that fitted over the wearer's

[34] Usually referred to as the "Texas."

[35] A few possessed but three, while an occasional craft, such as the *America*, towered to five decks.

[36] In the early days of the steam packets, professional gamblers were invariably tossed over the side or left stranded on some lonely shore, but when gambling became acceptable —and the packet companies and owner captains realized that during a card-manipulating session the players spent princely sums on liquor and wines ($791.50 is reputed to have been squandered on liquid refreshment during a saloon poker session that took place in 1858)—gamblers were treated with great respect, and many captains wouldn't cast off until they were sure they had one on board.

[37] Unconfirmed reports suggest that this may have led to much inelegant shuttling between cabins during the wee hours.

unshorn locks. Occasionally referred to as a cockscomb hairstyle or headdress.

ROADRUNNER A species of cuckoo that is confined to the Western Hemisphere, spends most of its time on the ground searching for the insects, small mammals, and reptiles, which make up its diet, and is also known as the "paisano," "churella," or "chaparral" bird. Long and strong of limb but curiously weak of wing, roadrunners seldom fly distances of more than a hundred yards. Plumage is mainly cream and black with a trace of blue in the long tail feathers and small patches of red on each side of the head.

ROBERTS, BILL   Alias sometimes used by Jesse Andrews, the "Buckshot" Roberts of the Lincoln County War. (See ANDREWS, JESSE.)

ROCK CREEK STATION   A stage and pony express station located on the Oregon Trail in southeastern Nebraska. Mainly remembered as being the setting for the Hickok-McCanles showdown. (See HICKOK, JAMES BUTLER, and MCCANLES, DAVID C.)

ROCKY MOUNTAIN FUR COMPANY Established in 1822 by General William H. Ashley as a competitive enterprise to the well-established American Fur Company. Unlike the American Fur Company, which possessed trading posts where furs could be collected, Ashley's company employed a large force of trappers who wandered into the wilderness with pack trains and returned to prearranged rendezvous where their pelts could be collected by agents of the company. Owing allegiance to Ashley were such men as Jed Smith, Jim Bridger, the brothers Sublette, and—for a short period—the insufferable Mike Fink. In 1834, after twelve years of competitive trading—the latter years of which had seen frequent armed clashes between Ashley's trappers and those of his rival —the Rocky Mountain Fur Company went out of business. (See AMERICAN FUR COMPANY; CARSON, CHRISTOPHER "KIT"; and FINK, MIKE.)

ROCKY MOUNTAINS
Multiple mountain system of the North American continent that on a relief map appears as crustated scar tissue puckering its way in a southeasterly direction across western Canada,[38] the United States' West and Southwest, and northwestern Mexico. Within the boundaries of the United States there are some twenty ranges that are embraced by the system, a few of the main ones being Wasatch (southeastern Idaho and central Utah), Laramie (southeastern Wyoming), Front (northern Colorado), Park (northwestern and central Colorado), Sangre de Cristo (southern Colorado and northern New Mexico), and San Juan (southwestern Colorado and northern New Mexico). Highest altitudes are attained in Colorado, where more than forty peaks tower to a height of fourteen thousand feet or more. Scenic beauty has led to four major national parks being established in the Rockies: Yellowstone and Grand Teton in Wyoming; Glacier in Montana; and Rocky Mountain in Colorado. When viewed from the Great Plains it is easy to understand how some unknown yet awe-stricken mountain man must have felt when he named this massive barrier of snow-tipped peaks the "Shining Mountains."

[38] If we ignore the Alaskan and Yukon ranges, whose admittance into the cordillera known as the Rocky Mountains is still under dispute.

ROCKY MOUNTAIN SHEEP
Alternative name for the bighorn sheep
of the Rocky Mountain region. (See
BIGHORN SHEEP.)

RODEO An exhibition of horse-riding,
roping, and cattle-working skills, the
Spanish term *rodeo*—which means a
roundup of cattle for branding purposes
—having been adopted into American
English to describe such a display. Organized rodeos, which are reputed to
have originated at Denver, Colorado, in
1876,[39] began to gain popularity toward
the close of the century, and nowadays
around five hundred such events are held
each year. Modern rodeos feature such
unlikely program fillers as brass bands led
by baton-tossing beauties with pulse-
thundering legs, singing cowboys, clowns,
and tight-panted cowgirls who must dread
the possibility of there being such a critter as a kinky Brahma bull. All reputable
rodeos are held under the benevolent
guidance of the Rodeo Association of
America, and annual events of national
fame are held at Cheyenne, Wyoming,
and Pendleton, Oregon.

ROGERS, ROBERT   Leader of a
gang of Cherokee nation robbers and
killers who terrorized this northeastern
area of the Indian-held lands of Oklahoma during the 1890s. Born near Nowata in the Cherokee nation in 1874,
Robert, together with younger brothers
Sam and James[40] and other assorted
deadbeats, began plaguing the region surrounding the Rogers homestead in the
summer of 1894, with horse theft, highway robbery, and store holdups being indulged in during this teething stage of the
game. In the late summer of 1894 young
James was arrested and shipped off to a

reform school, and in April of the following year Sam was picked up after being
wounded during a store robbery.

Robert, upon learning that Sam
wouldn't be around for some years, lay
low for a spell, but in the fall of 1895 he
rode to Adair with four other desperadoes and held up a train of the Missouri,
Kansas, and Texas Railroad. Failure to
blow the express car safe resulted in the
gang getting less than sixty dollars per
man for their efforts, a poor show that
no doubt provoked Robert into shooting
the train fireman dead before they made
their getaway. After this caper, rewards
totaling some three thousand dollars were
offered for the capture of Robert's four
accomplices, whether they be taken into
custody protesting or prone; Robert, for
some unknown reason, being left on the
shelf without a price tag. Robert dwelled
on this; it was kinda frustratin' not to
know one's own worth, but, by golly, it
was good to know what the quartet would
bring. Early in the New Year, skulduggery
worthy of any State Department got under way. Late in January Robert quietly
allowed four deputy U.S. marshals to enter the family homestead, indicated a
room in which his highly priced pals were
killing the Rogers' liquor supplies, then
ducked for cover as the lead began to fly.
When the smoke of battle cleared, three
of the bandits were ready for shipment to
the coroner's office, and the survivor was
en route to jail.

Reward money kept the stool pigeon
on the paths of righteousness for almost
a year, and it was not until December
that Robert found it necessary to form a
new gang. This mob held up a train of
the Missouri-Pacific at a tank stop known
as Seminole Springs on Christmas Eve,
murdered an express car guard, and

[39] State pride will not allow this to go undisputed, other claimants being Santa Fe, New
Mexico (1847); Cheyenne, Wyoming (1872); Winfield, Kansas (1882); and North
Platte, Nebraska (1883), a Buffalo Bill Wild West Show being held in that year.
[40] James was fourteen at this time, Sam about a couple of years older.

escaped with hardly enough folding stuff to buy a round of seasonal cheer. From then on train robbery was abandoned in favor of stock theft. This was profitable for but a short spell. A few weeks after "Happy New Years" had rung across the land, Deputy U. S. Marshal James Mays led a twelve-man posse[41] up to the Rogers home and thundered upon the door. The gunfire that followed kept the Cherokee nation awake for almost twenty-four hours. A posseman named McDaniels was killed during the early hours of the battle; Robert Rogers joined McDaniels at the deafening climax of the battle; and the family homestead was found to be structurally unsound as a result of the battle. The man who caused all this fuss is reputed to have gone down with more than twenty handgun bullets and a couple of charges of buckshot in his body, yet even so, there are no reports of anyone suggesting he should be melted down.

ROMAN NOSE   The white man's name for Sauts,[42] a Northern Cheyenne warrior chief who for the greater part of his lifetime adopted a policy of armed truce toward the troops and migrant trains using the Oregon and Bozeman trails, only becoming lethally hostile after the infamous massacre of Black Kettle's Cheyennes at Sand Creek had displayed to the tribes of the North Plains the depths of the white man's treachery. Roman Nose, 6 feet, 3 inches in his moccasins, wearing a red sash and a plumed war bonnet, which he believed would render him immortal if hands other than his own were never allowed to touch it,

face smeared with charcoal black and circles of yellow ochre[43] and pinto mounted, opened hostilities against the whites on January 7, 1865, a war party under his leadership ambushing a troop of cavalry on the morning of this day and killing eighteen troopers.

Within hours of this attack he had joined forces with Red Cloud's Sioux and was laying siege to Julesburg; three weeks to the day later he and his warriors wiped out a party of men who had been recently mustered from the ranks of Chivington's 3rd Colorado Volunteer Cavalry, a number of the victims being in possession of scalps they had lifted at Sand Creek. On July 27, a strong force of Indians under the leadership of Roman Nose and Crazy Horse attacked an Army stockade at Platte Bridge,[44] and a Lieutenant Caspar Collins and a number of troopers were killed.[45]

Other major engagements in which the hawk-nosed chief took part include an attack on a wagon train a few miles east of Fort Laramie in 1866 (twenty-two men of a cavalry escort of twenty-four troopers under the command of Sergeant James Custard being killed in this skirmish) and the derailment of a Union Pacific freight train and the murder of a number of track layers at Plum Creek, Nebraska,[46] on August 6, 1867. On the night of September 16, 1868, a squaw inadvertently touched the war bonnet of Roman Nose, and in the early evening of the following day he was wounded in the side while leading a charge against a force of civilian volunteers who were making a stand on a sandbar in the Arikaree of northeastern Colorado. The chief

[41] The dozen possemen were all members of the Anti-Horse Thief Association, a nononsense organization whose members probably used rustlers' "guts for garters."
[42] Cheyenne name for a bat (i.e., the flying mammal type).
[43] Representing death and joy, respectively.
[44] Sited where the Oregon Trail crossed the North Platte about forty miles due west of the Bozeman Trail.
[45] The stockade later became Fort Caspar in memory to the dead lieutenant.
[46] The present-day town of Lexington, Nebraska.

was carried from the field, but he died before the day was out. The location of his burial place is unknown.[47] (See BATTLE AT BEECHER'S ISLAND; JULESBURG FIGHT; and SAND CREEK MASSACRE.)

ROME, KANSAS
Probably the shortest-lived town on record. Promoted into existence in 1867 by Buffalo Bill Cody and William Rose, two men who had gone into partnership to purchase land that flanked the proposed right-of-way of the rapidly approaching Kansas Pacific iron in the hope that a fortune would soon be theirs. The ground was staked out into lots, corner lots being retained by the partners, who expected to realize about $250 each for these, and the remaining lots donated to anyone who wished to build. Cody and Rose erected a real-estate office and a saloon and named the place Rome, and one month later an instant settlement of more than two hundred buildings had risen from the plain—a mixed bag of prefabricated dwellings, stores, saloons, dance halls, and a two-storied hotel giving an air of permanence to this new town which was located on Big Creek about a mile northwest of the Army post of Fort Hays. Cody figured he was worth a quarter of a million dollars—on paper.

On returning from a three-day buffalo hunt but a short time after Rome had been established, Buffalo Bill had some difficulty finding the Cody-Rose half-a-million-dollar—on paper—prospect, for only the partners' original buildings and the hotel remained. Seems an advance agent of the Kansas Pacific Railroad, a certain Mr. Webb, had staked out a rail-road division town near the Army post which, being a railroad-backed site, offered better prospects, and the partners' friends, fellow Romans, and countrymen had moved their business premises and dwellings to the brand-new location of Hays City, leaving Cody and Rose with naught but vacant lots and even less on paper. (See CODY, WILLIAM FREDERICK, and HAYS CITY, KANSAS.)

ROSE, DELLA Described by many who met her as a quiet-spoken, slightly bucktoothed brunette of pleasant proportions who was always well groomed and well mannered, and as a "prostitute" by the Detective Division of the St. Louis Police Department who knew her. This Kentucky-born girl who was raised near San Angelo, Texas, became a camp follower of the loosely knit mob known as the "Hole in the Wall gang" in the fall of 1889, probably having been introduced into the gang by Edward Bullin,[48] a small-time owlhoot whom she had met earlier that year while working as a dance-hall girl in Wyoming. Sometime after her arrival in the "Hole," Della became a free roamer, changing straw-filled pads by becoming the common-law wife of a somewhat seedy-looking bank robber named Bill Carver, and from around 1896 this couple rode with Cassidy's Wild Bunch, Della—with hair piled under her stetson—having the distinction of being the only girl known to have ridden[49] with this gang until the magnificent Etta Place began eating Butch and Sundance's dust in 1899.

On April 2, 1901, Della became a common-law widow when Carver got

---

[47] Shortly after the battle a party of white men found the body of a tall Cheyenne male in an abandoned tepee and assumed that this was the corpse of Roman Nose; the Cheyenne, however, claimed this was the remains of another chief and that Roman Nose had been interred in secret at a location they would not divulge.

[48] Sometimes given as "Bullion." Ed and Della were most likely legally married on their arrival in the "Hole."

[49] Although numerous other girls frequented Hole in the Wall, Robbers Roost, etc., they did not take part in outlaw raids.

himself shot dead at Sonora, Texas, but her hazel eyes showed little grief, for a certain Ben Kilpatrick, who had been a childhood acquaintance of Della's, was now riding with the "Bunch," and within a matter of weeks of Bill's explosive exit, Della and Ben were chatting over old times in the snuggled warmth of a shared bedroll. In October 1901 this pair of torrid lovers visited St. Louis, Missouri, on a post-robbery spending spree, leaving a trail of easily traced currency that led to their arrests on November 5 and to the twenty-eight-year-old Della being sentenced to five years behind bars eight days later. After being released from prison Della may have readopted one of her many oft-used aliases,[50] for nothing more is known of her. One can only hope that the girl spent the rest of her days thumping a tambourine instead of a mattress. (See CARVER, WILLIAM; HOLE IN THE WALL GANG; KILPATRICK, BEN; PLACE, ETTA; and WILD BUNCH.)

ROSE OF CIMARRON A mysterious lass who is reputed to have lent a touch of glamor to the rough lives of the Doolin gang. Rose is alleged to have lost her innocence to "Bitter Creek" George Newcomb, and on September 1, 1893, during what was later to be referred to as the "Battle of Ingalls," Rose is reputed to have gone to his aid when he was brought down by a leg wound, dashing to his side with a bandolier of cartridges and shielding his rotten hide with her own sweet self when a bunch of unromantic United States deputy marshals were trying to make him dead.

So what's the mystery? Well, like some folk who were present on that gory day say "Rose of Cimarron" did as hitherto reported, while others who were ducking lead say that no female made any such appearance during the fracas—contradictory statements that give an "Angel of Mons" quality to the incident that no amount of fact-finding has yet dispelled. Most stories agree that Rose originally met up with George at a dance, period. After this the keyboards run wild: Rose was fourteen, fifteen, sixteen, or seventeen when she made her life-saving dash; her real name was Rosa Dunn, or Rose O'Leary;[51] and last, she was either a hard-bitten gun-moll, or an unchewed angel of mercy. (See DUNN, ROSA; INGALLS, OKLAHOMA; NEWCOMB, GEORGE; and O'LEARY, ROSE.)

ROUGH AND READY Located near Grass Valley in California's Mother Lode Country. Founded early in 1849 as a clapboard mining camp of rich potential,[52] Rough and Ready is mainly of interest because of the rebellious attitude adopted by its citizens when nearby Nevada City was granted ratification as county seat of Nevada County, a position of kudos that Rough and Ready had coveted, although the town was not one year old when this momentous happening occurred. The vigorous display of displeasure on the part of the majority of the Rough and Readyites—who claimed secession from the Union—drove all federal employees from the town in fear of grievous bodily harm; the post office was wrecked, all mail contained therein de-

---

[50] Known ones being Laura Bullin or Bullion, Laura Casey, and Clara Hays.

[51] Rosa Dunn being given an Oklahoma birthplace, while the O'Leary contender is reputed to have had her origins in Georgia. A third "suspect" who may have been given the name "Rose" (no other name) to prevent the repetitive "Hey, you!" from marring the flow of the story is alleged to have hailed from Texas.

[52] The potential wasn't overestimated; on one occasion digging a grave showed so much "color" that the "dear departed" was completely forgotten as all the mourners got as busy as ants staking out claims 'midst the graves and disinterring like ghouls.

stroyed, and the fittings and furnishings of all governmental offices burned.

After seventy-two hours of rioting, the saloons ran dry and all was forgotten and forgiven—by all but the United States Post Office Department, the latter evidently being of the opinion that the sins of the community were so immense that the progeny of these people should remain without benefit of a postal service for as long as stamps are licked. In 1954, however, the Post Office Department relented, and in that year a post office was re-established in the town, so that nowadays wish-you-were-here stuff, junk ad mail, and other metered rubbish flow into Rough and Ready's garbage cans as the hallmark of a Postal Service-approved community.

ROUNDUP   A gathering together of cattle, horses, etc., especially the semiannual cattle drives that are organized for branding or cutting-out purposes. The personnel engaged in an average cattle roundup consists of a wagon boss who is in charge of the operation; ten to fifteen cowhands; a horse wrangler who is in charge of the remuda; and a cook whose duties are manifold, for in addition to whipping up hot meals for the outfit, he has to find campsites—midday and evening—drive the chuck wagon, and take care of the men's bedrolls and equipment. (See CHUCK WAGON; REMUDA; and TRAIL DRIVE.)

RUDABAUGH, DAVE   Born in Missouri in 1841 and raised in Kansas from diaper days onward, Dave began hitting the outlaw trail around 1859, the small gang he is reputed to have led specializing in stock theft and highway robbery until 1870, after which they appear to have confined their attention to depleting the coffers of the Atchison, Topeka, and Santa Fe Railroad, robbing its pay trains and construction camps as its track-laying crews pushed their way through Kansas during the 1870s. In November 1877, after Rudabaugh and company had relieved a pay train of its wealth and their dust had hardly dispersed, the long-suffering railroad hired Wyatt Earp to track down the gang, but after a round trip that had taken him as far south as Fort Griffin in Texas, Earp was still following their pony tracks when they escaped with ten thousand dollars after robbing a pay train near Kinsley, Kansas. The gang had little time to spend any of this loot, for on January 28, 1878—just twenty-four hours after the robbery—Rudabaugh and a number of his men were taken into custody by a posse led by Sheriff Bat Masterson of Ford County.

While in jail Rudabaugh developed a no doubt latent mean streak, and when the gang's members were brought to trial, his turning state's evidence led to his being released as cell doors were opening to receive his onetime confederates. Shortly after becoming a free man, Rudabaugh turned up in Las Vegas, New Mexico, and for the next twelve months or more he was a member of a loosely knit mob of refugees from Kansas who were known as the "Dodge City gang." This membership led to Dave participating in the murder of jail turnkey Antonio Lino Valdez on April 2, 1880, when he and a fellow mobster were attempting to rescue a certain John J. Webb from the local calaboose and a possible appointment with the public hangman. This was a thoroughly frustrating excursion, for Webb—who was expecting a pardon or at least a commutation of sentence from the territorial governor—had no desire to be rescued, and Rudabaugh, no doubt cursing Webb, had to flee Las Vegas a few hoofbeats ahead of the local law.

Shortly afterward a gang of rustlers led by Rudabaugh were putting corrugations into the brows of New Mexico ranchers, and after Dave had joined his force with that of Billy the Kid's in the summer of 1880, the composite gang was suspected of nearly all the stock thefts occurring in the territory. On December 27, 1880, Stinking Springs became a nostril-wrinkling name to Rudabaugh and the Kid when they were arrested thereabouts by a party of lawmen led by Sheriff Pat Garrett, and in February of the following year Rudabaugh was given two consecutive terms of twenty years' imprisonment for robbing the United States mails while in transit by coach and train. With further charges relating to the murder of jailer Valdez still hanging over his head, Rudabaugh was lodged in the San Miguel County jail to await a further appearance in court, which was to result in his being sentenced to death on April 19, 1881. Appeals followed, but Dave had no intention of waiting around to find out whether his forty years were going to be reduced or encapsulated into a two-second drop, and after weeks of tunneling beneath the walls of the jail, he finally went absent on December 3, 1881.

A week after his escape, the fugitive dusted into the Mexican province of Chihuahua, and for the next five years Señor Rudabaugh led various gangs of displaced gringos and misfit greasers in a series of robberies and holdups that terrorized the region. By 1886 the outraged Mexicans had had a sufficiency of *bandido* Dave, and on February 19 of that year the villagers of Parral sewed up his career with a barrage of lead that left him quite dead. Events that followed give an insight into how fun-loving but impoverished peasants seize any opportunity to let a little free sunshine into their lives. Rudabaugh's head was lopped off, stuck on top of a pole, and an impromptu fiesta was held around this grisly totem in the village plaza.[53] (See EARP, WYATT BERRY STAPP; HOLLIDAY, JOHN HENRY; MASTERSON, WILLIAM BARCLAY; and McCARTY, HENRY.)

RULE, ANNIE Better known under her maiden name of Annie Ellis. (See ELLIS, ANNIE.)

RUNNING IRON A simple type of branding iron much favored by rustlers. (See BRANDING IRON.)

RUSSELL, MAJORS, AND WADDELL A famous staging and freighting company that began operating in 1854, William Hepburn Russell, Alexander Majors, and W. B. Waddell being the partners involved. (See HOLLADAY, BEN; MAJORS, ALEXANDER; and PONY EXPRESS.)

RUSSIAN BILL An ex-lieutenant of Russia's Imperial White Hussars who ended his days in New Mexico. (See TATTENBAUM, WILLIAM.)

RUSTLER A person engaged in the stealing of cattle, especially when the theft is accompanied by brand changing. Regarded in the early days as an almost legitimate method of building up a herd, rustling only became a serious offense when the big cattlemen—many of whom had built up their herds without troubling

[53] As many of the law-abiding citizenry appear to dislike having outlaws disposed of in the manner described—or in any other manner, for that matter—a pleasant "crime sure 'nough pays" ending has worked its wishful-thinking way into the record wherein, instead of a decapitated demise, Rudabaugh supposedly returned to the States in one piece, and after spending more than three decades as an honest rancher died from natural causes in Oregon at the age of seventy-seven.

to invest in a bull—decided that it was a threat to their existence. The stealing of horses was usually classed as "horse theft" rather than "rustling" and was, in most instances, regarded as a far more serious crime than the rustling of cattle. (See BRANDING IRON; JOHNSON COUNTY WAR; MAVERICK; and MAVERICKING.)

RYAN, WILLIAM   A small-time member of the James gang whose predilection for fiery waters led to his undoing. Ryan is known to have taken part in at least two of the escapades masterminded by Jesse: riding with the gang when they staged a train robbery at Glendale, Missouri, on October 7, 1879, and being identified as the bottle-waving and inebriated partner of Jesse when the latter held up a stagecoach traveling between Mammoth Cave and Cave City in Kentucky on September 3, 1880. In

March 1881 a drunken fracas in a saloon at White's Creek, Tennessee, led to a man who had given his name as "Tom Hill" being handed over to the Nashville police, and shortly afterward it was established that "Tom" was none other than William Ryan, a gentleman who was wanted in connection with the Glendale job of 1879. Tried and convicted at Independence, Missouri, in the fall of 1881, Ryan was sentenced to twenty-five years in the state penitentiary on October 15 of that year, but after serving less than a third of this term, he was released on April 15, 1889, on the grounds that he was dying of tuberculosis. Whether he was afflicted with this disease is debatable, for shortly after his release he went on a drunken riding spree during which he fell from his mount and cracked his head against a rock with fatal consequences. (See JAMES GANG.)

THOMAS E. MAILS

SACAGAWEA The young Shoshone girl who acted as guide and tribal intermediary for the Lewis and Clark Expedition. Born in the Lemhi Valley in 1787,[1] this Indian maiden was captured by the Hidatsa[2] while still in her early teens and taken to live within their stockaded villages along the upper Missouri, and it was here that she became the squaw of a French-Canadian fur trapper named Touissant Charbonneau sometime during the winter of 1803–4, the roughneck Charbonneau having either purchased her from the Hidatsa for trade goods or won her during a tribal gambling session.

In the fall of 1804 the Lewis and Clark Expedition located their winter camp in the vicinity of the Hidatsa and Mandan villages, and during the winter months Charbonneau and a fellow *voyageur* named René Jessaume were consulted by Meriwether Lewis regarding the best routes for further westward travel. During the course of these conversations it became apparent to Lewis that Charbonneau's squaw, the Snake woman named Sacagawea,[3] would be a greater asset to the expedition than either of the trappers, and shortly after she had given birth to a male child on February 11, 1805—whom Charbonneau christened Jean Baptiste—Sacagawea was per-

[1] An approximate date only.
[2] A minority group favors the Gro Ventres as being the kidnapers of Sacagawea, but the Hidatsa seem the most likely.
[3] There are numerous ways of spelling this Hidatsa word—meaning "Bird Woman"—but the pronunciation remains "Sa-KAKA-WE-a."

suaded to guide the expedition West on the understanding that she would not be parted from her child and her "husband" could accompany the party as a salaried interpreter.

The expedition pushed West on April 17, and it was not until sixteen months later, and after covering almost four thousand miles of virtually unexplored territory, that Sacagawea, Charbonneau, and Jean Baptiste were returned to their village home, on August 16, 1806. After this period the movements of Charbonneau and his squaw are sketchy, although the trapper is known to have traveled the Southwest on fur-hunting expeditions, and it is almost certain that Sacagawea would have accompanied him, and they were reunited with William Clark on the many occasions they visited St. Louis, Missouri. Sometime during 1812 Charbonneau traveled up the Missouri with Sacagawea and settled at one of Manuel Lisa's fur-trading posts located in what is now the north of South Dakota, and in the fall of that year Sacagawea gave birth to a girl whom they named Lisette. After this birth the Shoshone girl's health deteriorated, and she died at the post on December 20, 1812, "aged about twenty-five years."[4] (See BAPTISTE, JEAN; CHARBONNEAU, TOUISSANT; LEWIS AND CLARK EXPEDITION; and POMPEY'S PILLAR.)

SACRED BUNDLE   Alternative name for a medicine bundle. (See MEDICINE BUNDLE.)

SADDLE TREE   The framework of a saddle, originally made of wood, although modern trees may be manufactured from metal, Fiberglas, etc.

SAGEBRUSH   A type of vegetation that is common throughout the West, being especially plentiful in the arid regions. This silvery-gray shrub derives its name from the fact that it has a sagelike smell, although it is unrelated to the sage family.

SAGE HEN   Popular name for the sage grouse. This bird, the largest of the American grouse, has extremely long tail feathers, which give it an overall length of about 28 inches. Common in the dry sagebrush regions of the West. Sometimes called "Cock of the Plains." Should not be confused with the prairie chicken. (See PRAIRIE CHICKEN.)

SALMON RIVER   A river that is confined within the boundaries of Idaho. From its source in the Sawtooth Mountains in the southern half of the state the Salmon flows in a generally northerly direction until some twenty miles north of Salmon; here it swings abruptly west and sidewinds its way across the state to join the Snake River in the far west of Idaho. The fact that the Salmon has an extremely rapid current and is studded with rock-strewn rapids has led to it being dubbed the "River of No Return," for it is impossible to work any type of craft upstream. This turbulent stream has an overall length of 425 miles, and in some places its waters roar between canyon walls that tower to a height greater than those of the Grand Canyon of the Colorado.

SALOONS   Of the four basic places of entertainment that catered to the simple desires of the early Westerner, the saloon was probably the most popular, far more

---

[4] Other reports state that Sacagawea died on the Shoshone Reservation in Wyoming's Wind River Valley on April 9, 1884, at the age of one hundred years. Greater credulity should, however, be given to the postmortem documentation recorded by the clerk at Fort Manuel Lisa, an efficient German named Luttig.

time being spent in saloons than any of the competitive magnets for the somewhat obvious reasons that elbow bending requires far less skill than gambling, and marathon bouts may be indulged in without expending anything like the amount of energy that could be expected to be dissipated in but a short time within the confines of either dance hall or brothel. If we ignore the *cantinas* of the Southwest, which were dispensing strong liquids to siesta-loving peasants and peons well before the gringos started shooting streams of tobacco juice into spittoons, the Western saloon may be said to have had its origins in the log cabin grog shop of the pioneers and the tent saloons of the blossoming mining camps and end-of-track "towns."

If a saloon prospered in a newly established community that showed little signs of disestablishing itself overnight, the owner would usually improve his premises in an attempt to keep up with, or surpass, the "dump across the street"; but even so, the latent dread that his customers may relocate someplace else after hearing of a "strike" or receiving news that the railroad was going to bypass the town usually prevented him from investing in anything more elaborate than a prefabricated false front, which could easily be freighted elsewhere should his nightmares ever be realized. From these modest beginnings evolved the magnificent booze emporiums that reached their ultimate in opulence in the well-established cattle and mining centers. These palaces possessed massive mahogany bars, cut-glass chandeliers, an abundance of rococo work and plate-glass mirrors, a piano of modest or grand dimensions, and—frequently—in a place of honor behind the bar, a gigantic gilt-framed nude whom Rubens wouldn't have minded using as a model.[5]

As a general rule, and especially in those communities where members of the fair sex were beginning to make themselves heard, the railroad tracks separated the "respectable" saloons from those that lured customers with such disgusting gimmicks as pink-tighted nightingales singing tear-jerking ditties; low-cleavaged lovelies who scorned formal introductions and blew off the froth with long-practiced ease; and discreet, curtain-draped alcoves where one might retire to to count one's small change. Whether located on the quick or the dead side of the tracks, most saloons featured gambling tables, a generous number of spittoons, and sawdust-covered floors; many had one section of their floor space taken up with a tonsorial parlor, and an equal number were but part of a complex consisting of saloon, dance hall, and gambling room.

The fact that at any given time the average saloon could be expected to house a fair quota of pistol-packing *hombres* who had been long without women and a not-so-fair quota of provocative females, a few highly sensitive gamblers and the odd gent who crackled with hidden aces, a number of men who were fair-yoked with shoulder chips, and perhaps a twitchy-faced stranger who possessed a surfeit of armament and was obviously suffering from a plethora of undiagnosed neuroses, led to the saloons of the West erupting into violence at the

[5] At least one enterprising establishment had a mechanical bellows fixed behind such a painting, which caused the nude's abdomen to rise and fall most realistically. Around 1886 these stimulating masterpieces—whether breathing or otherwise—began to be replaced by prints of Cassily Adams' atrocious "Custer's Last Fight," which were being freely distributed by the Anheuser-Busch Brewery Company, a tragic aftermath of the Little Big Horn affair that no doubt overshadowed the original disaster in the minds of those who had developed a taste for the Anheuser-Busch suds.

drop of a garter or less. The affair in Tuttle's Saloon at Newton, Kansas, may rank as the greatest stand-up shootout on record. In the fall of 1872 a cowhand named Hugh Anderson, who harbored a grudge against the marshal of Newton, opened up with two .45s when he spotted Town Marshal McCluskie downing suds with friends, and when the fusillade ended, the marshal and three of his buddies lay dead, and five other Tuttle tipplers were seriously wounded. Before the smoke had cleared, Anderson had wandered off to the outhouse or someplace; but wherever, he was never arrested.

Names given to saloons were frequently grandiose, occasionally humorous, and sometimes suggestive of violence, Crystal Palace, Bella Union, Eldorado, Eyeopener, Road to Ruin, and Bucket of Blood being but a random selection of the type of nomenclature favored. Possibly the most ingeniously named saloon was located at Miles City, Montana. This was the First Chance–Last Chance, "First Chance" being painted on that side of the building that faced the wilderness, while "Last Chance" was on that side that faced the town center. (See HONKY-TONKS; NATION, CARRY A.; and WHISKEY.)

SALT LAKE CITY State capital of Utah. Located in the north of the state some twelve miles southeast of the Great Salt Lake, the city was founded in 1847 by Brigham Young, who had led his Mormon followers West to escape eastern persecution. Salt Lake City is the headquarters of the Church of Jesus Christ of Latter-day Saints, and more than half of its inhabitants are followers of the Book of Mormon. The sect's Tabernacle in Temple Square may be visited by nonsectarians, and the Seagull Monument—commemorating the birds' victory over a cloud of locusts—may be viewed by all, but the Temple of the sect may only be entered by members of the faith. (See GREAT SALT LAKE; LOCUST; MORMONS; and YOUNG, BRIGHAM.)

SAMPLE, COMER Member of the John Heath gang of outlaws, who were responsible for the Bisbee Massacre of December 8, 1883. After the robbery and killings at Bisbee, this red-headed lad fled North with fellow gunnie James "Tex" Howard, not stopping until they reached Clifton, some 120 miles to the north of the scene of the slaughter. Here they attracted attention to themselves by heavy spending and the hijacking of other men's girls, and early in January both men were arrested after an exchange of lead with a posse that left "Red" Sample seriously wounded. Sample recovered to stand trial and was sentenced to death, the hanging being carried out at Tombstone, Arizona Territory, on March 8, 1884. (See HEATH, JOHN, and HOWARD, JAMES.)

SAMUELS, ZERELDA M. The much-married gal from Kentucky who was the mother of the notorious James brothers. (See COLE, ZERELDA M.)

SAN ANTONIO, TEXAS Located on the headwaters of the San Antonio River in Bexar County, south-central Texas. One of the oldest settlements in the West, San Antonio was established by the Spaniards in 1718, having the Mission of San Antonio de Valero as its nucleus. In 1835 American settlers whom the Mexican Government had allowed to settle in Texas revolted against Mexican rule and captured San Antonio, but the following year General Santa Anna won back the city with his victory at the Alamo. Mexican repossession was short lived, for some six weeks after Santa Anna's success he was routed by a settlers' army at the Battle of San Jacinto. After this battle San Antonio became a city of the independent nation of Texas and took on the sobriquet of "The cradle of Texas liberty." San Antonio has been an important trading center from the early days and a cattle and mail-route center from the mid-1850s, a prosperity that was further reaffirmed with the arrival of the railroad in 1877. The city, which was, and is, the center of the Texas cattle industry, is sometimes referred to as "The cowboy capital." San Antonio's present (1970) population is around the 700,-000 mark and about 40 per cent of its inhabitants are of Mexican ancestry. (See ALAMO, THE; BATTLE OF SAN JACINTO; and TEXAS.)

SAN ANTONIO AND SAN DIEGO MAIL Better known under its unofficial title of "Jackass Mail." (See JACKASS MAIL.)

SAN CARLOS APACHE Apaches who were settled on the San Carlos Reservation[6] were given this name whatever their tribal affiliations; consequently members of any band who "jumped" the reservation were usually referred to as "San Carlos Apaches."

SAND CREEK MASSACRE During the closing days of November 1864, four hundred troopers of the 3rd Colorado Volunteer Cavalry,[7] supported by six hundred dismounted troopers and four cannon, and led by Colonel John M. Chivington, left Fort Lyon in Colorado Territory and plowed their way north to attack the village of Black Kettle's Cheyenne on Sand Creek.[8] In the freezing dawn of Tuesday, November 29, the Indians sighted the troops moving toward their village, but although dismayed at seeing such a large force of pony soldiers and walk-a-heaps they made no hostile move, Black Kettle merely going to the trouble of displaying the flag of the Union outside his tepee and reassuring his people that they had nothing to fear from the soldiers while the Cheyenne were displaying the white man's colors.[9]

Despite this action, cannon roared and tepees disintegrated, and soon the soldiers were within handgun range. John Simpson Smith, a "squaw man" living with the Cheyenne, slogged through drifts toward the troops in an attempt to halt the charge, but he died under a barrage of lead and the attackers overran the encampment. With snow muffling their hoofbeats and hindering their movements, the blue-uniformed host swept through the village like some phantom army enacting out a macabre ballet whose musical score was the crackle of small-arms fire and the screams of the dying. At close quarters sabers flashed before being dulled with carmine, women and children run through, bodies decapitated, and a head transfixed on the tip of a blade; smoldering tepees melted the snow, and rape and mutilation froze the brain as more than three hundred of Black Kettle's Cheyenne were

[6] Established in 1873 in the vicinity of the San Carlos River in the southeast of Arizona Territory.

[7] Known as "hundred dazers," a hundred days being their period of enlistment. This regiment of semidisciplined rabble, which had been recruited from the Colorado mining camps, are reputed to have been only too eager to instigate an Indian uprising in the hope that putting down such a "rebellion" would prevent them being shipped to the battlegrounds of the East, where they had a far better likelihood of being killed.

[8] Sand Creek was about thirty miles north of Fort Lyon. The site of the massacre may be located in Kiowa County, Colorado.

[9] Black Kettle and his friendlies had been given this flag by Major E. W. Wyncoop, who was commandant at Fort Lyon, the latter having assured the chief that it would be honored and that no harm would befall them from the soldiers while they were sheltering beneath it.

hacked, impaled, and shot to death. A
quarter of those who died were braves;
the remainder were women, children,
and old men. The infamous words of
Chivington, "We should kill and scalp
them all, big or little. Mites make lice,"
had been carried out to the letter when
the troops rode away with the frozen
scalps of the dead dangling from their
belts. The sound of cavalry trumpets
must have lost their undertones of hero-
ism from that day forward. (See BLACK
KETTLE; CHIVINGTON, JOHN M.; and
ROMAN NOSE.)

SANS ARCS SIOUX One of the
seven divisions of the Teton Sioux. Sans
Arcs literally translated meaning "No
Bows," or, in the more liberal translation
of the Sioux, "Those Who Have No
Bows People." (See SIOUX INDIANS.)

SANTA ANA A hot, dry wind that is
experienced in Southern California during the spring and summer months. An
unpleasant wind, for as it flows into California from the northeast it is laden
with dust which it has swept up during
its passage across the Mojave Desert.

SANTA ANNA The Mexican general
who led the attack on the Alamo. Santa
Anna being an abbreviation of Antonio
Lopez de Santa Anna. (See ALAMO, THE,
and BATTLE OF SAN JACINTO.)

SANTA CATRUDOS RANCH
The Texas spread of Colonel Richard
King; better known as the King Ranch.
(See KING RANCH.)

SANTA FE, NEW MEXICO
The state capital of New Mexico. Lo
cated in the north-central area of th
state, Santa Fe is one of the oldest citie
in the United States, having been estab
lished by the Spaniards in 1609 as L
Villa de la Santa Fe de San Francisco
From its early beginnings the settlemer
was the northern terminal of the Jornad
del Muerto; this "Journey of Death" be
ing the last ninety miles of the Camin
Real[10] which linked Santa Fe wit
Mexico City, some eighteen hundred tra
miles to the south. From 1821 until 188
the city was the western terminal of th
Santa Fe Trail and the eastern termina
of the Old Spanish Trail;[11] thus, wit
two-way traffic flowing in and out of th
city along trails spoking into the North
east, the West, and the South, Santa F
had the envious position of being th
trading hub of the Southwest. This cit
on the Santa Fe River, which still re
tains much of its Spanish origins an
culture, now classes tourism as its majo
industry. (See JORNADO DEL MUERT
and SANTA FE TRAIL.)

SANTA FE RAILROAD Abbreviate
version of the jaw-bustin' Atchiso
Topeka and Santa Fe Railroad. (Se
ATCHISON, TOPEKA AND SANTA FE RAI
ROAD.)

SANTA FE TRAIL The 780-mile
long wagon road that linked Independ
ence, Missouri, with Santa Fe, New
Mexico; two-way traffic flowing alon
this major trade route from 1821 unt
the 1880s. After leaving Missouri th
trail traveled west, passing through Coun

---

[10] The "King's Highway" or "Royal Road" linking Mexico City with the northern prov
inces. Despite its rather grand title, the Camino Real was little more than an ill-marked trai
[11] A trail that wound its way northwest from Santa Fe to pass through what is now south
western Colorado and eastern Utah, reached its most northerly limit in central Utah, then
blazed its way in a southwesterly direction to cross present-day Nevada and California's Mo
jave Desert to reach its terminal point at Los Angeles.

cil Grove and continuing in a generally westerly direction until meeting up with the Arkansas River near what is now Barton, Kansas. From here the trail kept to the north bank of the Arkansas until reaching Bent's Fort,[12] where it forded the river to follow a southerly direction, entering New Mexico via the Raton Pass and probing as far south as San Miguel before horseshoeing northwest for the last 40 miles of its journey to Santa Fe. The Cimarron cutoff of the Santa Fe Trail permitted travelers to bypass the Bent's Fort–Raton Pass section of the main trail if they so wished, the cutoff leaving the Santa Fe Trail proper at a point some 40 miles west of Dodge City[13] to arrow southwest in an almost direct line to rejoin the main trail about 50 miles northeast of San Miguel. (See SANTA FE, NEW MEXICO.)

SATANTA   The white man's name for Set-Tain-te,[14] a Kiowa chief who was frequently to be seen wearing the plumed brass helmet and epauleted jacket of a U. S. Army general's dress uniform, had a self-professed liking for activities in which scalping knives and breechloaders played major roles, and was adept in the art of kidnaping for ransom. During the 1860s and early 1870s Satanta's war parties were fully employed in hair-lifting and horse-stealing operations that were mainly confined to northwestern Texas, Satanta and his braves being in evidence at the Battle at Adobe Walls during this period. That Satanta was not without a sense of humor may be evidenced from the following: After stealing most of the regimental horse herd from Fort Larned, Kansas, he sent a message to the commanding officer requesting

that better mounts be made available when he paid a return visit, as the stolen horses were of inferior stamina.

All this hell-raising didn't pass unnoticed. Colonel G. A. Custer held him under tent arrest from October 1868 until the following February, and in July 1871 Satanta was sentenced to death for the murder of seven teamsters after a trial held at Jacksboro, Texas. This sentence was later commuted to life imprisonment, but after serving little more than two years behind bars, Satanta was released as a parolee in December 1871. Eleven months later—during which period he had joined forces with Quanah Parker and his Comanches to do his damnedest at Adobe Walls—Satanta was arrested for the murder of a white settler, and shortly afterward he was returned to the Texas State Penitentiary at Huntsville to complete his earlier sentence.[15] On October 11, 1878, after hearing that there was little hope of his ever being released, Satanta committed suicide by throwing himself from a second-story balcony. The chief was seventy years old at the time of his death, and he left four children in his wake—two sons and two daughters. The younger son, Mark Auchia, was later to see service as a trooper in the 7th Cavalry! His pa would've wept. (See BATTLE AT ADOBE WALLS and QUANAH PARKER.)

SAVAGE, JAMES
Frequently classed as a mountain man, although Jim, who was born in Indiana in 1823, didn't push West until 1846, when the genuine articles were already disappearing from the scene. Savage was a newly married man when he migrated

[12] Located in southeastern Colorado where the Purgatoire River joins the Arkansas.
[13] Or the "future site" of Dodge, if the route was traversed before 1872.
[14] Meaning "White Bear."
[15] This was one crime for which Satanta wasn't guilty, it later being learned that a Kiowa named Lone Wolf had done the deed.

from his home state, but his wife died during the last lap of their journey to the golden promise of California and was left in an unmarked grave at Truckee Meadows.[16] The Mexican War of 1846–48 was in progress when the widower arrived in California. He enlisted in the California Battalion, but he had seen less than a year in uniform when he was mustered out of service in the spring of 1847. Shortly after his becoming a civilian, Savage drifted into the San Joaquin Valley, and here he managed to accumulate enough gold dust to establish a trading post on the south fork of the Merced River and enough stamina to keep five Indian "brides" from becoming soured with frustration.

In the early days of 1850 the steady influx of mining types resulted in the "Digger" Indians of the area taking up arms, and by the late spring, mounting Indian problems of a nondomestic nature had forced Savage to relocate his post some twenty miles to the southwest. This move did naught but increase the belligerence of the war parties, and in the fall of 1850 the state governor appointed Savage commander-in-chief of a force of two hundred militiamen to deal with the problem. That Major Savage fulfilled his assignment admirably is evident from the facts that by the summer of 1851 all the renegades had been swept onto reservations and the militiamen were being mustered out of service. After this Savage returned to his trading post, and it appeared he would be left to prosper and procreate in peace, but in the late summer of 1852 a feud developed between Jim and a certain Judge Walter H. Harvey,[17] and in August of that same year His Honor shot Savage dead as the climax to a clash of

personalities that occurred in a Poole's Ferry tent saloon.

SCALPING   The art of lifting a person's cranium hair, whether the victim be dead or otherwise during the operation. Writers who appear to resent the idea that the Amerind brand of villainy may have been superior to anything the whites had to offer have been guilty of spreading the story that the Indians learned the art of scalping from the invaders from the Old World. This, of course, is incorrect, for all the evidence suggests that the "noble savage" knew all about hair lifting well before the arrival of the Europeans, although it must be admitted—if only in deference to the theory of racial supremacy—that the latter introduced the over-scalp philosophy which became rampant in the Southwest. Most tribes practiced scalping, although the area of scalp taken varied considerably from tribe to tribe, some merely removing a disk of hair-bearing skin of about 3 inches in diameter, while others took scalps of side-plate proportions, and an occasional tribe—notably among the Pueblos of the Southwest—left their victims' heads both nude and earless.

To lift a scalp one made a deft cut around the area coveted, then grabbed a handful of hair to assist in dragging the bloody mess from its owner. Scalps were usually dried out on scalp sticks and the skin side painted, after which the majority wound up as tepee decor or as embellishments to war bonnets and clothing. Contrary to popular belief, scalping did not necessarily prove fatal for the victim, for there are many cases on record of both males and females having survived the ordeal. Dried-out scalps lacking hair are not unknown, and a number of these

[16] On the California-Nevada line near the present-day town of Reno, Nevada.
[17] It would appear that Savage wanted the Indians to be left in peace on their allotted ground, while the judge, who coveted said ground, wanted them moved.

are still extant. These unimpressive-looking exhibits have puzzled learned men for years, the query being how the Indians removed the hair from these scalps without injuring the surrounding tissue, the idea that some kinky brave may have concentrated on removing his trophies from "baldies" evidently having been abandoned as too simple an explanation. (See GLANTON, JOHN J.; HOBBS, JAMES; KIRKER, JAMES; and MANGAS COLORADO.)

SCARBOROUGH, GEORGE Frontier peace officer who is best remembered as the man who killed the man who killed Wes Hardin. Born in Louisiana in 1858, George moved West with his parents while still a young boy and was raised to early manhood on the family's relocated homestead in McLennan County, Texas. While still in his teens, George left home and moved West along the San Saba River to take up employment as a cowhand in McCulloch County. At the age of twenty-seven, Scarborough moved North and settled in Jones County, where, over the next few years, he was elected sheriff for a twelve-month tour of duty on several occasions. In 1894 he accepted an appointment as a deputy U.S. marshal, a federal lawman job that necessitated him headquartering at El Paso and led to his becoming acquainted with John Selman (Hardin's nemesis), an aging pistoleer whom George shot to death in the early hours of Easter Sunday 1896. Some two years after Old John had been lowered beneath the sod, Scarborough took up employment as a cattle detective with the New Mexico Cattle Raisers' Association, a harassing of rustlers that was to lead to his death on April 6, 1900, from the effects

of a wound sustained during a long-drawn-out gunfight with four suspected rustlers[18] near San Simon, New Mexico. George Scarborough left a widow and six children. (See SELMAN, JOHN.)

SCARFACE CHARLIE A Modoc subchief who took part in the Modoc War of 1872. A photograph of Charlie depicts a split-visage personality, knife-work having sculpted the left (when viewing) side of Charlie's face into a sneering monstrosity, while the other half depicts a pleasant-faced individual displaying a Mona Lisa-type smile. (See MODOC WAR.)

SCHIEFFELIN, EDWARD L. The prospector whose name will be forever married to that of Tombstone, Arizona. Ed, who was born at Pittsburgh, Pennsylvania, in 1848, started his lifelong search for precious ores in southern Oregon sometime during the late 1860s, his parents having moved West and established themselves as farmers in the territory when Ed was but a small child. For almost twenty years he panned and picked his way through Colorado, Idaho, New Mexico, Arizona, and California before he made a succession of strikes that would bring him overnight fame and fortune. Sometime during the winter of 1876–77 Schieffelin arrived at San Bernardino, California, and in the spring of 1877 he attached himself to a regiment of cavalry that was leaving San Bernardino to take up duties at Fort Huachuca in southeastern Arizona—traveling with a cavalry escort being the safest method of traversing the Apache country of the Southwest during this period.

In the summer of 1877, accompanied by a seven-dollar burro named "Cactus,"

---

[18] Tentatively identified as Thomas Capehart, Max Stein, Frank Laughlin, and William Carver. If this identification be correct, the last-named of this quartet was a member of the Wild Bunch who was killed at Sonora, Texas, shortly after the San Simon fracas. (See CARVER, WILLIAM.)

Ed left the safety of the fort and worked his way northeast toward the Dragoon Mountains, having been duly warned by the post commander before leaving that he would find nothing in that Apache-infested wilderness but his tombstone. Man and burro crawled across the arid land; dehydrating heat and reflected glare, giant saguaro and prickly pear, smoke signaling upward from beyond a ridge, a couple of skeletons transfixed by Mescalero shafts, and then—in the last days of August—a "strike" that Schieffelin named "Tombstone." Other strikes followed: the "Graveyard," the "Lucky Cuss," and the "Tough Nut," whose silver ore ran twenty-two hundred dollars to the ton. Schieffelin became rich beyond his wildest dreams, and he traveled the major cities of the States living the life of Riley, red-carpeting between the best hotels and picking up a bride in California in the process.

By the middle 1890s this lush life had begun to pall, and in 1897 he reoutfitted himself for the lonely life of a prospector, left his wife in the social whirlpool, and moved back to his early stamping grounds in Oregon. Ed had found a mountain of silver, but he had yet to strike gold. In the summer of 1898 a fellow prospector found Schieffelin lying dead in a long-abandoned cabin that Ed had been using as a base while working an area a few miles south of Roseburg in Douglas County. Ed had died from natural causes, excitement probably having overtaxed his heart, for samples of high-grade gold ore were found lying around the body. Schieffelin was buried at Tombstone in Arizona Territory, and the Schieffelin Monument was erected to his memory a short distance to the west of the town limits. (See TOMBSTONE, ARIZONA.)

SCHONCHIM JOHN   A bearded Modoc Indian who played a leading role in the Modoc War of 1872. (See MODOC WAR.)

SCORPION Arachnid[19] that may be found in many areas of the United States south of the forty-fifth parallel, although they are at their most plentiful in the southern states. Scorpions possess a long segmented tail that terminates in a poison sting, four pair of multijointed legs, and a pair of large pincer-type claws, the latter being used to seize and hold their prey—usually spiders and insects and an occasional small animal—while the sting is whipped forward to dispatch or paralyze same. Should a human have the misfortune of being stung by a scorpion, severe pain, which may last for several hours, will be experienced, but the minute wound rarely proves fatal. Adult scorpions may reach a length of nearly six inches, about half of this length being taken up by the tail.

SCOTT, WALTER Better known as "Death Valley Scotty," a singularly successful desert rat who amassed his wealth in a manner that has yet to be satisfactorily explained—Scotty insisting that it came from his mine in Death Valley,[20] while some cynical folk suggested it may have been derived from Scotty's subrosa deals with a crippled millionaire named Albert M. Johnson.

Walter, who was born at Cynthiana, Kentucky, on September 20, 1875, probably became the youngest hobo to ever strike West when he left home in 1884 and managed to find employment as a horse wrangler at Humboldt Wells in Nevada before he had reached his tenth birthday. Two years later this well-muscled lad was driving twenty-mule-

---

[19] Member of a group that also includes spiders and mites.

[20] The "claim" was unrecorded, and since Scotty's death it has—as far as is known—never been relocated.

team borax wagons between Mojave and Death Valley, a grueling nine-mile trip across California's Mojave Desert that earned Walter the sobriquet of Death Valley Scotty. In 1888 Scotty made a trip to New York, and while staying in the city he paid a visit to Buffalo Bill's Wild West Show, and here a chance encounter with Cody led to Scotty being listed on the program as a "cowboy" for the next twelve years.[21] Over this period Scotty returned to Death Valley when the show was closed during the winter months, ostensibly prospecting trips which—as far as is known—resulted in naught but sand in his shoes. Even so, on being fired from the show in 1900, Scotty managed to persuade a certain Julius Gerard of New York to grubstake him for a Death Valley prospecting trip on the understanding that Gerard receive a fifty-fifty share of any profits that might result from Scotty's striking it rich.

Over the next three years Scotty spent most of his time prospecting the valley, paying occasional visits to New York to have his wallet reprovisioned by Gerard when he was getting short on victuals and liquor. By 1903 this unsuccessful prospector had worked some $8,000 of Gerard's money through his system and was a married man,[22] so when he visited New York in that year he was looking for a fresh backer, preferably one of unlimited means who would finance him to the extent of paying off Julius while still allowing him to continue his quest for gold. The hitherto mentioned Albert M. Johnson fulfilled these requirements, and twelve months later Scotty arrived in Barstow[23] loaded with gold certificates and folding money. "Big gold strike" was Scotty's explanation for

his sudden wealth, and as he took great delight in throwing money from hotel windows just to watch folk chase the stuff, no one worried too much as to whether he had found a bonanza or an excellent printing press.

That wealth went to Scotty's head cannot be denied, but as he remained supplied with a generous amount of negotiable paper for the rest of his days and was generous to the extreme; none but a Scrooge could call him a "fool." (N.B.: Any comments his wife may have made have been lost to posterity.) Possibly the most famous exploit of this extrovert character was his chartering of a special train of the Atchison, Topeka, and Santa Fe Railroad on July 9, 1905—paying $5,500 from a well-stocked wallet for the privilege of being transported from Los Angeles to Chicago in 44 hours, 54 minutes, and experiencing the thrill of traveling at 106 mph over a short lap of the journey.

In the early 1920s Scotty and Johnson commissioned top architect Frank Lloyd Wright to design a castle that they planned to erect at the northern end of Death Valley, but on seeing the finished plans the partners considered Wright to be way off the beam, and they discarded the pueblo-type building the architect had envisaged. This was probably a wise decision, for the flamboyant Moorish castle that was finally erected didn't blend into the landscape as Wright's may have done, and the exotic structure that became known as "Scotty's Castle" has been Death Valley's main tourist attraction since the day of its completion. When the number of tourists swelled to unforeseen proportions, Scotty moved into a nearby dwelling to savor a little

[21] The show was playing Staten Island at the time, and when Scotty was heard making disparaging remarks about a display of Cossack horsemanship, Buffalo Bill Cody invited him to "have a go," Scotty's subsequent performance resulting in his being given a contract.
[22] Walter married a Miss Josephine Millius at New York in 1902.
[23] About eighty miles southwest of the southern extremity of Death Valley.

peace, and he died here on January 5, 1954.

SCOTT'S BLUFF   A famous landmark and campsite on the Oregon Trail. Scott's Bluff is a free-standing cliff that rises some eight hundred feet above a treeless plain on the northern bank of the North Platte River in the extreme west of Nebraska. This old pioneer campsite, which is now the focal point of Scott's Bluff National Monument, is located near the city of Scottsbluff (spelled as one word), in Scotts Bluff (*sans* apostrophe) County, Nebraska. Old wagon ruts are still visible in the vicinity of the bluff. (See OREGON TRAIL.)

SELMAN, JOHN   Despite the facts that Selman is reputed to have had more than twenty kill counts to his credit and was pushing sixty when he became a notch on someone else's gun butt, spent all his adult life in the explosive cockpit of frontier settlements, and wore a lawman's badge for a number of years, he has never achieved anything like the mass-media coverage that has made the names of many of his contemporaries familiar to all who have ever read a Western or dialed a horse opera into life.

John Selman was born at Madisonville in northwestern Arkansas on November 16, 1839, one of four brothers who joined the Confederate armies at the outbreak of the Civil War, four years of strife that left John and brother Tom as the only surviving members of the Selman family—two brothers having been killed in action and both parents having died while their sons were in the service of a lost cause. When John and brother Tom returned to Madisonville in the summer of 1865, a couple of markers and the ruins of their family home were all that remained of family ties; so, rather than rebuild, the brothers pushed South-west, Tom settling in Bosque County, Texas, while John moved farther West to footloose around San Angelo, Abilene, Buffalo Gap, Fort Griffin, and other frontier settlements in the state. Sometime in 1867 Selman married a Miss Edna de Graffenreid, and for the next couple of years he worked for various cow outfits in the Fort Griffin area, after which he moved his wife and a twelve-month-old son whom they had christened Henry into New Mexico, settling in the northeast of the territory for a spell to allow his wife to give birth to a second boy, whom they named Bud before relocating in Lincoln County, where he established a small ranch.

Around this period New Mexico was a rustlers' cornucopia, and when Selman realized he would never become a second John S. Chisum, he formed a band of mercenaries who were prepared to clear running-iron specialists from any cattleman's range for a stipulated fee. This posse of unofficial lawmen was known as "Selman's Scouts." John employed a fast lad named Gus Gildea as his second in command, and within six months there wasn't a vertical rustler to be found on scout-patrolled range, Selman on one occasion being personally responsible for reducing four of a six-man gang to buzzard bait during a powdersmoke encounter that occurred while he was on lone patrol.

In the early months of 1870 the Selmans returned to Texas, squatting on land bordering the Clear Fork of the Brazos River for a time before moving to within a few miles of Fort Griffin, where John erected a crude rock-built home, which he named "Rock Ranch." Here Selman became acquainted with a fellow homesteader named John M. Laren, and when the latter was elected sheriff of Shackelford County, he appointed his newly found friend as his deputy, a twelve-month stint behind a badge durng which Deputy Selman is reputed to have gunned down a number of Fort Griffin hell-raisers in the course of his duties. In 1874, after Laren's term of office as sheriff had expired, he and Selman went into partnership and established a ranch, running their cattle under the registered Four of Clubs brand. This venture was a success, and although it is fairly certain that the partners increased their herds by means other than natural multiplication, there seems little evidence that the well-established ranchers' accusations of their being rustlers were ever justified.[24] These accusations, however, made the partners unpopular with some elements of Shackelford County, and a hired gun named Shorty Collins was only prevented from shooting Laren in the back while he was going about his business in Fort Griffin by the timely appearance of his partner, Selman killing Collins with one shot as the latter was leveling down on Laren.

Shortly after this attempt on his life Laren was arrested and placed in the Fort Griffin jail, where, later that same night, he was shot to death by a number of men who had succeeded in storming the jail. This action naturally infuriated Selman, and when a number of the county's more notable citizens began to die off from the effects of gunshot wounds, the man from Rock Ranch became the chief suspect. These suspicions led to a posse of cattlemen laying siege to Rock Ranch on an April evening in 1879 when the breadwinner happened to be absent, and Mrs. Selman and the children—now four in number—had to withstand a withering hail of gunfire throughout the hours of darkness, John's return with the dawn putting the mob to flight after he had killed one of their number. Mrs. Selman never recovered from the effects of this mob action, and she died before the month was out, a bereavement that Selman avenged by riding into Fort Griffin and shooting mob leader Fred Bates to death in a street-gun duel. This shooting got the Texas Rangers interested in Selman, so after he had made sure that his children were in the safe custody of friends he fled South and crossed into Mexico.

Sometime toward the close of 1879 Selman returned to the States with a newly acquired Mexican bride, and the couple settled at Fort Bayard in southwestern New Mexico, residing here until the early 1880s when they moved to El Paso where, having been assured that the Rangers were no longer interested in his whereabouts, Selman was persuaded into taking over the duties of marshal. During his first term of office he was baited into making fatal use of his six-gun, a shootout that was responsible for Selman being attacked shortly afterward by friends of the deceased, who left him in a dark alley in the belief they had killed him with multiple stab wounds. They hadn't, and shortly after his recovery, Selman was elected constable of El Paso's First District. Selman was to be re-elected constable for the remainder of his days, surviving for more than a decade behind a five-pointed lawman's star, which made a tempting target for any frontier troublemaker.

In 1894 the constable's six-gun felled ex-Ranger Bass Outlaw for keeps, and the following year John Wesley Hardin exhausted his last breath on a sawdust-covered floor while smoke still trailed from Selman's .45. On April 1, 1896,

---

[24] At this time and place mavericking and the appropriation of unbranded stock was regarded as an almost legitimate means of increasing one's herd; this the partners almost certainly indulged in, but that they went in for brand changing is doubtful, for they, like their neighbors, had rustler problems.

John Selman, Jr.,[25] tripped across the international border to Ciudad Juárez accompanied by a fifteen-year-old Mexican girl named José Maria Ruiz. John, Jr.'s intentions were most honorable, but the girl's parents objected to the association, and before he could take José Maria in legal matrimony he was arrested within twenty-four hours of crossing the Rio Grande and lodged in a Mexican jail on a charge of abduction.

When Constable Selman heard of his son's predicament he naturally made efforts on his behalf, and in the early hours of April 5 he met Deputy U. S. Marshal George Scarborough in the Wigwam Saloon, reputedly to persuade the federal officer to use his influence in an attempt to secure young John's release. Bystanders later reported that the conversation between the two lawmen appeared amiable, and when they left the saloon to carry on their talk in the privacy of an adjacent alleyway, there seemed little reason to suspect that within five minutes of their leaving Selman would be dying from the effects of four bullet wounds, and Scarborough would be admitting responsibility for the deed. The reasons for this shooting have never been satisfactorily explained, but it is worth noting that although no gun was found on Selman's person or in the immediate vicinity,[26] the shooting went down in the records as "justifiable homicide." (See HARDIN, JOHN WESLEY; OUTLAW, BASS; and SCARBOROUGH, GEORGE.)

SEVEN CITIES OF CIBOLA Seven legendary cities that the early Spanish conquistadors believed to be located somewhere north of the Rio Bravo in what is now New Mexico. In 1536 Alvar Nuñez Cabeza de Vaca, accompanied by his giant black slave Estevanico and a party of Indians, made contact with a party of Spanish soldiers near Culiacan in Mexico, De Vaca having spent much time wandering what is now Texas, New Mexico, and Arizona since his arrival in Florida some eight years previously. On reaching Mexico City, De Vaca and Estevanico recounted fabulous stories relating to a number of cities that lay more than three hundred leagues to the northwest—glittering golden cities whose many-storied apartment buildings had doors of turquoise and whose inhabitants regarded the possession of precious stones and metals as commonplace.

Spanish folklore regarding a domain known as "The Island of the Seven Cities"[27] may have been responsible for the Spanish colonists' ready acceptance of these stories, and the cities being labeled the "Seven Cities of Gold"; but whatever, in 1539 Friar Marcos de Niza, with Estevanico as guide, headed north at the head of a small party to either confirm or deny the existence of the cities. Friar Marcos confirmed the words of De Vaca and Estevanico, for although he had only seen the Zuni pueblos of Cibola[28] from a great distance, he returned from his mission with stories of a settlement that was larger than Mexico City, and in 1540 an army of conquistadors under the leadership of Francisco Vasquez de Coronado moved north to pillage what had now become known as the

---

[25] John Selman, Jr., was also a lawman, being employed as an El Paso policeman at the time of this escapade.

[26] The missing gun later turned up in the possession of a saddle tramp named Cole Belmont, Cole reporting that he had found the weapon, fully loaded, at the site of the killing.

[27] Name given to some legendary land where seven Catholic bishops took refuge during the Moorish domination of Spain. The seven bishops are reputed to have established a like number of cities within their province and to have made the place so attractive that all visitors were persuaded into becoming permanent residents.

[28] Located in what is now northwestern New Mexico.

"Seven Cities of Cibola." There was no gold. The Seven Cities were seven Zuni villages,[29] and although their dwellings may have glowed with a golden light at sunup and sundown, they were only built of adobe—just so much mud to Coronado and his warriors.

7TH CAVALRY Organized in 1866 at Fort Riley, Kansas, as one of four new cavalry regiments commissioned for service with the Department of the Missouri, Colonel Andrew J. Smith being appointed commanding officer of the new regiment with Lieutenant Colonel George A. Custer as his second in command. Custer whipped Civil War veterans and raw recruits into a cohesive whole, chose "Garryowen" as the regimental tune, and for the next ten years had the satisfaction of controlling the destiny of the 7th—said control only terminating on July 25, 1876, when Custer and five companies of the regiment were annihilated in the Valley of the Little Big Horn.[30] In 1877 the 7th helped contain Chief Joseph and his Nez Percés, and thirteen years later—under the command of Major S. M. Whitside—they took part in the infamous Wounded Knee affair. After this ghastly exercise with Hotchkiss guns, no more Indian blood was spilled by the 7th, and their next encounter with their old enemies wasn't until 1926, when they returned to the Little Big Horn for a friendly re-enactment of the Custer disaster. The 7th—which has been disbanded and reactivated over the years—is now an armored regiment,[31] but the spirit and costume of its plains period is still kept alive by E Company, 7th Cavalry Ghost Patrol, a civilian organization headquartered at Long Beach, California, which has been operating since 1954. (See BATTLE ON THE LITTLE BIG HORN; COMANCHE; CURLEY; CUSTER, GEORGE ARMSTRONG; HICKOK, JAMES BUTLER; JOSEPH; WASHITA MASSACRE; and WOUNDED KNEE MASSACRE.)

SHACKNASTY JIM Modoc Indian who took part in the Modoc War of 1872. (See MODOC WAR.)

SHALAM In 1884 a small group of spiritualists established a religious colony in Doña Ana County, New Mexico, after purchasing some twelve hundred acres of land on the banks of the Rio Grande a few miles north of Las Cruces. This was the Land of Shalam, the Rio Grande evidently substituting for the Shalam River mentioned in the group's bible.[32] Incorporated as the First Church of Tae, the movement had the laudable aim of the creation of a flawless society, their theory being that if they adopted unwanted babies and raised them to adulthood in pleasant and sinless surroundings, these

[29] The names of only six of these settlements are now known: Hawikuh, Halona, Kechipavan, Masaque (or Masaki), Kwakima, and Kiakima. Three- and four-storied apartments were common to all these "cities," whereas the occasional seven-story building was confined to Masaque. Hawikuh, which was surrounded by a stone wall, was probably the main "city" of Cibola.
[30] Charles Windolph, who died in 1950 at the age of ninety-eight, was the last survivor of those cavalrymen who fought in this battle. In 1958 the remains of an unidentified trooper were disinterred from beneath a few inches of turf after the buttons of his uniform jacket had activated a metal detector.
[31] While serving in Korea in 1958, men of the 7th Cavalry forwarded a hand-carved peace pipe to the great-great-grandson of Sitting Bull in the hope that the gesture would be regarded as a final peace treaty between the regiment and the Sioux.
[32] Oahspe, the sect's bible, is reputed to have been spirit-written, Dr. John Newbrough, the group's founder, having transcribed the message around 1880.

onetime foundlings would, in time, become the progenitors of a strain of humans whose behavior patterns would leave nothing to be desired. There was little wrong with this theory, and for a number of years the colony flourished, but in 1907 the project was abandoned, dissent among the colonists and hindrance rather than help from outside sources being the main reasons for the experiment's failure.[33] Although the Land of Shalam is a thing of the past, the First Church of Tae still has adherents in many parts of the world.

SHAMAN   A medicine man. Skills attributed to and required by a shaman were manifold; he had to possess the ability to communicate with the spirit world, be skilled in the art of healing, and adept in the performance of magical tricks. Paleface cynics would have us believe that all shamans were, and are, conjurers and charlatans; yet even so, reports of unbiased witnesses cause one to pause and ponder: Shamans have had success as rainmakers, and they have been known to cure malignant tumors and cause hair to grow on barren scalps; they have been observed plunging glistening knives into empty air to bloody the blades, addressing disembodied voices (ventriloquism?), and making apparitions appear through tepee smokeholes. Although many of the above examples that may be classed as "tricks" could be performed quite easily on a well-rigged stage, it is difficult to imagine what type of "rigging" could be attempted on a barren prairie. Shamanism could be either a heredity or vocational profession.

SHARP, JEBB   A convicted murderer whose neck was saved by the red tape of officialdom. (See MERRICK, DICK.)

SHARPS RIFLE   Breech-loading rifle that was developed by Christian Sharps in 1848. The 1st and 2nd regiments of U. S. Dragoons were issued with these percussion-type weapons in 1853, but it was not until the Civil War that the guns were to be manufactured in great numbers, some ninety thousand being supplied to the federal forces over the years 1861–65.[34] In 1869 the Sharps metal-cartridge rifles became available, the most famous of these being the .50-caliber model, which became the favorite killing tool of the buffalo hunters and the "shoots today, kills tomorrow" gun of the Indians. These rifles could have either round or octagonal barrels, and calibers other than those mentioned in this entry were available.

SHAWNEE TRAIL   The most easterly of the major cattle trails that had their origins in southern Texas. The Shawnee Trail fingered from San Antonio in a generally northeasterly direction, which took it across east-central and northeastern Texas, through the Choctaw and Cherokee lands of Indian Territory,[35] up into northeastern Kansas, and across the Kansas-Missouri line to the trail's terminal point at Kansas City, Missouri. The trail was about eight hundred miles in length.

SHEPHERD, MOLLIE   The only woman victim of the so-called Wickenburg Massacre. (See WICKENBURG MASSACRE.)

[33] The fact that the sect believed in the sharing of wealth, a belief that is regarded as a crime akin to heresy and high treason in many quarters, can have done little to help their cause.
[34] This military order was made up of rifles and carbines ranging in caliber from .36 to .54, many of the latter caliber being equipped with telescopic sights.
[35] Eastern Oklahoma.

SHERIFF   A lawman[36] whose jurisdiction extended over an entire county, the county seat usually being his headquarters. A sheriff was a political figure, and any man could offer himself as a candidate for the post in the hope that his backers, platform speeches, or past record would sway the electorate into voting him into office—usually a twelve-month tour of duty, although many were re-elected with such frequency that they rarely had to look for another job. The fact that these county lawmen did not have to tour the streets and saloons located within their bailiwicks damping down brawls and gun fights tended to keep their mortality rate far lower than that of town marshals. A sheriff could appoint parties of his own choosing to act as his permanent deputies, and he possessed the authority to deputize any number of men when the occasion warranted. Badges of office varied, but five- and six-pointed stars—usually of tin or silver, but occasionally of gold—were the most common. (See TOWN MARSHAL and UNITED STATES MARSHAL.)

SHINING MOUNTAINS
Name by which the Rocky Mountains were originally known—an obvious case of first choice being best. (See ROCKY MOUNTAINS.)

SHIRLEY, MYRA BELLE   Better known under her latter-day name of Belle Starr. (See STARR, BELLE.)

SHORT, LUKE   A ginger-haired, pint-sized, snappy dresser of a gambler whose prowess with both derringer and thumb-bustin' equalizer earned him the title of "The Undertaker's Friend." Luke, who was the sixth child to result from the legal union of John W. Short and Henrietta Brumley,[37] was born in Mississippi in 1854. Two years after his birth the family trekked westward and settled in Grayson County, Texas, and here Luke was to experience some fourteen years of belt-and-Bible upbringing before he decided to leave home for all time around 1870. For the next few years young Short worked as a cowhand, trailing cattle between Texas and Arkansas until he had accumulated sufficient capital to allow him to move North and establish a trading post on the Nebraska-Dakota border. Luke's stock was mainly bootleg whiskey, a product of paint-stripping quality that he peddled to the Indians at great profit; such being his success that he had to liquidate six pistol-point takeover specialists during the teething days of his business.

Sometime in 1875 the U. S. Army put an end to this illicit enterprise by arresting Luke and confiscating his stocks, but while en route for jail, the ex-trader managed to escape from custody, and shortly afterward he arrived at Leadville, Colorado, where, pockets bulging with a reputed sixty thousand dollars accrued from the sale of firewater, he set himself up as a professional gambler. Luke Short, dressed and armed to kill, had found his true vocation. During his Leadville days Luke was provoked into putting a derringer ball between the eyes of a trouble-maker named Isaac Brown when the latter had tried to break up Luke's faro game—a killing that may be termed the "highlight" of Luke's somewhat uneventful Colorado days.

[36] In the early days a sheriff was also expected to collect local taxes.
[37] Red-headed Scots-Irish Hetty gave birth to ten children. Martha was the first-born; then, in order of seniority, John, Joseph, Young, Mary, John L. (the subject of this entry), Henry, Belle, George, and William.

In the late 1870s Luke moved into Kansas and settled at Dodge City. Here he took over the gambling concession in Chalk Beeson's Long Branch Saloon, a faro-dealing period during which he became well acquainted with Wyatt Earp, Bat Masterson, and numerous other notables who handled cards and Colts with equal dexterity. In the spring of 1880 Short and Masterson moved to Tombstone in Arizona Territory to take over duties as dealers in Lou Rickabaugh's Oriental Saloon, a lush establishment that had "Buckskin" Frank Leslie dispensing liquor as it basked 'neath an umbrella of protection provided by Wyatt Earp. Wyatt, of course, wasn't always available, and on one occasion when he had left the Oriental to grab a quick lunch, the arrival of a hard case by the name of Charley Storms caused many a customer to drink up and drift.[38] Charley started the ball by calling Luke a cheat, and although Masterson intervened and escorted Storms to the door without incident, the evictee returned after lunch and began tracing the contours of Luke's mustache with the muzzle of his .45[39]— bully-boy tactics that provoked Luke into whipping out his Colt and putting three bullets into Storms which killed him before he realized where they'd come from.

Sometime in 1881 Short worked his way back to Dodge, and early in 1883 he purchased the Long Branch from Beeson and livened the place up by hiring an elegantly velveted lovely to play the saloon's piano—an instrument that had hitherto been abused by the fingers of various soused-up males. The Long Branch prospered as dwindling receipts became apparent in the nearby Alamo Saloon. Mayor Ab Webster, owner of the Alamo, immediately had an ordinance passed that forbade the employment of females in Dodge City saloons. This was political skulduggery of the lowest order, for when the girl left the Long Branch, Webster put her to work pounding out tunes in the Alamo, and when Luke protested, he was bounced onto an eastbound train with the promise that he would be shot dead if he ever had the temerity to return.

Luke was a mere 5 feet, 4 inches in height and light of build, but he didn't like to be pushed around. He dropped off the train at Kansas City, Kansas, and got the Morse keys clattering for help— Masterson being contacted first so that he might pass the message on to others. The "others"—Wyatt Earp, "Texas Jack" Vermilion, Johnny Green, John Millsap, and Daniel Tipton—arrived at Dodge City in June 1883, were immediately deputized by their old pal "Prairie Dog" Dave Morrow, who happened to be city marshal, and held their historic powwow with Mayor Webster in the city plaza under the watchful eye of Colonel Thomas Moonlight.[40] Wyatt's stipulation that "If Luke couldn't have a female piano player, no one could have a female piano player" was accepted by Webster, and Luke was invited back to Dodge after the "Dodge City Peace Commission" had

[38] Not surprisingly, for Storms had the reputation of being a gunslinger who toured frontier settlements whose limited resources and lack of law enforcement allowed him to practice his craft with little fear of the consequences. Storms was a "name" in Dodge when Bat and Luke were resident in the city, and the word was that he had killed men at Deadwood in Dakota Territory—his last known whereabouts prior to his arrival at Tombstone, which lay about one thousand miles to the southwest.

[39] A second-hand gun that Charley had purchased at the sale of the effects of the late Wild Bill Hickok.

[40] The adjutant general of the state of Kansas, who was acting as the state governor's observer.

been organized to look after his interests.[41]

From then on Luke had no further trouble while at Dodge. This lack of action may have palled, for in 1885 the little gambler sold out his interests at Dodge and moved South to take up residence at Fort Worth, Texas, where, shortly after his arrival, he opened the White Elephant, a luxurious drinking and gambling emporium located on Main Street. On the evening of February 8, 1887, "Big" Jim Courtright pressured Luke into a gunfight, a mad gamble that left Jim dead on Main Street and Luke on the way to the local jail. Friends of the deceased put lynch talk in the air, but this was soon forgotten when it was learned that Bat Masterson had volunteered to spend the night outside his friend's cell with his guns at the alert. As all the evidence branded Courtright as the aggressor, Luke was soon back at his place of business, and he was to remain unmolested for the remainder of his days. Sometime in the early 1890s Short moved his gambling layouts back into Kansas, and he died here, at Queda Springs, from natural causes on September 8, 1893. (See COURTRIGHT, JIM; EARP, WYATT BERRY STAPP; MASTERSON, WILLIAM BARCLAY; and MORROW, DAVE.)

SHOSHONE INDIANS
Plains-plateau tribe of the Uto-Aztecan language family that had roamed over what is now western Wyoming and the Snake River[42] Valley region of southern Idaho for at least two hundred years prior

to their acceptance of reservation life in 1868.[43] The Shoshone were originally plateau dwellers who lived in villages composed of grass houses,[44] but with the arrival of the horse in the Northwest in the middle of the eighteenth century, the Shoshone became far more mobile, venturing out onto the plains to become buffalo-hunting nomads whose main dwelling was the hide tepee of the true plains Indians. Clothing consisted of fringed buckskins and buffalo robes, and hair was worn long and usually braided. The Lewis and Clark Expedition established friendly relations with the tribe in 1806, and from that time on, the white man experienced little trouble with these Indians. This acceptance of the white man obviously stemmed from political rather than pacifist motives, for the Shoshone were lifting the scalps of their hereditary enemies, the Crow and the Blackfoot, until well into the latter half of the nineteenth century. Pronounced "Sho-SHOW-nee," and occasionally spelled "Shoshoni." (See LEWIS AND CLARK EXPEDITION; SACAGAWEA; and WASHAKIE.)

SHOTGUN So-called "sporting" gun, although anything less sporting can hardly be imagined. Single- or double-barreled shotguns, frequently with barrels sawed down to 18 to 20 inches, were fairly popular with frontier lawmen and overland express messengers, for not many owlhoots or gunslingers had the metal to face up to such a weapon when loaded with OO buckshot—a nine-balls-to-the-cartridge charge that was the favorite

---

[41] The "Peace Commission"—whose duties consisted of enforcing law and order until new peace officers could be appointed at Dodge—was composed of Charles Bassett, Neal Brown, Wyatt Earp, W. H. Harris, Bat Masterson, Frank McLane, William Potillion, and Luke Short, with Civil War veteran Colonel Thomas Moonlight acting as chairman.

[42] This being the reason for the tribe frequently being referred to as "Snake" Indians.

[43] These reservations being the Fort Hall and Wind River reservations, located in southeastern Idaho and west-central Wyoming, respectively.

[44] Hence their Sioux name of "Shoo-SHOO-nah," meaning "People Who Live in Grass Houses."

load of these old-timers. That these weapons were more often used as a threat—to cow mobs, etc.—rather than as murder weapons appears obvious from the fact that pistol and rifle bullets accounted for the majority of frontier firearm fatalities.

SHOTGUN CHAPS   Popular name for a type of chaparreras that has closed legs—i.e., they do not wrap around the leg to be fastened with buckles.

SHOTGUN MESSENGER   Name applied to any guard—whether Wells Fargo or otherwise—who rode the box[45] of a stagecoach when bullion or other valuable cargo was being carried. These guards usually carried a double-barreled shotgun, hence their name.

SHUMAN, JOHN
A French-Canadian trapper who ended his days as the victim in an early-day triangle drama. (See CARSON, CHRISTOPHER.)

SIBLEY STOVE   A conical-shaped stove with a detachable chimney that was invented by General Henry Hopkins Sibley and patented by him in 1857. Designed primarily as a heater for use inside Army tents—some sixteen thousand being in use with the Union forces during the Civil War—the Sibley later became popular with the trail-driving crews of the West.

SIDDONS, BELLE   Confederate spy of the Civil War years who became a lady gambler when her services were no longer required by the Confederacy. Under the adopted name of "Madame Vestal," Belle operated a faro and keno gambling establishment at Denver, Colorado, for some years until the gold strikes in the Black Hills persuaded her to move her layouts to Deadwood in Dakota Territory in 1876. During these boom years Belle was living with an ex-Quantrill raider named Henry McLaughlin, a gentleman who could usually be expected to be participating in some form of illegal violence when he wasn't by his paramour's side. While Belle was at Deadwood she received the news that her lover had been lynched by vigilantes after being taken into custody for a stage robbery that had occurred near Fort Laramie, Wyoming, and after this the girl who was known as the "Goddess of Chance" was never the same again, taking her grief and her layouts farther West via New Mexico and Arizona to find liquor-sodden relief in a San Francisco dosshouse, where she died some years later.

SIDEWINDER   A species of rattlesnake that is confined to the desert regions of the Southwest. (See RATTLESNAKES.)

SIEBER, ALBERT
Born in Germany in 1844 and raised as an American citizen in Minnesota, Al Sieber joined the Union forces in 1862, a husky 6-footer who was to be discharged after being wounded in the left leg at the Battle of Gettysburg in 1863. When his wound healed Sieber headed West, settling in Arizona where, for the next twenty years, he was to see service as civilian chief of scouts to various cavalry regiments stationed in the San Carlos region. In 1885 one of Al's scouts—an Apache who is usually referred to as the "Apache Kid"—put a bullet into Sieber's already scarred leg, and while he was

[45] The "box" being the forward boot, the driver's and guard's seat being built across the top of this.

hobbling around on crutches, he relinquished his command to Tom Horn, a hard-eyed man whom Al had taught all there was to know about scouting. With the surrender of Geronimo in 1886 the Apache wars came to a close, and Sieber was forced to look for another job. A little prospecting and a short spell behind a deputy U.S. marshal's badge kept him solvent over the next few years, and in 1906 he took up employment as a foreman in charge of a gang of laborers who were engaged on the Roosevelt Dam project in southeast-central Arizona. This was to be Sieber's last job, for on February 19, 1907, he was crushed to death by a fall of rocks that was the aftermath of a faulty blasting operation. (See APACHE KID and HORN, TOM.)

SIERRA An elongated range of mountains that possesses a sawtooth silhouette, a typical example being the Sierra Nevada of California.

SIGN LANGUAGE
An essential method of communication between peoples who are in frequent contact with other groups whose oral languages may be entirely different. When one considers that about three hundred languages were in use among the North American Indians, it is hardly surprising that most tribes were highly proficient in the use of "hand talk." Many gestures used in sign language are similar throughout the world, and as most of the Amerind symbolizations are readily understood by deaf mutes whatever their nationalities, the language may almost be classed as a manual Esperanto. Hand signs may be reduced to two basic types: those in which the hands are used to point out an object or person; and miming gestures, which indicate significant detail or details readily associated with a subject. A few examples of both nomenclature and abstract-type gesture are as follows:

Arapaho. The fingers of one hand are used to tap different points on the chest to indicate tattooing thereon.

Buffalo. Close the hands but allow the forefingers to remain extended and slightly curved, then place the hands against the temples so that the crooked forefingers appear to represent horns.

Cheyenne. Right hand used to make a chopping motion across the left forearm, the Cheyenne being noted for their removing of arms.

Crazy. Bring the extended fingers of the right hand close up to the center of the forehead and move the hand so the fingertips describe a small circle.

Crow (Indian). Move the arms in the flapping motion of wings.

Dog. Place the right hand with first and second fingers extended palm downward just below the left breast, then move the hand toward the right; this indicates a travois—originally drawn by dogs.

Good. The right hand is placed upon the left chest and then moved forward and to the right.

Greeting. Upraised palm of right hand held toward person being "addressed."

How?, What?, Where?, Why?, etc. (depending on the context of the "talk"). Right hand with fingers splayed held palm forward and agitated left and right.

Liar. A finger of the left hand is placed on the tip of the tongue, while two fingers of the right hand are splayed to indicate a forked tongue and pointed toward the observer.

Shoshone. Trace an invisible ripple motion with a forefinger. This indicates the crawling movement of a snake —"Snake Indians" being an alternative name for the Shoshone, as many of their villages were located in the Snake River area of southern Idaho. The same sign is also used to denote "Comanche," for this tribe was known as "The People from the Rattlesnake Country."

Sioux. The right forefinger is drawn across the front of the throat, the Sioux being noted for their practice of slitting the throats, or—in their early history—the decapitation of their enemies.

SIOUX INDIANS Name given to the Dakotah[46] Indians by the early French trappers and traders, the word being an abbreviated rendering of "Nadowessioux,"[47] a derogatory name applied to the Dakotah by their hereditary enemies the Chippewa. In the thirteenth century the Dakotah occupied an area that now embraces the eastern states of Ohio, Virginia, West Virginia, and North and South Carolina, but by the middle of the seventeenth century they had worked their way northwest to settle in what was later to be Minnesota and the Dakotas. By this time the Sioux nation was divided into three major divisions, the Santee, Teton, and Yankton, each of which spoke a different dialect, occupied separate territory, and was subdivided into a number of bands.[48]

The Dakotah originally lived in settled communities and derived their sustenance from farming and hunting, while "earth walking" and canoe travel were their only means of communicating with neighboring villages and distant tribes, and the dog travois their only means of overland freightage, but by the mid-eighteenth century the horse had arrived on the North Plains, and by the close of the century the Dakotah's canoes had been left to rot among the reeds, the horse travois was being used to transport heavy loads, and the tribe had become the tepee-dwelling nomads who were to cause the U. S. Cavalry so much grief over the latter half of the nineteenth century.

The tepees, buckskins, and robes of this major tribe of the Siouan language family were invariably decorated, horses, mounted Indians, buffalo, and geometric designs being painted on tepees, while beadwork, porcupine quills, and hair from scalplocks were used in a variety of ways to embellish clothing. The Sioux were probably the originators of "feather heraldry," for it was at its highest development among these peoples, the number of eagle feathers worn by a brave, and whether they were notched or sliced,[49] indicating his achievements and standing in the community far more reliably than the wearing of "the old school tie." Throughout the latter half of the nineteenth century the Sioux were in

[46] Meaning "Friends" or "Allies."

[47] Literally "Little Snakes," and by extension—as a snake is rarely regarded as anyone's friend—"Enemies."

[48] The Santee division was located in eastern Minnesota and consisted of four bands: the Leaf Shooter, Sisseton, Spirit Lake, and Wahpeton. The Teton, who roamed over North Dakota, were made up of seven bands: the Blackfeet (not to be confused with the Blackfoot Indians), Brule, Hunkpapa, Minnicoujou, Oglala, Sans Arc, and Two Kettle. The Yankton division of western Minnesota consisted of but two bands: the Yankton and the Yanktonai.

[49] The number of notches tallied with the number of enemies slain, while a sliced feather let an observer know that the wearer had slain an adversary by slitting his throat. The accumulation of a large number of these "coup" feathers made it possible for their owner to make a war bonnet.

constant opposition to the U. S. Army, and it wasn't until 1890 that they were finally subdued for all time. The majority of the Sioux who make up the various bands are now living on ten reservations in the Dakotas.[50] (See BATTLE ON THE LITTLE BIG HORN; BATTLE ON THE ROSEBUD; BLACK HILLS; CRAZY HORSE; FETTERMAN FIGHT; HORSESHOE STATION; JULESBURG FIGHT; RED CLOUD; SIGN LANGUAGE, subheading *Sioux;* SITTING BULL; SUN DANCE; WAGON-BOX FIGHT; and WOUNDED KNEE MASSACRE.)

SIRINGO, CHARLES A. Cowboy, Pinkerton operative, and author who was born in Matagorda County, southern Texas, on February 7, 1855. Charley was branding mavericks and skinning dead range cattle for their hides by the time he was fifteen, and he was the proud possessor of his own brand—the T5—some twelve months later, yet despite these promising beginnings the energetic Siringo was never to become the owner of anything but a meager spread, and throughout the 1870s he was trailing cattle to the railheads of Kansas for either "Shanghai" Pierce of Matagorda County or Beals and Bates, whose LX herds roamed some two hundred thousand acres near Tascosa in the Texas Panhandle. During these trail-herding days Charley was almost pistoleered into an early grave by a renegade cowhand by the name of Sam Grant,[51] and on more than one occasion Charley rode with posses that clouded into New Mexico after Billy the Kid when the little

villain's gang had made off with company stock.

In later life Charley left the bunkhouse life behind him and took up employment with the Pinkerton National Detective Agency, and for around twenty years he appears to have been in almost constant pursuit of various members of the Hole in the Wall community, risking his neck on one occasion by impersonating a fugitive and spending some time in the outlaw hideout after he had sweet-talked Elfie Landusky into betraying the whereabouts of her hard-boiled lover, Harvey Logan. Upon his retiring from the Pinkerton service, Siringo began pumping out prose, and although he did well out of this for a couple of decades with such books as *Lone Star Cowboy, A Cowboy Detective, Reata and Spurs,* and *History of Billy the Kid,* and a pamphlet entitled *"Two Evil Isms: Pinkertonism and Anarchism,*" the last few years of his life were spent watching rain pour through holes in his roof. This man of many talents died at Los Angeles, California, on October 19, 1928.

SISSETON SIOUX One of the four bands that made up the Santee division of the Sioux nation. (See SIOUX INDIANS.)

SITTING BULL Hunkpapa Sioux who was born in what is now southwestern South Dakota in 1831. Little is known regarding Sitting Bull's early life, but as a stocky veteran of some thirty-five "winter counts" who had been twice wounded during skirmishes with the

---

[50] These reservations being the Cheyenne River, Crow Creek, Flandreau, Fort Totten, Greenwood, Lower Brule, Pine Ridge, Rosebud, Sisseton, and Standing Rock.

[51] This shooting occurred in the summer of 1875. Grant, with a great show of incompetence, shot Charley through the knee instead of through the heart, as had been his intention, and before this error could be rectified, one of the victim's many friends had arrived on the scene and ruined Sam's plans; like even a gunnie like Grant didn't wish to commit a cold-blooded murder in front of a witness. Sam is reputed to have been employed to "fix Charley's wagon" by some unnamed cattleman who suspected that Siringo may have appropriated some of his stock.

Crows, he is reputed to have been nominated as paramount chief by the thirteen bands of the whole Sioux Nation sometime in 1866. Although Sitting Bull didn't lead any attacks against the enemy during the climactic North Plains Indian–U. S. Army engagements, by employing such noted warrior chiefs as Crazy Horse, Hump, Crow King, Gall, and Fast Bull as a multiplicity of fists, Sitting Bull was responsible for giving the white man a severe drubbing during the summer of 1876. After their victory on the Little Big Horn, the Sioux bands went their separate ways, Sitting Bull leading his Hunkpapas North to settle in Canada, where they remained for four years before returning South to surrender to the U. S. Army in July 1881. For the two years following his return to the States the chief was held as a prisoner of war at Fort Randall before being released into the custody of the Standing Rock Agency in South Dakota. In 1884 Sitting Bull was allowed a leave of absence to tour the country with the Alvaren Allen show, and the following year he was a star attraction with Buffalo Bill Cody's show for some months. Things appeared to be improving for the aging chief, but in 1890 during the Ghost Dance "uprising" he was shot dead by two Indian police who had been ordered to place him under arrest. (See BATTLE ON THE LITTLE BIG HORN; BATTLE ON THE ROSEBUD; CRAZY HORSE; SIOUX INDIANS; and WOUNDED KNEE MASSACRE.)

SKINNER, CYRUS
Member of Henry Plummer's band of "Innocents." Before his arrival in the Beaverhead diggings of what is now southwestern Montana, Skinner had been a saloonowner in both California and Idaho, and his first move on arrival in the gold fields was to purchase a clapboard saloon at Bannack

—an ideal business for learning the movements of bullion shipments, etc., so that the knowledge might be passed on to Plummer's "field workers." Although having the reputation of a fisticuff brawler rather than a pistoleer, Cyrus was not averse to helping fellow Innocent Bob Zachary in the holdup of a stagecoach and the killing of the driver so that they might loot the vehicle of around $250,000 in gold, and when gang member Buck Stinson killed a friendly Bannock Indian known as "Old Snag," Skinner didn't overlook the opportunity of lifting the old gent's scalp so that it might serve as bar decor.

The murder and robbery of Lloyd Magruder and a number of his employees was put into effect by a trio of men who are known to have been Innocents after Skinner had supplied them with information regarding Magruder and his pack train. About 1863 Skinner purchased a log-cabin saloon at Hell Gate,[52] and he was living here with a gal who is known only as Nellie when the Vigilantes of Montana arrested him as he was soaking up the morning sunlight at the front door of his premises on January 25, 1864. And that just about wraps up Cyrus, for before the day was out he had been hanged alongside two others who had possessed similar leanings.[53] (See BEACHY, HILL; INNOCENTS; MAGRUDER, LLOYD; PLUMMER, HENRY; and VIGILANTES OF MONTANA.)

SKULL, SALLY One of the many legally possessed names of the much-married Sarah Jane Newman—the "Juana Mestena" of the Old West. (See NEWMAN, SARAH JANE.)

SKUNK A New World member of the weasel family whose black-and-white fur coat and bushy tail make it one of the

---

[52] Located about two miles northwest of the present-day town of Missoula.
[53] The fellow sufferers being Aleck Carter and John Cooper.

most pictorially attractive of animals. There are four species of skunk, and representatives of all of these are to be found in the West, although the striped and little spotted varieties have a far greater range than either the hog-nosed or hooded skunks, the two latter varieties only being found in the extreme Southwest. All skunks possess a pair of scent glands beneath the tail, and when angered or frightened they can squirt a fine spray of one of the most evil-smelling liquids known to man for a distance of about ten feet.[54] Skunks feed on small mammals, birds' eggs, insects, and—occasionally—vegetable matter; they are very intelligent, and, with their scent bombs defused, make attractive pets. Sometimes referred to, erroneously, as "polecats." (See CARVER, WILLIAM.)

SLADE, JOSEPH A.
A well-educated gentleman of polished manners who became a hell-raising troublemaker when tanked up with spiritous liquids. Joseph Alfred Slade was born at Carlyle, Illinois, in 1828, the birth taking place in a mansion that his father, Congressman Charles Slade, had had built some eight years previously. Raised in a household dominated by his politically minded parent, Joseph left home in 1846 to fight in the Mexican War, and when he returned to Carlyle in the spring of 1848 he let it be known that he had been mustered out of the service with the rank of captain. Shortly after this homecoming, Captain Slade killed a man with a rock during a rough and tumble,[55] and although this could hardly be classed as "murder," the killer fled West, where, some years later, we hear of him working as a freighter along the Oregon Trail.

By 1859 Slade was married to a girl named Maria Virginia, had shot a fellow teamster named Andrew Farrar to death during a gun dispute in a way-station saloon, and was driving a six-in-hand stagecoach for the Central Overland, California, and Pike's Peak Express Company. Later that same year Russell, Majors, and Waddell promoted Slade to the post of station agent at Kearney, and early in 1860 he was elevated to superintendent of the Sweetwater Division, with headquarters at Julesburg, a post that led to his having a macabre encounter with the founder of Julesburg, which left the latter dead and earless. Early in the new year of 1861 four suspected stock thieves made their exits with the roar of Slade's guns still ringing in their ears, and in February of that same year a youth named Davenport was lynched near Fort Laramie after Slade had taken him into custody for stealing a few hundred head of Pony Express remounts.

Sometime in the summer of 1861 Slade went on a drunken spree and shot up the sutler's store at Fort Halleck, and although this display didn't result in any fatalities, pressure from the Army authorities persuaded Slade's employers to remove his name from the company payroll. By 1863 the Slades had moved up into Montana and were living in a stone-built house that Joseph had erected a few miles east of Virginia City. Here Slade operated a freighting business with moderate success and was fairly well liked in the settlements that littered the Grasshopper and Beaverhead diggings—when he was sober; when he was sloshed, he was unpredictable and addicted to vandalism. Riding into saloons and shooting out plate-glass windows or the ruination of a

54 The aroma is regarded as a sure-fire cure for headaches and catarrhal conditions in some regions of South America.
55 Some authorities state that this killing took place when Slade was only sixteen, but this seems very unlikely.

ballet dancer's performance by hollerin' for her to "Take 'em all off!"[56] can hardly be classed as crimes of a hideous nature; Slade, however, had the misfortune to be indulging in such practices during a period when that area of Montana was experiencing a wave of both outlaw and vigilante violence that had folks' nerves stretched to twanging point, a tenseness that Slade's actions did little to relieve.

Friends and vigilantes warned him to "Get his horse and begone!," but although Slade apologized for each of his misdemeanors after a session 'neath damp towels, he paid no heed to such advice. More's the pity, for by the end of January 1864 the vigilantes had cleared Henry Plummer's "Innocents" from the gold fields, and their nooses were lying idle as possemen screened the various mining camps for "customers." Such was the atmosphere in which Captain Slade made his last play. Over the night of March 3–4, 1864, Slade kept most of Virginia City awake by an explosive tattoo of gunfire and breaking glass, and on the morning of the fourth he topped off this display by presenting a derringer at the person of Judge Alexander Davis in the hope of inducing His Honor to grant him safe conduct from the town. Whether the judge would have granted this request will never be known, for while Slade was thus engaged a large force of vigilantes tromped into view and arrested him. Three hours later a box was kicked from beneath Slade's feet, and he was left to dangle his life away from the crosspiece of a corral gatepost. (See BENI, JULES; DALE, MARIA VIRGINIA; FARRAR, AN-DREW; INNOCENTS; PLUMMER, HENRY; and VIGILANTES OF MONTANA.)

SLAUGHTER, JOHN

John H. Slaughter, born in Louisiana on October 2, 1841, and raised in Texas from early childhood, never reached more than 5 feet, 3 inches in his stockinged feet, yet during the four years he was sheriff of Cochise County, Arizona, he cleared his bailiwick of outlaws by either giving them "twenty-four hours ter git!" or killing them on the spot. That John had seen much of life prior to his arrival in Arizona Territory in 1879 is evident; in 1861 he joined the Confederate forces, but after serving less than eighteen months he was discharged as medically unfit, an unnamed Army medic's diagnosis that Slaughter proved false by joining the Texas Rangers for a six-year stint of saddle-polishing before going on to establish a ranch in the Texas Panhandle in the early 1870s.

In the spring of 1879 Slaughter abandoned Texas and pushed his herds into the Southwest, it being of passing interest that one of his trail crew was young Billy Claiborne, an up-and-coming gunnie who was to find dubious fame and an oaken casket in Tombstone some years later. While herding across New Mexico, Slaughter gunned well-known herd cutter "Bittercreek" Jack Gallagher into a prairie grave in the vicinity of Fort Sumner, and he paused at Tularosa to marry a girl named Vida Howell before pushing farther West to establish what was later to become the one-hundred-thousand-acre San Bernardino Ranch of southeastern Arizona.[57]

[56] Her clothes, obviously. This happened to Kate Harper when she appeared at Virginia City's theater in 1863. Slade's "coarse remarks" are reliably reported to have emptied the theater of its audience of hard-bitten miners; if such was the case, it is evident that pink-tighted fantasies took precedence over pale-skinned realities.
[57] The ranchhouse was located about eighteen miles east of the present-day town of Douglas.

Over the next few years Slaughter is known to have given his "Git!" ultimatum to such known outlaws as Ike Clanton, Cap Stilwell, and Ed Lyle, and he is strongly suspected of having made buzzard bait out of numerous broncho Apaches and marauding Mexicans—no-nonsense tactics that were to lead to his being elected sheriff of Cochise County in 1887. Headquartered at Tombstone, Slaughter was to be re-elected on four consecutive occasions, and although Tombstone and its satellite camps weren't the hell-raising communities of their early years, the sheriff and his chief deputy—a man named Burt Alvord, who frequently cast a crooked shadow—managed to notch up a few adventures during their years in office. Slaughter and Deputy Alvord shot two train robbers of Mexican extraction to death when the latter pair failed to surrender after being tracked to their temporary hideout in the Whetstone Mountains,[58] and outlaw Juan Soto disappeared after he had been found not guilty of various charges that Slaughter considered to be well-deserved hanging offenses.

The sheriff, like most folk, did have his off days: The notorious Augustine Chacon holed up at Tombstone, but when Slaughter ferreted out his hideaway shack, the Mexican escaped after the lawman had fired two point-blank charges of buckshot at him, and missed! When his last term of office expired in 1891, Slaughter devoted himself to his San Bernardino spread, and in the early 1900s he and his wife adopted an Apache boy named Garcia, a happy-looking lad whom they raised as a *vaquero*. This was to turn out to be an unhappy choice for the foster parents, for in 1922 Garcia—

who was then twenty-two years old—teamed up with a couple of Mexicans and raided the Slaughter home, killing a storekeeper before they were driven off by the unsteady aims of old John and his wife.[59] That's about the last of the Slaughter saga, for old John died on December 15, 1922, at the age of eighty-one years. (See ALVORD, BURT; CHACON, AUGUSTINE; and CLAIBORNE, BILLY.)

SLOW ELK
Somewhat humorous term that was applied to cattle that were "rustled" for the sole purpose of keeping the family larder well stocked. Example: A hungry nester would say he was going "slow elk hunting" when he sneaked out to shoot the odd beef belonging to some neighboring cattleman. The cattlemen were not amused by this practice.

SMITH AND WESSON REVOLVER
Any model of the long line of revolvers produced at the Springfield, Massachusetts, factory of Horace Smith and Daniel Wesson. The first of these models appeared on the market toward the close of 1857. This was a .22-caliber, seven-shot, rim-fire revolver with a stud trigger and tip-up loading action; a pistol weighing around 1½ pounds and having an overall length of just over 10 inches, which was the first of the American metal cartridge revolvers. Four years later a six-chambered model became available in a choice of either .22 or .32 calibers. Although popular with officers during the Civil War years, frontiersmen considered these weapons as a "second gun" rather than as a substitute for the heavier-calibered revolvers that Smith and Wesson's competitors were placing

---

[58] The deceased—Guadalupe Robles and a man known only as Deron—had, with others, held up a train near Nogales, Mexico, in May 1888, killing three of the train crew and scooping up some fifteen thousand dollars in loot before hightailing North to lie low in Arizona.

[59] Garcia and his pals were arrested shortly afterward, and the trio were given life sentences in the Arizona State Penitentiary at Yuma.

on the market, and it was not until 1870 that the company attempted to fill this gap in their production by adding a heavy-calibered man-stopping revolver to their range. This was the Smith and Wesson No. 3 Revolver, a .44-caliber, single-action, six-shot weapon with a fluted cylinder and a break-down loading action that incorporated automatic ejection.[60]

In 1875 Smith and Wesson Schofield revolvers began to flow off the production lines. This model was similar in most respects to the No. 3 model, the main differences being that it was chambered for .45 ammunition and it had a frame-mounted barrel latch[61] instead of the latch being mounted on the barrel. The above are but a few examples of the Smith and Wesson Company's output; the entry does, however, cover most of their range that were available during the frontier years. These guns were very popular, and the writings of old-timers verify this, yet one rarely finds a Smith and Wesson mentioned in Western fiction; one wonders about this until it is realized that "He whipped out his trusty Colt" doesn't slow up the action as does "He whipped out his trusty Smith and Wesson." Smith and Wesson is still in production, and its large range of handguns is considered by many to embrace some of the finest defensive weapons available.

SMITH, "BEAR RIVER" TOM

The man who used his fists in preference to a thumb-bustin' piece of hardware to clean up Abilene in 1870. Thomas James Smith, who was born of Irish parentage in New York City in 1838, joined the

New York City Police Department in 1862, and for the next six years he was giving and receiving lumps on a tough Bowery beat—a seamy period that may have prompted him into turning in his badge in 1868 and pushing West to see what all the fuss was about regarding life on the other side of the Mississippi.

Sometime in 1868 Smith got a job with a Union Pacific construction crew headquartered at Bear River in southwestern Wyoming. Bear River was a nothing place until the Union Pacific's "Hell on Wheelers" arrived and proceeded to pump some life into the settlement. This they did to such good effect that the more sober-minded townies reacted by forming a vigilance committee that in no time at all had clashed with the railroad workers —a violent clash of arms that left some fourteen corpses scattered about the shattered community and was only quelled by the timely arrival of the U. S. Cavalry from nearby Fort Bridger. That Tom was in the thick of the fighting may be readily assumed from the fact that he was severely wounded by the vigilantes, and from then on he was to be known as "Bear River" Tom Smith.

For the next couple of years "Bear River" Tom spent varying periods as an end-of-track lawman, seeing service in this capacity with the Union Pacific as they pushed into Utah and then, later, moving East to pin on a badge at the Kansas Pacific base of Kit Carson in eastern Colorado. By the spring of 1870 constant wandering and the possession of a colorful nickname had made "Bear River" a household name throughout the plains, and in May of that year he rode

[60] The first 250,000 of this model were manufactured to fill a Russian order. These, which are known as Smith and Wesson Russian models, are easily identified from those produced for the American market by their having a finger grip that extends beneath the trigger guard. Hickok had a No. 3 model on his person at the time of his assassination.

[61] Patented by Major George W. Schofield in 1873—hence the name. In 1882 Schofield blew his brains out with a revolver of this model while stationed at Fort Apache, a macabre incident that put a damper on the Schofield's popularity. In his later years Jesse James favored this model revolver.

into Abilene, Kansas, to accept the appointment of town marshal. Smith's first move as marshal was to attempt the almost suicidal task of enforcing an ordinance that forbade the carrying of firearms, an ordinance that had hitherto been ignored. That "Bear River" accomplished this task without having to resort to the use of his twin-holstered guns seems incredible, yet it has been reliably reported that within forty-eight hours of his acceptance of Abilene's silver star, everyone was falling over themselves to hand in their hardware. This seemingly impossible task of transforming the lethally turbulent Abilene into a more or less respectable "flower power" community had been accomplished by using a pair of rock-hard fists against the chins and breadbaskets of a couple of truculent characters known only as "Big Hank" and "Wyoming Frank."

Over the next few months Smith had to use his solar-plexus and uppercut technique on a visiting Texan who was whooping it up in the Old Fruit Saloon, and on another occasion Smith had to wound three rowdies with gunfire when they jumped him in the same saloon, but otherwise he succeeded in keeping a tight lid on the town, and by the fall of the year he had accepted a U.S. deputy marshal appointment and was sporting two badges. On the second of November 1870 the sheriff of Dickinson County requested "Bear River's" help in arresting a settler named Andrew McConnell on a murder warrant,[62] and on that same day Smith rode out of Abilene and headed north to flush Andrew and a chum of his named Moses Miles out of their dugout. The marshal never got within fist range of his quarry. The two nesters brought him down with riflefire, and as he lay dying,

they finished him off with an ax.[63] With the passing of "Bear River" Tom Smith, Abilene reverted to its wild old ways, and it remained that way until Wild Bill Hickok became town marshal in the spring of 1871. (See ABILENE, KANSAS.)

SMITH, JEDEDIAH One of General William H. Ashley's "young men of enterprise" who was to develop into an outstanding trapper and mountain man whose abstinence from the use of tobacco, profanity, and attractive-looking squaws, and his possession of a high regard for the benefits that may be derived from the regular application of soap and water, made him unique among that buckskinned brethren.

Born at Jericho, New York, on January 6, 1799, and christened Jedediah Strong Smith by strong-minded Methodist parents who moved their family West around 1814 to finally settle in northern Ohio in 1820, Jed struck out on his own in 1821, and while in St. Louis the following year he joined Ashley's expedition to the upper Missouri after reading the general's "To Enterprising Young Men" want ad in the February 13 edition of the Missouri *Gazette*. The expedition was attacked by a large force of Arikaree Indians near the mouth of the Grand River, and many of the party were killed, but Jed survived to become a trapper for Ashley's Rocky Mountain Fur Company, and for the next three years he was "plew" hunting in what is now the Dakotas and Montana. During this period Smith was badly mauled by a grizzly while trapping in the bighorn country, an encounter that left him with a permanently mutilated ear, which he hid from view by allowing his hair to grow long.

[62] McConnell had killed a man named John Shea when the latter had herded cattle across Andrew's small holding.

[63] The two killers were arrested shortly afterward, and at a subsequent trial were given long prison sentences.

In 1826 Smith formed a company with fellow trappers William Sublette and Dave Jackson, and this trio hunted and trapped as far west as the Coastal Range of California[64] and as far north as the Hudson's Bay outpost at Fort Vancouver in the Oregon country, hard-traveling years during which they discovered South Pass and proved that the Great Salt Lake of Utah was the body of water that Jim Bridger had firmly believed to be the Pacific Ocean. In 1830 the partners sold out to the Rocky Mountain Fur Company, and when Jed paid a visit to Ohio that same year he had nearly eighteen thousand dollars in his parfleche.

The following year Jed rejoined Sublette and Jackson, and on April 10 they led a party of around eighty men out of St. Louis to move into the Southwest via the Santa Fe Trail. Sometime while journeying across an arid stretch between the Arkansas and Cimarron rivers, the party became short of water, and Jed volunteered to go off in search of a waterhole. Whether his quest was successful will never be known, for somewhere in that arid land[65] he disappeared, presumably the victim of Comanche lances. (See MOUNTAIN MEN; OREGON COUNTRY; ROCKY MOUNTAIN FUR COMPANY; SOUTH PASS; and SUBLETTE, WILLIAM.)

SMITH, JEFF Con man and gang leader who started his working life as a Texas cowhand, only shucking off his spurs when he had become adept at manipulating three halves of walnut shell so that one of them appeared to trap a fugitive dried pea. This was the shell game, a minor gambling activity from which a skilled operator could derive a good living by allowing any member of his audience to place a bet on which shell was hiding the pea, safe in the knowledge that the pea had been palmed and only an occasional "winner" need be allowed to revive flagging interest. Jefferson Randall Smith worked his first shell game pitch at San Antonio, Texas, but by the mid-1880s he had moved up into the Colorado gold fields, and was fleecing the miners of Leadville, a con man's paradise where he became acquainted with an aging gentleman named V. Bullock-Taylor, who was to introduce him into a far more lucrative line of business. This consisted of selling small cubes of soap that should have retailed at a nickel each for the inflationary price of one dollar, the con ploy being that the seller had wrapped hundreds of pieces of soap in full view of his audience while making a great show of placing a fifty-dollar or one-hundred-dollar bill in about 10 per cent of the packages, when in reality sleight of hand was steering the money back into the operator's pocket.

When old Bullock-Taylor died, Jeff became undisputed leader in this soap-swindle field, and "Soapy" was to be his nickname thereafter. So successful was "Soapy" that in the late 1880s he moved to Denver and opened a gambling hall with his profits, and within a short time he had extended his interests until he was skimming the cream from almost every illegal undertaking in Denver. This required an organization, and "Soapy's" was second to none. Con men of the caliber of "Judge" Norman Van Horn and the "Reverend" Charles Bowers

[64] This was a Mexican province, and on two occasions the party only escaped being thrown into jail by the timely interference of American seafaring types whom the Mexican authorities had no wish to offend for reasons of a commercial nature.

[65] As Smith's body was never found, one can only theorize as to where he met his death, somewhere in what is now Meade or Haskell counties of southwestern Kansas seemingly being the most likely bets.

masterminded the sales of gold bricks and phony mining stock, while an ex-safe blower named "Ice Box" Bernie Bolton[66] strawbossed a motley assortment of pickpockets, muggers, and burglars who bribed politicians, stuffed ballot boxes, and served as lawmen when not employed in their professional capacities.

In 1892 "Soapy" moved his headquarters to the booming mining camp of Creede in southwestern Colorado, and within a few weeks his gang of more than forty men had more or less taken over the town, Bob Ford's Creede Exchange Saloon being the only major attraction that remained beyond the gang leader's control. Whether "Soapy" had anything to do with Ford's place being burned to the ground is speculative, but within a few weeks of the Creede Exchange reopening as a tent saloon, it is strongly suspected that Bob had been forced into accepting "Soapy" as a business partner, and when a man named O'Kelly killed Ford, a goodly number of citizens figured that the king of the con men may have paid for the "hit."

Alaska got Jeff and his gang next, the entire mob descending on Skagway in the fall of 1897 with the express intention of relieving sourdoughs of their gold and making marionettes of the local politicians and lawmen, as they had in Denver and Creede. By the summer of 1898 Skagway was being run from the back room of Jeff's saloon, and con-man finesse had been abandoned in favor of allowing "Ice Box" to deploy his forces in simple mugging and thieving operations which required little skill but showed a quick profit. This removal of the velvet glove in

its entirety was to lead to "Soapy's" undoing.

Jeff, at the height of his power, led the Fourth of July parade in 1898, but four days later "Ice Box" and a few of his troopers robbed a miner named Lem Stewart of more than twenty-five hundred dollars in gold in a daylight mugging that broke the camel's back, and that same evening a large force of vigilantes gathered on Juneau wharf to take part in a major clean-up campaign. On hearing of this gathering, "Soapy" ordered "Ice Box" and his boys to break up the meeting, but on being confronted with a display of weapons sufficient to start a full-scale war, Bernie retired his forces from the field, leaving his boss to go down to the wharf to try to sort things out with a wide grin and a rifle. Smooth talk failed, and "Soapy" was shot dead by vigilante Frank Reid after the latter had taken a rifle bullet in the thigh.[67] This shooting whipped the vigilantes into full cry, and by the following dawn a half-dozen gangsters had been shot dead, and "Ice Box" and the remainder of the gang were being held under guard while nooses were being adjusted, a multiple lynching only being prevented by the arrival of a U. S. Infantry unit and the establishment of martial law. (See FORD, ROBERT.)

SMITH, JOSEPH   Founder of the Mormon religious sect. Born in Vermont in 1805 of a farming family, Joseph Smith claimed that when he was fifteen years of age he received divine revelations, and that seven years later further visions led to his finding a set of golden plates inscribed with "ancient Egyptian"

---

[66] Bolton's career as a safe blower was short-lived. While working illegally and after hours in a large meat mart, the low-browed Bernie had dynamited the ice box, mistaking it for the safe—hence the reason for his being an ex-safe blower and being the possessor of a way-out nickname.

[67] Reid died shortly afterward.

characters, which he translated[68] into a work that was published as the *Book of Mormon* in 1830. During the year in which his transcript was published, Smith established the Church of Jesus Christ of Latter-day Saints, and for the next thirteen years he was undisputed leader of the sect, but in 1843 he advocated a policy of polygamy, which split his followers, and when the printing presses of the defector group were destroyed on the orders of Smith, the rioting that followed led to Joseph and his brother Hiram being lodged within the Carthage, Illinois, jail for their own protection. This promise of protection was of little value, for in the late afternoon of June 27, 1844, an irate mob stormed the jail and shot the Smith brothers dead. Joseph Smith may never have crossed the Mississippi, but he most certainly left his mark upon the West. (See MORMONS.)

SMITH, "PEG LEG"   Mountain man and trapper who was dubbed "Peg Leg" after he had lost his right leg. (See SMITH, THOMAS L.)

SMITH, "SOAPY"   Probably the best-known confidence man of the frontier's closing years. (See SMITH, JEFF.)

SMITH, THOMAS J.   The fisticuff marshal of wild and woolly Abilene who is somewhat better known as "Bear River" Tom Smith. (See SMITH, "BEAR RIVER" TOM.)

SMITH, THOMAS L.
Born in Kentucky in 1797, young Smith started his working life on the flatboats of the Mississippi. Tom, however, was a footloose character, and he was soon roaming the wilderness learning the arts of beaver trapping, likker swillin', and squaw blanketing, which were to have him established as an all-around bounder of a mountain man by the time he signed up with a caravan leaving St. Louis for Santa Fe in the early months of 1824. The Southwest evidently appealed to Smith, for over the next three years he did his pelt gathering and supping in the Mexican-held territories that were later to become known as Colorado, Utah, Arizona, and New Mexico.

During this period Smith took part in the massacre of more than a hundred Papago men, women, and children when he, Milton Sublette, and about thirty lesser-known trappers attacked an Indian village in the spring of 1827 after receiving news that the Indians had almost annihilated a large force of French trappers but a few days previously. By the yardstick of the times this can hardly be classed as infamous conduct, yet one does feel that fate was trying to equalize when some unseen marksman placed a ball below Smith's right knee while Smith was trapping in the North Platte in the early days of 1828. Fellow trappers saved Smith's life by carrying out a crude amputation job, and while he was recovering, the victim fashioned himself an equally crude wooden leg, which resulted in his being dubbed "Peg Leg" just as soon as he was able to get about once more.

As the 1830s drew to a close, the price of beaver "plews" sank rapidly, and in order to keep himself supplied with likker, Smith resorted to stealing Indian children so that he might sell them as embryo

[68] That this text could be translated by Smith may seem remarkable. Smith, however, is reputed to have found the task easy, having in his possession the decoding stones known as "Urim" and "Thummim." The authenticity of all this cannot, unfortunately, be established, for the golden plates and the stones were given into the custody of a visiting angel whom only Joseph saw.

lave material to monied Mexicans. When things got too hot for him in this nefarious business, "Peg Leg" took up horse theft, and for almost a decade he was stealing mounts in California and trading them off at Bent's Fort near the mouth of the Purgatoire River in what is now southeastern Colorado. Sometime in the 1840s this buckskinned scallywag retired from his horse-stealing forays, and we next hear of him in northeastern Utah, where he is living in a community of shacks that lie within hailing distance of the Oregon Trail, the web of domesticity having enmeshed him to such a degree that he is surrounded by a number of snake Indian "brides" and an even greater number of half-breed kids that he has been siring over the years.

When domestic bliss threatened to drift into ennui, the aging "Peg Leg" moved out and drifted into California, and in 1865 he was at Fort Yuma swilling rum and other spiritous fluids prior to bumping his way West to reach San Diego. When he reached the coastal city, Smith was suffering from malnutrition, dehydration, and a no-doubt badly worn wooden leg, and he was rushed to the local hospital for treatment. Here "Peg Leg" began rambling about finding gold near some twin peaks that reminded him of "maiden's breasts,"[69] a story that was substantiated by the finding of gold-bearing ore in his pockets that was later sold for almost fifteen hundred dollars. Smith must have been released from the San Diego Hospital as more or less "fit to travel," for later that same year he was admitted to the San Francisco City Hospital, and he died here on October 25,

1866. It is now more than a hundred years since the old reprobate checked out, yet folk are still searching for the "Lost Peg Leg Mine."

SMOKE SIGNALS   A method of long-distance communication that was practiced by the Indians and was rarely, if ever, thoroughly understood by the white man. A signal could be nothing more than a lone column of smoke or a number of such columns, but more frequently a blanket was used to control the smoke's escape, the raising and lowering of the blanket allowing spherical or sausage-shaped clouds to rise into the air. By using combustibles that gave off a very pale smoke, the Indians could send out "invisible" messages when they didn't wish to give evidence of their whereabouts. These, of course, were only used when the sender knew that a friendly tribesman who was aware of what to expect had been stationed to watch for such sign. The art was mainly practiced by the plains tribes and the Indians of the Southwest, for smoke talk was of little use in well-timbered or mountainous regions where the range of vision was restricted.

SNAKE DANCE   A dance involving the use of live rattlesnakes that is performed each August by the Hopi Indians of northern Arizona. The ceremony is actually a prayer for rain in which the snakes act as couriers between the Hopi priests and the rain gods. The dance is the climax of the Hopi Snake Dance Ceremony, a religious ritual that extends over a period of a week to ten days in mid-August and is confined to one pueblo.[70] On the day of the dance, snakes[71] that

[69] It is worth noting that almost anything appears to have been capable of reminding these old rascals of the torrid zones of the female anatomy, for "Teton" nomenclature is common in the West. The shortage of women may have been responsible for this.

[70] No pueblo is expected to organize the Snake Dance Ceremony on two consecutive years, so each village takes its turn without adhering to any strict rotation.

[71] Usually rattlesnakes, other snakes only being used when a full quota of the former were unobtainable.

have been captured two or three days earlier and held prisoner in pottery jars are washed in readiness for the appearance of the dancers—priests wearing kilts and moccasins of a dark red color, a few head feathers, and much red and white paint. The dancers are divided into groups of three. One man places a snake in his mouth and grips it around the thickest part of its body, while a companion takes up a position slightly to his rear and waves a feather wand to hold the snake's attention as he rests his free hand on the foremost dancer's shoulder. The third member of each group brings up the rear, carrying a snake in either hand. These small bands jog their way around the village plaza four times, and then the snakes are dropped into a pile of sacred meal, after which they are collected and carried away into the open country to be released. The reptiles are then believed to communicate to the rain gods the story of their kind treatment at the hands of the Hopi, and the gods show favor to the Indians by opening the heavens. (See Hopi INDIANS.)

SNAKE INDIANS Alternative name of a regional nature that is often applied to the Shoshone. (See SHOSHONE INDIANS.)

SNOWSHED
Wooden, barnlike structure erected over a railroad right-of-way in regions where snowdrifts were a seasonal or permanent threat to traffic movement. Many snowsheds were only a few hundred yards in length, but the longest on record—the Central Pacific's snowshed at the summit of the Donner Pass in the Sierra Nevada—covered a continuous stretch of forty miles of track. A snowshed that housed a waiting room and cafeteria was a rarity, and prints, rather than the writings of the period, are the only proof of their existence. Rotary snowplows rendered snowsheds obsolete, and by the 1950s only a five-mile stretch of the Donner Pass structure remained.

SNOWSHOE THOMPSON
A fleet-footed mail carrier of the High Sierras. (See THOMPSON, JOHN A.)

SOAPY SMITH Top-line confidence man who worked the West during the closing decades of the nineteenth century. (See SMITH, JEFF.)

SODDIE A primitive dwelling that was erected by the early settlers in areas where timber was scarce or entirely absent. These buildings were composed of thick rectangles of turf, and although they are reputed to have been warm in winter and cool in summer they were verminous and a settler would quickly abandon one when other building materials became available. Windows were small, and as the supply of glass was usually as restricted as the supply of lumber, the light entered quite a few soddies via a pile of glass bottles that had been stacked lengthwise and cemented into place with whatever adhesive ingenuity could provide. A few precious planks or tree trunks were used as ceiling beams to support a sod and grass roof. The soddie was rarely inviting in appearance or entirely waterproof.

SOMBRERO Spanish name for a hat with a very wide brim that may be manufactured from straw, felt, or other suitable material. Much favored by the Mexican *vaquero* and the gringo cowhand.

SONTAG BROTHERS George and John Sontag, men in their thirties who owned a quartz mine at Visalia in south-central California, headed East in the spring of 1892 to commit train holdups at Kosota, Minnesota, and Racine, Wisconsin, which got them on the "wanted" list of the Pinkertons before they had time to get back to their home state. On August 3 of that same year the brothers robbed a Southern Pacific train near Collis Station[72] and escaped with five thousand dollars, but a sheriff's posse quickly ran the Sontags and fellow traveler Chris Evans to earth, and George was captured after a fierce gunfight in which a deputy sheriff was killed. After the capture of George and his subsequently being sentenced to a long stretch in the Folsom Penitentiary in November, John started an undeclared war against the Pinkertons, he and Evans even resorting to stopping stages to see if any "Pinks" were aboard. In June 1893, after a series of gunsmoke encounters with lawmen that had left seven of the latter severely wounded, a large force of officers discovered the outlaws' hideout near Visalia, and an eight-hour gunfight that was later to be known as "The Battle of Simpson's Flats" got under way. When the smoke finally cleared, two deputy sheriffs of Tulare County lay dead, and John and Chris were too shot up to squeeze a trigger. Evans recovered to stand trial, but thirty-three-year-old John Sontag died from the effects of his wounds on July 3, 1893.[73] (See EVANS, CHRISTOPHER.)

SOTO, JUAN   Mexican desperado who got himself shot dead by Sheriff Harry N. Morse. (See MORSE, HARRY N.)

SOURDOUGHS   Name applied to the miners and prospectors of the West and to all those who moved up into the Yukon gold fields via the Trail of '98. The name derives from the fact that many mining types—particularly the Yukon adventurers—subsisted mainly on sourdough bread, a bitter-tasting bread made from a mixture of malt, yeast, flour, sugar, and water. Sourdoughs have been immortalized by Robert W. Service's poems, which have been published as *Songs of a Sourdough*.

SOUTH DAKOTA
North-central state that is bounded on the north by North Dakota, on the east by Minnesota and Iowa, with Nebraska to the south and Montana and Wyoming to the west. First explored by the French in 1742 and its first settlement being a fur-trading post that was established some seventy-five years later, the region became the southern half of Dakota Territory in 1861 and was admitted to the Union as the fortieth state in 1889. Frequently referred to as either the "Sunshine" or "Coyote" state. Pierre is the state capital. (See BLACK HILLS; DEADWOOD, SOUTH DAKOTA; and NORTH DAKOTA.)

SOUTH PASS   Located in southwestern Wyoming. This twenty-mile-wide passage, which cuts its way through the Continental Divide at the southern end of the Wind River Mountains, was discovered by a party of trappers in the employ of the Rocky Mountain Fur Company in 1822. The trappers may not have realized its importance at the time, but as the pass offered an easily traversable route between the Great Plains and California and the Southwest, in later years it was to become part of the Oregon Trail. (See OREGON TRAIL; PONY EXPRESS; and SMITH, JEDEDIAH.)

[72] Located in Fresno County, California, Fresno being adjacent to the brothers' home base in Tulare County.
[73] The date given in this entry is taken from John's marker, yet most reports state that he died within a few hours of the gunfight.

SPADE BIT   A type of bit that has a more or less triangular-shaped piece of metal attached to the mouthpiece. When a rider who employs such a bit drags against the reins, the "spade" presses against the roof of the horse's mouth and causes pain. Not recommended. Used mainly on the Californian cattle ranges.

SPANISH PEAKS   Twin mountain peaks that are located in what is now the extreme west of Las Animas County, Colorado. Known by the Indians as "Wah-to-yah."

SPARROW, JOSEPH   The man who killed the objectionable "Print" Olive. (See OLIVE, I. PRENTICE.)

SPENCER RIFLE
A seven-shot lever-action rifle patented on March 6, 1860, by Christopher M. Spencer and manufactured by the Spencer Repeating Rifle Company of Boston, Massachusetts. The tubular magazine of the Spencer was located within the stock, a unique feature that protected the magazine and its contents if the rifle happened to be dropped or was subjected to rough usage. In 1863 less than four thousand of these repeaters were being used by the Union forces, but after they had turned the tide of battle at Gettysburg in the summer of that same year, the company was overwhelmed with military commitments, and by the end of the Civil War more than one hundred thousand Spencers were in the hands of Union troops. A change in the administration at Army Ordnance in 1866 resulted in the firm losing its military contracts; three years later the Spen-

cer Repeating Rifle Company went bankrupt, and on September 28, 1869, it was auctioned off to the Winchester Repeating Arms Company.

SPRINGFIELD RIFLE   Any of the rifled shoulder arms manufactured at the United States Armory at Springfield, Massachusetts, from 1795 onward. Springfield rifles saw service with the Lewis and Clark Expedition of 1804–6, and they were used in the War of 1812; the muzzle-loading .58-caliber percussion model was used in large numbers by Union troops throughout the Civil War; and the 7th Cavalry was equipped with the .45-caliber, single-shot model of 1873 when they rode to disaster on the Little Big Horn on July 25, 1876.[74] Toward the end of the era that may be described as the "Wild West" the Springfield Krag-Jorgensen made its appearance, and these .30-caliber magazine rifles were used during the Spanish-American War of 1898.

SQUARE DANCE   A type of folk dancing in which a "caller" leads the dancers through their paces while a fiddler scratches out some lively tune such as "Black Jack Grove," "Soapsuds over the Fence," "Shake That Wooden Leg," etc. Popular with the pioneers, square dancing has remained a part of the contemporary American scene.

SQUAW BOOTS   Term used by white men when alluding to an Amerind homosexual. (See BERDACHE.)

SQUAW MAN   Derogatory term used to describe a white man who marries, or lives with, an Amerind woman.

[74] In this model the cartridge case had a tendency to jam in the breech when the gun warmed up from continuous firing. When this happened it was recommended that a knife blade be used for the removal of the wedged case, the cases were, unfortunately, of such poor quality that the base usually ripped off before the remainder of the case could be removed, a misfortune that rendered the weapon inoperable.

STAGECOACH Any enclosed horse-drawn vehicle that has provision for the carrying of fare-paying passengers and their luggage on scheduled runs between distant towns or cities is usually classed as a stagecoach. This definition is, however, not entirely correct, for it ignores the differences between the stagecoach and the stage wagon. The true stagecoach had its skeleton concealed beneath the outside paneling and was somewhat elegant of design, whereas the stage wagon had its framework exposed to view and was of a more boxlike appearance than its more blue-blooded contemporary. The western-type mail or post coaches were mainly eastern products, being manufactured by such firms as Abbott, Downing & Company of Concord, New Hampshire; Gilbert and Company of Troy, New York; and the James Goold Company of Albany, New York. The Abbott, Downing "Concords" were by far the most popular, for although their competitors' products were more elaborate, they failed to capture but a small part of the western market, so that over the years "Concord" became synonymous with "stagecoach." Most coaches had front and rear boots and a roof rack for the carrying of luggage, etc., while the interior of a coach usually had seating provision for nine to twelve passengers, although this payload of humanity could be increased by allowing adventurous types to travel on the roof if space was available amidst the baggage. Coaches intended for short-distance travel could be ordered with additional omnibus-type seats fitted on their "top decks," and there was at least one Concord traveling the West that had an extra seat extending out over the rear trunk.[75] The size of the team employed to draw a vehicle was dependent on the type of terrain or dis-tance to be covered, a six-in-hand team —the maximum—being made up of three pairs of either horses or mules, and the pairs being known as "leaders" (fore-most), "swings" (center), and "wheel-ers" (rear). (See ABBOTT, DOWNING & COMPANY; CELERITY WAGON; and CON-CORD COACH.)

STAKED PLAINS A semi-arid and mainly treeless region that lies south of the Brazos River in western Texas and extends as far west as the Pecos River in eastern New Mexico. The overall area is usually referred to as the Llano Estacado, while the eastern half, which lies in Texas, is more often referred to as the Staked Plains.

STAMP IRON A branding iron that has the design of a full brand, or parts thereof, either welded or screwed to its shank, thus allowing livestock to be branded with one or more applications of the iron instead of the brand having to be "drawn," as is the case with a run-ning iron. (See BRANDING; BRANDING IRON; and BRANDS.)

STARR, BELLE Garbed in rich vel-vet and wearing a plumed D'Artagnan-type hat, the long-faced brunette with the cambered lips poses for the camera mounted upon a fine black mare named "Venus," the subject's preference for a Goodnight sidesaddle and the fact that a holstered .36-caliber Manhattan revolver is belted against her right hip being strong indications that an elegant upbringing may have been married to a violent na-ture. This was Belle Starr during the last decade of her life, when she was known as the "Bandit Queen" of Indian Terri-tory.

[75] This coach was employed on one of the longest runs in the West—between St. Louis, Missouri, and San Diego, California. Whether anyone rode the entire distance on this pre-carious seat is not recorded.

The girl who was to become known as Belle Starr was born in Washington County, northwestern Arkansas,[76] on February 5, 1848, the daughter of John and Eliza Shirley, a Virginia-born couple of substantial means who had settled in the Ozark region of Arkansas in the late 1830s. Shortly after the new arrival had been christened "Myra Belle," the Shirleys moved North, and by 1856 they owned a business complex consisting of livery stable, blacksmith's shop, and hotel at Carthage in Jasper County, Missouri. At the age of eight Myra became a pupil of the Carthage Academy for Young Ladies, where, over the years, she mastered the use of Latin, Greek, and Hebrew, became proficient in arithmetic and algebra, and absorbed such social assets as the possession of gracious manners, a good carriage, and the art of playing the piano. Plans for gracious living were shattered by the Civil War, for its vibrations shook many a noncombatant free of his substance, and after young Edward "Bud" Shirley[77] had been killed by federal troops and the Shirley Hotel had been razed to the ground in 1863, the family piled whatever belongings they could salvage into a couple of wagons and headed Southwest to settle near Scyene, a small settlement in Texas lying some nine miles east of Dallas. Four years after their arrival in Texas, John Shirley had recouped the family fortunes and was planning to build a hotel at Scyene with the monies accrued from the sale and breeding of horses.

During this period Myra Belle had blossomed into full flower while being cultivated by an ex-Quantrill guerrilla named Coleman Younger, so that when a onetime childhood sweetheart of her Carthage years arrived on the scene in the summer of 1868, the twenty-year-old girl was ripe for plucking. That this echo from the past was a man named James Reed who freely admitted to having ridden with the infamous Tom Starr and was strongly suspected of being allergic to anything resembling honest toil mattered little to Myra, and although her parents made efforts to halt the rake's progress, they rapidly changed their views and gave the couple their combined blessing when it became apparent that their loved one had been fertilized beyond controversy.

The newlywed Reeds took up residence in Bates County, Missouri, and here in the spring of 1869 Myra Belle gave birth to a girl child whom they christened Pearl. While his bride was rearing the new arrival, James Reed was riding with the Tom Starr band, a renewal of allegiance that led to Reed's killing a man named Shannon and his subsequent flight to California with his wife and child. While living in San Diego County, James Reed provided for his family by committing highway robberies, and Myra provided another mouth to feed when her second pregnancy terminated with the arrival of a boy in the early months of 1871. The infant had barely been christened Edward before the Reeds were fleeing back East to avoid the family breadwinner's imminent arrest on a charge of stage robbery. The fugitives didn't stop until they arrived at Scyene where, at some later date, they opened a livery stable, Myra looking after the business so that her husband might be free to engage in horse-stealing operations in Indian Territory. This arrangement worked well, for it kept the badly wanted Reed out of the public eye, and the family business was never without a good supply of remounts in its "used horse" lot.

[76] Not at Carthage, Missouri, as is often stated; it is worth noting that Belle's tombstone errs in this respect, as Belle always gave Carthage as her birthplace.
[77] One of Myra Belle's two brothers, the other being Preston.

On August 6, 1874, James Reed was shot dead by Deputy Sheriff J. T. Morris of Lamar County, Texas. The shooting occurred near Paris, and as far as Myra was concerned it probably happened at the right time, for shortly after learning of her new status she placed the children in the care of relatives, sold the livery stable, and headed for the glittering saloons and gambling halls of Dallas. The various exploits attributed to Myra during her stay in Dallas are of dubious repute; stories of her having shot a Dallas lawman to death are without foundation, and wild yarns that have her riding on cattle rustling sprees with a white man whose true identity will forever be obscured by the odd alias of "Blue Duck" are equally suspect.[78] The young widow did, however, work as a faro dealer and became acquainted with Jesse James while at Dallas.

Around 1877 Myra moved North and settled at rip-roaring Galena in the extreme southeastern corner of Kansas, and for the next couple of years she spent most of her time as the common-law wife of a medium-time gambler named Bruce Younger—an intimate relationship during which Myra displayed a remarkable touch of modesty by referring to her daughter as "Pearl Younger." By 1880 Myra left the bed and board of Bruce, although this interlude with a cousin of Coleman Younger was evidently not entirely forgotten, for when the widow became the legally wedded wife of old Tom Starr's twenty-three-year-old son Sam on June 6, 1880, and they settled on Sam's sixty-two-acre lot on a gooseneck bend of the Canadian River near Eufaula in Indian Territory, the new Mrs. Starr named their homestead "Younger's Bend." Honest folk were soon to know the Starrs' place as "Robbers' Roost," for the girl who was born Myra Belle Shirley was on

the threshold of becoming the infamous Belle Starr, a hatchet-faced trollop who was to attain such subtitling as "The Lady Desperado," "The Bandit Queen," and "The Petticoat Terror of the Plains."

Stories that "bill" Belle Starr as the undisputed leader of a gang of stock thieves and killers who either rallied to the banner of the Starrs or used Younger's Bend as a hideout cannot be disregarded, for at one time a reward of ten thousand dollars in gold was offered for ". . . the apprehension dead or alive of Sam and Belle Starr," yet when they were finally arrested by deputy United States marshals on horse-stealing charges in the late fall of 1882 they had little cause for worry, for when they were brought before "Hanging Judge" Parker in February of the following year, both Sam and Belle received comparatively light sentences, which allowed them to be back at "Younger's Bend" by the fall of 1883.

Shortly after their triumphal return to the "Bend," Belle's interest in Sam dropped well below freezing, and early in 1884 she transferred her affections to a twenty-three-year-old youth named Blue Duck who possessed a pencil-line mustache and a vacant expression and was an on-and-off member of the Younger's Bend community. What Sam thought of this has gone unrecorded, but he may have allowed a Cherokee sneer to crease his features when Blue Duck disappeared behind the walls of Menard Penitentiary in the summer of 1886. John Middleton, a fugitive who was wanted for the murder of Sheriff J. H. Black of Lamar County, quickly hopped into the saddle that had been vacated by Blue Duck, and a torrid affair developed between him and Belle. This may have led to something, but before Belle could decide whether to leave Younger's Bend for good with her new lover, news reached her that the re-

[78] If his reputed birth year of 1862 is anything to go by.

mains of Middleton had been discovered a few miles south of Younger's Bend. Most of Middleton's head had been shot away by a double blast from a shotgun. Sam may have smiled again; but not for long, for the smile was erased forever when he was shot dead in mid-December 1886 while engaged in a dance-hall brawl.

Sadly, Belle looked around for a replacement, but suitors were somewhat reluctant at becoming involved with such an obviously "jinxed" female whose face was as inviting as a clenched fist, but by the spring of 1888 one of Tom Starr's many nephews had stuck his neck out and taken up residence with Belle. His name was Jim July, and he had been a thorn in the side of the United States marshal's office at Fort Smith for some time, and on the morning of February 2, 1889, Belle persuaded him to surrender himself at Fort Smith to clear up a larceny rap that was hanging over his head. Belle accompanied July as far as San Bois, where they stayed overnight, parting the following morning so that Belle could return to Younger's Bend while Jim continued on his way to Fort Smith. Belle Starr never made it. Within but a short distance from her home a double blast from a shotgun lifted her out of "Venus'" saddle and left her dying in the dust.

The last of the big-time lady outlaws was buried in the yard of the Younger's Bend homestead, but the name of the person who killed her still remains conjectural; suspects are: (1) Edgar A. Watson, a fugitive from Florida justice who rented a small plot of land from Belle and was on extremely bad terms with her. Arrested and released for lack of evidence. Some years later Watson returned to Florida, where he was to be killed by a citizens' posse in the fall of 1910. (2)

Edward Reed. At the time of his mother's murder, Ed was a whiskey-sodden youth of eighteen who had peddled illicit whiskey to the Indians and spent time behind bars. The fact that Belle was always whaling the tar out of him with a bullwhip in an attempt to make him change his ways may have been sufficient motive. (3) Jim July. He may have suspected Belle's motives when she persuaded him to turn himself in. The fact that he arrived at Fort Smith does not constitute an airtight alibi, for he could have doubled back after parting from Belle at San Bois,[79] killed his "wife," then covered the 130 miles to Fort Smith with a stint of hard riding to make up for lost time. (4) In 1971 Mr. A. J. Robinson of Topeka, Kansas, claimed that sometime before her death in the 1930s his grandmother Mrs. Nana Devena had admitted to the killing of Belle Starr. The killing was a case of mistaken identity, for Mrs. Devena had been laying in wait for a neighbor whom she had been feudin' with when Belle came along to become a dead "innocent bystander" before the dry-gulcher realized her error. That Mrs. Devena was living near Eufaula at the time of Belle's death has been established, and although the confessor is reputed to have used the term "muzzle-loader" when referring to the weapon used, this may have merely been a memory lapse on Mrs. Devena's part or her misleading term for a shotgun. (See BLUE DUCK; STARR, TOM; and YOUNGER, COLEMAN.)

STARR, HENRY   Killer and bank robber who made his debut as a criminal during the Old West's twilight years and was still operating as such until well into the automobile era. Born on December 2, 1873, near Fort Gibson in Indian Territory, gurgling proof of the procreative

[79] San Bois was only fifteen miles east of Younger's Bend.

ability of George "Hop" Starr[80] and his Cherokee-Irish wife, Henry developed into a fine, upstanding youth who was well acquainted with the classics and possessed no obvious consumer vices such as an addiction to tobacco or alcohol. In 1889 young Henry started work as a cowhand, and for the next couple of years he was employed by various outfits with ranges in the northern half of the Cherokee nation, a period of honest effort that closed in the summer of 1891 with Henry being arrested—and subsequently fined—for trading whiskey to the Indians.

The following August saw him arrested on the far more serious charge of horse theft, but he jumped bond while awaiting trial and teamed up with a couple of miscreants named Edward Newcome and Jesse Jackson, and by the early days of December 1892 the Starr gang had held up a Missouri Pacific train at Nowata and committed at least two store robberies. Federal lawmen and railroad detectives scoured the territory for the band, a deadly game of cops and robbers during which Deputy U. S. Marshal Floyd Wilson was returned to Fort Smith draped across his saddle after he had been shot dead by Starr while attempting an arrest a few miles south of Lenapah. After being dubbed "killer," Starr increased his following by recruiting Frank Cheyney, Link Crumplin, Hank Watt, Bud Tyler, "Kid" Wilson, and a gunnie known only as "Happy Jack" to the colors, and over the next eighteen months this gang took part in three bank robberies, two store holdups, a train robbery, and a railroad depot stickup.

Toward the end of June 1893 Henry Starr and "Kid" Wilson moved into Colorado to lie low, and on July 3 of that year they were taken into custody by members of the Colorado Springs Police Department, Starr having been "jumped" in a restaurant while the "Kid" was being picked up in a brothel. On October 20, 1894, Starr was sentenced to death by Judge Isaac C. Parker for the murder of Floyd Wilson, but after a series of reversals and new trials, a manslaughter plea was allowed in 1898, and he was given the relatively light sentence of five years' imprisonment.

By 1904 Starr had returned to civilian life, found himself a bride, and became engaged in the real-estate business, but in March 1908 he returned to his old ways when he and recent payrolee "Kid" Wilson celebrated their reunion by robbing a couple of banks and escaping with more than three thousand dollars. Three months later the bank at Amity, Colorado, was visited by the pair, a crime that marked the end of the Starr-Wilson partnership, for after dividing the loot the "Kid" disappeared into the yonder and was never heard of again. The following year Henry fell into the eager hands of the Colorado authorities and wound up receiving a twenty-five-year stretch in the State Penitentiary at Canon City for his part in the Amity job, but in 1913 he was released on parole, and by the spring of 1914 it was strongly suspected that he was back in business as a bank robber. On March 27, 1915, these suspicions were confirmed, the accurate rifle fire of a seventeen-year-old youth named Paul Curry throwing Starr to the ground with a leg wound while he was attempting a getaway after he and his gang had staged a double bank job at Chandler, Oklahoma. This caper got Starr back behind walls to sweat out a twenty-five-year sentence in the Oklahoma Penitentiary.

Starr's luck, however, had not yet deserted him, and in April 1919 he was

---

[80] One of the many hard-bitten sons of an equally hard-bitten Cherokee Indian named Tom Starr, "Hop" was a brother-in-law of the infamous Belle Starr.

granted a full pardon. Within a short time of his release Starr appeared in a number of movies that laid great stress on the futility of a life of crime, thus garbing himself in the tatty raiment of pure hypocrisy, for when not required on the set, he was knocking off banks in Oklahoma.[81] On February 18, 1921, a well-dressed Henry Starr parked his automobile outside the People's Bank at Harrison, Arkansas, and entered the bank to stage a holdup. The caper misfired badly. Banker W. J. Myers' bellowing shotgun answered Starr's pistol-point request for a withdrawal of currency, and the bank robber *cum* film star was swept to the floor with a full load of buckshot lodged in his person. Starr died from the effects of his wounds on Tuesday, February 22, 1921. (See STARR, TOM.)

STARR, TOM   A full-blooded Cherokee Indian who was born in Tennessee in 1813. As a mature young man of more than 6 feet, 7 inches in height, Tom migrated to the Cherokee-allotted lands with his parents in 1837 and settled in what is now Adair County, Oklahoma. The Cherokee nation was a violent land in which to live, and by the time the Starrs had established themselves in their new home, Tom had used his bowie knife to cut short the career of a fellow tribesman named David Buffington. In 1845 a rival faction raided the Starr homestead and killed Tom's father and a twelve-year-old kid brother named Buck, a heinous crime that got the giant Cherokee on the trail of the thirty-two men whom he suspected of having taken part in the raid. This vendetta carried Tom far afield, but he did not fail in his self-allotted task, his only disappointment being that a handful of those whose names appeared on

his dead list had been scythed down by the Grim Reaper before Tom's blade could reach them.

Over the years Tom married and helped his wife Catherine raise a terrifying brood of eight boys and two girls, all of whom when fully growed became the nucleus of the "Starr gang," a legion of kinfolk whose ranks were constantly being swelled by the arrival of men on the run who were aware that Tom's domain on the south bend of the Canadian River had the reputation of being an outlaw's Eden. Throughout the Civil War years and for more than two decades after the roar of cannon had been silenced, Tom Starr's territory was avoided by most honest folk, as they regarded it as the most dangerous region in Indian Territory. By the time old Tom Starr died in 1890, he had built up a reputation of having killed more than a hundred men. This could well be, for as his predatory instincts are known to have taken him deep into Texas and as far west as California, the remains of many of his victims are doubtless still waiting to be dug up. In spite of all this, relatives of the deceased remembered him as a fun-loving gent who possessed a fine sense of humor. (See CHEROKEE INDIANS; STARR, BELLE; and STARR, HENRY.)

STETSON   In 1862, in an effort to while away the time while en route to the Colorado gold fields, John B. Stetson built a wide-brimmed *vaquero*-type hat from fur shavings, and this creation was so much admired that the Stetson Hat Company was formed to manufacture similar-style fur-felt hats in quantity. Stetsons are made from beaver, nutria, or coney fur, and a modern first-quality model retails at around twenty dollars.

[81] At least two banks—at Chandler and at Davenport, Oklahoma—are known to have been robbed by Starr and his associates in 1920.

The term "stetson" is often used when describing any of the wide-brimmed hats that were, and are, popular on the western scene.

STEVANS, BOB   Alias sometimes used by Robert Olive, brother of the infamous "Print" Olive. (See OLIVE, I. PRENTICE.)

STEVENS, JENNIE   Born in 1878 of poor dirt-farming parents whose ramshackle homestead was located on that portion of Indian Territory that was later to become Pawnee County, Oklahoma. Sometime in the early months of 1893 Jennie and a neighborhood lass named Annie McDougal became acquainted with members of the Doolin gang while attending a country dance, and both girls became camp followers of the mob, engaging in stock theft and whiskey peddling or acting as lookouts for the gang when they were not dispensing carnal comforts among the boys in the Pierce Hotel at Ingalls or some other favorite hideout. Over this period the 4-foot, 9-inch Jennie, attired in her all-male "outlaw" outfit, was known as "Little Britches," a juvenile delinquent who was to be run to earth by Deputy U. S. Marshal Bill Tilghman in 1894.

Jennie took flight when the lawmen arrived on the scene, but Tilghman shot her horse from under her and took her into custody after paddling the dust out of her buckskinned butt, and shortly afterward "Little Britches" had reverted to Jennie Stevens and was starting a two-year stretch in the Federal Reformatory at Farmington, Massachusetts. Released in 1896, the eighteen-year-old Jennie got a job as a domestic with a family domiciled at Boston, but after a few years of drudgery she moved to New York City, where she drifted into oblivion while reputedly engaged in religious work amidst the bums who frequented the Bowery.

Jennie Stevens may on occasion have used the name "Jean Metcalfe." (See DOOLIN GANG; INGALLS, OKLAHOMA; and McDOUGAL, ANNIE.)

STEWART, HENRI   A fully qualified medical practitioner who, after graduating from college, served as a ship's physician for a number of years before settling in Ohio to get married and raise a family. In 1877, at the age of thirty-three and with little more than six years of married life behind him, Henri left his wife and four children and moved West to exchange his thermometer for a .45 and take up the life of an outlaw. Stewart's crime career lasted less than two years, for although he is reputed to have learned the rudiments of train robbery while riding with the Sam Bass gang, he fared badly when going it alone, being picked up by federal lawmen shortly after he had killed a man named J. B. Jones during an abortive attempt to rob a train at Caddo in the Choctaw nation in May 1879. Placed on trial at Fort Smith, Arkansas, Stewart was sentenced to death by Judge Isaac C. Parker, and on August 29, 1879, the ex-doctor disappeared through the well-oiled trap of hangman George Maledon.

STILES, BILL   Occasionally come across as being the true identity of James gang rider Bill Chadwell, but this is incorrect. (See CHADWELL, BILL; STILES, BILLIE; and STILES, WILLIAM C.)

STILES, BILLIE   Joint leader of the Alvord-Stiles gang, which operated in Arizona Territory from early in 1899 until the beginning of the following year. Little is known regarding Stiles' early life apart from hazy reports that he was born near Casa Grande in Arizona Territory in the 1870s and that he was a patricide and had left home before he was out of his teens. Sometime in the early 1890s Stiles established a small ranch in southeastern Arizona where, over the years, he built up a good reputation, which was to lead to his seeing service as a deputy sheriff of Cochise County and as a local lawman at Pearce. In February 1900 Stiles' reputation was blown when it was learned that he and a fellow lawman named Burt Alvord had been arrested for a Southern Pacific train robbery that had taken place near Cochise on September 9, 1899. In the first week of April Stiles and Alvord escaped from the county jail at Tombstone, and Stiles headed for Nevada. Whether Stiles ever arrived in Nevada is doubtful, for although some reports would have us believe that he was shot dead shortly after having crossed the Nevada line, he was obviously in the best of health on March 9, 1902, for on that day he and his Mexican-born wife Maria were having their photograph taken at Naco, province of Sonora, Mexico. What may have happened to Billie Stiles after this date may never be ascertained with any degree of accuracy. (See ALVORD, BURT.)

STILES, WILLIAM C.
Shortly before he passed away at Los Angeles, California, on August 16, 1939, at the grand old age of eighty-nine, William C. Stiles had let it be known that he was the Bill Stiles who had ridden with the Jesse James gang from 1877 until the time of Jesse's death in 1882. As a man named Bill Stiles is known to have been an active member of the gang over this period, it appears quite likely that this old gentleman may have been speaking the truth and that he was the last surviving member of the gang at the time of his death. That William had the type of qualifications ad-

mired by Jesse is apparent from William's own admissions. These cover nearly half a century of ill-spent time that got off to a head start in 1865 when William started rolling drunks in his home state of New York and only drew to a close in 1913, in which year he was released from Sing Sing after serving a thirteen-year stretch for killing an unarmed man in the streets of New York City.

STILWELL, FRANK
Texas-born cowboy who became a member of the Clanton gang after his arrival in Arizona Territory in 1878. Stilwell's forte was stage robbery, and he is reputed to have held up the Tombstone-Bisbee stages on so many occasions that the stage teams obeyed his voice with the same show of alacrity as they exhibited when being hollered at by their drivers. During the greater part of 1881 Frank was carrying out these robberies while employed as a deputy sheriff by Sheriff John Behan of Cochise County, Frank's somewhat tarnished badge only being removed in mid-September of that year after he had been arrested on a charge of stage robbery.[82] Released shortly afterward on five thousand dollars' bond, Stilwell settled at Bisbee, where he soon established himself as a livery stable owner, an honest business image that was shattered when his mask slipped during a holdup of a Tombstone-Bisbee stage on January 6, 1882.

Two months later Frank took part in the assassination of Morgan Earp and got the Earp faction hot on his tracks. On the morning of March 21, 1882, and within seventy-two hours of Morgan's dying from his wounds, the body of Stilwell was discovered in the Southern Pacific Railroad yards at Tucson, Arizona. The remains contained "four rifle balls and two loads of buckshot." On the late eve-

---

[82] The Tombstone-Bisbee stage robbery that occurred at 10 P.M. on Thursday, September 8.

ning of the day preceding the discovery of Stilwell's body, shots had been heard while a train bearing the remains of Morgan and carrying Wyatt Earp, Doc Holliday, and Warren Earp as passengers had paused at Tucson on its journey to Colton, California. Frank Stilwell was twenty-seven years of age at the time of his death, and Wyatt and Doc are usually credited with the slaying. (See BEHAN, JOHN; CLANTON GANG; EARP, MORGAN; and EARP, WYATT BERRY STAPP.)

STINSON, BUCK Member of Sheriff Henry Plummer's gang of "Innocents." Whether Buck took part in any holdups while wearing a badge as one of Plummer's deputies is conjectural. That he was a killer is beyond all doubt. Early in 1863 he murdered a friendly Bannock Indian known as "Old Snag," and later that same year he and Haze Lyons assassinated a fellow deputy named J. W. Dillingham. Stinson and Lyons were arrested for the latter offense and sentenced to death by a people's court, but after being marched to the foot of the gallows, a masterly performance by Lyons and persuasive arguments put forward by "Innocents" Jack Gallagher and George Ives caused three women spectators to shed sufficient tears to bring about an abrupt change of public sentiment, and the two killers were released. On January 9, 1864, vigilantes arrested Buck, and he was hanged at Bannack the following afternoon, no ladies being allowed on this somber occasion. (See GALLAGHER, JACK; INNOCENTS; LYONS, HAZE; PLUMMER, HENRY; RAY, NED; SKINNER, CYRUS; and VIGILANTES OF MONTANA.)

ST. LOUIS, MISSOURI Major city lying on the west bank of the Mississippi River in western Missouri. Established as a French fur-trading center in 1764 and named after Louis IX of France, the city became the main provisional center for the fur trappers until the decline of the fur trade in the late 1830s, by which time the arrival of the river steamers on the Mississippi had guaranteed the city's continued prosperity and increased same by promoting it into becoming a key distributional center for numerous industries. To the pioneers St. Louis was the "Gateway to the West," and over the years of western expansion it became an intense focal point for stage and rail communications, a position it retains to this day. The town became part of the United States with the completion of the Louisiana Purchase in 1803. (See LOUISIANA PURCHASE.)

STONE BOILING A method of cooking in which red-hot stones are dropped into a container of water in which raw food has been placed. Practiced by Amerind tribes whose watertight baskets and pottery were far from fireproof. (See ASSINIBOINE INDIANS.)

STORMS, CHARLEY One of those unfortunate characters who only get their names in print on becoming the gun-law victims of more violent types. (See SHORT, LUKE.)

STOUDENMIRE, DALLAS A Civil War veteran and an ex-private of Company B, Texas Rangers, Alabama-born Dallas Stoudenmire arrived at El Paso in 1881 to accept the large shield that was to be his badge of office while employed as marshal of one of the toughest border towns in Texas. Shortly after he had pinned the badge onto a lapel of his long frock coat, the blond six-footer from Alabam' was involved in a gunfight of an all-embracing nature. On seeing a suspected killer named John Hale shoot Deputy Sheriff Gus Krempau dead in broad daylight, Dallas flipped a brace of Colts from the leather-lined back pockets of his pants and began tripping their hammers, and if we discount the fact that his first shot killed an innocent Mexican bystander, the marshal made a pretty good show, for his second and third shots killed Hale and a man named George Campbell—the latter being a friend of Hale's who was still undecided as to what course to adopt when Stoudenmire shot him dead. Friends of the defunct Hale sought to equate matters by employing a low-I.Q. gunnie named William Johnson to dry-gulch the marshal, but when Johnson, after a night of much drinking, attempted to fulfill his contract by sending two loads of heavy-gauge shot in the lawman's direction, he missed his target, and Dallas had killed him before Johnson had had time to realize that his aim had been faulty.

In February 1882 Stoudenmire took time out to travel back East to get married, leaving a brother-in-law named "Doc" Cummins and Deputy Marshal James Gillett in charge of the marshal's office during his absence. A few days after Stoudenmire's departure, "Doc" got himself shot dead while visiting the Coliseum Variety Theater. The Coliseum was one of two places of amusement owned by three brothers named Manning, three level-headed businessmen who assumed full responsibility for the gunning down of "Doc" on the grounds that the slaying had occurred on their premises and had been committed by one of their staff. On his return to duty, Stoudenmire made dire threats against the Mannings, but more sober minds, who had no desire to see El Paso deteriorate into a battleground of rival factions, persuaded him to reach an understanding with the brothers, and a "let bygones remain bygones" agreement was signed by both parties as an indica-

tion of their good intentions. It is possible that Stoudenmire regretted his signing of this agreement, for he became so cantankerous that he was relieved of his post, and James Gillett took over as marshal.

On the afternoon of Tuesday, September 18, 1883, Stoudenmire, suffering from the effects of a bad hangover, left home to go straighten himself out with a hair-of-the-dog tonic. Shortly afterward he appeared in a saloon that was owned by the Mannings and got into an argument with Dr. G. F. Manning, which led to both parties drawing guns and Manning getting a bullet in his arm as both men struggled to prevent his rival from aiming his weapon. James and Frank Manning came on the run as the combatants fandangoed through the batwing doors and out onto the street, and when Stoudenmire's head offered itself as a target, James Manning ended the affair by putting a bullet through the big Alabaman's right temple. Manning was subsequently acquitted of the offense on the grounds that he had been protecting the life of his brother when he killed Dallas Stoudenmire. (See GILLETT, JAMES BUCHANAN.)

STRANGLERS   Term sometimes used to describe a lynch mob or a posse of vigilantes. More specifically used when referring to the fourteen-man posse of "Regulators" organized by Granville Stuart in 1884. (See STUART, GRANVILLE.)

STUART, GRANVILLE   Gaunt-faced Virginia-born prospector and cattleman who in 1858, at the age of twenty-four, became one of the first white men to discover gold in the Deer Lodge Valley of the Oregon country.[83] Four years after making his strike, Stuart mar-

---

[83] Until 1862, in which year it became part of Idaho Territory. The Deer Lodge region became a permanent part of eastern Montana in 1864.

ried a Shoshone girl named Aubony, and over the 1863–64 period he was an active member of the vigilante movement that wrote "finis" to Henry Plummer and his gang of "Innocents." In the 1870s Stuart began touring the territory in search of a likely place to raise cattle, and in 1880 he established the DHS spread in the Judith Basin, a change of occupation that was to lead to Stuart forming a band of vigilantes that cleared the rustlers and stock thieves from the eastern ranges of Montana in the summer of 1884. This fourteen-strong civilian posse was known as the "Stranglers"—an apt name, for having seen service with the original Vigilantes of Montana, their leader was a strong advocate of the hempen sendoff when dealing with violators of other folks' rights. Although the "Stranglers" were strongly suspected of having hanged about seventy men who may have well deserved their fate, Stuart would make only rather oblique admissions to having lynched less than half this number. Shortly after the winter of 1886–87 had decimated his herds by more than 60 per cent, Stuart gave up ranching, and in his later years he began taking an active interest in politics, which resulted in his being appointed United States diplomatic representative to Uruguay and Paraguay in 1894, a position he held for just over four years. Granville Stuart died at Missoula, Montana, on October 2, 1918, and was interred at Deer Lodge. (See INNOCENTS and VIGILANTES OF MONTANA.)

STUDEBAKER WAGON Name that may be applied to any of the wagons produced by the H. & C. Studebaker Manufacturing Company[84] from 1852 until 1920, in which latter year the last horse-drawn vehicle came off the production line to make way for the Studebaker automobile, the latter having been first introduced as an electrically powered horseless carriage in 1901. The firm's horse-drawn output was not confined to the manufacture of wagons—landaus, broughams, phaetons, clarences, victorias, school omnibuses, tandems, and four-in-hand coaches all found their way into the firm's catalogue as an inducement to the carriage trade.

SUBLETTE, WILLIAM The most well known of the five Sublette brothers. William Lewis Sublette, born in Lincoln County, Kentucky, in 1779,[85] joined William H. Ashley's expedition to the upper Missouri in 1822, and for the next four years he was to be employed as one of a band of trappers who made up the field force of Ashley's Rocky Mountain Fur Company. In 1832, after spending some years as a business associate of Jedediah Smith, Sublette was wounded in the face by an Indian arrowhead during a trapper-Gros Ventre clash that occurred at the Pierre's Hole rendezvous, and from then on his name was to be prefixed by "Cut-face." During the year in which he acquired this grim sobriquet, Sublette teamed up with Robert Campbell in a business partnership, and two years later they established a fur-trading post within a log stockade they had erected on a site that was later to be occupied by Fort Laramie.[86] The Sublette-Campbell partnership was dissolved in 1842, and at some later date Sublette returned East and settled in Pennsylvania. William L. Sublette died at Pittsburgh on July 23,

---

[84] Established in February 1852 at South Bend, Indiana, by Henry and Clement Studebaker. In 1858 Henry sold out his interest in the company to another brother, named John.
[85] Not a definitive date.
[86] In 1835 the partners sold this trading post to fellow trappers Tom Fitzpatrick, Jim Bridger, and Milton Sublette—the latter being one of William's many brothers.

1845. Sublette's cutoff on the Oregon Trail[87] derives its name from one of William's trail-blazing trips. (See MOUNTAIN MEN; ROCKY MOUNTAIN FUR COMPANY; and SMITH, JEDEDIAH.)

SUCCOTASH   An Amerind dish that originally consisted of a boiled amalgam of corn, beans, and fish. At some later date the fish element was omitted, and succotash became a vegetarian dish.

SUN DANCE   A plains Indians' ceremony that was the culmination of a period of fasting and self-purification by males of the various tribes who wished to have powerful visions that might be of benefit to the whole tribe. Although the Sun Dance could take place with but one dancer, this was rare, for there were usually a number of males who had been cleansed and were eager to dance around a post that had been made from a ceremoniously felled tree trunk until they dropped into a trancelike stupor that usually had the desired effect of producing visions.

This was the somewhat mild version of the Sun Dance as practiced by most of the plains tribes. A far more barbaric form of Sun Dance enjoyed favor among tribes of the Siouan group. The Sioux dancers allowed sticks to be inserted through double cuts that had been made in either their pectorals or back muscles. Strings hanging from the central post were then attached to the sticks, and the dancers would strain against the pull of the strings until the tearing of their flesh allowed release.[88]

In the Mandan version of this ceremony the central post was replaced by a gallowslike structure, and the so-called "dancers" were suspended from the crossbeam until rupturing flesh or a sign from the tribal medicine man allowed them to be returned to the ground. The dance was almost invariably performed within the confines of a circular stockade made from brushwood. In the early 1900s the United States Bureau of Indian Affairs showed a complete disregard for the Bill of Rights by banning the Sun Dance ceremony, and it wasn't until 1934 that the ban was lifted on the condition that self-torture be omitted from the ritual.

SUNDANCE KID   Name that became firmly attached to Harry Longbaugh after he had spent some time sweating out a sentence for horse theft in the jail at Sundance, Wyoming. (See LONGBAUGH, HARRY.)

SUPERSTITION MOUNTAINS
A mountain mass in southern Arizona that rises abruptly from a flat wilderness of prickly pear and giant saguaro twenty miles due east of the town of Mesa, seemingly having punched its way up through the desert crust lying south of the Salt River when violent upheavals were sculpting the land a plethora of zeros ago. Within this amalgam of peaks, buttes, canyons, creeks, and pillars of rock have been found traces that indicate a Hopi Indian tenancy of the region during some period which, as yet, remains undated, while the ruins of abandoned mine shafts

---

[87] A short cut that left the Oregon Trail at the western end of South Pass and traveled in a generally westerly direction to rejoin the main trail as the latter worked its way north along the Bear River Valley.

[88] An alternative method was to suspend a buffalo skull or similar weighty object to the sticks; in this case a dancer would jog around until the jerking of his burden accomplished his purpose. Scar tissue resulting from this practice became self-awarded "medals" proclaiming bravery and endurance.

and smelters make it apparent that the Spaniards had penetrated the mountains in search of precious ores by the early 1800s.[89]

By this time the Apaches had infiltrated the Superstitions, and in 1848 Don Miguel Peralta, his son Pedro, and an army of employees—all of whom were probably unaware that they were trespassing on land the Apaches deemed sacred as being the source of their thunder god's gold—were massacred by tribesmen as the former were shipping gold out of the mountains by pack train. After wiping out this party of Mexicans, the Apaches may have camouflaged the location of the Peralta Mine, for as far as is known the workings have never been rediscovered. During the decade 1879–89 a man named Jacob Walzer—somewhat better known as "The Dutchman"—brought more than a quarter million dollars' worth of gold out of the mountains, and although it was assumed he had found the lost Peralta Mine, later evidence made this appear unlikely.

When Walzer died in 1891 without leaving any apparent clues as to the location of his mineral wealth, the legend of the "Dutchman's Lost Mine"[90] was born—a magnet that has been luring men into the Superstitions—and frequently to their deaths—ever since. Of the hundreds of prospectors and would-be prospectors who have ventured into the mountains, a good number have gone missing, permanently. But not all; over the years members of the Maricopa County sheriff's office have brought the remains of the following out of the Superstitions: Elisha

M. Reavis, known as "The Madman of the Superstitions," decapitated body and head recovered in April 1896; Adolph Ruth, a man who claimed possession of a map that gave the location of Walzer's hidden wealth, decapitated head with a bullet hole between the eyes found mounted on top of a cairn, with the remainder of corpse lying nearby, in December 1931; Hematite Frinck, a prospector who had a sack of pure gold lying by his side when he was found, at the point of death from a gunshot wound in the stomach, in November 1938 (Hematite died before he could make any statement regarding the gold); James Cavey, photographer turned prospector who disappeared into the mountains in August 1947, gut-shot, decapitated body found roped inside a bedroll, the head being discovered some distance away, in February 1948; a Dr. Burns, whose reasons for going into the Superstitions remain conjectural, body recovered with a gunshot wound in the stomach in February 1951; unknown human skeleton found in the shadow of Weaver's Needle in May 1954; body of a young hunter who had been shot between the eyes recovered in April 1955 (possibly a hunting accident). Theories as to who may have been responsible for all, or any, of these deaths range from some nameless prospector who wishes to keep the location of some rich find secret, to the possibility that some "Broncho" Apaches are still acting as guardians of the thunder god's gold.[91] In 1971 the United States Forestry Service made rumblings that suggest that the western region of the Superstitions[92]

[89] Possibly earlier.
[90] Alternatively—although somewhat ambiguously—the "Lost Dutchman."
[91] This latter theory, although seemingly "way out," still holds good in many quarters.
[92] This is the area in which the Peralta Mine and Walzer's "strike" are reputed to be located. Superstition Mountain, Black-top Mountain, Bluff Spring Mountain, Weaver's Needle, Needle Canyon, West Boulder Canyon, and East Boulder Canyon—all of which have found their way into the Peralta-Walzer legends—are located in the western and northwestern sections of the mountains. The site of the Peralta massacre lies at the northern end of the mountain that gives the range its name.

may become forbidden ground for prospectors in the near future. (See LOST MINES and WALZER, JACOB.)

SUTTER, JOHN AUGUSTUS

A Swiss cloth merchant who arrived in America in 1834, having fled his native Burgdorf and a wife and four children after much loose living had led him into bankruptcy and almost into debtors' prison. After settling at Independence, Missouri, shortly after his arrival, Sutter tried to establish himself as a Santa Fe trader, but he met with little success, and it wasn't until he arrived in Alta, California, in 1839 and fast-talked Governor Don Juan Bautista Alvarado into allowing him a land grant of forty-nine thousand acres that Sutter began to make much impression on the western scene. In August 1839 this man from the Mittelland proudly proclaimed that he had founded a colony and christened it New Helvetia, little knowing at the time that by 1854 the settlement would have been engulfed by Sacramento and would have become the state capital.

As the hub of this feudal domain Sutter erected a massive adobe fort, which contained barracks for his private army, workshops, a blanket factory, and had cannon mounted on its bastions.[93] This stronghold was a fitting background for Sutter, for he liked to parade around in a French officer's dress uniform he was not entitled to wear and be addressed as "Captain." Fremont commandeered the fort as his headquarters during the Bear Flag Revolution of 1846, and later that same year it became the center of operations when attempts were being made to rescue the ill-fated Donner party. By

1848 "Captain" Sutter had overextended himself and was more heavily in debt than when he had been forced to leave his native land, and James Marshall, Sutter's carpenter, was overseeing the building of a sawmill in the Coloma Valley[94] as the initial move in securing much-needed lumber which his boss was too impoverished to purchase.

On January 24, 1848, while he and his men were engaged in building a channel for the millrace, Marshall discovered a number of gold nuggets, and although every effort was made to keep the find secret, by May of that year the news had leaked out, and shortly afterward New Helvetia was being overrun by hordes of eager prospectors. After trying to remove the "squatters" from his land, and failing to do so, Sutter filed claim against 17,222 trespassers, but as the original land titles had been destroyed by fire while in the care of his lawyers, he first had to reestablish his legal ownership of the land. Over these troubled years Sutter opened a fruit-canning factory and nail and paper-manufacturing plants, but although he achieved a prosperity comparable with his early California years, most of this wealth was to be dissipated in fighting legal battles that were still unresolved at the time of his death at Lititz, Pennsylvania, in 1880. The "Captain" was survived by his wife, Annette, and their children. (See DONNER PARTY; and FREMONT, JOHN CHARLES.)

SUTTON-TAYLOR FEUD

The Sutton-Taylor feud of western history was but the final episode in a long-drawn-out series of lethal bickerings, the families involved having started the prac-

[93] Probably built more on credit than cash, for some years later, when the Russian-American Fur Company was pulling out of their Fort Ross base, Sutter purchased the firm's buildings and equipment for $2,000 in cash and a $28,000 promissory note, which he never redeemed.

[94] The sawmill being located on the American River about 40 miles east of Sutter's Fort.

tice of firing balls at each other's kinfolk in the Carolinas some twenty years before they decided to settle down as neighbors and fellow cattlemen in DeWitt County, Texas, in the 1860s. In the spring of 1868 William E. Sutton caused some tension by killing Charley Taylor,[95] and when he followed this up by shooting Buck Taylor to death in a Clinton saloon on Christmas Eve of that same year, the Taylors began reaching for their hardware to reactivate a family feud that was to develop into something like a small-scale war, with more than four hundred partisans trying to grab a "piece of the action."

For more than five years much of the bad blood existing between the opposing factions found release through bullet holes as more than forty men died in De-Witt County and adjacent Gonzales County, the feud only burning itself out with the killings of William E. Sutton and Gabriel Slaughter on March 11, 1874; both men having met their deaths —courtesy of James and William Taylor —on the deck of a river steamer that was tied up at Indianola receiving passengers for a trip to New Orleans. Over this period of strife the Sutton forces[96] included such men as Jack Helm and "Shanghai" Pierce, while the Taylors' ranks were stiffened by the Clements brothers and—toward the climax of the fracas—John Wesley Hardin. (See CLEMENTS, EMANUEL; HARDIN, JOHN WESLEY; HELM, JACK; and PIERCE, ABEL HEAD.)

SWAIN, J. H. An alias used by John Wesley Hardin. (See HARDIN, JOHN WESLEY.)

SWARTZ, ALFRED Names adopted by Alfred Packer while lying low in Wyoming after escaping from a Colorado jail. (See PACKER, ALFRED.)

SWILLING, JOHN W. Georgia-born prospector who arrived in Arizona Territory after seeing a brief period of service in the Civil War and became one of a party of miners who discovered rich placer deposits of gold near Wickenburg in 1863. In 1865, after more than five hundred thousand dollars' worth of pure gold had been winkled from this strike, Swilling pulled out of Wickenburg, and for the next couple of years he roamed the territory with a fellow prospector named Jacob Snively, reputedly searching for "lost" Spanish diggings. Sometime in 1867 Swilling paused from his wanderings and settled on the north bank of the Salt River to establish a small settlement which, after beginning life as "Stone-wall," was to be renamed "Phoenix."[97] Here John organized several irrigation schemes, remaining at Phoenix for a number of years before moving north to finally take up residence in the recently established mining camp of Gillette[98] in the early months of 1878.

Shortly after becoming domiciled at Gillette, Swilling and two of his cronies— Andrew Kirby and George Munroe—took a trip westward to dig up the remains of Jacob Snively, who had been killed by Apaches way back in '71, the trio being of the opinion that it was about time Jake's leavings were brought to Gillette so that they might enjoy the benefit of being reinterred in livelier surroundings. During the period in which these resurrection

[95] At the time of the killing Sutton was a deputy sheriff of DeWitt County, and Taylor was a fugitive from a stock-theft charge; the Taylors may therefore have grudgingly accepted this slaying as a line-of-duty affair.
[96] Usually referred to as the "Regulators."
[97] Later to become the state capital of Arizona.
[98] About thirty miles north of Phoenix. Gillette is now a ruined ghost of a town.

men were absent from Gillette, a stage-coach robbery in which two passengers were murdered occurred near Wicken-burg, and the three men had hardly had time to get Jake back underground on their return before Swilling and Munroe had been arrested as prime suspects in the robbery. After much legal dickering the two suspects found themselves inside the Yuma County jail awaiting trial, but the case was never to be resolved, for John W. Swilling died in the Yuma jail on August 12, 1878, at the age of forty-seven years. The deceased left a wife and five children.

SWING MEN Cowhands who ride on the flanks of a herd that is being kept on the move, "swing men" being positioned in rear of "point men" and ahead of "flank men."

SYDNEY DUCKS Of the horde of ex-penal-settlement rabble from Australia who invaded California during the early days of the gold rush, a large number settled in San Francisco and formed themselves into an organized society of thieves, muggers, burglars, and murder-ers; these were the infamous "Sydney Ducks." More than a hundred murders had been credited to the "Ducks" before vigilante action put an end to the mob in 1850, the public lynching of four well-known "Ducks"—John Jenkins, Robert McKenzie, James Stuart, and Samuel Whittaker—having the desired effect of either driving the remainder into re-spectability or from the city.

CHARLES M. RUSSELL

Tabor, Horace Austin Warner   Native of Vermont who had been prospecting in the Pike's Peak region of Colorado for almost twenty years with but moderate success before vast wealth began finding its way to his door in the spring of 1878. In April 1878 Tabor, recently elected mayor of Leadville[1] and owner of a four-room log building that housed his general store and post office, grubstaked a couple of prospectors to less than $20 worth of victuals and equipment for a third share in whatever they might find, and within a matter of weeks their strike—the "Little Pittsburgh" —was giving up silver ore at the rate of $20,000 a week. By the summer of 1878 much luck[2] in further speculations of a mining nature had jacked Tabor well into the millionaire class, and in the mid-fall of that year, after being elected lieutenant governor of the two-year-old state of Colorado, the "Bonanza King of Leadville" moved to Denver with his wife Augusta and their twenty-one-year-old son Nathaniel Maxcy to settle in a mansion that is reputed to have cost Tabor more than $60,000.

Tabor's spending escalated in direct ratio to the rise on his financial graph, and in 1881, at the peak of his success, he improved the cultural tone of Denver by erecting the Tabor Hotel and the Tabor Grand Opera House at a total cost of $1,350,000. In 1882, when Tabor was a graying fifty-two, fast living had led him into a torrid relationship with a twenty-six-year-old blond divorcee named Eliz-

[1] Known as "Slabtown" until January 1878.
[2] One "lucky" example: A shifty-eyed prospector known as "Chicken Bill" "salted" what he considered a worthless hole with silver ore stolen from the Little Pittsburgh and sold the site to Tabor for $40,000 as a going concern; the laugh, however, was on "Chicken," for the salted diggings became the fabulous "Chrysolite Mine."

abeth Bonduel McCourt,[3] and in March 1883, having obtained a divorce from Augusta, Tabor married his new light-of-love at Washington, D.C. Two girl children[4] were to be born of this union before Tabor's mines became barren and he was forced to sell out his holdings in various enterprises to retain the family living standards.

By the late 1890s the Tabors had been reduced to living in a rented room of the Windsor Hotel at Denver, and Tabor died here, from the effects of peritonitis, on April 10, 1899, his only remaining asset being a ramshackle shack located on his long-abandoned "Matchless Mine" workings. Elizabeth McCourt Tabor was to survive for more than thirty years amidst the ruins of the "Matchless," scraps of burlap keeping her warm as she waited for her husband's dying words —"Don't give up the Matchless, for it will make millions again"—to come true. They never did. Early in 1935 snow blanketed Leadville, and sometime during the first week of March the window-less shack on the Matchless became a mausoleum when Elizabeth sank into a cold-induced coma and froze to death, a tragic ending that will only be applauded by the most devout of moralists.

TALBOTTE, HENRY J.   A gold camp troublemaker who used the name "Cherokee Bob," reputedly because he was the offspring of a Caucasian father and a Cherokee mother. In January 1861 Georgia-born Talbotte established him-

self as a "somebody" on the western scene by taking part in a gunsmoke free-for-all that occurred in a Walla Walla playhouse, an offstage performance that left three dead men littering the stalls in its last act and got "Cherokee Bob" traveling East on a stolen hayburner shortly after the curtain had dropped. After putting seventy miles between himself and Walla Walla, Talbotte settled at Lewis-ton and became a saloonowner, but by the fall of 1861 gold strikes some two days' ride to the southeast of Lewiston had gotten his customers flowing thata-way, and early in 1862 he followed the trade and established himself as a saloon-owner in the boom camp of Florence.[5] Here Talbotte came into possession of a titian-haired lovely named Cynthia by scooping her up as the jackpot in a card game that left a cad named William Mayfield with naught to exercise his libido on.

On New Year's Eve 1862 Talbotte allowed Cynthia to be escorted to a local dance by a recently acquired pal named William Willoughby, an arrangement that allowed the saloonowner to remain at his post to keep the suds flowing. The dance was hardly a success, for before "Happy New Years" could be exchanged, a herd of green-eyed women of the town had persuaded the dance committee to eject Cynthia and William by threatening a mass walkout if the two remained. Incensed by this slight, "Cherokee Bob" and Willoughby strapped on their armament and went gunning for committee

[3] Affectionately known as "Baby Doe."

[4] Elizabeth Bonduel Lillie in 1885 and Rose Mary Echo Silver Dollar in 1889. Elizabeth left home in the early 1900s, to later marry and settle in Wisconsin. The younger daughter, who is usually referred to as "Silver Dollar," was to find employment with the Denver *Times* for some years before moving to Chicago around 1921, where she was to be scalded to death by a kettle of boiling water in September 1925—a mysterious death that was to result in a coroner's jury returning an open verdict on the remains of this thirty-six-year-old woman who, during her Denver years, had written a poorly received novel entitled *The Star of Blood.*

[5] Lewiston and Florence were at this time in Washington Territory, as was Walla Walla, but in 1863 the two former settlements became part of Idaho Territory.

members Jacob Williams and Orlando Roberts on New Year's Day. Jake and Orlando had been forewarned, however, and when the clash occurred, Talbotte and Willoughby were the ones to go down in the dust—the latter dying instantly, while "Cherokee" petered out in a back room of his saloon four days later. Talbotte's marker—which gives his age as twenty-nine at the time of his death—is located at Florence.[6]

TAMALES Mexican-Spanish name for a dish made from Indian corn that has been steamed in banana leaves or corn husks. Chopped meat—usually pork or chicken—that has been liberally seasoned with red peppers is mixed with the corn meal. Tamales (the plural of tamal or tamale) are a staple dish among the Mexican element of the American Southwest.

TAMARACK TREE Amerind name for the larch tree.

TANGLELEG
Humorous "trade" name applied to one of the many brands of spiritous liquids that were distilled by frontier traders and masqueraded as whiskey. (See TAOS LIGHTNING and WHISKEY.)

TAOS LIGHTNING
So-called whiskey manufactured from native wheat by Simeon Turley at his distillery and trading post on the Rio Hondo in New Mexico's Sangre de Christo Mountains. Turley's main outlet for his whiskey was Taos, which lay about twelve miles south of his plant, and during the early 1840s he found a lucrative market for his product among the local Pueblo Indians and the mountain men who used the town as a base and entertainment center. A

stone-built fort protected Turley's investment from possible Indian raids, but during the Taos uprising of 1847 the place was overrun by *insurrectos*, who left it a smoldering ruin. Turley escaped from the post before the final assault was mounted, only to be overtaken shortly afterward by a party of Indians, who killed and scalped him. The ruins of Simeon Turley's stronghold are still visible. (See TAOS, NEW MEXICO, and WHISKEY.)

TAOS, NEW MEXICO One of the oldest settlements in the American Southwest, the village known as "San Fernández de Taos" having been established for more than 200 years when the trappers and mountain men of the West began using the place as a rendezvous, supply base, and recreational center in the early 1800s. Located about 55 miles north-northeast of Santa Fe on a sage-dotted plain lying between the Rio Grande and the Sangre de Christo Mountains, with the Tanoan pueblos looming to the north of the town, Taos was the center of an Amerind-Mexican uprising that flared on January 19, 1847, exactly five months to the day after General Stephen Watts Kearny and his motley army of eastern riflemen had hoisted the Stars and Stripes above Santa Fe and proclaimed that all the surrounding region was United States territory. The *insurrectos*, suitably "juiced" on a local distillation known as "Aguardiente de Taos," killed newly elected Governor Charles Bent and used his scalp as a banner as they roamed the town and countryside killing a few local officials and a number of settlers, but their outbreak was short-lived, Colonel Sterling Price's army and a band of mountain men led by Céran St. Vrain bringing the rebellion to a close on February 4, 1847, after they had routed a

---

[6] Now a ghost town.

horde of Mexicans and killed some 150 Indians who had taken refuge in the old Spanish mission north of Taos. After the Mexican War of 1846–48 Taos came under the jurisdiction of the United States, and it is now the county seat of Taos County, New Mexico, and a major tourist and cultural center of the state. Pronounced "Touse." (See BENT, WILLIAM; NEW MEXICO; PUEBLO INDIANS; TAOS LIGHTNING; and TAOS TRAIL.)

TAOS TRAIL   Trail linking Taos with Santa Fe in the south and Bent's Fort on the Arkansas River in the north, the trail traveling north via the Raton Pass. (See BENT'S FORT; RATON PASS; and TAOS, NEW MEXICO.)

TAPADEROS   A leather covering that wraps around the front and sides of the stirrup. Useful in protecting a rider's feet from the elements and when riding through heavy brush, nettles, etc. Tapaderos is derived from the Spanish *tapadera*—literally meaning a lid or covering.

TARANTULA JUICE   Name of one of the many brands of "trade whiskeys" distilled in the West during the frontier years. (See WHISKEY.)

TATTENBAUM, WILLIAM
A young lieutenant of Czar Alexander II's Imperial White Hussars who deserted the colors in 1880 to avoid court-martial for striking a superior officer. Months later William entered the United States via California, and after outfitting himself in the finest of western-style raiment and armament, he rode into the interior, his identity cloaked beneath the tough-sounding alias of "Russian Bill." Tombstone in southeastern Arizona got this multilingual son of the wealthy Countess Telfrin when the Clanton gang was at the peak of its power, and within a short time of his arrival, Tattenbaum had

talked "Curly Bill" Brocius into accepting him as a member of the mob. Whether "Russian Bill" ever became deeply involved in any of the gang's escapades is open to doubt, but he did remain in the outlaw-infested camp of Galeyville for almost a year, no doubt grooming his long, lager-colored hair and amusing the boys with quotations from the classics when not engaged in running errands for the gang. In the fall of 1881 "Russian Bill" made a lone trip across the New Mexico line and was promptly arrested and tossed into the jail at Shakespeare for being in possession of a stolen mount. Law enforcement at Shakespeare was taken care of by a group of nononsense citizens who were known as the Law and Order Committee, and forty-eight hours after his arrest, Tattenbaum and a fellow prisoner named Sandy King were swinging from a ceiling beam in the banqueting hall of the Grant House hostelry; the double lynching being the sequel to a "court" hearing that had lasted as long as it takes to fashion a couple of nooses. In 1883 diplomatic inquiries made on Countess Telfrin's behalf elicited the information that William Tattenbaum had died in an accident. The town of Shakespeare has long been a ghost town, but as recent as the late 1950s a small marker indicated where the remains of "Russian Bill" lie buried.

TAYLOR, PEARL   Somewhat better known under her married name of Pearl Hart. (See HART, PEARL.)

TAYLOR-SUTTON FEUD   The explosive climax to an animosity of many years' standing. (See SUTTON-TAYLOR FEUD.)

TEN IN TEXAS RANCH
Recognized as the biggest spread in the West during the 1890s. (See CAPITOL SYNDICATE.)

TEPEE   Cone-shaped, hide-covered[7] tent that has adjustable smoke-flaps rising like a pair of ears at its apex. The framework of a tepee[8] consisted of 12 to 14 poles, each about 25 feet in length and tapering from an approximate 4-inch base to a 1-inch tip; these poles also served as travois poles when a tepee had been dismantled for transportation purposes. The largest of these dwellings—found mainly among the Blackfoot Indians—had a diameter of 20 feet, but a diameter of 15 feet was about average. The tepee, which was an invention of the plains tribes and is recognized as the most perfect form of tent, was used by the plains and plains-plateau Indians. Occasionally confused with the wigwam. (See WIGWAM.)

TEQUILA   An alcoholic drink of Mexican origin. Also known as mescal or mezcal. (See MESCAL.)

TETON SIOUX   One of the three main divisions of the Sioux nation, the others being the Santee and Yankton divisions. (See SIOUX INDIANS.)

TEXAS   Second-largest state in the union, Texas having dropped to second place when Alaska was admitted to the Union in 1959. Bounded on the northwest by New Mexico, on the north by Oklahoma, and having Arkansas as its northeastern and Louisiana as its eastern neighbor, the Gulf of Mexico gives it a coastline in the southeast, while its frontier in the southwest is established by that stretch of the U.S.-Mexico border that follows the winding course of the Rio Grande.

Originally a Spanish possession, the North Americans gained a foothold in the territory after Moses Austin had been granted permission to establish a colony on the lower reaches of the Brazos and Colorado rivers in the early days of 1821. Moses died before the colonization could be completed, but his son Austin continued the work, only to run into difficulties when Mexico won her independence from Spain in the summer of 1821 and the new administration took exception to the colonists' practice of slave ownership, opposing views that were not resolved until 1823, when both parties reached a compromise and the land grant was confirmed. English-speaking settlers, illegal squatters, and adventurers continued to filter into this Mexican province of Coahuila and Texas, and by 1830 clashes were occurring between the Mexicans and the Texas-Americans, and after six years of intermittent warfare the late arrivals proclaimed an independent republic on March 2, 1836.

On March 1, 1845, the Lone Star Republic of Texas joined the Union as the twenty-eighth state, an act that triggered off the Mexican War of 1846–48 and led to Mexico relinquishing all claim to the territory after the cessation of hostilities. During the Civil War Texas seceded from the Union and joined the Confederacy, and the state wasn't readmitted to the Union until 1870. After the Civil War Texas became the cradle of the West's cattle industry, and although the industry was later to become more decentralized, the King Ranch of Texas still has the reputation of being the largest spread in the world. The Texas Panhandle—punching its way north between Oklahoma and New Mexico—and the eastern half of the Llano Estacado or "Staked Plains" lie in the northwestern area of the state. Popularly known as the "Lone Star State,"

[7] Originally buffalo hides, later to be replaced with cow hides and later with muslin or burlap.
[8] Word used by the Sioux Indians which—roughly translated—means "a place used for dwelling."

Texas derives its name from the friendly Tehas Indians, who roamed the area during the days of Spanish occupancy. Austin is the state capital. (See ALAMO, THE; BATTLE OF SAN JACINTO; GOLIAD MASSACRE; KING RANCH; PANHANDLE; STAKED PLAINS; TEXAS RANGERS; and TEXIAN.)

TEXAS HAT Wide-brimmed *vaquero* type hat of the early days that had a flat crown and was made from inferior woolfelt. Wearers of these "Texas" hats usually threaded a rawhide thong through holes punched around the perimeter of the brim, the tightening of the thong causing the brim to curve slightly upward so that it didn't flop down in front of their eyes.

TEXAS JACK Popular alias or nickname adopted by—or dubbed upon—numerous owlhoots and long-haired Army scouts. A "Texas Jack" Vermillion lent muscle to many of Wyatt Earp's posses, while a onetime Confederate Army scout and Indian fighter known as "Texas Jack" Omohundro toured with Buffalo Bill's "Scouts of the Plains" and married the show's leading lady—the exotic Mademoiselle Morlacchi—but a short time before Omohundro died from natural causes. The above-named pair appear in numerous volumes devoted to the Wild West,[9] while "Texas Jack" Nathaniel Reed, whose infamous exploits make far more interesting reading, is often neglected. (See REED, NATHANIEL.)

TEXAS RANGERS Law enforcement in Texas had its origins in a constabulary of fifteen men that was organized by the governor of the Mexican province of Coahuila and Texas in 1823. This force can but vaguely be classed as

"Texas Rangers," for they were disbanded soon after their formation, and it was not until Stephen F. Austin established a force of between twenty and thirty men in 1826 to combat the ever-present Indian menace that the inspiration leading to a paramilitary force of lawmen being organized may be said to have been born.

The Texas Rangers were established as an organization with an initial strength of 150 men on October 17, 1835, their duties originally being the suppression of the Indians and the routing of bands of Mexican marauders. By 1840 the Rangers were being administered from permanent headquarters at San Antonio, and in the following year they introduced the Colt revolver into the West, making history by using their newly acquired Paterson five-shooters to rout a large force of Comanches at Plum Creek.[10] After the close of the Civil War a federally backed political structure disbanded the original Ranger force, and it was not until 1874 that they were reactivated under the benevolent influence of Governor Richard Coke. The Indian menace was by this time hardly sufficient threat to scare the pants off a two-year-old nervous wreck, and the newly organized force concentrated its energies on stamping out the gangs of Mexican bandits who splashed across the Rio Bravo to rustle the stock of the gringo *rancheros*.

Over this period each Ranger was usually in possession of a couple of books, which he consulted when in need of either spiritual comfort or incentive to continue. These were his "Bible 1" and "Bible 2"—the former being Holy Writ, and the latter a volume containing his list of wanted men. The Texas Ranger organization of the Wild West blazed its way well into the twentieth century, with

[9] Mainly in sequences of a space-filling rather than action-packed nature.

[10] Near the present-day town of Lockhart, Texas; not to be confused with the Plum Creek in Nebraska.

Rangers pumping automatic shotguns and pouring .45 slugs from the trembling muzzles of Thompson submachine guns with an expertise that would have brought a cheer from the veterans of the thumb-bustin' era. At nine-thirty on the Wednesday morning of May 23, 1934, on a dirt road near Arcadia in southern Louisiana, Ranger Captain Frank Hamer and Private Manny Gault were two of a party of six lawmen who fired more than 160 rounds of high-velocity ammunition through the bodywork of a Ford V8 sedan and cut Clyde Barrow and Bonnie Parker to pieces. On August 10, 1935, after a century of continuous service, the Texas Rangers of the frontier years were merged with the State Highway Patrol of Texas.[11] (See ATEN, IRA; GILLETT, JAMES BUCHANAN; HAYS, JOHN COFFEE; HUGHES, JOHN R.; JONES, FRANK; LEE, NELSON; McNELLY, LEE H.; OUTLAW, BASS; and TEXAS.)

TEXAS TRAIL   Alternative name for the Northern Trail. (See NORTHERN TRAIL.)

TEXIAN   Name used to describe an Anglo-Saxon colonist, or issue of same, who had been granted permission to dwell in the Mexican province of Coahuila and Texas. The term—most likely a contraction of TEXas-amerIcAN, remained popular until Texas became part of the United States, after which "Texan" began to find favor. Usage, however, dies hard, and "Texian" remained a close favorite of "Texan" until well into the 1870s, dying the death in direct ratio to

the passing of the old-timers. (See TEXAS.)

THIMBLERIG   Sleight-of-hand game that involves the use of three thimbles and a dried pea[12] and requires much skill in shuttling the pea into hiding beneath one of the thimbles. Half shells of walnuts were frequently used instead of thimbles, in which instance the game is usually classed as the "shell game." The game—however played—was much favored by the con men of the Old West. (See SMITH, JEFF.)

THOMAS, HECK   One of a trio of deputy U.S. marshals who were popularly known as the "Three Guardsmen."[13] Born at Atlanta, Georgia, in 1850, a dispatch rider for the Armies of the Confederacy at the age of twelve and a private in the reactivated Texas Rangers in the 1870s, Thomas later took up employment as an express messenger, and when Sam Bass and his gang staged a train robbery at Hutchins, Texas, on March 18, 1878, it was Messenger Thomas who managed to hide more than twenty thousand dollars of the cash-in-transit before a bullet from one of the outlaws' guns wounded him in the face and he was forced to surrender.[14] Thomas received a reward for his efforts, but the injury led to him giving up his job as a messenger.

Two years after his recovery from his wound, Thomas was appointed deputy U.S. marshal by Valentine Dell, marshal of the Western District of Arkansas, and in 1881 the new deputy began making

---

[11] A few years later the Rangers were re-established as a separate force, but the present-day organization can hardly be classed as a "Wild West" outfit.
[12] Or similar object.
[13] The others being Chris Madsen and Bill Tilghman.
[14] By a rather odd coincidence, Heck's brother, J. L. A. Thomas, had been the express messenger on the train that the Bass gang had robbed at Allen Station on February 24, 1878.

510510

Wild and WoollyWild and Woolly

a name for himself when he and his posse arrived at "Hanging" Judge Parker's Court at Fort Smith trail-herding a mixed bag of thirty-two owlhoots whom they had picked up in the Indian-held lands to the west. Four years later Deputy Heck Thomas tracked down and killed Tom Pink and James Lee but a short time after Pink and Lee had killed four federal lawmen and put a large posse to flight, and in January 1890 Thomas brought a badly shot-up Jim July into Fort Smith after the latter had been in a gun argument with deputies Bud Trainor and J. R. Hutchins, who wanted Jim for bond jumping—on a horse-theft charge—and as a prime suspect in the killing of the notorious Belle Starr.[15]

Shortly after the Jim July episode, Thomas turned in the star-and-crescent badge of a deputy U.S. marshal to accept the post of chief of police in the recently established town of Lawton in the equally recently established territory of Oklahoma, but by 1892 he was back behind a federal badge as a newly appointed deputy of Marshal E. D. Nix. The federal court at Guthrie was the seat of law administration in Oklahoma Territory, and Nix and his men were the field workers. Working out of Guthrie, Thomas was one of the many deputies who helped in the destruction of the Dalton, Doolin, and Buck gangs. Thomas teamed up with Deputy Bill Tilghman to bring Bill Raidler's career to a close, and Thomas was personally responsible for the tracking down of Ned Christie and for having the file on Bill Doolin marked "Closed." Heck Thomas died from natural causes at Lawton, Oklahoma, on August 15, 1912—five years after the ter-

ritory he had helped tame achieved statehood. (See BASS, SAM; BUCK GANG; CHRISTIE, NED; DOOLIN, BILL; MADSEN, CHRIS; PARKER, ISAAC C.; RAIDLER, BILL; STARR, BELLE; and TILGHMAN, WILLIAM H.)

THOMPSON, BEN Born at Knottingly in the West Riding of Yorkshire, England, in 1842, and possibly instilled with the county's unofficial motto of "If theau does owt fer nowt, do it fer thissen"[16] from an early age, Ben Thompson and his younger brother William were uprooted from their native soil and taken to the United States by their parents in 1849, the family eventually settling at Austin, Texas, where Thompson, Sr., a printer and typesetter from way back, found employment as a compositor on the staff of a local newspaper. In 1856 Ben was apprenticed to a New Orleans printer, and a couple of years later Ben was working in the composing room of the New Orleans *Picayune* and spending both his off-duty hours and his pay in the notorious Latin Quarter of the city. The Quarter was to be young Ben's finishing school. Its curriculum of whoring, boozing, and gambling, to which such unscheduled spectator sports as knife fights and pistol duels lent an added zest, were to siphon off what remained of his innocence, developing within this Yorkshire "tyke" a pathological interest in gambling, a biological interest in bawds, and a homicidal interest in weapons most deadly.

In 1859 an aristocratic Creole of French descent remonstrated with Ben for taking liberties with some unnamed female,[17] and Ben killed his first man, removing the aristo's blood from the

[15] Whether Jim July killed Belle remains conjectural, for he died from the effects of his wounds before he could be brought to trial on the horse-theft charge.
[16] "If you do anything for nothing, do it for yourself."
[17] According to Ben it was the other way around, Ben being the knight in shining armor in his version.

blade of his bowie as he disappeared into the labyrinth of the Quarter prior to fleeing back to Texas. When the Civil War had been raging for more than a year Ben joined the Confederate forces, became something of an asset to the Union by killing a mess sergeant and wounding an officer; then Ben went AWOL[18] and lost all interest in the struggle. Over the next two years Ben and his brother William spent much of their time in the gambling rooms of Laredo and Nuevo Laredo,[19] and although the brothers Thompson are reputed to have killed a few Mexicans over this period, it would be unacceptable to include these in either brother's "dead" list, for no self-respecting gunfighter kept a tally count of the greasers and Injuns he'd gunned out of existence.

In the summer of 1865 Ben was arrested at Austin for killing a man named Coombs, but he escaped from jail before he could be tried, and he fled to Mexico. Mexico was in turmoil at this time, and the fugitive joined the ill-starred Maximilian's army as a mercenary. Over the next two years Thompson was to be decorated for bravery and promoted to the rank of colonel, but in June 1867 Maximilian was captured by Júarez's men and executed by a firing squad, and Colonel Ben Thompson had to hightail back across the Rio Grande to preserve his hide. On returning to Texas Ben was rearrested for the Coombs killing and was tried and acquitted of the offense. In June 1868 he was back behind bars charged with an "intent to kill" assault, was found guilty, and on June 26 he started a two-year sentence in Huntsville Penitentiary.

Shortly after his release Ben moved up into Kansas with brother Bill. Here, at Abilene, Ben met up with an old Army pal by the name of Phil Coe, and he and Coe pooled their resources and opened the Bull's Head Tavern and Gambling Saloon. This establishment and the sign thereon became a source of dispute between the Thompson-Coe setup and the more sober-minded element, the latter faction objecting strongly to the tavern sign on the grounds that the bovine in the painting possessed certain overblown anatomical detail which fair threatened to bring the critter to its knees. Town Marshal James B. Hickok probably didn't give a toss about the sign or parts thereof, but as the duly appointed representative of the sober-minded element he was involved in the affair, and bad blood developed between the marshal and the owners of the "shame of Abilene," and on October 5, 1871, Hickok shot Coe into the cemetery while Ben was absent in Kansas City. When the news of Phil's passing reached Thompson at Kansas City he made dire threats against Hickok's welfare, yet he may not have given such a display of bluster had he not been housebound with a broken leg at the time,[20] for on his recovery he made no effort to meet up with Wild Bill Hickok, although the latter was hiding from no one.

Shortly after the first anniversary of Coe's death, the Thompson brothers opened a gambling concession in a back room of Brennan's Saloon at Ellsworth, Kansas. This enterprise kept the pair in fine store clothes and eating from the menu at the Grand Central Hotel until August 18, 1873, on which Monday twenty-six-year-old Bill Thompson killed Sheriff C. B. Whitney and fled the town as brother Ben held off a mob of would-be pursuers with a shotgun. One week later Ben was fined twenty-five dollars for aiding and abetting his brother, after

---

[18] Or, as Yorkshire-born Ben may have said, "joined out."
[19] A Mexican village across the Rio Grande from Laredo.
[20] A buggy overturned on Ben while he was showing his wife the sights of Kansas City.

which Ben left Ellsworth and moved into the Texas Panhandle where, some two years later, he was to step out of character; aligning his guns on the side of the angels when he prevented a gang of irate cavalrymen from doing grievous bodily harm to Bat Masterson after Bat had killed Sergeant Melvin King in a dancehall brawl at Sweetwater.

Over the next few years Ben did many things: The Texas Rangers had him for a brief spell, and he saw service as a gunfighter in the employ of the Atchison, Topeka, and Santa Fe Railroad during their dispute with the Denver and Rio Grande over possession of right-of-way through the Raton Pass; he caused disturbances at Dodge City and his home base of Austin through his constant imbibing of Hennessey Three Star but, oddly enough, there is no record of his having killed anyone over this period. Thompson was soon to make up for this oversight. On Christmas Eve 1879 he started some horseplay while a member of the audience in Mark Wilson's Senate Saloon and Variety Theater at Austin, and when Wilson prepared to evict him from the premises, Ben killed him with four well-aimed shots. A bartender who came to the assistance of his boss got Ben's fifth shot, receiving a wound in the neck that was to prove fatal a few weeks later. The fact that the citizens of Austin were scared stiff of this stockily built psychopath named Ben Thompson may have been partially responsible for his being acquitted of this double killing. This suckering-up-to-the-bully-so-he-won't-hit-you theory may also have been the spur that got the voters into a sufficiently crazy state of mind to elect Ben as city marshal in 1880.

For the next twelve months Thompson strutted around in a fancy uniform, an early-day example in both appearance and garb of the cop featured in Herriman's Krazy Kat cartoons of the early 1900s. In 1882 City Marshal Thompson left his uniform hanging in the closet and took a trip to San Antonio, intent on stirring up trouble at the Vaudeville Variety Theater, an establishment where one might ogle pink-tighted curves while blowing the froth from a schooner of suds. The proprietor of the Vaudeville, a one-armed hard case named Jack Harris, was to be Ben's target on this occasion. Harris[21] had been forewarned of the troublemaker's imminent arrival, a piece of intelligence that was to result in the fatal clash between Jack and Ben being afterward regarded as a fair contest, for Harris managed to blast off an ineffective round from his shotgun before three slugs from Ben's .45 killed him.

Ben resigned from his marshal's appointment on being indicted for the slaying of Harris, but in January 1883 he was released from custody after a five-day trial had resulted in a "Not guilty" verdict being returned. Shortly after his release, Ben received news that brother Bill was being held for murder in Refugio County down on the Gulf Coast. Bill, who had by this time gotten the reputation of being a gunnie who "liked to see 'em twitch," had little to worry about, for Ben was able to provide the best of legal talent from out of the profits of his gambling saloon at Austin, and the younger Thompson won an acquittal.

In 1884 this rapidly balding gunslinger, who had once blackened his tongue sucking pomfret cakes in his native Yorkshire, became friendly with a flashily dressed gunman named John King Fisher, and on March 10, 1884, they wandered into the Vaudeville Variety Theater while doing the rounds in San Antonio. This was

---

[21] Harris had been in the Confederate forces with Ben and had remained friendly with his old Army buddy, only becoming disenchanted with Ben after the latter had welshed on a bet while playing the tables in Harris' gambling saloon at Austin.

an unwise choice, for Joseph Foster and William Sims, partners of the late Jack Harris, still owned the theater, and it was a wide-open secret that they had sworn to get Ben Thompson. Sims and Foster confronted Thompson and Fisher within minutes of their arrival. Ben blustered and whipped out a revolver, but the theater's security officer grabbed the cylinder of the weapon, thus preventing the trigger being squeezed, and seconds later all hell had broken loose. Rifles and handguns appeared between the curtains of a darkened box as the theater owners whipped out pistols, and when the smoke lifted, both Thompson and Fisher were dead. Nine pieces of lead—all of which could have been fatal—were later recovered from the remains of bullyboy Ben. At the inquest it was discovered that Ben had managed to get off five shots, one of which may have found its way into Joseph Foster, for he died from a wound received in the affray shortly afterward. The killing of Thompson was regarded as an act of civic betterment, and the parties concerned in his removal never had to stand trial for the slaying. Thompson was survived by a wife, son, and daughter, and, of course, by brother Bill, the latter being killed on the streets of Laredo at some later date. (See COE, PHIL; FISHER, JOHN KING; FOY, EDDIE; HARDIN, JOHN WESLEY; HICKOK, JAMES BUTLER; KING, MELVIN; and MASTERSON, WILLIAM BARCLAY.)

THOMPSON, BILL Ben Thompson's younger brother William, sometimes referred to as "Billy." (See THOMPSON, BEN.)

THOMPSON, JOHN A.
The adopted name of Jon Torsteinson Rui, a Norwegian immigrant who has found his way into history as "Snowshoe" Thompson, the intrepid skiing mail carrier of the High Sierras. Born in Telemark on April 30, 1827, and a resident of the United States from the age of ten, John left his parents' farm in Illinois when he was twenty-four years old and pushed West to seek his fortune in the gold fields of California. Thompson didn't find much gold—just enough to allow him to buy a piece of land in Sacramento Valley and establish a small farm.

Total obscurity could easily have overtaken him here if he hadn't answered an advertisement for a mail carrier that appeared in the Sacramento *Transcript* early in 1856. Not just any mail carrier, but a man who could traverse the Sierras between Placerville, California, and Carson City, Nevada, during the winter months —ninety miles of hard traveling through blizzard-swept snowdrifts in subzero weather. Snowshoes were suggested, but Thompson went one better. The big blond Norwegian fashioned himself a pair of skis, strapped a sixty-pound pack of mail onto his back, and using a twelve-foot balancing pole, got under way. Three days later he was in Carson City, and history had been made. For the next twenty years every winter saw "Snowshoe" Thompson swishing his way across the Sierras with his sixty-pound pack. During this period there are no indications that Thompson ever destroyed, lost, mutilated, or made tardy delivery of mail, and although this would make it appear that he had a lot to learn about mail carrying, it most certainly adds to his uniqueness. John A. "Snowshoe" Thompson died on May 15, 1876, after a four-day illness, leaving in his wake a widow and a nine-year-old son.

THOMPSON, "SNOWSHOE"
Better if it had been "Skiing" Thompson, for this big Norwegian made his name on a pair of homemade skis; there we go fussin' about trifles ag'in. (See THOMPSON, JOHN A.)

THOMPSON, WILLIAM   One of
the numerous victims of Wild Bill
Hickok's marksmanship. No relation to
the notorious Ben Thompson. (See
HICKOK, JAMES BUTLER.)

THOMPSON, WILLIAM "BILLY"
No-good brother of the equally no-good
Ben Thompson. (See THOMPSON, BEN.)

THREE-FINGERED JACK   Mexican
desperado who is reputed to have been a
member of Joaquin Murieta's band of
Californian outlaws. (See MURIETA, JOA-
QUIN.)

THREE GUARDSMEN
Name dubbed upon a trio of federal lawmen who helped clear Oklahoma Territory
of outlaws during the closing years of the
nineteenth century. (See MADSEN,
CHRIS; THOMAS, HECK; and TILGHMAN,
WILLIAM H.)

THUNDERBIRD   The gigantic bird of
Amerind mythology. This was the
winged creature that caused thunder by
flapping its wings and lightning by blinking its eyes, while its hollowed-out back
held a reservoir of water, which could be
released as a deluge of rain. The thunderbird could carry a whale in its claws
after killing the leviathan with arrows
fired from the bow of its wings. Although
the thunderbird is featured as a bird in
stories and drawings, the Indians made
offerings of such unlikely objects as tobacco and moccasins to this god of the
elements. Each tribe had its own unique
method of depicting the thunderbird, yet
all these designs are obviously ornitho-
logical in character and have the reputation of being able to ward off the attentions of evil spirits. Stylized drawings of
thunderbirds were frequently to be seen
on shields and tepees and the wooden
houses of the Northwest Coast tribes.

TILGHMAN, WILLIAM M.   Best
known in his role of a deputy U.S. marshal who helped clear the outlaws from
Oklahoma Territory during the 1890s,
although Bill had seen service behind
lawman badges well before this period.
Born at Fort Dodge, Iowa, on July 4,
1854, and christened William Matthew,
young Bill was dropping buffalo on the
plains of Kansas by the time he was
eighteen, and five years later he was en-
rolled as a deputy at Dodge City by
Sheriff Charlie Bassett of Ford County.
This was to be the start of Tilghman's
long career as a peace officer. Over the
next ten years, while serving a succession
of law-enforcement appointments at
Dodge, Bill established a small ranch between Fort Dodge and Dodge City, but
in 1889, when the Indian lands of Oklahoma were being opened to white settlement, he abandoned his Kansas homestead, resigned from his current job as
city marshal, and followed the rush.
Twelve months later he was the possessor
of a number of lots in the newly staked-
out townsite of Guthrie and had been
elected marshal of the rapidly growing
community.

In 1892 Tilghman became one of the
150 deputies appointed by U. S. Marshal
William Grimes of the two-year-old territory of Oklahoma, and over the years
Tilghman was to form friendships with
fellow deputies Chris Madsen and Heck
Thomas that were to lead to the triumvirate being dubbed the "Three Guardsmen." Bill's most highly publicized adventures during these hard-riding years
were his capture of Bill Doolin and his
shootout arrest of Bill Raidler, while a
certain amount of light relief was added
by the "Little Britches–Cattle Annie"
affair.

In 1900, when most of the outlaws had
been swept from the brush, Tilghman
was elected sheriff of Lincoln County,
Oklahoma, and while working out of his

office at Chandler he met an attractive young girl named Zoe Agnes Stratton, who was to become his wife in 1903. The couple settled at Chandler for a few years before moving to Oklahoma City, where Bill was appointed chief of police in 1911. After serving for three years, the aging lawman resigned in 1914 to supervise the production of a moving picture entitled *The Passing of the Oklahoma Outlaws*. This movie purported to tell the truth about many of the ne'er-do-wells who had plagued the U.S. marshal's office during the 1890s, and when it was finally in the can in 1915, Tilghman went on tour with the finished product as a publicity buildup.

Bill's last call to duty as a lawman came in 1924, when the state governor, M. E. Trapp, persuaded the seventy-year-old veteran to serve as a peace officer in the new oil-boom town of Cromwell. The blight of Prohibition now lay across the land, but on the Saturday evening of November 1, 1924, there was no shortage of drunks in Cromwell, and Prohibition Agent Wiley Lynn, a shifty-eyed badge-toter whom Tilghman strongly suspected of being in league with numerous bootleggers, was not of the sober element. At about 10 P.M. Agent Wiley fired his gun at a pink elephant after stepping from a sedan parked outside Murphy's eatery and dance hall. The shot brought Tilghman to the scene within seconds, and he grappled the gun from Lynn's grasp; then, believing he had disarmed the rowdy, Bill relaxed. This was to be a fatal error. Lynn whipped out a small automatic pistol and put two bullets into Tilghman's chest, which killed him within minutes. When he had sobered up Agent Lynn surrendered to the authorities, but Tilghman's murder was not to be avenged by judicial means, for the jury who tried the accused returned the amazing verdict of "Not guilty," and Lynn was acquitted to return to his duties of Prohibition agent.[22] (See CIMARRON COUNTY SEAT WAR; DOOLIN, BILL; MADSEN, CHRIS; McDOUGAL, ANNIE; RAIDLER, BILL; STEVENS, JENNIE; and THOMAS, HECK.)

TIN CUP, COLORADO   A gold-mining camp in Gunnison County, Colorado, that was jerked into existence when prospectors and parasites began throwing up rickety shacks and tent premises in 1880. Tin Cup never developed into a substantial bricks-and-stone community, but the camp is of interest if only as an indication of the manner and speed by which these embryo mining settlements removed their duly appointed town marshals from office. Out of a total of four daredevils who were to pin five-pointed targets to their chests over the 1881–83 period, three were to be shot dead shortly after taking office, while the fourth was to be driven into a straitjacket by "battle fatigue," and he ended his days in a lunatic asylum.[23] In 1883 a forty-odd-year-old Kansan named Dave Corsaut was appointed marshal. Dave was evidently the toughest man around, for from then on Tin Cup was to runneth over with law 'n' order. Uninhabited traces of this village may still be found.

[22] In August 1932 Prohibition Agent Wiley Lynn and State Patrolman Crockett Long shot each other to death in a drugstore at Madill, Oklahoma. This shootout—which also caused the death of a customer who had probably only wanted to purchase some aspirin—is reputed to have been the climax of a feud of long standing.
[23] The quartet of luckless lawmen: Frank Emerson, shot dead by ex-Marshal Thomas Lahey; Harry Rivers, derringered to his doom by a gambler; Samuel Mickey, the "battle fatigue" badge; and Andrew Jameson, shot dead by a man named Taylor during the course of a private argument.

TIPI   Sioux word which—roughly translated—means "a place used for dwelling." Usually spelled "tepee." (See TEPEE.)

TISWIN   An intoxicating beverage that is produced by the Apache Indians, fermented corn, maize, wheat, or mesquite beans all being regarded as a suitable base. Sometimes spelled "tizwin," and frequently referred to as "Apache beer."

TOMAHAWK   Amerind name for a heavy war-club that was roughly hatchet-shaped and had a spike or round stone fitted into its striking edge, or, alternatively, a much lighter weapon consisting of a flat or round stone that had been attached to the head of a wooden handle. At a later date iron hatchets were introduced to the Indians by the French and Anglo-Saxon fur-trading companies. These "trade" tomahawks usually had a pipe bowl incorporated in their design so that tobacco or herbal mixtures could be smoked between sessions of skull splitting, the handle of the weapon serving as a pipe stem.[24]

TOMBSTONE, ARIZONA   Mining town in southeastern Arizona that had its birth pangs shortly after Ed Schieffelin had discovered silver in the area in 1877. By 1880 there were about five hundred buildings in the town, two of which housed pioneer newspapers, while more than a hundred had been granted licenses to sell hard liquor, and probably half this number were operating as "businesses of Ill Fame."[25] Tombstone was laid out in square town-blocks, with its grid of streets running north to south and east to west; the former group, reading from the west, being First, Second, Third, Fourth, Fifth, Sixth, and Seventh streets, while the four main intersecting thoroughfares, reading from the north, were Safford, Fremont, Allen, and Toughnut streets. To the west of the town center—in the block bounded by Fremont and Allen, and Second and Third streets—lay the Mountain Maid Mine[26] and the Chinese community, which was locally known as "Hop Town." With an estimated population of ten thousand in the first half of the 1880s, these were Tombstone's boom years, and had the town possessed a chamber of commerce to publish a promotional brochure over this period, one may well have culled the following lists from between its pages.

Hotels. The Grand, Cosmopolitan, American, Noble's, and Exchange hotels.

Boardinghouses. Palace Lodgings, San Jose House, Inez McMartin's Boardinghouse, Russ House, Aztec House, and Fly's Lodginghouse.

Restaurants, etc. Fashion Restaurant, New Orleans Restaurant, Maison Doree Restaurant, Can Can Restaurant, Elite Restaurant, Sam Chung's Chinese Restaurant, New York Coffee Shop, and Tom Walker's Wine Rooms.

Corrals and Livery Stables. Dexter Livery and Stables, Tombstone Livery and Feed, Dunbar's Corral, Pioneer Livery, West End Corral, O. K. Livery and Corral, Lexington Livery, and Arizona Corral.

---

[24] The use of a heated piece of wire was the favorite method of "drilling" a smoke channel through the length of the handle.

[25] These premises were not overlooked by the license tax collector's office. City License No. 116, issued at Tombstone, Cochise County, A.T., on August 1, 1894, was made out to "Augustine" on receipt of "the sum of Seven dollars for license on the business of Ill Fame for the month ending Aug. 31st. 1894." This document was signed by City Auditor Tarbell and Mayor Fitts.

[26] This mine tunneled its way beneath the settlement.

Saloons. Willows, New Orleans, Capitol, Oriental, Hafford's, Hatch's, Vogan and Flynn's, Occidental, Alhambra, Moses and Mehan's, Arcade, Dragon, Deel's, Headquarters, Pony, and the Eagle Brewery (the latter having been originally known as the Crystal Palace Saloon).

Theaters. Bird Cage Theater, Schieffelin Concert Hall, Crystal Palace Concert Hall, and the Elite Theater.

Stores, etc. Bauer's Meat Market, Addie Bourland's Millinery, Summerfield Brothers' Store, Eastman's Carpentry Shop, Kearney's Drugstore, Brown's Grocery, Schuenfeld and Hayman's Furniture Store, Langenberger's Tin Shop, Fly's Photographic Gallery, Thompson's Saddle Shop, Hart's Gun Store, Seamans and Sons' Jewelry Store, Spangenburg's Gun Shop, Papago Store, Sydow and Kieke's Clothing Store, Vogan's Bowling Alley, and Safford, Hudson, and Company's Bank.

Miscellaneous Buildings. City Hall, County Courthouse,[27] Masonic Hall, Mining Exchange, Fire House for Engine Company No. 1, and four churches—Roman Catholic, Methodist, Episcopal, and Congregational.

The above lists are not comprehensive, for Tombstone had its fair share of tonsorial parlors, gambling rooms, Chinese laundries, ice cream vendors, small-time businesses, and big-time brothels that any C. of C. might be expected to overlook. The brothels and cribs were mainly to be found east of Sixth Street, and although this area was hardly frowned upon, cyprians bearing such names as Diamond Annie, Shoo-fly, Dutch Annie, Margarita, and Gold Dollar could be expected to pay a fine of twenty dollars if caught soliciting on the streets.

Tombstone survived two disastrous fires—in 1881 and 1882—but when water flooded the mines in 1886, the population began to shrink, and although attempts to reactivate the mines were made in 1900, these met with failure,[28] and the town became a semighost. In 1930 the surviving residents staged a three-day festival in the hope that tourists might revitalize the town. This event was named "Helldorado," and the townies worked hard at re-enacting many of the clashes of arms that had occurred during the town's frontier years, but although this met with some success, more than two decades were to elapse before Tombstone was to become a major tourist attraction of the Southwest. The town now stages its "Helldorado" annually during October, and when all the blanks have been fired, visitors may visit such ancient buildings as the Bird Cage Theater, Bob Hatch's Billards Saloon (where Morgan Earp died), the Crystal Palace Saloon, Nellie Cashman's Russ House lodgings, the *Epitaph* offices, Vogan's Bowling Alley, and the City Hall. Other favorite attractions are the site of the O. K. Corral gunfight, the "Wyatt Earp slept here" places, and the Boot Hill cemetery. (See BREAKENRIDGE, WILLIAM MILTON; CLAIBORNE, BILLY; CLANTON GANG; CLUM, JOHN P.; EARP, MORGAN; EARP, VIRGIL; EARP, WYATT BERRY STAPP; GRAHAM, WILLIAM B.; HEATH, JOHN; HOLLIDAY, JOHN HENRY; HUNT, ZWING; JOHNSON, GEORGE; KILLEEN, MIKE D.; LESLIE, FRANK; O. K. CORRAL; SCHIEFFELIN, EDWARD L.; TOMBSTONE EPITAPH; and TOMBSTONE NUGGET.)

[27] At this time Tombstone was the county seat of Cochise County, a position it enjoyed until 1931, when it was voted that Bisbee should take over the honor.
[28] The silver is still there, the problem being how to get it out of the flooded tunnels at nonprohibitive cost.

TOMBSTONE EPITAPH
Pioneer newspaper established by John Philip Clum at Tombstone, Arizona Territory, in 1880, the twenty-nine-year-old Clum being of the opinion that "every tombstone should have its epitaph." The first issue of this daily and weekly publication made its appearance on May 1, 1880, all editing, composing, and printing having been accomplished by Clum on premises located on the north side of Fremont Street between Third and Fourth streets. The *Epitaph* backed law and order and the Earp faction in no uncertain terms, and its columns were sprinkled with black humor of an inoffensive variety, and although the editor took frequent swipes at various parties who had occasioned his displeasure, none of these comments possessed the extreme "cattiness" that is the tawdry hallmark of the unisex journalists of the 1970s.

The paper covered gunfights, mine disasters, and holdups of a major nature at great length, but violent death was such a permanent feature of everyday life in Tombstone that scores of fatalities resulting from stabbings, shootouts, fisticuff brawls, poisonings (both alcoholic and otherwise), and accidents on the streets and in the homes, merely found their way into a column entitled "Death's Doings." Various merging of interests resulted in the paper being renamed *Epitaph and Republican* in 1884 and *Daily Record-Epitaph* in 1885, and it didn't regain its original masthead until 1887. In the spring of 1887 Clum sold out his interest in the *Epitaph* and moved to California, where he died in 1932, but the paper that he created survives to this

day, accepting subscriptions from all over the world at its original office on Fremont Street. (See CLUM, JOHN P.; TOMBSTONE, ARIZONA; and TOMBSTONE NUGGET.)

TOMBSTONE NUGGET The first of Tombstone's pioneer newspapers.[29] Established as a weekly in 1879, but later becoming a daily when the rival *Epitaph* arrived on the scene in 1880, the democratic *Nugget* invariably slanted its coverage in favor of the "cowboy" element[30] —a partisan choice that led to numerous typeset skirmishes occurring between the *Nugget* and the republican *Epitaph*, which occupied premises on the opposite side of Fremont Street. The *Nugget* went out of business in May 1882, this short life span of less than three years making it appear that the early settlers in Tombstone were rather more in favor of the law-and-order element than present-day disparagers of the Earp brothers would have us believe. (See TOMBSTONE, ARIZONA, and TOMBSTONE EPITAPH.)

TONKAWA INDIANS
Minority group of the Caddoan language family who are known to have been settled in southeastern Texas from at least 1600. By 1840 there were a bare 350 Tonkawa Indians, tepee-dwelling buffalo hunters who sought allegiance with the white man as protection from their hereditary enemies the Kiowa and Comanche. These enemies named the Tonkawa "the eaters of human flesh," a gruesome but well-deserved title, for they were one of the few tribes[31] of Indians who removed choice cuts from the bodies of slain ene-

[29] Other Tombstone newspapers that had brief histories: *Evening Gossip* (1881); *Independent* (1882); *Daily Tombstone* (1883–86); *Arizona Kicker* (1892); and *The American* (1903).
[30] The Clanton–Curly Bill Brocius mob and their followers.
[31] Other tribes practicing cannibalism were the Karankawa (living south of the Tonkawa on the Gulf Coast between Matagorda Bay and the Nueces River) and some of the Northwest Coast tribes.

mies for postbattle feasting. This tribe numbered about 250 when they were established on the Brazos Agency in 1854, and by 1900 a head count gave a total of only 59 survivors. Now extinct. (See CANNIBALS.)

TONTO APACHE   Apache tribe that located east of the Mazatzal Mountains between Tonto and Cibecue creeks in southeast-central Arizona. Tonto means "fool."

TONTO BASIN WAR   Alternative name for the Pleasant Valley War. (See PLEASANT VALLEY WAR.)

TORNADO   The term tornado, as used in the West, describes a whirlwind that travels at an average of thirty miles an hour and usually lasts for about forty to fifty minutes. The center of such a wind may reach a velocity of more than two hundred miles an hour. (See DUGOUT.)

TORTILLA   A flat cake of unleavened maize that has been baked on a hot stone or an iron stove. A staple food of the Indian tribes of the Southwest.

TOTEM POLE   A pole that has been carved into the stylized form—or forms—of one or more tribal or personal totems.[32] These brightly colored heraldic devices—some of which were 70 feet in height—were an exclusive product of a number of Northwest Coast tribes[33] living north of the forty-ninth parallel, the use of such totems being unknown to the Amerinds of the American West.

TOWN MARSHAL   A duly appointed representative of law and order whose jurisdiction did not extend beyond town or city limits. A town marshal was far more likely to have his career terminated by gunshot wounds of a fatal nature than either a federal or county lawman, for the rowdy element were to be found in great numbers within the saloons, gambling houses, and brothels of the settlements, and a town marshal would be rubbing shoulders with such types for the greater part of his waking hours. Five- or six-pointed stars made of tin or silver[34] usually served as badges of office, although shield-type badges were not unknown. (See SHERIFF and UNITED STATES MARSHAL.)

TRACY, HARRY   Thin-lipped, slit-eyed, and jug-eared thug who left his bloody handprint on the West during its twilight years. Born Harry Tracy Severns at Pittsville, Wisconsin, in 1875, Harry discarded his surname shortly after leaving his home and heading West at the age of twenty. In 1896, after killing a man in Utah, Tracy fled North and settled in Wyoming's Hole in the Wall country for a spell. Here he met such vaguely likable characters as Butch Cassidy and the Sundance Kid, the unsavory Harvey Logan, and other lesser-known long riders who frequented the Hole. By this time Tracy could stay on the back of a horse and he could put a .45 slug into a man-sized target without too much concentra-

[32] Animals venerated by a tribe or group of tribes. Such creatures could be imaginary (the thunderbird) or real (whales, ravens, wolves, beavers, eagles, etc.)

[33] Mainly the Tlingit, Kwakiutl, and Haida tribes of southwestern Alaska and the Queen Charlotte Islands.

[34] A town marshal wearing a gold badge could occasionally be found, but such a man would rarely have a pocketful of these to hand out to his deputies.

tion,[35] attributes that helped him to survive as a cattle rustler until his killing of a deputy sheriff in the fall of 1897 had him fleeing into the Far Northwest.

Sometime in 1898 Tracy arrived in Seattle, Washington, and within a short time he had teamed up with an ex-convict named David Merrill, and the pair were soon engaged in the daredevil business of rolling drunks. After accumulating little more than five hundred dollars from this form of outlawry, the local police began taking an interest in the activities of Tracy and Merrill, and the two thugs left Washington and headed for the mining camp of Cripple Creek in Colorado. Cripple Creek's new arrivals had no intention of mining. Shaking the dust from the miners when the latter left the safety of their "burrows" was to be their method of prospecting, and when they had built up a gun-point kitty of more than five thousand dollars in gold dust, they mounted a trusty train to Denver to spend their "winnings." When the gambling halls, booze joints, and bordellos of Denver had relieved the big spenders of their loot, Merrill was overcome by a rare bout of homesickness, and he and Tracy confiscated the takings of a Denver saloon to raise the train fare to Merrill's home in Portland, Oregon.

The pair arrived in Portland in the early days of 1899, and here Tracy met Dave's sister Mollie, a gal who evidently admired thin-lipped, slit-eyed bums, for in less time than it takes to load a six-gun a torrid liaison had developed be-

tween Miss Merrill and Tracy, and they were married in the last week of January 1899. Mrs. Tracy was still struggling to master the technique of boiling Harry's eggs to the degree of toughness required by her newly acquired spouse when the marriage ended in disaster: On February 6, 1899, Tracy and Merrill were arrested and charged with a series of local hold-ups, and seven weeks later they were on their way to the Salem Penitentiary—Tracy having been sentenced to twenty years, while Dave had drawn an unlucky thirteen.

Once behind bars Tracy began plotting a break, but it was not until June 9, 1902, that a rifle and a sawn-off shotgun, which had been smuggled into the jail inside a toolchest,[36] were to get into the eager hands of Harry and Dave and cause a bad day at Salem. Within minutes of their coming into possession of the weapons Tracy had killed two guards named Ferrell and Jones, and the two felons had used a strategically placed ladder to scale the wall. Having escaped the walls, Tracy wounded an outside guard named Tiffany, and the two escapees used the wounded man as a shield and hostage as they made their way toward a nearby stand of timber. On reaching the safety of the woods Tracy put a bullet through the back of the luckless Tiffany's head, and the pair of zebra-striped figures made good their escape.

Within twenty-four hours of their escape Harry and Dave had forcibly procured a change of clothing and were

---

[35] It is sometimes claimed that Harry was a very efficient cowhand and that he was probably the fastest and deadest shot in the West. It is equally likely that this is a load of poppycock, for Harry missed his targets on many occasions, and there is no record of his ever having needed to employ a fast draw, while most of the full-time rangehands of the West could have ridden circles around the lad.

[36] Two felons who had been released early in 1902 were responsible for getting the guns into the prison, their efforts reputedly having been financed by a certain Miss Warrington, an old flame of Harry's who was a resident of Chicago. If we take into account that Tracy married Mollie Merrill and he only appears to have gotten in touch with Miss Warrington when in dire need of assistance or "mad" money, the girl from Chicago was evidently a much-abused filly.

headed North. On June 14 they crossed the Columbia River, and on the evening of that same day Tracy killed a lawman during a clash with a posse in Clark County, Washington. Two weeks later the fugitives escaped after engaging in a gun duel with officers some fifty miles south of Tacoma, and sometime during the next seventy-two hours Tracy put a couple of fatal bullets into his partner's back, thus dispelling a pathological suspicion that Dave might be entertaining ideas of "shopping" him to the cops. The following day Tracy was run to earth by Sheriff Cudihee and his posse of King County lawmen, but Tracy once more escaped after killing Deputy Sheriffs Raymond and Anderson, after which Tracy began working his way East, bumming and commandeering meals and lodgings as he moved across country until he reached Lincoln County early in August.

On August 5, 1902, a force of local and county officers, their ranks stiffened with civilian volunteers, got Tracy bottled up in a wheat field near Creston in Lincoln County. The battle raged long and hard, and by nightfall Tracy had sustained serious arm and leg wounds, which made any attempt at escape out of the question. The "Mad Dog" of the Northwest had reached the end of the line, and he knew it. Sometime during the hours of darkness he placed the muzzle of his Colt .45 against his reddish-blond hairline and blew his dinosaur-type brain into a mass of disconnected thoughts. (See HOLE IN THE WALL GANG.)

TRADE BLANKET   Any blanket used as an article of barter by the various fur-trading companies of North America in their dealings with the trappers, whether Indian or European. The Hudson's Bay Company of Canada was the first to introduce blankets as an item of exchange, and this company's blankets were the finest in the field. Manufactured in England from the best quality of wool, the largest size in Hudson's Bay blankets measured 6 feet by 15 feet and weighed about 12 pounds. The red, white, green, or multi-striped Hudson's Bay trade blankets possessed a wide Prussian blue band, which ran the full width of the blanket about 6 inches from either end, a trademark that made them readily identifiable. At the height of the fur trade—1815–35—there were around 5,000 white trappers working and trading among more than 250,000 Indians—relative figures that make it apparent why trade blankets were to become so readily associated with Indians throughout the West. (See TRADE GUN.)

TRADE GUN   Weapons purchased by the fur-trading companies as trade goods, the companies exchanging the guns with the Indians in return for pelts. In the early years of the 1800s the Hudson's Bay fusil—more commonly known as the "Hudson's Bay Fuke" or "Northwest Gun"—was the original "trade" gun. These guns were of British manufacture and were readily identifiable by having the figure of a squatting fox engraved on both lock plate and barrel. By 1807 various American gunsmiths were turning out copies of the Hudson's Bay trade piece, and by 1810 the U. S. Government had shipped around five hundred weapons described as "Indian muskets" into the Indian lands. By the 1830s numerous types of rifled caplocks and flint-locks were finding their way into the hands of the Indians, but as these had not been specifically manufactured for barter purposes, they may only loosely be classed as "trade" guns. (See FUSIL and TRADE BLANKET.)

TRADE RAT   Popular name for wood-rats which possess the habit of substituting an article to replace anything they may have been tempted to pilfer. Also known as pack rats. (See WOODRATS.)

TRAIL DRIVE   The handling of a herd of cattle that is being moved to some distant pasture or trailhead shipping point. For the trailing of a herd of around three thousand head, a trail crew would consist of a trail boss; some fifteen to twenty cowhands; a cook, who drove the chuck wagon and established campsites; and a horse wrangler, who was in charge of the remuda. Once on the move, with the trail boss, chuck wagon, and remuda some three or four miles in the van, the herd would be led by a "lead" steer, with the following cattle stringing out behind, reaching greatest density at the rear of the herd. On either side of this movement rode three cowhands: the first pair, riding slightly in rear of the "lead" steer, were known as "point" men; the second pair were known as "swing" men; and the third pair were known as "flank" men. The remainder of the trail crew were strung out in a semicircle in the herd's dust cloud and were known as "drag" men.

A trail herd might cover about twelve to sixteen miles during the hours of daylight; then each evening the cattle would be bedded down for the night, the night watch keeping their charges tranquil during the hours of darkness by crooning softly to the animals as the watchmen rode slowly around the perimeter of the herd. Stampedes were an ever-present menace during the night watch, for although cattle rarely took off on headlong flight during the hours of daylight, the least thing could "booger" them when darkness limited their range of vision. A few thousand head of stampeding cattle swept everything from their path, and the only way to curb such a panic rush was for the riders to gallop alongside one flank of the herd and slowly turn the leading animals, working them around until they were eating their own dust in the drag and the herd was milling in a complete circle. This milling could continue for hours, but at least the cattle weren't going anyplace. (See CHISHOLM TRAIL; CHUCK WAGON; NIGHT HAWK; NORTHERN TRAIL; OLD BLUE; REMUDA; TRAIL TOWN; and WESTERN TRAIL.)

TRAIL TOWN   Town located on a railroad line and that owed its existence or economic growth to the fact that it had been established as, or evolved into, a major cattle shipping point. The main feature of a trail town was an extremely wide main thoroughfare through which, should it become necessary, a herd of cattle could be trailed. Most of the true trail towns—all of which were located in Kansas—experienced boom years that lasted for much less than a decade. (See ABILENE, KANSAS; BAXTER SPRINGS, KANSAS; DODGE CITY, KANSAS; ELLSWORTH, KANSAS; HAYS CITY, KANSAS; NEWTON, KANSAS; and WICHITA, KANSAS.)

TRAPPERS   The legion of hard-bitten characters of many nationalities who invaded the unchartered West in search of furs[37] in the early 1800s and only faded into history with the death of the fur trade in the middle 1840s. Many of these men worked as loners, misanthropist types who only gathered in large numbers to meet supply caravans at prearranged rendezvous.[38] Trappers who worked west of the 104th meridian are usually classed as mountain men. (See AMERICAN FUR COMPANY; BEAVER;

---

[37] Mainly beaver.

[38] With the exception of a couple of rendezvous that occurred in Pierre's Hole, just across the Idaho line, all the sites were confined to what is now western Wyoming, mainly on the Green and Wind rivers and tributaries thereof.

BECKWOURTH, JAMES P.; BRIDGER, JIM; CARSON, CHRISTOPHER ("KIT"); CHARBONNEAU, TOUISSANT; GLASS, HUGH; MÉTIS; MOUNTAIN MEN; ROCKY MOUNTAIN FUR COMPANY; SMITH, JEDEDIAH; SUBLETTE, WILLIAM; TRADE BLANKET; TRADE GUN; VOYAGEURS; and WILLIAMS, BILL.)

TRAVOIS Mode of transport used by the North American Indians. A travois consisted of two crossed poles that had been fastened to the shoulders of a dog or, later, a horse, so that the free ends of the poles trailed behind the animal and could be used to support fairly heavy loads.

TUALISTO A full-blooded Creek Indian who was hanged at Fort Smith, Arkansas, on June 29, 1883, after being found guilty of the robbery-murder of a white man named Cochran. Tualisto is mainly of interest for his unique method of keeping a tally count of his victims; this cheeky Creek being in the habit of sewing a button onto his hatband to remind himself of each unfortunate whom he had sent to the Happy Hunting Grounds. When Tualisto dropped through the trap there were four buttons on his hatband, but the names that may have been attached to three of these disks of bone will never be known.

TULSA JACK Alias used by a small-time member of the Doolin-Dalton gang. (See BLAKE, JACK.)

TUMBLEWEED Any type of worthless herbaceous plant which, on becoming brittle through drought, easily snaps off from its roots and takes up a wind-propelled nomadic existence of seed scattering. The American West has always been plagued by a native thistle that has these characteristics, but in 1873 a Russian immigrant of a similar but tougher species invaded the West via a packet of flax seeds, and this "fifth column" variety of tumbleweed is now far more plentiful than its far less obnoxious American cousin. Giant balls of tumbleweed rolling merrily across the land can spook horses and booger cattle, bring farming machinery to a gear-clogged halt, and cause havoc with drainage systems. As it apparently thrives on weed killers, tumbleweed is evidently here to stay. The native variety is sometimes referred to as "pigweed."

TUMPLINE A large band made from a strip of either hide or woven material that was used as a carrying aid by many of the Amerind tribes; the tumpline was looped across the forehead and around any load which the wearer wished to support between his or her shoulder blades.

TUNSTALL, JOHN HENRY A much-traveled multilingual Englishman who was to become the first fatal victim of a clash of commercial interests that was to escalate into the sanguinary feud known as the Lincoln County War. Born in London on March 6, 1853, Tunstall arrived at the town of Lincoln, New Mexico, in the fall of 1876 with the intention of becoming a rancher and businessman, and within a short time of his arrival in the territory he had established a cattle and horse ranch on the Rio Feliz some forty miles south of Lincoln and become a business partner of John S. Chisum and Alexander A. McSween. The fact that the enterprises which Tunstall was associated with were in direct competition with the longer established Murphy-Dolan setup—details of which may be found elsewhere in this volume —was to lead to the Englishman's death. At around 5 P.M. on February 18, 1878, an eighteen-man posse of so-called sheriff's deputies who were intent on ar-

resting Tunstall on a trumped-up charge
of stock theft intercepted their quarry
about ten miles south of Lincoln, and
after the Englishman had surrendered his
six-gun, he was shot to death by possemen Jesse Evans and William Morton.
(See DOLAN, JAMES J.; EVANS, JESSE;
LINCOLN COUNTY WAR; MCCARTY,
HENRY; MCSWEEN, ALEXANDER A.; and
MURPHY, LAWRENCE G.)

TURKEY   A potential Thanksgiving
dinner that is still on the gobble. These
large ground-nesting game birds are only
to be found in their wild state in the
Americas, ranging at one time from the
Canadian line to Guatemala in the south
and as far west as Colorado's eastern
boundary. In the 1880s, when the buffalo herds had been decimated to near
extinction, turkey hunting became a
highly popular method of making money,
east of the Cimarron in northern Oklahoma being regarded during this period
as "the best turkey range in the world."
By 1900 wild turkeys had become very
scarce, but before they could join the
dodo, the small flocks that remained became a protected species.[39] An adult tom
turkey may reach a length of 48 inches,
be 36 inches in height, and weigh as
much as 45 pounds. Benjamin Franklin
at one time suggested that the turkey
should replace the eagle as the emblem
of the United States. Serious or business
conversation is often referred to as
"talking turkey." (See TURKEY GOBBLE.)

TURKEY GOBBLE   Eerie sound that
the braves of some of the plains tribes
made as a warning of their intention to
kill. (See FRIEND, JOHN.)

TURLEY, SIMEON
A onetime trapper who was indirectly responsible for a large number of bloodshot
eyeballs. (See TAOS LIGHTNING.)

TUTT, DAVE   Gambler and gunman
who crossed paths with Wild Bill Hickok
on numerous occasions during the Civil
War prior to their final shootout in the
summer of 1865. Tutt, who was born
near Yellville in the Ozark's Boston
Mountains of northern Arkansas and
came from a long line of feudin' folk,[40]
is reputed to have had a fisticuff fracas
with Hickok in the summer of 1881 when
Bill was serving as a Union spy behind
the Confederate lines. Shortly after this
encounter Dave joined the Confederate
forces, but by the tail end of 1862 he
had shucked off his uniform and was
back playing the tables in various
Arkansas settlements. In November 1863
Dave was shuffling the pasteboards at
Fort Smith in western Arkansas, and
here he banged into Wild Bill once again,
a further display of fisticuffs between the
two men being occasioned by Dave's borrowing of Bill's mount—the renowned
Black Nell—without first obtaining permission to do so.

Sometime in the spring of 1865 Tutt,
together with his mother, sister, and
brothers, left Arkansas and moved North
to settle at Springfield in southwestern
Missouri. Hickok was spending much
time in the gambling rooms and saloons
of Springfield at this period of his career,
but in spite of their earlier explosive
meetings, Dave and Bill became good
friends in Missouri; Dave having been
known to loan Wild Bill money when the
latter hadn't the wherewithal to pay for

---

[39] Wild turkeys may be hunted during one week in the spring and one week in the fall if
the hunter first obtains a hunting license (for five hundred dollars, as of 1969). A wild
turkey sandwich must work out fairly expensively.

[40] During the 1850s more than forty-five men are reputed to have died in the Ozarks from
gunshot wounds as a direct result of the Tutt-Everett feud.

urgently needed booze, bawds, and powder and shot. The fact that Tutt's sister was a comely wench and Bill had a passion for damsels who could be so described may have been partially responsible for the much improved relationship between Tutt and Hickok. But whatever, shortly after the Tutts' arrival in Springfield a heroine in homespun named Susanna Moore made her appearance in the town, and the lass had the seeds of disaster in her stays.

Miss Moore had been born and raised about twelve miles south of Yellville, and on many occasions she had served Wild Bill his victuals when he had been lodging with her parents during his cloak-and-dagger days, a propinquity from which passion doth ofttime bloom, so it is hardly surprising that Susanna and Bill knew each other, but well. This must have been a tiresome time for Hickok, for being well aware that Susanna had attempted to put a leaden projectile between the whalebone supports of a rival on at least one occasion, he can have only regarded her arrival as an harbinger of doom. Hickok made a valiant attempt at keeping both girls happy in an effort to prevent violence, but playing two violins at the same time rarely results in harmony, and Bill soon had a quadrangle drama to contend with: Tutt frowned upon Hickok's two-timing, while Susanna, who wasn't too happy with a mere 50 per cent of Bill, began running her fingers through Dave's locks as a buildup to having him fill the gap in her love life.

By the middle of July there was a lot of green in the pupils of Wild Bill Hickok's eyes, and he and Dave were no longer friends. On the evening of July 20 in that year of 1865, Tutt confronted Hickok in the gaming room of the Lyon House on South Street and let everyone within hearing know that Bill owed him thirty-five dollars. Hickok claimed that ten dollars must have been lousy interest, whereupon Dave snatched up a fancy gold Waltham watch that Bill had left lying on the gambling table and said he would keep the timepiece as security. Bill replied that he had no wish to start a ball in the Lyon House, but that if Dave should embarrass him by wearing the watch in public, he would sure enough shoot Dave dead. Tutt sneered, then he tromped from the room after a parting shot which informed Hickok that he would be able to ask Dave the time from his Waltham if they should meet during the course of the following day.

At nine o'clock on the morning of the twenty-first, Hickok stepped from the Lyon House, and minutes later he spotted Tutt wearing the Waltham. Dave had probably seen Bill first, for he started walking across the town square with a pistol hanging from his grasp. When a distance of about seventy-five yards separated them, Hickok warned Tutt not to come any closer, but Tutt's only reply was to raise his gun and send a ball humming past Bill's head. Wild Bill's reply was far more definitive. In a twinkling he had taken careful aim (mustn't ruin the Waltham!) and put a shot through Tutt's heart. When they gathered around the fallen gambler the Waltham was the only thing still ticking, so Bill scooped it up and retired from the field. Shortly afterward Hickok stood trial for the killing and was acquitted. (See HICKOK, JAMES BUTLER.)

TWAIN, MARK Nautically inspired pen name of Sam Clemens. (See CLEMENS, SAMUEL LANGHORNE.)

FREDERIC REMINGTON

U NDERWOOD, HENRY
Leading member of the Sam Bass gang.
Underwood, who was born in Jennings
County, Indiana, on January 10, 1846,
and was a fairly well-educated youth,
served in the Union forces during the
Civil War, after which he settled in
Labeck County, Kansas, where he married a Miss Mary Emory on the day of
his twenty-first birthday. While in Kansas
Henry had the reputation of being an
honest farmer, but on moving to Denton
County, Texas, in September 1871, he
took up other employment, hauling wood
over the forty-mile trip between Denton
and Dallas for a spell before meeting with
a certain amount of success as a pistol-
point bill collector.

Sometime in 1874 Underwood became
acquainted with Sam Bass, and shortly
afterward Henry got into a gun dispute
with a party of vigilantes regarding the
morality of their actions; the fracas occurred in a Fort Concho saloon and
resulted in Henry and a couple of vigilantes occupying adjoining beds in the
local military hospital. It was considered
that Henry had a mortal wound, but he
managed to sneak from the premises one
night to return back to Denton County,
where he was nursed back to health by
his wife. On recovering, Underwood
started a period of blameless existence,
but ill luck evidently dogged his heels,
for he had hardly gotten back into his
stride before he was arrested on suspicion of having burned down the Presbyterian Church at Denton, and he was
held in jail for six months before being
released for lack of evidence. Within but
a short time of his release he was un-
justly accused of stealing a yoke of oxen,

a final straw that led to Henry fleeing his home and becoming a member of the Sam Bass band in November 1877.

On December 24 of that same year Underwood was arrested for complicity in the Big Springs train robbery[1] and lodged in the Kearney, Nebraska, jail to await trial. Before he could be brought to trial Underwood broke jail, rejoining the Bass gang in time to take part in the Eagle Ford and Mesquite train robberies of April 4 and 10, 1878, respectively. Exactly two weeks after the Mesquite job Underwood left Texas and was never heard from again in that region. Shortly after his disappearance Mrs. Underwood pulled up stakes and left for parts unknown, rumors having it that she moved to Kentucky, where her husband is thought to have started a new and unsullied life. (See BASS, SAM.)

UNION PACIFIC RAILROAD
Chartered in 1862 with the passing of the Pacific Railroad Act of July 1 of that same year, the Union Pacific's track-laying crews began pushing west from Omaha, Nebraska,[2] early in 1864, government-subsidized to the same extent as the rival Central Pacific, which had started laying its iron east from Sacramento, California, some months earlier. The UP tracks followed the Platte across Nebraska, meandered through southern Wyoming, then pushed across northern Utah until they reached Promontory Point where, on May 10, 1869, they linked up with the tracks of the Central Pacific. (See CENTRAL PACIFIC RAILROAD and PROMONTORY POINT.)

UNITED STATES MARSHAL
A federal lawman whose appointment came directly from the President and who was charged with the enforcement of federal laws only. A United States marshal's jurisdiction could extend over a whole territory (e.g., Arizona), or part of a territory (e.g., Western District of Arkansas), and he was empowered to appoint as many deputies as he thought necessary.[3] A marshal's term of office could last for as long as he remained in presidential favor, but as presidential elections were, and are, held every four years, this was the maximum length of time a marshal could be expected to remain in his post. Insignia of office varied from time to time, badge designs of either a six-pointed star or a five-pointed star embraced within the down-sweeping horns of a crescent[4] being the most common. (See SHERIFF and TOWN MARSHAL.)

UPSON, ASH Abbreviated pen name used by Marshall Ashmun Upson, a nomadic newspaperman and writer who was born in Connecticut on November 23, 1828, and started his working career as a member of the journalistic staff of the New York *Tribune*. During the early 1860s Upson moved West and settled in New Mexico where, over the years, he was to find employment with many of the territory's pioneer newspapers, serve as acting postmaster at Roswell, and hand out fines as a justice of the peace in Lincoln County. Over these years Upson became friends with Pat Garrett, and shortly after the latter had been elected

---

[1] If persecution wasn't involved this was a clear case of mistaken identity, for Underwood played no part in this robbery, it having occurred before he joined the gang.

[2] Designated as the eastern terminus and starting point of the Union Pacific by President Abraham Lincoln on November 17, 1863.

[3] Example: James F. Fagan, United States marshal for the Western District of Arkansas from July 2, 1874, to July 10, 1876, employed two hundred deputies. A deputy U.S. marshal was at liberty to stand for election as sheriff or take on the duties of town marshal while serving as a federal officer.

[4] This latter type of badge frequently occurs in the photographs of old-time U.S. marshals.

sheriff of Lincoln County in 1880 he employed Ash to keep his official records straight, an association that led to their jointly producing *The Authentic Life of Billy the Kid* in 1882. Marshall Ashmun Upson died at Ulvalde, Texas, in 1894, having remained a friend of Garrett's until his death.[5] (See BAKER, FRANK; BILLY THE KID; and GARRETT, PATRICK FLOYD.)

UTAH Western state that is bounded on the north by Idaho, on the northeast by Wyoming, has Nevada and Colorado to the west and east, respectively, and has Arizona as its southern neighbor. First settled by the Mormons in 1847, Utah still remains a Mormon stronghold, with some 70 per cent of its churchgoing population bearing allegiance to the Church of Jesus Christ of Latter-day Saints. Originally Mexican territory that was ceded to the United States in 1848, Utah was organized as a territory in 1850 and was admitted to the Union as the forty-fifth state in 1896. Tourist attractions in the state include the Bryce Canyon and Zion National Parks, historic Promontory Point, and the largest salt

lake in the Americas. Salt Lake City is the state capital, and the state is popularly known as either the Mormon State or the Beehive State. (See GREAT SALT LAKE; MORMONS; MOUNTAIN MEADOWS MASSACRE; and PROMONTORY POINT.)

UTE INDIANS Plains-plateau tribe of the Uto-Aztecan language family who have been resident in what is now Utah and western Colorado since at least 1600. Originally seed gatherers and hunters of small game, by the late 1700s the earlier arrival of the horse had made it possible for the Ute to develop into nomadic tepee-dwellers who could use the buffalo herds of the Great Plains as their commissariat. The Ute were culturally inferior to most of the plains tribes and reputedly more savage, yet they gave the white man relatively little trouble, for after a few outbreaks of violence in the mid-1860s and the late 1870s the Ute resigned themselves to living on the Uintah-Ouray Reservation in northeastern Utah. (See BLACKHAWK WAR; MEEKER MASSACRE; MEEKER, NATHAN C.; and OURAY.)

[5] Ash being interred in a plot of consecrated ground that Garrett owned at Ulvalde.

CHARLES M. RUSSELL

VALLEY TAN Name given to an intoxicating beverage that possessed more of the qualities of an embalming fluid than the "whiskey" it was professed to be. Valley Tan was made in the Henry Mountains of Utah. (See WHISKEY.)

VAQUERO Spanish or Mexican herdsman. The American cowboy's style of dress, horse furnishings, and stock-handling equipment have all been influenced by the *vaquero*.

VASQUEZ, TIBURCIO California *bandido* of the post-gold-rush years. Tiburcio was born in Monterey County, California, in 1837, one of a family of six children born to parents of Mexican extraction, and like most of the greaser *bandidos* of the period, he is reputed to have been forced into a life of crime after having supposedly killed a gringo who had insulted either his sister or his mistress or—alternatively—abused some bawd who worked in a *cantina cum* bagnio that Vasquez may have owned at the tender age of eighteen. That he was never sought or arrested for this "killing" makes it appear far more likely that Tiburcio joined the forces of disorder to get *mucho dinero* with the loss of as little sweat as possible.

In 1857, after two or three years of undetected crime as a member of various bands of brigands, Vasquez was arrested in Los Angeles on a charge of cattle theft. The charge stuck, and this half-pint outlaw who was mustachioed most fearsome was not allowed back among the righteous until 1863. Over the next seven years, during which time he had formed an association with outlaws Juan Soto and "Red-handed Dick" Procopio, Vasquez was to receive short terms of imprisonment for stock theft, his third session behind bars ending with his being released from San Quentin in the early months of 1870. From this time onward Tiburcio's depredations became much wider in scope, this three-time loser leading a motley band of peon-class cutthroats in a series of wayfarer, stage-coach, store, and mission robberies which, over the next four years, were to leave an Italian butcher as dead as his mutton at Enriquita in Santa Clara County, and three equally dead citizens at Tres Pinos in San Benito County.

In common with all such legendary owlhoots of hot-blooded Latin extraction, Tiburcio is reputed to have had an extremely full love-life, California at this time evidently being full of *señoritas*—and *señoras*—who could be aroused to a fair pitch on being serenaded by the staccato tune of a Colt .45. Such dalliance was to lead to this "Don Juan's" downfall, for despite the fact that large rewards dangled over his head, it was a cuckolded husband and not a bounty hunter[1] who led a posse to Tiburcio's hideout near San Francisco on May 14, 1874. On noting the arrival of the law, Vasquez made a break, but before he could reach his horse, he was wounded by a shotgun blast fired by posseman George Beers, and Vasquez surrendered —some say "gracefully." On March 19, 1875, Tiburcio Vasquez did his last tango on the gallows at San Jose, California. For the record, some reports state that Vasquez was entitled to 4½ dozen notches at the time of his passing. (See MORSE, HARRY N.)

VEGA, CRUZ   A mail carrier of Mexican descent who on September 20, 1875 helped to waylay and murder the Reverend F. J. Tolby as the minister was riding the twenty-mile trip between Elizabethtown and Cimarron in New Mexico Territory. A friend of the deceased, the Reverend O. P. Mains, became convinced of Vega's guilt, and although the suspect had been arrested and released for lack of evidence, eye-for-an-eye Mains persuaded a non-choirboy acquaintance named Clay Allison that it might be a good idea to beat a confession out of Cruz. On the night of October 30 Vega was dragged from his home by a gang of roughs led by Mains and Allison, and after the prisoner had been roughed up into admitting being present at the slaying of Tolby and had fingered a fellow Latin American named Manuel Cardenas as the triggerman, they hanged him from a convenient telegraph pole. Shortly afterward Cardenas was arrested. He was, however, never to be brought to trial, for on November 10 a number of masked men stormed the jail and shot him to death.[2] One wonders if the Reverend Mains was behind one of the

masks. (See ALLISON, CLAY, and GRIEGO, FRANCISCO.)

VERMILLION, "TEXAS JACK"
One of those mysterious characters who make brief appearances on the western scene but of whom hardly anything is known. Colorado, Kansas, and Tombstone all had Jack for varying periods during the 1870s and early 1880s, and he did serve as a deputy lawman—local, county, and possibly federal—under both Masterson and Earp, but no definitive incidents have ever been attributed to Vermillion, and although he is invariably classed as being a gunfighter of great dexterity, there is no record of his having fired anything but the twisted ends of cylinders of Bull Durham. Vermillion was riding behind Wyatt when the latter terminated the careers of Indian Charlie and Curly Bill Brocius, and in 1883 Vermillion rode the rails to Dodge City with Earp to give Luke Short a hand in his clash with Mayor Webster, but after this year little more was heard of the man, for shortly after Luke's problems had been sorted out, this genie known as "Texas Jack" Vermillion seems to have disappeared back into his bottle. Jack's regional nickname does not necessarily mean he was a product of Texas, there being numerous "Texas Jacks" around who had most likely never visited the state. (See CRUZ, FLORENTINE; GRAHAM, WILLIAM B.; SHORT, LUKE; and TEXAS JACK.)

VICTORIO   Mimbreño chief who left a bloody trail across the Southwest and the Mexican province of Chihuahua during the twilight years of the Apache wars. Born near Ciudad Juárez in the province

---

[1] The informant could have been both.
[2] Manuel Cardenas was a man with a record; in 1864 he had been sentenced to death for murdering a gringo, but the sentence was later commuted to a life term which—unfortunately for Tolby, Vega, and Cardenas—didn't last long enough.

of Chihuahua in 1830,[3] Victorio had spent many years as a warrior under the leadership of Mangas Colorado and had fought alongside Cochise's Chiricahuas before being accepted as chief of the Warm Springs band in the late 1860s. In the spring of 1877, after nearly seventeen years of spasmodic warfare with the white man, Victorio's band settled on six hundred square miles of land that had been reserved for them on the headwaters of the Gila River in southwestern New Mexico. This area of land embraced the band's favorite campsite at Ojo Caliente, and had they been allowed to remain here little more may have been heard of Victorio, but in the April of 1879 it was decided to remove the band to the dreaded San Carlos Reservation in southeastern Arizona, and rather than submit to this, Victorio broke camp and left New Mexico at the head of a war party of thirty braves. In western Texas the fleeing Mimbreños received reinforcements when some eighty Mescaleros placed themselves under Victorio's leadership, and this united force crossed the Rio Grande to push west and establish a stronghold in the Candelaria Mountains of Chihuahua.

On September 4, 1879, Victorio led his warriors back north and attacked a company of the 9th U. S. Cavalry camping near Ojo Caliente, the Apaches killing eight troopers and escaping with more than forty cavalry mounts before the soldiers knew what was happening. Over the next two weeks Victorio's warriors were to kill a further eighteen of their enemies during clashes with a miner's posse and details of the pursuing 9th Cavalry, after which the Apaches disappeared into Mexico. Over the next few months Victorio concentrated on raiding

rancheros within easy reach of his retreat in the Candelarias, and when two posses from the village of Carrizal trailed the Mimbreños into the mountains, they never returned, twenty-nine Mexicans thus being added to the list of the raiders' victims.

For months Victorio continued to make successful raids into western Texas and as far north as Ojo Caliente, but by the summer of 1880 more than two thousand U.S. troops and a like number of Mexican soldiery, plus a hundred Texas Rangers, had forced the Mimbreños to leave the Candelarias, and by early October Victorio and his warriors were bottled up in the Tres Castillos Mountains in northwestern Chihuahua. On October 14, 1880, a large force of Mexican troops under the command of Colonel Joaquin Terrazas trapped the Apaches in the Tres Castillos, and after a long-drawn-out engagement Victorio and seventy-eight of his band lay dead and some sixty-eight surviving Mimbreños had been taken prisoner. (See COCHISE and MANGAS COLORADO.)

VIGILANTES
Group of public-spirited individuals bearing allegiance to a self-appointed organization that had been formed to maintain public order and deal with outlawry in a community or region that lacked official law enforcement or possessed an obviously corrupt regime of such public officials. The Vigilantes of San Francisco (1851 and 1855–56) and of western Montana (1863–64)—not to mention many smaller and lesser-known groups, cleaned up violence in their bailiwicks with a speed and expertise that might well be employed to advantage in the present-day jungles of New York, San Francisco, and London.

[3] If we accept the published statements of Don Jesus Tarin—which are extremely convincing—as being reliable, this would be Victorio's approximate year of birth if he was indeed a Mexican named Francisco Cedillos, who had been captured by the Mimbreños while still a small child, the name "Victorio" being adopted at some later date.

The members of a well-organized vigilance committee signed a covenant of their intentions and ideals, and although their "courts" left much to be desired,[4] the innocent were rarely dragged before them. Malefactors of a nonviolent or merely suspect nature were usually given adequate warning to leave the area, but if this failed to achieve its purpose, a "trial" could be a speedy affair—a show of hands (or similar type vote) leading to acquittal, banishment, or a "suspended sentence" being carried out at the nearest crossbeam or local hanging tree. A posse of vigilantes may have occasionally deteriorated into a lynch mob, but a lynch mob should never be classed as a group of vigilantes. The so-called vigilantes and regulators formed by the big cattlemen were little more than lynch mobs. (See INNOCENTS; STUART, GRANVILLE; and VIGILANTES OF MONTANA.)

VIGILANTES OF MONTANA
A vigilance committee that was organized at Virginia City in western Montana during the last week of 1863 with the initial object of clearing a gang of outlaws known as the "Innocents" from the gold-mining towns and camps lying to the east of the Bitterroot Mountains. The covenant of the Vigilantes of Montana —in its original spelling—read as follows: "We the undersigned uniting ourselves

in a party for the laudible purpos of arresting thievs & murderers & recovering stollen propperty do pledge ourselvs & and our sacred honor each to all others & solemnly swear that we will reveal no secrets, violate no laws of right & and not desert eachother or our standerd of justice so help us God. As witness our hand and seal this 23 of December A D 1863."

The Montana organization had chapters in Bannack, Junction City, Pine Grove, Nevada City, Summit, Highland, and Fairweather, among other towns, and between December 21, 1863 (two days before the articles of the Vigilantes had been signed), and January 11, 1864, twenty-four "Innocents" had been found guilty of a variety of crimes and been hanged. The Montana Vigilantes were organized on a basis similar to that of the San Francisco Committee of Vigilance of some twelve years earlier,[5] and although the Montanans were equally as successful as the California organization, the Montana group usually went to greater lengths in warning a public nuisance or non-homicidal malefactor that his actions were under scrutiny before hauling him before one of their "courts."[6] As vigilance committees had no penal institutions or personnel to operate same, a felon who had been taken into custody for a quick "trial"

[4] The legal profession, deriving as it does its livelihood from the courts, will no doubt support this view.

[5] The San Francisco Committee of Vigilance, which was established on June 9, 1851, on the instigation of a onetime Mormon elder named Samuel Brannan, gave each of its vigilantes a certificate of membership. This group was disbanded in August 1851 after their hanging of four habitual criminals had driven the lawless element from the city. By the spring of 1855 San Francisco was once again as corrupt as a rotten apple, and in May of that year a second Committee of Vigilance was organized, with Sam once more at the helm. This second movement, which headquartered at Fort Vigilance (popularly known as "Fort Gunnybags"), was active for fifteen months, had a membership of five thousand, and had hanged four miscreants by the time they were dissolved in August 1856.

[6] A paper bearing the numerals 3-7-77 was often tacked to a suspect's door or cabin wall as a warning for him to quit the region. What 3-7-77 means is anyone's guess. Many suggest that the numbers may refer to the measurements of a grave—3 feet wide, 7 feet deep, and 6 feet, 5 inches long—but this writer likes to think they are a reference to some long-forgotten text. Drop us a line and we'll sort it out yet.

didn't have to worry that he might be placed behind bars, for only three verdicts were possible: acquittal, banishment, or hanging. The Vigilantes of Montana rarely, if ever, wore masks, and they never indulged in night-riding activities of a terrorist nature. (See BANNACK, MONTANA; BEIDLER, JOHN XAVIER; DIMSDALE, THOMAS J.; INNOCENTS; SLADE, JOSEPH A.; STUART, GRANVILLE; and VIGILANTES.)

VILLA, PANCHO
Well-known Mexican *insurrecto*. (See ARAMBULA, JOSÉ FRANCISCO VILLA.)

VINEGARROON   Name that Roy Bean gave to a tent village in southwestern Texas[7] on his establishing a grog shop in the vicinity in July 1879. Vinegarroon is also the popular name for a scorpion in Texas. (See BEAN, ROY, and SCORPION.)

VIRGINIA CITY, MONTANA
Mining town that blossomed into existence in the Tobacco Root Mountains of southwestern Montana within weeks of gold being discovered along Alder Creek in 1863. Within but a short time the town had a population of around ten thousand, and before it was six months old it had nearly two hundred murder victims to its discredit—statistics that suggest that a citizen had a roughly 2 per cent chance of winding up dead if he stepped out for a beer. After giving its inhabitants just over four years of easy come, easy go and easy dead excitement, Virginia City went into a decline, and it was only saved from becoming a complete "ghost" by

the timely arrival of a successful farmer named Charles Bovey who, in 1946, bought up much of the near-deserted and dehydrating town and began restoring it to its former glory. Thanks to Mr. Bovey, Virginia City is now one of Montana's main tourist attractions. (See VIGILANTES OF MONTANA.)

VIRGINIA CITY, NEVADA
Mining town that mushroomed from the barren ground of western Nevada shortly after silver- and gold-bearing ore had been discovered in the area early in 1859.[8] Unlike many mining towns, Virginia City developed into a thriving business metropolis of some twenty-five thousand souls, most of whom were dressed in the latest of fashion and indulged but rarely in the rowdyism that was the usual hallmark of such communities. Multistoried hotels graced its streets as did magnificent saloons, luxurious brothels, and the offices of the *Territorial Enterprise,* a pioneer newspaper that has been in continuous production since 1858.[9] By 1879 the mines were almost played out, and a general depression set in that soon began to drive the population elsewhere and reduce the opulence into a condition of seediness. By the turn of the century, decay had reduced Virginia City to a third of its size, yet even so, the town was not to become a "ghost," for although its present population is only around the five hundred mark, the town is a major tourist attraction of the state. (See BULETTE, JULIA, and COMSTOCK LODE.)

VOLCANIC PISTOL
Any of the lever-action[10] magazine pistols

---

[7] On the northern bank of the Rio Grande a few hundred yards west of the Pecos River.
[8] This was the fabulous Comstock Lode.
[9] Samuel Clemens first used his "Mark Twain" by-line while working for the *Enterprise.*
[10] A large-ringed trigger guard was used for this purpose.

manufactured by the Volcanic Repeating Arms Company from 1855 to 1857 and by the New Haven Arms Company from 1857 to 1859. Pistols listed by Volcanic are as follows: 4-inch pocket pistol, .300-caliber six-shot; 6-inch target pistol, .300-caliber ten-shot; 6-inch Navy pistol, .394-caliber eight-shot; and 8-inch Navy pistol, .394-caliber ten-shot. Calibers given are approximate. All Volcanic firearms—both rifles and pistols—had tubular magazines running the full length of their barrels, and all used the same type of ammunition: conical bullets containing 7½ grains of powder and a primer in their hollowed-out bases. This low-velocity ammunition was the reason for the Volcanic's short history. (See VOLCANIC RIFLE.)

VOLCANIC RIFLE Any rifle having the same history as the Volcanic pistol. Rifles[11] listed by Volcanic are as follows: 16-inch carbine, .394-caliber, twenty-shot; 20-inch carbine, .394-caliber, twenty-five shot; and 24-inch carbine, .394-caliber, thirty-shot. The Volcanic was the forerunner of the Henry rifle.

(See HENRY RIFLE and VOLCANIC PISTOL.)

VOYAGEURS Fur company employees who transported furs, trade goods, and trappers to and from outlying posts by waterway. *Voyageurs* were usually of French-Canadian extraction, although Scots, South Sea islanders, and Amerinds were also found within their ranks. Canoes or *bateaux*[12] were employed for this work.

VULTURE Large carrion-eating bird, two species of which—the turkey vulture and the black vulture—may be found in the American West. The turkey vulture, which has a length of about 30 inches and may be readily identified by its bright red head, is found in most areas of the West, but the black vulture, which is about 5 inches smaller and has a black head and plumage, is mainly confined to the Southwest. Neither of the American species builds nests—caves, hollows in the ground, etc., being used as nesting places. In North America vultures are frequently called "buzzards." (See BUZZARD.)

[11] Volcanic—and New Haven—classed the weapons as "carbines" whatever the barrel length.

[12] A long, narrow, flat-bottomed craft that is only suitable for use on inland waterways.

FREDERIC REMINGTON

WADSWORTH, MICKEY
Better known as Mickey Free. (See FREE,
MICKEY.)

WAGNER, JOHN
One of Sheriff Henry Plummer's band
of road agents who sported one of
Henry's deputy badges and was popularly
known as "Dutch John." Wagner was suspected of many crimes, but he is only
known to have taken part in one of Plummer's unofficial capers. In the fall of 1863
the sheriff detailed deputies Wagner and
Marshland to waylay a caravan reputedly transporting some seventy-five
to eighty thousand dollars in gold. The
owlhoot deputies made their play near
Junction City, but the holdup was unsuccessful, and Wagner and Marshland
were driven off after Wagner had been
wounded in the shoulder and Marshland
had copped a ball in his chest. As both
his deputies had been recognized during
their abortive attempt at robbery, Sheriff
Plummer advised them to leave the territory, but Wagner was arrested by vigilantes while he was still shopping around
for a good mount, and on January 11,
1864, shortly after being allowed to write
a last letter to his mother in New York
City, Dutch John was hanged at Bannack. (See INNOCENTS and PLUMMER,
HENRY.)

WAGON-BOX FIGHT On August 2,
1867, a detail of the 9th U. S. Infantry
under the command of Major J. W.
Powell was attacked by a thousand-strong
force of Red Cloud's Sioux while acting as escort to a party of woodcutters
who were operating a few miles southwest of Fort Kearney. This was a bad
day for Red Cloud and Crazy Horse, for
the woodcutters managed to get back to
the fort, and the major and his thirty-
man detail were forted up within an
impenetrable corral of wagon-boxes,
Powell having had the foresight to remove the wheels from fifteen freight
wagons and arrange the boxes in a circle
in anticipation of such an emergency.[1]

[1] Removal of the wheels prevented any attacker from gaining entrance to the corral via a
beneath-the-wagons route.

536

Wild and Woolly

The troops had also been recently issued with breech-loading Springfields, weapons that were capable of far more rapid fire than the old muzzle-loaders, which Red Cloud expected them to be using. The Sioux, making massed attacks behind such leaders as American Horse, Crazy Horse, and Crow King, had three of their charges repulsed with heavy losses, and before they could regroup for a fourth attack, a howitzer shell exploded some distance away, a detonation that signaled the imminent arrival of a large relief force from the fort and persuaded Red Cloud to withdraw his warriors from the field. Major Powell's losses were seven dead and three wounded, while the Sioux losses have been estimated at near the two hundred mark.

WAIGHTMAN, GEORGE Reputed to have been found wandering on Cowboy Flat in what is now Payne County, Oklahoma, after being abandoned by his parents and raised to adulthood by a foreman of Oscar D. Halsell's HX Ranch, the man known as "Red Buck" Waightman joined the newly formed Doolin gang in the fall of 1892, having until this time probably only engaged in stock theft and other minor crimes. During the Doolin robbery of a Rock Island train at Diver, Oklahoma, in May 1895, Waightman's horse was shot from beneath him, and he had to escape riding tandem behind "Bitter Creek" George Newcomb, a misfortune that was to result in the death of an aged preacher *cum* farmer within hours of the robbery, Waightman shooting the man down when the man came to the door of his shack while the outlaw was stealing one of his horses. This cold-blooded murder didn't set well with Doolin, and after giving the killer his cut of the take, Doolin banished him from the gang.

Shortly after being driven into the wilderness, Red Buck established himself in a dugout in Dewey County, Oklahoma, and here he became acquainted with three men who were to appear onstage during the last act of his saga, the parties being Joseph Ventioner, George Miller, and a small-time rancher known only as Glover. Sometime in the summer of 1895 Waightman began to suspect that Glover was harboring thoughts of turning informer, and on seeing a posse in the vicinity while sheltering in the suspect's home, the onetime orphan erased these suspicions by shooting Glover dead.

There is no evidence to suggest that Ventioner took part in any of the store robberies associated with Waightman during this period, but it may be assumed that the killing of Glover prompted Ventioner into laying information before Sheriff C. L. Bradley of Dewey County, for shortly after Miller and Waightman had holed up in their hideout after returning from a store holdup at Arapaho in adjacent Custer County, Ventioner was a conspicuous member of the Bradley posse that began pumping lead into the dugout after the two outlaws had failed to heed a call to surrender. As this was an era when sendees' names could not be attached to flying lead with any degree of accuracy during a multigun shootout, it is impossible to state whose bullets wounded Miller into surrender and Red Buck into his grave.[2] (See DOOLIN GANG, and INGALLS, OKLAHOMA.)

WAIGHTMAN, "RED BUCK" Nickname attached to gunman George Waightman. (See WAIGHTMAN, GEORGE.)

WALKER COLT Largest of the Colt handguns. (See COLT FIREARMS, subheading *Walker*.)

[2] A bullet in the back was the cause of death, and it could have been fired by Ventioner. After the battle Miller was to be known as "Three-finger" George.

WALLACE, "BIG FOOT"
An early-day frontiersman who was big in every way. (See WALLACE, WILLIAM ALEXANDER ANDERSON.)

WALLACE, WILLIAM
ALEXANDER ANDERSON
Born at Lexington, Virginia, on April 3, 1817,[3] Wallace started making tracks for Texas in 1837, a 6-foot hunk of manhood weighing 240 pounds who settled at San Antonio de Bexar in 1838 to make a name for himself the following year through his efforts to track down a thievin' Injun known as "Big Foot"; Wallace never got the red-stick in his sights, but from then on he was to be known as "Big Foot" Wallace. Two years after his arrival at San Antone he joined the Texas Rangers, and over the next couple of years he was involved in skirmishes with Indians and battles with the troops of Mexico, the highlight of this period being the escapade in which Big Foot cannily cut down a Mexican soldier of similar build to his own so that he might procure a change of pants.

In the last week of 1842 Big Foot was one of a large number of prisoners taken by the Mexicans, and although the greater part of these escaped over the next few months, Wallace and 159 other prisoners were still wearing irons on March 27 when General Santa Anna sent down the order for all of them to be shot. The officer in charge of the prisoners would not agree to this, and it was decided that 144 white beans and 16 black beans would be placed in a gourd and each prisoner would be allowed to withdraw one of same on the understanding that anyone finding himself with a black bean would be shot without further ado. When it came to Big Foot's turn he spent so long trying to feel "color" that the Mexicans urged him to "Hurry up!" with much *pronto* prompting, but the big man took his time and finally came up with a white bean, thus insuring return to the comfort of a roach-infested cell rather than the cold comfort of the long trench that awaited those whose luck ran out that day. What passions assailed this giant during his incarceration can be readily imagined, and on one occasion when two nubile *señoritas* visited the jail to see the Americanos, Big Foot managed to seize one of the dark-haired lovelies and it took the might of a number of soldiers and the prison chaplain to release the no doubt mentally ravaged girl from his embrace.

On August 5, 1844, this man who the Mexicans knew as the *"loco* Americano" was released, and the following year he settled on the banks of the Medina River west of San Antone. Big Foot left his mark in the Medina region by decimating the puma population of the area, reputedly having killed 142 of the fearsome critters with a club during one short season—a seemingly heroic feat until one realizes upon turning the page that the pumas were young cubs that were still in the "kitten" stage.

In 1846 Wallace rejoined the Texas Rangers to fight in the Mexican War, and two years after his term of enlistment had expired in 1848 he managed to secure a contract to carry mail between San Antonio and El Paso, a 1,200-mile round trip that was accomplished by Big Foot's stagecoach and its six armed outriders in about thirty days, come high water or Comanches. This job lasted until 1852, in which year Governor P. H. Bell commissioned Wallace to raise a company of 76 Rangers to protect southwestern Texas from the depredations of marauding bands of Indians, a 12-month stint of "whuppin'" Comanches during which Big Foot killed himself a chief.

[3] Reputedly having maternal links with Robert Bruce of Scotland.

Wild and Woolly

By this time Wallace had relocated on Chicon Creek, and on his return from Ranger service he settled down to raise a few horses and cattle, at the same time making a fat income on the side by tracking down runaway black slaves for the reward money; Big Foot employing a pack of hounds when engaged in the latter task. When the Civil War came around, Wallace chose to remain on the frontier, the forty-four-year-old veteran being of the opinion that the protection of Confederate enlistees' womenfolk was far more important than donning a uniform. In later years Wallace was to see a small settlement named "Big Foot,"[4] and he was to spend the last few years of his life at the home of some friends who lived a few miles north of the village that bore his nickname, dying here on January 7, 1899, while in his eighty-second year. (See TEXAS RANGERS.)

WALTZ, JACOB   Frequently come across when reading articles about the Superstition Mountains of Arizona, although Walzer is correct. (See WALZER, JACOB.)

WALZER, JACOB   The mysterious "Dutchman" who is the central figure in the legends of the so-called "Lost Dutchman Mine," a source of vast wealth that has been in the "Lost" category since 1891. The year of Walzer's arrival in the United States cannot be verified, but it was most likely during the late 1850s, for in 1861 he became a naturalized American citizen at Los Angeles, California, the immigration authorities recording Jacob von Walzer as being a graduate of Heidelberg University and a professional mining engineer who had been born in the province of Württemberg, Germany, in 1810. Over the next decade Walzer's trail is dim, but although the census records of 1864 merely pinpoint him as being a resident of Prescott, Arizona Territory, in that year, it may be safe to assume that he never strayed from this territory for the remainder of his days.

Early in 1873 he got a job as consulting engineer with the Vulture Mine at Wickenburg, but before the year was out he left this employment,[5] and in 1874 he had set up house with a young Apache girl at the five-year-old settlement of Phoenix. Forty miles due east of Phoenix lay the grim natural fortress of the Superstition Mountains—legendary site of the Apaches' thunder god's gold and an area in which small bands of Tontos still roamed[6]—and sometime in the summer of 1874 Walzer's squaw led him into these mountains with a couple of pack burros, and a few days later they returned to Phoenix with about $70,000 in pure unworked gold.[7] Three days after their return an Apache war party raided Phoenix, and although Walzer escaped harm, his squaw was captured so that her tongue might be torn out—a grisly operation that requires no comment.

---

[4] Located in Frio County, Texas.

[5] Rumors abound that he was fired after being caught stealing high-grade ore, but there is no evidence to support this.

[6] The United States 5th Cavalry under the command of Major William H. Brown cleared most of Chuntz' band of Tonto Apaches from the Superstitions in January 1873, but small remnants of the band were still roaming the mountains well after this date.

[7] It appears certain that Walzer's squaw must have led him to the source of the "Thunder God's Gold"—some secret Apache cache that had probably been accumulated over the years when the Indians were making murderous raids on Mexican pack trains that were freighting smelted gold out of the Superstitions en route to Mexico. Two points may be worth noting: The remains of many Spanish smelters may still be found in the mountains, and it is on record that Mimbreño chief Mangas Colorado told a party of miners that he could lead them to a vast hoard of gold—an offer that was disbelieved when it was made in 1847.

538

Undeterred by this tragedy, Walzer continued to visit the Superstitions and return with varying amounts of raw gold, and in 1877, evidently having decided that he required aid, he took a carpenter named Jacob Wisner[8] into his confidence, and over the next two years he and Wisner made numerous profitable trips into the mountains. In February 1879 Apaches raided the partners' campsite in the Superstitions during Walzer's absence, and when he returned, he found Wisner dead, staked out across their campfire and burned to a crisp.

This experience failed to curb Walzer's lust for gold, and over the next ten years he shipped a recorded $250,000 of the smelted metal to the U. S. Mint at Sacramento, California. Some of the more rugged residents of Phoenix were not without curiosity as to the source of the "Dutchman's" wealth, and attempts were made to follow in his tracks when he pushed out toward the Superstitions, but of the twenty-six men who managed to trail him well into the mountains, none survived their trip, their dead bodies being recovered after they had been made that way by either Walzer's gun or the guns of the Apaches. Jacob Walzer, who was probably better known as "The Dutchman," died at Phoenix on October 25, 1891, and as little money was found in his effects, it appears he must have spent the last seventeen years of his life working in a vicious circle, transforming his gold into cash via the U. S. Mint, then burying the currency in some remote place. Folk are still searching for the "Lost Dutchman Mine,"[9] but, oddly enough, no one appears to be interested in trying to trace Walzer's assumedly hidden wealth. (See LOST MINES and SUPERSTITION MOUNTAINS.)

WAMPUM Contraction of *wampampeog*, an Algonkin word that may be roughly described as meaning "a string of beads." These beads were originally made from shells, stones, animal claws, and other suitable materials and were used for decorative purposes, but shortly after the arrival of European settlers they became acceptable as items of trade, and glass beads that the English and Dutch colonists had imported for this purpose began to find their way into the hands of the various tribes. When used as articles of trade, colored wampum was classed as having greater value than the white variety. Wampum, however, never became exclusively connected with barter, and belts made of wampum were frequently used as treaty covenants, geometric designs and/or the stylized figures of humans and animals being woven into such belts to remind a tribe of "clauses" in any such agreement.

[8] A man whom Walzer had become acquainted with during his stay at Prescott in 1864.
[9] As "Dutchman" Walzer stated he "picked the gold off the ground," it can hardly be classed as a mine. Most of this gold may have been cached by the Apaches after the Peralta pack-train massacre of 1848, for as this was a "large pack train," it may well have been transporting well in excess of $3,000,000 worth of smelted gold out of the mountains. From time to time headlines proclaim that the "Lost Dutchman" has been found, but none of these reports has been reliable. Minor earth tremors occurred in the Superstitions in 1879, and these may have blotted out all trace of Walzer's "find" forever, for although the western area of the Superstitions contains numerous as yet undeciphered pointers to the whereabouts of the Peralta mines—giant saguaros encircled by iron bands or mutilated by blaze marks—there are no such clues to the location of Walzer's gold, the only worthwhile clue in the case of the "Lost Dutchman" being Jacob's statement that "The mine can be seen from Weaver's Needle." The debunkers of Walzer claim that it is possible to have an uninterrupted line of vision for twenty-five miles in any direction if one climbs to the top of this landmark (which had been named after some little-known mountain man); could be—but Walzer most likely meant from "ground level."

WAPITI Large species of deer that could be found in most areas of the West during the first half of the nineteenth century. Regarded as the New World representative of the red deer of Europe, the wapiti is the second-largest deer in the world,[10] a fully grown male standing 5 feet at the shoulder, having a length of almost 10 feet, and weighing in the region of 1,000 pounds. Coloring is mainly grayish-black, with almost black undersides and a yellowish rump patch. Antlers are multipointed and may have a span of around 5 feet. Usually referred to as the "elk" in North America.

WAR BONNET
The spectacular, feathered headdress that had its origins among the plains tribes[11]—most likely the Sioux—during the first half of the nineteenth century. About thirty-six eagle feathers were used in the making of a Sioux *wa-pa-ha,* a further fifty being required if the bonnet had a trailer. As the wearing of feathers could only be sanctioned after authenticated acts of valor had been performed, only the greatest of warriors could ever hope to possess sufficient feathers to make a full bonnet. This feather heraldry had become much abused by the tail end of the 1800s as more and more tribes began making war bonnets in their efforts to catch up with the white folks' idea of what an Indian should look like, and nowadays with war-bonnet kits retailing at less than twenty dollars each, it's a mighty poor Indian who can't pose for his photograph or sit behind his curio stall wearing one of these feathered creations. (See ROMAN NOSE.)

WARD, MICKEY
A villainous-looking half-breed whom Al

Sieber employed as a scout. Better known as Mickey Free. (See FREE, MICKEY.)

WARPAINT   Facial and/or body makeup applied by the braves of many tribes prior to going on the warpath, possibly in an effort to appear fearsome. Iron oxide, kaolin, copper ore, and charcoal were the bases used to produce red, white, green, and black, respectively—a palette that could be further enlarged by the addition of yellow and blue clays. A supply of these was usually carried in a small bag, and they were mixed with animal fat before they were applied. Generally speaking, colors represented the fairly obvious: white for virtue, red for life, blue for melancholy, black for death, green for fruitfulness, and yellow for happiness.

WARREN MASSACRE Name given to an Indian outrage that occurred near Salt Creek in northern Texas[12] on May 18, 1871. At three o'clock on the afternoon of that day a mixed band of some 150 Kiowa, Kiowa-Comanche, and Comanche led by Satanta attacked a ten-unit wagon train that the firm of Warren and Duposes was using to freight grain from Weatherford to Fort Griffin, and although wagonmaster Nathan C. Long managed to corral the wagons and offer sufficient resistance to allow five of his men to escape, he and his six remaining teamsters were killed. On May 19 a detail of the 4th Cavalry recovered the bodies of the slain teamsters. All had been mutilated. Two Indians are known to have been killed in this fight. (See SATANTA.)

[10] The largest being the moose.
[11] War bonnets were only suitable for wearing on the plains, for such a headdress would soon have been "snarled" from the head of a brave if he had attempted to ride through a thicket or a stand of timber.
[12] About 35 miles west of Fort Richardson and 12 miles east of the ruins of Fort Belknap.

WAR SACK Bag in which a cowboy carries a change of clothing, personal articles, and washing equipment. Usually used as a pillow when in camp, and sometimes referred to as a "war bag."

WASHAKIE One of the few Indian chiefs who never warred against the white settlers. Born of a Chinook father and a Shoshone mother in 1798 in a Shoshone camp located somewhere in what is now northeastern Idaho, and known as Shoots Straight until he acquired the name Washakie[13] sometime during his late teens, this mixed-blood Indian became a chief of the Shoshones in the early 1840s. Chief Washakie led his warriors in frequent battles against both the Crow and Blackfoot tribes, but when white settlers began pushing into the Northwest, he let it be known that the new arrivals were not to be molested, and when other tribes attacked caravans using the Oregon Trail, any Shoshones who might be in the vicinity usually went to the aid of the whites.

In 1868 the Great White Father showed his appreciation by reserving the Wind River region of west-central Wyoming[14] for Washakie and his Shoshones, and on various occasions during the U. S. Army's North Plains campaigns of the 1870s Washakie and a number of his braves showed their gratitude by serving as scouts with the forces of Uncle Sam. When Washakie had reached his three-score years and ten, some of the young braves of his band suggested he was getting soft. The old chief replied to this by going on a lone hair-raising trip, and when he returned after an absence of two moons with seven recently lifted Blackfoot otakans, the scurrilous talkers became silenced. Washakie of the Shoshones died during the early hours of February 21, 1900, and Uncle Sam gave his remains a full military funeral. (See SHOSHONE INDIANS.)

WASHINGTON State located in the extreme Northwest that has a coastline on the Pacific Ocean, is bounded by Canada on the north, and has Idaho and Oregon to the east and south, respectively. Originally known as the Oregon country, Washington was organized as a territory in 1853 and was admitted to the Union as the forty-second state in 1889. The state capital is Olympia. Popularly known as the Evergreen State. Many Europeans confuse this state with Washington, D.C.[15] (See OREGON COUNTRY.)

WASHITA MASSACRE Started at dawn on November 27, 1868, when the notes of a trumpet heralded General George Armstrong Custer's cavalry attack on the winter camp of Black Kettle's Cheyenne. Snow blanketed the landscape when the 7th Cavalry made its four-pronged assault against this unsuspecting village on the Washita,[16] and most of the

---

13 A loose translation being "Rattler"—derived from the fact that Washakie liked to shake a rattle he had made from the pate hide of his first buffalo.

14 The Wind River Reservation covered an area of 4,297 square miles; this made it rather more than twice the size of the state of Delaware, or—as a more readily acceptable comparison for European readers—more than 2½ times the area of the county of Lancashire, England. Over the years the reservation has been whittled away by the U. S. Government, and now only about a fifth of its original acreage remains.

15 The District of Columbia is 61 square miles of federal land that was established at the confluence of the Potomac and Anacostia rivers in 1790 as the federal capital of the United States. This federal land was taken out of the eastern states of Maryland and Virginia.

16 The site of the massacre may be located on the north bank of the Washita River, approximately fourteen miles northwest of the present-day town of Cheyenne in Roger Mills County, western Oklahoma.

Indians had barely time to leave the huddled warmth of their tepees before sabers and small-arms fire was spilling them to the ground—an orgy of killing that was played out to the accompaniment of the strains of "Garryowen" and was to continue until 10 A.M. When "Recall" had been sounded, Chiefs Black Kettle and Little Rock and more than a hundred Cheyenne men, women, and children were lying dead in the raspberry-tinted ice cream of their ravaged village, and the 7th had taken sixty female and juvenile prisoners. General Custer was pleased with this exercise, which had been accomplished for the loss of but two officers and nineteen enlisted men, and after he had witnessed the slaughter of the Indian pony herd of more than eight hundred animals, he retired his 7th from the field with guidons streaming and the band playing "Garryowen." (See BLACK KETTLE; CUSTER, GEORGE ARMSTRONG; and 7TH CAVALRY.)

WATSON, ELLA   Also known as Kate Averill and Kate Maxwell and frequently referred to as "Cattle Kate." Born in Canada in 1861, Ella crossed into the United States with her parents while still a young girl, and by the mid-1860s her father, Thomas Watson, had established his family on a small farm in Smith County, Kansas. By the late 1870s the Watsons were classed as "well-to-do," and Ella had developed into a good-looking, nubile brunette who had reached the stage where she was looking around for something to do, preferably with the boys. Sometime during 1879 Ella contracted a marriage with a man named Maxwell,[17] but shortly thereafter, upon hearing that her husband was doing

much sparking in pastures other than marital, the little-used bride severed all family and boudoir ties by deserting Smith County, and we next hear of her unraveling her string across Nebraska, Colorado, and Wyoming, reputedly demanding cash on the barrelhead before allowing any male to cross her drawbridge.

By 1883 Ella was settled at Rawlins, county seat of Carbon County, Wyoming, and here she met James Averill, a saloon *cum* storeowner and postmaster whose business premises and homestead were located on the Sweetwater River some fifty miles north of Rawlins. In 1884 Ella[18] gave birth to a male child who looked sufficiently like Averill to justify his being christened Tom Averill, and four years later Averill requested Ella to join him on the Sweetwater, the postmaster being of the opinion that the ruffians who purchased his whiskey and filled his spittoons were in need of a little female companionship. Ella and young Tom arrived at Averill's place in the spring of 1888, and after filing claim to a homestead site about a mile from her lover's business complex, Ella had a cabin and a corral erected with monies supplied by Averill.

Within twelve months of her arrival on the Sweetwater it was being rumored around that Ella would accept cattle in return for her favors and that cowhands, rather than dip into their wallets, were making withdrawals from company herds to pay for such pleasures. In the early days of the game the ranchers regarded this as being the price they could be expected to pay for having a few laughs over their beers, and they merely dubbed her "Cattle Kate," but when all the puns

---

[17] The name Maxwell being conjectural, the fact that Ella used the name "Maxwell" on various occasions after this date having led to this assumption.

[18] Ella is usually described as having deteriorated into an uncouth 160 pounds of blowzy womanhood by this time, but photographs taken during this period make it quite obvious that such a description is far from valid.

revolving around "cows" had grown stale, a few hotheads decided that Ella had been given enough rope, and on July 20, 1889, they used what hemp they had left to hang both "Kate" and her lover from the branch of a cottonwood tree in Spring Creek Gulch. (See AVERILL, JAMES, and AVERILL, TOM.)

WATTLE   Type of brand mark that is made with a knife. (See BRANDING.)

WEASEL   A short-legged, long yet slim-bodied carnivore that possesses scent glands and is extremely vicious in its hunting habits. All true weasels are some shade of brown with white or cream undersides, possess slim tails, and have comparatively small ears. Numerous species of true weasel are to be found west of the Mississippi. These range in size from the least weasel, which has an average length of a bare 7 inches and is found only in the Northwest, to the five varieties of long-tailed weasels, which may reach a length of 19 inches and are common to the Rocky Mountains and the Great Plains. The black-footed ferret is a distinct species of weasel whose range is confined to the plains regions that extend from the Canadian line to southern Texas. This carnivore, which may also be classed as a polecat, is of a light ocher color, possesses a distinctive black mask and an extremely offensive scent, and may reach a length of 2 feet, of which 6 inches is taken up by the tail. Other, less obvious, members of the weasel family that are to be found in the West are: martens, confined to the densely forested regions of the Far West; minks, common to all but the most arid regions; badgers, found on most of the plains; and skunks and otters, both of which are to be found in most areas.

Wolverines, the largest members of the weasel family, may occasionally venture into the American West, but in the New World they are mainly confined to Canada.[19] (See SKUNK.)

WEBB, JIM Known alias of Wild Bill Longley. (See LONGLEY, WILLIAM P.)

WEIGHTMAN, GEORGE
Frequently come across as a misspelling of Waightman. (See WAIGHTMAN, GEORGE.)

WELCH, ED A native of San Angelo, Texas, who was an ex-con and a man of many aliases[20] when he teamed up with the better-known Ben Kilpatrick to commit a train robbery that ended in disaster. (See KILPATRICK, BEN.)

WELLS FARGO & COMPANY
An express company that had its origins in the minds of the directors of the American Express Company during the latter months of 1851 and was organized as a subsidiary of the American Express to begin operations in the gold fields of California on March 18, 1852. Two months later, Wells Fargo opened a banking and express office in San Francisco, and by the following year further offices had been established in Oregon, Hawaii, and Australia. By 1855 Wells Fargo had offices throughout the Mother Lode country and it was the major express company of California, although it was merely renting space on the vehicles of various stage lines and possessed no transport of its own, Wells Fargo Concords and celerity wagons only making their appearance on the western scene in 1860, when the company's acquisition

---

[19] An adult wolverine can have a length of 3 feet and weigh as much as 38 pounds.
[20] H. O. Beck, Ole Hobeck, and Howard Benson reputedly being three of these.

of the Pioneer Stage Line and the purchase of an interest in the Overland Mail Company resulted in two fleets of coaches being at the company's disposal. Wells Fargo continued to expand, and by 1863 they had nearly 180 depots throughout the West and had established a foothold in Mexico. The firm rode the crest of prosperity and weathered short periods of slump until 1918 when, as a national emergency measure, it was merged into the American Railroad Express Company, and only the banking interests of the company retained the "Wells Fargo" designation. In 1923 Wells Fargo banking interests were integrated with those of the Union Trust Company, and the Wells Fargo Bank and Union Trust Company is now the only remaining link with the express company of the Wild West era. "Stand and deliver!," shotgun messengers, burned-out relay stations, "Wells Fargo never forgets," Superintendent John J. Valentine's reward notices, company detectives, "Throw down the box!," Wells Fargo "markers," and dust-clouding coaches embedded with arrows are all part of the Wells Fargo saga, much of which may be found elsewhere in this volume. (See ADAMS & COMPANY; AMERICAN EXPRESS COMPANY; BLAIR, EUGENE; BOLTON, CHARLES E.; BUTTERFIELD OVERLAND MAIL COMPANY; CELERITY WAGON; CONCORD COACH; FARGO, WILLIAM G.; MONK, HANK; OVERLAND STAGE LINE; PACIFIC UNION EXPRESS; PANAMINT; PONY EXPRESS; and WELLS, HENRY.)

WELLS, HENRY
A native of Vermont whose name will forever be linked with that of William G. Fargo. Born at Thetford in 1805, Wells started his working career as a speech ther-

apist at Rochester, New York, in 1827, but by the early 1830s he was considering entering the express business, a change of interest that was to lead to his forming an association with William Fargo and their partnering the firm of Wells and Company's Western Express into existence in 1845. Within twelve months Wells had sold his interest in this embryo company, and some two years later he was operating as Wells and Company, but in 1850 he again became a business associate of Fargo's when the firms of Butterfield, Wasson and Company; Livingstone and Fargo and Company; and Wells and Company united to become the American Express Company. Two years later the American Express Company launched the subsidiary company of Wells Fargo and Company, and Henry Wells was to be connected with this firm until he retired from business in 1869. Henry Wells, pioneer expressman, died on December 10, 1878. (See FARGO, WILLIAM G., and WELLS FARGO & COMPANY.)

WEST, "LITTLE DICK"
A half-pint owlhoot who saw service with the Doolin mob and others. (See WEST, RICHARD.)

WEST, NATHANIEL
Sometimes given, incorrectly, as being the name of an outlaw known as "Texas Jack" Reed. (See REED, NATHANIEL.)

WEST, RICHARD   Oklahoma outlaw whose diminutive stature earned him the title of "Little Dick." Orphaned or abandoned while still a child and adopted by cowhands of the Halsell Ranch after being found living a gypsy-type existence on their range in Indian Territory,[21] Texas-

[21] Fellow owlhoot "Red Buck" Waightman—with whom "Little Dick" is oft confused—is reputed to have had foster upbringings of a similar nature to West's; unfortunate beginnings for both of the lads, for Oscar D. Halsell's HX spread on the Cimarron was an outlaw hatchery of some renown.

born Dick had spent some years as a horse wrangler with this outfit when he became a member of the Dalton gang in the summer of 1892. After the Coffeyville disaster West joined the newly formed Doolin mob, and he saw service with this gang until it fragmented into history in the latter half of 1895. Two years later Dick took part in the one and only robbery committed by the so-called Jennings gang, a near-fruitless caper that profited "Little Dick" to the tune of a mere sixty dollars. At some later date West became employed as horse wrangler at the Arnett Ranch near the town of Guthrie, and on the Thursday of April 7, 1898, while thus employed on the Arnett premises, he was shot dead by county and federal lawmen when he attempted to resist arrest. (See DALTON GANG; DOOLIN GANG; and JENNINGS, AL.)

WESTERN TRAIL
Nearly nine hundred miles of cattle trail that linked Bandera, Texas, with the cattle-shipping points of Dodge City, Kansas (Atchison, Topeka, and Santa Fe Railroad) and Ogallala, Nebraska (Union Pacific Railroad), the latter settlement being the Western Trail's northern terminal.

WESTPORT LANDING One of the two mustering places used by migrants who wished to push West via the Oregon Trail. Westport Landing was later to become known as Kansas City, Missouri. (See OREGON TRAIL.)

WHISKEY Although many reputable brands of domestic whiskey and a few imported Scotch and Irish whiskies found their way into the early West, these were well outnumbered by brands of so-called whiskies that had often been produced without recourse to distillation, and it is with this latter group of mind-bending beverages that this entry will briefly deal. In the Ozark regions of Missouri and Arkansas, whiskies were[22] produced by time-honored methods at illicit stills in the mountains, and while some of these "hillbilly brands" had no more adverse effect on an imbiber's system than had the proprietory brands, others have been known to make a devotee's eyeballs bleed but a short time before his kinfolk could be expected to be giving the coroner's office notification of their loss. Even so, Ozark whiskey was usually far less lethal than most of the spiritous liquids that found favor farther west.

Whiskey peddlers who manufactured their own products and knew nothing about the processes of distillation invariably produced their liquors from barrels of raw alcohol, adding various ingredients to achieve "bite," tang, and color until satisfied that they could sell their mixtures as whiskey. That many of these peddlers showed a callous disregard for the palates and internal workings of their clientele may be deduced from the following "whiskey" recipes: (1) Mix one pint of creosote with one barrel of raw alcohol. (2) Add liquid coffee to a barrel of alcohol until the desired shade of gold has been achieved, then add red pepper and chewing tobacco to give extra "bite." (3) Fill a barrel to the halfway mark with water and then add one pound of burned sugar, one plug of chewing tobacco, and one ounce of sulphuric acid before topping up the barrel with raw alcohol.[23]

An occasional peddler might add further ingredients to any of these basic recipes in an effort to give his liquor an individual touch—a quest for more exotic blends that reached its ultimate expression in "Snakehead" Thompson's six-rattlesnake-heads-to-the-barrel "whiskey,"

---

[22] Were—and still are; illicit distillation being a way of life in the Ozark Mountains.
[23] The product was often classed as "brandy" if grape juice was added to any of these mixes.

which was tickling the palates of plains dwellers during the 1870s and 1880s. Tangleleg, Tarantula Juice, Lightning, Forty-rod, Rookus Juice, Tanglefoot, Valley Tan, and Taos Lightning are but a few of the names conferred upon the rotgut whiskies of the frontier years. It has been said that the drinking of these explosive liquors rarely led to addiction, death usually intervening before any such distinction could be achieved. (See FORTY-ROD; TAOS LIGHTNING; and VALLEY TAN.)

WHISKEY BILL   Alias of a member of Henry Plummer's "Innocents." (See GRAVES, WILLIAM, and INNOCENTS.)

WHITE, CARLOS   A native of New York who settled at Natchez, Mississippi, in the early months of 1804 and achieved some renown during the summer of that year by instigating an antivice crusade against a gang of white slavers led by a villain named Samuel Purdy. Purdy's gang stole nubile merchandise from as far north as St. Louis, Missouri, for sale at waterfront auctions that were held at Natchez and were attended by local brothelkeepers and their counterparts from Baton Rouge and New Orleans, and it was after viewing one of these sordid sales that White persuaded a local newspaper owner to start a crusade against Purdy, which was to lead to the violent dissolution of the gang.

Carlos, reputedly heavily disguised and most certainly loaded for bear, was personally responsible for rescuing a couple of girls whom Purdy had sold to a New Orleans bagnio, but whether he had a hand in the violent deaths that encompassed Sam and five of his band must remain conjectural. By the end of 1805 all the Purdy mob had been dealt with by

means lethal and legal, and Carlos, his zeal probably having been sapped as he crusaded through a chain of brothels in search of the lasses hitherto mentioned, retired from the crime-busting scene. White settled in Louisiana, got himself a wife and, at some later date, established himself as the owner of a prosperous cotton plantation, which could only have been run on slave labor. (See BECKETT, ROSE, and PURDY, SAM.)

WHITE-EYES   Name used by both the Apache and the Ute Indians to describe anyone of Caucasian origin.

WHITE MOUNTAIN APACHE
Apache band that ranged the Arizona–New Mexico border region between the Salt and San Francisco rivers.

WHITE-TAILED DEER
A medium-sized deer that has a wide distribution in most wooded regions of the West. Coloring is reddish-brown with white undersides. A fully grown buck is usually about 6 feet in length (almost a foot of which is taken up by the tail), some 3½ feet tall at the shoulder, and may weigh in the region of 300 pounds. Antlers are only borne by the males, but both sexes raise their tails to display the white undersides of same when alarmed.

WHITE, WILLIAM   Alias of Bill Gristy, a member of the Thomas Hodges gang. (See HODGES, THOMAS J.)

WHITMAN MASSACRE
Name given to a series of killings committed by Cayuse Indians at the Waiilatpu Mission in northern Oregon[24] over the period November 29 to December 6, 1847. Dr. Marcus Whitman and his wife Narcissa had been in charge at Waiilatpu ever

---

[24] The mission was located just a few miles southwest of Walla Walla, Washington, the site being but a short distance within the Oregon boundary.

since they had established the mission on Cayuse land in 1836, and their relations with the Indians had been good until but a short time before the tragedy; said rapport having deteriorated after an outbreak of measles and dysentery in the summer of 1847 had caused a 50 per cent mortality rate within the ranks of one band of the tribe and some of the survivors had become obsessed with the notion that Dr. Whitman had been spreading poison among them so that he might come into possession of their crops, etc.

Sometime around midday on Monday, November 29, 1847, subchiefs Tomahas, Tilaukait, and Tamsucky, and a number of their followers who were within the mission grounds, pushed their way into the home of the Whitmans, hatcheted the doctor to death, and killed his wife with musketfire. During the remainder of that day the mission's schoolmaster, plus two youths who had been adopted by the Whitmans, and four male employees, were to be dispatched by various weapons employed by the Cayuse, and on the thirtieth a man named Kimball was killed as he was attempting to get water for his wife and five children. By December 6 three more white men had been murdered, and fifty-seven men, women, and children were being held prisoner by the Indians. The Indians' blood lust had now been appeased, and they released their captives after receiving five hundred dollars in trade goods for the safe return of the prisoners.[25] (See CAYUSE INDIANS and NEZ PERCÉ INDIANS.)

WHITNEYVILLE WALKER REVOLVER The heaviest of the Colt handguns. (See COLT FIREARMS, subheading *Walker*.)

WICHITA INDIANS Plains tribe of the Caddoan language family whose range extended from the Texas Panhandle to well into Kansas, the tribe having established themselves in this region sometime prior to 1600. Elements of the tribe made use of the tepee during buffalo-hunting expeditions, but as the Wichita were a farming people who were not entirely dependent on the buffalo for sustenance, they spent most of their lives raising crops of maize and melons that had been laid out around permanent settlements whose dwellings consisted of beehive-shaped grass houses. The Wichita were culturally akin to the Plains Caddo and—like the latter tribe—they gave the white man little trouble. The Wichita were established on the Wichita-Caddo reserve in what is now western Oklahoma in the late 1860s, and they remained in control of this land until it was opened to white settlement on July 9, 1901. (See CADDO INDIANS and WICHITA, KANSAS.)

WICHITA, KANSAS A Kansas trail town that had its beginnings in 1864, when a trading post was erected near a Wichita Indian village located at the junction of the Arkansas and Little Arkansas rivers. Over the years other dwellings began to group themselves around the post, but it was not until the Atchison, Topeka, and Santa Fe Railroad probed a branch line into the town in 1872[26] that Wichita had the key to lightning expansion within its grasp. By 1873 herds that had been pushed North along the Chisholm Trail were being shipped East via the Wichita loading pens, and by the following year the town was the recognized cattle-shipping center of Kansas,

---

[25] The Hudson's Bay Company of Canada intervened on behalf of the captives, and the company paid the ransom after its representative had hurried south from Fort Vancouver and reached agreement with the Cayuse renegades at a powwow held at Fort Walla Walla (about thirty-five miles west of the town of Walla Walla).

[26] This twenty-six miles of branch line linked Wichita with the main-line town of Newton.

nearly a quarter-million beef steers passing through the Wichita railroad depot during the 1874 season. Signs proclaiming "Everything goes in Wichita" were erected on all major approaches to the town, and every type of low-down taste known to man—be it whoring, imbibing, or the pop-eying of shows most lewd— could be appeased in the red-light area of the town.[27] By 1875 Dodge City had become the acknowledged "Queen of the Cowtowns," but the decline of Wichita never became serious, and today this one-time trail town has a population nearing the three hundred thousand mark and is the county seat of Sedgwick County. (See TRAIL TOWN.)

WICKENBURG MASSACRE
Occurred on the Sunday morning of November 5, 1871, when a party of "Broncho" Apaches waylaid the Wickenburg–La Paz stage on a blind bend a few miles west of Wickenburg, Arizona. Stagedriver John Lanz had seven passengers riding his Concord on that day—Messrs. Hamel, Adams, Salmon, Loring, Shosholm, and Kruger—and an attractive young woman named Mollie Shepherd, but the attack came without warning, and within seconds of the lead horses being killed, only Kruger and Miss Shepherd remained alive. Kruger and Mollie, although severely wounded, managed to escape from the coach, Kruger keeping pursuers at bay with his six-gun until the Apaches abandoned their quarry, and two hours after the massacre these two survivors were picked up by the La Paz–Wickenburg stage and whisked back to Wickenburg for treatment. Kruger survived his wounds, but Miss Shepherd was to die from an infected arm wound within days of her return to Wickenburg. In 1937 a monument was erected on the site of the massacre.[28]

WICKEYUP or WICKIUP
An Apache dwelling composed of a light framework of branches that has been "thatched" over with dried grasses or other bird's nest-type materials. Wickeyups may be either dome-shaped or conical.

WIGWAM An Algonkin word used to describe an Indian dwelling composed of a dome-shaped framework of semiflexible poles to which a covering of rushes, rush mats, or peeled bark had been affixed. Frequently confused with the tepee, possibly because conical-shaped wigwams were not unknown.

WILD BILL HICKOK The most spectacular pistoleer who ever trod a boardwalk. (See HICKOK, JAMES BUTLER.)

WILD BUNCH Name given to a loose-knit gang that operated from the outlaw strongholds of Hole in the Wall, Brown's Hole, and Robber's Roost over the years 1896–1901. Although the hard core of this gang probably never exceeded ten long riders and such delectable fellow travelers as Della Rose and Etta Place, it is quite likely that more than a hundred outlaws spent brief periods as "Bunchers" during the gang's five years of existence. However much the roll of membership may have fluctuated over the years, leadership of the Wild Bunch remained within the firm grasp of Butch Cassidy, a friendly-looking ex-cowhand whose authority was buttressed by the Sundance Kid—a well-chosen second-in-command whose draw was re-

[27] An area known as "Delano."
[28] Located in the Vulture Mountains some six miles west of Wickenburg.

puted to be as fast as the movement of a snake's tongue.[29] Major operations of a criminal nature committed by the Wild Bunch or splinter groups of the gang include the following successful and unsuccessful robberies: April 1897, appropriation of an $8,000 mine payroll at Castle Gate, Utah; June 1897, attempted holdup of a bank at Bella Fourche, South Dakota; June 1899, held up a Union Pacific train at Wilcox, Wyoming, and rode away with about $30,000; August 1900, made $5,014 profit from a Union Pacific train robbery at Tipton, Wyoming; July 1901, held up a Great Northern train at Malta, Montana, and escaped with an estimated $40,500. The Malta robbery was the gang's last known job. (See CARVER, WILLIAM [second entry under this name]; HANKS, CAMILLA; HOLE IN THE WALL GANG; KILPATRICK, BEN; LAY, ELZA; LOGAN, HARVEY; LONGBAUGH, HARRY; O'DAY, TOM; PARKER, ROBERT LEROY; PLACE, ETTA; ROSE, DELLA; and TRACY, HARRY.)

WILLIAMS, BILL   Large-framed, ginger-haired, and gaunt-faced mountain man of great renown. Born at a settlement on Horse Creek in Western North Carolina on January 3, 1787, and christened "William Sherley" by Baptist-inclined parents who moved West and settled in southeastern Missouri while their son was still in his teens, Bill started his wanderings in the fall of 1806 when he pushed West on a stolen mount with his pappy's flintlock cradled across his arms. Before the year was out he had established himself with the Osage Indians by taking a young Indian girl as his squaw and was doing his living and loving in a tribal village in southwestern Missouri.

Williams was to use the Osage settlement as his base for the next eighteen years, years during which he made exploratory trips that took him as far west as the Texas Panhandle; fought alongside his adopted kinsmen in their frequent clashes with the Comanche; become twice a widower; and had fathered two red-headed half-breed girls who were in their late teens when he left the tribe in the summer of 1825 to act as guide and interpreter for a survey party which, escorted by a squadron of United States Dragoons, intended mapping out the region traversed by the Santa Fe Trail. The following year Bill parted company with Dragoon commander Major G. C. Sibley at Santa Fe, and over the next few years Bill began to make a name for himself as a trapper and mountain man, his numerous loner expeditions into regions that would later be known as Arizona, Utah, Colorado, and Wyoming earning him the sobriquet of "Old Solitaire."

In the summer of 1832 Williams was one of an army of trappers who signed up with Captain Bonneville to go on a fur-hunting expedition into the Far West. This was a typical mountain man "outing," which got off to its sordid start while the band was plew hunting in the Uintah Mountains and Bear Lake regions,[30] eight of the buckskinned bullyboys dying in knife fights shortly after Old Solitaire's introduction of a dozen flat-faced Bannock squaws into the camp had fanned passions to killing heat. After twelve months of not very successful trapping, the Bonneville party loaded up its pack train and headed for Alta California. The journey was not without incident. Before their arrival at Monterey in mid-November 1833, the Bonneville brigade had stolen pelts and maidens from the so-called savages who lived along the Snake

[29] Probably faster, for a very fast gun could draw his weapon and get a bullet on its way during the brief period when an eyelid cuts off vision during the normal process of blinking.
[30] Straggling the tristate junction of Colorado, Wyoming, and Utah.

River Valley,[31] and the brigade had killed some two dozen Paiute braves near Lake Winnemucca so that the squaws of a number of the deceased might experience the delights of paleface penetration before being dispatched to join their menfolk.

After soaking up both the liquid and lewd delights of California for some months, Old Solitaire teamed up with a couple of fellow scallywags named Joe Meek and "Peg Leg" Smith, and they organized a band of "hoss" thieves who preyed on the California *ranchos,* occasionally herding as many as three thousand head back East to sell them at Bent's Fort or among the Apache tribes of the Southwest. This profitable enterprise lasted for a number of years, and during the 1838 season the infamous James Kirker and James Hobbs joined the mob for a spell, but by 1840 age was altering Old Solitaire's behavior patterns, and in 1841 he established a trading post in Brown's Hole,[32] got himself a passel of nubile Ute maidens, and settled down for a spell of suppin' and so on. Completely revitalized by the spring of 1842, Bill made a trip back East with Kit Carson to see how his red-headed offsprings were making out and look in on his kinfolk back in Missouri, and over the next six years Bill made frequent appearances at Bent's Fort in between ventures that included trading probes into the Wind River country and acting as guide and interpreter to various civilian and military expeditions.

In the fall of 1848 General John C. Fremont hired Bill to act as his guide on a railroad survey expedition, and on November 19 the party left Bent's Fort to start on a journey of disaster that was to leave eleven dead men in the La Garita Mountains of Colorado and result in Williams being accused of incompetence and cannibalism when the survivors finally managed to reach Taos, New Mexico, on January 20, 1849.

Fired by Fremont, Old Bill remained behind when the party pushed on toward California, and within a few weeks of his fall from grace he was hired to lead a squadron of Dragoons up into Colorado via the Raton Pass. It was now the month of March; Old Solitaire was two months past his sixty-second birthday, and he would be buzzard bait before the month was out. A few days after he had led the mounted infantry through the Raton Pass, guide and interpreter Williams went missing, and it wasn't until the following day that a search party discovered the reason for his absence: Their guide was dead, his buckskinned and fly-covered remains porcupined by Ute-fletched shafts. The town of Williams, Bill Williams Mountain, and the Bill Williams River insure that Old Solitaire's name will be long remembered. (See CARSON, CHRISTOPHER ("KIT"); FREMONT, JOHN CHARLES; HOBBS, JAMES; KIRKER, JAMES; MOUNTAIN MEN; and SMITH, THOMAS L.)

WILSON, BILLY
Small-time outlaw of Texas origins who rode with Dave Rudabaugh from around 1877 and became an associate of Billy the Kid when Dave and the Kid joined forces sometime during the late fall of 1879. Wilson was with the Kid when the latter gunned down James Carlyle,[33] and he was present when the gang rode into an ambush that left Tom O'Folliard dying in the snow. On December 27, 1880,

---

[31] The Shoshone Indians.

[32] A region encompassing parts of what are now southwestern Wyoming, northern Utah, and southeastern Idaho.

[33] As Carlyle had a number of bullets in his remains, some of these pieces of lead may have come from the guns of both Wilson and Rudabaugh.

Wilson, the Kid, Rudabaugh, and Tom Pickett were arrested at Stinking Springs after a shooting match with a posse had caused the death of fellow owlhoot Charlie Bowdre. Although warrants relating to the possession of counterfeit currency and robbery of the U.S. mails are reputed to have been hanging over Wilson's head at this time, he was only charged with the relatively minor offense of horse theft. Wilson was speedily convicted, but within a few weeks of his being given a cell in the jail at Mesilla he had tunneled his way to freedom, and over the next five years he appears to have left little track on the records.

In 1886 Wilson and his old *compadre* Tom Pickett were working as cowhands with the Hashknife Outfit up on the Little Colorado, and at some later date Wilson got himself a wife and settled down in Terrell County, Texas, under the assumed name of Anderson. Over the years "Anderson" achieved prosperity as a rancher, a success that was only marred by the knowledge that old warrants were still waiting to be served should federal or New Mexico lawmen ever discover his whereabouts. During the early 1900s the man known as Anderson was elected sheriff of Terrell County, and shortly afterward, while visiting El Paso on official business, he was recognized in his true identity by Pat Garrett—the onetime nemesis of the Kid and his gang who had recently been appointed collector of taxes at El Paso by President Theodore Roosevelt. Wilson feared the worst, but Garrett went to great lengths on his behalf and finally succeeded in persuading the President of the United States and the governor of New Mexico into granting pardons to Wilson for such antisocial behavior as interfering with the U.S. mails and tunneling his way out of jail.

The fact that Anderson and Wilson were one and the same person never became public knowledge, and it was as Sheriff Anderson that Wilson was to reach the end of the track in 1911 when he was shot dead by a drunken reveler whom he had been attempting to arrest. Wilson was about fifty-three years of age at the time of his death. (See GARRETT, PATRICK FLOYD; McCARTY, HENRY; and RUDABAUGH, DAVE.)

WINCHESTER RIFLE Any of the rifles manufactured by the Winchester Repeating Arms Corporation of Connecticut.[34] The first Winchester rifle was the Model 1866, a brass-framed, seventeen-shot, lever-action weapon with either an octagonal or round barrel that had been designed to fire .44–28 rim-fire ammunition and was to remain in production for 25 years in spite of the fact that much-improved models became available over this period. In 1873 an iron-framed model with a strengthened mechanism that allowed the more powerful .44–40 center-fire ammunition to be used came off the production lines. This latter model had a magazine capacity of 15 rounds, it weighed 9 pounds against its predecessor's 9½ pounds, and 6 years after its introduction it was being chambered to accept .38–40 or .32–20 center-fire ammunition or .22-caliber rim-fire ammunition. In 1876 the Centennial Model made its appearance, a rugged .45–75 lever-action rifle that in later years was to be chambered for even heavier loads. The Model 1873 ("the gun that won the West") and the Centennial Model were two of the most popular guns of the frontier years, and 136 of the former and 51 of the latter were engraved with either "One of One Thousand" or "1 of 1,000" after factory tests had proved that the

---

[34] Founded in 1866 by Oliver Fisher Winchester, a manufacturer of dress shirts who had hitherto been associated with the Volcanic Repeating Arms Corporation and the New Haven Arms Company.

rifles so described had barrels of exceptional merit.[35] In 1885 a single-shot rifle was introduced that could be had in models ranging from .22 to .50 caliber, and the following year a lever-action chambered for a wide range of ammunition became available. Model 1892 was a thirteen-shot lever-action that came in .25–20, .32–20, .38–40, and .44–40 calibers, and in 1893 a .22-caliber, pump-action repeater found its way into the Winchester catalogue. During the 1870s the company produced about ten experimental designs for revolvers, but none of these handguns went into production. Other weapons produced by Winchester during the latter half of the nineteenth century include bolt-action rifles and lever-action shotguns capable of holding five cartridges. The corporation's present-day range of firearms is extremely extensive. (See HENRY RIFLE and VOLCANIC RIFLE.)

WISNER, JACOB   Ill-fated partner of Jacob "Dutchman" Walzer. (See WALZER, JACOB.)

WOLF   Large member of the dog family that at one time could be found throughout the West but is now confined to those areas that are more or less inaccessible to man. There are many regional variations, and coloring may range from almost pure white through brownish-gray and reddish-tan to near black. A fully grown male may reach a length of 4 feet plus 18 inches of tail and weigh in the region of 140 pounds. Dependent on habitat, they are sometimes referred to as timber or prairie wolves. The coyote is a small species of wolf. (See COYOTE.)

WOODCHUCK   American name for a species of marmot. (See MARMOT.)

WOODRATS
Large, immaculate-looking rats with comparatively hairy tails whose unique habit of collecting almost any type of object and replacing it with an "exchange" article[36] has led to them becoming known as trade or pack rats. Woodrats make their nests of twigs in trees, caves, cacti, and abandoned dwellings, and all are nocturnal in their habits. The largest variety of woodrat has a length of about 20 inches—almost half of which is taken up by tail.

WOODSON, BEN   Sometime alias of Frank James. (See JAMES, ALEXANDER FRANKLIN.)

WOOTTEN, RICHARD   Born in Virginia in 1816 and christened Richard Lacey, Wootten began moving West in his middle teens, and by the time he was twenty years old he had established himself as a meat hunter at Bent's Fort on the Arkansas. Two years later he began operating as a trapper, and in the fall of 1838 he was one of a party of twenty of such men who went on a plew-hunting trip that took them across parts of what are now the states of Wyoming, Montana, Idaho, Washington, Oregon, California, Arizona, Utah, and Colorado. In January 1847 Wootten joined up with Ceran St. Vrain's band of mountain men to take part in a punitive campaign against the Taos *insurrectos,* and Dick tomahawked at least one "Injun" to death before the rebellion was crushed.

By the spring of 1848 Dick had acquired himself a wife and become resi-

---

[35] In 1950 three replica "One of One Thousand" rifles were manufactured to "star" in Anthony Mann's *Winchester '73*—an epic Western that had James Stewart and Dan Duryea as "goodie" and "baddie," respectively.

[36] Many a prospector has had his watch or eating utensils replaced with an empty can, nuts, or a few pebbles.

dent at Taos, and as the demand for beaver pelts had declined to an extent where trapping was no longer economical, he moved into the freighting business, first along the Santa Fe Trail and later as an Army contractee moving supplies between frontier posts in New Mexico Territory. When the Colorado gold rush got under way in 1858, Wootten began shipping "Taos Lightning"[37] up North to sell to the miners, a profitable enterprise that persuaded the onetime trapper to erect premises at Auraria for use as a saloon *cum* store.

For some obscure reason Wootten was now being called "Uncle Dick," and in 1866, after having acquired a charter to build a toll road through Raton Pass, Uncle Dick Wootten rough-graded about twenty-seven miles of mountain path, erected premises that incorporated a toll booth, an eatery, and a crude boardinghouse, and began raking in the *dinero*— probably around seven thousand dollars per annum, even though he allowed Indians to use his road for free. In 1877 Wootten sold out his interests in Raton Pass to the Atchison, Topeka, and Santa Fe Railroad and retired to Trinidad, Colorado. Uncle Dick Wootten died at Trinidad in 1894 and was survived by a wife (his fourth) and eight children. (See RATON PASS and TAOS, NEW MEXICO.)

WOOTTON, DICK Sometimes come across as an incorrect spelling of "Wootten." (See WOOTTEN, RICHARD.)

WOUNDED KNEE MASSACRE
As an aftermath of the murder of Sitting Bull at Standing Rock on December 15, 1890, many bands of Hunkpapa and Miniconjou Sioux left their Dakota reservations and moved toward the Badlands south of the Cheyenne River, a nonviolent flight occasioned by fear that caused General Nelson Miles, commander of the Department of the Missouri, to order more than 3,000 well-equipped troops into the field to act as disciplinarians. Waters gurgled beneath a thick coating of ice, and crunching whiteness blanketed the land as fur-hatted troops equipped with Hotchkiss guns began rounding up the so-called renegades, and on the morning of December 29, eight troops of the 7th U. S. Cavalry had surrounded a Hunkpapa village on Wounded Knee Creek[38] and were preparing to herd the Indians back to the Standing Rock Agency. The Sioux encampment sheltered the aged Big Foot, who was grievously ill with pneumonia, and 350 of his followers,[39] while the U.S. military contingent consisted of 500 troopers who were under the command of Colonel James W. Forsyth and who had four Hotchkiss guns at their disposal; the dice were thus heavily loaded against Big Foot's band, but prior to breaking camp, Forsyth trained his rapid-firing cannon onto the village and ordered a thorough shakedown of the Indian tepees and baggage in a last-minute search for hidden arms.

Whether the Indians had any guns in their possession has never been definitively established, but suddenly on that breath-clouding morning a shot rang out, and within seconds the Hotchkiss guns were pouring two-pounder fragmentation shells into the village at the combined rate of 200 rounds a minute. Tepees disintegrated and burst into flame, and the Indians who hadn't been riveted into the snow by the first scything burst of fire scattered like quail. But there was nowhere to hide. Pursued by blood-

---

[37] Not the original "Taos Lightning" as distilled by Simeon Turley (see TAOS LIGHTNING); Wootten's eyeball reddener was a product of Ceran St. Vrain's distillery located near Taos.
[38] Approximately 25 miles west of the present-day town of Martin, South Dakota.
[39] Totals of 120 adult males of various ages and 230 women and children.

crazed cavalrymen, men, women, and children fell before a barrage of small-arms fire, some of the fugitives managing to cover two and three miles before they were overtaken and either clubbed or shot to death. When the guns stopped firing, Big Foot and more than 200 of his followers lay scattered over the frozen ground,[40] and 29 troopers had been clubbed and manhandled to death. The frozen bodies of the Indian dead were collected and buried in a communal trench. This massacre is sometimes referred to as the "Battle of Wounded Knee." (See 7TH CAVALRY; SIOUX INDIANS; SITTING BULL; and WOVOKA.)

WOVOKA   Paiute Indian who was born in 1854 somewhere in the region of what was later to be known as Mineral County, Nevada. In 1889, while suffering spells of delirium occasioned by some unspecified malady, Wovoka experienced visions in which the Great Spirit ordained him in the role of the new Indian Messiah, and on recovery he began to spread an inoffensive gospel of the love-thy-neighbor variety. Converts to this new religion were expected to perform a dance that Wovoka taught them—the so-called Ghost Dance, which spread across Nevada and up onto the North Plains like wildfire. The performers of this dance probably only experienced a lunatic light-headedness such as may be encountered at any modern pop festival, but short-on-copy newspapers and short-on-glory Army commanders were soon giving out type and hot-air mutterings about a "Ghost Dance uprising" and laying the blame for a lot of nonhappenings at the door of Sitting Bull's tepee. The Hunk-

papa chief was around fifty-nine years old at this time, and there was no proof that he had ever engaged in the five-day ritual called the "Ghost Dance," but on December 15, 1890, orders were given for his arrest. The fact that Sitting Bull was murdered while being placed under arrest did cause an Indian exodus from the reservations in the Dakotas, and the fact that many tribesmen were wearing Ghost Shirts,[41] which they believed rendered them immune to the firepower of the soldiers, may have led some of the Indians to adopt a truculent attitude, but there seems little justification for the 7th Cavalry's massacre of Big Foot's band on Wounded Knee Creek, a mass execution that caused the Ghost Dance to become an out thing overnight. After this grisly affair little more was heard of Wovoka,[42] and he died in obscurity at Walker Lake, Nevada, on October 4, 1932. (See SITTING BULL and WOUNDED KNEE MASSACRE.)

WYATT, ZIP   Small-time outlaw who only took to a life of crime after losing his job as a cowhand during the temporary suspension of ranching activity that took place when the Cherokee Strip was opened to white settlement on September 16, 1893. Wyatt, using the alias of Dick Yeager, joined up with a like-inclined character named Ike Black, and for a couple of years they committed a number of store robberies that caused little attention to be turned their way, but in the spring of 1895 they killed a settler, and a big manhunt got under way. Ike was shot dead by lawmen on August 1 near Canton, Oklahoma, and three days later Zip was taken into custody after he had

[40] The official figures for Indian dead were: 64 males, 44 women and girls, and 18 very young children. Most authorities, however, give the number of dead as being in excess of 200.

[41] Buckskin shirts upon which buffaloes and thunderbirds had been painted.

[42] Also known as Jack Wilson, a name given to Wovoka on his being adopted by a white family at the age of fourteen.

been wounded in a shootout with Garfield County officers that occurred near Enid, Oklahoma. Wyatt-Yeager died from his wounds while being held in the county jail. Rumors abound that Wyatt sometimes rode with the Doolin gang; he may have, but there is no evidence to support this.

WYOMING Plains-plateau state that is bounded on the north by Montana, on the east by South Dakota and Nebraska, has Colorado to the south, and has Idaho and Utah as its neighbors in the west and southwest, respectively. Originally part of that vast region that came under U.S. dominion with the completion of the Louisiana Purchase of 1803, and having the fur-trading post of Fort Laramie as its first permanent settlement in 1834, Wyoming was organized as a territory in 1869 and became the forty-fourth state of the Union in 1890. Tourist attractions include Yellowstone National Park,[43] Grand Teton National Park, Fort Laramie National Monument, and the "Frontier Days" Rodeo, which is held annually at the state capital of Cheyenne. Popularly known as the Equality State, it being the first state to grant women voting rights.

[43] Established in 1872 as the first of the national parks.

CHARLES M. RUSSELL

X

Highly abbreviated form of address occasionally bestowed upon John X. Beidler. (See BEIDLER, JOHN XAVIER.)

XIT RANCH   The Ten in Texas Ranch, XIT being the brand used by this spread. (See CAPITOL SYNDICATE.)

THOMAS E. MAILS

Y AGER, ERASTUS Member of Henry Plummer's gang of "Innocents" whose mop of red hair and facial whiskers led to his being nicknamed "Red." As far as is known this thin little man may never have killed anyone, but on being arrested by a band of vigilantes in the last week of December 1863 he did admit to having carried messages for the gang—a confession that resulted in Yager being hanged from a cottonwood tree in Stinkingwater Valley on January 4, 1864. Before being lynched, Yager gave the vigilantes information regarding the gang's structure, password ("Innocent"), and the names of Plummer and twenty-five of his key men—a session of stool-pigeoning that was to lead to the breaking up of the gang. (See INNOCENTS.)

YAGER, RED Small-time member of the "Innocents." (See YAGER, ERASTUS.)

YAKIMA INDIANS Plains-plateau minority group of the Penutian language family who have been living in what is now the Washington-Oregon border region for at least three centuries. Berry gatherers and hunters of small game who dressed in deer skins and lived in crude tepees or wickeyups, the Yakima gave the white man trouble along the Columbia River stretch of the Oregon Trail for a short period in 1858, but by 1859 they had been settled on the Yakima Agency in southern Washington, a reservation on which they still remain.

YANKEE Originally a New Englander or progeny of same, but later used to describe an inhabitant of any of the northern states. The term is reputed to have been derived from an Amerind corruption of "English" (or the French equivalent, Anglais). Outside the United States the term is loosely used to refer to any citizen of that country.

YANKTON SIOUX One of the three main divisions of the Sioux nation. (See SIOUX INDIANS.)

YEAGER, DICK Alias of a small-time owlhoot named Zip Wyatt. (See WYATT, ZIP.)

YELLOW HAIR Name by which General George A. Custer was known among the Indians of the North Plains. (See CUSTER, GEORGE ARMSTRONG.)

YELLOW HAIR A Cheyenne sub-chief who was killed by Buffalo Bill Cody at War Bonnet Creek. Better known under his possibly incorrect name of Yellow Hand. (See YELLOW HAND.)

YELLOW HAND A Cheyenne warrior leader who achieved typeset immortality by becoming the victim of Buffalo Bill Cody's Winchester. On July 16, 1876, some forty braves of Little Wolf's Northern Cheyenne followed Yellow Hand from the Red Cloud Agency at Fort Robinson in northwestern Nebraska and moved west with the intention of visiting the site of the Indian victory on the Little Big Horn, completely unaware that two troops of the 5th Cavalry under the command of Colonel W. Merritt were camped on War Bonnet Creek—about forty miles WNW of Fort Robinson and directly across the Indians' line of march. Buffalo Bill Cody—attired in an impressive *vaquero* costume of black and red velvet[1] —and the somewhat less splendid Chris Madsen were serving as scouts with Merritt at this time, and when Yellow Hand led his warriors along a dry wash leading to the east bank of War Bonnet Creek, this intrepid pair and a number of troopers under the command of Captain Charles King were watching their every

move from the concealment of a small hill on the Indians' right flank.

Suddenly King gave an "Up and at 'em!" command, and Cody and company spurred their mounts forward. The so-called Battle of War Bonnet Creek had commenced. Cody wounded Yellow Hand, then Cody was thrown from his saddle as his horse stepped into a gopher hole and he and the Cheyenne more or less hit the dust at the same time. The velvet-draped plainsman was the first to recover both his feet and his rifle, and before Yellow Hand knew what was happening, Cody's second shot had killed him. Tossing aside his Winchester, Buffalo Bill withdrew a tremendous bowie, whipped off the fallen Cheyenne's trailer war bonnet, and scalped his victim to the accompaniment of what was later to be regarded as his most famous line of dialogue—the famous "First scalp for Custer!" yell, which ended the so-called Battle of War Bonnet Creek. Yellow Hand[2] was the only casualty. Despite the numerous slanted writings of the Cody debunkers, there is no doubt whatsoever that the plainsman *cum* showman killed and scalped Yellow Hand, ample confirmation of this being available in the statements of Colonel Merritt, Captain King, and Chris Madsen. (See BATTLE ON THE LITTLE BIG HORN; and CODY, WILLIAM FREDERICK.)

YELLOWSTONE KELLY Colorful name bestowed upon a well-known Army scout. (See KELLY, LUTHER SAGE.)

YELLOWSTONE RIVER Major tributary of the Missouri River. The

---

[1] Cody had been appearing in "Scouts of the Prairie" at Wilmington, North Carolina, when he received a telegram from General Philip Sheridan's headquarters requesting him to join Merritt's command, and Cody had ridden the rails West without taking time out to change from his theatrical costume.

[2] On the monument erected at the site the name is given as "Yellow Hair." This could well be correct, for the white man's translations of Indian names were often monumentally inaccurate.

Yellowstone rises in the Rocky Mountains of northwestern Wyoming, takes a north-easterly course across southeastern Montana, and joins the Missouri immediately after crossing the North Dakota boundary. The river is about one thousand miles in length.

YOUNG, BRIGHAM

A onetime house painter and glazier who joined Joseph Smith's newly established Mormon sect in 1832 at the age of thirty-one; saw service in England as a missionary of the sect over the years 1839–41, and became the accepted leader of the Church of Jesus Christ of Latter-day Saints on the death of Smith in 1844. In 1847 Brigham organized the Mormon exodus from the persecutions of the East and settled his followers near the Great Salt Lake, which lay to the west of the Wasatch Mountains, and when the territory of Utah was organized in 1850, he became the first territorial governor. Young preached polygamy, and he evidently practiced what he preached, for when he died at Salt Lake City on August 29, 1877, he was survived by seventeen wives and about fifty children. (See MORMONS; SALT LAKE CITY; SMITH, JOSEPH; and UTAH.)

YOUNGER, COLEMAN

Born near Lee's Summit in Jackson County, Missouri, on January 15, 1844, the seventh child of the union of transplanted Kentuckian Henry Washington Younger and a Missouri girl named Bersheba Fristoe. Christened Thomas Coleman Younger, but evidently having decided to drop "Thomas" at an early age, Cole joined Quantrill's guerrillas in the fall of 1861, and over the next four years he killed at least three men; achieved the rank of first lieutenant of cavalry when Quantrill's band was mustered into the Confederate forces on August 15, 1862; took part in the Battle of Lone Jack within twenty-four hours of being promoted from the ranks; and was holding the rank of captain when Quantrill made his bloody raid on Lawrence in the summer of 1863.

After the close of the Civil War Cole teamed up with Frank and Jesse James, and he was riding the owlhoot trail as co-leader of the James-Younger band until the eleven bullets he got in his person during the Northfield debacle prompted him into surrendering to the law on September 21, 1876. Two months after being arrested, Cole, together with his brothers Jim and Bob, pleaded guilty to indictments that included two murder counts,[3] and they were each given life terms in the Minnesota State Penitentiary at Stillwater. After spending twenty-five years as Convict No. 699, it was decided that Cole be given his freedom on condition that he remained in Minnesota, and after being released from prison on July 14, 1901, he settled at St. Paul and took up employment as a tombstone salesman. Two years later he was given a full pardon and he returned to Lee's Summit, and soon afterward he and Frank James organized the "Cole Younger–Frank James Wild West Show," a short-lived venture that had Cole as its arena manager. When this show folded, the aging Cole joined the Lew Nichols Carnival Company, a freak and daredevil-act show that billed Cole's attraction as "Cole Younger's Coliseum." Cole Younger died at Lee's Summit on February 21, 1916. (See JAMES GANG; LAWRENCE MASSACRE; NORTHFIELD, MINNESOTA; QUANTRILL, WILLIAM CLARKE; STARR, BELLE; YOUNGER, JIM; YOUNGER, JOHN; YOUNGER, ROBERT; and YOUNGERS.)

[3] All arising out of the foulup at Northfield: the murders of Heywood and Gustafson, the wounding of Bunker, and the robbery of the First National Bank.

YOUNGER, JIM Out of a family of fourteen children, Henry and Bersheba Younger had four bad apples, and James was one of this quartet. Jim, who was born near Lee's Summit on January 15, 1848, joined Quantrill's guerrillas during the closing years of the Civil War, and he remained with the band until their leader got his death wound in Kentucky in the fall of 1865. After the war Jim's career followed the same pattern as brother Cole's: ten years of robbery and murder; capture after the Northfield fiasco;[4] and subsequent sentence of life imprisonment, which ended with his being released with Cole in the summer of 1901. On being pardoned Jim helped Cole sell tombstones for a few weeks and then he tried selling insurance, but he was successful at neither, and on October 19, 1901, he blew his brains out in a St. Paul, Minnesota, hotel room. (See JAMES GANG; NORTHFIELD, MINNESOTA; QUANTRILL, WILLIAM CLARKE; YOUNGER, COLEMAN; YOUNGER, JOHN; and YOUNGERS.)

YOUNGER, JOHN Younger brother of the far better known Cole, Jim, and Bob. Born near Lee's Summit in 1853, John is reputed to have helped his brother Jim kill four Union soldiers when he was but ten years of age and to have pistoleered a civilian to death some five years later.[5] Having thus established himself as a hard boy, he was inducted into the James-Younger mob in his late teens, and he rode with the gang until March 16, 1874, on which day he and brother Jim got into a gunfight with lawmen near Monegaw Springs, Missouri, and John was shot dead.[6] (See JAMES GANG; YOUNGER, JIM; and YOUNGERS.)

YOUNGER, ROBERT On September 26, 1872, eighteen-year-old Bob Younger aided the James brothers in their robbery of the pay office at the county fair that was being held at Kansas City, Missouri—an introduction to outlawry that was to lead to Bob following in the footsteps of brothers Cole and Jim until the threesome were arrested on September 21, 1876. In November of that same year the three Younger brothers began serving life sentences in Stillwater Penitentiary—"life sentence" being literally correct in the case of Robert, for he died in the prison hospital from the effects of tuberculosis on September 16, 1889. (See NORTHFIELD, MINNESOTA, and YOUNGERS.)

YOUNGERS Owing to the depredations of the James-Younger gang, members of the Younger family have become the victims of a number of misconceptions, which this brief entry will attempt to dispel. The members of the family were not all scallywags: Henry W. Younger and Bersheba had a family of eight boys and six girls, and of these only Cole, Jim, John, and Bob triggered their way into the annals of western banditry. Henry W. Younger possessed a prosperous farm of some thirty-five hundred acres in Cass County, Missouri, and he served a term as mayor of Harrisonville (county seat of Cass County) in 1859; he was also a Union sympathizer;[7] yet even so, he was murdered and robbed by a band of Union irregulars in the summer of 1862. The Youngers had no blood links with the James family, but they did have a remote kinship with the Daltons. (See YOUNGER, COLEMAN; YOUNGER,

[4] When arrested Jim had been wounded five times.
[5] The victim on this latter occasion is alleged to have slapped John across the face with a wet and very dead fish just prior to his demise—a rash act that resulted in John being acquitted on a self-defense plea.
[6] Before John had gotten his death wound and before the escape of Jim, the brothers had fatally wounded Pinkerton detective L. Lull and Sheriff E. B. Daniels of St. Clair County.
[7] Despite the fact that he had two black slaves.

JIM; YOUNGER, JOHN; and YOUNGER, ROBERT.)

YOUNTIS, OLIVER Member of the Doolin gang whom very little is known about. Yountis, using the alias of "Crescent Sam," joined the gang shortly after its being organized in the fall of 1892, and he is known to have rode with the mob when they looted a bank at Spearville, Oklahoma, in the spring of 1893. Within a few days of the Spearville job Yountis was run to earth at the home of his sister near Orlando, Oklahoma, and when he resisted arrest he was shot to death by Deputy U. S. Marshals Madsen and Houston. (See DOOLIN GANG.)

YUCCAS Large treelike plants that have their very thick stems covered with tough, dagger-shaped leaves. Blooms consist of long flower stems adorned with a mass of pale yellow, bell-shaped flowers. Yuccas may reach a height of 40 feet and are only found in the southwesterly regions of the United States. Also known as the Joshua tree. As some plants rely on bees for fertilization, the yucca depends on the co-operation of the female of the night yucca moth.

YUMA INDIANS Tribe of the Uto-Aztecan language family who have lived along the Colorado River in what is now southwestern Arizona since at least 1650. Essentially a farming people who hunted small game as a dietary supplement and clothing source, the Yumas lived in settled communities, their dwellings consisting of rectangular, flat-roofed houses, which usually had a patio attached.[8] Tribesmen frequently went naked and

their womenfolk nearly so, and when clothing was worn it rarely consisted of little more than a rough jerkin made from the woven skins of rabbits, etc., to which the women would often add a pectoral of beadwork. The tribe practiced the art of tattooing and the cremation of their dead —the latter being unusual in Amerind societies. The Yuma, although extremely tough when aroused, gave the white man little trouble, and they have been allowed to remain on the land that their ancestors roamed. (See GLANTON, JOHN J.)

YUMA PENITENTIARY
The Arizona territorial prison at Yuma, and the most hated penal institution in the Southwest. Erected in 1876 on a 10-acre plot of ground on the east bank of the Colorado River where it is joined by the Gila River, the prison had adobe walls that were 18 feet high, stone-built cellblocks, four corner guard towers, a gate tower (the latter being equipped with a deadly Gatling gun), and bucket-brigade toilet facilities. Cell doors were a latticework of ironwork, and many of the 9-foot-square cubicles were exposed to the direct rays of the desert sun, and although the inmates were allowed to exercise in the prison yard during the daytime, they were chained to the stone floors of their cells from sundown to dawn. At any given time about 275 felons could be expected to be taking the cure at Yuma under the watchful eyes of a warden and about 20 guards. This owlhoot hell was abandoned as a prison in 1909, and the crumbling remains are now used as a museum. Since 1909 the Arizona territorial prison[9] has been located at Florence. (See GATLING GUN.)

[8] These houses were made from a framework of poles over which a latticework of twigs and vegetable fibers had been laid.
[9] State prison since 1912.

FRANK TENNEY JOHNSON

ZACATE   Mexican-Spanish name for grass that has been grown for provender purposes. The term is mainly confined to the Southwest.

ZACHARY, ROBERT   Small-time member of Henry Plummer's band of road agents. During the last week of November 1863 Zachary, George Ives, and Bill Graves robbed the Virginia City–Salt Lake City mail coach near Point of Rocks, Montana.[1] This may have been Zachary's only crime of a major nature, but the Vigilantes of Montana considered it a capital offense, and after they had taken Robert into custody during the early hours of Monday morning January 25, 1864, they gave him a quick trial, allowed him to write a letter to his mom, then hanged him before they went to lunch. (See INNOCENTS and VIGILANTES OF MONTANA.)

ZEBU   A large humped ox with a heavy dewlap that is domesticated in India,

China, and Africa. A number of these animals have been imported into the United States for breeding purposes, and as ranch stock they are somewhat better known as Brahma cattle. (See BRAHMA CATTLE; and PIERCE, ABEL HEAD.)

ZOUAVES   Originally Arab infantry recruited from the ranks of Zouaoua tribesmen, Zouave regiments of light infantry became a feature of the French Army after the French conquest of Algeria in 1847. Zouave regiments fighting in the Crimean War (1853–56) attracted the attention of military observers, and soon afterward other countries began to organize similar regiments—the attractiveness of the Zouaves' musical-comedy-style uniform of loose, harem-type trousers, short blue tunic, white gaiters, and bright red *chéchia*[2] evidently outweighing the fact that the costume was anything but practical for wear in more temperate regions. A number of such regiments, all bearing   a   striking   resemblance   to

[1] In the Beaverhead Mountains of southwestern Montana.
[2] Probably best described as looking like a "limp fez."

the original Zouaves, were formed in the United States to see service in the Civil War (1861–65) in both the armies of the Union and the Confederacy, but few of these saw any action west of the Mississippi.

ZUNI INDIANS The foremost tribe of pueblo Indians. The Zuni still remain on land that their ancestors settled more than a thousand years ago, they have their own language family—the Zunian—and their pueblo at Zuni on the river of that name in northwestern New Mexico is the largest Amerind apartment dwelling still extant. The Spaniards gave the Zunis a rough time in 1540 when searching for the fabled "Seven Cities of Cibola,"[3] but the tribe never became converts of the Spanish missionaries, as did many of the Indians of the Southwest. Agriculturalists whose clothing has always been of woven materials, the Zunis are skilled pottery-makers and silversmiths, and they produce much turquoise jewelry. The wealth and social status of a Zuni Indian is dependent on how much turquoise he possesses. (See PUEBLO INDIANS and SEVEN CITIES OF CIBOLA.)

[3] *Cibola* being Spanish for "buffalo."

EDWARD BOREIN

Bibliography

Books

Adams, Andy. *The Log of a Cowboy.* London: Archibald Constable & Co., 1903.

Amber, J. T., ed. *The Gun Digest.* Chicago: Gun Digest Co., 1954.

Asbury, H. *The French Quarter.* New York: Pocket Books, Inc., 1955.

Beebe, Lucius, and Clegg, Charles. *The American West.* New York: E. P. Dutton & Co., Inc., 1955.

——. *U.S. West: The Saga of Wells Fargo.* New York: E. P. Dutton & Co., Inc., 1949.

Bowman, H. W. *Antique Guns.* Greenwich, Conn.: Fawcett Publications, Inc., 1953.

——. *Antique Guns from the Stagecoach Collection.* Greenwich, Conn.: Fawcett Publications, Inc., 1964.

——. *Famous Guns from the Winchester Collection.* Greenwich, Conn.: Fawcett Publications, Inc., 1957.

——. *Famous Guns from Famous Collections.* Greenwich, Conn.: Fawcett Publications, Inc., 1957.

——. *Pioneer Railroads.* Greenwich, Conn.: Fawcett Publications, Inc., 1954.

Breihan, Carl W. *Great Gunfighters of the West.* London: Arrow Books Ltd., 1964.

——. *Great Lawmen of the West.* London: Arrow Books Ltd., 1964.

——. *Outlaws of the Old West.* London: John Long Ltd., 1959.

Brewer, Rev. E. Cobham, LL.D. *Brewer's Dictionary of Phrase and Fable.* London: Odhams Press Ltd., 1932.

Brisbin, Gen. James A. *The Beef Bonanza.* Norman, Okla.: University of Oklahoma Press, 1959.

Brown, Dee, and Schmitt, Martin F. *Trail Driving Days.* New York: Charles Scribner's Sons, 1952.

Brown, Ivor. *Chosen Words.* England: Penguin Books Ltd., 1961–64.

Brown, Mark H., and Felton, W. R. *Before Barbed Wire*. New York: Henry Holt & Co., 1956.

Brown, Mark H., and Felton, W. R. *The Frontier Year*. New York: Henry Holt & Co., 1955.

Burgess, F. H. *A Dictionary of Sailing*. England: Penguin Books Ltd., 1961.

Burns, W. N. *The Saga of Billy the Kid*. London: MacDonald & Co., 1951.

Byam, M. *Discovery of North America*. London: Hamlyn Publishing Group Ltd., 1970.

Cary, Lucian. *Completely New Lucian Cary on Guns*. Greenwich, Conn.: Fawcett Publications, Inc., 1959.

———. *The New Lucian Cary on Guns*. Greenwich, Conn.: Fawcett Publications, Inc., 1957.

Catlin, George. *Catlin's Indians*. London: Garr and Inglis, 1896.

———. *Letters and Notes on The Manners and Customs of the North American Indians*. London: Published by the author at Egyptian Hall, 1841.

Chalfont, W. A. *Gold, Guns and Ghost Towns*. Stanford, Calif.: Stanford University Press, 1947–54.

Chase, Richard. *American Folk Tales and Songs*. New York: Signet Key Books, 1953.

Children's Animal World Encyclopedia. London: Paul Hamlyn, 1967.

Chilton, Charles. *Discovery of the American West*. London: Hamlyn Publishing Group Ltd., 1970.

Collier, Jolin. *Indians of the Americas*. New York: Mentor Books, 1956.

Connelley, W. E. *Quantrill and the Border Wars*. New York: Pageant Book Co., 1956.

Cook, Gen. D. J. *Hands Up! or Twenty Years of Detective Life in the Mountains and on the Plains*. Norman, Okla.: University of Oklahoma Press, 1958.

Cooke, David C. *Fighting Indians of the West*. New York: Dodd, Mead & Co., 1954–55.

Cooper, Jeff. *Fighting Handguns*. Los Angeles: Trend Books, Inc., 1958.

Crockett, Davy. *The Life of Davy Crockett*. New York: The New American Library, Inc., 1955.

Croft-Cooke, Rupert and Meadmore, W. S. *Buffalo Bill*. London: Sidgwick and Jackson Ltd., 1952.

Croy, Homer. *Last of the Great Outlaws*. New York: The New American Library, Inc., 1958.

Cunningham, E. *Triggernometry*. Caldwell, Ida.: The Caxton Printers Ltd., 1952.

Daraul, Arkon. *Secret Societies*. London: Tanden Books Ltd., 1965.

De Zavala, Adina. *The Alamo*. San Antonio, Tex.: The Naylor Co., 1956.

Dimsdale, Prof. Thomas J. *The Vigilantes of Montana*. Norman, Okla.: University of Oklahoma Press, 1957.

Eaton, Frank. *Pistol Pete*. London: Arco Publishers Ltd., 1953.

Edwards, Frank. *Strange People*. London: Pan Books Ltd., 1966.

———. *Stranger Than Science*. London: Pan Books Ltd., 1963.

Elliott, Florence, and Summerskill, Michael. *A Dictionary of Politics*. England: Penguin Books Ltd., 1964.

Evans, I. O., F.R.G.S. *Flags*. London: Frederich Warne & Co., Ltd., 1959.

Fast, Howard. *The Last Frontier*. London: Bodley Head, 1948.

Forrest, Earle R. *Arizona's Dark and Bloody Ground*. London: Andrew Melrose Ltd., 1953.

Frantz, J. B., and Choate, J. E. *The American Cowboy*. London: Thames & Hudson, 1956.

Gardiner, Dorothy. *The Great Betrayal*. London: Transworld Publishers Ltd., 1957.

Garrard, Lewis H. *Wah-To-Yah and the Taos Trail*. Norman, Okla.: University of Oklahoma Press, 1955.

Garrett, Pat F. *The Authentic Life of Billy the Kid*. Norman, Okla.: University of Oklahoma Press, 1954.

Garst, Shannon. *Wild Bill Hickok*. New York: Julian Messner, Inc., 1957.

Gilmore, M. G. *Prairie Smoke*. New York: Columbia University Press, 1929.

Golden Encyclopedia of Geography. London: MacDonald and Co., 1960.

Grant, Paul War Cloud. *Sioux Dictionary*. Pierre, S. D.: Paul War Cloud Grant, State Publishing Co., 1971.

Greeley, Horace. *An Overland Journey*. London: MacDonald & Co., Ltd., 1965.

Hale, Will. *Twenty Years a Cowboy and Ranchman*. Norman, Okla.: University of Oklahoma Press, 1959.

Hamlin, W. L. *The True Story of Billy the Kid*. London: Panther Books Ltd., 1965.

Havighurst, Walter. *Annie Oakley of the Wild West*. London: Robert Hale Ltd., 1955.

Hooper, Bill. *Odd Facts*. London: New English Library Ltd., 1965.

Horan, James D. *The Great American West*. New York: Crown Publishers, Inc., 1959.

——. *Mathew Brady*. New York: Crown Publishers, Inc., 1955.

Horan, James D., and Sann, Paul. *Pictorial History of the Wild West*. London: Arco Publishers Ltd., 1955.

Horan, James D., and Swiggett, Howard. *The Pinkerton Story*. London: William Heinemann Ltd., 1952.

Howard, Robert West, ed. *This Is the West*. New York: The New American Library, Inc., 1957.

Hueston, Ethel. *Star of the West*. London: Transworld Publishers Ltd., 1956.

Hunt, F. *The Tragic Days of Billy the Kid*. New York: Hastings House, 1956.

Hunt, W. Ben. *Indian Crafts and Lore*. London: Paul Hamlyn Ltd., 1967.

Hunter, Hy. *Hand Guns of the World*. Los Angeles: Trend Books, Inc., 1956.

Hunter, J. Marvin, and Rose, Noah H. *The Album of Gunfighters*. Bandera, Texas: Hunter and Rose, 1951.

Irving, Washington. *A Tour of the Prairies*. Norman, Okla.: University of Oklahoma Press, 1956.

Jackson, J. H. *Gold Rush Album*. New York: Charles Scribner's Sons, 1949.

James, Don. *Folk and Modern Medicine*. Derby, Conn.: Monarch Books, Inc., 1961.

James, Marquis. *The Cherokee Strip*. London: Phoenix House Ltd., 1947.

Kellett, E. E. *A Short History of Religions*. England: Penguin Books Ltd., 1962.

Koller, Larry. *Popular Hand Guns*. New York: Maco Magazines Corp., 1957.

Lake, Stuart N. *He Carried a Six-shooter*. London: Peter Nevill Ltd., 1953.

Lavender, David. *Bent's Fort*. London: Transworld Publishers, 1959.

———. *The American West.* England: Penguin Books Ltd., 1969.

Lee, Nelson. *Three Years Among the Comanches.* Norman, Okla.: University of Oklahoma Press, 1957.

Leslie, Desmond, and Adamski, George. *Flying Saucers Have Landed.* London: Werner Laurie, 1953.

Lomax, Alan. *The Penguin Book of American Folk Songs.* England: Penguin Books Ltd., 1964.

Longstreet, S. *War Cries on Horseback.* London: Sphere Books Ltd., 1972.

Manfred, F. *Lord Grizzly.* London: Transworld Publishers Ltd., 1970.

Martin, Charles L. *A Sketch of Sam Bass the Bandit.* Norman, Okla.: University of Oklahoma Press, 1956.

Martin, Douglas D. *Tombstone's* Epitaph. Albuquerque, N.M.: University of New Mexico Press, 1951–53.

Mason, F. van Wyck. *The Fighting American.* London: Jarrolds Publishers Ltd., c. 1944.

Mercer, A. S. *The* Banditti *of the Plains.* Norman, Okla.: University of Oklahoma Press, 1959.

Merington, Maguerite. *The Custer Story.* New York: Devin Adair Co., 1950.

Miller, David Humphreys. *Custer's Fall.* London: Transworld Publishers Ltd., 1965.

Moore, W. G. *A Dictionary of Geography.* England: Penguin Books Ltd., 1964.

Morton, C. O. Sylvester. *Dictionary of Foreign Terms.* New York: Bantam Books, Inc., 1961.

Myers, John Myers. *Doc Holliday.* London: Jarrolds Publishers Ltd., 1957.

Neihardt, John G. *Eagle Voice.* London: Andrew Melrose Ltd., 1953.

Nordyke, Lewis. *John Wesley Hardin.* New York: William Morrow & Co., 1957.

North, René. *Military Uniforms.* London: Hamlyn Publishing Group Ltd., 1970.

Nye, Col. W. S. *Carbine and Lance.* Norman, Okla.: University of Oklahoma Press, 1937–57.

Nye, Russel B., and Mopurgo, J. E. *A History of the United States.* England: Penguin Books Ltd., 1964.

O'Connell, John. Popular Mechanics *Railroad Album.* Chicago: Popular Mechanics Co., 1954.

O'Connor, Richard. *Bat Masterson.* London: Alvin Redman Ltd., 1958.

———. *Wild Bill Hickok.* London: Mayflower Books Ltd., 1966.

Olsson, Jan O. *Welcome to Tombstone.* London: Elek Books Ltd., 1956.

Palmer, A. W. *A Dictionary of Modern History.* England: Penguin Books Ltd., 1964.

Parkman, Francis. *The Oregon Trail.* New York: Mentor Books, 1955.

Penfield, T. *Western Sheriffs and Marshals.* New York: Grosset and Dunlap, 1955.

Pratt, Fletcher. *Civil War in Pictures.* New York: Henry Holt & Co., 1955.

Prettyman, W. S., and Cunningham, Robert E. *Indian Territory.* Norman, Okla.: University of Oklahoma Press, 1957.

Purnell's New English Encyclopedia. London: Purnell & Sons Ltd., 1965.

Radin, Paul. *The Story of the American Indian.* New York: Liveright Publishing Corp., 1944.

Raphael, Ralph B. *The Book of American Indians.* Arco Publishing Co., 1960.

AN ENCYCLOPEDIA OF THE OLD WEST

Ridge, John Rollin. *The Life and Adventures of Joaquin Murieta.* Norman, Okla.: University of Oklahoma Press, 1955.

Roget's College Thesaurus. New York: The New American Library, Inc., 1962.

Sanders, Helen Fitzgerald, and Bertsche, William H., Jr., eds. *X. Beidler: Vigilante.* Norman, Okla.: University of Oklahoma Press, 1957.

Sanderson, Ivan T. *How to Know American Mammals.* New York: Mentor Books, 1951.

Sandoz, Mari. *Crazy Horse.* New York: Hastings House, 1942–55.

———. *The Buffalo Hunters.* New York: Hastings House, 1956.

Schaefer, Jack. *Heroes Without Glory.* London: Mayflower Books Ltd., 1968.

Schmitt, Martin F., and Brown, Dee. *Fighting Indians of the West.* New York: Charles Scribner's Sons, 1948.

———. *The Settlers West.* New York: Charles Scribner's Sons, 1952.

Shirley, Glenn. *Law West of Fort Smith.* New York: Collier Books, 1961.

Short, Luke, ed. *Frontier: 150 Years of the West.* London: Transworld Publishers Ltd., 1957.

Smith, Decost. *Red Indian Experiences.* London: George Allen and Unwin Ltd., 1949.

Stanek, V. J. *Pictorial Encyclopedia of the Animal Kingdom.* London: Paul Hamlyn Ltd., 1962.

Starr, Frederick. *American Indians.* Boston: D. C. Heath & Co., 1898.

Stidworthy, J. *Snakes of the World.* London: Hamlyn Publishing Group Ltd., 1969.

Summerhays, R. S. *Horses of the World.* London: Frederick Warne & Co., Ltd., 1949.

Thorp, R. W., and Bunker, R. *Indian Killer.* London: W. Foulsham & Co., Ltd., 1958.

Tibbles, Thomas Henry. *Buckskin and Blanket Days.* London: Oldbourne Book Co., Ltd., 1958.

Vestal, Stanley. *Dodge City, Queen of the Cow Towns.* London: Peter Nevill Ltd., 1957.

Ward, Fay E. *The Cowboy at Work.* New York: Hastings House, 1958.

Weybright, Victor, and Sell, Henry Blackman. *Buffalo Bill and the Wild West.* London: Hamish Hamilton Ltd., 1956.

Wilkinson, Frederick. *Guns.* London: Hamlyn Publishing Group Ltd., 1970.

Willison, G. F. *Here They Dug the Gold.* London: Eyre and Spottiswoode, 1950.

Wilson, C., and Pitman, P. *Encyclopedia of Murder.* London: Pan Books Ltd., 1964.

Winther, Oscar O. *Via Western Express and Stagecoach.* Stanford, Calif.: Stanford University Press, 1947.

Magazines

Castle of Frankenstein. New York: Gothic Castle Publishing Co., Inc., Issue 15, "Witches' Brew."

Frontier Times. Austin, Tex.: Western Publications, Inc. Issues 1 to 78.

Old West. Austin, Tex.: Western Publications, Inc. Issues 1 to 34.

Real West. Derby, Conn.: Charlton Publications, Inc. Issues 7, 13, 72, 79, 83, 84, and 86.

Saga. New York: McFadden Publications, Inc. Vol. 13, No. 5, 1957.

The Life and Trial of Frank James. New York: Frank Tousey Wide Awake Library, Special Number Sept. 28, 1883.

The West. Freeport, N.Y.: Maverick Publications, Inc. Issue 5.

"True Life of Billy the Kid," by Don Jenardo. New York: Frank Tousey Wide Awake Library, No. 451 Aug. 29, 1881.

True West. Austin, Tex.: Western Publications, Inc. Issues 3 to 113.

Maps

Map 2-A. Washington, D.C.: U. S. Department of the Interior Geological Survey. Stanford's General Map of the United States. Edward Stanford Ltd., London. Tombstone 1881. Tucson, Ariz. Don Bufkin.

Pamphlets, etc.

Civil War Scrapbook and Americana Catalogues Published by Thomas Woroniecki Corp. 1960/ 19th Century Advertising Literature Published by E. Remington and Sons; Volcanic Repeating Firearms Co.; J. Stevens and Co.; the Gatling Gun Co. of Hartford, Conn.; Wanted Posters, and various Buffalo Bill Wild West Show advertisements.